The Community of *Nuchi Du Takara*
("Life is the Ultimate Treasure")
in Postwar Okinawa

The Community of *Nuchi Du Takara* ("Life Is the Ultimate Treasure") in Postwar Okinawa

Local Subjectivity within and against Empire

MASAMICHI (MARRO) INOUE

University of Michigan Press
Ann Arbor

Copyright © 2025 by Masamichi (Marro) Inoue
All rights reserved

For questions or permissions, please contact um.press.perms@umich.edu

Published in the United States of America by the
University of Michigan Press
Manufactured in the United States of America
Printed on acid-free paper
First published February 2025

A CIP catalog record for this book is available from the British Library.

Library of Congress Cataloging-in-Publication data has been applied for.

ISBN: 978-0-472-07714-4 (hardcover : alk. paper)
ISBN: 978-0-472-05714-6 (paper : alk. paper)
ISBN: 978-0-472-22202-5 (e-book)

DOI: https://doi.org/10.3998/mpub.12473365

This book will be made open access within three years of publication thanks to Path to Open, a program developed in partnership between JSTOR, the American Council of Learned Societies (ACLS), University of Michigan Press, and The University of North Carolina Press to bring about equitable access and impact for the entire scholarly community, including authors, researchers, libraries, and university presses around the world.

Learn more at https://about.jstor.org/path-to-open/

Whenever we look at the actualities of the Battle of Okinawa, we are convinced that there is nothing as brutal, nothing as dishonorable as war. In the face of our firsthand experiences, no one will be able to speak out for or idealize war.

To be sure, it is human beings who bring about wars. But more importantly, it is also we human beings who can make efforts to prevent wars.

Since the end of the Battle of Okinawa, we have abhorred all wars, yearning to create a peaceful island.

This is the unwavering principle of life that we have obtained in exchange for the too heavy price that we paid.

—The concluding statement of the exhibition at the Okinawa Prefecture Peace Memorial Park

I dedicate this book to my daughter, Momo, my wife, Katie, and my mother, Teiko. To them I will always owe more than I can express.

CONTENTS

Acknowledgments — xi

Note on Japanese/Okinawan Names and Translations and Okinawan Pronunciations — xv

Introduction — 1

Part I. Anti-base Struggles in Henoko and the Formation of the Community of *Nuchi Du Takara* by the Okinawan Multitude

Introduction to Part I — 33

1. Anti-base Struggles in Henoko, 2004–2023 — 38
2. Protest as a Life-Form of the Okinawan Multitude: Internal Workings of the Community of *Nuchi Du Takara* — 65

Conclusion to Part I — 101

Part II. Money and Taboo: Okinawan Subjectivity as "a *Changing* Same" and the Construction of the Community of *Nuchi Du Takara*

Introduction to Part II — 107

3. Ambivalence toward the US Military: Formation of the Androcentric Community by the Okinawan "People" (1945–1972) — 112
4. Money and the Development of Okinawan Citizenship in Post-reversion Okinawa (1970s–1990s) — 157

Conclusion to Part II — 196

Part III. Empire in the Asia-Pacific Region:
Between American/Global and Japanese/National

    Introduction to Part III   201

5. American/Global/Postmodern Tendencies of Empire:
Five Historical Moments of Its Formation and Transformation   206

6. *Dojin* and Okinawa: Official Nationalism Versions 1, 2, and 3   249

    Conclusion to Part III   273

Part IV. A Paradigm beyond Self and Other: The Okinawan Multitude within and against Empire in the Asia-Pacific Region

    Introduction to Part IV   277

7. The Mimetic Production of the Okinawan Multitude
in the Planetary Time-Space   281

8. Conclusion: Collective Security from an Okinawan Perspective   322

    References   339

    Index   419

Digital materials related to this title can be found on the Fulcrum platform via the following citable URL: https://doi.org/10.3998/mpub.12473365

ACKNOWLEDGMENTS

This monograph has been a long time in the making. I gratefully acknowledge the kind support of many individuals who have helped me bring this project to completion.

I thank my colleagues in the Japan Studies Program at the University of Kentucky—Doug Slaymaker, Akiko Takenaka, Keiko Tanaka, Miyabi Goto, Joannah Peterson, Atsushi Hasegawa, Koji Tanno, and Yoko Horikawa—together with those in the Department of Modern and Classical Languages, Literatures & Cultures and across the University of Kentucky campus—Luo Liang, Jeff Peters, Jeanmarie Rouhier-Willoughby, Cindy Ruder, Leon Sachs, Jianjun He, Lisa Cliggett, Sue Roberts, Sarah Lyon, Donna Kwon, Yujia He, and Karen Slaymaker, among others—for their advice, insight, and encouragement at various stages of my research. I also deeply appreciate the generous financial support for my research that the University of Kentucky's College of Arts and Sciences has provided over the years.

I greatly benefited from conferences and workshops where I presented my findings. The Okinawa workshop held on the University of Sheffield campus in March 2009 and the two panels on Okinawa organized for the Association for Asian Studies annual conferences in Toronto in March 2017 and in Washington, DC, in March 2018 were particularly helpful for me in developing ideas, perspectives, and concepts for this book. I am grateful for the inspiring dialogues with organizers, participants, and audience members at these venues, including Glenn Hook, Mika Ko, Lisa Yoneyama, Yasuhiro Tanaka, Kimiko Miyagi, Kozue Akibayashi, Christopher Ames, Rick Siddle, Chihiro Minato, Eiichi Hoshino, Aaron Gerow, and Patrick Beillevaire (at the 2009 Okinawa workshop), Masakazu Tanaka, Sabine Frühstück, Carl Gabrielson, Nan Kim, Wendy Matsumura, Rebecca Forgash, and Leo Ching (at the 2017 AAS conference), and Mire Koikari, Tze Loo, Christopher Nelson, Yuan-Yu Kuan, Noriko Horiguchi, Davinder Bhowmik, and Annmaria

Shimabuku (at the 2018 AAS conference). I am also indebted to esteemed teachers of mine—Anne Allison, Orin Starn, Charlie Piot, Catherine Lutz, Steve Rabson, Mark Selden, and Mariko Tamanoi—for their insight, support, and encouragement during various phases of this project.

I fondly remember the time that I spent together with informants, friends, scholars, activists, and intellectuals based in Okinawa, Japan "proper," and the United States. To maintain their anonymity, however, I can mention only a limited number of names here: the late Kinjō Yūji, Kinjō Hatsuko, Oyafuso Ai, Ashitomi Hiroshi, Kawano Jyunji, Motoyama Jinshirō, the late Yakabi Osamu, the late Arasaki Moriteru, Nozoe Fumiaki, Mike Mochizuki, Tadatomo Keishi, Takazato Suzuyo, Yamashiro Hiroji, Kitaueda Takeshi, James Roberson, Satō Manabu, Maetakenishi Kazuma, Medoruma Shun, and Ishikawa Mao.

I express my heartfelt appreciation to Christopher Dreyer of the University of Michigan Press. A perceptive editor with vision and experience, he offered skillful guidance to help me prepare and produce this book. Excellent editorship has been extended by Katie LaPlant, who took over Christopher's position at the press and brought this project to completion. Two anonymous readers commissioned by the press provided astute comments and criticisms for the improvement of my descriptions and analyses. In particular, one of the readers read three different versions of my manuscript from beginning to end and offered invaluable suggestions, including the idea of bringing the local everyday notion of *nuchi du takara* ("life is the ultimate treasure") to center stage in my book. With heartfelt gratitude, I have implemented that idea. I also appreciate feedback received from the members of the Executive Committee of the press. In addition, I owe a debt of gratitude to each of the following individuals of the press: Mary Hashman for her splendid knowledge and skills in managing the book's production process, Richard Isomaki for his beautiful copyediting, Danielle Coty-Fattal and Sarah Berg for their effective promotion and marketing, Juliette Snyder for her artful editorial assistance, Heidi M. Dailey for her fantastic designing of the cover of this book, and Marcella Landri for her gracious finishing touch on the whole process of publication of the book. And my deep appreciation goes to Greg Epp, my personal copyeditor-cum-friend over twenty-plus years. He spent countless hours sharpening this manuscript's prose.

Three intellectual giants—Takara Kurayoshi, Karatani Kōjin, and Tomiyama Ichirō—have helped shape my scholarship, for which I am eternally grateful. A noted historian of the Ryukyu Kingdom and a former lieutenant governor of Okinawa (2013–2014), Takara wrote a statement on peace in 1978 for the renewal of exhibits in the older Okinawa Prefectural Peace Memorial Museum (Kuroshima 2022), which I have used for the cover and epigraph of this book and discussed in the introduction to this book. Though leftist scholars viewed his openly pro-base position critically (as I once did), personal interactions with him over the years have allowed me to recognize the importance of something in Okinawa that one fails to grasp if one approaches it with an anti-base/pro-base (or progressive/conservative) dichotomy. Exploration of this "something" forms one of the central themes of this book.

I met Karatani Kōjin once in the late 1990s, when he came to Duke University to deliver a paper for a conference. Then a graduate student of cultural anthropology, I happened to see him in the restroom of the conference venue. "Karatani sensei!" I said to introduce myself, but the next words did not come out of my mouth due to nervousness. "Have I met you?" he asked, softly. "No, sir, but I am an admirer of your work," I barely responded. In the evening, I had a blessed opportunity to share a meal with him in a small group setting in what I remember to be a guest room of a hotel. He told me about his ongoing project about Kant and Marx and I told him about my interest in Okinawa. Before the end of this gathering, Karatani wrote down his name together with his home address and telephone number on a piece of paper and gave it to me, adding, "Feel free to contact me when you are in Japan." I said yes with gratitude, but I have remained too intimidated to do so. Informed by Karatani's articulation of the Kantian notion of the "World Republic," this book, I hope, may perhaps serve as a substitute for my broken promise, even if he does not remember me or that piece of paper that I keep as a treasure of my life.

Tomiyama Ichirō has played a leading role in setting the agenda of Okinawan studies since the 1990s by providing a series of brilliant, in-depth analyses of Okinawa's position in Japan from the perspective of postcolonial studies, broadly defined. I partially criticize his writings in this monograph, precisely because of the excellence and integrity of his scholarship, which is truly worth engaging. Developing a criticism of his works pains me, however. I hope that this book reveals my continued appreciation and respect of Tomiyama as a scholar, an individual, and a friend.

NOTE ON JAPANESE/OKINAWAN NAMES AND TRANSLATIONS AND OKINAWAN PRONUNCIATIONS

Throughout this book, I follow the Japanese/Okinawan convention in which given names follow family names. In case of the Japanese/Okinawan authors who have published in English, however, I follow the English convention in which given names precede family names. Macrons (e.g., Kinjō, Satō) indicate long vowels. However, macrons are omitted in the case of place-names (e.g., Tokyo). While the names of political and public figures (e.g., Governor Onaga, Prime Minister Abe) are real, informants' names are mostly altered (e.g., Mr. B, Ms. S) to maintain their anonymity except where specified; the real name is provided if this individual has been publicly known and/or this individual agrees to the full name revealed. Translations of Japanese and Okinawan "dialect" are mine throughout this book unless noted otherwise.

I provide Okinawan pronunciations in Romanized form for terms that have specific local cultural/historical significance. The basic rules of Okinawan pronunciation that I have learned by visiting Okinawa over the years are that (*a*) "a, i, u, e, o" (five vowel sounds in "standard" Japanese) correspond to "a, i, u, i, u" (three vowel sounds) in the system of Okinawan pronunciations, and (*b*) the Japanese "ai" and "ae" sounds correspond to "ē" in the system of Okinawan pronunciations, and (*c*) the Japanese "ki" and "wa" sounds correspond to "chi" and "ā," respectively, in the system of Okinawan pronunciations, among other differences (Takeuchi A. 2020). It should be emphasized that the system of Okinawan pronunciations has undergone historical changes and has its own local variations. The Okinawan pronunciations I provide in this study are only approximations.

Introduction

Toward the end of World War II,[1] Okinawa—discarded by the Imperial General Headquarters in Tokyo as a sacrifice to protect Japan "proper"[2]—became the site of a fierce battle, the Battle of Okinawa. In the process, Okinawa lost an estimated 150,000 residents, a quarter of the prefectural population, due to the US military's barrage of indiscriminate bombing and artillery fire along with other causes such as the atrocities of the Japanese Imperial Army against Okinawans, shortage of food, and spread of diseases.

After the war, the US military occupied Okinawa, transforming it into the "Keystone of the Pacific" as part of a broader security structure to contain the threat of communism. Okinawa was thus used for logistical and other purposes during the Korean and Vietnam Wars. The administration of Okinawa reverted to Japan in 1972, but, under the framework of US-Japan security cooperation, Washington demanded Okinawa for a concentration of military bases during and following the Cold War, and Tokyo acceded, an arrangement that enabled the US military to deploy troops to, for instance, the Middle East during the Gulf War. Most recently, Washington and Tokyo have broadened and deepened their collaboration to restructure Okinawa as a fortress against China's maritime expansion. Although Okinawa constitutes just 0.6% of Japan's total landmass, areawise, approximately seven-tenths of the US military's exclusive-use facilities in Japan are concentrated in Okinawa at the time of this writing (December 2023).[3]

The disproportionate and prolonged presence of the US bases generated a range of social problems in post–World War II Okinawa (hereafter "postwar Okinawa"), such as crimes and accidents attributable to US service personnel, the ear-splitting noise of fighter airplanes, and land and ocean pollution on and around the bases. Among these social problems, the rape incident in 1995—painful and tragic though it is—must be noted here, as it constitutes an important background for the descriptions, analyses, and arguments this book presents.

On the night of September 4, 1995, a twelve-year-old Okinawan schoolgirl—who happened to be on her way back from a local general store after shopping—was raped by three US servicemen in northern Okinawa. A seething anger at the crime was anchored in the pain of historical experiences involving the war, the bases, and the servicemen, helping Okinawa express a strong anti-base attitude. For instance, several weeks after the rape incident, Governor Ōta Masahide (1925–2017; in office 1990–1998)[4] declared his refusal to renew the soon-to-expire lease with Tokyo that would allow the US military to continue to use Okinawa's land, and eighty-five thousand residents gathered to protest in October 1995, demanding the reduction and reorganization, if not the outright removal, of the US bases in Okinawa. In April 1996, in an attempt to calm the anger of Okinawa that threatened to undermine US-Japan security cooperation, Washington and Tokyo announced the closure and return of Futenma Air Station, a US Marine Corps facility located in a congested residential area of Ginowan City in central Okinawa.

Although this announcement was welcome, Okinawa was torn by an accompanying provision calling for the construction of a new military facility *within* Okinawa in return for Futenma's closure. In its final report issued in December 1996, the Special Action Committee on Okinawa (SACO 1996), a bilateral consultative body created by Washington and Tokyo, announced that a sea-based US military facility would be constructed "off the east coast of the main island of Okinawa." It soon became clear that the waters off the beach of Henoko—a sparsely populated eastern coastal district (population: fourteen hundred) of Nago City (population: fifty-five thousand) in northern Okinawa that had been home to the Marine Corps' Camp Schwab since the late 1950s—would be the site of the "Futenma Replacement Facility" (FRF), a term invented by Washington and Tokyo that obscured the facts that what would be created was a *military* facility and that Okinawa was to continue to shoulder a disproportionate share of the burden of the US bases.

In my book published in 2007, entitled *Okinawa and the U.S. Military: Identity Making in the Age of Globalization*,[5] I explored, from an anthropological perspective, a social tension in Henoko and elsewhere in Nago City generated by the planned construction of the FRF, a tension between edu-

Figure 1. Futenma Air Station
In April 1996, in an attempt to calm the anger of Okinawa (caused by the rape of an Okinawan schoolgirl by three US servicemen in 1995), Washington and Tokyo announced the closure and return of this facility within five to seven years, conditional on the construction of a new military facility, the Futenma Replacement Facility (FRF), on the shore off Camp Schwab. The US military continues to use Futenma Air Station as the construction of the FRF remains incomplete.
Source: Okinawaken Chijikōshitsu Kichitaisakuka 2017a.

cated, middle-class residents who mobilized movements to oppose the FRF based on progressive ideals centered on unarmed peace, environmental protection, and gender equality, on the one hand, and working-class residents who expressed their willingness, enthusiastically or reluctantly, to accept the FRF in light of Tokyo's promise to provide money for the development of economically depressed northern Okinawa, on the other. At work behind this promise of money, however, was Tokyo's discriminatory intention of continuing to concentrate US bases in Okinawa, as its residents—even pro-base residents—clearly saw. Accordingly, while it might have softened and complicated anti-base sentiments among Okinawans on the surface, money also led them, at a deeper level, to renew collective cultural sensibilities against Tokyo informed by the agony of historical experiences. Having ethnographically

4   THE COMMUNITY OF *NUCHI DU TUKARA*

Figure 2. Camp Schwab
This picture was taken before the construction of the FRF gained momentum in 2018.
Source: Okinawaken Chijikōshitsu Kichitaisakuka 2017b.

confirmed Okinawa's broad anti-Japanese sentiment overlapping with a critical attitude toward the US bases, I concluded my first book with hope that the protests in Henoko and Nago against the FRF construction would continue to receive collective support in Okinawa in spite of its internal division and would eventually push Washington and Tokyo to abandon the FRF construction plan altogether.

Nearly two decades have passed since 2004, when I completed my data collection activities for the first book. The conditions in Okinawa today at once fulfill and crush my hope. At one level, my hope has been fulfilled because of the formation of the so-called All-Okinawa movement against the FRF construction, a movement, led by Governor Onaga Takeshi (1950–2018; in office 2014–2018), that united the anti-base and pro-base sectors of Okinawa and embraced individuals with diverse backgrounds—including those from Japan "proper" and beyond—in this unity. At another level, however, my hope has been crushed because the determination of Washington and Tokyo to construct the FRF at any cost has increasingly drained the oppositional political energy of Okinawans and caused a decline of the anti-base protests in Henoko and Nago, though this is not to be confused with a decline of the anti-base voices and sentiments in Okinawa. In this second book on the US military base issues in Okinawa, I thematize Okinawa's enduring anti-base voices intertwined with critical sentiments against Japan in reference to the notion of the "Okinawan multitude," on the one hand, and the sustained will of Washington and Tokyo to construct the FRF no matter what in terms of the concept of "Empire," on the other. In so doing, I explore the contradiction between the Okinawan multitude and Empire as the most recent manifestation of the broader historical struggle between the constituent power (the "power of life") of Okinawan social actors and the constituted power (the "power over life") of the ever-growing global sovereignty founded upon the US-Japan alliance in the Asia-Pacific region (Hardt and Negri 2009, 57).

As I demonstrate in this study, however, the contradiction between constituent power and constituted power has rarely led to revolution—a radical, systemic, and potentially violent restructuring of an existing social-political order, or the overthrow of Empire by the multitude, as Michael Hardt and Antonio Negri envision it (e.g., 2009, part 6)—in postwar Okinawa. To be sure, this does not mean that revolutionary moments have not occurred in postwar Okinawa. For instance, the island-wide movement against the US military's land seizure procedures in the 1950s (which I explore in chapter 3) has been widely recognized as an example of revolutionary resistance (e.g., Ahagon 1973, 1992; Arasaki M. [1986] 1995, chap. 2; Mori 2010b; Kokuba [1973] 2019). In the realm of Okinawan literature, Medoruma Shun's controversial novella, *Hope* (*Kibō*) (1999), introduces a revolutionary notion of counter-violence by expressing the hope of Okinawa through the description of the killing of a three-year-old American boy living on a US base by the protagonist, an Okinawan man; in so doing, the novella reverses the positions of the US military and Okinawa and reveals what Okinawa has experienced ever since 1945 in a radically inverted literary context. In a novel titled *A Bird of Rainbows* (*Niji no Tori*) ([2004] 2017) that is filled with descriptions of even more gruesome violence perpetrated by a teenage *girl* against men, both Okinawan and American, extended into the murder of the five-year-old American daughter of a serviceman, Medoruma radicalizes the rejection of the social order of postwar Okinawa in a manner that reminds us of what Walter Benjamin called "divine violence" (Kinjō M. 2010, 323–326).

However, by carefully examining varied phenomena and events across the levels of everyday life, national politics, and international relations in postwar Okinawa, this study suggests that revolutionary actions and notions have typically been balanced by a broader social tendency to control, regulate, and even undermine them from within. In other words,

6   THE COMMUNITY OF *NUCHI DU TUKARA*

Figure 3. The location of the Island of Okinawa
Source: This map is secondary work by the author using the file titled "Map of the World with Countries—Single Color" (author unknown, n.d.), available from FreeVectorFlags.com.

"resistance" or "revolution," which remains an important perspective for the explanation of certain aspects of postwar Okinawa, is only a part, not the whole, of what I seek to explore in this book. Rather, I demonstrate that the contradiction between the constituent power of Okinawan social actors (Okinawan multitude) and the constituted power of US-Japan alliance (Empire) has been mediated by a cultural "cushion" in between, which allows a series of complex negotiations that, though they often involve compromises and concessions of constituent power vis-à-vis constituted power, nonetheless have helped the community of postwar Okinawa develop an internal capacity to embrace diverse and often contradictory attitudes, experiences, and perspectives regarding the US military and bases for small yet significant and incremental social changes. I explore the mechanism of such negotiations and social changes by using Okinawa's indigenous notion of *nuchi du takara* ("life is the ultimate treasure"). More specifically, employing methods of anthropology and cultural studies, this book provides descriptions and analyses of specific social movements and cultural practices to highlight *nuchi du takara* as an organizing principle of everyday life in postwar Okinawa. In so doing, I also develop and refine this local principle into a "concept" to generate a global policy proposal in the realm of international relations.

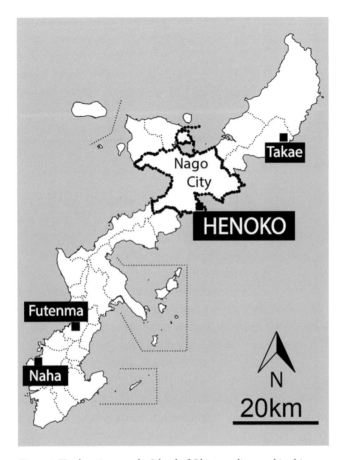

Figure 4. Key locations on the Island of Okinawa discussed in this book, including the locations of the existing base (Futenma) and the planned base (Henoko in Nago City).
Naha is the capital of Okinawa Prefecture. Takae is the site of the construction of new heliports, an issue to be discussed in chapter 6. Dotted lines represent the boundaries of the municipalities.
Source: This map is secondary work by the using the file titled "Map of Okinawa Island 02.svg" (author unknown, 2021) available from Wikimedia Commons, the free media repository.

This introduction explicates the notions of "Empire," the "Okinawan multitude," and *nuchi du takara*, in that order, to present the conceptual framework within which this study develops its descriptions, analyses, and arguments. I then explain the organization of this book. I conclude the introduction by commenting on and responding to potential critiques of this study.

Empire in the Asia-Pacific Region

Following the thesis of Hardt and Negri, I conceptualize Empire as a form of global sovereignty, "a *decentered* and *deterritorializing* apparatus of rule that progressively incorporates the entire global realm within its open, expanding frontiers" (2000, xii). A movement within and against "modern" European colonial imperialism—which was "really an extension of the sovereignty of the European nation-states beyond their own boundaries" (Hardt and Negri 2000, xii)—Empire was born out of the New Deal in the United States, spread across the capitalist states after World War II, and was perfected during the 1970s and beyond across the globe (Hardt and Negri 2000, chap. 3.2). Empire has expressed a "postmodern" mechanism of rule based on perpetual internalization of new frontiers, the "outside" (Hardt and Negri 2000, chap. 2.5). Accordingly, Empire "does not annex or destroy the other powers it faces," like modern European colonialist/imperialist nation-states, "but on the contrary opens itself to them, including them in the network" (Hardt and Negri 2000, 166). Similarly, Bruce Cumings notes that what was established by the United States in Asia in general and in Japan in particular in the wake of World War II was "not a colonial or neocolonial imperialism, it was a new system of empire begun with Wilson and consummated by Roosevelt and Acheson. Its very breadth—its nonterritoriality, its universalism, and its open systems . . .—made for a style of hegemony that was more open than previous imperialisms to competition from below. Indeed, we may eventually conclude that this was its undoing" (1984, 6–7). Naoki Sakai and Hyon Joo Yoo (2012, 12) use the term "global sovereign state" to capture this new form of power, writing that it is "irreducible to any single state of old imperialism, for it is the very systematicity of international relationships in which national states are sustained in complicity. This is to say that the global sovereign state does not coincide with any sovereignty of a single existent nation-state." Following the insights of these scholars, this study traces how an "imperial"—not "imperialist" (or colonialist)—paradigm of rule has been developed by the United States as the avatar of Empire, as it were, in the Asia-Pacific region across the Cold War and post–Cold War periods.

Therefore, I investigate how Empire in the Asia-Pacific has continued to internalize the constituent power of the "outside"—Japan from 1945 on, China from the 1970s on, and the former Soviet Union and its satellite states from the 1990s on—to establish the ever-enlarging world market as its sovereign territory. More specifically, I examine how, in the 1950s through the 1960s, the logic of the social contract as explained by Thomas Hobbes (via the concept of "Leviathan") was applied transnationally to develop the US-Japan alliance for the formation of what I call "Empire version 1," a process whereby US hegemony and violence in the Asia-Pacific region was materialized. I also explain how, in the 1970s through the 1990s, Empire v.1 was modified or "democratized" through the logic of reciprocity among the United States (core), Japan (semi-periphery), and other Asian nations (periphery) for the formation of "Empire version 2." Furthermore, I demonstrate how, in the twenty-first century, Empire v.2, with no more outside to internalize, has been transformed into "Empire version 3" with a broader security mechanism that has aimed but failed to manage omnipresent threats from within—such as "terrorism," North Korea's missile programs, China's maritime expansion, climate change, the Covid-19 pandemic, Russia's invasion of Ukraine, and the Israeli-Palestinian conflict. In analyzing Empire v.3 in the Asia-Pacific region, I underscore the process whereby the rise of postwar Japan under the hegemony of the United States in the Cold War period has been replaced in the post–Cold War period by the fall of Japan and the rise of China, together with the emerging conflict, or really the "civil war" (Hardt and Negri 2004, 3), between the United States and China—or between the so-called democratic and authoritarian states more broadly (often with the "Global South" situated in between)—within the same world market as the shared sovereign territory of Empire v.3.

One of the key contributions this book makes concerns the historical elucidation of the roles postwar Okinawa has been forced to play in the formation and transformation of Empire. Accordingly, I explore complex negotiations between John Foster Dulles (winner) and Hirohito, Emperor Shōwa (loser), in the wake of World War II, in order to examine how the same Japanese state that had discarded Okinawa as a sacrifice to protect

Japan "proper" in that war separated Okinawa from Japan "proper" to assist the United States in transforming Okinawa into the "Keystone of the Pacific" for the development of Empire v.1 between 1945 and the 1960s. I also show how this separation—or the alienation of Okinawa from Japan "proper"—was reinforced for the development of Empire v.2 from the 1970s to the 1990s through what I call "split governance" cogenerated by Washington and Tokyo, a form of rule enabled by the economic development of Japan "proper" as the "great workshop of Asia" and the military abuse of Okinawa as the "Keystone of the Pacific." In addition, I describe and analyze how the mechanism of split governance has been transformed in the twenty-first century into a generalized system of biopolitical control over everyday social life—the global security apparatus—across Japan "proper" *and* Okinawa while perpetuating the unequal relations of power between them, a process that coincided with the formation of Empire v.3.

In effect, Empire as a "new," postmodern, global sovereignty in the Asia-Pacific region has been fused into "old," modern, internal post/colonialism, producing continued domination of Okinawa by Tokyo across the colonial past and the postcolonial present. In other words, Empire in the Asia-Pacific region reveals a double-sided or hybrid character, both new (postmodern) and old (modern), imperial and colonialist, and American/global and Japanese/national.

Fundamental to the development of this hybrid character of Empire in the Asia-Pacific region is the notion of "collective (or regional) self-defense"—of defending the interests, safety, and security of ever-diversifying friends (Self) against enemies (Other). Defined as an "inherent right" of the state by the United Nations Charter's Article 51, collective/regional self-defense indeed helped Empire in the Asia-Pacific region to continually internalize the "outside" and hybridize itself, reframing the Self/Other (friend/enemy) binary across the Allies and the Axis during World War II into one across the capitalist and communist states during the Cold War period. The paradigm of collective/regional self-defense has reproduced and multiplied this binary anew in varied conflicts—"civil wars" within the single sovereign territory of Empire—today, including Russia's invasion of Ukraine and the Israeli-Palestinian conflict.

Showing that the existing scholarly interventions into Empire, while valuable, are ultimately insufficient to overcome the Self/Other binary underlying the notion of collective/regional self-defense as well as the current crisis that notion has brought to the world, this book proposes an alternative paradigm of "collective security"—a paradigm adopted by the United Nations as its fundamental principle of operation and one to which collective/regional self-defense is deemed secondary and an exception. Collective security involves the process whereby all states transfer their "inherent right" of collective/regional self-defense (but not their right of individual self-defense) to a democratic supranational power, which in turn collectively prevents, suppresses, and removes threats to the peace by complementing the right of individual self-defense of all states on the basis of the notion that the security of one state is the concern of all and the security of all is the concern of each state (United Nations, n.d.). I argue that collective security is possible and necessary under new historical circumstances of globalization that already connect us as earthlings beyond the paradigm of Self and Other, friend and enemy. Developing the insight of Karatani Kōjin (2006, [2010] 2014), I call this democratic supranational power the World Republic of *nuchi du takara*—currently approximated by but also disrupted by the United Nations. Grounded broadly in the premise that "life is the ultimate treasure"—a premise shared by Okinawan and other social actors across the globe—the World Republic of *nuchi du takara* helps to envision how we could (*a*) restore the principle of unarmed peace stipulated in Article 9 of the Constitution of Japan, (*b*) link that principle to shared management and use of military forces by the democratic supranational power against common threats, and (*c*) reconcile, from a fresh perspective, modern Asia's "history issues" (Dower 2014, 12)—the Nanjing massacre, "comfort women," Okinawa, and other problematic legacies of Imperial Japan's colonial dominations across Asia before and during World War II that have been long silenced by postwar American hegemony.

The Okinawan Multitude—or Okinawan Subjectivity as "a *Changing* Same"

My attempt to explore the formation and transformation of Empire in the Asia-Pacific region is complemented by a key argument of this book concerning a historical shift of Okinawan social actors from the poor, oppressed "people" in the age of Empire v.1 to increasingly affluent and confident "citizens" in the age of Empire v.2 and to the multitude with diverse backgrounds in the age of Empire v.3. In particular, struggles in Henoko in the twenty-first century bring to light an emerging Okinawan social actor that I call the "Okinawan multitude" (Inoue 2017a, xxv–xxx; Inoue 2017b), consisting of not only the Okinawan "people" (or *minshū*, in local parlance) who as the first postwar generation had experienced the Battle of Okinawa in 1945 and the "citizens" (or *shimin*, in local parlance) who as the second generation experienced the US rule of Okinawa in 1945–1972 without undergoing the war but also increasingly the third generation who experienced neither the war nor US rule. Extending Hardt and Negri's notion of the multitude as "singularities that act in common" (2004, 105), I demonstrate that the protest to block the construction of the FRF in Henoko—when considered with a range of cultural and social practices in postwar Okinawa at large, ranging from literature, dance, photography, music, and prayer to debates over reversion, gender, and the Okinawa-Tokyo relationship—allows us to explore the Okinawan multitude as an multigenerational network of singularities that has stretched across regions, countries, and continents connected historically and generationally through the issues of the US military presence in Okinawa. It is a process or a movement that produces *not* an "essence" or an "identity" of Okinawa that is shared by everybody *but rather* what Ludwig Wittgenstein called "family resemblances" ([1953] 2001, 27e), a web of overlapping similarities and crisscrossing differences whereby some experiences, visions, and perspectives are shared by *some* (but not all) social actors in postwar Okinawa.

Accordingly, the Okinawan multitude expresses similarities and differences of the ways in which Okinawans are situated in postwar history, including, for instance, those killed in the war, those who survived the war, and those who did not experience the war but have heard the stories of the war, as well as future children and grandchildren who are not yet born but will hear, directly or indirectly, such stories. The Okinawan multitude also includes US servicemen stationed in Okinawa and long-marginalized mixed-race Okinawans as well as their mothers, together with sexual minorities such as gay US servicemen and queer Okinawans, among others. The Okinawan multitude even includes dugongs, sea turtles, common terns, corals, and other creatures whose habitats are affected by the construction of the FRF and the presence of the US bases in Okinawa. What emerges from family resemblances of the Okinawan multitude, I suggest, is a broader desire for universal peace, global democracy, and shared affluence, a desire that overlaps with grievances expressed in the twenty-first century in the Arab Spring, the Occupy movement, the Me Too movement, the Black Lives Matter movement, the climate movement, and other social movements, as the Okinawan multitude marshals local historical experiences—the war, the bases, the servicemen, and the rape—not only as a way to remember the past but also as a method for presaging and reimagining the future through the explosive communication it produces in both physical spaces and cyberspace.

Lest the reader judge that my periodization of the three types of social actors (the "people," "citizens," the multitude)—which roughly correspond to the three versions of Empire—is too linear and mechanical and lacks necessary nuance and complexity, I note that my analysis in this book shows that the languages and actions of the Okinawan multitude in the twenty-first century are often preceded by those of the Okinawan "people" and/or "citizens." For instance, a draft of the "Constitution of the Ryukyu Republic Society," released in 1981 by local critic Kawamitsu Shin'ichi ([1981] 2014), heralded the concept of the Okinawan multitude by emphasizing radical openness to and acceptance of everyone regardless of race, nationality, gender, class, and other attributes in what he called the Ryukyu Republic Society, as discussed in chapter 8, section 2. I conduct my analysis, however, without losing sight of the broader historical shift of Okinawan subjectivity by highlighting "tendency," as explained in reference to Marx by Hardt and Negri (2004, 141). Specifically, Hardt and Negri argue that even though the numbers of the industrial working class worldwide have not declined, a growing tendency in contemporary society is that "industrial labor has been displaced from its hegemonic position over other forms of labor by immaterial labor, . . . [which transforms] all sectors of production and society itself in line with its qualities" (2004, 223). Similarly, I argue that while it has continued to provide important inspirations for contemporary struggles in Henoko and other places in Okinawa, the social movement of the Okinawan "people" and "citizens"—of the older generations—may have "been displaced from its hegemonic position" over other modalities of protest and resistance, which transform forms of life in Okinawa and Okinawan society itself "in line with [their] qualities." In other words, I articulate both a paradigmatic shift of Okinawan subjectivity *and* the nuance and complexity associated with this shift.

As such, my approach is aligned with Michel Foucault's notion of "genealogy" (1977)—historicization of what we tend to believe is without history, such as subjects he studied: madness ([1961] 1988), punishment ([1975] 1977), and sexuality ([1978] 1990). This study, for one, explores a genealogy of Okinawan subjectivity; I do so by examining the intersection of race, gender, and class in a manner that underscores what Paul Gilroy called "a *changing* rather than an unchanging same" (1993, 101).

On the one hand, I explore the "same" of postwar Okinawan subjectivity by tracing it to the experience of victimization during and following the Battle of Okinawa, a period when Okinawa was constructed as the object of direct military attack and control by the US military. Specifically, in their struggle to survive in the ruins of the war, the Okinawan "people" were placed in a contradictory situation: they needed to depend on the very US military that had destroyed their forms and ways of life with absolute power—political, legal, economic, material, ideological, and sexual—exercised over them. Emerging from this contradiction is what Sigmund Freud called "ambivalence," that is, "the simultaneous existence of love and hate toward the same object" ([1913] 1950, 157)—the US military—among the Okinawan "people." And yet, while Freud attributed ambivalence to a sense of guilt derived from a primordial patricide, an act by the son who displaced the father to become the father himself, the position of the Okinawan "people"—gendered as male, racialized as non-White, and class-bound as oppressed—was defined by their *in*ability to become the father, the impossibility and prohibition of patricide. The positional difference between the ultimately empowering Freudian son and the forever victimized Okinawan "people" has an important theoretical implication for grasping the "same" in Okinawan subjectivity—a form of androcentric nationalism, expressed as "fraternal" solidarity against the US military externally *and* as "fratriarchal" oppression of Okinawan women and others internally—across the postwar period.

Yet, on the other hand, I also show how social actors in postwar Okinawa have negotiated, as a subject, their status as an object of US military control from within and without to actualize "a *changing . . . same.*" Attention is paid to how money—explained by Marx as the generator of relations of equality across all forms of labor—has set Okinawan subjectivity in motion. Indeed, turning the originally androcentric structure of Okinawan subjectivity into a constituent movement, money has engaged the Okinawan social actors—including not only men ("people") but also women ("citizens") and other minorities ("multitude")—in the expansion of peace, actualization of democracy, and realization of shared affluence externally vis-à-vis the US military *and* internally within increasingly diversified Okinawa, even though this double-sided movement has always been complicated and curtailed by the configuration of politics at the local, national, and global levels. To explore the workings of Okinawan subjectivity as "a *changing* same" further in the planetary time-space of the twenty-first century, I also analyze the "mimetic faculty" of the Okinawan multitude—the faculty of becoming and behaving like the Other, of producing overlapping similarities and crisscrossing differences across the Asia-Pacific region and beyond rather than divisions and identities of Self and Other within it.

My approach to the genealogy of Okinawan subjectivity—a search for "a *changing* same"—is a response to two essentializing tendencies in Japanese/Okinawan postcolonial scholarship even as I draw on the insights of this scholarship throughout this study. First, Japanese/Okinawan postcolonial scholarship—not unlike some English-language scholarship on Okinawa (e.g., McCormack and Oka Norimatsu 2018)—tends to portray Okinawa solely as a site of resistance. For instance, studies conducted by Mori Yoshio (2010a, 2010b, 2016) generalize the homogeneously subordinated Okinawan "people" (*minshū*) as an underlying essence of revolutionary protests across postwar Okinawa, from the 1950s to the present. While insightful in capturing the importance of social movements for attainment of sovereignty and citizenship against Empire, his approach addresses the "same" of Okinawan subjectivity without paying enough attention to its internal differentiations and historical changes.

Second, the works of Japanese/Okinawan postcolonial scholarship tend to generalize experiences and perspectives of Okinawan men as the Okinawan experience and perspective. For instance, Tomiyama Ichirō (2002) analyzes lived experiences of noted Okinawan male intellectuals such as Iha (or Ifa) Fuyū, Higa Shunchō, Yamanokuchi (or Yamanoguchi) Baku, and Nagaoka Chitarō without doing so for a single woman. When he explores violence against Okinawans in his critique of Japanese colonialism-capitalism from the 1920s through the 1940s, Tomiyama's analysis also implicitly represents Okinawans (*Okinawajin*) through male figures and from their perspectives, as in the cases of Okinawan workers in major Japanese cities such as Osaka (1990) and in a mandate in the "South Seas" (previously German territories) given to Japan by the League of Nations following World War I (2006, 90–113; see also 2002, chap. 3). In addition, while Tomiyama (2002) thematizes how perceived presentiments of violence led Okinawans—represented by men—to take defensive postures (*migamaeru*) against the Japanese state and Japanese capital from the 1920s through the 1940s (chaps. 1, 2, and 3) and the US military after the war (247–302), he does not explore—except in brief sections (e.g., 157–165)—how Okinawan men's defensive posture has shaped relations of gender within Okinawa, leaving the problems of Okinawan androcentrism largely unexamined.

My exploration of the Okinawan multitude—and of Okinawan subjectivity as a *changing* same, more generally—may reflect my own positionality as a *changing* same. The "same" of my positionality is derived from a Japanese background. Indeed, even though I was born in the United States, I was raised in Japan from an early age: I was educated in Japan from elementary school to college and worked there for a few years before returning to the United States in 1989 for graduate education. My first language remains Japanese; I still speak English with an accent and write it with sometimes awkward turns of phrase. Nonetheless, together with the fact that I have been less familiar with Japan from the 1990s on, this sameness has been increasingly complicated and uncertain due to new changes brought into my life, represented by scholarly commitment to Okinawa's US base issues over the past twenty-five-plus years, on the one hand, and by work and family, which I have established in the United States, on the other. For instance, Kinjō Yūji, an informant-friend in Okinawa, profoundly changed my life by taking care of me during my 1997–1998 fieldwork in Henoko and Nago and afterward as if I were his own son. His premature death in 2007 at age seventy-two—news that I received in the United States—brought further changes to my life, as certain aspects of my connection to—and distance from—him/Okinawa have become frozen through his absence. Changes have also occurred through my work in the United States, when, for instance, a student veteran who had been stationed in Okinawa to serve in Iraq killed himself, apparently due to post-traumatic stress disorder, in the midst of the semester in which he took my Japanese cultural studies course, and immediately after he—a courteous and dedicated marine through and through—had spoken with me in my office about his profoundly pleasant experiences in Okinawa. These examples show the ways in which my positionality as a *changing* same—or as a Japanese and something else—intersects with and traverses other *changing* sames such as Yūji and the student veteran across a global network of the Okinawan multitude.

Nuchi Du Takara ("Life is the Ultimate Treasure"): The Unwavering Principle of Life across and beyond the Anti-base/Pro-base Divide

My attempt, noted above, to overcome the standardized (and often masculinized) view of Okinawa as a site of revolutionary resistance will be reinforced by the development of an indigenous everyday notion of *nuchi du takara* ("life is the ultimate treasure") as a concept in this study. Functioning as a cultural logic inserted like a cushion between the constituent power of Okinawan social actors and the constituted power of Empire, this concept will help highlight the presence of complex sentiments in postwar Okinawa that cannot be classified either as "anti-base" or "pro-base" (or that really are at once anti-base *and* pro-base)—a conundrum one would fail to grasp solely through the lens of "resistance" or "revolution."

For instance, the sociologist Kishi Masahiko (Kishi and Manabe 2022) discusses his interview experience with an Okinawan man. Having wept bitterly when talking about the loss of his younger brother in a "compulsory group suicide" (Field 1991, 61) of residents carried out at the order of the Japanese military during the Battle of Okinawa (see chapters 3 and 6 of this book on this issue), this interviewee nonetheless supported the US military presence because it had provided the social environment of postwar Okinawa in which he raised his family on what he earned as a worker on a US base during the day and as a taxi driver at night. Younger Okinawans often articulate a similar sense of complexity regarding the US military presence under contemporary circumstances. Hentona Issa, the leader of a popular dance/vocal group named Da Pump, grew up in Koza—a district adjacent to Kadena Air Base where one could hear the humming and noise of fighter jets around the clock—with a US serviceman as his grandfather. In a way that reflects Issa's upbringing, Da Pump features a powerful American style of hip-hop, while his pro-Americanism (i.e., pro-base attitude) is offset by and grounded in stories of cruelty and horror during the Battle of Okinawa that he heard from his Okinawan grandmother. Issa's pro-base attitude thus overlaps with an antiwar/anti-base sentiment. He commented, "There is a history in Okinawa where precious lives were lost. It is precisely because of that history that we live" (Issa and Hikarizumi 2022). In my fieldwork in the late 1990s, I too had an experience that exposed the complexity of Okinawan attitudes toward the US military presence. I was talking with a number of pro-base residents in Henoko in an old bar used as an office for their lobbying activities to invite the Futenma Replacement Facility to the community; one of them, a middle-aged man, in the midst of explaining to me the economic benefits of the new base, commented, "But I don't want my daughter to marry an American" (Inoue 2007, 123). Everybody nodded.

I sensed then and sense now that there is something in postwar Okinawa that one fails to grasp if one approaches it with an anti-base/pro-base (or progressive/conservative, good/bad) dichotomy—a dichotomy that has been framed conceptually by a tension between the pacifist perspective that views the military as a root of the evils of war and the realist position that recognizes practical or possible uses of the military for peace in actual circumstances of international politics (e.g., Takara 2017). It is to grapple with this "something" generated across the anti-base/pro-base divide and to assess the impact of this "something" on the negotiations between Okinawan social actors and Empire that I utilize the local notion of *nuchi du takara* in this study. This notion approximates what former Okinawan governor Yara Chōbyō (1902–1997; in office 1972–1976) called *donkakuteki taisei*, or an "obtuse-angle attitude" that he thought would be needed to solve the US base problems in post-reversion Okinawa (Ryukyu Asahi Hōsō 2017). By this he meant that Okinawa should employ an approach based not on a sharp, revolutionary, "acute-angle" confrontation between Okinawa and Tokyo/Washington, which would result in bitter disappointment and resentment among all parties involved, but on a soft, resilient, inclusive, and "obtuse-angle" attitude that would make the confrontation manageable for the achievement of small steps productive of steady, incremental progress.

I view *nuchi du takara* as an expression of the "obtuse-angle" attitude, a cultural cushion inserted between the power of life of Okinawan social actors from below, on the one hand, and the power over life of Empire from above, on the other—or between subject and structure. This cushion, I suggest, has helped Okinawan social actors externally engage not in revolution but in complex negotiations with Empire on the basis of the internal capacity of their community to embrace diverse and often contradictory attitudes, experiences, and perspectives regarding the US military and bases across and beyond the anti-base/pro-base divide.

It should be added that this internal capacity has been generated because the cultural logic of *nuchi du takara* can be mobilized by both the anti-base and pro-base positions for the common purpose, the care of life as the ultimate treasure. For, as this study shows, the anti-base position promotes *nuchi du takara* often from a pacifist perspective by rejecting the military and its bases as an institution created to annihilate this treasure through wars, while the pro-base position affirms *nuchi du takara*, typically from a realist perspective, by viewing the military and its bases as economic opportunities and resources, as a deterrent to enemy attacks, or as a site of intercultural/interracial communication, friendship, and marriage, all of which help protect and support this treasure. Under normal circumstances, the cultural logic of *nuchi du takara* thus allows these two contradictory attitudes to coexist in the collective mind of Okinawan social actors. However, under unusual circumstances, it also sways these actors toward the anti-base or pro-base position or leads them to prioritize one position over the other, as in the cases of the 1972 reversion and the 1995 rape incident (when Okinawa expressed a strong anti-base attitude for the care of life) or moments following the Battle of Okinawa (such as the period between 1945 and 1949, when "love and trust" of the US military as the new ruler at least partially permeated Okinawa for the care of life), as I will elaborate in this book.

A historical perspective helps underscore the centrality of life underlying *nuchi du takara* across the anti-base/pro-base divide in postwar Okinawa. For the notion of *nuchi du takara* expresses the shared "unwavering principle of life" against killing based on the collective experience of the Battle of Okinawa. Note that the following *anti*war (pacifist) statement—written by Takara Kurayoshi, a noted historian of the Ryukyu Kingdom and a former lieutenant governor of Okinawa (1947–present;[6] in office 2013–2014) whose *pro-base* (realist) position is well known (Takara, Ōshiro, and Maeshiro 2000)—has been adopted by the Okinawa Prefectural Peace Memorial Museum (hereafter OPPMM), a center and mecca of Okinawan pacifism, since 1978 when its exhibits were renewed (OPPMM, 2000, 98–99,[7] Kuroshima 2022).

> Whenever we look at the actualities of the Battle of Okinawa, we are convinced that there is nothing as brutal, nothing as dishonorable as war. In the face of our firsthand experiences, no one will be able to speak out for or idealize war.
>
> To be sure, it is human beings who bring about wars. But more importantly, it is also we human beings who can make efforts to prevent wars.
>
> Since the end of the Battle of Okinawa, we have abhorred all wars, yearning to create a peaceful island.

> This is the unwavering principle of life that we have obtained in exchange for the too heavy price that we paid.

In its unwavering rejection of killing/war, *nuchi du takara* echoes, I suggest, the planetary consciousness, or a perspective in the planetary time-space, conveyed, for instance, by what Archie Johnson (2023), an undergraduate student of the University of Kentucky, noted in my class: "One day a few billion years from now, the earth will be swallowed by the sun as it begins to die. What is the point of killing innocents [in wars] when we can just live our lives in peace? Life exists for an impossibly short amount of time [in the context of Earth history]." With the concept of *nuchi du takara*, this study historically and ethnographically explores the ways in which Okinawan social actors have coped with the anti-base/pro-base divide; in so doing, ultimately, it seeks to generate a policy proposal for the care of life by overcoming this divide from a planetary perspective.

• • •

The origin of *nuchi du takara* is not known. A leading hypothesis is that in 1932 Okinawan actor Iraha Inkichi (1886–1951) improvised a traditional Okinawan poem (*ryūka*) that included this phrase for the first time, when he acted the part of Shō Tai (1843–1901)—the last king of the Ryukyu Kingdom—who had surrendered Shuri Castle to the Meiji government rather than putting up do-or-die resistance against it, a historical event that occurred in 1879 (National Diet Library 2020). When mediated by the collective experience of the war and the US military's rule, the phrase—though it may have originally connoted submission to and passivity toward power—began to allow postwar Okinawa to actively express its "unwavering principle of life" against power. Specifically, as the notion of *nuchi du takara* was woven into the popular myth of Okinawan pacifism—that Okinawa, ever since the age of the Ryukyu Kingdom, had renounced the military to seek and establish peace[8] (Uezato T. 2007)—this "unwavering principle of life" helped Okinawan social actors express their strong anti-base attitude. For instance, starting in the 1950s, Ahagon Shōkō (1901–2001), a larger-than-life antiwar Okinawan landlord on Ie Island (off the coast of the Motobu peninsula of northwestern Okinawa), explicitly and implicitly advocated *nuchi du takara* as the "heart of Okinawa's pacifism" (1992) (see chapter 3, section 2). Similarly, from the late 1990s through the early twenty-first century, Inochi o Mamoru Kai (the Society for the Protection of Life)—a Henoko-based grassroots organization that Kinjō Yūji organized to oppose and stop the planned construction of the FRF (Inoue 2007, chap. 5)—nurtured a nonaggressive yet forceful attitude to life by including *inochi* (life)—the Japanese translation of *nuchi*—as part of its name and building its movements on that attitude.

Meanwhile, the prolonged presence of the US military has generated complex and often conflicting relations of power and history within postwar Okinawa, and, in the process, *nuchi du takara* has been employed and appropriated across and beyond the anti-base/pro-base divide, as vignettes presented above in this section indicate. In 2000, the former US president Bill Clinton (2000) mentioned *nuchi du takara* in a speech delivered at the Cornerstone of Peace in the Peace Memorial Park in Okinawa (of which OPPMM is part) (on this park, see chapter 4, section 5) in order to justify the continued presence of the US military in Okinawa. In addition, the term has been used as the name of one of the nine gems protected by Ryujin Mabyer, an Okinawan superhero for children (Ryujin Mabyer Official Website, n.d.) An *awamori* (Okinawan distilled liquor) company has also promoted a vessel used for brewing and storing its product by engraving *nuchi du takara* on its surface (Kariyushi Okinawa, n.d.).

Against the background of the complex genealogy of *nuchi du takara*, I deploy this notion as a *concept* with which to ethnographically and historically describe, analyze, and explain complex negotiations between constituent power and constituted power across the levels of everyday social life, national politics, and international relations, a process that goes hand in hand with the formation of an internal capacity of the community of Okinawan social actors to embrace diverse and often contradictory attitudes, experiences, and perspectives regarding the US military and bases. The deployment of *nuchi du takara* as a concept helps avoid reproducing a Western-white-male-centric scholarship, as it enables me to exercise something similar to—and even beyond—the "creolization of theory," the multiplication of analytical frames of reference through perpetual dialogue across binaries of the West and the rest, the universal and the particular, theories and examples (Chen 2010; Shih and Lionnet 2011). While the creolization of theory, couched in the West/rest and other binaries, might end up reinforcing these binaries in its very attempt to deconstruct them, this study—by developing the local everyday notion of *nuchi du takara* into a concept—controls, relativizes, and decanonizes Western theories in more fundamental ways. Specifically, this book addresses how theoretically deep and conceptually rich the everyday notions—such as *nuchi du takara*—and associated life-forms of Okinawan social actors have been. In so doing, I subvert the hierarchical binary between theoretical/immaterial work in the academy (historically dominated by Western men) and physical/practical/material work at the level of everyday social life (to which many varied Others were limited in the past).

In case the reader suspects that the use of the local notion in this study risks a reductionism of *nuchi du takara*, wherein all social phenomena are conveniently explained away in reference to this concept, I note that in the introduction to each part of this book, I place the concept of *nuchi du takara* in critical conversation with the main Western theoretical framework used in that part—that is, the "community" in Part I, money and taboo in Part II, the state in Part III, and mimesis and the general will in Part IV. This procedure helps articulate how *nuchi du takara* has been deployed, practiced, and materialized by Okinawan social actors in specific historical and social contexts—in the "community," through money and taboo, within and against the state, and through mimesis and the general will—thereby safeguarding against a reductionism of *nuchi du takara*.

In effect, by developing the Okinawan everyday notion into a concept and placing that concept in critical dialogue with Western theories, this study highlights postwar Okinawa's universality *and* local specificity. On the one hand, this study underscores that specific insights of Western theorists are relevant to understanding postwar Okinawa in the broader geopolitical context of the Asia-Pacific region because the basic economic, social, and political principles of modernity and postmodernity, analyzed and expressed in their works—for example, the "community" in the cases of Nancy, Blanchot, and Derrida, money in the case of Marx, taboo in the case of Freud, the state in the cases of Hobbes and Locke, mimesis in the case of Benjamin, and the general will in the case of Rousseau—have moved outside Europe to permeate the entire world today. Accordingly, their theoretical insights allow me to emphasize the universal aspects of postwar Okinawa. But, at the same time, in deploying *nuchi du takara* as a concept with global explanatory potential, I also explore how such economic, social, and political principles of post/modernity have been countered, subverted, and rearticulated in particular local contexts of postwar Okinawa by varied social actors, rather than simply imposed from above by the West.

Organization of the Book

This book has four parts. Chapters 1 and 2 comprise Part I, titled "Anti-base Struggles in Henoko and the Formation of the Community of *Nuchi Du Takara* by the Okinawan Multitude." More specifically, chapter 1 explores how the community of the Okinawan multitude structured by the notion of *nuchi du takara* has engaged externally in complex negotiations with and against Empire, while chapter 2 examines how this "unwavering principle of life" contributes to the development of an internal capacity of the community of the Okinawan multitude to embrace diverse and often contradictory attitudes, experiences, and perspectives regarding the US bases. Taken altogether, Part I aims to demonstrate how the community of *nuchi du takara*, as a cultural cushion, mediates two processes—external negotiations with the constituted power of Empire (chapter 1) and internal articulations of the constituent power of Okinawan social actors (chapter 2). This task is facilitated in the introduction to Part I, wherein the concepts of "constituent power" and "constituted power" are elaborated and theoretical insights into "community" developed by Jean-Luc Nancy, Maurice Blanchot, and Jacques Derrida are articulated.

Part II, titled "Money and Taboo: Okinawan Subjectivity as 'a *Changing Same*' and the Construction of the Community of *Nuchi Du Takara*" consists of chapters 3 and 4. Examining everyday social life in terms of what Ludwig Wittgenstein called "the whole, consisting of language and the actions into which it is woven" ([1953] 2001, 4e), it explores varied life-forms in postwar Okinawa up through the 1990s, such as the stage performances of an all-female troupe, protests on the street, and literary works in US-ruled Okinawa (chapter 3) and a social debate on women's status, Ishikawa Mao's photography, Henoko's "friendship" with Camp Schwab, and protests against the above-mentioned rape incident in post-reversion Okinawa (chapter 4). Chapter 3 specifically shows how the Okinawan "people" in US-ruled Okinawa were gendered as male, racialized as non-White, and class-bound as oppressed vis-à-vis the US military, a process whereby they developed two taboos—a homosocial taboo (forbidding friendship with the US military) and a heterosocial taboo (forbidding sexual relationships between US servicemen and Okinawan women)—to constitute the androcentric community of *nuchi du takara*. Chapter 4 explores how the affluent and confident Okinawan "citizens"—women in particular—undermined these taboos to rearticulate the community of *nuchi du takara* and renew a critical attitude toward the US bases through the collective memory of the war established against Tokyo. The introduction to Part II discusses insights of Freud and Marx in some detail to explain the ways in which the language and actions of *nuchi du takara* were mediated by taboos and money up through the 1990s. Varied life-forms of the Okinawan multitude as the new social actor beyond the 1990s are examined in Part IV, which, in combination with the analysis of anti-base protests in Henoko in Part I, helps extend the investigation of the community of *nuchi du takara*—together with Okinawan subjectivity that has constituted it—as "a *changing same*" into the present.

Part III—entitled "Empire in the Asia-Pacific Region: Between American/Global and Japanese/National"—consists of chapters 5 and 6. Chapter 5 focuses on how Empire in the Asia-Pacific region has continued to internalize the "outside"—Japan from 1945 on, China from the 1970s on, and the former Soviet Union and its satellite states from the 1990s on—to establish the ever-enlarging world market as its sovereign territory, a process that has accompanied continued conflicts and wars. This analysis will specifically shed light on American/global/postmodern/new/imperial characteristics of Empire generated in the Asia-Pacific region after World War II. Meanwhile, chapter 5 also serves as a background against which the analysis of chapter 6 is presented; that analysis explores continued colonialism exerted over Okinawa by Tokyo. Drawing on Tomiyama Ichirō's insight that "in Okinawa, colonialism never ends" (2010, 15), I accomplish this task historically and ethnographically by analyzing how the term *dojin*—"a savage and inferior native race"—has been woven into Japanese nationalism against Okinawa across the colonial (or prewar/wartime) past and the postcolonial (or postwar) present and how this nationalism, as it is expressed digitally today, is fused with the rule of Empire. In so doing, chapter 6 highlights the Japanese/national/modern/old/colonialist characteristics of Empire constructed in the Asia-Pacific region after World War II.

In combination, the components of Part III establish the thesis that

Empire in the Asia-Pacific region has dual tendencies, both American/global and Japanese/national, new (postmodern) and old (modern), and imperial and colonialist. The introduction to Part III discusses the insights of Thomas Hobbes and John Locke to highlight the Japanese state as the key mediator between these two tendencies, outlining how it has shaped actions of Empire externally and predicaments of Okinawa internally. Special attention is paid to the roles the Japanese emperor (Hirohito) played in the Japanese state from the prewar period through the early phase of the Cold War and then to the process whereby different forms of capital have displaced the power of the emperor in the Japanese state from the 1960s to the 1970s and into the post–Cold War period.

Part IV is titled "A Paradigm beyond Self and Other: The Okinawan Multitude within and against Empire in the Asia-Pacific Region." Pulling together key threads of analysis developed in Parts I, II, and III, Part IV investigates how the Okinawan multitude constructs its community and subjectivity and deploys a specific institutional mechanism in the planetary time-space to confront and negotiate with Empire. Two notions—"mimesis" (as developed by Walter Benjamin) and the "general will" (as developed by Jean-Jacques Rousseau)—will conceptually structure my descriptions, analyses, and arguments in Part IV to seek a paradigm beyond Self and Other. While the notions of mimesis and the general will will be fully elaborated in chapter 7 and chapter 8, respectively, the introduction to Part IV explains the passage to this paradigm—a paradigm beyond Self and Other—from the argument that I have developed in Part II.

Whereas Part I explores protest movements in Henoko from 2004 to 2023, chapter 7 aims to expand my analysis by looking at other cultural and social practices in the twenty-first century to identify varied expressions of *nuchi du takara*—the unwavering principle of life against war and killing—by the Okinawan multitude. To this end, I examine, for instance, the music and other artistic endeavors of the Okinawan artist Cocco, experiences and perspectives of US servicemen stationed in Okinawa, struggles of mixed-race Okinawans in their search for who they are, and the experience of the former Japanese emperor, Akihito (r. 1989–2019), and his wife, Michiko, in postwar Okinawa. My description and analysis in chapter 7 is structured by the concept of the "mimetic faculty"—the faculty of becoming and behaving like the Other, of producing family resemblances of *nuchi du takara* across the community of the Okinawan multitude rather than divisions and identities of Self and Other. The concluding chapter (chapter 8) expands the general will of the Okinawan multitude into the realm of international relations by presenting a policy proposal, from an Okinawan perspective, to actualize collective security by a yet-to-come, democratic supranational power that I call the World Republic of *nuchi du takara*.

Conclusion: A Revisionist Approach to Empire and the Multitude?

The reader may readily point out that the Okinawan multitude is less radical or revolutionary than the multitude conceived by Hardt and Negri, who present it as a new form of subjectivity that rejects all transcendental authority by arguing, "People don't need bosses at work. They need an expanding web of others with whom to communicate and collaborate; the boss is increasingly merely an obstacle to getting work done" (2009, 353). In other words, "The multitude . . . is able to act in common and thus rule itself" (2004, 100). In contrast, I propose that the Okinawan multitude should critically engage in the United Nations—in particular, with regard to its potential capacity to exercise collective security—even though Hardt and Negri dismiss the United Nations, in the final analysis, as "a fantastic utopia" (2000, 6), due in part to a mechanism of representation that forever suspends democracy of all by all (Hardt and Negri 2004, 291–293). In addition, I argue that the state will not wither away, which is contrary to the view that Hardt and Negri advance in reference to revolution (e.g., 2009, 355); rather, I theorize the state as an institution with a propensity to violence that cannot be eradicated but must be regulated by the multitude from below and by the World Republic of *nuchi du takara* from above (Karatani 2006, esp. 219–225; [2010] 2014, part 4, chap. 2). Furthermore, I give a positive evaluation to the former emperor, Akihito, and former empress, Michiko, who support and become part of the Okinawan multitude, in spite of the fact that the Japanese Imperial House constitutes an example of what Hardt and Negri call "an external authority imposing order on society from above" (2004, 337) in modern Japan. The reader could charge that this study is an example of a revisionist approach to Empire and the multitude, significantly diluting fundamental premises advocated by Hardt and Negri.

I justify my approach on the basis of empirical evidence as much as theoretical premise, arguing that the cultural logic of *nuchi du takara* employed by Okinawan social actors has facilitated negotiations for small yet significant and incremental social changes across the levels of everyday social life, national politics, and international relations vis-à-vis the constituted power of Empire in the Asia-Pacific region, rather than violent confrontations for a large-scale revolution. Focusing on life-forms that express "something"—the unwavering principle of life—that cannot be captured by the anti-base/pro-base (or progressive/conservative, good/bad) binary, however, I actually follow a line of thought created within the project of Hardt and Negri, who note that "today the historical processes of transformation are so radical that even reformist proposals can lead to revolutionary change" (2004, 289). Indeed, through a range of "reformist" articulations and rearticulations of their life-forms, the Okinawan social actors may revolutionarily subvert the Western myth of Oedipus (Deleuze and Guattari 1983), a homosocial myth of perpetual struggles between the son and the father, the hero and the villain, good and evil, a struggle that may have been preserved theoretically by Hardt and Negri in the dichotomy between the multitude and Empire. For Okinawan social actors do not or cannot eradicate/kill the US military even if they dream of it. Instead, they have pursued, ever since the Battle of Okinawa and well into the twenty-first century, the potentiality of *nuchi du takara* to stop the cycle of killing through small yet significant and incremental social changes. I present this study to underscore this concept in light of the wars that we witness today, both actually (the Russian invasion of Ukraine and the Israeli-Palestinian conflict) and possibly (the Chinese invasion of Taiwan), as well as other forms of violence that prevent us from actualizing universal peace, global democracy, and shared affluence.

• • •

This monograph deploys methods of anthropology (participant-observation and interviews), cultural studies (critical analysis of cultural products/texts and social phenomena/events), and international relations (historical exploration of relations of states with one another and with international organizations such as the United Nations). Data and information are drawn from a range of sources available through the internet and/or print media, including but not limited to newspapers, magazines, pamphlets, video clips, TV programs, governmental documents, literary works, music, photography, and scholarly writings, as well as from participant-observation and interview procedures that I have conducted at various times between 2004 and 2022. At the beginning of each part of this book, I provide brief "methodological notes" to explain key sources of information used in that part. My descriptions and analyses in this book are based on data up to December 2023.

Notes

1. The Battle of Okinawa in 1945 is often discussed in the context of the "Asia-Pacific War" or the "15-year war" to highlight the unique historical circumstances in the Asia-Pacific region. For instance, the Okinawa Prefectural Peace Memorial Museum (2001, 19) notes: "What started in 1931 as the 'Manchurian Incident' escalated into all-out war in China, Asia, and the Pacific, with Okinawa becoming the site of the final, decisive battle in this 15-year [war]." However, in this book, I use the term "World War II" instead of the "Asia-Pacific War" or the "15-year war" to explore the Battle of Okinawa and postwar Okinawa. This is not meant to downplay the unique historical circumstances in the Asia-Pacific region. (The main thrust of the book is an ethnographic-historical exploration of local social conditions and cultural sensibilities in postwar Okinawa situated in that region.) Rather, I use "World War II" to shed light on two important global issues that the other terms tend to obscure. First, "World War II" serves to highlight the Battle of Okinawa, along with Hiroshima and Nagasaki and the holocaust, as the culmination of a series of global conflicts that marked the dead end of modernity as it had unfolded in Europe and the Asia-Pacific region. In other words, the term helps underscore that the Battle of Okinawa is an integral part of modern world history. Second, the term "World War II" also helps emphasize the Battle of Okinawa as the beginning of a new, *postmodern* global order, Empire (Hardt and Negri 2000), in the Asia-Pacific region (see Part III of this book). In effect, by using "World War II" instead of the "Asia-Pacific War" or the "15-year war," this book highlights, from a global perspective, how Okinawa has been embedded in the passage from one historical epoch (modernity) to another (postmodernity).

2. This term—Japan "proper"—is a translation of *hondo*, and in this book it designates all areas of Japan except Okinawa. Put differently, this term underscores Japan from the perspective of Okinawa. The term *wider Japan* (together with *the rest of Japan* and *elsewhere in Japan*) is used somewhat interchangeably with Japan "proper," even though the latter conveys a sharper sense of distinction, opposition, or contrast between Okinawa and other areas of Japan.

3. The number of the US military's exclusive-use facilities in Okinawa is thirty-one, three of which are used by the Army, five by the Navy, six by the Air Force, thirteen by the Marine Corps, and four by two or more service branches. These facilities occupy 45,984 acres, or 8.2% of the land of Okinawa prefecture. As of June 2011, US service persons in Okinawa numbered 25,843, consisting of 1,547 soldiers

(6.0%), 2,159 sailors (8.4%), 6,772 aviators (26.2%), and 15,365 marines (59.5%) (Okinawa Prefectural Government 2018, 6; Okinawaken Sōmubu Chijikōshitsu Kichitaisakuka 2022, 13).

4. Throughout this book, the title of a particular individual is the one held by this individual at the time referred to in each instance.

5. In 2017, I published an updated version of the same book with a new preface (Inoue 2017a).

6. Throughout this book, "present" refers to December 2023, when I finalized the manuscript for the book.

7. I have slightly modified the original translation. I use this statement on the cover of this book and provide this translation as the epigraph.

8. In actuality, the Ryukyu Kingdom reinforced the military to unify its territories in the sixteenth century (Uezato T. 2007).

PART I

Anti-base Struggles in Henoko and the Formation of the Community of *Nuchi Du Takara* by the Okinawan Multitude

Introduction to Part I

Following the insights of Michael Hardt and Antonio Negri, I define constituent power and constituted power as the "power of life" and the "power over life," respectively (2009, 57). More specifically, "The constitutive practice of [social actors] is not the means to anything but its own power" (Hardt and Negri 1994, 295). Like what Walter Benjamin called "divine violence" ([1921] 1996, 249), constituent power "expresses life in itself in a nonmediate way, outside of law, in the form of the living" (Hardt and Negri 1994, 294). In contrast, constituted power "is empty; it merely falls back on, contains, and recuperates the constituent forces" (Hardt 2009, vii) through mechanisms of biopolitical control such as the law (Hardt and Negri 1994, 294), the police (Hardt and Negri 2000, 17–18), and the assembly (Negri 1999, 2). As "a parasite that draws its vitality from [social actors'] capacity to create ever new sources of energy and value" (Hardt and Negri 2000, 361), constituted power cannot constitute itself but is only made possible and constituted by constituent power.

Hardt and Negri suggest further that "the conflict between active constituent power and reactive constituted power is what characterizes . . . [modern] revolutionary experiences" (Theory Out of Bounds Series Editors 1999, viii) in England in the 1640s–1650s, the United States in the 1770s–1780s, France in the 1780s–1790s, and Russia in the 1910s, among other instances. Complicating and challenging, as much as expanding, their insight, I suggest that negotiations for small yet significant and incremental social changes, not revolutions, have occurred between Okinawan social actors and Empire in postwar Okinawa, because the conflict between constituent power and constituted power has been mediated by the cultural logic of *nuchi du takara* ("life is the ultimate treasure") that has acted as a cushion in between. This cultural cushion has also enabled social actors of postwar Okinawa to develop an internal capacity of their community—the community of *nuchi du takara*—to embrace diverse and often contradictory positions and perspectives regarding the US bases across and beyond the anti-base/pro-base divide, even though under specific historical-political circumstances it would prioritize one position over another, as explained in the introduction to this book.

The local debate regarding the construction of the Futenma Replacement Facility from 2004, a debate that has not been settled at the time of this writing (December 2023), is an example of such "specific historical-political circumstances." Thus, Part I shows that the community of *nuchi du takara* generated in Henoko—while embracing diverse social actors with both anti-base and pro-base positions to constitute themselves as the "Okinawan multitude"—has nonetheless prioritized the former over the latter. In the process, my description reveals a horizontal expansion and a historical depth of Okinawa's community of *nuchi du takara*. On the one hand, Part I shows the horizontal expansion of this community by examining how the logic of *nuchi du takara* brings together the two processes—external negotiations of the Okinawan multitude with the constituted power of Tokyo and Washington (chapter 1) and internal articulations of the constituent power of the Okinawan multitude (chapter 2). On the other hand, Part I (together with other parts of this book) also demonstrates the historical depth Okinawa's community of *nuchi du takara* by deploying theoretical insights into "community," developed by three French critics, Jean-Luc Nancy, Maurice Blanchot, and Jacques Derrida.

In an article entitled "The Inoperative Community," Jean-Luc Nancy situated "community" on a metaphysical level by stating that "community is revealed in the death of others" (Nancy [1983] 1991, 15). In particular, by way of commenting on the writings of Georges Bataille,[1] Nancy shows how the death of a fellow being exposes the finitude of the living being: finitude divides the dying other and the living self as much as it connects them as mortal beings. It is this division-as-connection that he calls "communication" (28–29): "Finitude passes 'from' the one 'to' the other: this passage makes up the sharing" (35). The community generated by such communication or sharing is "inoperative" because it is not something we invent or construct; rather, it is metaphysically "given to us with being and as being, well in advance of all our projects, desires, and undertaking" (Nancy [1983] 1991, 35). As such, the inoperative community is "resistance itself" (Nancy [1983] 1991, 35) to the invented, imagined, or constituted community such as "homeland, native soil or blood, nation, a delivered or fulfilled humanity, absolute phalanstery, family, or mystical body" (Nancy [1983] 1991, 15). To borrow from Karatani Kōjin, this metaphysical realm represents the "'power of God'" (kami no chikara) or divine power, appearing and reappearing in world history "not so much as something deriving from human desires or free will, but in the form of a categorical imperative that transcends them" ([2010] 2014, 14). I draw on Nancy's insight—enhanced by Karatani's thought—to articulate how the community of *nuchi du takara*, founded upon the death of Okinawans in the Battle of Okinawa, expresses "resistance itself" to Empire often beyond human desires or free will.

Maurice Blanchot traced, expanded, and complicated Nancy's metaphysical analysis by exploring how specific life-forms are produced at the everyday/social level as an *effect* of the inoperative community (cf. Nishitani 2001, 288). In *The Unavowable Community* ([1984] 1988), in particular, Blanchot underscored a social layer of everyday life centered on face-to-face communication beyond the metaphysical layer, with specific examples of life-forms such as the copresence of the people in May 1968.[2] With the definition of the unavowable community as what Georges Bataille called "the community of those who do not have a community" ([1952] 1973, 483, cited in Blanchot [1984] 1988, 1), his writing helps me underscore that postwar Okinawa, perpetually denied citizenship and sovereignty, has never had a national community to which it could belong. The concept of the unavowable community also helps to articulate the multiplicity of "those who do not have a community" in postwar Okinawa and to explore how the community of *nuchi du takara* has embraced diverse sentiments, positions, and perspectives within and against the constituted power of global sovereignty: "Without project, without conjuration, in the suddenness of a happy meeting, like a feast that breached the admitted and expected social norms, *explosive communication* could affirm itself . . . as the opening that gave permission to everyone, without distinction of class, age, sex or culture, to mix with the first comer as if with an already loved being, precisely because he [sic] was the unknown-familiar" (Blanchot [1984] 1988, 29–30). While remaining cautious about a subtle androcentric tendency in Blanchot's writings, Part I (along with other parts of this book) explores what he called "explosive communication" in everyday social life as a basic characteristic of the community of *nuchi du takara* in postwar Okinawa.

Furthermore, I radicalize Blanchot's understanding of community through Jacques Derrida's insights. Specifically, in a manner not unlike Derrida's problematization of Emmanuel Levinas's emphasis on face-to-face (i.e., everyday/social) communication that privileges oral discourse between Self and Other (1978, esp. 92–109),[3] I note that the unavowable community theorized by Blanchot tends to privilege face-to-face, everyday/social communication among those who are copresent at the same time-space, leaving unexamined the possibilities of communication among those separated from each other across time and space. Part I (together with other parts of this book) explores such unexamined possibilities, showing how Okinawan social actors have developed explosive communication in the global/virtual layer so as to actualize what Derrida calls "a friendship without presence" ([1994] 2005, 155) in the community of *nuchi du takara*. I pay attention to how "a friendship without presence" has emerged in that community as a life-form straddling absence and presence, "composing itself only as it decomposes itself constantly" (Blanchot [1984] 1988, 6). In so doing, I underscore the roles digital technologies and media have played in the development of such a life-form (Derrida [1994] 2005, 222).

In sum, underscoring the "unwavering principle of life" in postwar Okinawa, Part I explores how the community of *nuchi du takara* has developed in the protest movement in Henoko across its three ontological layers—the metaphysical, the everyday/social, and the global/virtual. In so doing, Part I examines the basic characteristics of the community of *nuchi du takara*—integrality against constituted power, explosive communication, and the absence/presence of structural permanency—that have been expressed by an expanding network of Okinawan social actors for small yet significant and incremental social changes in spite of compromises and concessions with Empire that they have often made in the process.

Methodological Notes

In Part I, I draw on data and information taken from a range of sources including but not limited to (*a*) my own fieldwork in Okinawa in August 2015, July 2016, June 2019, January 2020, and December 2022; (*b*) *No Base*, a newsletter edited and published by a Japanese woman, Ms. S., who observed as much as helped the anti-base struggles in Henoko for a period of fifteen years, as I discuss in chapter 2; (*c*) a book written by local activist/thinker Urashima Etsuko entitled *Henoko: Umi no Tatakai* (Henoko: A Struggle on the Sea) (2005); (*d*) a documentary titled *Umi ni Suwaru: Hankichi 600 nichi no tatakai* (Sitting In on the Sea: 600 Days of an Anti-base

Struggle in Henoko) that was directed by Mikami Chie and was broadcast in March 2006 by the television station Ryukyu Asahi Hōsō (Mikami 2006; sunao999 2012a, 2012b, 2012c, 2012d); and (*e*) two local newspapers, the *Okinawa Times* and *Ryukyu Shimpo*.[4]

Notes

1. In a way that captures a theme explored in, for instance, his *Madame Edwarda* ([1956] 1989), Bataille noted that "if it sees its fellow-being die, a living being can subsist only *outside itself*. . . . Each one of us is then driven out of the confines of his person and loses himself as much as possible in the community of his fellow creatures" (Bataille [1949] 1976, 245, cited in Nancy [1983] 1991, 15).

2. Other examples include Acéphale, a secret society Bataille created in the second half of the 1930s (Nishitani 1997, 129–130) and the world of lovers described in Marguerite Duras's 1982 novella titled *The Malady of Death* ([1982] 1986).

3. Blanchot's thought on Self and Other was shaped under the influence of Levinas (Blanchot [1984] 1988, 40–41; Levinas [1954] 1998; see also Derrida [1994] 2005, 296).

4. As for (*d*), an anonymous reviewer of the original manuscript that I submitted to the University of Michigan Press graciously informed me that the English subtitles for this documentary were provided by an Okinawan woman who was an activist, a retired English teacher, and a founding member of the Okinawa "Kichi/Guntai o Yurusanai Kōdōsuru Onnatachi no Kai" (Association of Women Acting against Military Bases and Forces in Okinawa), an organization established in 1995 after the rape incident that I will discuss in chapter 4. She apparently enlisted the help of a US scholar conducting research in Okinawa for the subtitles, an act that has helped the documentary to reach a wider international audience as well as to receive a Galaxy Award for TV programs in Japan—a system that overlaps with the Emmy Awards in the United States in scope and purpose—in 2006 (Ryukyu Asahi Hōsō 2006). As this reviewer insightfully noted, the ways in which this documentary was disseminated signal how the Okinawan multitude horizontally expands itself as a network through complex negotiations across borders, an issue that will be explored in chapters 2 and 7, among other chapters.

CHAPTER 1

Anti-base Struggles in Henoko, 2004–2023

> The opposing force [i.e., Tokyo and Washington] that we are dealing with is like a monster who comes back to life, no matter how many times it is destroyed, to become an ever-larger figure.
> —Urashima Etsuko (2005, 236)

I explore how the Okinawan multitude—often referred to as "protesters"[1] in this chapter—have formed the community of *nuchi du takara* ("life is the ultimate treasure") through their collective negotiations with Washington and Tokyo from 2004 up to the time of this writing to stop the construction of a Futenma Replacement Facility (FRF) in Henoko. I do so by focusing on two distinct periods. After presenting background on the FRF proposals, my description focuses on the first period, from April 2004 to September 2005, when protests developed to thwart a specific FRF construction plan. Then, after analysis of debate that developed from 2006 to 2012 over the rationale for building the FRF in Okinawa, the next part of chapter 1 describes the second period, from 2013 to 2023, which encompasses a series of local struggles to stop an updated FRF construction plan—which I call the Camp Schwab fortification plan—to build a military airport with two 1,800-meter runways in a V-formation through reclamation of 160 hectares of land from the seabed adjacent to Camp Schwab.

1. The First Period of Anti-base Protest in Henoko (2004–2005) and Its Aftermath (2006–2012)

If the 1995 rape incident represented the infringement of constituent power by constituted power "in a nonmediate way, outside of law [in the form of men's violence against the body and soul of the girl]," to modify the words of Hardt and Negri (1994, 294), political discourse in Okinawa that developed thereafter exhibits complex negotiations between constituent power and constituted power as mediated by the community of *nuchi du takara*. United by the indignation at the US servicemen who raped the girl, this community affirmed its internal capacity to embrace diverse and often contradictory attitudes regarding the US military and bases, as exemplified by the ways in which both the pro-base and anti-base perspectives were represented in the resolution that included a demand for reorganization and reduction—not the outright removal—of the US bases, adopted in the protest rally attended by eighty-five thousand people after the rape incident.[2] In response, while making the concession of returning Futenma Air Station to Okinawa, Washington and Tokyo, as "parasites," also appropriated Okinawa's cultural logic of *nuchi du takara* to advance their own security agenda in the post–Cold War world, because "Okinawa was indispensable for the strategies of the United States that desired the expansion of the scope of activities of the US military in Japan" (Fujita and Matsuyama 2021).

Accordingly, toward the end of 1996, Washington and Tokyo announced the original plan for the FRF, proposing to build a sea-based military facility with a 1,500-meter runway off the coast of Henoko (SACO 1996). In so doing, they also promised projects to develop economically underdeveloped northern Okinawa, an act that aimed to induce tensions between the anti-base and pro-base positions and control the anti-base voices within the community of *nuchi du takara*. In 1998, however, they abandoned this plan because of sustained local protests (Inoue 2007, chaps. 5 and 6). After this setback, Washington and Tokyo intervened in the community of *nuchi du takara* by directly collaborating with center-right Okinawan leaders of the time, in particular Governor Inamine Kei'ichi (1933–present; in office 1998–2006) and Mayor Kishimoto Tateo (1943–2006; in office 1998–2006) of Nago City, together with leaders of the Henoko community. Tokyo and Washington did not impose their plan from above, as in the case of the original FRF construction plan; rather, manipulating the subjectivity of these Okinawan leaders, Tokyo and Washington had them "voluntarily," so to speak, propose an alternative FRF plan—to build a bifunctional commercial-military airport with a 2,000-meter runway on the coral reef off Henoko, work that would involve reclaiming more than 230 hectares of land from the ocean (Inoue 2007, 201–207). In a way that expressed and retained the anti-base spirit of the community of *nuchi du takara*, however, this apparently "pro-base" proposal also specified that Okinawa would accept the construction of this facility on the condition that use of its military portion would be restricted to a period of fifteen years, after which Okinawa would use it for commercial activities only.

Regrettably, after the plan was finalized toward the end of 1999, the balance between constituent power and constituted power tipped toward the latter due to the continued manipulation of the community of *nuchi du takara* by Washington and Tokyo. For instance, Tokyo organized the G-8 summit in Nago in 2000 in order to publicize the appearance of collaboration between Okinawa, Tokyo, and Washington and thus to contain the anti-base protest/sentiment in Okinawa. Additionally, Washington rejected outright Okinawa's proposal to restrict the use of this facility as a military base to fifteen years. Before and after Inamine was reelected as governor in 2002, Tokyo said repeatedly to Okinawa, including Nago City, "We will discuss the matter with the US government," but that never happened. Instead, Tokyo chose to proceed with the construction plan by ignoring Okinawa's request for restricting the military use of the airport altogether (Inoue 2007, 206–207; cf. McCormack and Oka Norimatsu 2018, chap. 5).

• • •

In the early morning of Monday, April 19, 2004, officials of Naha Bōeishisetsukyoku (Naha Defense Facilities Administrative Agency; NDFAA), together with contractors working with the NDFAA, arrived with more than twenty vehicles, including some large trucks, at the fishing port of Henoko, in order to begin preparatory work for a boring survey of Henoko's seabed, the very first step toward building the commercial-military airport. Confronting NDFAA officers and contractors were one hundred or more protesters, many of whom had been involved in the movement against the construction of the FRF in Henoko since 1997. After some brushes, protesters drove the visitors away; then they set up a tent for sit-ins on the beach adjacent to the fishing port of Henoko in order to block the boring survey, or for that matter any other construction-related work (Urashima 2005, 54–57; Mikami 2006; sunao999 2012a, 1:00–2:45). This marked the beginning of sit-ins that have continued at the time of writing (December 2023), a proof of the interminable power of life actualized by Okinawan social actors (Herikichi Hantaikyōgikai, n.d.).

In a broader historical context, sit-ins were employed by Okinawan social actors as a method to protect life and to create and recreate the community of *nuchi du takara* against the US military. For instance, in the mid-

1950s, farmers in various parts of Okinawa sat in to protest seizures of their land by the US military, as I will discuss in chapter 3. From 1966 to 1971, residents of Gushikawa Village, an eastern coastal village in central Okinawa, used sit-in demonstrations and successfully stopped the planned requisition of their land by the US military (Nahashi Rekishi Hakubutsukan 2015); similarly, from 1989 to 1992, residents of Onna Village, a western coastal village in central Okinawa, staged sit-ins and eventually stopped the US military's attempt to develop an Urban Warfare Training Facility within the village boundaries (Ryukyu Asahi Hōsō 2014a). Participants in sit-ins in Henoko in 2004–2005, consciously or unconsciously, renewed the constituent power of the community of *nuchi du takara* against the constituted power of the US military (Mikami 2006; sunao999 2012a, 2012b, 2012c, 2012d).

It should be noted, however, that the protest that began in 2004 was also different from previous movements, as it revealed a historical depth and a horizontal expansion of Okinawa's community of *nuchi du takara*. On the one hand, the historical depth of this community was indicated by the participation of diverse generations, represented by, for instance, (*a*) those belonging to the first generation of Okinawan social actors, who experienced the war and US rule of Okinawa, such as old Henoko residents, mostly women, who were the members of a Henoko-based anti-base organization called Inochi o Mamoru Kai (Society for the Protection of Life); (*b*) those belonging to the second generation, who experienced US rule but not the Battle of Okinawa, such as Ashitomi Hiroshi, in his mid-fifties, a long-term leader of Herikichi Hantaikyōgikai (Coalition for Opposing the Offshore Base Construction; COOBC), a network of grassroots organizations in greater Nago City; (*c*) those belonging to the third generation, who experienced neither the war nor US rule, such as Higashionna Takuma, in his early forties, then an activist and later a Nago City assemblyman, and Taira Natsume, a pastor in his thirties; and (*d*) local women's organizations representing different generations, such as Jannu-kai (Group of Women/Dugongs) and Kokoroni Todoke Onnatachi no Nettowāku (Women's Network to Reach the People's Heart) (Hattori 2014; Mikami 2006; sunao999 2012a, 2012b, 2012c, 2012d). On the other hand, the horizontal expansion of the community of *nuchi du takara* was confirmed by the participation in the 2004–2005 protest of individuals from Japan "proper" and beyond with varied backgrounds, as will be discussed below in this chapter. The historical depth and the horizontal expansion of the community of *nuchi du takara* observed in Henoko in 2004 signaled the formation of the Okinawan multitude, an open network of singularities that has stretched across regions, countries, and continents connected generationally through the issues of US military presence in Okinawa.

Before the NDFAA's first visit to Henoko on April 19, 2004, protesters' anger had already been running high because of the perceived arrogance of the NDFAA and, by implication, the Japanese government. In particular, the NDFAA did not release the "scoping document," meant to set out the scope, goals, and methods of an environmental impact assessment, prior to its visit to Henoko. Protesters' frustration was intensified as the NDFAA blocked the "scoping document," finally released on April 28, 2004, from public reading—it was only perusable at eight locations in Okinawa, where copying was prohibited. A local environmental group managed to publish it on its home page, which was accessed more than 5,000 times in three days (Urashima 2005, 67–68). Subsequently, criticisms erupted because, as the World Wildlife Fund–Japan (2004) put it, the "description of the project" was "absolutely insufficient" and the "methods of investigation, prediction, and evaluation" of environmental impacts of the construction work were "unclear," as it did not specify what species, exactly, the NDFAA would choose to assess, and where, how, and when the assessment would occur. In effect, it did not deserve the name of an official "scoping document."

On the spot, NDFAA officials and contractors assumed a low profile so as not to antagonize protesters further (Mikami 2006; sunao999 2012a, 5:50–7:10). They indeed tried to obtain permission from them to begin the boring survey by returning to the fishing port of Henoko a total of 32 times between April and September 2004 (Kanegae 2007, 104). Meanwhile, in spite of their anger, protesters kept their emotions well under control. On one spring day, for instance, protesters invited six NDFAA officials to the tent in order to dissuade them from initiating the boring survey. These officials took off their shoes and sat down on the blue tarp covering the ground of the tent, as a Henoko woman in her nineties quietly but eloquently admonished them: "We were able to raise our children during and after the war because of the wealth of this sea. What good does it create to reclaim land from this sea? Do you want to kill us?" Kinjō Yūji, the leader of Inochi o Mamoru Kai (Society for the Protection of Life) in his late sixties, was also assertive and reasoned: "In Okinawa, there is a saying: *ichariba chōdē*; it means that we are all brothers once we meet [and therefore we should treat each other like brothers, not like enemies]" (Mikami 2006; sunao999 2012a,

7:50–9:05).[3] Hearing statements like these from older residents whose age must have been similar to that of their own parents and grandparents, the NDFAA officials fell silent, with their faces down. Some even shed tears (Urashima 2005, 78).

The state of abeyance did not last long, however, in part because of the crash on August 13, 2004, of a US Marine Corps CH-53D Sea Stallion helicopter on the campus of Okinawa International University (OIU), located about 300 meters from the southern fence line of Futenma Air Station and situated in a congested residential area of Ginowan City in central Okinawa (D. Allen 2004). On the day of this accident, a protester who had visited Henoko regularly from her house adjacent to the OIU campus called the tent, screaming, to report the incident (Kanegae 2007, 107). Futenma Air Station was working at full stretch then for the Iraq War that had started in March 2003; even though no students, faculty, or staff were killed or injured, the US military's control over information was particularly tight, so that no Okinawans—even the president of the university, the mayor of Ginowan City, or the Okinawa Prefectural Police—were allowed to enter the site of this accident as a zone of extraterritoriality, as it were, an act that was justified by the Status of Forces Agreement stipulating the privileges of the US military (Tanaka 2010, 132–137).

The NDFAA's somewhat conciliatory attitude toward the protesters changed after this incident. Though it had constantly refused to have a public meeting to explain the construction plan for the bifunctional military-commercial airport, the NDFAA, all of a sudden, held one on September 3, 2004, in a community hall near Henoko, enacting a thin pretext to initiate the construction work for the FRF. The meeting ended in utter confusion because the NDFAA did not show any sense of human decency, revealing itself as a representation of the constituted power to suppress the voice of opposition from the residents altogether (Mikami 2006; sunao999 2012b, 2:55–5:55).

The high-handed attitude of the NDFAA, combined with the crash of a helicopter at OIU, prompted the appearance of a large number of protesters, approximately 500, near Henoko's fishing port on the morning of September 9, 2004, when construction personnel (NDFAA officials, workers, and contractors) were expected to forcefully initiate the preparatory work for the boring survey. It was their first attempt after the failed one on April 19, 2004. A protesters' action plan had been created under the leadership of Taira Natsume, a young Okinawan pastor; they had decided to use boats and canoes to obstruct activities of the NDFAA construction personnel on the sea, presumably deployed from Henoko's fishing port. Prior to this date, Natsume had noted Okinawa's responsibility to stop the construction work in light of ordinary residents in Iraq and elsewhere killed by troops sent from US bases in Okinawa; he felt that he and Okinawa had been involved in the killing (Mikami 2006; sunao999 2012b, 9:10–10:20).

The NDFAA sabotaged this action plan simply by sending materials as well as workers from the port of Matenkō, located in southern Okinawa 50 kilometers away from Henoko, without using the fishing port of Henoko at all. The appearance of a squadron of fourteen NDFAA ships near Henoko thus came as a bolt from the blue. Protesters, caught off guard, hurriedly rowed out with their dozen canoes and two small powerboats to block these ships, but it was too late. The priest was in tears as the NDFAA ships swiftly threw buoys out onto the water to initiate the preparatory work for the boring survey (Mikami 2006; sunao999 2012b, 6:00–7:40; Urashima 2005, 101–102).

For the following two months, a tug-of-war between the NDFAA workers and contractors and protesters continued, as the former, with a large number of ships, attempted to conduct the preparatory work needed for the boring survey and the latter, with two boats and a dozen canoes, attempted to stop the work (Mikami 2006; sunao999 2012c, 0:00–2:20), to be performed at a total of sixty-three points both inside and outside the coral reef off Henoko. When contractors dove to investigate conditions on the seabed, protesters tried to obstruct the work by diving under the water or sending canoes and boats above them (Mikami 2006; sunao999 2012b; Urashima 2005). On land, too, protesters tried to prevent NDFAA officials, workers, and contractors from creating a job site yard near the fishing port of Henoko—an attempt that led, ironically, the NDFAA to create such a yard inside Camp Schwab, an area to which protesters had no access.

Then, on November 16, 2004, a huge pontoon, together with a number of NFDAA ships, came into view; it was loaded with machinery and materials needed for building single-pipe scaffolds, to be used for the boring survey inside the reef offshore from Henoko. Ten or more boats owned and steered by local Henoko fishers also appeared on the scene, hired by the NDFAA as lookout guards who were expected to thwart protest activities. Henoko's old women in the tent responded to this situation by initiating their prayers on the beach near the tent. Some protesters tried to block the passage of the pontoon with canoes and boats; others wrestled with NDFAA officials, workers, and contractors to physically stop the creation of the scaffolds; still others dove into the sea to do the same (Mikami 2006; sunao999 2012c, 3:55–5:05). In spite of these and other desperate attempts by the protesters, a total of five single-pipe scaffolds were built inside the reef by November 20, 2004. On that day, a clumsy spudding-type pontoon was also set up in the open sea outside the reef. The preparation for the boring survey was thus complete both inside and outside the reef (Urashima 2005, 119–128).

Protesters were disappointed at the progress they had not prevented but did not give up. They initiated sit-ins on the scaffolds (Urashima 2005, 123–134). Typically, at 9:00 a.m., NDFAA ships picked up governmental officials, together with contractors and their employees, from Camp Schwab's job site yard and then went to the scaffolds, where the protesters stood ready. The protesters—some on the beach and others on the scaffolds—carefully observed all of these actions with binoculars and transmitted information by radio among themselves, though, of course, NDFAA officials also tapped these radio communications. Both parties used video cameras to record each other's actions. Encounters at the scaffolds were sometimes confrontational to the extent that protesters were injured, particularly when the construction personnel tried to do the work hurriedly in order to make up for the delays—as of November 20, 2004, the NDFAA still intended to complete the boring survey at sixty-three points by the end of the year, that is, in little more than one month (Kanegae 2007, 112–113; Miyasaka 2005).

Okinawa's waters in late fall were not warm, and sit-ins on the scaffolds on the sea were particularly exhausting. However, protesters' activities to block the boring survey were well sustained. The thrust of protest activities was reinforced on December 13, 2004, when local fishers from across northern Okinawa began to come to Henoko with their fishing boats, helping the protest activities by besieging the scaffolds. On December 21, 2004, in particular, the spectacle of an ocean parade was performed by twenty-four fishing boats (Mikami 2006; sunao999 2012c, 5:30–6:55). Yamashiro Yoshikatsu, a man in his early sixties—the first generation of the Okinawan social actors—with more than forty years of experience as a fisher, was the key facilitator of these fishermen's involvement. To dramatize his solidarity with protesters, he on one occasion wore a red loincloth—a traditional Okinawa fishermen's tool to drive sharks away, which was here intended to drive the governmental ships away—and dove into the sea in front of a TV camera (Mikami 2006; sunao999 2012c, 6:55–7:50). When a Henoko fisher hired by the NDFAA yelled at him, "Don't come to Henoko's waters! You don't have a license to enter our waters!" Yamashiro Yoshikatsu replied, "The license is provided to protect the sea; those who destroy it do not have any qualification to talk about licenses" (Urashima 2005, 137).

In the midst of the confrontation between protesters supported by sympathetic fishers, on the one hand, and the NDFAA construction personnel, on the other, there were also moments of friendly (though somewhat sexist) engagement. An Okinawan NDFAA officer, on a ship lying at anchor, said, "Mr. Yamashiro, your performance today [referring to his diving with a red loincloth] was awesome. Your diving must have been well captured by a TV camera." A contractor chimed in, "A lot of young girls are on your boats these days," adding, "We cannot push through our plan of work in the presence of these women." Yamashiro Yoshikatsu on a different ship replied, "That's exactly what we aimed for." People on both sides chuckled (Mikami 2006; sunao999 2012c, 7:50–8:30). The presence of these young women, combined with the fact that protesters and governmental workers and contractors saw each other every day, contributed to the construction of a relationship of a kind, a sense of homosocial trust, across the divide (Miyasaka 2005, 30; Urashima 2005, 122, 140, 170, 182–183, 207–209).

As the year 2005 began, the local media began to report that the US and Japanese governments were reviewing the existing plan (Urashima 2005, 153; Watanabe Ts. 2008, 13–14). Officially, however, the Japanese government under the leadership of the popular prime minister Koizumi Jun'ichirō (1942–present; in office 2001–2006) of the Liberal Democratic Party (LDP)—a conservative, pro-American party in power in much of post–World War II Japan after 1955 (when it was formed)—continued to express a will to push on with the existing plan to construct the military-commercial airport in Henoko, as scheduled ("Kiteihōshindōri Kyōchō . . ." 2005). By March 2005, however, protesters had gained some control over the construction, as their actions were supported by additional individuals and organizations from outside Okinawa (Urashima 2005, 136, 148). Mr. M., a protester from Nagano Prefecture in his thirties, was one of these. He came back to Henoko during the second period of protest (see section 2 of this chapter) in the summer of 2015 and wrote to me in an email about what he had experienced back in 2004–2005: "I was very happy when they [Okinawan protesters] said that 'this struggle could not be fought by Okinawans only; we are thankful for participants from Japan "proper."'"

In addition, in March 2005, the *Rainbow Warrior* of Greenpeace arrived to demonstrate solidarity with protesters (Urashima 2005, 162–166). An order by the San Francisco Federal Court issued in March 2005 was also encouraging, because it "declared that the Okinawa dugong did indeed constitute historically significant 'property,' rejecting the DoD's claim that it did not" (Tanji 2008, 480). This court order was issued in reference to a lawsuit that had been filed in October 2003 by a network of NGOs from across Okinawa, Japan "proper," and the United States against the secretary of the US Department of Defense. The dugong, an endangered marine mammal related to the Atlantic-inhabiting manatee, was one of the primary plaintiffs; the claim was that the planned construction of a new airport in Henoko should be canceled because it violated the National Historic Preservation Act of the United States by not protecting the dugong.[4] The local activist Higashionna Takuma was one of the plaintiffs and a driving force behind the dugong lawsuit (Mikami 2006; sunao999 2012b, 0:50–1:30; sunao999 2012d, 0:00–0:35). Furthermore, the foreign media—such as the BBC—came to Henoko in response to sympathetically cover the protests (Mikami 2006; sunao999 2012d, 2:50–3:00).

As if to punctuate Tokyo's final gesture toward the completion of the boring survey, the NDFAA began to have the construction personnel work twenty-four hours a day, seven days a week beginning in April 2005 (Mikami 2006; sunao999 2012c, 9:10–12:45; Urashima 2005, 184). Protesters responded by sitting in on the scaffolds around the clock, an arduous task. One young woman, apparently from Japan "proper" (judging from her accent), said as she was sitting in on the scaffold at night, "What do I want to do now the most? [Take] a bath" (Mikami 2006; sunao999 2012d, 0:40–1:45). Nonetheless, protesters continued to coordinate activities effectively with fishers, divers, and other supporters to cope with Tokyo's maneuvers. On September 2, 2005, the NDFAA removed all the scaffolds, citing the arrival of the typhoon season as the reason. The boring survey was not completed at any of the sixty-three planned points after all. This marked a successful conclusion of the first period of protest in Henoko, from 2004 to 2005, which clearly demonstrated the constituent power of Okinawan social actors (Mikami 2006; sunao999 2012d, 3:15–3:30; Urashima 2005, chap. 5).

The participation of several generations of protesters in the struggles, together with the enduring method of nonviolent resistance, sit-ins, was a reminder of the depth of Okinawa's historical experience—the excessive, prolonged burden of the US bases, originating in the history of the war (1945) and the US rule (1945–1972), as will be elaborated in Part II. Meanwhile, protesters also collaborated with supporters from Japan "proper" and beyond to renew their protest strategies (e.g., introduction of canoeing, use of video cameras to monitor the behavior of the NDFAA officers, swimming performance in a red loincloth for TV, the lawsuit in the United States), in a way that revealed creativity and innovation shared with newly emerging social protests to confront globalization at that time (Castells 1997; Hardt and Negri 2004). What emerged at the intersection between the specificity (historicity) and universality (contemporaneity) of the first period of protest in 2004–2005 is the community of *nuchi du takara* structured by the Okinawan multitude through the unwavering principle of life against the military.

• • •

In 2005, Washington and Tokyo thus abandoned their second plan for the FRF—to construct a commercial-military facility in Henoko—in addition to giving up the original sea-based military facility plan pursued in 1997–1998. However, they did not remain idle. Washington and Tokyo responded to the integrality of the community of *nuchi du takara* among the Okinawan multitude by proposing what I call the "Camp Schwab fortification plan" in October 2005 through a document titled *US-Japan Alliance: Transformation and Realignment for the Future* (US-Japan Security Consultative Committee 2005), resurrecting an old plan crafted by the US Navy back in 1966 to build a military harbor around Camp Schwab (McCormack and Oka Norimatsu 2018, 92–95). The finalized plan—agreed to by Nago City's new pro-Tokyo mayor (and others) in April 2006 and made official in May 2006 through a document titled *United States-Japan Roadmap for Realignment Implementation* (US-Japan Security Consultative Committee 2006)[5]—was to build a military airport with two runways of 1,800 meters each in a V-shaped configuration (instead of L-shaped, as originally proposed in 2005), together with an aircraft parking apron, a naval harbor, and other functions that do not exist at Futenma, a process that would involve offshore land reclamation to create 160 hectares adjacent to Camp Schwab from coastal waters known as a pristine locale on the migration route of the dugong.

The execution of the Camp Schwab fortification plan, however, was drawn out. Indeed, even though the governmental environmental assessment started in March 2008 and was completed in December 2011, with additional data submitted in December 2012, overall, only relatively minor progress was made from 2006 through 2012, because, first of all, the plan met with sustained opposition from the community of *nuchi du takara*—including the new center-right Okinawa governor, Nakaima Hirokazu (1939–present; in office 2006–2014), who succeeded the aforementioned Inamine Kei'ichi. Second, the cabinets led by leaders of the LDP such as Abe Shinzō (1955–2022; in office 2006–2007 and 2012–2020), Fukuda Yasuo (1936–present; in office 2007–2008), and Asō Tarō (1940–present; in office 2008–2009) were all short-lived, unable to proceed with this plan. Third, and perhaps most significant, the Camp Schwab fortification plan was virtually suspended by Prime Minister Hatoyama Yukio (1947–present; in office 2009–2010) of the Democratic Party of Japan (DPJ)—a center-left party that came to power in 2009 by defeating the conservative and pro-America LDP with a vision of establishing autonomous diplomacy for the nation. Specifically, he aimed to limit US global strategies by constructing what he called Higashi Ajia Kyōdōtai (Community of East Asia), including China (Democratic Party of Japan 2008; Hatoyama Cabinet 2009); in the process, Hatoyama put forward an idea to build the FRF elsewhere, *outside* Okinawa (McCormack and Oka Norimatsu 2018, chap. 6; Miyagi and Watanabe 2016, chap. 3). The community of *nuchi du takara*, mediating the constituent power of Okinawan social actors, actively and effectively collaborated with Hatoyama to (almost) subvert the constituted power of Tokyo and Washington.

Indeed, Hatoyama's idea, a significant departure from the LDP's traditional diplomatic policy depending on and subservient to Washington, was enthusiastically received in the community of the Okinawan multitude at large to reinforce its cultural logic of *nuchi du takara*, to the extent that (*a*) anti-base candidate Inamine Susumu won the mayoral election in Nago City in January 2010 to succeed three conservative, pro-base mayors who had administered Nago City since 1998, and (*b*) ninety thousand Okinawans gathered in a rally in April 2010 to express Okinawa's will to support Hatoyama's idea. Unfortunately, Hatoyama failed miserably in actualizing his idea because of the pressure of US officials serving in the Obama administration and the dearth of assistance from his own subordinates—ministers and bureaucrats of the Ministry of Defense and Ministry of Foreign Affairs who resisted the change to the basic framework of US-dependent postwar diplomacy (McCormack and Oka Norimatsu 2018, chap. 6; Miyagi and Watanabe 2016, chap. 3; NHK Shuzaihan 2011, 186–192). In the end, Hatoyama awkwardly returned to the Camp Schwab fortification plan in May 2010, a decision that deeply disappointed Okinawans, and then he resigned in June 2010 due to this mishandling of the Futenma relocation issue. Successive DPJ administrations fell short of the expectations of Japanese constituencies—for example, mishandling the aftermath of the great earthquake and tsunami in eastern Japan in 2011 and making an unpopular decision to increase the consumption tax in 2012—and, toward the end of 2012, the LDP returned to power with Abe Shinzō as prime minister. Abe became prime minister for the first time in 2006, but he resigned in 2007 due to health problems apparently triggered by the money-related scandals of his own cabinet members, along with other political problems, and did not really engage in issues of US bases in Okinawa then, even though he revealed his nationalist tenets by, for instance, proposing the vision of *Utsukushī Kuni, Nippon* (a beautiful nation, Japan) (Abe S. n.d.). During his second term, from the end of 2012 until September 2020, however, he was adamant in his pursuit of the once-suspended Camp Schwab fortification plan, committed to renewing the constituted power of Washington and Tokyo by deepening the US-Japan security alliance against China and North Korea. It is by confronting and negotiating the constituted power of Washington and Tokyo that the community of *nuchi du takara* among the Okinawan multitude has taken a specific form in Henoko.

2. The Second Period of Anti-base Protest in Henoko (2013–2023)

In 2013, a number of political processes paved the way for executing the Camp Schwab fortification plan. First, in February, Prime Minister Abe came to Okinawa to declare his intention to proceed with the plan. Then, second, in the same month, President Obama directly pressed Abe at the White House to advance construction of the new base in Henoko by suggesting that Okinawa submit a land reclamation permit (Suzuki et al. 2015). In November 2013, five national assembly members from Okinawa, who as the members of the Okinawa chapter of the LDP had been elected by pledging themselves to oppose the Camp Schwab fortification plan, were forced by the secretary-general of the LDP, Ishiba Shigeru (1957–present; in office 2012–2014), to accept it. What is more, they were brought to a press conference organized by Ishiba as a punishment, as it were, where they publicly acknowledged their change of position. Images of their faces, rigid with distress, were broadcast across the nation, in a manner that made the unequal relations of power between Okinawa and Tokyo crystal clear ("Futenma Isetsu de . . ." 2013). Then, in December, in spite of his earlier public promise to oppose the Camp Schwab fortification plan, Governor Nakaima Hirokazu, right before he left office, approved a land reclamation permit in exchange for an increased amount of governmental aid to Okinawa. In the summer of 2014, the boring survey began.

Activities during the second period of anti-base protest have been organized at two sites around Camp Schwab: one area in front of the main gate and another on the ocean surrounding the camp. For protesters, these sites, located outside the residential area of Henoko, are crucially important to disruption of the Camp Schwab fortification plan, as materials and machinery for the construction-related work were first accumulated in the job site yard inside Camp Schwab and then deployed onto the sea. In the meantime, the original tent area established in April 2004 near the fishing port of Henoko, noted above, came to be commonly referred to as "Tent Village" (*tentomura*), becoming a hub for protest activities at large by serving as an information booth, a learning center, a rest station, a chat space, a meeting room, a press conference site, a lunchroom, and so forth for protesters coming from Okinawa, Japan "proper," and abroad. One can think of these three sites—the gate area of Camp Schwab, the ocean nearby, and Tent Village within Henoko—as a "triangle" of protest activities, where varied life-forms have been generated through language and actions into which it is woven for the construction of the community of *nuchi du takara*, as will be detailed in chapter 2. The rest of this chapter focuses on political actions of the protesters as embodiment of the constituent power of the Okinawan multitude, exploring the basic contour of the community of *nuchi du takara* vis-à-vis the constituted power of Washington and Tokyo.

• • •

With the land reclamation permit finally issued, Okinawa Bōeikyoku (Okinawa Defense Bureau; ODB), formerly the NDFAA, announced, in the spring of 2014, its intention to begin the boring survey as a step toward the construction of the FRF according to the Camp Schwab fortification plan ("Henoko Isetsu . . ." 2014). The ODB reduced the number of points of drilling from sixty-three (as in 2004–2005) to twenty-four, apparently with the intention to expedite the construction of the new base at the risk of cutting corners. The boring survey was to be completed by the end of November 2014 ("Kussakusagyō..." 2014).

Sit-in demonstrations in front of the main gate of Camp Schwab began on July 7, 2014, in response to the news that the ODB was likely to initiate the boring survey soon. Protesters, numbering thirty to fifty, pitched tents (blue tarps) during the day—and removed them at night—on the sidewalk along the chain-link and barbed-wire fence near the main gate, with the intention to check the entrance of vehicles carrying materials and machineries needed to initiate the boring survey. On July 20, 2014, at around 2:30 a.m.—when the tents were gone and no protesters were present—the ODB conducted the first major delivery by having contractors carry buoys and floats, to be used for establishing a restricted area offshore, through the gate with more than forty heavy vehicles ("Bui, Henoko..." 2014). A strong anti-Tokyo sentiment surfaced, resulting in a protest rally on August 23, 2014, in front of the Camp Schwab gate, where as many as thirty-six hundred people gathered (Medoruma 2014a) in a manner that made the oppositional will of the community of *nuchi du takara* clear.

The progress of the boring survey was slow for the remainder of 2014, however, because the sea is often rough during the typhoon season in Okinawa, which typically runs from May to October. In November and December 2014, the ODB did not perform much of the survey either, taking into consideration the possibility that continuing the survey against the will of Okinawans would "negatively" (from the governmental point of view) influence the results of the upcoming gubernatorial election (November 2014) and general elections (December 2014).

Meanwhile, by January 2015, protesters had established a capability to monitor the Camp Schwab gate at all times by always having someone in the tent area. The Japanese government responded, in February 2015, by ordering the removal of the tents altogether ("Henoko Kōgitento..." 2015). Protesters evacuated the area near the fence to at least partly obey the order, but at the same time they occupied the other side of the road—away from the fence—to continue their protest (No Base 3/5/2015, #1161b). Around the same time, protesters, numbering thirty to two hundred and often more, began sit-in demonstrations in front of the camp gate. The goal of this action was to directly and systematically delay the entrance of dump trucks and other heavy vehicles, numbering thirty to three hundred, and nearly four hundred at times (No Base 5/9/2018, #1576a). These trucks/

vehicles typically came to the gate three times a day (morning, early afternoon, and late afternoon) carrying materials and machinery for the boring survey and related work, aided by employees of private security companies who stood ready at the gate all day long, as I observed in August 2015.

Protest activities met persistent and often violent interventions by the riot squad of the Okinawa Prefectural Police as a vehicle of the constituted power exercised by Washington and Tokyo. Based on his observation of and participation in protest activities in front of Camp Schwab in January 2015, Douglas Lummis (2015, 3) wrote:

> Japanese riot police have a different mode of operation from, for example, American riot squads. If this action [i.e., sit-ins in front of Camp Schwab] were happening in the US probably the police would be smashing heads and making arrests by now. Japanese riot police dominate with numbers. When they come, they come by the hundreds. If one person, say, stands in front of a truck and refuses to move, five or six policemen will crowd around and immobilise her (at Henoko, most likely her)[6] in a kind of human strait jacket, then move her out of the way. It looks a little like a rugby scrum. It doesn't make as violent a picture as pounding heads with nightsticks, but people get hurt.

After the ODB began actual reclamation work on October 29, 2015 ("Bōeikyoku Henoko . . ." 2015), more members of the riot squad were used to control the ever-intensifying protests. For instance, on November 4, 2015, more than one hundred riot police officers from the Tokyo Metropolitan Police Department—together with one hundred members of the riot squad of the Okinawa Prefectural Police—joined security in front of the main gate, where one protester was arrested and another protester was injured and taken to the hospital ("Keishichō . . ." 2015).

In spite of the often violent police intervention, protesters resisted more forcefully by attempting to "dominate with numbers," to use Lummis's words. On November 11, 2015, for instance, five hundred protesters participated in a sit-in protest in front of Camp Schwab and drove the riot squad away ("Henoko Saidaikyū . . ." 2015); on November 15, 2015, the number swelled to twelve hundred ("11gatsu15nichi . . ." 2015). In January 2016, assembly members across Okinawa began to come to the gate area on Wednesdays and Thursdays, an effort that increased the number of protesters at Camp Schwab. Their efforts to re-dominate the consti-

Figure 5. Members of the riot squad forcibly removing demonstrators from the gate in front of Camp Schwab
Source: Ryukyu Shimpo 2015.

tuted power also came in the form of piling concrete blocks in front of the gate. On January 30, 2016, for instance, a fourteen hundred concrete blocks were stacked up, paralyzing the efforts of the ODB to proceed with the boring survey, although this, together with other acts, led the police to arrest Yamashiro Hiroji, a leader of protest activities in front of the camp ("Henoko de . . ." 2016).

Concurrent with the reinforcement of the community of *nuchi du takara* together with its constituent power in front of Camp Schwab, protesters also organized activities offshore by creating a canoe team in order to directly obstruct the boring survey and the construction work at large. On any particular day, the team typically consisted of ten to twenty—sometimes as many as fifty or more—canoeists (Medoruma 2014b). The canoe team was usually joined by one to three small powerboats, which took visitors—researchers like myself, journalists, and activists and so forth from wider Japan and abroad—on board, as needed. In addition, a group of divers were often taken on the powerboats; they dove into the ocean and took photos of the marks made by the dugongs as they ate algae on the bed of the ocean or of damage to the coral reef caused by the ODB's boring survey, as evidence of the destructiveness of their work (No Base 1/16/2015, #1138a).

Meanwhile, Tokyo established a number of hardline tactics to confront, control, and remove protesters on the sea. First, in July 2014, it created the "no admittance" zone, a vast area (561.8 hectares, to be precise) extending from the coastlines of Camp Schwab to the water 2.3 kilometers (at the maximum) offshore. In so doing, Tokyo tried to avoid the error it had made in 2004–2005, when the "no admittance" zone extended only 50 meters off the beach ("Henoko Niramiau Umi . . ." 2015), allowing protesters to enter the site of the boring survey and to occupy the scaffolds on the sea.

Second, while protesters on the canoes and boats approached, and climbed over if they could, layers of buoys and oil fences that demarcated the "no admittance" zone, officers of the Japan Coast Guard (JCG)—the police force deployed in the sea—used advanced equipment to block the protesters. Like the riot squad at the gate of Camp Schwab, the JCG tried to "dominate with numbers," mobilizing as many as twenty high-speed rubber boats and twenty large patrol ships. As I myself observed from a powerboat in June 2016, these vessels enabled the JCG to swiftly approach protesters as soon as they came close to the buoys that demarcated the zone and deliver a polite yet intimidating warning: "Entering the no-admittance zone is dangerous. Leave immediately. Thank you for your cooperation." The sense of domination was fortified by the attire of JCG officers, who wore black wetsuits, yellow life jackets, and black sunglasses, in a way that projected the constituted power of the state and suppressed any sense of individuality among officers. These officers often became violent; they dragged the canoeists into the JCG's boats or ships, overturned the canoes, towed the canoes into a nearby port, or, worse, into the open ocean as far as several kilometers away from the port ("Kaiho, Seigensui'ikigai . . ." 2014). They also swarmed into the powerboats to threaten those on board, turn off the engine, or even tip it over for what they called "safety reasons." While the JCG denied the use of excessive force, some protesters on the sea were injured and taken to the hospital ("Kaiho no Bōryoku . . ." 2014; Kudō and Shimizu 2015). Protesters thus called the JCG "Kaijō Hakaichō" (Japan Coast Demolisher) rather than Kaijō Hoanchō (the Japan Coast Guard). In an interview conducted by journalists in 2015, Mr. I., a farmer from Chiba Prefecture in his thirties who as a canoeist frequently participated in the first and second periods of anti-base protest in Henoko, stated, "What is different from the past [i.e., the first period] is that the JCG comes to the fore [to control protesters]. Their role in the past was simply to mediate the confrontation between those who protested and those [governmental workers and contractors] who did the work" (Iwata, Kashiwabara, and Gigi 2015).

・・・

In effect, since the summer of 2014, implementing the tactics cited above and other uncompromising measures, Tokyo and Washington made clear a

56   THE COMMUNITY OF *NUCHI DU TUKARA*

Figure 6. Officers of the Japan Coast Guard in a high-speed rubber boat approaching protesters to give a warning, one of them video-recording protesters
Source: Herikichi Hantaikyōgikai 2022.

political will of the constituted power to construct the FRF in Henoko no matter what. Given the enormity of this political will, acts of the protesters such as blocking the gate of Camp Schwab on land with sit-ins or obstructing the boring survey on the sea with canoes and boats may seem futile. In actuality, when carried out every day, the effects of such "weak" protest activities generated in the community of *nuchi du takara* by the constituent power of protesters were profound. For instance, the small size of a canoe provided a protester with the ability to go to a narrow spot behind a buoy where a governmental ship could not enter (Medoruma 2016a). Removing such a protester took time and drained the resources of the JCG and the ODB. In addition, the effects of protest activities were also manifested at a subtle psychological level. A prefectural police officer in front of Camp Schwab reportedly "wiped away his tears and looked up at the sky" ("Kokusaku . . ." 2015) due to the repeated requests by a college student that he listen to the voices of the protesters, and to accusations that the police should protect, not the government, but the Okinawans. One activist, a social worker from Japan "proper" in her thirties whom I interviewed in June 2016, noted that protest activities had made some JCG officers on the sea—and by extension, police and ODB officers on land as well—increasingly uncertain about the ethics of their own behavior; they might resort to violence in order to suppress the sense of guilt, an act that would, ironically, intensify their uncertainties. Some truck drivers who transported sediment, materials, and machinery to Camp Schwab expressed similar uncertainties (Hikarizumi and Itō 2022).

Repeated typhoons in Okinawa made the government's work even more difficult, to the extent that the boring survey, originally expected to be completed at the end of November 2014, was "tentatively" finished in February 2016, when one point of survey—evidently, of the soft ground 90 meters deep to the east of Camp Schwab (see below)—remained incomplete. Moreover, in 2015, in the midst of the survey, prehistoric earthenware was discovered along the coastline at the planned construction site within Camp Schwab, leading the Nago City Board of Education to investigate the entire boundary of Camp Schwab, in accordance with the Cultural Property Protection Act. This investigation set back part of the boring survey and construction work until November 2018 (Okinawa Kenritsu Maizō Bunkazai Sentā and Nago City Kyōiku Iinkai 2020). It seems as if Okinawa's nature and culture supported the community of *nuchi du takara* in delaying the construction of a new military base.

It should be added that activities during the second period of anti-base protest in Henoko from 2013 on were supported by residents across Okinawa in a manner that revealed the contour of the community of *nuchi du takara* arrayed against the Abe cabinet, which kept saying, "Henoko is the only solution to the Futenma relocation problem" ("Henoko Kyōgiketsuretsu . . ." 2015), a position Washington pressed (Henna 2016a). In January 2014, for instance, the anti-base mayor of Nago City, Inamine Susumu, won a second term as mayor, reconfirming the will of Nago constituencies to oppose the Camp Schwab fortification plan. Then, in July 2014, by unifying broad political and business sectors of Okinawa, the All-Okinawa Council to Realize the "Okinawa Petition"—submitted in 2012 to Tokyo to stop the deployment of V-22 Ospreys, tilt-rotor military aircraft with vertical takeoff and landing capabilities, at Futenma, on the grounds of potential safety and noise problems (No Osprey Okinawa Kenmintaikai Jimukyoku 2013)—was created to oppose Camp Schwab fortification, functioning as a driving force behind the victories of candidates who opposed the FRF construction in Henoko in many of the elections in Okinawa thereafter. These included the gubernatorial election in November 2014, the nation's general election in all four electoral districts in Okinawa in December 2014, the prefectural assembly election in June 2016, and the national House of Councilors election in July 2016. Public opinion polls during the time the boring survey was in progress (September 2014 through February 2016) consistently showed that an overwhelming 70% to 80%—often more—of Okinawans opposed the plan ("Osupurei 'Kiken' . . ." 2017).

This continuing popular opposition—a concretization of the constituent power of the Okinawan multitude mediated by the formation of the community of *nuchi du takara*—was intertwined with actions of the charismatic Okinawa governor, Onaga Takeshi (1950–2018; in office 2014–2018). He repeatedly pledged, "I will use all available measures to stop the construction of the base in Henoko." True to his word, in September 2015, Governor Onaga delivered a speech at the United Nations Human Rights Council to highlight the problems of the US military presence in Okinawa (Onaga 2015a). On October 13, 2015, furthermore, he revoked (*torikeshi*) a land reclamation permit that the previous governor (Nakaima Hirokazu) had issued back in December 2013, as noted above. Legal battles continued between Okinawa and Tokyo, resulting in the suspension of the construction work in March 2016. Eventually, however, on September 16, 2016, the Naha branch of Fukuoka High Court handed down a decision that the Okinawa Prefecture's revocation of the land reclamation permit was illegal. On December 20, 2016, the Supreme Court rejected the appeal lodged by Okinawa Prefecture. On December 26, 2016, Governor Onaga accepted the decision of the court and canceled the revocation he had issued. On the following day, after a halt for approximately three hundred days, the ODB resumed preparation for the construction work ("Henoko Kōji Saikai" 2016). After all, the Japanese court system had been created not so much to protect the community of *nuchi du takara* of the Okinawan multitude as to reinforce the constituted power of Washington and Tokyo, for the reasons that will be historically explored in Part III.

• • •

Meanwhile, in April 2016, a twenty-year-old Okinawa woman was assaulted, raped, and murdered by a former marine who at the time held a job related to computer and electrical wiring at Kadena Air Base. "Following the discovery of the victim's dead body [in May 2016], a deep sense of sadness and anger permeated Okinawa, triggering a series of grassroots activities that led to an all-Okinawa rally of protest and mourning attended by 65,000 Okinawans on June 19, 2016" (Inoue 2017a, xii). In July 2016, as if to ignore the sadness and anger of the Okinawan multitude, Tokyo began to push through another construction project to create helipads in Takae Village, adjacent to the Northern Training Area north of Camp Schwab, in exchange for returning 4,000 hectares of the training area to Okinawa (see chapter 6 for further analysis). In December 2016, a V-22 Osprey crashed into the ocean off the east coast of Nago City; Okinawa's demand for the cessation of the operation and of the deployment of Ospreys was simply ignored; the US military resumed operations in six days after the incident ("'Okinawa-kenmin mo . . .'" 2016).

From 2017 on, Tokyo more aggressively proceeded with the land reclamation procedure to build the FRF in Henoko. From February through March 2017, the ODB dropped more than two hundred concrete blocks (weighing up to 13.9 metric tons each) into the waters off Henoko ("Henoko Umetate Chakkō . . ." 2017). In April 2017, the artificial shore construction work was initiated, aiming to enclose the ocean for land reclamation ("Henoko Umetate Hajimaru . . ." 2017). Even though protests continued, the construction of the artificial shore had progressed in June 2018 to the point that the ODB was ready to deposit soil in the reclamation area ("Henoko 8gatsu . . ." 2018).

In response, in late July 2018, Governor Onaga—two weeks before his death from cancer at the age of sixty-seven—publicly declared his intention to withdraw (*tekkai*) approval for land reclamation issued by the previous governor back in December 2013, a legal action different from the revocation (*torikeshi*) that the court had denied, as discussed above. His intention—or his will, indeed—to halt the construction work was executed by the vice governors in August 2018 immediately after his death. Meanwhile, Tamaki Denny (1959–present; in office 2018–present), a fifty-eight-year-old former disc jockey with a mixed-race background (i.e., with an Okinawan mother and a US service member father) who had declared that he would continue the policy of the former governor and oppose the construction of the FRF in Henoko, was elected governor in September 2018. In November 2018, however, Tokyo resumed the work, suspending Onaga's withdrawal of the approval (Yamashita R. 2018). In the same month, Tamaki went to New York and Washington, DC, to assert Okinawa's position by meeting with US politicians, United Nations staff members, and university faculty and students ("Kyokuchōkyū ..." 2018), but despite all of his efforts, Tokyo began to dump sediment into the water for the first time in December 2018 ("Seifu Henoko ..." 2018). The Supreme Court legally supported Tokyo's action by rejecting in March 2020 and December 2022 two appeals lodged by Okinawa Prefecture (by Governor Tamaki) seeking to withdraw (*tekkai*) the approval for land reclamation (Sasagawa, Tajima, and Watanabe 2023).

The Japanese government has justified the disproportionate and prolonged presence of the US military in Okinawa on the basis of "military usability" consisting of, among others, (*a*) the geographic advantage of Okinawa in case of emergencies and (*b*) the US bases in Okinawa as a deterrent (Bōeishō 2016, 257). Extending this line of reasoning, in May 2022, which marked the fiftieth anniversary of Okinawan reversion ("Henoko Suishin ..." 2022), Tokyo and Washington reconfirmed their commitment to completion of the construction of the FRF no matter what; yet, the changing security environment of the Asia-Pacific region since the 2010s, characterized by the rise of China and other "threats," has led the US military/Marine Corps to transform themselves into a "globalized security apparatus" (see chapter 5, section 5, for further analysis), a process that contradicts the very logic of military usability of Okinawa upon which the current FRF construction plan, finalized back in 2006, was founded. I point out four issues to consider partial or potential misfiring of the existing FRF construction plan from a security perspective.

The first issue concerns consolidation of the US bases in Okinawa. Together with Futenma Air Station, the US military has returned or plans to return to Okinawa (*a*) facilities sprinkled through central-southern Okinawa, often in exchange for the construction of replacement facilities within and/or outside Okinawa (Bōeishō 2013a), and (*b*) a large portion of the US Marine Corps' Northern Training Area (approximately 4,000 hectares) in exchange for the construction of a total of six new helipads for V-22 Ospreys in Takae (an issue to be discussed further in chapter 6). Consequently, a significant number of US military facilities would be removed from south-central Okinawa—where over 80% (1.19 million) of Okinawa's population (1.42 million) resides (Nanseichi'iki Sangyō Kasseika Sentā 2015, 13)—and consolidated in less-populated northern Okinawa. This would reduce contacts and conflicts between US military operations and Okinawan civilian lives and thus increase "usability of Okinawa." However, consolidation of the US bases in Okinawa would also compromise the deep-seated historical desire of the US military/Marine Corps to use the entire area of Okinawa, an island gained in the hard-fought Battle of Okinawa, forever for military purposes. Even though (or precisely because) the US military returned Okinawa to Japan in 1972, this historical desire may have been rekindled due to China's maritime expansion and other "threats" in the Asia-Pacific region since the 2010s.

The second issue involves expanding the functions of Japan's Self-Defense Forces and integrating them in the operations of the US military. Though officially not acknowledged, the top officers of the US Marine Corps and Japan Ground Self-Defense Force secretly agreed in 2015 on the shared use of the FRF (Abe T. 2021).[7] Also, the FRF construction has gone hand in hand with increased presence of Self-Defense Forces on islands near Taiwan such as Miyako, Ishigaki, and Yonaguni (Fujiwara 2020), accompanied by the planned deployment of the newly established "Japanese" Marine Corps in the Ground Self-Defense Force to US Marine Corps Camp Hansen in Okinawa in the first half of the 2020s (Doi Taka. 2017). However, enhanced integration of the functions of the US military and Japan's Self-Defense Forces in Okinawa has drawn resentment from China and other potential adversaries and has increased, rather than deterring, the danger of war.

The third issue involves decentering of the US military/Marine Corps. FRF construction has been combined with plans (*a*) to relocate approximately nine thousand (out of approximately sixteen thousand) marines of the Third Marine Expeditionary Force to Guam and Hawaii (US-Japan Security Consultative Committee, 2005, 2006), (*b*) to utilize Australia as a new site of rotational deployment for the Marine Corps (A. Wilson 2023), and (*c*) to develop training areas in Guam and the Commonwealth of the Northern Mariana Islands for the US Marines and Japan's Self-Defense Forces (Tan 2023). Ironically, constructing the FRF in Henoko goes against the project of decentering, as this construction does not change perpetual concentration of the US military facilities in Okinawa, making this island prefecture even more vulnerable to the "enemy's" attack today precisely because of its geographical proximity to the potential sites of conflicts.

The fourth issue concerns upgrading the military capabilities of the Marine Corps and the US military as a whole. *Force Design 2030* (United

States Marine Corps [hereafter USMC] 2020) suggests that, in response to the development of the A2/AD technologies and "smart" weapons by China and other adversaries, the Marine Corps pursue a radically flexible, mobile, expedient, and lighter—yet more lethal and "reportedly 'commando-like'" (Cancian 2020, 5)—system of operations through concepts such as "Littoral Operations in a Contested Environment" and "Expeditionary Advanced Base Operations (EABO)" (USMC, n.d.-d). Accordingly, in November 2023, the Marine Corps transformed the existing Twelfth Marines in Okinawa into the Twelfth Marine Littoral Regiment to develop EABO capacity (Yamashiro 2023b). Yet, how the FRF construction will help (or hinder) the Marine Corps' newest upgrades is not clear, because the FRF will be smaller than Futenma and will obstruct radar visions of the "enemies" due to its location (on the east coast of Okinawa, behind the mountains) (Tanahashi et al. 2023). Nor is it clear how the FRF construction will be aligned with similar upgrades implemented by other units of the US military as well as the Department of Defense as a whole (Makino Y. 2023).

In effect, the above issues (consolidating US bases in Okinawa; integrating Japan's Self-Defense Forces into the US military; and decentering and upgrading the US military) reveal how the FRF construction plan, together with the notion of military usability of Okinawa upon which it was based, may conflict with changing security needs of the US military/Marine Corps in the 2020s. Accordingly, from the perspective of the US military/Marine Corps, the plan begins to look somewhat outdated at the time of this writing (December 2023) (Tanahashi et al. 2003).

The actions of Washington and Tokyo as the constituted power to construct the FRF no matter what have also revealed the enormity of the task required to complete it. For instance, while approximately 20 million cubic meters of sediment are needed for the planned land reclamation of 160 hectares, as of December 2019, one year after the deposits began, little more than 1% of the needed soil had been deposited ("Shinkichi 100nen..." 2019); a year later, in December 2020, to Tokyo's dismay, only 3.8% of the needed soil had been deposited ("K8..." 2020). As of July 2023, about 15.6% of the soil needed to cover 98% of the shallow water area south of Henoko had been deposited, but the existence of soft and fragile ground ninety meters deep prevented Tokyo from conducting any work in the eastern side of the sea, part of the area that needs to be reclaimed (Sasagawa, Tajima, and Watanabe 2023). A Japanese engineer-activist monitoring the construction work in Henoko, Kitaueda Takeshi, obtained information about the soft ground in March 2018 from the ODB through a request-for-information disclosure, but Tokyo did not publicly acknowledge it until January 2019 (Kitaueda 2018). This inconvenient truth has had a substantial impact upon the construction schedule. As of 2015, the boring survey was to be followed by land reclamation work (five years) and a variety of follow-up projects (three years), placing the earliest possible completion date in early 2024 (Henna 2016b). However, due to the additional work necessary to improve this soft ground, the revised estimate of the earliest completion of the FRF has now been pushed back to the 2030s. Expected cost has also swelled from 350 billion yen, as announced by Tokyo in March 2014, to 930 billion yen, as announced by Tokyo (as opposed to the estimate of 2.55 trillion yen by the Okinawa prefectural government) in December 2019 ("Henoko Kōki . . ." 2019), in spite of the ever-worsening national debt of Japan, which was more than 1,000 trillion yen even before the Covid-19 crisis ("Kunino Shakkin . . ." 2020).

Meanwhile, experts have pointed out that improvement of soft ground this deep underwater has never been carried out. The Subcommittee on Readiness of the Armed Service Committee, House of Representatives, expressed concerns over the issue in June 2020 ("Bei, Nanjyakujiban . . ." 2020). Similarly, in July 2021, two (of five) judges of the Supreme Court of Japan pointed to the problem of soft ground and supported the position of the Okinawa prefectural government, which had been sued by Tokyo due to its refusal to follow Tokyo's order to approve a plan to transplant the coral from this area to another location (Ōshiro and Kara 2021). Furthermore, on November 25, 2021, Okinawa Prefecture, led by Governor Tamaki, officially rejected Tokyo's plan to improve the soft ground, proposed by the ODB on April 21, 2020 ("Henoko no Shin'kichi . . ." 2021). Even though in September 2023 the Supreme Court ultimately endorsed Tokyo's proposed plan (Sasagawa, Tajima, and Watanabe 2023), Mark F. Cancian (colonel, USMCR, ret.), a senior adviser with the International Security Program at the Center for Strategic and International Studies in Washington, DC, states: "This project continues to have difficulties, with the completion date pushed out again, to [the] 2030[s], and the price skyrocketing. It appears unlikely that this will ever be completed" (2020, 12). In an interview that I conducted in Tent Village in June 2019, Mr. T., an activist-analyst from Japan "proper" who has been working for the COOBC since 2004, stated that the new base will "never be made." In the face of Governor Tamaki's refusal to cooperate, Tokyo is expected to forcefully start improving the soft ground in early 2024 through the administrative procedure of subrogation—also known as "execution by proxy" (Tajima et al. 2023)—approved by the Japanese court in December 2023 (Arakaki and Agarie 2023). However, whether and when Tokyo will be able to complete this project remains unclear.

Notes

1. Their individualities and singularities will be fully articulated as this book develops its descriptions and analyses more fully in other chapters, chapters 2 and 7 in particular.

2. See chapter 4, section 5, for further analysis of the community of *nuchi du takara* constructed in the late 1990s after the rape incident.

3. The translations from Mikami's (2006) *Sitting In on the Sea* are those provided in sunao999 (2012a, 2012b, 2012c, and 2012d) as subtitles for the video; they have been occasionally modified by the author.

4. After twists and turns, the plaintiffs lost the case in the San Francisco federal court in August 2018, but appealed to the Ninth Circuit Court of Appeals in September 2018. That hearing was concluded in February 2020. Even though the plaintiffs lost the case on May 6, 2020 ("Jyugonsoshō Genkoku Haiso" 2020), the significance of this lawsuit was undiminished.

5. The US-Japan Security Consultative Committee is a highest-level bilateral committee on security held at a ministerial level. *US-Japan Alliance: Transformation and Realignment for the Future* (US-Japan Security Consultative Committee 2005) and *United States-Japan Roadmap for Realignment Implementation* (US-Japan Security Consultative Committee 2006) will be discussed again in chapter 5.

6. I am not sure that I agree with this observation.

7. This agreement was shared by Washington and Tokyo, even though Tokyo has denied it. The idea that the FRF is to be used by both the US Marine Corps and Japan's Self-Defense Forces emerged within the Japanese government at least by 2010 (Fujita and Teramoto 2021).

CHAPTER 2

Protest as a Life-Form of the Okinawan Multitude

Internal Workings of the Community of *Nuchi Du Takara*

Whereas chapter 1 explored protest activities in Henoko in the twenty-first century to grasp how the community of *nuchi du takara* has shaped and has been shaped by the negotiations between the constituent power of the Okinawan multitude and the constituted power of Tokyo and Washington, chapter 2 ethnographically examines the same protest activities—in particular, activities in the second period beginning in 2013—in terms of the development of an internal capacity of this community to embrace diverse and often contradictory positions and perspectives regarding the US base issues. In other words, it explains the formation of the community of *nuchi du takara* by the Okinawan multitude from within.

The internal capacity of this community is indicated, first and foremost, by the extraordinary diversity of backgrounds and experiences of those who have participated in the struggles in Henoko. On a certain day in August 2015, for instance, I encountered various individuals at the "triangle" of protest activities—the gate area of Camp Schwab, an ocean area surrounding Camp Schwab, and Tent Village within the community of Henoko—including but not limited to a group of children and their teachers from central Okinawa; a couple and their two-year-old child from central Okinawa; an environmental activist from central Okinawa; a number of residents of Henoko; reporters and members of the camera crew of Okinawan newspapers and TV stations; a TV director from Tokyo and her son, a student in junior high school, together with her two friends who work for an NGO; a reporter and his assistant from a TV station in Tokyo; a comedian from Osaka; the wife of a Japanese actor, the late Sugawara Bunta, who passed away in 2014; a group of college students from Aichi Prefecture; a high school teacher and her partner from Tokyo; members of a teachers' union from Yokohama; members of a medical workers' union from Japan "proper"; a movie director from Tokyo; a Japanese singer whose song was featured in a documentary film on Okinawa; a retired chemistry teacher from Osaka; a poet-activist from Nagano; a university professor from Kyoto; a *furītā* (underemployed person) who was a college dropout; and a Buddhist monk from Kyoto. I also saw an American college student and his friend, a skilled translator, at the gate area on that day.

Indeed, visitors to Henoko are not limited to those coming from within Okinawa and those from wider Japan. Over the years, individuals from Australia (No Base 9/4/2017, #1498b), Canada (No Base 6/27/2015, #1208a), China including Hong Kong (No Base 1/14/2015, #1137b; 1/17/2017, #1416b; 8/12/2017, #1490b), France (No Base 11/30/2017, #1528a), Germany (No Base 1/16/2015, #1138b; 4/29/2017, #1454b), India (No Base 11/7/2014, #1113b; 4/24/2017, #1452a; "Sekai no . . ." 2015), Nepal (No Base 2/13/2018, #1551b), the Philippines (No Base 2/18/2015, #1153b), Rwanda (No Base 11/11/2017, #1521b), South Korea (No Base 1/31/2017, #1422b; 2/13/2017, #1427a; 9/4/2017, #1498b; 1/11/2018, #1541b; 1/27/2018, #1546a; 2/14/2018, #1554b), Switzerland ("Sekai no . . ." 2015), Taiwan (No Base 2/19/2019, #1429a; 4/4/2017, #1445b; 11/14/2017, #1522b; 3/22/2018, #1562b), Thailand (No Base 11/7/2014, #1113b), Uganda (No Base 11/7/2014, #1113a), the United Kingdom (No Base 12/11/2014, #1126b; 9/4/2017, #1498b; "Sekai no . . ." 2015), and the United States (No Base 1/16/2015 #1138b; 3/31/2016, #1314b; 5/9/2017, #1457b; 12/3/2017, #1529b; "Sekai no . . ." 2015), to mention only an incomplete list, have visited Henoko to express and share their sympathy with protesters. Members of the Veterans for Peace and of Greenpeace are regular visitors-cum-participants of the protest in Henoko (e.g., No Base 11/7/2014, #1113b; "Taieki Beigunjinra . . ." 2015).

In chapter 2, I use the radical diversity of protesters as an entry point to a "life-form"—that is, what Ludwig Wittgenstein called "the whole, consisting of language and the actions into which it is woven" ([1953] 2001, 4e)— of the Okinawan multitude. More specifically, first, I examine how the language of resistance and peace has been woven into actions of the Okinawan multitude in the triangle of protest activities from 2013 on, to trace the formation of the community of *nuchi du takara* across the everyday/social and the global/virtual layers. Then I explore a specific mechanism by which the Okinawan multitude has anchored this community in the metaphysical layer, where the life-form of the Okinawan multitude is shaped by collective memory of the Battle of Okinawa and the death of others. Regarding the three ontological layers (or levels)—the metaphysical, the everyday/social, and the global/virtual—of the community of *nuchi du takara*, the reader is advised to consult the introduction to Part I.

1. The Triangle of Protest Activities and the Community of *Nuchi Du Takara*

1.1. In Front of the Gate at Camp Schwab

As noted in chapter 1, twelve hundred protesters participated in a rally in front of the gate of Camp Schwab on November 15, 2015, and successfully blocked the construction-related work of the day. One participant in this rally—Mr. B., who revealed, in an interview with me conducted in August 2016, his identity as a retired math teacher in his sixties from Osaka with Korean background—described what happened on that day in a blog published by the canoe team ("11gatsu15nichi Henoko . . ." 2015).

The gate area was overflowing with protesters. At around 6:45 a.m., according to the blog, leader Yamashiro Hiroji, in his sixties, delivered a succinct yet reassuring speech, in order to provide a sense of direction, comradeship, and unity to participants gathering from across Okinawa and wider Japan, some of whom—particularly first-timers—were excited but also nervous and scared. As Douglas Lummis (2015, 2) notes: "[Yamashiro Hiroji] has earned himself the awkward but appropriate name Mister Before-the-Gate (Misutaa Geetomae). He stays at the gate twenty-four hours a day, sometimes, it is said, for weeks at a time. During the day he often holds the microphone for hours on end, making speeches, haranguing the police and guardsmen, singing, leading the group in the chanting of slogans." In that morning, too, Yamashiro confidently stated, according to the blog: "The basics of our action is nonviolence and disobedience. We will not allow a single one of us to be injured or arrested. But by the same token, we will not tolerate any violence from the riot squad. Let us confront the power in an orderly way but adamantly." After Yamashiro's speech, the blog continues, protesters anxiously waited for the arrival of the riot squad.

Surprisingly, however, the riot police were not able to come, because the large number of protesters occupying the area showed the power of presence of the Okinawan multitude. Afterward, as the blog notes, "We realized that a collective will shared by those of us who sat in had begun to turn into a clearly defined *political will*. We did not feel any worries or fears. I felt as if I was embraced by warm friendship and strong courage. A powerful sense of confidence among us ruled over the area." Songs and dances spread spontaneously among the protesters. As the blog states, "The individual words [of the song] disappeared and the sound of the song as a whole embraced us, unified us, and led us to an explosion of joy. I wondered if this was an artistic experience by itself.... All participants collaborated to shape a specific expression of [a political will]."

The blog entry, and in particular the description of songs and dances, shows that, by weaving the language of resistance into the actions of nonviolence and disobedience, protesters in Henoko expressed their power of life, developing the community of *nuchi du takara* through specific modes of face-to-face cooperation and collaboration at the everyday/social level. More specifically, in spite of the subtle androcentrism of such cooperation and collaboration—represented by the fact that the leader of the rally in Henoko was a male, as was the writer of the blog entry—protesters in Henoko fostered unconditional friendship through Blanchot's "explosive communication," which enabled the rally in Henoko to exhibit the power of presence of the Okinawan multitude against the constituted power of Tokyo and Washington. The significance of this rally was enhanced when participants did not seek to replace the existing structure of power with another; they dispersed, like a gust of wind, after this rally. In so doing, the protesters in Henoko produced a life-form of the Okinawan multitude distinguished by the absence/presence of structural permanency, a life-form based on the ability to constitute, dissolve, and reconstitute itself continuously (cf. Blanchot [1984] 1988, 6).

The construction of the community of *nuchi du takara* at the everyday/social level—characterized by explosive communication generating (androcentric) friendship, integrality against power, and the absence/presence of structural permanency—was observed in front of the gate of Camp Schwab on various occasions. For instance, a public entertainment show was held there on New Year's Eve 2014, in which 180 protesters participated, enjoying the impromptu performances (No Base 1/3/2015, #1134b). Similarly, March 4 is celebrated as the day of *san-shin* (a three-stringed musical instrument) in Okinawa—the pronunciation of "March 4" is *san-shin*—and therefore supporters played the *san-shin* together as an expression of their protest in front of the gate on that day every year from 2015 to at least 2018 (No Base 3/2/2015, #1159a; 3/7/2017, #1435b; 3/8/2018, #1558a). In addition, the participants organized "Henoko University" in August and September 2015, at which experts delivered ten free lectures, often followed by performances and concerts that elated everybody (Kitaueda 2015). On other occasions, including the dates when I visited the area in the summers of 2015, 2016, and 2019, photo exhibitions, dance performances, lectures, concerts, stand-up comedy, and other activities were continually underway. I stood up to deliver a speech of support on these occasions, so as to be part of the community of *nuchi du takara* mediating the constituent power of the Okinawan multitude.

In the process, this community has increased its extraordinary diversity. I have already noted the presence of Others from outside—such as individuals from Japan "proper" and foreigners—who have joined the protest in Henoko. It should be added that the community of *nuchi du takara* has also embraced Others from within, such as Okinawans in business and related circles who used to support the construction of a Futenma Replacement Facility (FRF) in Henoko for economic development. For instance, on April 9, 2015, a group of 130 employees of Kanehide Holdings (including its CEO), a powerful Okinawan company conducting business widely in construction, retail, insurance, and other sectors, came to the gate to show their solidarity with protesters ("Henoko Shinkichi: Kanehide . . ." 2015). They subsequently revisited Henoko at least three times (No Base 4/7/2018, #1567b). Okinawa Ham and Kariyushi Hotel Group, two influential companies in Okinawa, also expressed their support of the protests. The recognition shared among them is that US bases in Okinawa, which neither undertake economic activities nor produce any wealth, depress the full potential of Okinawa's economic and social development. The creation of a world-class resort after the return of Camp Schwab to Okinawa has been suggested by some business leaders in Okinawa (Taira C. 2014). Ashitomi Hiroshi, a long-term leader of the Coalition for Opposing the Offshore Base Construction (COOBC) in greater Nago City, told me in an interview that I conducted in June 2016 that the diversity of participants who acted together to stop construction of the FRF in Henoko "is something that I never expected to happen. In particular, the business circles now have a new way of thinking about the US bases [seeing them as a factor that hinders, rather than promotes, the development of Okinawa]. They think that Henoko's coastal waters are needed for the future of Okinawa."

The collaboration between anti-base and pro-base sectors of Okinawa has not been without problems. In September 2021, for instance, part of this collaboration officially ended. The president of Kanehide Holdings withdrew himself and his companies from the anti-base movement, citing negative impacts on his business, which had been made possible by cooperation with the Japanese state ("Onaga Takeshi-shi . . ." 2021). The withdrawal of Kanehide was part of a broader process whereby protest movements in Okinawa, at least in their current form, may have lost their hegemonic position, as will be elaborated in the conclusion to Part I. Of course, this is not to be confused with the evaporation of the constituent power of the Okinawan multitude itself: as will be explored in other chapters of this book, the power of life of Okinawan social actors has found expression in diverse life-forms, including but not limited to social movements.

1.2. On the Sea

Protest activities on the sea around Camp Schwab reveal no less dramatically the ways in which face-to-face everyday social activities have shaped life-forms of the Okinawan multitude for the production of the community of *nuchi du takara*. Higashionna Takuma—the activist and Nago City assemblyman—originally came up with the idea of using canoes in 2000 after hearing a story about activists in Sasebo, Nagasaki Prefecture, who had used canoes in their protests against the US military presence there.[1] Discovering that canoes do not require boat licenses—that is, the legal status of canoeists on the sea is similar to that of pedestrians on the street—he sought volunteers from wider Japan who would allow him to use their canoes. Eventually, Takuma secured five canoes for the double purpose of performing protest activities and establishing ecotourism as a means of livelihood; in so doing, he made the owners of these canoes happy because (*a*) they could support Okinawa's protest and protect its environment, even from Japan "proper," (*b*) they were relieved of the burden of storing the canoes in their small homes, and (*c*) they were entitled to use their canoes when they visited Okinawa (Higashionna and Gigi 2015).

During the second period of protest in Henoko. beginning in 2013, a canoe team was created in a way that extended Takuma's vision. A parking and storage zone for canoes, powerboats, and other equipment, together with a small prefab structure, was created as an annex of Tent Village, an arrangement made possible by the establishment of nationwide support organizations such as Henoko Kikin (Henoko Fund) (section 2 of this chapter provides further detail). In the process, an increasing number of volunteers came from Okinawa and from wider Japan to join the canoe team. Though most of them had no prior canoeing experience, they were trained under the leadership of experienced instructors, themselves protesters, before paddling out to sea from a Henoko beach called Matsuda nu Hama, adjacent to Camp Schwab (Kanū Chīmu Henoko Burū, n.d.-a, n.d.-b). The membership of the team has been fluid (though often androcentric in leadership); some members actively participated in the protest every day, others contributed on weekends, and still others joined for a limited period of time, from a few days to several years ("Ankēto . . ." n.d.).

In effect, the canoe team as a life-form of the Okinawan multitude has concretized the three features of the community of *nuchi du takara* through face-to-face social actions: integrality against power (exemplified by the disruption of the governmental construction work with canoes), friendship/fraternity founded upon explosive communication (created across Okinawa and Japan "proper" through canoes), and the absence/presence of structural permanency (enabled by the fluidity of membership of the team). Canoe protests share these features with other tactics developed by participants who surfed and windsurfed near Henoko or paddled out with *sabani*, traditional Okinawan boats without engines (No Base 2/18/2015, #1153b; 5/4/2016, #1326b). These tactics, combined with other innovative practices and ideas employed on land, such as having a wedding ceremony in front of the gate of Camp Schwab (No Base 7/7/2015, #1212b), let us catch a glimpse of the constituent power, the power of life, of the Okinawan multitude that has sustained the community of *nuchi du takara* from within the sites of protest in Henoko.

An ethics of togetherness was formulated in the process. For instance, when Okinawan writer and anti-base activist Medoruma Shun was detained by a military policeman and subsequently arrested by the Japan Coast Guard (JCG) for entering the "no admittance" zone in April 2016, as many as 150 participants showed up in front of the JCG building to display solidarity with him and demand his immediate release ("Akutagawashō Sakka . . ." 2016); in March 2019, Naha District Court handed down a decision that the arrest by the JCG was illegal (Itō Kaz. 2019). Along the same lines, to request the acquittal of Yamashiro Hiroji, detained since October 2016 in part because of the concrete blocks piled in front of Camp Schwab (as noted in chapter 1, section 2), as many as 210,000 signatures—obtained from individuals living in Okinawa or wider Japan and fifty other countries—were submitted to Naha District Court in March 2018 (No Base 3/11/2018, #1559b).[2] On a related note, on the day a new powerboat was launched to support the protests on the sea, its owner spoke about the ethics of togetherness permeating the Okinawan multitude and its community of *nuchi du takara*:

> Actions of individuals who went out on the sea, even though they may be weak, create circles [of cooperation] across the nation. Some people take time off from work, others interrupt their schoolwork to save money, and still others are sent from organizations and workplaces. . . . We think about these comrades precisely when we cannot go out to the sea due to prior engagements, physical conditions, and other reasons. . . . Everybody supports and is supported by everybody through an invisible network. . . . Reflecting on countless individuals who have participated in the movement at the gate, on the sea, and on the beach, I cannot help feeling something hot welling up. I know I am not the only one who feels this way. . . . It is these countless individuals who are the owner of this boat. (Medoruma 2015)

1.3. In Tent Village

Meanwhile, before the Covid pandemic, people from all walks of life from across Okinawa, Japan "proper," and beyond, anywhere from twenty to more than one hundred on any given day,[3] came to Tent Village, as it provided daily (typically from 8:00 a.m. to 4:00 p.m.) an intimate space of sharing, communication, and collaboration, a process whereby a specific lifeform was created in a manner that facilitated the construction of the community of *nuchi du takara* for the Okinawan multitude at the level of everyday/social activities. For instance, Tent Village became the site of a miniconcert: a young Japanese with Korean background, after having addressed issues of discrimination against minorities in Japan, sang her songs; eight people (visitors and volunteers) who happened to be in the tent listened, deeply touched (No Base 10/11/2017, #1511b). On another occasion, a woman from central Okinawa discussed her experience of voting in her neighborhood. Many of her neighbors belonged to the conservative pro-base faction, and when an election drew near, she explained, members of this faction often gave voters in the community money to influence their voting. This woman once accepted that money to avoid tension with this faction, but the money drove her to vote for a candidate against her true desire. Since then, she had stopped accepting money from them, which made her feel so free and happy that she came to Tent Village to share this story (No Base 2/9/2015, #1154b). On still another occasion, protesters shared a joke in Tent Village that they would shop at Kanehide Supermarket, buy products of Okinawa Ham, and stay at Kariyushi Hotels because all of those companies supported protests (No Base 8/4/2014, #1072b). Also, on the morning of July 20, 2014, one protester was in tears as he reported, in Tent Village, on what he had seen the night before at the Camp Schwab gate—the first major transport of the materials for the boring survey by the Okinawa Defense Bureau (ODB) (No Base 7/21/2014, #1065b). He felt as if Okinawa had been violated; Tent Village became a site of shared mourning, as it were. On another occasion, Tent Village became an instant classroom for elementary school children, who visited it to conduct their summer projects (No Base 8/8/2016, #1360b). On still another occasion, it became a counseling room: a young Okinawan junior-college student, Ms. M., talked about her uncomfortable experience with her friend. Criticizing Governor Onaga, who had declared a stop to the construction of a new base in Henoko (as noted), this friend had told her, "I want to say to him, 'Mind your own business.'" Ms. M. wanted to say something to her friend in response but did not know how. A senior protester in the tent advised her, "What about asking your friend why she said such a thing?" thereby helping Ms. M. open up opportunities for further conversation and dialogue with her friend about base issues (No Base 12/27/2014, #1132b).

Somewhat magically, Tent Village, perhaps due to its setting that allows visitors to see Henoko's beautiful seas, induces a deep-seated desire for face-to-face communications among visitors, in a manner that questions our ways of life with smartphones and other electronic gadgets that deprive us of opportunities for such communications. I myself have sensed that magic whenever I have visited Tent Village over the years. This description itself is one of the results of such magic.

74   THE COMMUNITY OF *NUCHI DU TUKARA*

Figure 7. Tent Village
Source: Masagata, n.d.

The life-form—the whole consisting of language and the actions into which it is woven—at Tent Village has been coordinated through face-to-face communication by a number of dedicated volunteers who greet visitors, explain to them the situation of Henoko using photos, newspapers, and printed matter hung on the wall of the tent, answer their questions, and receive donations from them for the expansion of the community of *nuchi du takara*. Ms. S. was one of them. As she explained to me in an interview that I conducted in July 2016, Ms. S., in her fifties, moved from a cold, mountainous prefecture in Japan "proper" to Nago City in 2004 simply to seek a warmer place to live; she came to learn about the base issues in Henoko after settling in Nago City. Her sympathies led her to frequent Tent Village, where she eventually began to work, in October 2004, as a part-time assistant for the COOBC. Since then she had edited *No Base*, a two-page newsletter usually published every two to four days (but sometimes every day) to provide descriptions and analyses of base-related issues from the perspective of Tent Village. Her descriptions and analyses were handwritten. Starting in 2004, 1,581 issues of *No Base* were published until May 29, 2018 (the last day of her work) as a form of explosive communication.[4] In addition, in 2012 Ms. S. began the project of tying, with other protesters, red ribbons and banners with written messages onto the fence of Camp Schwab located along Henoko's beach, Matsuda nu Hama, near Tent Village. She named this fence "No Base Gallery," creatively remaking the fence of a military base into a space for public visual art as a form of communication and collaboration, a form of life. The total number of banners provided by supporters reached 2,736 on May 29, 2018, even though each and every one was removed by US service members living on the opposite side of the fence and by others. Referring to these banners, Ms. S. said in my interview, with laughter, "They must be thinking that I am excessively obstinate." Ms. S. also noted that she really harbored no ill feelings toward US service members, as occasional conversations with them across the fence made her realize that they themselves might be victims of the larger system that disposed of their lives by sending them off to battle. I share that view, arguing that US service members are an integral part of the Okinawan multitude and develop specific life-forms for the community of *nuchi du takara*, as will be explored in chapter 7.

1.4. Digital Resistance in Cyberspace and beyond Okinawa

As discussed in the introduction to Part I, the concept of community theorized by Blanchot, in spite of its power to help capture life-forms of the Okinawan multitude at the everyday/social level discussed above, tends to privilege face-to-face communication among those who are copresent in the same time-space, ignoring the possibilities of communication among those separated from each other across time and space. In contrast, social actors in Henoko often "*do* things with words" (Hammersley and Atkinson, 2007, 170) differently, urging me to explore what Jacques Derrida calls "a friendship without presence" ([1994] 2005, 155), a life-form that has been made possible by the development of digital technologies (Derrida [1994] 2005, 222). Indeed, if in the 1990s struggles of the constituent power of Okinawan "citizens" against the constituted power of Washington and Tokyo over the US base issues (e.g., the 1995 rape incident) demonstrated the significance of the analog media for the formation of the community of *nuchi du takara*, as will be further elaborated in chapter 4, the struggles today over the US base issues (e.g., the FRF construction) have revealed the significance of digital media for the expansion of that community into the global/virtual realm.

For instance, crew members on the private patrol boats—chartered by a security company the ODB hired—were instructed to take digital pictures of canoeists participating in protest activities to check whether any of them matched about sixty faces of individuals on a list the company had created as a reference. The information collected was, ultimately, transmitted to the ODB (Abe and Akamine 2016). Similar surveillance mechanisms have been implemented by the ODB in front of the gate at Camp Schwab. The US Marine Corps has also gathered information about protesters ("Okinawa Beigun, Kōgisankasha . . ." 2016). Surveillance activities by digital technologies have been connected to police actions in physical space, such as criminalization of legitimate protest activities, as represented by the arrests of leaders of the movement such as Yamashiro Hiroji and Medoruma Shun, noted above, or the use of razor wire to block the activities of protesters within construction-related sites in Okinawa (Onosaka 2019). In addition, the house of Miyagi Ayano, an Okinawan butterfly researcher, was investigated by the Okinawa Prefectural Police in June 2021 because her action of placing waste left by the US military in the Northern Training Area in northern Okinawa (also the site of her research) in front of the gate of this training area was seen as potentially "criminal" ("Jitakunai . . ." 2021). Furthermore, also in June 2021, Tokyo passed the so-called *tochikiseihōan* (Land Control Act), purporting to control the use of land near facilities deemed important for the security of Japan—such as the bases of the Self-Defense Forces and the US military. While the government justified the introduction of this law as a precaution against the purchase of land near such facilities by foreigners (e.g., Chinese developers), Okinawa viewed it as still another method of surveillance introduced by the government to suppress anti-base movements in Henoko and elsewhere ("Tochikiseihō . . ." 2021).

In response, the Okinawan multitude—in particular, tech-savvy members of the younger generations—has developed skills for digital resistance, in a manner that concretizes explosive communication, integrality against power, and the absence/presence of permanent structure of the community of *nuchi du takara* at the global/virtual level. For instance, aforementioned Ms. S. in Tent Village took pictures of all banners she received from supporters and had these pictures uploaded on her blog, titled *Days at No Base Gallery*,[5] rescuing in cyberspace banners that were removed and destroyed physically. Her blog is indeed part of the explosive communication of the Okinawan multitude, which—like participants in the Arab Spring, the Occupy movement, and the BLM movement—has appropriated advances in information technologies to expand networks of a "friendship without presence" in a manner that enhances the integrality of the multitude against power (Arce and Rice 2019; Castells 2015; Hardt and Negri 2017, esp. part 1).

Accordingly, both on land and on sea, events, activities, and incidents—such as the progress of the boring survey and the use of excessive force against protesters by the riot squad on land and against canoeists by JCG officers on the sea—have been diligently captured by protesters with their cameras and disseminated in real time across Okinawa, Japan "proper," and beyond as pictures and videos and as detailed texts through their blogs, YouTube, Facebook, Twitter (which became X in 2023), and other forms of social media platforms. Examples include Medoruma Shun's *Uminari no Shimakara: Okinawa/Yanbaru yori* (The Island Filled with Sea Roars: From Yanbaru, Okinawa) (n.d.), Kitaueda Takeshi's *Choisan no Okinawa Nikki* (Mr. Choi's Okinawa Diary) (n.d.), the blog (n.d.-a) and Facebook page (n.d.-b) of Kanū Chīmu Henoko Burū (Canoe Team Henoko Blue), a series of blogs titled *Yamahide no Okinawadayori* (Yamahide's Letters from Okinawa) created by Yamamoto Hideo (n.d.-a, n.d.-b, n.d.-c), the blog of COOBC (Herikichi Hantaikyōgikai, n.d.-a, n.d.-b), and a blog titled *Uchinā Kana Nikki* (Okinawan Diary) (n.d.). When I was aboard a powerboat of the anti-base coalition COOBC in June 2016, JCG officers constantly took photos and videos of us all for the record, but we took photos too, an act loathed by these officers, particularly when they took their sunglasses off, as one activist explained to me in an interview in June 2016. In effect, the digital literacy of the Okinawan multitude has helped to express its constituent power and extend networks of the community of *nuchi du takara* beyond the physical sites of struggles—the gate area of Camp Schwab, the ocean area around Camp Schwab, and Tent Village (and other places) in Okinawa—as they "occupy" cyberspace as well. Following the insights of scholars of security studies (Mann, Nolan, and Wellman 2003), I call this ability of the Okinawan multitude "sousveillance"—a term originally created from the French words *sous* (below) and *veiller* (to watch)—to analyze the ways in which watching from below, or inverse surveillance of those in power by the weak, has spread within the new media space and without (Inoue 2019).

By making digital images of struggles in Okinawa available for a large, unspecified number of individuals across Okinawa, Japan "proper," and beyond through the internet, sousveillance directly and indirectly produces social awareness and political actions among these individuals in the ever-expanded community of *nuchi du takara*. Put differently, it helped to generate a new life-form of the Okinawan multitude. A grassroots student group, Students Emergency Action for Liberal Democracy (known primarily by the acronym SEALDs), is a good example of this new life-form as an effect of Okinawan multitude's sousveillance. Members, who in July 2014 had contributed to building nationwide movements against the Abe administration's reinterpretation of Article 9 stipulating unarmed peace (which is discussed in chapter 5, section 5), responded to and supported protests in Henoko in 2015 by skillfully combining political action with elements of youth pop culture (e.g., rap, hip-hop, dance, eccentric fashion) in the physical spaces and cyberspace of Japan (e.g., Toyoshima 2017). In the process, they became a driving force behind the mobilization of a large number of Japanese citizens (7,000 in January 2015, 15,000 in May 2015, 22,000 in September 2015, 28,000 in February 2016, and 18,000 in June 2017) who showed up in front of the Diet Building in Tokyo to oppose the FRF construction in Henoko ("'Henoko Shinkichi Soshi' . . ." 2015; "Kokkai . . ." 2016; No Base 2/25/2016, #1301a; 6/13/2017, #1469a). These demonstrations, in turn, generated new nodal points for sousveillance, stimulating similar demonstrations as a new form of social life in Sapporo, Sendai, Osaka, Kyoto, Kobe, Nagoya, and other major cities in wider Japan. Some members of SEALDs from Okinawa eventually played a leading role in realizing the prefecture-wide referendum held in February 2019 to express the opinion of Okinawans regarding the FRF.

Other examples of sousveillance as a cause or effect of "a friendship without presence" in the community of *nuchi du takara* across Okinawa, Japan "proper," and beyond are as follows:

(a) Film directors produced documentaries such as *Assatsu no Umi: Okinawa, Henoko* (The Ocean Where Freedom Is Suppressed: Henoko, Okinawa) (dirs. Fujimoto Yukihisa and Kageyama Asako, 2014), *Ikusabanu Tudumi* (Bringing the War to an End) (dir. Mikami Chie, 2014), and *Okinawa: Urizun no Ame* (Okinawa: The Rain of Early Summer) (dir. John Junkerman, 2015).

(b) Noted individuals in Japan expressed their opposition to the construction of the FRF in Henoko, including writer Ōe Kenzaburō ("Ōe . . ." 2015), the late musician Sakamoto Ryūichi ("Rola . . ." 2019), rock singer Sano Motoharu ("Sano . . ." 2015), comedy duo Bakushōmondai ("Bakushōmondai . . ." 2009), comedian Muramoto Daisuke ("Amerika yori..." 2017), writer Ochiai Keiko (No Base 3/14/2018, #1560b), critic Kang Sang-jung (No Base 5/28/2015, #1196a), politician Yamamoto Taro ("Kenmin wa..." 2019), anime director Miyazaki Hayao ("Miyazaki..." 2015), pop idol group Seifukukōjō-Īnkai ("Aidoru..." 2015), and the late actor Sugawara Bunta (mentioned above) (Shibasoromon 2019).

(c) Several groups of scholars have issued statements in opposition to the FRF construction in Henoko, including historians in November 2015 (Kano et al. 2015), legal scholars in December 2015 (Kitano 2015), October 2018 ("Henoko Shinkichi: Gyōseihō..." 2018), and January 2019 ("Henoko Shinkichi Kensetsu no..." 2019), social scientists in November 2015 (Peace Studies Association of Japan 2015) and September 2016 (Futenma-Henoko Mondai o Kangaeru Kai 2016), and natural scientists in August 2019 (Chigakudantai Kenkyūkai 2019); from a slightly different perspective, critics, scholars, journalists, and others began an online journal, *OKIRON* (2017) in November 2017 to create a critical space for discussion about Okinawa across Japan.

(d) Residents in prefectures of Japan that provide gravel for the land reclamation work in Henoko have jointly voiced their opposition since 2015 (Henoko Dosha Hanshutsu Hantai Zenkoku Renraku Kyogikai 2019).

(e) A right-wing nationalist group, Issuikai, and a right-wing female activist, Nakamura Midori, both of whom have become well known through the Japanese digital media, have declared their support for the protests in Henoko ("Aikokusha..." 2016; Yasuda 2018).

(f) Tsūhan Seikatsu, a company that provides mail-order and online shopping services, has since November 2016 openly supported Okinawa's anti-base protest despite receiving threats from customers saying, "We will not buy your products" ("'Sayokuzasshi'..." 2016).

Finally, sousveillance from Okinawa has multiplied the community of *nuchi du takara* in a broader planetary time-space of the Asia-Pacific region and beyond in a way that allows the Okinawan multitude to reimagine its network itself as a method of emancipation. One important example is a feminist global network of anti-base movements created among scholars and activists in Okinawa, South Korea, the Philippines, Guam, Hawaii,

Vieques, and other countries and areas that host the US military. Originating in part in the Okinawan women's protest against the rape of an Okinawan schoolgirl by three US servicemen in 1995, this network has evolved to hold many international conferences, some of the most recent ones having been held in Okinawa in 2019 and on the web in 2021 (Akibayashi 2017; Okinawa "Kichi/Guntai o Yurusanai Kōdōsuru Onnatachi no Kai" 2021). Overlapping this network are grassroots intellectual-political-cultural exchanges between Okinawa and South Korea, which, after having developed from the 1980s up until the early twenty-first century through the efforts of the late Okinawan intellectual Arasaki Moriteru and others (Arasaki M. 2014; Takahashi S. 2017), have been reinforced during the second period of struggles in Henoko since 2013 through varied discourses and practices. In January 2018, for instance, the COOBC in Nago received a peace and justice award from a South Korean Christian organization ("Herikichi Hantaikyō . . ." 2017).

The foreign media, such as Al Jazeera (No Base 4/28/2015, #1184a), the BBC ("Henoko o . . ." 2005), ARD (a consortium of public broadcasters in Germany) (No Base 10/23/2014, #1107a), ARTE (a Franco-German free-to-air television network) (No Base 7/4/2015, #1211b), Korean Broadcasting System ("Kyō no Henoko . . ." 2015); *Le Figaro* (No Base 11/21/2017, #1525b), New China News Agency (No Base 5/16/2015, #1191b), *New York Times* (No Base 6/1/2016, #1335b), PBS ("On Okinawa . . ." 2017), Radio France (No Base 9/30/2017, #1507a), Reuters (No Base 2/26/2016, #1301a), and Reporters without Borders ("Kisha Kōsoku . . ." 2016), among others, came to Henoko and reported situations back to their respective countries/regions/continents and beyond in a way that reinforced the community of *nuchi du takara* through the network of global sousveillance. In addition, movie director William Oliver Stone, linguist Noam Chomsky, and other noted figures mostly living outside Japan—a total of twenty-nine individuals in January 2014 ("Okinawa/Henoko . . ." 2014) and 109 individuals in August 2015 ("Ōbeishikisha . . ." 2015)—issued a statement of opposition to the construction of a new base in Henoko. Further, on December 8, 2018, when the ODB was prepared to deposit soil in the reclamation area, Robert Kajiwara, a fourth-generation Okinawan living in Hawaii who is a singer-songwriter and activist, initiated a movement to submit signatures to an online petition system, We the People, established by the White House, in order to halt the construction of the FRF in Henoko. Within two weeks the number of signatures exceeded 100,000, the threshold that requires the

White House to respond. The total number of signatures reached 203,800 in a month, "making it the fifth most signed petition on the 'We the People' site" (Miyagi and Abe 2019).

These digital networks concretize the potentiality of "a friendship without presence" in the community of *nuchi du takara* at the global/virtual level by way of promoting sousveillance.

2. The Mechanism for Incorporating Others into the Community of *Nuchi Du Takara*

The above descriptions unveil the presence of two "Others" who, by directly and indirectly joining the protests in Henoko, have contributed to the formation of the community *nuchi du takara* by the Okinawan multitude. The first is non-Okinawans, particularly those from Japan "proper," who have committed themselves to the protest for a prolonged length of time. Indeed, in addition to Mr. M., Mr. I., Mr. Kitaueda, Mr. T., Mr. B., and Ms. S., mentioned in my discussion thus far, other long-term participants from Japan "proper" in the protest include a young truck driver sent by a labor union who joined the canoe team from 2015 to 2016 (Kenheiwa Sentā 2015); a Buddhist monk in his thirties who once led the canoe team (MMproton 2015); a photographer from Tokyo in his fifties volunteering in Tent Village; a diving instructor and social worker in her thirties who pilots a powerboat; another social worker in her thirties on the canoe team; a yoga instructor in her fifties on the canoe team; retired social studies and math teachers in their sixties, both on the canoe team; an activist in his forties with disabilities who joined the movement by putting his disability pension into it; a documentary film director in his seventies running a cram school in Nago; and a high school dropout in his twenties who became an active member of the movement, to mention only a sampling (see also MMproton 2014; ages of informants in this passage are as of the summer of 2016). The blog of Henoko Blue (the canoe team) (Kanū Chīmu Henoko Burū 2018) confirmed the contribution of participants from Japan "proper" to sustaining the protest; one-half (twenty-nine) of the canoeists who participated in the protest activities on April 25, 2018, were from Okinawa, and the other half came from Japan "proper" (see also Kudō and Shimizu 2015, No Base 11/20/2014, #1118a).

The second Other is a group of Okinawans in business and related circles who used to support the construction of a new military facility in Henoko but now oppose it. The boundaries of this group are also extensive, and it is not limited to the employees of Kanehide Holdings, Kariyushi Hotels, and Okinawa Ham—even as some of them later withdrew from the movement, as explained above. For instance, in August 2015, I met Mr. O., in his fifties, in Takae, north of Henoko, where Tokyo pushed through the construction work for helipads in July 2016, an issue to be discussed in chapter 6. He used to be employed by a company in Nago that was mobilized for base construction in the late 1990s. He told me that when he had a drink with his colleagues, the most common topic of conversation was how much they detested what they had to do—pressing friends and acquaintances to vote for approval of the base in the 1997 Nago City referendum by saying that the base would make Nago affluent. When the majority of Nago residents collectively expressed their "no" to the base in the referendum, Mr. O. was happy even though he was not allowed to express his happiness. Now that he runs his own construction company, Mr. O. is dedicated to stopping the construction of the FRF in Henoko. Higashionna Takuma, the activist and Nago City assembly member mentioned earlier, was once in a similar position. An episode at Tent Village provides another example; a Henoko fisher who had been hired by the ODB to police the anti-base protest with his boat came to Tent Village to support the protest (No Base 1/31/2018, #1547b).

Often, even some of the openly pro-base residents of Henoko do not hide their frustration at the ways in which Tokyo has treated them, thereby helping the community of *nuchi du takara* engage ever more diverse Okinawan subjects and make the voice of resistance louder. For instance, an owner of a local grocery store in Henoko said on a TV program, "Until recently, it was the Okinawa Defense Bureau and the government who asked for our cooperation. But after the former governor [Nakaima] gave a land reclamation permit [in December 2013, as noted] the tables have been turned. When we bring a list of requests to them, it looks as if we were asking favors of them, even though they get us into trouble. They do not even try to gain our understanding, let alone having any dialogue with us. We are really mortified because they began the construction work [i.e., the boring survey] under such circumstances" (Ryukyu Asahi Hōsō 2014b, 3:06–3:51). To the comment made by Chief Cabinet Secretary Suga Yoshihide in December 2015 that local communities to be affected by the FRF construction—including Henoko—have conditionally approved the plan to build the base, leaders of these communities publicly complained by saying that they remain opposed to the plan, adding that they are simply willing to receive monetary compensation for the damage the government will cause ("Suga-shi Hatsugen..." 2015).

The presence of varied Others—individuals from Japan "proper" and (formerly or presently) pro-base Okinawans who oppose or question the FRF construction, in particular—in the community of *nuchi du takara* requires explanation, as this reveals something in Okinawa that cannot be captured by an anti-base/pro-base (or progressive/conservative, good/bad) dichotomy, as noted in the introduction to this book. When I studied the protest activities in Henoko and Nago City back in 1997–1998, this "something" was existent—as exemplified by the comment of a pro-base Henoko male resident who stated, "I don't want my daughter to marry an American" (see the introduction to this book)—but not clearly observable. For one thing, the power of life of Okinawan "citizens" generated a deep divide between the anti-base and pro-base residents to the point where there was no room for collaboration across it in the 1990s (Inoue 2007, chaps. 4–7). For another, the protest movement against the FRF—that is, the power of life of Okinawan "citizens" then—extended the collective anger at the 1995 rape incident that had occurred in the fiftieth year after of the end of the Battle of Okinawa, a process that encouraged the formation of Okinawan identity that tended to categorically exclude the "Japanese," whom Okinawans then—and some Okinawans now—often designated, with a subtle sense of aversion, with vocabulary such as *naichā*, *yamatonchu*, and *yamato no ningen*.

I suggest that the presence of these Others in the community of *nuchi du takara* in the twenty-first century is the consequence of a double-sided mechanism. More specifically, on the one hand, the general decline of the pro-base logic in Okinawa has blurred the pro-base/anti-base division in Okinawa; on the other hand, this process has encouraged the participation of an increasingly large number of individuals from Japan "proper" in anti-base protests in Okinawa, against the background of the formation of shared cultural sensibilities between Okinawa and Japan "proper." I will explain this mechanism below.

2.1. The Decline of the Pro-base Logic and the Rise of the Unity of Okinawa against Japan

The announcement made by Tokyo and Washington in late 1996—that they would build the FRF in Henoko—generated an island-wide protest, which threw into relief collective memory concerning the Battle of Okinawa through universalist citizenry discourses and actions for establishing peace, problematizing gender violence, and promoting environmental protection. However, it is also true that such universalist discourses and actions were countered by a local cultural logic and sentiment of the business and conservative political circles that, whether reluctantly or enthusiastically, advocated the acceptance of the FRF construction in exchange for the jobs it would generate (Inoue 2007, chaps. 4 and 7). In particular, against the background of Henoko's history of "international goodwill" (*kokusai shinzen*) about Camp Schwab since the late 1950s—that is, it allowed a vast plot of its land to be taken by the US military for the construction of Camp Schwab in exchange of economic development of the community (Inoue 2007, 98–105; see also Part II of this book for details)—leaders of Henoko at that time showed their willingness to accept the proposal to construct the FRF, while criticizing the activities of Inochi o Mamoru Kai (Society for the Protection of Life), a group of local residents who opposed the construction, as being influenced or hijacked by "outsiders" (*yosomono*), such as progressive politicians and researchers, labor unionists, student activists, environmentalists, extremists, and communists from Okinawa outside Henoko and from Japan "proper" and elsewhere. As one of such "outsiders," I was asked, or really accused, by some pro-base Henoko residents back in 1997: "Whose lives are more important!? We humans' or the dugongs'!?" As noted in chapter 1 and elaborated further below, the dugong, an endangered marine mammal, became in the late 1990s a key symbol of Okinawa's anti-base movement, to which this question (or really accusation) expressed an antipathy by highlighting the fact that "we" would lose a way to make a living without the construction work the FRF project would generate. In other words, these Henoko residents expressed the notion of *nuchi du takara* ("life is the ultimate treasure") from a pro-base perspective that viewed the FRF construction as an economic opportunity, a perspective that was excluded from the anti-base community of *nuchi du takara* Okinawan "citizens" in the late 1990s constructed against Tokyo and Washington.

Since the early twenty-first century, however, Okinawa has witnessed an overall decline of the pro-base logic and sentiment, as the Okinawan critic Arasaki Moriteru noted (2014, 169)—even though the determination of Washington and Tokyo to construct the FRF at any cost, when combined with the Covid-19 crisis in Okinawa, has often drained the oppositional political energy of Okinawa in general and of Nago in particular. I will elaborate on how this sapping of oppositional energy has diversified Okinawa's constituent power into other life-forms beyond anti-base movements in the conclusion to Part I. Here I wish to focus on the overall decline of the pro-base logic and sentiment in the twenty-first century, which has occurred for a number of reasons.

The first reason concerns the Okinawan economy; as stated above, there is a growing consensus in Okinawa that US bases in Okinawa, which neither conduct economic activities nor produce any wealth, depress the full potential of Okinawa's economic and social development. The background against which such a consensus has emerged is that even though indicators of Okinawa's economic status (e.g., poverty rate, average per capita income) have continued to lag behind those of Japan "proper," Okinawa has gained economic autonomy and confidence vis-à-vis the US military in the twenty-first century by developing tourism and related industries. Indeed, while the US bases accounted for 34.4% of Okinawa's total income in 1965, 15.5% in 1972, and just about 5% since the mid-1990s (Shigemori 2000, 90; Shimada 2011), the annual number of tourists to Okinawa has increased from 440,000 in 1972, to 3 million in 1992, 6 million in 2008, and 10 million (larger than the number of annual tourists to Hawaii) in 2019, including nearly three million international tourists from mainland China (including Hong Kong), Taiwan, South Korea, and other places, who use a growing number of airlines and cruise lines originating in these increasingly affluent countries (Ishikawa and Chinen 2022) and stay in luxurious hotels in Okinawa—including the Ritz-Carlton (opened in 2012), Hilton (opened in 2014), and Hyatt (opened in 2018). Due to the Covid-19 pandemic, the Okinawan tourist industry—and thus the Okinawan economy at large—suffered a severe downturn, but it has also seen a sign of recovery since 2022 (Kuniyoshi T. 2023). In effect, Okinawans feel today that they can make do without US bases.

Meanwhile, problems derived from the US military presence in Okinawa (e.g., the ear-splitting noise, land and ocean pollution, crimes and accidents attributable to US service personnel) have continued to occur, in a way that has made the traditional pro-base logic—of overcoming Okinawa's economic situation by relying on income from the US military—increasingly unconvincing. Also, examples of global environmental deterioration—for example, hotter summers, continuing rise of ocean temperatures, and increasingly strong typhoons—have directly impacted Okinawa's everyday life to such an extent that it sounds anachronistic to criticize the anti-base movement by asking, for instance, which is more important, humans or dugongs. In light of the notion of *nuchi du takara*, many Okinawans today—the Okinawan multitude—would argue that dugongs are just as important as humans. These reasons have made the traditional pro-base argument less viable in the eyes of contemporary Okinawans. It is not surprising that, until the late 2010s, poll results consistently showed that 70% to 80% of Okinawans opposed the current FRF plan ("Osupurei 'Kiken' . . ." 2017, Yoshioka 2021, 87) even though the Covid-19 pandemic has complicated their collective psyche, as I will explain in the conclusion to Part I.

It is against the background of the general decline of the pro-base logic that a former Okinawa governor advocated "identity rather than ideology." Onaga Takeshi, sixty-four years of age when he became Okinawa governor in December 2014, was an influential conservative politician born in Okinawa under US rule who had once played a leadership role in the Okinawa chapter of the Liberal Democratic Party to *promote* the construction of the FRF in Henoko by citing the economic benefits it would bring. Having served as Naha City assemblyman (two terms, 1985–1992), Okinawa prefectural assemblyman (two terms, 1992–2000), and mayor of Naha City, the capital of Okinawa (four terms, 2000–2014) before running for Okinawa governor, however, his political trajectory was characterized not by a rigid pro-base position but by flexible conservatism, a profile meant to at once develop Okinawa economically and control US base problems politically, with the help of the Japanese government on both (Matsubara 2016, 113–121).

Meanwhile, in January 2013, Onaga had a shocking encounter with the new Japanese nationalism that showed that his flexible conservatism would no longer work in the twenty-first century. Specifically, when Okinawan leaders from both conservative and progressive sectors—including Onaga, then mayor of Naha City—came to downtown Tokyo for a rally to express their opposition to the deployment of V-22 Ospreys in Okinawa (based on potential safety and noise problems of this aircraft),[6] they heard bystanders yelling at them: "Traitors!"—aiming to remove the bases in Okinawa to make Japan vulnerable to outside threats such as China. "You are selling the nation!" "Spies of China!" Some even screamed, "Get out of Japan!" (Yasuda 2016). This encounter with wider Japan's hate speech against Okinawa, combined with Onaga's experience with the Abe cabinet, which would never listen to the voices of Okinawa, became a key prompt for Onaga to drop flexible conservatism and to move to unify Okinawa against Tokyo to stop the FRF (Matsunaga 2016, 145–150).

On December 2, 2015, Governor Onaga made a court appearance—in reference to his legal decision to revoke the land reclamation permit that the previous governor had issued back in December 2013 (noted in chapter 1)—in order to state, "My view is that in Okinawa, conservatives are not the enemy of progressives and progressives are not the enemy of conservatives either. Our enemy is to be found somewhere else" (Onaga 2015b). This enemy, as I see it, is the Japanese government as an integral part of Empire, to be discussed in Part III. Meanwhile, Onaga added that in order to confront this enemy, Okinawa must promote "identity rather than [pro-base/anti-base] ideology" (Onaga 2015b; 2015c, chap. 4) by overcoming its internal divisions and solidifying its unity. In so saying, he appealed, indirectly if not directly, to the notion of *nuchi du takara* as a key method for achieving Okinawan "identity." His localist vision was strongly supported by Okinawans, and he was deeply admired as governor from 2014 to 2018. When he passed away due to cancer in August 2018 at the age of sixty-seven—a death that might have been caused indirectly by the arduous work of confronting Tokyo—70,000 Okinawans participated in a memorial to commemorate Onaga's work and life ("Shinkichi Hantai . . ." 2018).

2.2. The Increasing Participation of Japanese in the Protest in Henoko and Its Mechanism

The general decline of the traditional pro-base logic in Okinawa has interacted with two social changes, one occurring in Henoko and the other happening in wider Japan, in a manner that has enabled the Okinawa multitude to embrace but move beyond Onaga's localist vision and to incorporate non-Okinawans into the community of *nuchi du takara*.

Let me explain the social change in Henoko first. Back in 1997, Inochi o Mamoru Kai, a grassroots organization created to oppose the FRF, built the "struggle hut" (*tōsōgoya*) in front of Henoko's fishing port, in the heart of the Henoko district. The struggle hut then became a key contact zone between Henoko's anti-base residents, mostly the elderly born before the Battle of Okinawa, on the one hand, and supporters of their struggles from across Okinawa, wider Japan, and beyond, on the other (Inoue 2007, 137–142). However, after a candidate opposing the FRF in Henoko was defeated in the mayoral election of Nago City in February 1998, members of Inochi o Mamoru Kai were weakened by criticisms (that they were influenced by *yosomono*, or "outsiders," as noted above) coming from within their own neighborhood, such as relatives and friends, as well as bosses of Henoko, to the point that they adopted a policy to shut down contacts with outside supporters. Consequently, the atmosphere of the struggle hut became unfriendly, if not hostile, to outside supporters (Inoue 2007, 187–193). After the death of leader Kinjō Yūji—who actually continued to welcome and engage with all the visitors, against the insular policy—in May 2007, Inochi o Mamoru Kai became increasingly disorganized and, together with the struggle hut, was dismantled in 2013.

In contrast, Tent Village, created in 2004 in Henoko during the first period of protest (noted in chapter 1), was located close to but remained separate from the original struggle hut, which has made it possible for the anti-base movement in Henoko to restore the link to the broader outside world. To be sure, the pro-base position of Henoko leadership has remained unchanged; today, more than 50% of Henoko residents are said to support the current FRF plan ("Kaiketsusaku . . ." 2016), which reveals the idiosyncrasy of the Henoko district, as it intends to continue to depend on US-base-related income to survive economically ("Shuwābu Ichibu . . ." 2015). However, unlike in Henoko in the late 1990s, "outsiders" can join protest activities with ease because such activities are conducted today not around the struggle hut within Henoko but at the Camp Schwab gate and the ocean near Camp Schwab, a few kilometers away from the heart of the Henoko district. As a result, the influence of pro-base Henoko leadership (or, the influence of the pro-base Henoko district) upon the anti-base movement (or, upon activities at the gate and the ocean near Camp Schwab) is limited, a situation that can be seen as a symbolic (or, spatial) expression of the temporal process of the decline of the pro-base logic and sentiment in Okinawa at large. Meanwhile, by anchoring globalized protest activities at the gate and the ocean, Tent Village has expressed the presence of a larger community of *nuchi du takara*, an open, inclusive, and nonviolent realm of solidarity of the Okinawan multitude, while also becoming a reminder of local initiatives as the origin of Okinawa's ongoing anti-base struggles because of its location, that is, inside Henoko.

The incorporation of non-Okinawans into Okinawa's protest occurs when local social change in Henoko (i.e., restoration of the link to the broader world) has combined with a national social change, that is, the formation of the underclass, the precariat, in Japan, together with the development of a language of environmentalism—or translation of the local notion of *nuchi du takara* into a universal premise—shared between Okinawa and Japan "proper" (and beyond), as explained below.

Against the background of the global penetration of neoliberalism characterized by privatization, deregulation, free markets, and a lifting of governmental protection for workers (Harvey 2005), the cabinet of Koizumi Jun'ichirō (1942–present; in office 2001–2006) responded to Washington's demand (e.g., Armitage et al. 2000) for neoliberalist reform by privatizing postal services and the public highway corporation, reforming the public pension system and public health care system, and reorganizing governmental financial agencies. In the process, established labor policies and practices in Japan—including the lifelong employment system and labor-management cooperation originated prewar Japan (Noguchi 2015)—have become more or less a thing of the past.

Consequently, the middle class has dramatically thinned (Komamura 2015), a process accompanied by the spread of the "personal responsibility" narrative, which has been utilized to justify both the formation of a select class that enjoys unprecedented wealth—with *tawā manshon* (expensive, high-rise condominiums) in downtown Tokyo as their gated community and status symbol—and the appearance of large numbers of people belonging to the "underclass" (Hashimoto 2018) or "precariat," deprived of stability or guarantee of safety in work and life (Allison 2013; Amamiya and Kayano 2008; Standing 2011).[7] In particular, the latter consists of an increasing number of Japanese who have become contingent workers, who do part-time, temporary, contract, freelance, gig, and other kinds of work. Such workers were an exception in the past but are a part of the norm now. They accounted for approximately 15% of the entire labor force in 1984, but 20% in 1994, 25% in 1999, 31% in 2004, 34% in 2009, 37% in 2014, 38% in 2019, and 37% in 2022 (Kōsei-Rōdōshō, n.d., 1). Understandably, one of the earnest dreams of the Japanese youth of today is thus to find a so-called full-time job. However, the life of full-time workers is often hellish, because they are pressured to overwork under the tacit threat of being fired if they do not. An increasing number of workers in present-day Japan thus end up becoming mentally ill and in some cases kill themselves due to work-induced depression and stress—Japan's per capita suicide rate is the highest among G7 nations (Chiba 2016; Okazaki and Sakaguchi 2020). Women and children are particularly vulnerable. Women are exploited as cheap laborers without full-time status—70% of non-full-time workers in Japan are women (Esashi and Miyashita 2015)—while also being expected, implicitly or explicitly, to play the role of "good wife, wise mother" in a continually male-centered society. In 2018, one of seven children in Japan lived in poverty (Tanaka and Itō 2020). The Covid-19 pandemic has made the situation of women and children of the underclass even more difficult (Takahashi M. 2020).

In effect, under the regime of neoliberalism, biopolitical oppression of everyday life has been reinforced. Dictated by the technology of evaluation and assessment, everyone—even an individual with a full-time job—has been placed in perpetual competition against everyone. No one is safe. An irony is that biopolitical control of everyday life, having functioned as the foundation of prosperity for postwar Japan and its middle-class consumer lifestyle until the 1990s or so, has been intensified to such an extent that it no longer provides the prosperity that it is supposed to generate for the majority of the populace. Biopolitical control and oppression of life in Japan is intensified even as (or perhaps precisely because) Japan becomes increasingly poor.

As this situation—no job is safe or secure in ever-declining Japan—has been associated with the rise of China, a significant portion of the constituent power of the precarious Japanese has been ideologically absorbed in a new form of nationalism (as will be discussed in chapter 6); the other portion, however, seems to have managed to develop critical consciousness about how society is organized. Protesters in Henoko coming from wider Japan have shared this critical consciousness.

For instance, Ms. Y., a former civil servant from Yokohama in her fifties, explained to me in an interview that I conducted in Henoko in June 2016 that she quit her job as a civil servant after she witnessed how workers, herself included, were "dehumanized" (*ningensei ga ushinawareteiku*) and "worn out" (*hiheishiteiru*) due to the increase of workloads combined with personnel reductions—that is, due to the penetration of the neoliberal ideology of "efficiency" that systemically denies and manipulates life, to use more theoretical terms. In Okinawa, she joined the canoe team while becoming a yoga instructor to restore her humanity. Even though her salary was 10% of what she used to earn in Yokohama, she had "no regrets" (*kōkai wa nai*) because of an invaluable human network she was able to create by participating in the protest, an act of affirming *nuchi du takara*. The experience of Ms. Y. is not an isolated example. At the beginning of this section (i.e., section 2), I cited a sample of those from Japan "proper" who have participated in protests in Henoko; they represent singularities with irreducible backgrounds, seeking meanings and purposes in life that they, as the "precariat," find it increasingly difficult to experience in the empty time-space of Japan, regulated by the logic and spirit of capital and technology, of neoliberal efficiency. Still another participant from Japan "proper," a retired chemistry teacher in his sixties, whom I met in June 2016 in Henoko, summarized the sentiment of Japanese participants by noting that he had not felt so alive in years as he did when he confronted the police together with anonymous comrades.

2.3. The Language of Environmentalism and the Fusion of the Okinawa/Japan "Proper" Interface

In effect, participants from within Okinawa and those from elsewhere in Japan have generated a cultural interface due to the decline of the pro-base influence in Henoko and elsewhere in Okinawa, on the one hand, and the formation of the underclass across Japan, on the other. This interface has been solidified by, among other things, shared sensibilities about the environment, broadly defined. In response to various developmental projects, such as the construction of a crude-oil staging terminal in Kin Bay in northern Okinawa in the 1970s and the construction of a new airport on the pristine coral reef of Ishigaki Island (more than 400 km away from the main island of Okinawa) in the 1980s, global discourses on environmental conservation were powerfully mobilized in oppositional movements in Okinawa, a process that assisted the interactions between intellectuals and activists from Okinawa such as Arasaki Moriteru and those from Japan "proper" such as Ui Jun (Arasaki et al. [1989] 2016; Asato 2009). Emerging from the collaboration between Okinawa and Japan "proper" in the 1970s–1980s is what Manuel Castells called "*the creation of a new identity, a biological identity, a culture of the human species as a component of nature*" (1997, 126)—in other words, a culture of *nuchi du takara*. In the late 1990s, when anti-base protests emerged in Henoko, a merging of singularities in Okinawa and those from Japan "proper" occurred through an expansion of this culture founded upon the unwavering principle of life. The dugongs played a crucial role in this process.

For instance, I witnessed a gigantic billboard with a cartoon figure of a dugong in front of the struggle hut in Henoko in 1997–1998, which served as a background against which supporters from elsewhere in Japan took pictures as a memory of their visit to Henoko. Dugong T-shirts were also created by Inochi o Mamoru Kai and sold to these supporters. In the process, discourses as well as actions for protecting the dugong were generated by local organizations such as Okinawa Kankyō Nettowāku (Okinawa Environmental Network, established in 1997) ("Okinawa no Kankyō..." 2018) and Jyugon Hogo Kikin (Dugong Protection Fund, established in 1999) (Jyugon Hogo Kikin, n.d.), as well as by national/international organizations such as the World Wildlife Fund–Japan (involved in Henoko issues since 1997) (Inoue 2007, 177; World Wildlife Fund–Japan, n.d.), the International Union for Conservation of Nature (involved in Henoko issues since 2000) (Nihonshizenhogo Kyōkai 2001, 2004), and other organizations directly and indirectly linked with the protest in Henoko. In the process, the biological identity—the culture of *nuchi du takara*—became an integral part of Okinawan citizenship in the 1990s.

In the twenty-first century, the culture of *nuchi du takara* has continuously been reinforced across Okinawa and wider Japan in a manner that helps constitute a life-form of the Okinawan multitude, a process intertwined by the efforts of organizations such as Henoko Kikin (Henoko Fund), created in April 2015 jointly by economic and cultural leaders of Okinawa (including the president of Kanehide Holdings) to support the protest in Henoko. In May 2015, Miyazaki Hayao of Studio Ghibli, who directed globally acclaimed films such as *My Neighbor Totoro* (1988), *The Princess Mononoke* (1997), and *Spirited Away* (2001), joined the Henoko Fund as a codirector. The contributions to the fund have increased steadily. As of April 2015, 4,577 donors had contributed a total of 119,150,698 yen (approximately $1 million in 2015 dollars); as of November 30, 2020, the contributions made by 120,015 donors had reached 745,829,327 yen (approximately $7 million in 2020 dollars); 70% of contributions come from Japan "proper" (Henoko Kikin, n.d.; "Henoko Kikin..." 2015). Donations have been used for publishing protest advertisements in newspapers and magazines within Japan and without, as well as for providing items such as boats, canoes, wet suits, and tents in order to support protests on the sea and on land.

Of course, it is possible to argue that these contributions, as a form of charity, represent nothing other than an extension of the old "Orientalism" (Said 1978)—a structure of discourses and actions that perpetuates the domination of wider Japan over Okinawa by allowing the former to hijack and distort cultural sensibilities (such as *nuchi du takara*) of the latter for the promotion of its own interests. Indeed, a touristic trend in wider Japan from the 1990s to constitute Okinawa as the Other endowed with culture that Japan lacked—mythic spirituality, blue sky and ocean, exotic foods, and distinctive music (see chapter 4)—may have now simply merged into the environmental discourses to praise and consume Okinawa as the Other endowed with nature that Japan lacks. My own take, however, is that by rearticulating this old Orientalism, singularities in Okinawa and wider Japan (and often others from abroad) have come to share a similar life-form in the planetary time-space, as exemplified by the experience of one participant from Japan "proper," a diving instructor and social worker in her thirties, who noted in an interview that I conducted in June 2016 that she had never experienced being differentiated or discriminated against as *yamato no ningen* (an individual from elsewhere in Japan) in Okinawa. In other words, situated directly or indirectly in the beauty of Henoko's emerald-green sea, known as a pristine spot of biodiversity where dugongs, sea turtles, corals, common terns, and other creatures—more than fifty-eight hundred species—live or migrate, participants in and supporters of Henoko's protest, in spite of their differences, have come to produce a shared environmental consciousness—life is the ultimate treasure—as an expression of their constituent power against the planned construction of a new military facility. After all, singularities from Okinawa and wider Japan, networked as the Okinawan multitude deprived of stability or a guarantee of safety in work and life, are included or contained in the system of constituted power but excluded from protection—as in "bare life," defined by Giorgio Agamben as "something that is included [in the system] solely through an exclusion" (1998, 11)—for broad historical reasons that I will trace in Part III.

3. The Depth of the Community of *Nuchi Du Takara* and the Transformation of Historical Experiences of the Okinawan Multitude through Postmemory

Intertwined with the formation of the interface across Okinawa and Japan "proper" outlined above is the historical actuality in Okinawa characterized by the declining population of those who experienced the Battle of Okinawa (1945) or the US rule of Okinawa (1945–1972), a process that has lowered the hurdle of establishing friendship between Okinawa (which had experienced them) and Japan "proper" (which did not). In 2010 (taken as a reference point) the third generation—born after reversion and then under thirty-eight years old—constituted a primary segment (47%) of the prefecture's population (which totaled approximately 1.38 million) and the first generation (sixty-five years old or older, who experienced the Battle of Okinawa and the US rule of Okinawa) and the second generation (thirty-eight to sixty-four years old, who experienced the US rule of Okinawa but not the war) accounted for 17% and 36% of the population, respectively (e-Stat 2010).

However, this does not mean that collective memory of the war and alien rule has simply evaporated. I suggest that postmemory—defined as "a *structure* of inter- and trans-generational transmission of traumatic knowledge and experience" (Hirsch 2008, 106)—helps the Okinawan multitude "vertically" rearticulate and marshal Okinawa's historical experiences, not only as a way to remember the past but also as a method for presaging and reimagining the future at the depth of the community of *nuchi du takara*. If my analysis thus far helps us grasp the ways in which the Okinawan multitude "horizontally" expands its constituent power by embracing Others for the construction of this community, my experiences during fieldwork in September 1997 and in August 2015, when combined with a number of voices of the Okinawan multitude from diverse generations, shed some light on the specificity—historical depth—of the constituent power that permeates this community, the depth defined by the death of the others.

In September 1997, I met a ghost, or what I believe is a ghost, a spirit of a dead person, perhaps a woman, in Henoko. After assisting with anti-base activities of Inochi o Mamoru Kai, I was sleeping alone in the struggle hut. It was warm in the pitch-dark room without air conditioning. As the night went on, I felt something heavy placed on me. The more I struggled to move, the heavier the pressure became, to the point that I could no longer move any part of my body, even my eyelids. I had a high-pitched noise in my ears that muffled the sounds of ocean waves enveloping the struggle hut. I had difficulty breathing and was scared. Earlier, in an attempt to initiate this young Japanese doctoral student from the United States into the Henoko community, some residents talked to me, half-jokingly and half-seriously, about a woman with troubles in love who, a long time ago, had thrown herself into the sea in front of where I slept. I regretted that I had laughed at the story. Though the experience probably lasted only a few minutes, it felt as if the heaviness on my body would never end. When it eventually disappeared, I turned on the miniature light bulb in the room and fell into sleep even as I remained fearful of the ghost's return. The sun was bright the next morning when I woke up. Villagers came to the struggle hut for the day's activities and asked if I had slept well. I lied by saying yes.

I never slept in the struggle hut after this experience. I am aware that what I experienced is scientifically explainable as sleep paralysis, but I believe that was a ghost, the spirit of the woman who taught me, the researcher from outside, that death should never be taken lightly in Okinawa. Together with crucial significance of the spirit in Okinawan social life as explicated by Matthew Allen (2002, chaps. 5 and 6; 2017), the fact that multiple friends and informants of mine in Okinawa are able to see and communicate with ghosts and spirits, to straddle between a secular time-space of the living and a sacred, planetary time-space of the dead, confirms my belief. Kinjō Hatsuko is one of them.

In August 2015, I spent substantial time with Hatsuko, a resident of Henoko in her seventies; she was the widow of Kinjō Yūji (1935–2007), a leader of the local anti-base organization Inochi o Mamoru Kai. One hot afternoon, I was visiting her house, where she was interviewed by a TV station in Tokyo. Referring to the renewed articulation of the voice of opposition to the construction of the FRF across Okinawa through Governor Onaga's leadership at that time, she emphasized in the interview the contributions made in the past by a number of people whose names had been almost forgotten, such as her late husband, by saying, "What he did is finally bearing fruit."

In fact, Yūji—who took care of me as if I were his own son when I conducted fieldwork in Henoko and greater Nago City in 1997–1998 and after— laid the foundation of today's anti-base protests in Henoko by developing, often all by himself, Inochi o Mamoru Kai from its inception in 1997 until his death in 2007.[8] The motivation behind his involvement was his grounded anger at and critique of the violence of the war and of Japanese discrimination against Okinawans, both of which he experienced, as he was born and grew up in communities in Osaka with a large number of Okinawan migrants (cf. Rabson 2012; Tomiyama 1990, chap. 2). For instance, when he was little, Okinawans and Koreans were often lumped together and discriminated against by Japanese in Osaka, a fact confirmed by studies by Tomiyama (1990, 139) among others. Yūji also talked to me about his experience of a US air raid in 1945 as a ten-year-old child. At that time, Yūji had been evacuated with his family (except his father, who needed to work at an ironworks) to a less populated and safer part of Kyoto to avoid the war, but he went to Osaka to let his father know of the birth of his youngest sister. Due to the air raid that happened on his way to Osaka, it took him three days to see his father. He saw Osaka reduced to ashes and dead people floating in the river. The chickens he had raised were also killed; he told me that since then, he had never been able to eat chicken. As he grew up, Yūji, together with his father and older brother, established a successful transportation company in Osaka. In 1971, right before the reversion of Okinawa, Yūji came back to Henoko, where his family originated, in order to provide a better living environment for one of his daughters who had asthma. Since then, he had been an active participant in and then a leader of labor movements as a bus driver for an Okinawan bus company before getting involved in the anti-base movement in Henoko upon retirement from his job. When he was alive, Yūji, in a manner that expressed Okinawa's grounded "identity" in the sense Onaga used it, talked to me about wider Japan's continuing discrimination against Okinawa, citing as the primary example the disproportionate burden of the US bases imposed on Okinawa in general and the planned construction of a new base in Henoko in particular. To such discrimination Yūji responded by often stating: "The poor people [like us Okinawans] have our way of fighting" (*binbōnin niwa binbōnin no tatakaikataga aru*). For Yūji, and for the Okinawan multitude at large, the protest is deeply anchored in the Okinawan sensibilities to "the death of others" as Jean-Luc Nancy ([1983] 1991, 15) called it, sensibilities constituted as "resistance itself" (Nancy [1983] 1991, 35) against the war and against Japan.

As I was reflecting on the trajectory of Yūji's life, Hatsuko, still being interviewed by a TV reporter from Tokyo, noted that she prayed every day that the plan to construct a base in Henoko would be revoked. In light of my encounter with the ghost, I knew that I must take the word "pray" seriously within the context of Okinawan cultural practices. In our conversation, Hatsuko told me that Yoji, more than seven years after his death, still appeared in her dreams as if he wanted to communicate something to her before moving into the world of the dead permanently. Her prayer was a response to the call from the dead. In a way that confirms the importance of prayer, I will add that, during my fieldwork in Okinawa in August 2015, Hatsuko and I visited the newly opened community center and museum of the Airakuen Sanatorium—established in 1938 for leprosy and ex-leprosy patients in Sumuide on Yagaji Island of Nago City. Photos, objects, and stories in the center/museum reveal the most excruciating experiences of the patients before and during the war—for example, confinement as a form of deprivation of basic human rights and dignities and forced labor to create underground shelters during the war as the expansion of such deprivation (Okinawa Times 1971, 140–146; Yoshikawa 2017); they cast light on the impacts the war in Okinawa had on the lives of the most vulnerable in a manner that induced deep prayer in her and me.

In effect, what I experienced with my informant and friend Kinjō Hatsuko in August 2015, when placed against the background of anti-base protests in Henoko in which I have been involved intellectually and politically over the years, was a form of postmemory: "It is a *consequence* of traumatic recall but (unlike post-traumatic stress disorder) at a generational remove" (Hirsh 2008, 106). What is recalled in the context of Okinawa, more specifically, is *nuchi du takara*, the unwavering principle of life. I wrote earlier that it looks as if Okinawan nature and culture wanted to support the protests in Henoko; having caught a glimpse of the depth of the community of *nuchi du takara* thorough a series of postmemorial acts—that is, fieldwork, interviews, and other forms of data collection for this research—I add that I feel as though the dead—such as Kinjō Yūji, those confined in Airakuen before, during, and after the war, and the war dead at large, together with the ghost I met—did the same in their invisible contribution to the production of this community against Tokyo and Washington. In the process, postmemory became a life-form of the Okinawan multitude, leading me to confront "the death of others"—or the finitude of the living being—that divides the dying Other and the living Self as much as it connects them as the metaphysical foundation of the community of *nuchi du takara*. The ways in which the Okinawan multitude experiences the death of others and the finitude of life are, of course, diverse because, as Christopher Nelson, an anthropologist who has explored how memories of the war and US rule have shaped Okinawan society (e.g., 2008), insightfully notes, "In Okinawa, the memory of death haunts everyday life" (2015, 143). I cite three examples below.

After the Okinawa Defense Bureau (ODB) furtively initiated construction work in July 2014, as noted, numerous dump trucks and heavy vehicles entered the gate of Camp Schwab to deliver materials for the boring survey. On one sweltering summer day in 2015, Shimabukuro Fumiko, a woman from Henoko in her eighties, stood in front of one of the vehicles, with her cane, addressing from the street the driver sitting behind the windshield: "Look at me. Listen to me. I will not let you pass. I will stop you. I am not simply a person who survived the war. I survived by drinking [water in a pond mixed with] blood [of those Okinawans who were killed and injured in the war]" (LunaticEclipseHenoko5 2015, 8:30–9:00; cf. *Ikusabanu*

Tudumi program production editor 2015, 7). During the Battle of Okinawa, Fumiko, then fifteen years old, was in the south of Okinawa where the fiercest battles took place. She ran around this way and that with her mother and brother trying to escape bombs falling like rain; in a cave where she was hiding, Fumiko was burned on her shoulders and other parts of her body by a flamethrower the US military used. Back in 1998, when I was conducting fieldwork in Henoko, she showed me that burn during my interview. Her message of *nuchi du takara* was simple, strong, and straightforward—she could not possibly let what she had experienced, the death of others, happen again by allowing a new military facility to be built.

When Nakamura Sugako, then a high school student, delivered a statement in 1995 at the rally organized to protest the rape of an Okinawan schoolgirl by three US servicemen, she in one sense transmitted the traumatic knowledge and experience, together with the commitment to the notion of *nuchi du takara*, of numerous Okinawans, including Shimabukuro Fumiko, by addressing the audience of eighty-five thousand: "Since the bases arrived in Okinawa, crimes have repeatedly been committed. I would like us to be liberated from the agonies caused by the bases. For Okinawa belongs to nobody other than us Okinawans.... Allow us, the younger generation, to start a new Okinawa. I wish Okinawa to become a peaceful island in the true sense of the word.... Please return Okinawa to us. Return Okinawa without the military, without tragedies" (Ryukyu Shimpo 1995, 12). In an interview by *Asahi Shimbun* conducted twenty years after the rally ("Hankichi..." 2015), Sugako stated—in a way that allows us to see the sustained presence of the community of *nuchi du takara* through a fuller development of postmemory in Okinawa—that the return of Futenma, proposed by the US and Japanese governments in the name of reducing and removing "risks" associated with its presence in a congested residential area, obscures the essence of the base problems, the continuing domination of Okinawa by the US military as mediated by the Japanese government, which will be detailed in Part III. Now a wife and the mother of a child, she noted that, as an ordinary Okinawan, continuingly discussing the base issues with people around her is a step toward changing the situation, adding that "Okinawa should not and will not give up."

A similar, yet more incisive, structure of intergenerational recall emerged in Henoko when, for instance, Okinawan writer Medoruma Shun began joining the canoe team in the summer of 2014 to stop the construction of the FRF (Medoruma 2014c). Back in 2005, Medoruma wrote:

When I think about sixty years after the war, a question of how I define and transmit [experiences of] the Battle of Okinawa—which is the starting point of postwar Okinawa—emerges as an important task for me. . . . I was born in 1960. . . . I probably belong to the last generation that is able to hear the stories of parents who have [experienced] the Battle of Okinawa. In light of this, I think of myself as part of a nodal generation that inherits war experience [from their parents' generation, the first generation] and transmits it to the next generation [the third generation]. (2005, 20–21)

In 2014, almost seventy years after the Battle of Okinawa, he views, from the perspective of a nodal generation practicing postmemory to extend the community of *nuchi du takara*, the construction of a new base in Henoko as a clear indication that the war seventy year ago has not ended, or rather, another war has perhaps already begun: "We must imagine. This sea is . . . connected to the battlefields far away" (Medoruma 2014d). Taira Natsume, an Okinawan priest who led activists during the first period of protest in Henoko in 2004–2005 when he was in his thirties (see chapter 1, section 1), also extends the community of *nuchi du takara* by exercising postmemory on his blog as follows: "It would be okay even if this happens just one day before my death. I want to live the postwar. Okinawa has been always in the war and in the new prewar as well" (Taira N., n.d.). In other words, the Okinawan multitude across generations—such as Kinjō Yūji (first generation, having experienced the war and US rule of Okinawa), Kinjō Hatsuko (first generation), Shimabukuro Fumi (first generation), Medoruma Shun (second generation, having experienced US rule but not the war), Yamashiro Hiroji (second generation), Ashitomi Hiroshi (second generation), Yamashiro Yoshikatsu (second generation), Onaga Takeshi (second generation), Taira Natsume (third generation. having experienced neither the war nor US rule), Nakamura Sugako (third generation), Higashionna Takuma (third generation), and others who have appeared in Part I—shows the continued presence of the community of *nuchi du takara* outside and against the constituted power of Tokyo and Washington. In the process, postmemory—that "life is the ultimate treasure"—serves not only as a mechanism to remember the past but also as a method to presage and reimagine the future of the community of *nuchi du takara*. For the constituent power underlying the Okinawan multitude's postmemory is resistance itself, appearing and reappearing "not so much as something deriving from human desires or free will, but in the form of a categorical imperative that transcends them" (Karatani [2010] 2014, 14).

Notes

1. For information about Sasebo's US Navy base, see Rimpeace, n.d.
2. Yamashiro Hiroji was sentenced to two years in prison, the sentence suspended for three years (No Base 3/18/2018, #1561a); the judgment became final at the Supreme Court in April 2019 (Kitazawa 2019).
3. During 2016, a total of 20,062 supporters, or approximately 55 supporters a day (No Base 1/11/2017, #1414b), came to Tent Village.
4. A total of 1,347 issues of *No Base* (from #235 to #1581) are digitally archived at http://henoko.blog110.fc2.com/blog-category-1.html
5. Pictures of these banners are digitally archived at http://www.rimpeace.or.jp/jrp/okinawa/galleryindex.html
6. In December 2016, an Osprey crashed into the ocean off the east coast of Nago City, as noted in chapter 1, section 2.
7. This new class composition is evidenced by the fact that the while the average household income in Japan was 5,419,000 yen in 2014 and 5,523,000 yen in 2018, in both 2014 and 2018, income for more than 60% of the households was below average and 45% of the households had income between 1 million yen and 4 million yen (Kōsei-Rōdōshō. n.d.; 2015, 10–11; 2019, 9–10). Furthermore, annual household income below 1,220,000 yen—which represents the "relative poverty rate" (the percentage of those whose annual income was less than half of the median income)—reached 16.1% in 2012 (a record high), 15.7% in 2015, and 15.8% in 2018 (Kōsei-Rōdōshō 2019, 14).
8. Part of the following description about Yūji's life is taken from Inoue 2007, 148–149. It is also informed by a documentary on his life directed by Koshi'ishi Tadashi (2009), in particular, chapter 3.

Conclusion to Part I

Describing struggles in Henoko during the first period of protest and its aftermath (2004–2012) and during the second period of protests (2013–2023), Part I has explored how the logic of *nuchi du takara* mediates two processes—external negotiations of the Okinawan multitude with the constituted power of Tokyo and Washington (chapter 1) and internal articulations of the constituent power of the Okinawan multitude (chapter 2)—for the formation of the community of *nuchi du takara*. Part I has also shown that it is only by trying to accomplish something that may not ever be accomplished—construction of the FRF, hampered by the presence of the soft ground—that the constituted power of Washington and Tokyo can sustain itself. The effect of this self-contradictory exercise of power—accomplishing the unaccomplishable—by Washington and Tokyo upon the community of *nuchi du takara* should not be underestimated, however. For the unity of Okinawa against the FRF seems to be waning, particularly since the death of the charismatic governor Onaga Takeshi in August 2018, a process that may have been accelerated by the Covid pandemic.

At one level, to be sure, Okinawa's protest was well sustained in spite of Onaga's death. One could argue that his death reanchored Okinawa in the metaphysical foundation of the community of *nuchi du takara*, in a manner that invigorated the language of protest and the actions into which it is woven, as evidenced by the victories of candidates opposing the FRF in Henoko in the gubernatorial election in November 2018 and in the nation's House of Councilors election in July 2019. In addition, in 2018, a group of young Okinawans initiated a movement to realize a prefecture-wide referendum to express the opinion of Okinawans regarding the FRF; in spite of attempts to sabotage it by conservative political circles in Okinawa influenced by Tokyo, the referendum was successfully held in February 2019 (as noted in chapter 2, section 1), and more than 70% of those who voted expressed opposition to the construction of the FRF. In front of Camp Schwab, too, a rally was organized on the first Saturday of every month beginning in October 2017 ("Henoko Shinkichi Kensetsu Soshi! . . ." 2017); even though this activity was suspended from November 2020 to September 2021 in response to the Covid-19 pandemic ("Koronagono Henoko . . ." 2020), the rallies were often attended by more than one thousand after Onaga's death ("Kenmin wa . . ." 2019).

Even in the midst of the pandemic, the number of protesters in front of the Camp Schwab gate and on the sea around Camp Schwab remained steady. For instance, from June 12 to July 12, 2020, the average number of participants in sit-in activities in front of the gate each day was 123 ("Koronagono Henoko . . ." 2020). It should be added that the prefecture-wide antipathy to the US bases has also intensified due to instances of Covid-19 spreading into Okinawa (apparently) from the US bases ("Okinawa Beigun de . . ." 2020). Furthermore, since 2021, the issue concerning the PFAS (per- and polyfluoroalkyl substances)—which, apparently originated from the US bases, contaminates drinking water for Okinawans—has become another source of prefecture-wide frustration against the US military ("Suidōsui . . ." 2021). Last but not least, protest spread across Okinawa and beyond from March 2021 on after Tokyo announced that part of the soil to be used in land reclamation for the FRF construction in Henoko would come from southern Okinawa, where the fiercest combat took place during the Battle of Okinawa. Okinawans shared the sentiment of protest that uncollected bones of those killed during the battle would likely be mixed in with the sediment, an act that would profane the victims (Fujiwara 2021).

In spite of all the indications of sustained anti-base sentiments in Okinawa, it has also become increasingly evident at another level that the gesture of Washington and Tokyo to construct the FRF at any cost has drained the oppositional political energy of Okinawa in general and of Nago in particular, as is exemplified by the victory of Toguchi Taketoyo—a conservative politician who, following the will of Tokyo, has remained silent about FRF construction—in two mayoral elections in January 2018 and January 2022. A poll conducted before the January 2022 mayoral election in Nago specifically showed that the percentage of Okinawans who oppose the FRF construction decreased from 63% in 2018 to 54% in 2022 (Kuniyoshi M. 2022). Yoneda Sachihiro shows statistically that Okinawans in their thirties or younger—that is, the third generation of Okinawan social actors who experienced neither the Battle of Okinawa nor US rule of Okinawa—tend to distance themselves from the anti-base movement (see also Kumamoto et al. 2023). While further investigation is needed, it is possible that this generation shares the sentiment that (*a*) the US military presence might be needed in light of increasingly volatile international security conditions and (*b*) the US military might contribute to economic well-being of Okinawa in light of the Covid-19 pandemic since 2020, which has hit tourism, the foundation of Okinawa's contemporary economy, hardest (Yoneda and Tanizu 2022). Back in 2000, a heated intellectual debate occurred in reference to the so-called Okinawa Initiative, a policy proposal by three influential professors at the University of the Ryukyus asserting that Okinawa should accept the US military presence to actively participate in its management for the peace and prosperity of the Asia-Pacific region (Takara, Ōshiro, and Maeshiro 2000). While critics—including myself (Inoue 2002)—vehemently opposed this proposal at that time, I must at least admit that the Okinawa Initiative in a way was a harbinger of the sentiment of the new generation in today's Okinawa not openly opposing the US military presence (cf. Sakurazawa 2015, 333).

Does this mean that the protest activities in Henoko, after continuing for well over twenty-five years, have been abating? Relatedly, has the community of *nuchi du takara* been disappearing? On the one hand, I reluctantly say yes to the first question because, in line with Yoneda's observation cited above, my own interviews of five younger Okinawans conducted in January 2020 unveil their reluctance to come to Henoko and participate in the direct action of protests due to their fear of confrontation with the police or riot squad, dislike of yelling at US servicemen, the somewhat outdated style of singing and chanting slogans together, and the androcentric hierarchy in the protest activities (cf. Kawakita 2011); in effect, they felt as though the community of protesters, in spite of (or precisely because of) its internal cohesiveness, was somewhat closed to outsiders such as younger generations. These young interviewees shared opposition to the FRF, but they suggested that there should be other methods for protest other than simply coming to Henoko. The movement to realize the prefectural referendum on the FRF in Henoko in February 2019, noted above, was indeed initiated and led specifically by a group of younger Okinawans reluctant to come to Henoko in spite of their fundamentally anti-base position, as I confirmed through my interview with a leader of this group, Motoyama Jinshirō, in January 2020 (cf. Yamamoto A. 2018).

More generally, younger Okinawans seem to share a perception or a sentiment that the presence of the US bases is, after all, part of "scenery" (*fūkei*) into which they were born and which they accept as a given—they would go to flea markets in the US bases to look for and purchase American-made jeans or would have mixed-race Okinawans born to US servicemen and Okinawan women as friends in school. Thus, they may not have a clearly defined anti-base consciousness that would prompt them to participate in protest activities in Henoko. Through their indecisiveness, it should be added, younger Okinawans also shed light on an important contradiction or dilemma of the anti-base protest in Henoko. That is, given that Futenma Air Station will not be returned unless the FRF is constructed, the protest in Henoko may have unwittingly contributed to the continued presence of Futenma Air Station to benefit the US military.

On the other hand, I say no to the second question: "Has the community of *nuchi du takara* been disappearing?" For Okinawan social actors have continued to constitute and reconstitute the community of *nuchi du takara*—together with their subjectivity as "a *changing* same"—through diverse life-forms in addition to social movements, as essays collected in *Islands of Discontent: Okinawan Responses to Japanese and American Power*, edited by Laura Hein and Mark Selden (2003), have perceptively demonstrated and as my explorations in other chapters of this book will reveal. Indeed, by situating anti-base protests in Henoko in a broader historical-social context, this book—in particular, Parts II and IV—will historically and ethnographically investigate specific mechanisms that have enabled the community of Okinawan social actors and their subjectivity to continue to grow in diverse forms across the Cold War and post–Cold War periods. Ultimately, my investigation (see chapter 8) will help shed light on how the Okinawa multitude in the twenty-first century has rearticulated the logic of *nuchi du takara* through which to assert that construction of the FRF in Henoko is unnecessary *and* that Futenma is to be returned unconditionally. It is through this logic that the community of *nuchi du takara* engages in and overcomes the above contradiction/dilemma—the ani-base protest in Henoko may have contributed to the continued presence of Futenma Air Station—for the trans/formation of itself within and against Empire.

PART II

Money and Taboo

Okinawan Subjectivity as "a *Changing* Same" and the Construction of the Community of *Nuchi Du Takara*

Introduction to Part II

Part II explores the community of *nuchi du takara* up through the 1990s—together with the subjectivity of Okinawan social actors who constituted that community—as what Paul Gilroy called "a *changing* rather than an unchanging same" (1993, 101), inscribed with struggles and memories of the Battle of Okinawa in 1945, Okinawa reversion in 1972, and the rape incident in 1995, among others. Toward this end, Part II links a segment of the insights of Freud that help highlight the "same" of the Okinawan community and subjectivity (androcentrism) (chapter 3) with a segment of the insights of Marx that help explain "changes" of the community/subjectivity in terms of the class and gender structure (chapter 4). In other words, I reconcile Freud/Marx with postwar Okinawa/Japan, so as to underscore a particular social mechanism—centered on taboos and money—that enabled the community of *nuchi du takara* ("life is the ultimate treasure") to be articulated and rearticulated by the constituent power of the poor and oppressed Okinawan "people" (1945–1960s) (chapter 3), on the one hand, and by increasingly affluent, educated, and confident Okinawan "citizens" (1970s–1990s) (chapter 4), on the other.

In *Totem and Taboo*, Sigmund Freud ([1913] 1950) traced the origin of ambivalence to the sons' act of killing the violent primal father—who "[kept] all the females for himself and [drove] away his sons as they [grew] up" (141)—at the earliest yet unspecifiable stage of human history. The result of this killing is ambivalence, "the simultaneous existence of love and hate toward the same object" ([1913] 1950, 157). For "After they had got rid of him . . . , the affection which had all this time been pushed under was bound to make itself felt. . . . A sense of guilt made its appearance, which in this instance coincided with the remorse felt by the whole group" ([1913] 1950, 143).

Exercising the absolute power over Okinawan life, the US military dominated postwar Okinawa politically, economically, socially, culturally, and sexually like the Freudian father. Yet, unlike the Freudian sons, the Okinawan "people" were deprived of the power to "get rid of" the father; they were forced to depend on the very US military that had destroyed Okinawa's life-forms through the Battle of Okinawa and its control over Okinawa that followed. The result was "ambivalence in reverse." That is, the "simultaneous existence of love and hate"—ambivalence—toward the US military was defined by the *in*ability of Okinawan "people" to kill the father, the impossibility of "revolution." This *in*ability-cum-impossibility shaped the community of *nuchi du takara* and the subjectivity of the Okinawan "people" who constituted it in specific ways.

For—as I will explicate in chapter 3—the community of *nuchi du takara* developed specific "taboos" as a mechanism to cope with this ambivalence, a mechanism that was also "in reverse." The Freudian sons revoked their deed of murdering the father by forbidding the killing of the totem animal (the substitute for their father) and by renouncing sexual relations with the father's women (i.e., the mothers). Accordingly, the Freudian model of totemism is structured by a homosocial command—"not to kill the totem [the totemic animal]" (Freud [1913] 1950, 132), which represents the father—on the one hand, and a heterosocial command—"not to have sexual relations with a woman of the same totem" (Freud [1913] 1950, 132), who represents the mother—on the other. The underlying thesis of totemism is, of course, the Oedipus complex: "If the totem animal is the father, then . . . the two taboo prohibitions which constitute its core . . . coincide in their content with the two crimes of Œdipus, who killed his father and married his mother" (Freud [1913] 1950, 132). Through the two taboo prohibitions, Freudian sons identified with, internalized, and restored the father they had eliminated, or made the absent present. Put differently, they became the father.

In contrast, the Okinawan "people" could neither kill the father nor identify with the father, the US military; they needed to engage in a different task, that of revoking their deed of accepting the violent and omnipotent father in exchange for money. Their task, in other words, was to minimize, if not entirely eliminate, the power of the foreign ruler who had intruded into Okinawa's local time-space, that is, to make the present absent (to the extent that was possible). Toward this end, on the one hand, the community of *nuchi du takara* developed the first taboo that served as the principle of external negotiations with the US military: "Don't develop friendship with the US military." This taboo was homosocial in nature, like Freud's first taboo, but its command was reversed to separate the Okinawan "people" from the US military, in a manner that helped the former to establish a more equal and democratic relationship with the latter. The second and related taboo, which served as the principle of regulating the power of life of Okinawan women (and others) internally, was "Don't allow sexual relations between Okinawan women and US servicemen." Like Freud's second taboo, this taboo is heterosocial in nature, but its command is, again, the opposite of Freud's in that it promotes intimacy and sex with women of the same "totem" (Okinawan women). When combined, these taboos show the ways in which the community of *nuchi du takara*—together with the subjectivity of the Okinawan "people" who constructed it—was structured by androcentrism consisting of fraternity against the US military externally *and* fratriarchy over Okinawan women and others internally.

The contradiction between fraternity (a search for democracy and equality) and fratriarchy (a denial of democracy and equality) in the community of *nuchi du takara* by the Okinawan "people," however, posed obstacles to the development of this community that eventually had to be overcome, at least partially, in post-reversion Okinawa, as I will show in chapter 4. I suggest that one of the key driving forces of this development is money as the "universal equivalent," as Karl Marx ([1887] n.d., 46) called it. More specifically, Marx (49) stated: "Whenever, by an exchange [through money], we equate as values our different products, by that very act, we also equate, as human labour, the different kinds of labour expended upon them." In other words, the subordination of varied forms of living labor (or the power of life) to money and capital as "human labour in general" (Marx [1887] n.d., 40) also contributed, positively and constructively, to the process whereby "the notion of human equality ... acquired the fixity of a popular prejudice" (Marx [1887] n.d., 41).

Applying Marx's insight to post-reversion Okinawa, chapter 4 shows that (*a*) the huge sum of Japanese money paid as compensation for the continued presence of the US military after the reversion of Okinawa in 1972 encouraged Okinawan women to participate in the ever-expanding labor market even as it subsumed them under the system of capitalist exploitation, and (*b*) women's participation in the labor market, in turn, contributed to the process whereby "the notion of human equality ... acquired the fixity of a popular prejudice" among increasingly affluent, educated, and confident Okinawan "citizens," particularly women. I will investigate, with a number of specific examples taken from post-reversion Okinawa of the 1970s through 1990s, how this "popular prejudice" provided Okinawan "citizens," particularly (though not exclusively) women, with the power to critically undermine, if not entirely dissolve, the two androcentric taboos produced by the Okinawan "people" after the war through the 1960s. In effect, "money" would have an ambiguous role to play in undermining one form of Okinawan subjectivity founded upon the constituent power of the "people," or men while generating another based on the constituent power of "citizens," or women. In so doing, Okinawan "citizens" (i.e., women) contributed to a rearticulation of anti-base sentiments less through androcentric taboos against the US military and more by grounding such sentiments in the collective memory of the Battle of Okinawa against Tokyo, a process that resulted in the formation of the community of *nuchi du takara* by Okinawan "citizens" in post-reversion Okinawa.

To clearly grasp the development of Okinawan subjectivity and the specific forms that the community of *nuchi du takara* took in postwar Okinawa up through the 1990s, Part II introduces (and Part IV extends) the term "time-space" by incorporating David Harvey's theoretical insights. Specifically, as will be shown in chapter 3, the local time-space developed in postwar Okinawa through the 1960s by the US military refers to "a relative autonomy of social relations and of community inside roughly given territorial boundaries" (Harvey 1990, 240). In this "local time-space," there was no longer any influence from the emperor of Japan as in prewar Okinawa; instead, during this period, the US military promoted Okinawa's traditional culture so as to separate Okinawa from wider Japan. It was in this local time-space that the community of *nuchi du takara* was constructed by the Okinawan "people." In contrast, as will be shown in chapter 4, formation of the "national/Japanized time-space" refers to the process whereby Okinawa's basic framework of social life was realigned with the Japanese political, legal, economic, and cultural system so that "a new landscape was to emerge" (Harvey 1990, 249) for Okinawan "citizens" in the 1970s–1990s, a process that involved redefinition of Okinawan subjectivity in the context of "historical contradictions and imbalances in power *between* [American, Japanese, and Okinawan] men [and women]," to use Anne McClintock's words (1995, 197). It was within this national/Japanized time-space that the community of *nuchi du takara* was renewed by Okinawan "citizens."

Meanwhile, as will be fully explored in Part III, Empire constructed the "globalized time-space" across and beyond the Asia-Pacific region, where "time-space compression" became predominant, accompanied by the process whereby "the world sometimes seems to collapse inwards upon [the lived world of the Okinawan multitude]" (Harvey 1990, 240). Part IV will show that the Okinawan multitude has constructed the "planetary time-space" in which to assemble a new community of *nuchi du takara* within and against Empire.

Methodological Notes

Part II uses the methods of cultural studies, broadly defined, which involve critical analysis of cultural products/texts and social phenomena/events. Data and information for analysis come from diverse sources, such as newspapers, pamphlets, literary works, photography, prior scholarly works, and my own conversations and interactions with certain informants such as Ishikawa Mao. I also reanalyze some of the participant-observation that I conducted in Henoko in the late 1990s.

CHAPTER 3

Ambivalence toward the US Military

Formation of the Androcentric Community by the Okinawan "People" (1945–1972)

In light of the theoretical framework presented in the introduction to part II, I will examine in this chapter the formation of the community of *nuchi du takara* by the Okinawan "people" under US-ruled Okinawa. I will do so in terms of the following four phases. In phase 1 (1945–1949), a vague sense of "love" toward the US military was generated in the wake of the Battle of Okinawa, as US forces rescued, in the very act of destroying Okinawa, its residents from the violence of the Japanese Imperial Army. In phase 2 (1950–1957), the seizure of Okinawa's land generated a deep resentment and "hate" toward the US military, a process that, situating Okinawa in "the simultaneous existence of love and hate toward [the US military]," led to the formation of the "people" as the key social actor in the community of *nuchi du takara*. In phase 3 (1958–1966), as the ambivalence toward the US military was deepened due to the policy of persuading Okinawa to accept the US bases with the power of money (US dollars), the Okinawan "people" also developed a set of taboos—one homosocial and the other heterosocial—to cope with it. In phase 4 (1967–1972), the Okinawan "people," against the background of the intensification of the Vietnam War, overcame, if temporarily, the ambivalence by enacting the two taboos through the reversion movement, a process that paved the way for the rearticulation of the community of *nuchi du takara* by affluent, confident, and younger Okinawan "citizens." The beginning and closing years specified for these phases are meant to be guideposts, rather than a strict periodization, to facilitate the analysis of the formation and transformation of the community of *nuchi du takara* together with the subjectivity of the Okinawan "people" who constituted it in postwar Okinawa. At times, I overstep the closing year of a particular phase in order to indicate the full impact of particular events and incidents that happened during that phase.

1. Love and Trust toward the US Military in the Shadow of Violence (1945–1949)

The Japanese Imperial Army consisting of 110,000 troops was not able to defend Okinawa when the US military deployed fifteen hundred ships and 540,000 troops for the Battle of Okinawa, code-named Operation Iceberg, which began on March 26, 1945. In May 1945, the Japanese Imperial Army fled in disorderly retreat; and in late June, its systematic military operations more or less ended.[1] In the process, an estimated 150,000 Okinawans, or a quarter of the population of Okinawa Prefecture at that time, were killed under the "typhoon of steel"—the barrage of bombs, shells, and artillery fire used by the US military—together with other causes such as spread of diseases and shortage of foods (Arashiro 1994, 241, 253–254). What was shared by surviving Okinawans was the ultimate experience of violence that divided them from as much as connected them to fellow Okinawans who had died in the war. Situated in this metaphysical foundation of the community of *nuchi du takara*, these Okinawans established the common saying, *Guntai wa Jyūmin o Mamoranai*, or "The military [the emperor's military at that] does not protect the lives of local residents," due to the atrocities of the Japanese Imperial Army during the battle.

For instance, Miyagi Harumi (2008a, 2008b) shows how "compulsory group suicide" (Field 1991, 61) occurred on Zamami Island, one of the Kerama Islands cluster,[2] when the US invasion began (see also Okinawan Times 1950, 32–41 and Yakabi 2009, chap. 1). While the Japanese government claimed later that Okinawans had died out of the "sublime spirit of self-sacrifice" (Bōeichō Bōeikenshūjo Senshishitsu 1968, 252, cited in Miyagi 2008b, 102), Miyagi shows—on the basis of her fieldwork since the 1970s in general and of experiences of her own mother who survived the war in particular—that it was due to direct or indirect orders from the officers of the Japanese Imperial Army that many heads of the families in Zamami—men—took the lead in killing their own wives, children, and other family members as well as themselves with grenades, razors, rat poison, sickles, ropes, and other available instruments, in order to avoid a fate worse than death—according to these officers—that "men would be torn

Figure 8. American battleships gathering around the Island of Okinawa
Source: OPPMM, n.d.-a.

limb from limb and women would be killed after being raped" (Miyagi 2008b, 80) by the US military should they be ever captured. The total number of deaths by "compulsory group suicide" was 135 out of 242 residents on the island. *Tetsu no Bōfū* (The Typhoon of Steel and Bombs) (Okinawa Times 1950), a book narrated from the perspective of ordinary Okinawans, also reveals that Japanese imperial soldiers, in the name of the emperor, obtained food from Okinawans by force (112, 322, 323, 400), exploited them sexually (150, 293), kicked them out of shelters (116, 154), fled to Japan "proper" (83, 320, 402), and in some cases executed them after accusing them of being spies for the US military (117, 322) or saying that the cries of children would enable the US military to locate where they were and to attack them (263).

Meanwhile, when the invasion of Okinawa began, Admiral Chester W. Nimitz, commander in chief, Pacific, issued Navy Military Government Proclamation Number 1 (Okinawaken Kōbunshokan, n.d.) to establish the US Military Government of the Ryukyu Islands (USMGR), declaring its administrative and judicial power over Okinawa. This marks the appearance in Okinawa of the *father*, the law of law, who suspended the prewar regime centered on the emperor of Japan to institute a new social order centered on the US military.

One of the most dramatic expressions of the US military's "power over life" was the construction of sixteen temporary internment camps across the island of Okinawa and beyond (Fisch 1988, 45–60),[3] in which approximately three hundred thousand residents, or more than 85% of surviving Okinawan civilians, were accommodated as of the end of June 1945 (Kabira N. 2011, 42–44; Okinawa Times 1971, 117–118 and 2014, 50). A vague sense of love for and trust in the US military was generated in these camps, in spite of the violence it exercised. For the US military behaved paternalistically as a liberation army, that is, an army rescuing Okinawa from the oppression of Japan, even though it also behaved as an occupier punishing Okinawans as Japanese and the enemy with draconian measures (Miyagi Et. 1982, 63). In the process, the community of *nuchi du takara* began to take shape as a cultural cushion between the constituent power of the surviving Okinawans and the constituted power of the US military. During phase 1, indeed throughout the period of US direct rule of Okinawa (1945–1972), this cultural cushion, I suggest, helped the Okinawan "people" externally engage in complex negotiations with and often against the occupier on the basis of the internal capacity of their community to embrace diverse and often contradictory attitudes, experiences, and perspectives regarding the US military. Let me grasp the initial phase of this crucial process by discussing the violence of the US military as the occupier first, to establish a background for the love and trust among Okinawans developed in the context of paternalistic acts of the US military as the liberation army that I analyze afterward.

For instance, the construction of refugee campus went hand in hand with the enclosure of vast plots of Okinawan land. Specifically, after seizing former Japanese bases created by the Imperial Army in prewar times (1,410 hectares) for the creation of US bases to be used as staging grounds from which to attack Japan "proper" (before Japan's surrender) and to watch over the situation in Japan "proper" (after Japan's surrender) (Nakano 1969, 1), the USMGR continued to enclose vast plots of Okinawan land including fertile farmland (18,200 hectares) until 1947 (Sakurazawa 2015, 9–10, 168) without any clearly defined purposes. It was done under an equivocal notion of America's national interest in the postwar world.[4] Futenma Air Station was one of the military bases created by the USMGR in 1945 through this enclosure (Okinawa Prefectural Peace Memorial Museum [hereafter OPPMM] 2001, 126). As a result, many Okinawans found their land used by the US military when they returned from the refugee camps to their home villages from October 1945 to April 1946 (OPPMM 2001, 108). The number of residents who could not return to their land due to enclosure had reached 150,000 as of October 1946 (Kabira N. 2011, 63–64). These residents were dispersed to nearby communities, and some of them, mobilized to participate in the expansion and creation of US bases, ended up working on their own land, now held by the USMGR (OPPMM 2001, 109).

Another form of violence the construction of the refugee camps introduced and reinforced was sexual violence by US troops against Okinawan women (Miyagi H. 2006, 46–52; Okinawa "Kichi/Guntai o Yurusanai Kōdōsuru Onnatachi no Kai" 1996). For instance, in June 1945, in a tent inside a refugee camp in Gushikawa Village in central Okinawa, Ms. H. was resting with a baby she had recently delivered, when a Black serviceman snuck into this tent. Ms. H. screamed for help. Ms. T., her younger sister, rushed in and banged the oxygen gas cylinder used as a bell—an item that had been placed for emergencies of this kind (OPPMM 2001, 110)—to summon help from those in the camp. Fortunately, this serviceman did not have a weapon and when surrounded by villagers he ran away. Nine months later, however, it was Ms. T., the younger sister of Ms. H. who had helped her, who was raped by three White servicemen after she was released from the refugee camp. Ms. T., then aged thirty, was digging for sweet potatoes together with other women and elders in her community.

> At first, [three servicemen] held her hand firmly. As she tried to escape, they hit her in the face. Her two front teeth were broken. She screamed for help, but the people around her did not have any means to rescue her. There was an Okinawan civilian policeman, but he too was helpless without a weapon. . . . Meanwhile, the three servicemen continued their act of violence together against Ms. T. who resisted desperately. They hit her in the face more and her mouth tore. Still, she tried to get up and leave, but then they knocked her from behind with the butt of a rifle. The joint of her right foot was fractured and she fell, no longer able to move. (Fukuchi [1977] 1995, 114)

Violence against women continued beyond the immediate postwar rehabilitation period, due in part to the low level of discipline and morale among US troops: "In the later 1940s the islands became, as bitter Army officers put it, 'the end of the Army's logistical line,' a junk heap of discarded World War II equipment and human cast-offs from the Far East Command" (Fisch

1988, 81). *Time* magazine correspondent Frank Gibney (1949) therefore called postwar Okinawa of this period a "Forgotten Island." In 1949, in order to control sexual violence of US servicemen and to protect Okinawan women (but to sacrifice a specific group of Okinawan women), Okinawan leaders (men) sent a proposal to the USMGR to set up "comfort facilities," an act that resulted in the formation of the entertainment districts in Koza adjacent to Kadena Air Base and other areas (Miyagi H. 2006, 52–56)

In spite of these forms of violence by the US military as the occupier, the construction of the refugee camps also played a positive role in postwar Okinawa's phase 1, generating a vague sense of love for and trust in the US military in the emerging community of *nuchi du takara*, because the US military provided—like Freud's primal father—"protection, care and indulgence" (Freud [1913] 1950, 144) to utterly helpless Okinawans (Kabira N. 2011, 47–50). To begin with, the refugee camps protected the lives of Okinawans as the US military encouraged them to surrender in defiance of the Japanese Imperial Army, which told Okinawans to fight until they died or to commit suicide when faced with capture. The release of materials and supplies to the camps by the US military, such as food (rations), clothes (military uniforms), homes (tents), and medicine, albeit in a limited quantity (Fisch 1988, 45–60; Kabira N. 2011, 131–138), were experienced by Okinawans as a fatherly act of generosity (Miyagi Et. 1982, 44–45). In addition, the US military "cleaned out" the Japanese soldiers outside the enclosures or put them into a separate camp created for them; they were then used as longshoremen handling military goods (Nakachi 2001, 88; Wakabayashi 2015, 99).

Furthermore, in these camps, the USMGR liberated Okinawa from the grip of Japan sociopolitically and culturally. Sociopolitically, it introduced liberal policies emphasizing self-governance (e.g., the establishment of the Okinawa Advisory Committee in August 1945) and democracy (e.g., the introduction of women's suffrage to choose members of this committee in September 1945), in a manner that rewrote the prewar Japanese ideology that had fostered patriarchy and forced sacrifice for the emperor (Hokama 2007, 35–36; Kabira N. 2011, 65–67). This was particularly true until the fall of 1945 when the USMGR was run by civil affairs officers of the US Navy such as George Murdock (Wakabayashi 2015, 40–48, 70–76), an anthropologist from Yale who wrote—together with Clellan S. Ford and John W. M. Whiting, both of whom were then Murdock's colleagues at Yale (cf. Fisch 1988, 14)—*Civil Affairs Handbook: Ryukyu (Loochoo) Islands* (US

Navy Department 1944), to assist the occupier in exercising the power over life to administer postwar Okinawa. The USMGR also promoted the traditional "Ryukyuan culture," to help Okinawa establish an identity outside of the Japanese counterpart. Well known in Okinawa are the activities of Lieutenant Commander Willard Anderson Hanna, a scholar of Southeast Asian history and a teacher of English, and Lieutenant Commander James Thomas Watkins, a scholar of international relations, who together contributed to the creation of a museum of Okinawan culture in 1945 in Ishikawa—the temporary capital of postwar Okinawa until October 1946, which experienced a population surge, from eighteen hundred before the war to more than thirty thousand after the war—by collecting traditional artifacts that had survived the war (Loo 2014, 159–160; Yonaha K. 2016). To be sure, cultural policies like this was shaped, at least in part, by a calculated insight developed by *Civil Affairs Handbook* as an administrative tool of the constituted power; accordingly, the handbook stated that, in spite of official Japanese policy, "The Ryukyu islanders have not become wholly assimilated to the culture of the Japanese, by whom they are generally regarded as somewhat uncouth rustics" and added, "Inherent in the relations between the Ryukyu people and the Japanese, therefore, are potential seeds of dissension out of which political capital might be made" (US Navy Department 1944, 69, 43). Nonetheless, positive impacts of such policies on the formation of the community of *nuchi du takara* by surviving Okinawans should not be underestimated.

Indeed, between 1945 and 1949, the sense of love for and trust in the US military among the Okinawans who survived the Battle of Okinawa—"who felt a strange sense of liberation and hope in spite of the confusion and inconvenience in the blazing brightness of the ruins" (Miyagi Et. 1982, 57)—was reinforced in an emerging social environment where they could express their power of life. For instance, the US military allowed Okinawans to establish political parties from 1947 on, including the Okinawa People's Party, which played a significant role in the island-wide resistance to the US military in the 1950s (Mi. Higa 1963, 27; Toriyama 2013, chap. 3; Wakabayashi 2015, chaps. 4 and 7), as will be discussed below. I cite two additional examples of the expression of their power of life for the construction of the community of *nuchi du takara*, a community that protected, nurtured, and celebrated life even as it risked dependence on the violence of the US military.

The first concerns the performing arts in the refugee camps, where "using empty cans and parachute cords, Okinawan performers of music and dance put together makeshift versions of Okinawa's traditional *sanshin*, the three-stringed banjo-like musical instrument played with a finger pick. The US military government encouraged the performing arts as an important component in postwar recovery" (OPPMM 2001, 106).[5] Particularly well known was an event on Christmas 1945, when thousands of Okinawans witnessed performances in the refugee camp in Ishikawa. One of the programs presented then was a play titled *Hanaui nu In* (Connections of the Flower Vendor), which thematized family love by highlighting a dramatic reunion between a husband, an impoverished aristocrat in the age of the Ryukyu Kingdom—unified in the fifteenth century but abolished by Meiji Japan in the 1870s—who chose to travel to northern Okinawa to peddle goods and make money, and his wife and child, who waited for his return in Shuri, the capital of the kingdom in southern Okinawa. Members of the audience in the refugee camp are said to have wept bitterly when the wife and child traveled to find the husband, who had become a flower vendor, and the three made their way back to their home in Shuri together, because the story overlapped with the difficulties of their own families—separation, loneliness, and reunion—in the wake of the war (Kabira N. 2011, 100–103; see also Miyagi Et. 1982, 60–62; Okinawa Times 1971, 152–158).

Another well-known example is the so-called *senkwa-agiyā*, or the people who engaged in obtaining "war booty" (Fisch 1988, 81; OPPMM 2001, 109; Okinawa Times 1971, 162–164), a process that occurred within the context of increased aid from the United States, such as the US Government Appropriation for Relief in Occupied Area (GARIOA) Fund, which beginning in 1946 contributed a total of $185 million to provide food, medicine, vehicles, roads, ports, and electricity, among other things, to postwar Okinawa (Keizai Kikakuchō 1972; Ryukyu Ginkō Chōsabu 1984, 152–155). Motivated by the need to survive, men and women stole food, clothes, construction materials, and other necessities from facilities and supply yards of the US military (Toriyama 2007, 92). The US military acquiesced in Okinawans' diversion of goods, which they did without a sense of committing crimes. Stolen items were not only consumed by those who acquired them but also traded in markets (Hokama 2007, 38). Testimonies reveal that truck drivers who carried these items were able to build homes quicker than anybody else in postwar Okinawa because they were in the position of collecting, using, and selling them (Toriyama 2007, 92–94). A saying for young Okinawan women then was, "Instead of marrying a public servant or a teacher," two highly respected occupations in prewar Okinawa, "marry a truck driver" (Okinawa Times 1998, 60; see also Okinawa Times, 1971, 158–164).

The construction of the community of *nuchi du takara*—founded upon that notion that "life is the ultimate treasure"—indicated by the above examples in postwar Okinawa led its social actors to reexamine what had been taken for granted before the war, that Okinawa was part of the Japanese state. For instance, Okinawan critics discussed what Okinawa was like immediately after the war by reporting on "the sense of liberation from things like the [Japanese] state" and "a situation in which there are no bureaucrats or governmental offices and everybody is liberated and stands on the same footing" (Makiminato et al. 1975, 99, cited in Fukuma 2010, 35). In a manner that reflected the shared sense of liberation, the majority of Okinawans in this phase (1945–1949) supported the independence of Okinawa under the guidance of the United States, not reversion to Japan, as the most viable option concerning its future (Sakurazawa 2015, 31 and 41–47).

The shared sense of liberation was also expressed in the realm of literary works at that time, even though authors wrote not in English but continuingly in "standard Japanese," an important aspect of the prewar Japanization program (Bhowmik 2008, chap. 3).[6] For instance, in a novella titled *Kami no Shisha* (A Messenger of God) (1950), Miyara Tamotsu described despair and hope as he, a leper, experienced them in postwar Okinawa. In particular, the treatment he received at Airakuen Sanatorium[7] was depicted in terms of the ideals of Christianity and a belief in the progress of American/modern medicine, the opposite of the discrimination he received from his own family. Women writers joined the idealistic spirit in the fledgling community of *nuchi du takara* at that time by exploring new ways of life. In *Sumire Niou* (A Violet That Smells Good), Kameya Chizuko (1950), for instance, described how a former fiancé of Kumiko—the protagonist of the novella—abandoned her in accordance with the will of his aging parents in the conventional village, while presenting a new dream that Kumiko—who had relationship with an American officer—found: "In order to live my own life, I must seek freedom and love all by myself" (24) without denying a desire to "purchase beautiful clothes, have a lot of money, and eat a lot of delicious foods" (21). In a novella titled *Azami to Seppun* (Thistles and Kisses), Yae Sakura (1950) conducted a similar search for truth from a woman's perspective.

It should be noted that the celebration of "freedom and love" often went hand in hand with reproduction of the ruler's views and values. For instance, Okinawan novellas in this phase communicated admiration of US servicemen driving jeeps, playing golf, and living in luxurious houses on Okinawa as the occupier, none of which Okinawans, the occupied, could then do. In addition, the ruler's views and values on race were reproduced as well as rearticulated in these novellas, which often depicted Black servicemen negatively, equating them with an animalistic Other with insatiable sexual instincts (e.g., Torikobori Jo's *Iwa'ana no Tenshi* [An Angel in a Cave] [1949]). In a book entitled *Post-war Okinawa* (1955, 214), geographer Forrest Pitts, anthropologist William Lebra, and anthropologist Wayne Suttles noted that the Okinawan attitude toward Black servicemen were shaped by Japanese racial attitude that Okinawans had internalized before the war, together with white discrimination against Black servicemen and the behavior of Black servicemen that Okinawans witnessed in US-ruled Okinawa. Arnold Fisch (1988, 83–85) discussed the violence, sexual violence included, that Okinawans experienced from Black servicemen—and from members of the so-called Philippine Scouts brought over to Okinawa to replace "violent" Black servicemen—in the wake of the war, which may partially explain negative descriptions about non-White servicemen in some of the novellas produced in the late 1940s.

Meanwhile, toward the end of phase 1, residents began to feel the decline of "freedom and love" in the emerging community of *nuchi du takara* as a result of the transformation of the US occupation policy. More specifically, the intensification of the Cold War in the Asia-Pacific region, especially the rise of Communist China and the political instability of South Korea, prompted the US government to decide, between 1948 and 1949, on the long-term occupation of Okinawa, finalized by President Truman's approval of NSC 13/2 (October 1948) and NSC 13/3 (May 1949) (Eldridge 2001, chap. 6; Foreign Relations of the United States [hereafter FRUS] 1948b, 877 and 1949, esp. 731–732; Wakabayashi 2015, chap. 5). Accordingly, 1948–1949 was a time when frustrations of Okinawans with the US occupation rose, because they were left abandoned in the "forgotten island," where food prices increased, income tax was introduced, desire for political representation was suppressed, and land was seized and kept by the US military. These and other sources of frustrations led to the formation of the first major protest against the US military in postwar Okinawa (Mori 2016, 62–72; Sakurazawa 2015, 14–15; Toriyama 2013, chap. 3; Wakabayashi 2015, chap. 7).

Major General Josef Robert Sheetz, who served as the military governor of the USMGR from October 1949 through July 1950 and was remembered by Okinawans for his "just rule" (*zensei*) (Miyagi Et. 1982, 94–97), implemented new policies to control these frustrations of Okinawans (Wakabayashi 2015, chap. 6); he did so, however, not so much to liberate Okinawans as to pave the way for the long-term occupation of Okinawa. Specifically, Sheetz tried to improve the economic conditions of postwar Okinawa by reducing food prices, increasing aid (e.g., the GARIOA fund), and expanding imports from elsewhere in Japan (Toriyama 2013, chap. 4). In addition, he tried to democratize the local governing structure by establishing a system of four regional "archipelago" (*guntō*) governments within Okinawa, each led by popularly elected governors. He also tried to reduce crimes by US service members and to improve higher education of Okinawans by introducing the system of sending Okinawan students to US universities (July 1949) and establishing the University of the Ryukyus (May 1950) (Miyazato 1975, 22–24), as if he wanted to reinforce the sense of love and trust in the community of *nuchi du takara* before the anger of Okinawan "people" would overwhelm it, as will be discussed next.

2. Formation of the Okinawan "People" and Ambivalence toward the US Military (1950–1957)

In phase 2 of the US rule over Okinawa (1950–1957), love for and trust in the US military that had been generated in the nascent community of *nuchi du takara* in phase 1 (1945–1949) receded into the background, while outrage and resentment against its violence, which had constituted the background for phase 1, became prominent in that community. The background of this change was Washington's decision to occupy Okinawa for the long term in 1948–1949 to confront the rise of communism in Asia, noted above.

Accordingly, the United States began to take on the task of transforming the "forgotten island" into an extensive fortress called the "Keystone of the Pacific" (Ogden 1954) in the 1950s, a process that led the US military to exercise its power over life for a dramatic transformation of Okinawa in terms of its landscape, economy, and governance. In terms of landscape, for instance, from early 1950 on, new military barracks, shops, theaters, schools, libraries, and churches, among other structures, were built within the existing US bases in Okinawa. The outbreak of the Korean War in June

1950 confirmed the military utility of Okinawa as a launching base, a process that made the confiscation of Okinawan land by the US military during and after the Battle of Okinawa a permanent and irreversible condition (Toriyama 2013, chap. 4). The change of landscape went hand in hand with the process whereby Okinawa's economic system was irreversibly transformed from an agriculture-based one to a base-dependent one in the 1950s. Accordingly, the number of Okinawans working in agriculture decreased by 43.2%, from 259,217 in 1950 (e-Stat 1950, 11) to 147,481 in 1960 (e-Stat 1960, 205), while those pushed out of agriculture and other industries, statistically speaking, ended up entering the tertiary (service) industry targeting the US military as its key client, which increased its labor force by 435%, from 15,749 in 1950 (e-Stat 1950, 11) to 68,524 in 1960 (e-Stat 1960, 205). In the process, former owners (farmers) of the confiscated land—numbering an estimated eighty thousand as of October 1949 (Toriyama 2013, 106)—now abandoned their hope of returning to their land to cultivate it; instead, they needed to accept the semipermanent use of their land by the US military.

In the sphere of governance, Washington restructured the USMGR into a new body of military administration called the US Civil Administration of the Ryukyu Islands (USCAR) in December 1950. Entrusted with the office by General MacArthur, the deputy governor—a US Army commander—represented the authority of the USCAR beyond and above the provisional Okinawan government (established in April 1951 above the four archipelago governments), which became the Government of the Ryukyu Islands (GRI) in April 1952, headed by the chief executive appointed by the USCAR (Nakano 1969, 55). Throughout the US occupation, which lasted until 1972, the GRI remained subordinate to the USCAR, even though it was, on paper, the self-governing body of, by, and for the Okinawan "people." In fact, the GRI often consisted of the older generation of Okinawan leaders born in the 1890s and earlier, who—after having played a key role in enforcing the emperor-centered social order in Okinawa before and during the war—were chosen by the US military as the community leaders immediately after the Battle of Okinawa (Wakabayashi 2015, 139–141),

The USCAR, while transforming Okinawa's landscape, economy, and governance, also implemented a number of increasingly oppressive policies over the power of life of Okinawans. For instance, in 1952, the USCAR announced the beginning of payment of rent for the Okinawan land used for military purposes (i.e., for almost seven years, the US military did not pay any rent), even though the rent was so low that only a small fraction of Okinawans (less than 2% of landowners, numbering nine hundred or so) signed leases (Nakano 1969, 105; Okinawa Times 1973, 185). Similarly, in 1952–1953, when the wage discrimination against Okinawans and their extremely poor working conditions prompted workers to mount strikes against major Japanese construction companies involved in building facilities for the US bases in Okinawa, the USCAR responded by suppressing labor movements altogether through a number of ordinances (Toriyama 2013, chap. 6). In 1953, with "bayonets and bulldozers" (as Okinawans described them), the USCAR began to seize land at Aja and Mekaru in Mawashi Village (April 1953) and Gushi in Oroku Village (December 1953) on the island of Okinawa for the construction of new bases and for the expansion of existing bases (Miyazato 1975, 24–25), using the notorious Land Acquisition Ordinance (Ordinance 109), which in effect deprived landowners in Okinawa of any right to say no to the USCAR's decision to seize their land (Nakano 1969, 105–107; Toriyama 2013, chap. 7). In the process, the contradiction between the constituent power of postwar Okinawa and the constituted power of the US military reached a breaking point. The community of *nuchi du takara*—a cultural cushion that had allowed surviving Okinawans to embrace the US military in phase 1—now swayed them toward the anti-base position.

Those who effectively mobilized the anti-base spirit in the community of *nuchi du takara* in phase 2 were not older Okinawan leaders active since the prewar/wartime period (i.e., the members of the GRI), but new Okinawan leaders (men) born in the early twentieth century—such as Senaga Kamejirō (1907–2001) of the Okinawa People's Party, Yara Chōbyō (1902–1997) of the Okinawa Teachers' Association, Nishime Junji (1921–2001) of the Okinawa Socialist People's Party, and Kokuba Kōtarō (1927–2008) of the Okinawa People's Party. They represented the first generation of social actors in postwar Okinawa, the Okinawan "people," united by the shared hardships of the war and the US military rule. Critical of the older generation of Okinawan leaders in the GRI subservient to the USCAR, these younger leaders outside the GRI contributed to shaping new political sensibilities among the Okinawan "people" in the 1950s. The year 1955—at which point approximately 58% of the population (approximately eight hundred thousand) had been born in the twentieth century but before the war (and were between ten years old and fifty-five years old), 32% were children born after the war (and were under ten years old), and 10% had been born in the 1890s or earlier (and were fifty-six years old or older) (e-Stat 1955)—is a useful reference point for when the Okinawan "people" established themselves as the new social actor. Specifically, those between ten years old and fifty-five years old became a key constituent of the Okinawan "people"; their political vision was established against the older prewar generation (fifty-six years old or older) while it also shaped the consciousness of the younger generation (ten years old or younger) who did not experience the war. Ideologically, against the background of increasing oppression by the USCAR, the Okinawan "people" sought the reversion of Okinawa to Japan (not the independence of Okinawa under US guidance, as in phase 1) as a method for regaining political autonomy, a process that involved idealization of Japan as a democratic nation defined by the new constitution and postwar economic recovery (Sakurazawa 2015, 42–43; Wakabayashi 2015, 44 and 139–141).

The USCAR responded to the formation of the community of *nuchi du takara* with an increasing anti-base thrust in the early 1950s by, for instance, arresting and jailing thirty-plus activists of the Okinawa People's Party, including Senaga Kamejirō, its charismatic leader, in 1954 (Mori 2016, 114–117). The USCAR also declared off-limits to military personnel the entertainment quarters formed around the US bases, as a means of draining Okinawa's power of life economically, and it also suppressed public discussion on reversion by designating it communist propaganda (Toriyama 2013, chap. 8). It should be added that from the early days of occupation until 1965, the US military controlled, through a licensing system, the publication of newspapers and magazines to suppress Okinawan's freedom of speech (OPPMM 2001, 120; Wakabayashi 2015, 134–135); in the 1950s, the USCAR reinforced this suppression by targeting literary and political activities of students of the University of the Ryukyus (Gabe S. 2013). Meanwhile, the USCAR announced the seizure of additional land in areas such as the Isahama community of Ginowan Village,[8] in central Okinawa.

As the announced date of land seizure, July 18, 1955, approached, activists and sympathizers—eventually numbering ten thousand—came to Isahama to support the villagers. One reason for this massive mobilization is related to the Okinawan Communist Party as an amorphous, illegal, underground network of activists and sympathizers across Okinawa, of which Kokuba Kōtarō of the Okinawa People's Party was a central organizer (Mori 2010, chap. 3; 2016, 113–122). In a grounded description of the land seizure in Isahama in a book he published in 1973 (republished in 2019, 237–242), Kokuba noted that the US military did not do anything during the day to avoid confronting the community of *nuchi du takara* formed by the Okinawan "people." The land seizure actually started after midnight, when most of the protesters had gone back home:

> Around 3 a.m., . . . I heard an ominous noise coming from the military road right across the paddy fields. But I could not yet see what it was [due to darkness]. When the noise approached, I looked hard, and found that trucks and bulldozers filled with armed soldiers were slowly coming one after another with their headlights off. By dawn, the 40-hectare area of paddy fields was completely surrounded by the armed soldiers; then, the bulldozers rushed into the community of 32 families. . . . Things having come to this, the farmers could not do anything. They sat in the houses, now surrounded by barbed wires, to show their last resistance. After turning these farmers out of doors by pointing guns and pistols at them, U.S. soldiers started destroying the houses. First, a giant axe was driven into the roof of a variety store at the entrance of the community. The exposed crossbeam was then tied with a rope, which a bulldozer pulled, and the store fell down. Chopped wood was collected by bulldozers, put on trucks, and dumped on the nearby beach. In this way, all 32 houses were destroyed. Against such cruel treatment by the U.S. military, women protested with their hair disheveled. Watching all this [happen], I . . . could not stop something hot from welling in my eyes. (Inoue 2007, 42–43)

The USCAR exercised similar violence in Maja on Iejima Island, a small island located approximately three miles west of the Motobu Peninsula of the island of Okinawa (March 1955) (Nakano 1969, 122–125); its cruelty was highlighted when peasants and farmers on Iejima Island called themselves "beggars"—who lost everything due to the land seizure—to make public their plight by performing sit-ins in front of the GRI building from March to July 1955, and by marching on the main island of Okinawa from July 1955 until February 1956 under the leadership of Ahagon Shōkō, a larger-than-life anti-base activist mentioned in the introduction to this book (Ahagon 1973; Mitchell 2010; Mori 2016, 132–133). The cruelty of the constituted power was underscored more generally in the community of the Okinawan "people" when the report submitted in June 1956 by a Special Subcommittee of the Armed Services Committee, House of Representa-

Ambivalence toward the US Military 127

Figure 9. Okinawans joining a rally to protest the US land seizures
This picture was taken on June 20, 1956.
Source: Okinawa Prefectural Archives 1956.

tives, chaired by Congressman Melvin Price (D-Illinois), following an inspection tour of Okinawa from October 14 to November 23, 1955, supported the USCAR's land seizure procedures, including the lump-sum payment method, which meant that the United States would have the right to use the land semipermanently for military purposes (Nakano 1969, 177–179; Purves 1995–2019). Furthermore, in September 1955, a six-year-old girl was raped and murdered by a US serviceman.[9]

The Okinawan "people" confronted the USCAR by reinforcing the antibase thrust in the community of *nuchi du takara* through varied forms of protest. For instance, in June 1956, in a manner that revealed the absence/presence of structural permanency of that community by constituting and reconstituting itself only as it disintegrated itself continuingly, more than three hundred thousand Okinawans—approximately 40% of the population—participated in a series of protest rallies against the Price report held in fifty-six municipalities across US-controlled Okinawa.

In addition, this community's integrality against power together with its ability to generate explosive communication from within was shown when one hundred thousand residents attended a rally held in a schoolyard in Naha starting at eight o'clock in the evening, the atmosphere of which is conveyed in a quotation from a newspaper article below. Significantly, against the background of the support of the idea of reversion among the Okinawan "people" for the solution of political predicament of Okinawa in phase 2, the notion of Okinawa as part of the Japanese state, together with blood ties and historical bonds of the Okinawan "people" in the community of *nuchi du takara*, was highlighted against the rule of the US military, an institution from a "foreign country":

> Yara Chōbyō, president of the Okinawa Teachers Association, whose passionate eloquence is well known, then rushed out of his seat to take the microphone: "160,000 brethren died glorious deaths for defense of our homeland [Japan] and for peace. In order to repay their sacrifice, we cannot possibly give even a piece of land to a foreign country.... If we compare the benefits Okinawa has gained from the United States and the benefits the United States has gained from Okinawa, which is bigger is as clear as day." The eloquence of President Yara, convincing and squared with reason, threw the whole audience into a state of feverish excitement. Dignified faces in the [nearby] amusement park, in the [adjacent] stadium, and on the rooftops of the school buildings shouted "Yes! Yes!" again arousing a storm of handclapping. ("Yowagoshi..." 1956, cited in Nakano 1969, 192)

In a manner that complicated Okinawa's initial love for and trust in the US military in the community of *nuchi du takara* in phase 1, local novels published during phase 2 also depicted the US military with a sentiment of disillusionment, a tendency that was particularly noticeable in the radical journal *Ryūdai Bungaku* (University of Ryukyu Literature). For instance, in a novel titled *Nagaregi* (Driftwood), Kawase Shin (1954) depicted the life of protagonist Keizo, who, having fought the war in Manchuria and been detained in Siberia by Soviet Russia for two years, came back to Okinawa only to find that a military base was newly created in his village, his mother had been killed in the Battle of Okinawa, and a woman resembling his wife walked the streets like a prostitute. In a novel titled *Kurai Hana* (A Dark Flower), Kishaba Jun (1955) explored the relationship between Joe, a Black serviceman, and Nobuko, a prostitute, by writing that Nobuko felt that Joe's attitude toward her could not mask an obvious sense of superiority, expressed in the name of love. In another radical journal, *Shin-Nihonbungaku* (New Japanese Literature), published in Tokyo, Okinawan writer Shimota Seiji ([1952] 2005, [1954] 2005) wrote a series of novels that thematized the humiliation felt by old Okinawan farmers who, having experienced the Battle of Okinawa, had their land seized by the US military.

To overcome the crisis of governance, the USCAR used money; this tactic worked, at least on the surface, as exemplified by the way the island-wide protest died down and disappeared in the late 1950s because of the "reactionary" actions of Henoko and other pro-base communities.[10]

In January 1955, the USCAR notified Henoko of its plan to use the community's mountain area for military training purposes; then, in July 1955, the USCAR notified Henoko of another plan to conduct land surveying for expropriation of 500 acres of its land to build a new base (Nakano 1969, 217; Henokoku Hensan Īnkai 1998, 631; Ōshiro Y. 2013, 111). Throughout, Higa Takahiro—mayor of Kushi Village (of which Henoko was a part until 1970)—and Henoko leaders (men) relied on the Village Assembly to request that the GRI, the self-governing body of, by, and for the Okinawan "people" on paper, prevent the implementation of the land seizure plan (Henokoku Hensan Īnkai 1998, 575–587, 631). Caught between the USCAR, which had power to override the GRI's decisions, and the Okinawan "people," who demanded the cancellation of the land seizure procedures, the GRI was paralyzed, incapable of carrying out its job as a mediator. Meanwhile, between the summers of 1955 and 1956 (i.e., in the midst of the rise of the island-wide protest), the USCAR negotiated behind the scenes with landowners in Henoko and upper echelons of the Kushi Village administration. The attitude of these Okinawans appears to have softened in the process (Ōshiro Y. 2013, 111). In fact, the USCAR offered higher bids to these landowners than it had originally proposed, while suggesting that if these bids were not accepted, residents would be ordered to evacuate without receiving compensation (Henokoku Hensan Īnkai 1998, 632).

Tragic stories of the Okinawan "people" in other communities, such as Isahama and Iejima Island, whose land had been forcefully expropriated by armed US troops, were well known to residents of Henoko. Fearful that the same fate would befall their community, Henoko leaders negotiated with the USCAR over the plan, persuading the occupier to promise to provide electricity and water to Henoko, to preferentially employ residents on the base when completed, and to allow residents to grow farm products in fields that the base would rent but not use. There had been an unarticulated desire in this poor community for a modern, urban life with electricity and sanitary water; residents also hoped that the problem of depopulation in Henoko at that time—the youth had left Henoko to look for employment opportunities in central Okinawa, where new bases were being constructed— would be solved by accepting the base (Henokoku Hensan Īnkai 1998, 631– 640). Some Henoko leaders summed up these desires in a Far East Network radio broadcast in November 1956. One of them stated, "In northern Okinawa, in particular, in Henoko, . . . the benefit for residents derived from letting the US military use their land is as clear as the day."

He added, "If we are unaware of not only their way of thinking and their power but also our own power and position, then the result of our struggles [over the land issues] is uncertain no matter how much we fight" ("Watashi . . ." 1956; see also Kumamoto 2014, 257, and NHK Shuzaihan 2011, 48; cf. Ōshiro Y. 2013). In so saying, he threw into relief the enormous imbalance between the power of life (postwar Okinawa, the occupied) and the power over life (the US military, the occupier) from an economic perspective, an imbalance that unmistakably existed in spite of the "success" of the island-wide protest. Indeed, in 1957, receipts derived from US bases—from wages of base workers, rent of land used for bases, and service, entertainment, and sex businesses surrounding the bases—constituted 56.8% of Okinawa's gross income (Tomikawa, n.d., 28), which showed that, at least from an economic perspective, Okinawa's autonomy was a "myth" and did not exist, to employ the words of High Commissioner Paul Caraway (1905–1985; in office 1961–1964) in 1963 (Miyagi Et. 1982, 260–261; see below for further analysis of this statement). Following as much as materializing and reinforcing the irreversible trend toward the development of a base-dependent economy in postwar Okinawa, on December 20, 1956, Henoko, Kushi Village, and the USCAR sealed the deal for construction of a new American base—named Camp Schwab—in Henoko that would use 628 acres of its land. The mayor of Kushi Village apologetically stated that, given that military land issues had not been resolved at the higher political level, it required a lot of courage for him to sign the lease agreement on behalf of landowners in Henoko, adding, "I am prepared for the criticism against this measure from all directions." Nonetheless, he justified his decision by noting, among other things, that "Kushi Village, an out-of-the-way corner which has been economically ill-fated in all respects as compared to other towns and villages in Okinawa, could attain development by having a base" ("Sonmin . . ." 1956).

In 1957, Kin Town, just south of Henoko, followed suit by accepting the construction of Camp Hansen (Kinchō to Kichi Henshū Īnkai 1991, 32–33). This move, combined with the USCAR's decision to withdraw the proposed idea of lump-sum payment, among other factors (Sakurazawa 2015, 62–64), contributed to bringing the island-wide protest to an end in 1958

(Miyazato 1975, 41). Subsequently, Henoko and Kin—together with Koza, a community created in the late 1940s adjacent to the Kadena Air Base, noted above—each developed within their boundaries a special entertainment district for US servicemen, a process that helped residents experience unprecedented, if precarious, prosperity (Henokoku Hensan Īnkai 1998, 624–625; Katō M. 2014; Kinchō to Kichi Henshū Īnkai 1991, 32–33; Shimabuku 2019, 89–93). Specifically, as I noted in my first book (Inoue 2007, 103), "Henoko in the 1960s was seething with its excitement for money-making, happiness, and a better life. Payments made by servicemen in a bar would fill up, in a day, a big cardboard box used as a cash register, and the bar owner would have to trample down the money just to keep it from flowing out of the box." What Henoko residents then called the "rain of American dollars" (*doru no ame*) enriched their community, until the Vietnam War came to an end.

• • •

One could dismiss the compromises and concessions made by Henoko and other pro-base communities in the late 1950s as "reactionary," arguing that they simply dampened and destroyed the revolutionary thrust of the island-wide protest by the Okinawan "people" against the US military. However, I also wish to pay attention to what was produced in the process. I suggest that in spite of the "sin" of imploding the island-wide protest, the actions of these neighborhoods indeed contributed to generating something in postwar Okinawa that cannot be fully grasped by a good/bad (anti-base/pro-base or progressive/conservative) dichotomy. The concept of ambivalence, "the simultaneous existence of love and hate" (Freud [1913] 1950, 157) toward the US military, is helpful in approaching this "something"—the community of *nuchi du takara*—as a manifestation of constituent power that social actors have mediated to develop a mechanism of negotiation with the US military by inserting pro-base sentiments, positions, and perspectives into it. For, unlike the Freudian sons, the Okinawan "people" were deprived of the power to "get rid of" or overthrow the father; they were forced to depend on the very US military that had destroyed Okinawa's lifeforms, as exemplified by the transformation of the Okinawa economy, noted above. This contradiction was captured at the level of everyday life by, for instance, Kyan Yukio (1943–present), a noted bassist/singer for many Okinawan rock bands in the 1960s, including the legendary Whispers, who grew up in Koza—a mecca of the "service" industry for US servicemen created outside Kadena Air Base; he explained what he experienced when he was eight or nine years old in the early 1950s as follows:

> One day, somebody knocked on the back door of my house [which was a brothel]. As I opened it, I found a shabby-looking man holding a baby, with a little girl standing next to him. He asked me to call a woman.... As she came out, he told this woman that he needed ten dollars for the little girl's school excursion. The little girl was looking at the woman from behind. He received ten dollars, shouldered the baby, and took the little girl home with him. The woman kept crying while watching this. I did not understand what had happened until later, when I realized that this man had his wife work [as a prostitute]. (Kyan 1994, 137–138)

In light of Kyan's description, I modify Freud's idea that killing of the father generated ambivalence among the sons (see the introduction to Part II for details); rather, I suggest that after the Okinawan "people"—represented by "a shabby-looking man"—received money from the father/the US military (via Okinawan women working as prostitutes), the hatred, rather than the affection or "love," that had all this time been pushed under was bound to make itself felt. A sense of guilt made its appearance, which in this instance coincided with the remorse felt by the whole group of the Okinawan "people." In other words, money provided by the US military in various forms, while it had helped the Okinawan "people" reconstruct their lives after the war and develop their "love" toward the US military, also became a constant reminder of the US military's absolute power and violence over Okinawan social life, thereby generating "hate" toward the US military. In the process, the Okinawan "people" were suspended in the ambivalence between love (pro-base) and hate (anti-base) toward the US military. The community of *nuchi du takara* helped them contain, if not resolve, this ambivalence.

The Okinawan people's attitude toward so-called *konketsuji*, mixed-race children born to Okinawan women and US servicemen in postwar Okinawa, can also be explained in reference to ambivalence. In the refugee camps created in the midst of the Battle of Okinawa, many rapes occurred, as noted above, which—together with other forms of interracial sexual relations—became one of the origins of the births of mixed-race children in Okinawa (Pitts, Lebra, and Suttles, 1955, 111, 120; Fukuchi 1980); in the

1950s and beyond, as entertainment quarters developed in Koza, Henoko, and Kin, among other places, mixed-race children were continually born.[11] On the one hand, their presence was a testimony to the power over life exercised by the US military that also revealed the political, economic, and sexual incompetence of the Okinawan "people," who were unable to "protect their women." As a result, negative feelings ("hate") toward the US military was projected onto mixed-race children. Indeed, mixed-race children were often barred from family gatherings; their right of inheritance was often denied; and their desire to marry Okinawans was often rejected; depending on their physical characteristics, they were discriminated against with varying labels such as *amerikā* (American), *kuronbō* (Black), *akabū* (red hair), *chijirū* (frizzy hair), and *hījyāmī* (goat eyes = blue eyes) (Fukuchi 1980, 156–157; Okinawaken Kyōikushinkōkai 1976, 35).Yet, on the other hand, presence of mixed-race children—in and around the entertainment districts adjacent to the US bases, in particular—also was a constant reminder that the Okinawan "people" needed to depend on the money provided by the US military; as a result, negative feelings toward mixed-race children were also balanced by positive feelings ("love") toward the US military of which power mixed-blood children represented. In effect, presence of mixed-race children tended to tear the mind of Okinawan "people" in the ambivalence toward the US military; I suggest that the community of *nuchi du takara* was called into being in response, helping the Okinawan "people" develop an internal capacity to embrace and contain, if not resolve, conflicting emotions of love and hate for—ambivalence toward—mixed-race children as an embodiment of the power of the U.S. military.

• • •

The varied experiences of the Okinawan "people" included in this section—such as leaders of the island-wide protest, negotiators in Henoko, the wife of the shabby-looking man in Koza, and mixed-race Okinawans—show that the key to understanding the complex practices in the community of *nuchi du takara* is gender, or the androcentrism of this community and the subjectivity of those who constituted that community.

Historically speaking, the Ryukyu Kingdom, established in the early fifteenth century and abolished by Meiji Japan in the 1870s, instituted Okinawan androcentrism by fusing power of the male-centered court with a religious authority of priestesses who, in the image of *unai-gami* (meaning sister-goddess), served as the spiritual guardians of her brother who was the king (Takara 1987, 176–192). Okinawan androcentrism was fortified in prewar Okinawa due in part to the introduction of the Japanese legal system. For instance, it considered women in Okinawa (as elsewhere in Japan) to be "incompetent" and without any legal capacity. The local androcentrism was acutely expressed in the "compulsory group suicide" during the Battle of Okinawa, in which the heads of the families, men, killed their own wives, children, and other family members as well as themselves under the orders of the Japanese Imperial Army (Miyagi H. 2008b), as discussed earlier. The local androcentrism was then retained in Okinawa after the war, because (in spite of limited efforts of the US military to improve women's conditions by, for instance, giving them voting rights) the gender-sensitive constitution of postwar Japan was not applied in Okinawa due to US rule (Sawada 2014, 110–113). Even though the more gender-equal new Civil Code (created in reference to the postwar Civil Code of Japan, adopted in 1948, as the model) was introduced to US-ruled Okinawa in 1957 (Horiba 1990, 192; Kugai 1990), social expectations and pressure for women to produce male offspring remained strong in postwar Okinawa to compensate for the loss of a large number of males who had been killed in the war. Shaped by a myriad of historical currents, androcentrism was crystalized at the core of subjectivity of the Okinawan "people" when they confronted and negotiated with the US military in phase 2 (1950–1957).

Indeed, the experiences of the Okinawan "people" discussed in this section show that the local androcentrism not only constituted the Okinawan "people" as the oppressed in terms of race and class vis-à-vis the US military but also subordinated women and mixed-race Okinawans in terms of gender and race. In other words, androcentrism—an organizing principle of the community of *nuchi du takara* constructed by the Okinawan "people" at the intersection of race, gender, and class—developed two faces, as it were, in relation to the US military externally and in relation to Okinawan women and mixed-race Okinawans internally. For the notion of *nuchi du takara* helped the Okinawan "people" externally engage in complex negotiations with the US military on the basis of the internal capacity of their community to contain and accommodate (if not resolve) tensions among diverse and often contradictory attitudes, experiences, and perspectives regarding the US military. In the next section, I will analyze the ways in which these two faces developed as the Okinawan people's ambivalence toward the US military deepened in the community of *nuchi du takara*.

3. Okinawa's Deepening Ambivalence toward the US Military and the Formation of the Two Taboos (1958–1966)

If the division between the pro-base and anti-base sectors—or between the economic desire for a better life anchored in the presence of the US military (e.g., Henoko, Kin, and Koza) and the political logic of justice grounded in the yearning for returning to Japan (e.g., the island-wide protest against the US military)—highlighted Okinawan people's emerging ambivalence in the community of *nuchi du takara* during phase 2 of the US rule (1950–1957), the contradiction deepened in phase 3 (1958–1966).

On the one hand, Okinawa's antipathy to the US military intensified in that community due to accidents and crimes such as the following, to mention only six examples: (*a*) in 1959, a US fighter plane crashed into an elementary school and killed seventeen people (including eleven children) and injured 210 people (including 156 children); (*b*) in the same year, a US serviceman shot a farm woman he mistook for a wild boar; (*c*) in 1961, a serviceman committed a hit-and-run, killing two girls and injuring two others; (*d*) in 1962, a US Air Force cargo plane crashed into a local house, killing five crew members and two Okinawans and injuring eight people; (*e*) in 1963, a US serviceman driving a military truck went through a red light, killing an Okinawan junior high school student; and (*f*) in 1965, a military trailer fell from a fighter plane and crushed a local girl to death (OPPMM 2001, 132–133). It should be added that under US rule, "Okinawa was allowed to arrest US military personnel only for crimes committed in the presence of a [police officer]; it had no legal right to investigate or to otherwise exercise jurisdiction over them" (Inoue 2017a, xiv–xv).

Meanwhile, a new administrative position, high commissioner, was created in the USCAR in 1957. While Washington hoped that this position would bring order and stability to Okinawa after the disquieting dispute over land seizure procedures, its effects were limited. In particular, representing the will of the US military, High Commissioner Paul Caraway (in office 1961–1964) behaved in a way that concretized the aforementioned statement he made in 1963—that political autonomy of the Ryukyu Islands is a "myth" (Miyagi Et. 1982, 260–261)—by suppressing, for instance, Okinawa's demand for popular election of the chief executive of the GRI, who had been appointed by the USCAR since 1952 (Miyagi Et. 1982, 262–275; Nakano 1969, 359; Miyazato 1975, 62–63). Overall, Okinawa's resentment toward the US military remained strong in the community of *nuchi du takara* during phase 3, which was reflected in the formation of Okinawaken Sokoku Fukki Kyōgikai (also known as Fukkikyō, or the Association for the Reversion of Okinawa Prefecture to the Homeland) in 1960 (Miyazato 1975, 62) and the rise of its movement. The desire of the Okinawan "people" for reversion had taken shape first in the mid-1950s, but the USCAR had suppressed this desire by viewing it as communist propaganda, as noted. However, in the 1960s, in spite of the continuation of the Cold War, the USCAR was no longer able to suppress the power of life of the Okinawan "people" desiring reversion as it had in the 1950s. So widespread had that desire become, that "reversion appear[ed] to be the preference of some 90% of the Okinawans," as political scientist Higa Mikio[12] stated in his book published in 1963 (92).

On the other hand, however, the love for and trust in the US military also increased in the community of *nuchi du takara* during phase 3, because of the reinforcement of the base-dependent economy: base-related receipts remained 40%–50% of Okinawa's gross income in the first half of the 1960s (Tomikawa, n.d., 28). In addition, while B-yen had been used in postwar Okinawa since 1948 for the development of the base-dependent economy (see chapter 4, section 1, for further analysis), in 1958, the USCAR discontinued the B-yen and introduced the US dollar in Okinawa instead in order to bring about a shift from the controlled, base-dependent economy that discouraged innovation and reform of business practices to the more liberalized, free-trade-oriented market economy that would encourage entrepreneurship, or really to contain Okinawa's frustrations at problems caused by the US military within the dream of Americanization (Ryukyu Ginkō Chōsabu 1984, chap. 8). Furthermore, in a manner that would allow the Okinawan "people" to witness the arrival of the "high-growth era" in an Okinawan version (Sakurazawa 2015, 105–106), Washington increased its financial support for Okinawa to counter and control the multiplying voices calling for reversion to Japan. The love for and trust in the US military resulted in the expansion of the power of pro-USCAR assemblymen in the Okinawa Congress in the first half of the 1960s, exemplified by the merging of the conservative parties in 1959, their victory in the general elections for the Okinawa Congress in 1960 and 1962, and the reinforcement of their power in 1964 (Miyazato 1975, 52 and 72; Sakurazawa 2015, 92–94, 98–100, and 105–106).

I analyze Ōshiro Tatsuhiro's *The Cocktail Party* ([1967] 1989, translated by Steve Rabson)—the first Okinawan novel to receive in 1967 the prestigious Akutagawa Prize, the gateway for success in the literary world in Japan—as a work that most clearly captured the sense of intensified ambivalence of the oppressed Okinawan "people" toward the US military in the changing community of *nuchi du takara* during phase 3. I do so by building on critics who analyzed this novel to interrogate the intersectionality of gender, race, language, nation/state, post/colonialism, and other issues (e.g., Bhowmik, 2008, 100–104; Matsushita 2011; Molasky 1999, chap. 1; Motohama 2003; Okamoto K. 1986; Rabson 1989, 1993; Yoneyama 2016, chap. 1). Originally written in 1965, the novel was published in 1967, situated in a transitional period between phase 3 (1957–1966) and phase 4 (1967–1972) of the US occupation of Okinawa. Accordingly, significantly, the novel also depicted the mechanism—the two "taboos," as explicated below—the Okinawan "people" developed to cope with the intensified sense of ambivalence toward the US military, in a manner that anticipated the reversion movement during phase 4.

The novel is divided into two parts. The first part is described from the perspective of "I" (the protagonist), the second part from a perspective that objectifies the protagonist as "you." In so doing, the novel helps us probe how the subjectivity of the Okinawan "people" is constructed through reflexivity, "the turning-back of the experience of the individual upon himself [sic]" (Mead 1934, 134), through which "I" (the protagonist) as a subject becomes also an object to himself and vice versa.

In the first part of the novel, the protagonist, an elite Okinawan man working for the GRI who has a wife and a daughter attending high school, is invited to a cocktail party organized by Mr. Miller, an American officer who will later turn out to work (as a "spy," so to speak) for the Army Counter Intelligence Corps, and his wife at their house, located in a gated community reserved for US military personnel and separated by fences from the Okinawan community. Also invited, in addition to the protagonist, are Mr. Sun, a Chinese lawyer practicing in US-ruled Okinawa who had fled from mainland China to escape atrocities of the Japanese Imperial Army during World War II; Mr. Ogawa, a newspaper reporter from Japan "proper" (and possibly from a *buraku*, a discriminated community of outcast people); and Mr. Miller's other friends from the US military. The protagonist, Miller, Sun, and Ogawa know each other because they are the members of a "Chinese-Language Research Group" that they unofficially created to practice Chinese; they meet once a month at a club on the base to build international friendship. In effect, this friendship is created and maintained by the presence of the US military, toward which Okinawa's "love" is expressed in the following way:

> We'd been introduced once to Mrs. Miller at the club, and my first thought now [after receiving the invitation] was that I could have another look at her beautiful face and voluptuous figure. And, of course, we'd be able to enjoy the fine liquor none of us local people could ever afford on our salaries. Almost before I realized it, I had begun to take pleasure in things that had nothing to do with our Chinese conversation fellowship. Not the least of these was the military club where we gathered every month. Meals there were tax-free, so we could eat and drink quite cheaply. It was also a place to which only a few local people were admitted. My pleasure was somehow enhanced by the feeling that I'd been chosen to enjoy these privileges. (37)

The party is cordial. Even as participants talk about sensitive political issues—such as the reversion of Okinawa, the independence of Okinawa, the relations among Okinawa, Japan "proper," China, and the United States, the war, and communism—the conversation never goes beyond the limit of "friendship," in a manner that helps maintain the love for and trust in the US military in the community of *nuchi du takara*. In its midst, there is an announcement that a three-year-old son of one of the participants in the party, Mr. Morgan, an American officer, is missing. And yet, this small disturbance, too, is resolved when it is discovered that his Okinawan maid took the boy along to her house on her day off without informing anybody, after which the facade of friendship is maintained to the end of the party.

However, the second part, written from a perspective that objectifies "I," highlights "rage" (53) and "outrage" (80) toward the US military as it revolves around the protagonist's struggle to seek justice for the rape of his own daughter by an American serviceman, Robert Harris, at Cape M. This rage is intense because of the contradiction in his own and Okinawa's life, that he depended on the very father who oppresses him. That is, in addition to working as an employee of the GRI, an organization subordinate to the USCAR, the protagonist rented an apartment in the rear of his house to the very serviceman who, while using this room to keep an Okinawan mistress, raped his daughter as he—the protagonist—took pleasure in the cocktail party. A sense of guilt made its appearance, which in this instance coincided with the remorse felt by the protagonist. The power differential is absolute, however, because of the law that the ruler, the US military, instituted in

Okinawa, the ruled: the daughter has been detained due to her "crime" of pushing the rapist over an embankment of the cape and causing him to be hospitalized, a situation that was no less unsettling than the action of Mr. Morgan, mentioned above, who later decided to sue the Okinawan maid for her "crime" of taking his son along to her house. Meanwhile, it was "impossible to prove the defendant's claim of self-defense because the Okinawan judiciary has no authority to summon US military personnel—such as Robert Harris—as witnesses" (55).

In the process, "international friendship" falls apart into conflicts and differences among the American, Japanese, Chinese, and Okinawan "people"—even though certain experiences (e.g., statelessness) are shared by somebody (e.g., the protagonist and Mr. Sun) (Yoneyama 2016, chap. 1). The novella highlights such conflicts and differences by revealing that (*a*) the protagonist was a soldier in the Japanese Imperial Army deployed to China during the war; (*b*) a soldier of the Japanese Imperial Army raped Mr. Sun's wife; (*c*) Mr. Sun declines to assist the protagonist in bringing an accusation against the rapist Robert Harris, citing as the reason his delicate residential status as a Chinese refugee in US-ruled Okinawa; (*d*) Mr. Ogawa's (Japan's) willingness to help the protagonist (Okinawa) was complicated by Okinawa's collective memory of the Japanese Imperial Army's atrocities against Okinawans during the Battle of Okinawa; and (*e*) Mr. Miller refused to help the protagonist, highlighting the importance of US-Okinawa friendship. Interlacing these and other subtexts, the novella brings forward the ways in which the category of the Okinawan "people"—gendered as male, racialized as non-White, and class-bound as oppressed—is crystalized within the protagonist in his absolute helplessness. It should be added that the protagonist constructs the category of the Okinawan "people" by disavowing (subjectively, as "I") yet also being implicated in (objectively, as "you") the historical process whereby he has been complicit in the very institution—the Japanese military then and the US military now—that exercises violence against him and Okinawa.

In depicting the simultaneous existence of love and hate toward the US military, this novel also elaborates on two specific "taboos" constructed as a mechanism to cope with this ambivalence. On the one hand, *The Cocktail Party* expresses a homosocial taboo—"Don't develop friendship with the US military"—as a *fraternal* command to unite the Okinawan "people's" community of *nuchi du takara* against the US military by showing that the protagonist, against all odds, decided to file charges against Robert Harris to seek justice for his daughter; he declared to Mr. Miller that the international friendship is "only a disguise. This great friendship you talk about is nothing but a mask [you, as a member of the Army Counter Intelligence Corps who spy on me, have] all put on" (77).

The second and related taboo is "Don't allow sexual relations between Okinawan women and US servicemen." This Okinawan taboo registers a heterosocial command by the community of *nuchi du takara* of Okinawan "people," a *fratriarchal* command to protect (or control, depending on one's perspective) "pure" Okinawan women—like the protagonist's daughter—from the US military. The closing paragraphs of the novel, which describe the inspection of the protagonist's daughter at Cape M conducted according to a judge's instruction, give the sense of purity to be protected by this command: wearing "a one-piece dress" as "her hair fluttered in the breeze" (79), the daughter "stretched one of her light-brown arms out over the cliff and held the other above her head. In the background was a sea so blue it seemed to soak into the pupils of your eyes. She might have been reenacting the moment of desperation when she pushed her tormentor over the cliff. In the ocean, a white bank of wave crests glided toward a distant reef. You stared at your daughter and held your breath, praying that she would be able to fight her case openly and vigorously at a trial" (80).

In the process, significantly, this taboo—"Don't allow sexual relationships between Okinawan women and US servicemen"—also enabled the community of *nuchi du takara* of Okinawan "people" to internally construct a class hierarchy by marginalizing "impure" women in the entertainment quarters who worked to satisfy the needs, sexual needs included, of US servicemen, a process that extended an act of Okinawan leaders (men) in the late 1940s who tried to protect Okinawan women (but to sacrifice a specific group of Okinawan women) by setting up "comfort facilities" for US servicemen, noted above. In this novel, the behavior of Robert Harris's mistress, the "impure" woman, who apparently came from a remote island within Okinawa, an island that historically had been the object of discrimination by Okinawans themselves, is described as follows: "She immediately began to pack her belongings, and by the next day she had moved out. . . . She left no message to give [Robert Harris] when he returned. You felt then how remote this girl's world was from your own" (53). The marginalization of "impure" women in this phase (1958–1966) is also exemplified by an episode that I wrote in my first book on the basis of a fieldwork experience that I had in 1998:

In a deserted, small bar in the commercial area of Henoko where she worked, a woman in her fifties told me ... that she was from a poor village in central Okinawa and had moved to Henoko in the 1960s to work as a bar hostess. The oldest of five siblings (two younger brothers, two younger sisters, and herself), she needed to support her family by sending home $200 a month, as her mother was blind and her father had died at an early age. Sleeping with her would cost a U.S. serviceman $5. The money she made enabled the family to remodel their thatch-roofed house and her sisters and brothers to attend and graduate from high school; she was very proud of the financial contributions she had made to her family. Nevertheless, one day, the elder of her two brothers during a quarrel disdainfully called her *panpan*, a derogative term meaning prostitute, which so chagrined her that she immediately grabbed a kitchen knife and shouted, "Say that word again! I will kill you!" As the privileged, protected oldest son in the [androcentric] Okinawan kinship system called *munchū* [see chapter 4, section 2], "He would not understand how I felt when I had to sell myself," she said, half crying. "I would never forgive my brother, never." (Inoue 2007, 111–112)

In effect, *The Cocktail Party* revealed the ways in which the Okinawan "people" coped with their ambivalence toward the US military by synchronizing the homosocial taboo with the heterosocial taboo, a process that helped them to constitute, externally, a fraternal autonomy of their community of *nuchi du takara* against the US military, on the one hand, and to reinforce, internally, fratriarchal control over women and others such as mixed-race Okinawans in that community, on the other.[13] The duality—fraternity and fratriarchy—of the androcentrism of the Okinawan "people" is the basic characteristic of their community of *nuchi du takara* in this phase.

4. Completing the Construction of the Community of *Nuchi Du Takara* by the Okinawan "People" in a Transition from the Local Time-Space to the National Time-Space (1967–1972)

This section explores how the duality—fraternity and fratriarchy—of the androcentrism of the Okinawan "people" was developed socially and politically beyond the realm of literary works in phase 4 (1967–1972) of US-ruled Okinawa. I so doing, I examine how their community of *nuchi du takara* would be completed precisely when it began to break down from within. I accomplish this task in two steps. First, I look at activities of a women-only theater company, the Otohime Troupe (Otohime Gekidan), from the days of the refugee camps through the early 1960s, in order to retrace the formation of the heterosocial taboo ("Don't allow sexual relations between Okinawan women and US servicemen") at the level of everyday social life in postwar Okinawa, a process that highlighted the significance of fratriarchy in the community of *nuchi du takara* constructed by the Okinawan "people." Then I explore how this heterosocial taboo, against the background of the dramatic change of material conditions in Okinawa, was synchronized with the homosocial taboo ("Don't develop friendship with the US military") in an institutional political process—the reversion movement—in the 1960s through 1972, a process that underscored the power of fraternity in the community of *nuchi du takara* of the Okinawan "people." In so doing, I also explore how the Okinawan "people" shifted the site of construction of their community from the local time-space regulated by the US military, beginning to redefine it as a new community of confident and affluent "citizens" in the national time-space produced by Japan.

4.1. The Otohime Troupe and the Formation of the Heterosocial Taboo

Noted for its exuberance and elegance, the Otohime Troupe—a women-only theater company—originated in the refugee camps created in the midst of the Battle of Okinawa, where "the U.S. Military Government encouraged the performing arts as an important component in postwar recovery" (OPPMM 2001, 106; cf. Barske 2010, 16–21). Many (but not all) members of Otohime—meaning "young princesses"—were from a special entertainment district, Tsuji (Chīji in Okinawan pronunciation). Allow me to discuss the significance of this place first, to pave the way for analyzing Otohime's activities in postwar Okinawa.

Located near Naminoue Beach in Naha City, Tsuji—though destroyed as a result of a US air raid on Naha in October 1944—was established in the late seventeenth century by the Ryukyu Kingdom, as a place where women called *juri* entertained male guests—such as envoys, officials, merchants, travelers, and others—from China and Japan "proper" for "comfort," as Miyagi Eishō (1967, 141) noted. Such practices were established against the historical background of the double subordination of the Ryukyu Kingdom to China and Japan in premodern times.[14] Local worthies, such as court officials, merchants, and sailors (in the age of the Ryukyu Kingdom) and

Figure 10. The Otohime Troupe
Noted for its exuberance and elegance, the Otohime Troupe—a women-only theater company—originated in the refugee camps created in the midst of the Battle of Okinawa. The troupe's popularity peaked in the late 1950s but declined thereafter because of commercial TV broadcasting that began in 1959 in Okinawa; instead of going to the theaters, the Okinawan people watched performances aired by TV stations. In 1970 the Otohime Troupe announced its dissolution. Earlier members were often from Tsuji, a special entertainment district in Naha.

politicians, bureaucrats, businessmen, journalists, and school administrators (in prewar Okinawa), were also important patrons (Miyagi Ei. 1967, 181, 294–302; Yonaha S. 2016, 17–18). Typically, *juri* were from rural families afflicted with poverty; many of them had been sold by their own parents for monetary reasons when they were little, as exemplified by Uema Ikuko, the founder of the Otohime Troupe, who came to Tsuji when she was eight due to the death of her father, which had put her mother—with four children to raise—in great difficulty (Uema I. 1981, 107–108), and by Uehara Eiko, the model for Lotus Blossom in the novel, play, and movie *The Teahouse of the August Moon* ("Uehara Eiko," n.d.),[15] who came to Tsuji at the age of four due to the poverty of her farming family (Uehara 1976, 14–53). These girls lived in the teahouses—functioning as at once inns, restaurants, meeting places, and brothels—owned and/or managed by older women (former *juri*) called *anmā* who bought the girls. *Anmā* trained young girls in "performing arts," which included not only dance and music but also sex work, in addition to a range of housekeeping duties such as cooking, waiting, and cleaning, in order to help them become *juri* so that they would repay the amount of money the *anmā* had paid to buy and raise them. *Anmā* and *juri* are said to have been united by a special family-like love stronger than family love. *Juri* were not sexual slaves; while bound in unequal gender and economic relations, they had the power to choose their customers. *Anmā* were the administrators of this special district; men were excluded from the governing body of Tsuji (Kinjō Y. 1977, 20–33).

At one level, *juri* were idealized in Okinawa through the image of "flowers of Tsuji," a presence carrying the torch of the culture of the Ryukyu Kingdom with the capacity to provide men a kind of cultural (including sexual) experience that ordinary life centering on work and family could not offer. And yet, as Valerie Barske (2013, 70–71) notes, women in Tsuji—but not the men who frequented this pleasure quarter—were often seen as the source of venereal diseases, a social "threat" to the existing order (cf. Miyagi Ei. 1967, 299–302; Ōta M. 1976, 279–289). The Japanese military exploited and reinforced the marginalized status of such women during the war by setting up "comfort stations" across Okinawa where women from Tsuji as well as Korean women, among others, served soldiers sexually (Akutibu Myūjiamu Onnatachi no Sensō to Heiwa Shiryōkan (wam) 2020, Kawada 1987). Accordingly, as Uema Ikuko noted, "in times of peace, women in Tsuji were denounced as those who 'destroy happy families,' while in times of emergency, they were forced to offer sexual services 'for the nation, for the soldiers' through the order of authorities" (Uema I. 1981, 119).

Former *juri* such as Uema Ikuko and Uehara Eiko infused their power of life into the refugee camps, the metaphysical foundation of the community of *nuchi du takara* that divided as much as connected the dying other and the living self through the shared experience of the war; they performed dance and music to give a sense of hope to those Okinawans who had survived the war. I noted earlier the extraordinary presentation of a program in a refugee camp in Ishikawa on Christmas Day in 1945. Other programs presented on that day included dances by women from Tsuji (Inagaki 1990, 55–56), a process that constituted the starting point for the establishment in 1949 of the first women-only theater company, the Otohime Troupe, consisting of some twenty members (Ōshiro et al. 1990, 47). The problem was that in prewar Okinawa female performers were marginalized within an established male-centered system of Okinawan performing arts originated, at least in part, in the court culture of the Ryukyu Kingdom (Hosoi 2014).[16] *Juri* thus performed mostly in the "teahouses" in Tsuji for their patrons (men) or occasionally in the playhouses around Tsuji together with established male performers (Yonaha S. 2016, 15–17). After the Battle of Okinawa, however, ideas of gender equality, democracy, and freedom were "imposed" by the US military, as exemplified by the universal suffrage introduced to the refugee camps in 1945 in spite of the opposition of Okinawan men (noted in section 1 of this chapter). In a manner that concretized these ideas at the level of everyday social life, women in Tsuji transformed the refugee camps into a new "public space" in postwar Okinawa, in a manner that showed the development of the community of *nuchi du takara* at the everyday/social level beyond the metaphysical level of life and death that the refugee camps represented.

Indeed, while the refugee camps were mostly closed in 1946, this public space did not disappear but spread across the entire social realm of postwar Okinawa. Due to the desire of the Okinawan "people" for re-experiencing what they had seen in the refugee camps, outdoor stages, often without roofs, made out of articles disposed of by (or stolen from) the US military numbered as many as forty-four across Okinawa in 1948 (Kabira C. 1997, 107), and the number of performance troupes, including Otohime, was at least twenty-seven in 1950 as compared to three that traveled among the refugee camps immediately after the war (Kabira C. 1997, 75–76; Inagaki

1990, 67–68). Otohime's popularity became particularly explosive in the 1950s. For instance: (*a*) when visiting Hawaii in 1951 in response to the earnest request of Okinawan immigrants in Hawaii, they continuously drew full houses for four months (Uema I. 1981, 126–127); (*b*) they received the "best theatrical company" award (competing against other established companies with famous male actors) in 1955 (Miyagi Ei. 1967, 360); and (*c*) Kawabata Yasunari (1899–1972), a noted Japanese writer who received a Nobel Prize in Literature in 1968, visited Okinawa in 1958 in order to watch the performance of the Otohime Troupe (Makishi 2016). The majority of the audience of Otohime, it should be added, consisted of women (Ikemiya 1990, 43).

And yet one should not exaggerate the agency of women in the early phases of postwar Okinawa, which was embedded in the local time-space controlled by the US military (men). The US military's goal of separating Okinawa from Japan "proper" in early phases of its rule, noted earlier, was translated into a cultural policy wherein the Okinawan "people" were encouraged to reclaim an authentic "Ryukyuan" culture (Kano 1987, 3–112, esp. 53–68), a policy that persisted until the mid-1960s (Binnendijk 1973, 50; Miyazato 1975, 37; see also Loo 2014, chap. 5 and Miyagi Et. 1982, 371). It should be added that before the war Okinawan culture, as an embodiment of its "backwardness" vis-à-vis progressive Japan "proper," was often identified by the Okinawan "people"—and particularly by its leaders—as something that needed to be eradicated to stop Japanese discrimination against Okinawa, a topic that will be discussed further in chapter 6. The US military turned this same "culture" into a source of pride and identity for "Ryukyuans" (Inoue 2007, 49). Otohime's performance—utilizing Okinawan dialect, the *sanshin* music, and traditional hairstyles and costumes—as in the case of Okinawa's performing arts at large, was a crystallization of the production of authentic Okinawan culture as the US military wanted to see it (Ōshiro T. 1990a, 191).

Meanwhile, the Okinawan "people" (men) appropriated Otohime to shape the heterosocial taboo—"Don't allow sexual relationships between Okinawan women and US servicemen"—by celebrating Otohime as "the representation of good old Okinawa" (Kojima 1990, 42), "a form of renaissance of Okinawan culture" (Yano Te. 1974, 420), and "an expression of a culture shared by the [Okinawan] race" (Inagaki 1990, 151). Reflecting the energy they invested in the appraisal as well as in the protection, production, and control of Otohime, the list of praise for Otohime by Okinawan "people" (men) is long, including writers such as Ōshiro Tatsuhiro (1990b), Funakoshi Gishō (1990), Kayō Yasuo (1990; also cited in Inagaki 1990, 151), and Nagadō Eikichi (1985), politicians/administrators such as Kabira Chōshin (GRI administrator, in office 1946–ca. 1953) (cited in Inagaki, 1990, 151), Ōta Seisaku (GRI chairman, in office 1959–1964) (1990), Oyadomari Kōsei (Naha City mayor, in office 1984–2000) (1990), Inamine Kei'ichi (Okinawa governor, in office 1998–2006) (1999), and other noted males in postwar Okinawa's leadership positions such as Onaha Būten (performer) (Otohime Gekidan 1999), Koiso Kazuo (president of Okinawa Television Broadcasting) (1990), and Oroku Kunio (president of Ryukyu Broadcasting) (1990).

Such appraisals—conducted in Japanese, the language the ruler did not comprehend—helped the Okinawan "people" (men) to regulate the constituent power of Okinawan women internally, by asserting *fratriarchal* control over Otohime as "their" women, on the one hand, and by establishing the community of *nuchi du takara* that excluded the US military from the very realm, authentic Okinawan culture independent of Japan "proper," that it had constructed in the island it ruled, on the other. Equally important, it is the above-cited men who contributed, directly and indirectly, to the *fraternity* of the reversion movement against the US military externally. For instance, in the early 1960s, as the GRI chairman, Ōta Seisaku—included on the list of Otohime supporters above—played a key role in unifying Okinawa with Japan in the domains of economy and politics (Ōta S. 1980). Another Otohime supporter, Ōshiro Tatsuhiro, from a cultural and literary perspective, endorsed as much as facilitated the reversion of Okinawa to Japan by stating, "I anticipate that after reversion, various social conditions [such as middle-class Okinawan children understanding standard Japanese better than Okinawan dialect] today will facilitate the true 'unification of [Okinawa with Japan] in spirit'" ([1970] 1992, 59). In the 1960s, Ryukyu Broadcasting (Ryukyu Hōsō Kikakubu 1965) and Okinawa Television Broadcasting (Okinawa Terebi Hōsō Sōgōkikakushitsu 1989), whose leaders enthusiastically supported Otohime, as noted above, also powerfully contributed to integrating Okinawa into Japan by transforming the media environment of postwar Okinawa, as discussed below. By playing a leadership role in the reversion of Okinawa across the levels of politics, literature, and media culture, these men—the Okinawan "people"—materialized the homosocial taboo, "Do not develop friendship with the US military," to constitute the community of *nuchi du takara* externally against the ruler.

In effect, the same Okinawan male leaders who reinforced *fratriarchy* within Okinawa by supporting Otohime in the 1950s contributed to the *fraternity* of the reversion movement against the US military in the 1960s. The process of mediation between fratriarchy (internal control of the constituent power of Okinawan women) and fraternity (external negotiation with and against the constituted power of the US military) also highlights how the poor and oppressed Okinawan "people" confined in the local time-space reinforced and completed the community of *nuchi du takara* toward the end of US control of Okinawa, while at the same time beginning to rearticulate it into a community of affluent and confident Okinawan "citizens" in the national/Japanized time-space. I trace this complex formation and transformation of the community of *nuchi du takara* in reference to the reversion of Okinawa below.

4.2. The Construction of the National Time-Space in Okinawa and the Reversion Movement as a New Life-Form in the Community of Nuchi Du Takara

In the 1960s, economic and cultural exchanges between Okinawa and wider Japan in various forms rapidly shortened the psychosocial distance between them. The Akutagawa Prize given to Ōshiro Tatsuhiro's *The Cocktail Party* in 1967 was one example. In addition, the number of Japanese pilgrims/tourists visiting war memorials, which had begun in the 1950s, increased in the 1960s (Figal 2012, chap. 2). Similarly, interactions between women's associations of Okinawa and the rest of Japan increased in the 1960s, as Mire Koikari analyzes (2015, 20; see also chap. 6 of her book). Furthermore, in 1961, President John F. Kennedy permitted Tokyo to contribute financial aid to Okinawa (Miyazato 1975, 57–58; Sakurazawa 2015, 116); the amount of support from Tokyo exceeded that from Washington in 1967 (Miyazato 1975, 71).

In a way that reinforced these and other cultural and economic interactions, commercial TV broadcasting began in 1959 in Okinawa (Miyagi Et. 1994, 165), which caused a proliferation of TV sets there—the number of TV sets increased from 10,000 in 1960 to 100,000 in 1965 and to 168,940 in 1969 (Binnendijk 1973, 56), as a growing number of Japanese programs was watched locally. In contrast, the Otohime Troupe's popularity, which peaked in the late 1950s, declined thereafter because, instead of going to the theaters, the Okinawan "people" watched Okinawan performances aired by

TV stations (Asato K. 1989, 172–177). As a result, the number of Okinawan theater groups decreased dramatically. Otohime could not avoid the effects of this shift. Financial circumstances were particularly difficult, and in 1970 Otohime announced its dissolution.[17]

Furthermore, in 1964, the year of the Tokyo Olympics, a microwave circuit was established between Okinawa and wider Japan, enabling the Okinawan "people" to watch this national event in real time on TV (Miyagi Et. 1994, 221). This was an important media event that constituted a sharp contrast with the environment in place until the 1950s, in which "the population—some 882,000 by 1960—lived in island isolation . . . with communications entirely in the hands of the occupying power" (Binnendijk 1973, 23). Meanwhile, the microwave circuit also made it possible for NHK's public (i.e., noncommercial) news and other programs to be broadcast via Okinawa's two commercial TV stations, a process that contributed to introducing the Okinawan "people" to the lifestyles of increasingly affluent Japanese through commercials for electronic appliances, foods, medicines, and cosmetics offered by Japanese companies such as Matsushita (today's Panasonic), Lion (noted for its toothpaste), and Ajinomoto (Asato K. 1989, 104–113; Odagiri 2012).

Influence from elsewhere in Japan increased in terms of the print media, too, not only because "all full-time foreign correspondents in Okinawa were Japanese" and "a large proportion of the hard news for Okinawan consumption was drawn from Japanese wire services" (Binnendijk 1973, 51) but also because of a doubling of the combined daily circulation of two major newspapers, *Okinawa Times* and *Ryukyu Shimpo*, that incorporated the hard news drawn from Japanese wire services: circulation increased from 110,000 in 1960 to 223,000 in 1969 (Binnendijk 1973, 56 and 66). Similarly, the number of radio sets increased from 100,000 in 1960 to 317,700 in 1969 (Binnendijk 1973, 56). In addition, the value of books and magazines shipped from elsewhere in Japan to Okinawa increased dramatically in the 1960s (Binnendijk 1973, 64).

It is within this newly emerging Japanese time-space that the reversion movement was articulated for the completion of the community of *nuchi du takara* by the Okinawan "people." As Yara Chōbyō, now the leader of Fukkikyō (the Association for the Reversion of Okinawa Prefecture to the Homeland), stated in 1970 in an interview conducted by foreign policy analyst Johannes Binnendijk, "The press and TV in Okinawa played a pivotal role in spreading the reversion movement. Without the help of the mass communications media, reversion would not have developed into a political movement" (cited in Binnendijk 1973, 49).

As noted, reversion became the preference of more than 90% of Okinawans in the first half of the 1960s. During this period, a collective opinion of the Okinawan "people" in favor of reversion was expressed economically in terms of their desire for a better life, for an improvement of their material conditions, with wider Japan imagined "as the model, indeed the ideal, to emulate," to borrow from Koikari (2015, 20). Consequently, political issues related to the US bases were temporarily put on the back burner (Sakurazawa 2015, 86). Indeed, as Japan thrived in the age of high growth (approx. 1955–1972), economic conditions in pre-reversion Okinawa remained relatively dismal in spite of continuing financial aid for Okinawa from the US and Tokyo, although Okinawa's GNP grew substantially during the same period. For instance, (*a*) the average per capita income of an Okinawan worker remained in the range of 50%–60% of that of a worker in the rest of Japan during the 1960s (Kurima 1998, 27); (*b*) as of 1965, the average monthly salary of a manager of the GRI, $43.70, was about one-third that of a private (the lowest-ranking serviceman) in the US military, which was $125.10 ("Kichi Nakunaruto . . ." 2019); and (*c*) the number of medical facilities in 1972 (right before reversion) was about one-half that of other prefectures in Japan "proper" (Miyamoto 2000, 8). The power of life among the Okinawan "people" desiring a better material life resulted, in the first half of the 1960s, in the reversion movement that highlighted not so much hatred toward the US military as a renewed sense of attachment to and dependence on Japan, the "mother"-land, through the enthusiastic display of the rising sun flag in public spaces across Okinawa (Oguma 1998, chap. 22, esp. 569–577)—an act made possible by President Kennedy, who had allowed the Japanese flag to be hung in public buildings in Okinawa on holidays (including the birthday of the emperor) in 1961. Critics Miyagi Etsujirō (1982, 233) and Ōmine Sawa (2008, 155), among others, also noted that Okinawa in the 1960s represented the relationship between itself and the rest of Japan through the *image* of the mother-child relationship (cf. Doi Take. 1971)—though the *actuality* of the relationship was defined by the imbalances in power between men, Japanese and Okinawan. Somewhat ironically, Okinawa's attachment to Japan "proper"—or, really, the imbalances in power between Japanese and Okinawan men—was also revealed in the revival of the prewar educational practice of *hōgenfuda*—hanging a small tablet from the neck of a student who uttered Okinawan dialect as a punishment—at schools across Okinawa (Oguma 1998, chap. 22; Okinawa Times 1998,

165–171). These and other nationalist acts in Okinawa were performed in part to show the US military that the reversion movement did not intend to promote communism and should not be suppressed as it had been in the 1950s.

One of the turning points of the reversion movement was the first visit of a prime minister of Japan to postwar Okinawa, in August 1965 (Arasaki M. 1969, 233–234; Oguma 1998, 602; Ryukyu Ginkō Chōsabu 1984, 703–707), a visit that corresponded with the intensification of the Vietnam War. This prime minister was Satō Eisaku, and his visit revealed Tokyo's basic strategy about how to handle Okinawa reversion, that is, to promote Okinawa's unification with the rest of Japan administratively, financially, and educationally, while at the same time allowing the US military to continue to use its bases in Okinawa in light of the Japanese state's imperatives to help the US military prosecute the Vietnam War and contain the "threats" of communism to the peace and security of Japan and the "Far East" (Miyazato 1975, 73–75).

After Satō's visit, the reversion movement went through a "qualitative change" (Sakurazawa 2012, esp. 20–22), a process that went hand in hand with the radicalization of the OTA, the Okinawa Teachers Association, as the key constituent of Fukkikyō (Arasaki M. 1969, 250–255; Sakurazawa 2015, 127–132). Members of OTA—public school teachers, more specifically—displaced praise of the rising sun flag with praise of the Japanese constitution, in particular its Article 9 (stipulating unarmed peace), against the background of a growing number of social problems caused by US service members stationed in Okinawa on their way to Vietnam (Oguma 1998, 601–609).[18] The average number of crimes committed by US service members per annum in 1965–1969 increased to 1,202, as compared to 516 in 1955–1959 and 930 in 1960–1964 ("Sōdōmae..." 2020). In addition, as I stated in my previous book:

> In 1966 a tanker airplane crushed and killed one local resident and ten servicemen, and a taxi driver was stabbed to death by a serviceman; in 1967 a hostess was strangled by a serviceman, a male high-school student was killed in a military vehicle's hit-and-run, and a four-year-old girl was run over by a military trailer and died; in 1968, four Okinawans were injured and three hundred houses were damaged by an explosion of a B-52 in Kadena Air Base; in 1969 poison gas leaked in a military facility and twenty-four servicemen were hospitalized, and a housewife was killed in a hit-and-run accident caused by a serviceman; and in 1970 a female high-school

student was stabbed by a serviceman on her way from school. (Inoue 2007, 50–51)

The OTA played a critical role in the victory of Yara Chōbyō, leader of the reversion movement at large, in the first popular election for GRI's chief executive, conducted in 1968 (Oguma 1998, 602–604), as well as in the promotion of the slogan that he advanced as the chief executive: "immediate, unconditional, and entire removal" (*Sokuji, Mujyōken, Zenmen Henkan*) of the US bases upon reversion. In so doing, the reversion movement sharply expressed the homosocial taboo of the Okinawan "people"—"Don't develop friendship with the US military"—for the construction of the community of *nuchi du takara* externally at the institutional political level.

In 1969, as Washington and Tokyo finalized the details of reversion— including its timing, 1972—the Okinawan "people," while rearticulating their material status in the direction of middle-class "citizens" via the money from Tokyo and Washington, reclaimed their identity as the "people" with the method of resistance developed in the 1950s, direct action. In so doing, the Okinawan "people" generated the reversion movement as a new life-form in their community of *nuchi du takara* with the anti-base trust. For instance, from 1968 through 1969, the movement to remove B-52s—numbering more than one hundred at some points during the Vietnam War (Takamine 1984, 101)—was mobilized with demonstration as its basic method. In December 1970, triggered by a traffic accident (in which a car driven by a US serviceman hit an Okinawan man) near the Kadena Air Base, five thousand Okinawans clashed with several hundred military police and burned more than seventy cars owned by US servicemen in the so-called Koza riot (Inoue 2007, 53–55). Journalist Takamine Chōichi (1984, 68–69) noted that Okinawan men with skill in karate, a martial art that originated in Okinawa, often beat up US servicemen in bars and restaurants around the time of this "riot." Together with two general strikes in 1971, direct action concretized and achieved the *fraternal* language of reversion against the US military.

In the process, the community of *nuchi du takara* of the Okinawan "people," having been constructed through the heterosocial taboo ("Don't allow sexual relations between Okinawan women and US servicemen") in the local time-space through the 1950s via the fratriarchal control over women such as (for instance) Otohime and mixed-race children, was synchronized with and amplified by the homosocial taboo ("Don't develop friendship with the US military") through the political vision of "immediate, unconditional, and entire removal of the U.S. bases" in the national time-space. By mediating these two androcentric taboos through the political act of reversion, the Okinawan "people" brought their community of *nuchi du takara* to completion, as it were, across the local time-space controlled by the US military and the national time-space controlled by the nation-state of Japan, with the metaphysical foundation of that community constituted by the death of others in the Battle of Okinawa, even though "immediate, unconditional, and entire removal" of the US bases upon reversion did not occur. On the day of reversion—May 15, 1972—Chief-Executive-turned-Governor Yara thus stated: "Now, the day of Okinawa's reversion has come. Still, when we look at the details of reversion compared with what we had hoped for, it is also true that we can hardly say our aspirations were realized. We returned to Japan despite the existence of many problems, such as the base situation. Therefore, our hardships continue and we may face new problems" (OPPMM 2001, 138). It should be added though that the desire of the Okinawan "people" for a better life, for an improvement of their material conditions—which had been foregrounded in the first half of the 1960s—did not disappear in their community *of nuchi du takara* in the second half of the 1960s through 1972, even as it might have receded into the background due to the "qualitative change" of the reversion movement, as noted above.

Beneath the politicization of the reversion movement in the second half of the 1960s through 1972, indeed, the Japanese money continued to be injected to Okinawa to control its anti-base sentiment, paving the way for shaping a new historical-material context in which a different social actor—the affluent, confident, educated, gender-sensitive, Okinawan "citizens" of younger generations who did not experience the Battle of Okinawa—would eventually construct a new community of *nuchi du takara* in post-reversion Okinawa, as will be discussed in chapter 4.

Notes

1. The US military declared the end of its operations on July 2, 1945, and the Japanese Imperial Army signed the instrument of surrender on September 7, 1945 (Arashiro 1994, 247).
2. The Kerama Islands cluster consists of more than twenty islands of various sizes located approximately 40 kilometers west of Naha, the capital of Okinawa Prefecture, on the main island of Okinawa.

3. The number of refugee camps changed over time. In August 1945, there were twenty-one camps. In September–October of 1945, there were eleven on the island of Okinawa and five on the surrounding islands of Henza, Aguni, Iheya, Kerama, and Kumejima (Onga 2017, 412–413; OPPMM 2001, 103; Yui 2007, 27).

4. This notion was broadly shared by the Joint Chiefs of Staff but not by the Department of State, which formulated different ideas built on the principle of territorial nonexpansion originated in the 1941 Atlantic Charter (Eldridge 2001, chaps. 2 and 3; Miyazato 1975, 5–6). The violence of land seizure in Okinawa after the Battle of Okinawa was concomitant with the deferral of the creation of clearly defined polices with regard to Okinawa in Washington, an effect of equivocal international relations before the intensification of the Cold War, which will be explored in part III.

5. This quotation is from the book titled *Okinawaken Heiwakinen Shiryōkan Sōgōan'nai* (Okinawa Prefectural Peace Memorial Museum Comprehensive Guide). All translations of this book were made by OPPMM.

6. Issues concerning the prewar Japanization program are explored in chapter 6.

7. Airakuen, at that time operated under the authority of the USMGR, is still in existence today on the west coast of Nago City, where I, together with my friend-informant Kinjō Hatsuko, paid a visit (see chapter 2, section 3).

8. Ginowan Village was reorganized as Ginowan City in 1962 due to population growth (Ginowan City 2020).

9. As I wrote in a different publication (Inoue 2017a, xii): "On the evening of September 3, 1955, Nagayama Yumiko, a six-year-old kindergartner living in what was then Ishikawa City in central Okinawa, went missing while she was watching *eisā*, an Okinawan folk dance that marks the end of the Bon festival. On the following day, she was found dead in a vacant field near a military dumping ground in then Kadena Village. The September 4, 1955, edition of *Okinawa Times* describes 'her slip sliding down to her left arm and her lips tightly held' (quoted in Asato E. 2000). The victim's dead body, beaten by heavy rain before it was discovered, showed signs of sexual assaults. The suspect was a sergeant in his early thirties who belonged to Kadena Air Base. In a resolution addressed to the US military, the Ryukyu Legislative Council expressed Okinawans' indignation in the strongest terms: 'As it became clear that the girl was [sexually] assaulted [before being murdered], the entire Okinawan population has developed animosity and resentment [toward the U.S. military]' (1955, quoted in Nakano 1969, 126)."

10. What follows here is a description consisting of a summary of what I provided in my first book (Inoue 2007, 99–102) and pieces of new information that became available after the publication of that book.

11. The estimated number of mixed-race children was three to four thousand around the time of Okinawan reversion (Namihira 1970, 80; Okinawaken Kyōikushinkōkai 1976, 69).

12. He later served as the vice governor of Okinawa Prefecture from 1979 to 1984.

13. The two taboos, as a coping mechanism for Okinawa's ambivalence toward

the US military, were a long time in the making. In the 1950s, for instance, the Okinawan "people" discriminated against mixed-race Okinawans, as noted, an issue that can be explained more clearly in light of these two taboos. That is, Okinawa's discrimination against mixed-race Okinawans occurred because their presence violated these taboos in the eyes of the Okinawan "people"—the presence made possible by the entertainment business for US servicemen (established against the homosocial taboo forbidding friendship with them) where sexual encounters between Okinawan women and US servicemen were promoted (against the heterosocial taboo forbidding them). Also, in 1954, the Okinawan "people" had acted out these taboos by blocking presentation of *The Teahouse of the August Moon*, a comedic play. However, analysis of this incident has been omitted due to space limitations. The basic information of *The Teahouse of the August Moon* is provided in note 14 below. The important point is that in the earlier phases of postwar Okinawa, these taboos were not yet clearly articulated but were expressed through the somatic, almost instinctive, rejection of *The Teahouse of the August Moon* and the mixed-race Okinawans by the Okinawan "people." In the second half of the 1960s, in contrast, *The Cocktail Party* articulated these taboos more fully through language.

14. On the one hand, the Ryukyu Kingdom, a tributary state of China, was subordinated to China, participating in the maritime trade network across Asia organized by the Ming dynasty (1368–1644) and Qing dynasty (1644–1912). On the other hand, the kingdom was subordinate to Tokugawa Japan, because it had been conquered by Satsuma, the southmost feudal domain of Tokugawa Japan, in 1609.

15. *The Teahouse of the August Moon*, a novel, was written by Vern Sneider in 1951, on the basis of his experience in 1945 in the Okinawan landing operations and in the administration of a refugee camp in the Tōbaru area of central Okinawa that accommodated approximately five thousand Okinawans (Azusawa 2012, 320; Yonaha S. 2019). The novel was adapted for the stage by John Patrick in 1952 and was performed on Broadway more than one thousand times from 1953 to 1956 (Azusawa 2012, 325). In addition, the play was made into a film in 1956 with Marlon Brando (as Sakini), Glenn Ford (as Captain Fisby), and Kyō Machiko (as Lotus Blossom) playing the lead characters. The basic plot of the film, based more on John Patrick's play than on Vern Sneider's original novel (Azusawa 2012, 326; Masubuchi 2013, esp. 18 and 26–29), is as follows.

Captain Fisby is sent to the village of Tobiki to undertake the task of postwar recovery; Sakini, an Okinawan translator, works for him. Although the captain is expected to implement a plan to build a pentagon-shaped thatched school for children, villagers give Fisby, among other gifts, Lotus Blossom, a woman from the Tsuji pleasure district, convincing him to build a "teahouse" instead on the basis of the "democracy" (decision by majority, in this case by the villagers) that he teaches in representing the US military as the father. Due to this teahouse, together with a brewery business Fisby also initiates, Tobiki is successfully revitalized; friendship and trust grow between Fisby and the villagers, and a romance develops between Fisby and Lotus Blossom, both of which are facilitated by the work of Sakini the translator. Meanwhile, Fisby's boss, Colonel Purdy, becomes furious at the "immorality" of the teahouse and brewery business and orders Fisby to destroy them. However, Washington misconstrues Tobiki as an example of the success of the US military's efforts for postwar recovery in Okinawa, sending a congressional committee for inspection. Colonel Purdy ends up ordering Fisby to rebuild the teahouse for these legislators after he too is struck by the beauty and mystery of the Orient (Nakazato I., n.d.).

16. Historically, one of the origins, if not the origin, of Okinawan performing arts is the classical court performance called *kumiodori* (or *kumiudui*, in Okinawan pronunciation)—presented during the age of the Ryukyu Kingdom by male performers-cum-officials for envoys from China. These performers, when they lost a kingdom to serve and were deprived of their jobs, started to perform outside the court beginning in the 1880s, incorporating the needs and desires of the common people into their art to establish it as a popular entertainment in Okinawa before the war (Hosoi 2014; Yano Te. 1974, 243–261). In the process, the sense of locality was also added by the use of distinctive Okinawan "dialect," costumes, and hairstyles onstage and by the settings and subject matter of everyday Okinawan life centering on family, community, and love. In effect, Okinawan plays can be grasped as a fluid cultural practice wherein an established tradition (*kumiodori*) was rearticulated by the "people" under new historical circumstances introduced by the establishment of Meiji Japan. In a way that extended the tradition—that *kumiodori* was performed by men—however, Okinawan plays in prewar Okinawa were also controlled by men.

17. Enthusiastic voices of support from its fans emerged after Otohime announced its dissolution in 1970, and, from 1971 to 2001, Otohime, while no longer traveling to perform at theaters across Okinawa as in the 1950s, presented one to three regular performances a year in a theater in Naha (Uema I. 1981, 134–137). In 2001, the troupe's second leader, Hazama Yoshiko (1928–2001), an original member of Otohime from Tsuji who had succeeded Uema Ikuko as leader in 1990 (Yonaha S. 2016, 22; Otohime Gekidan 1999, 141), passed away. With the death of Hazama, Otohime ended its celebrated career.

18. Writers such as Arakawa Akira, Kawamitsu Shin'ichi, and Okamoto Keitoku explored an alternative possibility beyond and against reversion, as will be discussed in chapter 8.

CHAPTER 4

Money and the Development of Okinawan Citizenship in Post-reversion Okinawa (1970s–1990s)

1. The Relevance of Marx to the Analysis of Postwar Okinawan History: From the "People" to "Citizens"

In *Capital*, volume 1, Karl Marx ([1887] n.d., 40–41) explained differences between ancient Greek society and a capitalist society as follows:

> Greek society was founded upon slavery, and had, therefore, for its natural basis, the inequality of men and of their labour powers. The secret of the expression of value, namely, that all kinds of labour are equal and equivalent, because, and so far as they are human labour in general, cannot be deciphered, until the notion of human equality has already acquired the fixity of a popular prejudice. This, however, is possible only in a society in which the great mass of the produce of labour takes the form of commodities, in which, consequently, the dominant relation between man and man, is that of owners of commodities.

Not unlike ancient Greek society, premodern Okinawa, having existed as the Ryukyu Kingdom until the 1870s, had been founded upon the feudalistic class system determined by birth and "had, therefore, for its natural basis, the inequality of men and of their labour powers." In other words, different kinds of labor were not seen as equal and equivalent in the Ryukyu Kingdom, a situation that made it impossible to construct a shared social world founded upon "human labour in general." As Tomiyama Ichirō (1990) and Wendy Matsumura (2015), among others, have shown, however, Okinawa since the late nineteenth century had increasingly been incorporated into a global market economy as a production site of sugar as well as into a national market economy as a supply base of cheap laborers sent to Osaka and other major cities in Japan. Accordingly, Okinawa became gradually but unmistakably homogenized as a collective of "human labour in general," a process that went hand in hand with the penetration of the money economy that equates "all kinds of labour."

The arrival of the US military at Okinawa through the war accelerated this general process, the development of the commodity-centered money economy in Okinawa in a manner that reinforced "the notion of human equality [that had] already acquired the fixity of a popular prejudice." Even if the US military saw Okinawans as different, calling them derogatorily "Gooks" and "Okies" (Miyagi Et. 1982, 53–58), the ruler and the ruled had already shared the common ground of the capitalist mode of social life ever since they encountered, as exemplified by strong desire of the Okinawan "people" for the restoration of the money economy to replace the economy in the wake of the war in which everything was provided by the US military or bartered with American cigarettes as the "universal equivalent" (Marx [1887] n.d., chapter 1; Ryukyu Ginkō Chōsabu 1984, 30–71).

This desire was solidified by the introduction of B-yen in Okinawa in July 1948,[1] with which the US military tried to accomplish three different yet related goals: (*a*) the B-yen was pegged to the US dollar and thus detached the Okinawan economy from the postwar Japanese economy; (*b*) the fixture of the exchange rate at $1 = 120 B-yen = 360 Japanese yen enabled Okinawa to import materials needed for construction and maintenance of the US bases from elsewhere in Japan, and the B-yen thus helped wider Japan develop the export-oriented postwar economy; and (*c*) the arrangement increased the buying power of the Okinawan "people" and improved their standard of life. In its combined effect, the B-yen contributed to development of the so-called base-dependent economy—an economy founded upon the seizure of Okinawa's land by the US military in the 1950s—and deprived US-ruled Okinawa of the ability and opportunity to develop productive export-oriented industries as Japan did elsewhere in its postwar territories (Makino H. 1987, 145–183; Ryukyu Ginkō Chōsabu 1984, 265–273).

In this historical context somewhat artificially shaped by the B-yen, Yara Chōbyō's statement at the rally protesting the land seizure procedures in 1956 (cited in chapter 3, section 2) expressed awareness of the equality of different kinds of human labor between the ruler and the ruled in postwar

Okinawa: "If we compare the benefits Okinawa has gained from the United States and the benefits the United States has gained from Okinawa, which is bigger is as clear as day." It is also significant that this awareness was linked to the anger of the Okinawan "people" at systemic exploitation of the ruled by the ruler: data from 1955 show that an Okinawan man working as a laborer at a base construction site earned 9.5–20.0 B-yen an hour, a Japanese worker under similar working conditions received 25.0–45.0 B-yen an hour, a Filipino worker/foreman 48.0–196.8 B-yen an hour, and an American worker/supervisor 125.2–752.0 B-yen an hour (Inoue 2007, 235; Nakano 1969, 146). The injustice was also made obvious in the exceedingly low amount of rent set by the USCAR before the land seizure—in 1952, the rent of one *tsubo* (approximately 3.3 square meters) of land for a year was less than the price of a pack of cigarettes (Okinawa Times 1973, 185). In effect, against the background of the restoration and expansion of the economy based on money as the universal equivalent, "The notion of human equality already acquired the fixity of a popular prejudice" in postwar Okinawa, where the "people" developed a critical consciousness that the equality of different kinds of human labor was not adequately expressed or realized by the ruler.

It is this consciousness that led to the establishment of Tochiren (Military Landowners' Association) in 1953, a group that played a pivotal role in organizing the island-wide protest against the USCAR's land seizure procedures (discussed in chapter 3, section 2). More specifically, Tochiren acknowledged and established money as a general mechanism for handling, addressing, and resolving political problems of inequality by proposing the so-called four principles to protect Okinawa's land: (*a*) opposition to the proposed lump-sum payment method (i.e., advocacy of the annual payment method), (*b*) adequate annual payment of rent for the land already used, (*c*) adequate compensation for all the damages caused by the US military, and (*d*) opposition to new land acquisition (Arasaki M. [1986] 1995, 30–31). It should be noted that these principles—in particular, (*a*)—revealed an assumption of the Okinawan "people" about the continuous presence of the US military in postwar Okinawa in the foreseeable future. It was not a matter of supporting or opposing the US bases; the US bases constituted a reality that they would have to accept, from which emerged the basic strategy of Henoko and Kin for securing economic gain from the US bases for the stability and improvement of their everyday (Toriyama 2013).

While Henoko and Kin discarded principle (d), the island-wide protest in the mid-1950s was a watershed moment; thereafter, it became increasingly difficult for the U.S. military to merely exercise oppression and violence to control the constituent power of the Okinawan "people." As a result, the US military ended up balancing its oppression and violence with the compensation mechanism of money. Beginning in the early 1960s, against the background of the rise of the reversion movement, Washington thus gradually allowed Tokyo to introduce a series of financial programs and media-cultural strategies, as discussed in chapter 3. However, the irony is that the more the US military provided money to Okinawa, the more strongly it generated the notion of human equality in Okinawa, which was expressed politically in the form of the reversion movement, a movement for eliminating inequality between Okinawa and the US military (via "immediate, unconditional, and entire removal" of the US bases, as noted in chapter 3) and actualizing equality between Okinawa and the rest of Japan (through the actualization of a better material life, as also noted in chapter 3). And, in the late 1960s, Washington decided to return Okinawa to Tokyo when it could no longer contain the contradiction—that the very money expected to control situations in Okinawa actually let them get out of control—while Tokyo, from 1972, was tasked to help the US military to continue to use the bases in Okinawa and at the same time to control Okinawans' frustrations over the continuing US presence with the power of money.

Accordingly, immediately after the reversion, Tokyo increased land rent for the US bases in Okinawa by more than 600% while also implementing a law that practically made it impossible for military-base landowners in Okinawa to refuse renewing lease contracts (Arasaki M. [1973] 1992, 17; NHK Shuzaihan 2011, 90; Nozoe 2016a, 81). More broadly, a series of Okinawa Development Plans crafted by Tokyo (the Okinawan Development Agency) played a key role in promoting "development"—a Japanese style—in post-reversion Okinawa. For instance, in the name of *hondonami* (catching up with the rest of Japan), Tokyo provided a huge sum of subsidies to improve social infrastructure, from roads and schools to hospitals and sewage systems, in post-reversion Okinawa (Miyamoto 2000, 6–7).[2] Similarly, an examination by sociologist Tada Osamu (2004) of the Ocean Expo held in Okinawa in 1975–1976 reveals the ways in which the Japanese state and capital—Mitsui, Marubeni, Itōchū, Mitsubishi, and Sumitomo (140)—constructed the image of Okinawa as a semitropical resort with blue ocean water.[3] Okinawa tourism thrived in the process; the number of tourists visiting Okinawa annually increased from 440,000 in 1972 to 3 million in 1992 (Ishikawa and Chinen 2022). The reconstruction plan for Shuri Castle, which had been burned down during the Battle of Okinawa, was finalized by Tokyo in the mid-1980s as part of its post-reversion development scheme of "Ryukyu Restoration" (Figal 2012, chap. 4; see also Loo 2014, 185–186 and Naikakufu 2013) to attract more tourists from wider Japan as well as to reinforce Okinawa's historical identity. As Miyume Tanji and Daniel Broudy (2017, 41) note, "In Okinawa, the state introduces market dependence within the scope of the 'Okinawa development regeneration' policy, which has traditionally been Tokyo's core administrative principle for the prefecture."

In the realm of culture, an Okinawan-born female pop singer by the name of Minami Saori, whose debut in 1971 nearly coincided with the reversion of Okinawa in 1972, radiated an exoticized image of Okinawa through analog media such as radio broadcasting, TV song shows, records, and popular magazines and gained immense popularity in wider Japan in the 1970s (Nagai 2011). Linked to the reconstruction of Shuri Castle, a historical drama entitled *Ryukyu no Kaze* (The Wind of the Ryukyu Kingdom) that narrated the rise and fall of the Ryukyu Kingdom was broadcast by NHK, Japan's public TV/media station, across the nation in 1993. In the 1990s, an exoticized view of Okinawa as a place of spirituality (*iyashi*), family, and relationship was added to its established image as a semitropical resort with blue ocean water through, for instance, Okinawan actress Taira Tomi (1928–2015), featured as a kindhearted yet resilient *obā* (grandma) in films such as *Nabī no Koi* (Nabī's Love) (dir. Nakae Yūji, 1999), TV drama series such as *Churasan* (Beauty) (NHK 2001), and other cultural products thematizing Okinawa sold in wider Japan. Together with the increasing acceptance of Okinawan music, Okinawan food, and Okinawan artwork (e.g., Ryukyu glass) across Japan, Okinawan culture, broadly defined, contributed to the reinforcement of Okinawa's "market dependence" in the 1980s–1990s and beyond.

The strategies of Washington and Tokyo worked: vaguely defined pro-base sentiments spread—or explicitly anti-base sentiments disappeared—in post-reversion Okinawa, particularly during the era of a pro-Tokyo governor, Nishime Junji (1921–2001; in office 1978–1990) (Nozoe 2016a, 198–205; 2016b, 106–108; Sakurazawa 2105, 195–198). For instance, there were no large-scale social movements against the US bases for the first twenty years after reversion[4] in spite of the prolonged US military presence, together with continuing problems of accidents and crimes committed by the US troops; between 1972 and 1995, indeed, indictments for a total of 4,790 crimes were processed by the Okinawa Prefectural Police, including twenty-one murders, 355 robberies, and 111 rapes (Arasaki M. [1986] 1995, 232). In addition, there emerged a growing reluctance among Okinawa's military landowners—in particular, Tochiren (Military Landowners' Association), which led the island-wide protest against the US land seizures in the 1950s—to agitate for the return of their land, which begot an ever-increasing amount of rent—12.3 billion yen in 1972, 31.1 billion yen in 1980, 44.7 billion yen in 1990, and 72.8 billion yen in 2000 (Nozoe 2016a, 139–141; Okinawaken Chijikōshitsu Kichitaisakuka 2020, 58–68). Furthermore, paid to established companies in the construction, tourism, retail, and finance industries and to the public sector, the subsidies Tokyo invested enabled these companies and the public sector to provide employment opportunities to post-reversion Okinawa at large, thereby contributing to reinforcing, if subtly, a broader pro-base sentiment there (Higuchi 2014).

In effect, in addition to being continuously oppressed by the presence of US bases, post-reversion Okinawans, on the surface, were "disciplined" by Tokyo, as *docile subjects* (Foucault [1975] 1977); in exchange for money, Okinawa seems to have accepted the US bases for the "peace and prosperity" of the Japanese state of which it became part.

This superficial observation, however, must be complicated by the fact that this very money paid as compensation for the continuing US military presence also became "a constant reminder of the prolonged violence of power, the US military presence, thereby helping Okinawa to renew cultural sensibilities . . . enmeshed with the pain of local historical experiences— the war, the bases, the servicemen, and the rape" (Inoue 2007, 27), as I stated in my first book. In the context of post-reversion Okinawa from the 1970s through the 1990s, indeed, money set Okinawan subjectivity in motion, turning its androcentric structure and norms into a historical-social-cultural movement for the expansion of equality and actualization of democracy, externally vis-à-vis the US military *and* internally within increasingly diversified Okinawa. Okinawan "citizens" are the social actor who concretized and achieved this movement for the rearticulation of the community of *nuchi du takara* in post-reversion Okinawa.

The second postwar generation born during US rule of Okinawa (1945–1972)—the "postgeneration" (Hirsch 2008, 103) having not directly experienced the war like the Okinawa "people"—constituted the core of Okinawan "citizens." Demographically, 1985 can be taken as a reference point at which we can clearly recognize the formation of "citizens" when the second generation (thirteen to thirty-nine years old) became a prominent majority of the population (approximately 1.18 million) at approximately 43% and the first generation (forty years old or older, i.e., the key component of the Okinawan "people")[5] and the third generation (under thirteen years old, who experienced neither the war nor the US rule) accounted for approximately 34% and 23%, respectively (Okinawaken Kikakubu Tōkeika, n.d.-a). Against the background of this new intergenerational configuration where the first generation became a minority, Okinawan "citizens" in the 1970s through the 1990s expressed their subjectivity as individuals with new economic backgrounds, cultural sensibilities, and political practices vis-à-vis the Okinawan "people."

To begin with, in contrast to the poor and oppressed Okinawan "people" in postwar Okinawa up through the 1960s who had developed a style of resistance by weaving the language of land (1950s) and reversion (1960s) into political actions, Okinawan "citizens" of the 1970s–1990s were affluent—in the late 1990s Okinawa's per capita GDP exceeded that of some of the Group of Eight nations, including Italy and Canada (Inoue 2002, 264)— with an expanded ability to resist power through language mediated by the analog media (newspapers and TV, among others). To be sure, in the 1960s through the early 1970s, the analog media had already played a vital role in mobilizing the reversion movement of the Okinawan "people," as stated in chapter 3, section 4. However, in the 1970s–1990s, Okinawan "citizens" expanded the use of the analog media by actively incorporating the position and perspective of women, undermining, if not dissolving, the heterosocial taboo—"Do not allow sexual relationships between Okinawan women and US servicemen"—created by the Okinawan "people" in the 1950s–1960s. In addition, in the 1970s–1990s, against the background of the stronger yen vis-à-vis the weaker dollar, the US service members were increasingly included and managed by Okinawan "citizens" at the level of everyday social life, a process that weakened, if it did not dissolve, the homosocial taboo, "Do not develop friendship with the US military." The decline of the two taboos helped Okinawan "citizens" to rearticulate their anti-base sentiments less through the taboos created in the local time-space of US-ruled Okinawa and more through "collective memory" constructed in the increasingly national/Japanized time-space in post-reversion Okinawa. As a result, unlike the Okinawan "people," whose subjectivity was shaped against the US military, Okinawan "citizens" expressed their subjectivity more in relation to Japan "proper" than to the US military per se in post-reversion Okinawa.

In an attempt to explore these features of Okinawan "citizens," first, I examine the dispute over the so-called *tōtōme*—a distinctive Okinawan-style mortuary tablet—in the early 1980s as a symptom of the development of citizenship led by women at the level of everyday social life. Second, I examine a cultural event in Henoko, on the one hand, and photographer Ishikawa Mao's work, on the other, to further explore the ways in which Okinawan citizenship was developed in relation to the two androcentric taboos with which it negotiated. Third, I analyze the protest against the rape of an Okinawan schoolgirl by three US servicemen in 1995 as Okinawa's attempt to consummate Okinawan citizenship. When these events are combined, we will see that in post-reversion Okinawa, money functioned as a driving force to restructure the community of *nuchi du takara*, where life-forms of the "people" were transformed by those of "citizens" to develop Okinawan subjectivity as "a *changing* same."

2. Women's Constituent Power in the Dispute over *Tōtōme*

Typically placed in the center of a house, a *tōtōme* is an Okinawan-style mortuary tablet that represents the spirit of ancestors, as it incorporates wooden plates with the names of dead members of a patrilineal descent group called *munchū* (also known as a *yā*) side by side. A mortuary tablet typically measures 27–32 centimeters (width) by 7–8 centimeters (depth) by 32–35 centimeters (height). As such, *tōtōme* expresses Okinawa's distinctive ancestor worship, which this section explores as a fusion of the political-economic power controlled by men and the spiritual-social beliefs embraced by women. More specifically, on the one hand, a range of political-economic practices concerning *tōtōme* can be explained by the principle of primogeniture, which dictates that a *tōtōme* must be inherited and taken care of by the oldest son—or the next oldest son or even an adopted son if the oldest son is dead or unavailable, but never a daughter—of the main family of the descent group and that the person who inherits the *tōtōme* will also inherit the property of the descent group. On the other hand, the spiritual-social dimension of *tōtōme* practices can be grasped in reference to the role that a woman plays as the spiritual guardian of a *munchū* into which she was born in protecting its oldest son (i.e., her brother); the spiri-

Figure 11. A *tōtōme*
Source: Obutsudan no Akamine, n.d.

tual power of the woman, invoked through the image of sister-goddess, *unai-gami*, is often shared and expressed by other women, including the mother of the oldest son of that *munchū* (Higa Ma. 1987; Iha F. [1927] 1973a, [1936] 1973b; Itō Kan. 1962; Nakamatsu 1990, 152–164; (cf. Sered 1995, 1999) and *yuta*, local female shamans (Ōhashi 1983, 1998). As I show below, the debate over *tōtōme* in the early 1980s—which problematized gender inequality with the slogan "What's wrong about women inheriting *tōtōme*!?"—allowed Okinawan "citizens"/women to critically rearticulate *tōtōme* practices from within; they subverted the political-economic domain of the *munchū* system but protected its spiritual-social domain. In so doing, they undermined *and* reinforced Okinawan androcentrism. Before discussing the debate and its implications, however, I need to provide a broader historical context in which it occurred.

• • •

Originally, *tōtōme* customs were introduced from Ming China—with which the Ryukyu Kingdom had a tributary relationship—to the royal families of this kingdom in the fifteenth century and then came to be imitated by and spread across its ruling aristocratic class in the late seventeenth century (Ryukyu Shimpo 1980, 126–134). In 1899–1903 (i.e., after abolishing the kingdom to recreate it as Okinawa Prefecture), the Meiji government eliminated the old customs such as the *jiwari* system of premodern Okinawa—wherein a significant portion of the village land had been owned in common and co-used by villagers and the remainder of the land divided, allocated to villagers, and reallocated after a certain period (Uechi 2008)—in order to introduce the modern system of private property for taxation purposes. Political-economic practices surrounding *tōtōme*, involving the transfer of property through a line of the eldest sons, of course, could not be "invented" until the system of private property had been introduced and established in Okinawa. It is in the process of invention that the prevention of women from inheriting property was formalized; it aimed to preempt a situation in which the property given to a daughter would be taken by the family to which she was married out.

Such an androcentric "tradition" may have made sense in Okinawa before 1945, because prewar Japan adopted, particularly through the old Civil Code implemented in 1898, primogeniture as a basic legal framework of family inheritance. A process of recovery from the devastation of the Battle of Okinawa also assisted the maintenance, and indeed the reinforcement, of *tōtōme* practices at the level of everyday social life in postwar Okinawa because social expectations for women to produce male offspring remained strong to compensate for the loss of the large number of males during the war, as noted in chapter 3, section 2. However, *tōtōme* practices as an expression of the political-economic power of males generated increasing tensions in post-reversion Okinawa due to the rise of critical gender awareness. I consider the transformation of the labor market as one of the principal factors that accelerated the process whereby "the notion of [gender] equality . . . acquired the fixity of a popular prejudice" in post-reversion Okinawa.

Due in part to various *hondonami* and other Tokyo-led development projects (noted above), Okinawa's gross prefectural income expanded from 501 billion yen in 1972 to over 2.8 trillion yen in 1982, and to almost 3.2 trillion yen in 1992 (Sakurazawa 2015, 351). The expansion of the money economy in post-reversion Okinawa facilitated the participation of an increased number of women in the Okinawan labor market, from 136,000 in 1975 to 236,000 in 2000 (Okinawaken Kikakubu Tōkeika, n.d.-b).[6] In the process, women advanced into various economic fields, as indicated by a decline in the number of women employed in the primary industry (e.g., farming, fishery, forestry, and other industries that produce wealth by directly engaging in nature) in post-reversion Okinawa (24,000 in 1975,

22,000 in 1980, 20,000 in 1985, 21,000 in 1990, 14,000 in 1995, and 13,000 in 2000), on the one hand, and by an increase in the number of women employed in the nonprimary industry (e.g., manufacturing and construction industries that utilize materials produced in the primary industry, as well as financial, retail, service, and other industries that produce immaterial wealth) in post-reversion Okinawa, on the other (112,000 in 1975, 132,000 in 1980, 160,000 in 1985, 189,000 in 1990, 199,000 in 1995, and 223,000 in 2000) (Okinawaken Kikakubu Tōkeika, n.d.-c; cf. Miyagi Ei. 1967, 337–379). To be sure, the participation of women in the labor market involved the subordination of women's living labor to the capitalist mode of production—exploitation of women's power of life. Yet this very subordination also enabled Okinawan women to gain a social awareness that "all kinds of labour are equal and equivalent" (to reuse Marx's words ([1877] n.d., 40) that I quoted at the beginning of this chapter) regardless of the gender of laborers. This awareness—"popular prejudice," if you will—was concretized by women's engagement in the public sphere of discussion and deliberation as Okinawan "citizens."

For instance, Yui Akiko (1933–2020), a journalist who had been involved in a range of Okinawan women's issues, edited in 1977 a pioneering biography of Kinjō Yoshiko, a social welfare activist from Okinawa, and she became the first female managing editor of the *Okinawa Times*, one of the two major newspapers in Okinawa, in 1991 ("Yui Akiko-san . . ." 2020). Photographer Ishikawa Mao, whose life and work I discuss below, began her professional career in the 1970s. Okinawan literary critic Okamoto Keitoku (1990, 421) also pointed out the appearance of a large number of women writers—such as Nakandakari Hatsu ([1981] 1993), Yamazato Teiko ([1984] 1990, [1989] 1994), Yoshida Sueko ([1984] 1990), Yamanoha Nobuko ([1984] 1990, [1985] 1990), Kishaba Naoko ([1985] 1990), Taba Mitsuko ([1985] 1990), Shiraishi Yayoi ([1986] 1990, [1987] 1990), Sakiyama Tami ([1989] 1994), and Tokuda Tomoko (1989)—in Okinawa in the 1980s, as compared to Okinawa before 1945, when there were few women writers (e.g., Kushi Fusako [1932] 1993; cf. Matsumura 2015, conclusion). In the 1980s, also, women began to address contemporary social issues such as the impact of resort tourism upon women, as well as historical issues such as that of the comfort women in Okinawa. Unai Fesutyibaru (Okinawa Sisters' Festival), initiated by Naha City in 1985 (and continuing today), was one result of these varied engagements of Okinawan women (Akibayashi 2004, 77). The debate over *tōtōme* was situated in this broader trend in post-reversion Okinawa, where women increasingly asserted their agency as affluent, confident, and educated "citizens."

• • •

When *Ryukyu Shimpo*, the other of the two major newspapers in Okinawa, took up the issue of *tōtōme* as part of a larger series, titled "Okinawa, Women and Men," in January 1980, the editorial office received endless calls and numerous letters of support (Ryukyu Shimpo 1980, 1). In time, the issue of why women were not allowed to inherit *tōtōme*—an issue involving the political-economic power of men in the androcentric descent group— became a topic of public debate in which a wide range of "citizens," particularly women, became involved. For instance, the predicament of women was expressed on the newspaper as follows.

> My mother was a wife of an oldest son. She gave birth to three girls but not a boy, and soon my father had a relationship with a different woman, who gave birth to a boy. When my mother berated my father, her mother-in-law said, "It cannot be helped because you did not give birth to a boy. Without a boy, who would continue the family succession?" Ashamed, my mother left the family and raised us all by herself [implying that the father remarried to the woman who gave birth to the boy who would continue the family succession]. (Ryukyu Shimpo 1980, 56)

> Our family is in uproar because the property of my older brother (the oldest son) is about to be taken by the second oldest son and his child. My older brother has four daughters but no boys, and the son of the second oldest son, taking advantage of the authority of a local shaman's suggestion [on this, more below], claims the right to all the property of my older brother. Four daughters and their elderly mother will be kicked out of the house. Members of my *munchū* do not listen to opinions of these daughters and their mother and said that it is natural to give [the property] to the son of the second oldest son. (Ryukyu Shimpo 1980, 46)

> Merely because I became the wife of an oldest son, I have to take care of a few hundred people coming to our house whenever seasonal events [to worship the ancestors] are held. [The number of such events could go

beyond one hundred a year (Horiba 1990, 207).] They cost a lot of money, and we are bankrupt. (Ryukyu Shimpo 1980, 46)

> We have five daughters. . . . We were planning to have one of them inherit the *tōtōme*. But one of the members of our *munchū* put a stop to this, saying that there would be a curse if a woman holds the *tōtōme*. From that moment on, relatives [in the *munchū*] have given us lectures day in and day out. One of them even said, "We have a daughter (who has become a widow). You can have her as a mistress [of your husband]; have my daughter give birth to a boy." That they try to persuade us by all possible means is unbearable. Out of fear that they would destroy my family, I have reluctantly begun to think about having another child. (Ryukyu Shimpo 1980, 28)

In a manner that responded to the problems cited above, in 1981, the court delivered a judgment on this matter in support of women's rights to inherit *tōtōme*. In this case, Ms. A., fourth of six daughters, had taken care of the *tōtōme* together with the family tomb after the death of her father, whom she had looked after. However, this family tomb became part of an area to be developed as a park in Naha City and needed to be relocated with compensation to be paid by the city. Then a male member of the descent group insisted on his right to inherit the *tōtōme* and the tomb on the basis of *tōtōme* customs. Part of the background of this claim was the fact that after reversion, land prices rose due to the impact of a range of *hondonami* development projects and thus the stakes of property inheritance—including inheritance of the tomb—became higher (Shimanaka 1982, 48). The Naha Family Court ruled that the custom of prohibiting a woman from inheriting *tōtōme* violated the Constitution of Japan and the Civil Code of Japan—both introduced to Okinawa after reversion to emphasize the principle of equality between men and women—acknowledging Ms. A. as the rightful person to manage the *tōtōme* together with the family tomb. This implied that the compensation to be paid by Naha City should be received by Ms. A. (Wakao 2012, 119–126). The decision was enthusiastically received by Okinawan women.

In effect, ordinary women in post-reversion Okinawa—as "citizens" situated in improved material conditions of life, involved in the commodity economy as "human labour in general," and informed by legal (rational) discourses—extended, appropriated, and rearticulated the ongoing process of Japanization of their lived time-space (e.g., the introduction of the Constitution of Japan and the Civil Code of Japan to post-reversion Okinawa), by highlighting the injustice of gender inequality from the margins of Okinawa's androcentrism. Women's constituent power, when articulated through the analog media/newspapers, prevailed in a way that transformed the *political-economic* domain (i.e., inheritance) of the Okinawan family long controlled by men.

And yet women's "victory" became murkier when the *spiritual-social* domain of *tōtōme* customs is considered, a domain regulated by Okinawan women in collaboration with local female shamans called *yuta*. In the *tōtōme* debate in the early 1980s, *yuta* were criticized publicly as the root of the evil, because they reinforced the androcentrism of *tōtōme* practices by giving "absurd" and "backward" advice and judgments (called *hanji*)—such as "If the rules of *tōtōme* are violated, an evil consequence will follow" or "Misfortunes happened because these rules had been violated"—while charging clients, mostly women, a lot of money to handle each and every case: from 50,000 yen to 300,000 yen (from $467 to $2,804 in 2020 dollars) (Ryukyu Shimpo 1980, 115–116). Historically, the "absurdity" and "backwardness" of their practices had always been the reason for continued suppression of *yuta* by the authorities who sought to Japanize and modernize Okinawa. In the age of the Ryukyu Kingdom, for instance, the court repeatedly attempted to eradicate them precisely for this reason (Takara 1983; 1987, 176–192) and in prewar Okinawa, the Japanese state hunted them as a challenge to the totalitarian national order (M. Allen 2016). Nonetheless, the commoners, particularly women, widely accepted, protected, and used *yuta* as a "folk counselor" (*no no kaunserā*) (Ōhashi 1983, 14; cf. Barske 2013), who would heal, console, and support women in distress by uniting the living with the dead, humans with nature, and here with there through the act of possession. After the Battle of Okinawa, as Matthew Allen insightfully (2016, 230) notes, "It appears that *yuta* were revived and/or reinvented, mostly for pragmatic reasons," such as the need for mourning the war dead. Similarly, I suggest that in postwar Okinawa, in a way that retained and reclaimed the spiritual-social power—or the constituent power—women had held ever since the era of the Ryukyu Kingdom, *yuta* helped them to cope with continuing social crises, punctuated by the Battle of Okinawa (1945), alien rule (1945–1972), and reversion (1972). Although their exact number has never been certain, it is estimated to have been six hundred in postwar Okinawa (Ryukyu Shimpo 1980, 107–125).

In the context of post-reversion Okinawa, specifically, *yuta* may not only have financially exploited but also spiritually and socially helped Okinawan women as "citizens," by providing interpretations (language) about newly emerging, "unfamiliar" historical circumstances—characterized by the ever-increasing power of Japanese money, commodities, and ideas (such as "development")—through old and "familiar" actions of ancestor worship for Okinawa at large. Indeed, 64% of 269 housewives (172 housewives) in Nago City that Ōhashi Hideshi (1998, chap. 6) studied from 1976 to 1982 had hired *yuta* for a variety of reasons. Among those who were responsible for managing *tōtōme* (182 housewives), about 40% of them (72 housewives) experienced troubles over *tōtōme*, and 83.3% of those (60 housewives) relied on *yuta*'s advice or judgments in order to resolve these troubles (Ōhashi 1998, 373 and 393–394). In so doing, in their very exploitation of Okinawan women, *yuta* may also have contributed to rearticulating the existing life-form for them under new historical circumstances of Japanization in post-reversion Okinawa. Their outrageous fee scale (50,000–300,000 yen) itself can be seen as a method *yuta* employed to help situate Okinawan women in post-reversion Okinawa saturated by Japanese money. Accordingly, while ordinary women wished to change certain aspects of *tōtōme* practices, in particular the prohibition of women inheriting *tōtōme*, they also hesitated to radicalize the debate in fear of exterminating the system of *yuta* itself on which they depended for their social and spiritual lives; their reluctance, ultimately, brought the entire debate over *tōtōme* to an end (Horiba 1990, 241–243).

In short, the debate over *tōtōme* shows "something" in Okinawa that one fails to grasp if one approaches it with a dichotomy of good and bad, progressive and conservative. As stated in the introduction to this book, I seek to grasp this "something" in terms of the local notion of *nuchi du takara* ("life is the ultimate treasure"), a notion that Okinawan social actors developed in their community to cope with and embrace contradictory perspectives, views, and sentiments. In this case, Okinawan "citizens"/women critically transformed *tōtōme* practices from within, challenging the political-economic power of men in the *munchū* system by appropriating a broader transformation of post-reversion Okinawa (e.g., gender equality) induced by Japanization at the level of everyday life, while at the same time protecting the spiritual and social domain of *tōtōme* from Japanization at the metaphysical level of the community of *nuchi du takara*. In effect, the debate over *tōtōme* helps us catch a glimpse of the ways in which

Okinawan "citizens" and women reorganized the community of *nuchi du takara* as "a *changing* same" by at once criticizing *and* embracing androcentrism in post-reversion Okinawa.

The following two examples help us examine further the questions of androcentrism in the changing community of *nuchi du takara* as well as subjectivity of Okinawan "citizens" who redefined it in post-reversion Okinawa. The first example, taken from Henoko (cf. Inoue 2007, 98–125), shows the decline of the homosocial taboo, "Don't develop friendship with the US military," a process that corresponded to the preservation of androcentrism in the post-reversion community of *nuchi du takara* that we have seen in the debate over *tōtōme*. The second example is photographer Ishikawa Mao's work from the 1970s through the 1990s, which illustrates the decline of the heterosocial taboo, "Don't allow sexual relationship between Okinawan women and US servicemen," a process that corresponds to the undermining of androcentrism in that community that we have also seen in the debate over *tōtōme*.

3. Friendship as a Life-Form to Control the US Military: Rewriting the Homosocial Taboo to Preserve Androcentrism in the Post-reversion Community of *Nuchi Du Takara*

In August 1970, President Richard Nixon announced the ending of the gold standard against the background of amassed debt, a trade imbalance, and rampant inflation in the United States, a decision that allowed the value of the dollar to fluctuate against other currencies. The value of the yen rose sharply against the US dollar thereafter, and the buying power of the US dollar in Japan dropped over the period from 1970 ($1 = 360 yen) to the late 1970s and early 1980s ($1 = approximately 200–250 yen), and to the late 1980s and early 1990s ($1 = approximately 125–150 yen); 79.75 yen on April 19, 1995, marked the lowest value of the US dollar against the Japanese yen then (Kobayashi 2014). Consequently, after the 1972 reversion of Okinawa to Japan, that is, after the Japanese yen was introduced to Okinawa in place of the US dollar that had been circulated in US-ruled Okinawa from 1958 to 1972, it was often Okinawan "citizens" who became wealthier than US service personnel (Inoue 2007, xxx; Iha Y. 1993, 153). For instance, in the 1960s, the sexual service of the Okinawan women in the entertainment quarters had been abstracted as "human labour in general";

for a "short" period (fifteen minutes) of sexual service, Black servicemen paid three dollars and White servicemen paid five dollars (Fujii S. 2018, 40, 168; Murase 1970, 93–94), the equivalent price of one matchbox full of marijuana, which costed three to five dollars (Takamine 1984, 29). But, in the 1990s, the salaries of the US service personnel would not allow them to buy many bottles of beer (five dollars each) a night in Okinawa. For instance, even though a lance corporal with two years of experience in the Marine Corps earned about $900 a month after tax (with room and board provided), he saved $400—apparently out of worries about the financial stability of his future after retiring from service—and spent a substantial amount of money for night snacks because the supper was provided in the base only from 4 p.m. to 6 p.m. As a result, what he could spend on drinking was limited (Ishikawa, Kuniyoshi, and Nagamoto 1996, 89–90). They could no longer hire Okinawan women as entertainers; it was Okinawan men who hired Filipinas and others as such (Nakazato K. 2013). In a broader macroeconomic perspective, the influence of the US military declined in postreversion Okinawa; percentage of gross prefectural income that base-related receipts accounted for was 15.5% in 1972, 10.1% in 1975, 7.1% in 1980, 6.4% in 1985, and about 5% in the 1990s (Sakurazawa 2015, 351) as compared to 40%–50% (often beyond 50%) in US-ruled Okinawa.

A 1980 Okinawan novel by Arasaki Kyōtarō titled *Kanettai: Ōbāhīto Zōn* (Exceedingly Tropical: An Overheated Zone) captures this "reversal" of the economic relationship between Okinawa and the US military by showing how, in a bar in Henoko, a number of hostesses sit around the two customers from elsewhere in Japan. As I noted in my first book (Inoue 2007, 103), as the Vietnam War came to an end, "once-booming Henoko [enriched by the "rain of American dollars"] sharply contracted as the number of [US] servicemen in Camp Schwab decreased. By the late 1970s, hundreds of [Okinawan] employees in Camp Schwab were laid off," and in the process, bars, restaurants, and other businesses were closed. The novel was situated in this specific historical context. Guided by a male Okinawan sex broker, these Japanese customers seek an opportunity to sleep with a White woman—the wife of a US serviceman without money—at one of the surviving bars in Henoko. This serviceman is depicted in the following manner (Arasaki K. 1980; see also Nakahodo 2008, 263–265).

"Hey, don't you need to wait on the American customer over there?" asked one of the customers.

"It's okay; he does not have much money in any case," a woman said after releasing a puff of smoke from her nose.

"Mama-san [meaning "a woman in charge"], beer, give me one more beer," said the American, as if he had heard the voice of the woman. Judging by appearance, he was a US serviceman.

"Pshaw!" The woman, irritated, put out her cigarette and stood up.

"Hummmm." The two [Japanese] customers strained their eyes.

"Half dollar." The woman slapped a small bottle of beer onto the table. The US serviceman, without a word, gave coins to the woman. He kept looking down all along. . . .

"Though he has no money, he stays as long as one or two hours in the bar over a bottle of beer. With his low salary, he cannot play around here. This place is for mainland Japanese only. Americans are no good anymore." The woman quaffed beer.

The "reversal" of the economic relationship between Okinawa and the US military captured in this novel involved subversion of the homosocial taboo, "Don't develop friendship with the US military," where Okinawan "citizens"—the bar hostesses as well as the sex broker—actively asserted their agency to control and manipulate the US serviceman through a particular relationship (approximating a "friendship") shaped by the power of the Japanese yen. I ethnographically observed a similar reversal in the late 1990s, where "friendship" (*shinzen*) was actively promoted by the Henoko community.

On May 10, 1998, hundreds of US Marines and their families and Henoko residents of all ages jointly participated in *hārī*—the dragon boat festival in which boats made in the images of dragons are raced—on Henoko's beach. Originated in the age of the Ryukyu Kingdom, *hārī* is a festive event that evokes and confirms Okinawan "tradition" as a site of male performance. It is an invented tradition; *hārī* was introduced in the mid-1970s in Henoko for revitalizing the spirit of the community that had declined economically after the Vietnam War and for rebuilding friendship (*shinzen*) between the community and the US military.

In the early afternoon, prominent Okinawan political figures (men)—including Kishimoto Tateo (mayor of Nago City), Kakazu Chiken (national assembly member of the Okinawa Liberal Democratic Party), and a number of pro-base Nago City assembly members—arrived and were ushered into a tent set up to protect against the already scorching early summer sun.

Next to them, leaders of Camp Schwab sat in uniform. The invited Okinawan politicians delivered speeches, and then the male commander of Camp Schwab spoke, thanking the community for "this special opportunity to let us participate in local cultural activities." The political meaning of the presence of influential figures from Okinawa and the US military was obvious; the 1998 Henoko *hārī* was a stage upon which their friendship was to be performed to generate support for the construction of a new Futenma Replacement Facility (FRF) in the waters off Henoko. Especially, leaders (and often residents as well) of Nago and Henoko saw the FRF construction as an opportunity to develop economically depressed northern Okinawa, as noted in chapter 2, section 2. Music, both Okinawan and American, played pleasantly. Translation work by an Okinawan interpreter, a public relations officer of Camp Schwab, was excellent. Members of the Henoko Women's Association worked busily to provide free food and drinks for the participants, in a manner that showed the financial power of Henoko, made possible by the payment of rent by Tokyo. Everybody looked happy.

Henoko as a whole formed a total of twenty-four teams—each of Henoko's twelve residential units called *han* formed two teams—while Camp Schwab sent marines to create fourteen teams. Races began at around three o'clock in the afternoon among Henoko teams in the format of inter-*han* competition. Each race used four dragon boats owned by Henoko. Typically consisting of eight men, each team rowed its way to the turning point created a couple of hundred meters away from the beach and then returned to the beach to reach the finish line. Henoko men were not only experienced in paddling; for the honor of their *han* they rowed very seriously to secure first place. Residents, both men and women, gave enthusiastic encouragement to the teams from their *han*. Several races were held, one after another, amid great excitement among the residents. Young marines looked pleased to be allowed to come and watch an exotic Okinawan cultural practice, though at the same time they seemed a bit frustrated and bored because they were not included as equal partners.

Then, as a sideshow, as it were, races among the marines were conducted. Most of them had not been on board a dragon boat before. Some of them had difficulty moving the boat forward, others fell from the boat, and still others had their boat capsize. Watching these events, Henoko men and women on the beach exploded with laughter, as if wanting to assert their power over unskilled, absurd foreigners in the realm of culture. One member of the Henoko administration told me that Camp Schwab had expressed marines' desire to race with and/or against Henoko residents, but residents, knowing that marines were no match for them, refused this request, preferring to hold separate races for the residents and for the service personnel.

At about six o'clock, prizes—including *awamori* (Okinawan liquor) and fish caught locally—were presented at the post-race ceremony, wherein the Henoko administration/men became a giver ("above"), and the US Marines (as well as residents) a recipient ("below"). The tent was then struck by members of the Henoko Youth Association, and the dragon boats were put away by the marines and Henoko men. By seven o'clock in the evening, Henoko's beach became dark and quiet, but an area off the beach, located in front of the community storehouse in which the dragon boats were kept, became lively as a gathering began. Okinawan food was served, a *kanpai* (cheers) toast was made, and attendees—both the guests (marines) and the hosts (Henoko men, not women)—ate, drank, and attempted to talk with each other. Command of the Japanese language among marines was, however, minimal at best, and command of the English language among residents was no better; as a result, marines simply started to talk with the interpreter or among themselves in English, while residents spoke to each other in their own language. The gathering ended relatively early because the marines had training the following day. The Henoko men, in contrast, had the freedom to stay up late drinking among themselves.[7]

As a whole, *hārī* as an everyday/social event became an occasion where subordinated Henoko residents/men came together, symbolically and temporarily subverting the unequal relations of power and history in the forms of collective laughter, collective separation of the races of marines as a sideshow, and collective construction of a language barrier that marines could not overcome. In addition, by arranging the entire event as men's business (i.e., no women attended *hārī* or the gathering afterward), Henoko cunningly established homosocial bonds with the marines in a masculinized sphere of intercultural communication and subtly prohibited them from making advances toward local women. Last but not least, *hārī* in Henoko confirmed Okinawan androcentrism centering on *munchū* (patrilineal descent groups), a system the debate over *tōtōme* challenged but ultimately maintained, as noted above. As I analyzed in my first book (Inoue 2007, 105–116), Henoko's communal politics in the 1990s had been built on the basis of a balance of power among several *munchū*; the twelve residential units (*han*) were each and as a whole organized in a manner that replicated, conformed, and complicated that balance of power. One of the reasons that *hārī* generated an intense sense of rivalry, noted above, was that the event implicated this *munchū*-centered power structure of Henoko.

In sum, *hārī* in the 1990s enacted "friendship" with the US military as a life-form in the community of Okinawan "citizens," a community that, against the background of the stronger yen vis-à-vis the weaker dollar and of the political issues of the FRF construction, expressed the cultural logic of *nuchi du takara* ("life is the ultimate treasure") through the pro-base attitude. As noted in chapter 3, section 1, the US military exercised its power over life by promoting as much as manipulating the "Ryukyuan culture" in the local time-space for the broader administrative goal of separating Okinawa from the rest of Japan after the war and through the 1960s. In post-reversion Okinawa, in contrast, Henoko—and the post-reversion community of *nuchi du takara*, more broadly—appropriated the military as economic opportunities to support its social life, negotiating and, to a certain extent, subverting and regulating the constituted power of the US military in an increasingly Japanized time-space, through the very "Ryukyuan culture" (such as *hārī* in Henoko) that it had once promoted/manipulated. In the process, significantly, with a sense of androcentric confidence and power of life, Henoko men actively defined and controlled the terms of "friendship" in a manner that undermined and rewrote the homosocial taboo—"Don't develop friendship with the US military"—that the Okinawan "people" had formerly established.

4. Representing "Citizens" through Photography: Rewriting the Heterosocial Taboo in the Community of *Nuchi Du Takara* from the Perspectives of Women

Christopher Ames (2010), Rebecca Forgash (2020), and Miyanishi Kaori (2012), among others, provide insightful ethnographic descriptions of how US servicemen were increasingly incorporated into post-reversion Okinawan society through marriages with Okinawan women; in so doing, these studies show the process whereby the heterosocial taboo—"Don't allow sexual relationships between Okinawan women and US servicemen"— was negotiated within the context of the formation of Okinawan citizenship. This section provides yet another example of negotiation of this taboo by analyzing the work of photographer Ishikawa Mao (1953–present), whom I have befriended since the late 1990s, when we worked in the same location, Henoko; there I conducted an ethnographic study and she took pictures, engaging in the overlapping project of capturing the predicament of its residents, who were as much divided as connected by pro-base and anti-base sentiments in the community of *nuchi du takara*. Incorporating information derived from conversations and interactions that I had with her in January 2020, this section examines the transformation of that community in the newly appeared national and Japanized time-space from the 1970s through the 1990s. This time-space was at once liberating and oppressive: liberating because it helped Okinawan "citizens" like Mao to progressively upend the Okinawan fratriarchy that had maintained the heterosocial taboo, but oppressive because it also made the liberation of Okinawan "citizens" impossible through commodification of culture now extended from Japan as a whole to Okinawa. Indeed, through a specific medium of expression—photography—Mao, as an Okinawan "citizen" *and* as a woman, captured the contradiction and complexity of life-forms shaped in the community of *nuchi du takara* in post-reversion Okinawa.

In the 1960s, as an elementary school student, Mao had already witnessed symptoms of Japanization of the local time-space as her teachers made students purchase and own Japanese flags to confirm that Okinawans are Japanese (Ishikawa 2002, 16–17), an episode that pertains to the reversion movement centered on the rising sun flag described in chapter 3, section 4. The process of Japanization, however, took an increasingly violent political form as the date of reversion drew near. On November 10, 1971, for instance, a demonstration was held in Naha in which more than one hundred thousand Okinawans participated to protest the Japanese government's decision to maintain US bases in post-reversion Okinawa. Mao, then a rebellious young girl who had just graduated from high school, participated in this demonstration in which protesters clashed with the police force. In the midst of the struggle, an Okinawan riot police officer was struck by a Molotov cocktail a demonstrator threw and burned to death (Nakao 1990, 50). Mao saw this dead police officer with her own eyes. He had convulsions, with smoke coming out of his body "like a volcano" (Ishikawa 2002, 21). She was confused, scared, and angry all at once, as she did not understand why "Okinawans had to kill each other" (Ishikawa 2002, 21; see also PMG5 2016, 14:15–15:15)—a contradiction manifested because the Ryukyuan Police, established in 1952 in the local time-space to cope with local crimes and incidents caused by Okinawans (i.e., as a rule, the Ryukyuan Police were not allowed to arrest US service personnel, as noted in chapter 3, section 3), was being repositioned into the national time-space as part of the Japanese/state police system to represent the will of the state to confront and control Okinawans. Mao's photography, originating in social conditions of post-reversion Okinawa in the 1970s, was situated and shaped precisely in this liminal time-space that was at once local and national.

The heterosocial taboo—"Don't allow sexual relations between Okinawan women and US servicemen"—was intensely rearticulated in this liminal time-space, as illustrated by the experience Mao had in a project that she, together with Higa Toyomitsu (a noted male Okinawan photographer), developed from 1975 to 1977. This project involved taking photos of intimate interactions, including sexual interactions, between Black servicemen and Okinawan women—such as herself—at segregated GI bars or what seem to be their residences in Koza near Kadena Air Base and in Kin near Camp Hansen. Pictures of mixed-race children born to them were also taken.

I noted in chapter 3, section 1, that Black servicemen had often been represented extremely negatively in postwar Okinawan society before reversion. Murase Haruki, a Japanese writer who visited pre-reversion Okinawa in the late 1960s, also stated that "in Okinawa, sleeping with Black people means that [a woman] becomes a person of a different class. . . . Women who sold their bodies to Black people were despised by even prostitutes" (1970, 94–95). Mao confirmed that a discriminatory view of Black servicemen continued by stating that "women at the bars who dated Black servicemen were looked down on by [Okinawan] society. I was one of them" (Ishikawa 2002, 76). Nonetheless, a significant difference in post-reversion Okinawa is that Mao, together with women working at the bars as living labor, expressed a voice of dissent as younger, affluent, gender-conscious "citizens." Situated in a specific political-economic context of post-reversion Okinawa, this gendered, generational voice challenged the existing heterosocial taboo forbidding sexual relations between Okinawan women and US servicemen by saying: "What's wrong with loving a Black man! What's wrong with working at a Black bar! What's wrong with celebrating our freedom! What's wrong with enjoying sex!" (Ishikawa 2017, back cover). In so doing, this dissent extended the voices of women contemporaneously expressed from within the "pure" institution of Okinawan descent groups in the debate over *tōtōme* into the realm of "impure" pleasure quarters.

Mao's act of subverting the taboo within the context of established Okinawan fratriarchy, however, backfired, due to Japanese commodification of this very subversion—that is, due to the commercial appropriation of the local Okinawan time-space by the national/Japanized time-space. To be sure, bar girls in Koza and Kin "lived freely without restraint" (Ishikawa 2002, 76), and yet, in light of Okinawa's discriminatory view of women having relationships with Black servicemen, it is also true that these women did not want their intimate photos to be seen by the public. Mao was in her early twenties when she was involved in this project; due in part to her youth, she apparently did not understand the significance of the complex feelings of these women as the photographic subjects. Even though some of the women asked Mao not to release their photos, Mao imposed her view—that it is wrong to suppress or regret the fact that you dated Black servicemen and to do so would participate in discrimination against Black people—and she published these photos in her first photo book, titled *Atsuki Hibi in Kyampu Hansen!!* (Blazing Days in Camp Hansen!!), in 1982 (Ishikawa 2002, 101).

The problem surfaced immediately, because photos included in the book, such as those that showed sex between Black servicemen and Okinawan women—herself included—were sensationally broadcast across Japan through two TV stations in Tokyo. Note that the 1970s and 1980s was the time when literary works in Japan "proper" such as Murakami Ryū's *Kagirinaku Tōmei ni Chikai Burū* (Almost Transparent Blue) (1976) and Yamada Eimi's *Beddotaimu Aizu* (Bedtime Eyes) (1985, sensationally cinematized by director Kumashiro Tatsumi in 1987) explored relationships between Japanese women and Black men, in a manner that presented an antithesis to the dominating discourse of "homogeneous" Japan at that time. Mao's photo book was, in a way, also a critical and serious intervention in such a discourse. As Laura Kina (2017, 165) notes, "Through Okinawan eyes, her work extends the visual archive of the Black Pacific by centering Black bodies within Japanese history." However, unlike the works of Murakami and Yamada, which were debated and respected, more or less, as new forms of literary "high culture," Mao's work was commercially sensationalized by the Japanese mass media of which Okinawa, due to reversion, had become an integral part. To borrow from Annmaria Shimabuku, the Japanese nation-state disseminated the norms of monoethnicity in the very act of "securing Okinawa for miscegenation" (2019, 32)—that is, commodifying Okinawa as an exotic or "impure" site of mixing.

After the TV broadcasts, Mao received complaints from the women who had appeared in the book together with demands for compensation;

she responded by not only paying money but also discontinuing the publication of that book (until 2017, when many of the pictures from *Atsuki Hibi in Kyampu Hansen!!* were released in the book titled *Red Flower: The Women of Okinawa* (Ishikawa 2017; cf. Silveria 2017)). Mao stated: "I was only thinking of my own freedom of expression then. I was forced to realize that I am not allowed to publish private photos without permission. I came to understand both the pleasures and risks of doing photography. This was an important lesson that I learned, which has become a basic principle that has regulated my behavior as a photographer" (2002, 103). In other words, Mao began to see photography not simply as a form of self-expression but also as a form of communication between the photographer and the photographed, a process that would implicate viewers—that is, "citizens"—in the community of *nuchi du takara* where the anti-fratriarchal critique of the heterosocial taboo was to be shared, rather than imposed, in the expanded national time-space and beyond.

A book titled *Korega Okinawa no Beigunda: Kichi no Shima ni Ikiru Hitobito* (This Is the US Military in Okinawa: People Living on the Island of Bases) (Ishikawa, Kuniyoshi, and Nagamoto 1996) is what I see as one of the best examples of photography as a communicative act that Mao implemented in the increasingly Japanized time-space of post-reversion Okinawa. Particularly important for my own analysis are the ways in which Mao's photos taken between 1988 and 1995 (mostly) in Okinawa, together with her stories and descriptions supplementing these photos, engaged in the heterosocial taboo in a liminal time-space created as a result of communication between Tokyo (Kōbunken, a progressive publisher) and Okinawa (authors, including Mao).

For example, Ms. B., a twenty-six-year-old Okinawan woman married to a US serviceman—who could not let her relatives know about her marriage—said in an interview with Mao, "My father was born in Taiwan before the war, where he saw his parents and younger brother die in a US air raid. He returned to Okinawa after the war and underwent a lot of hardships. Therefore, he hates not so much Americans as the military. . . . When my grandmother died, my parents told me not to bring [my husband] to her funeral" (Ishikawa, Kuniyoshi, and Nagamoto 1996, 174). Comments like this help us to understand the depth of history from which the heterosocial taboo emerged in the community of *nuchi du takara* in postwar Okinawa. But at the same time, Mao's pictures and descriptions of Okinawan women married to US servicemen revealed, from the perspective of women, the newly emerging, complex, ambiguous, yet powerful life-forms in that community that subverted this heterosocial taboo—forbidding sexual relations between Okinawan women and US servicemen. Examples include (*a*) an Okinawan woman who worried whether or not her husband with whom she lived in Okinawa would go to a battlefield somewhere in the world (177), (*b*) an Okinawan woman who watched TV together with her husband, a former member of the Black Panther Party, as well as her mixed-race son and daughter, in their small house in central Okinawa (180–181), and (*c*) an Okinawan woman living in North Carolina who received a will from her husband, right before he went to Somalia as a marine in 1993, that stated that all of his property and rights will pass to her upon his death (187), as well as (*d*) Ms. B. who, after the interview with Mao, brought herself to talk with her parents and obtained their approval of her marriage (177). These actualities were made visible through Mao as she situated herself in the liminal time-space for a double criticism: criticism of the fratriarchal heterosocial taboo within Okinawa from women's perspectives, on the one hand, and criticism of Japan (a site of monoethnicity) from an Okinawan perspective (a site of hybridity), on the other. These two criticisms were united by Mao's specific political-economic position and perspective. For clarity, let me call the former "internal criticism" and the latter "external criticism."

Projects Mao completed from the 1970s through the 1990s (and beyond) advanced this double criticism by reinforcing her vision of photography as a communicative act. In a project titled *Hinomaru o Miru Me* (Here's What the Japanese Flag Means to Me) (2011) that she originally developed in the 1990s (and revisited in the following decade) (Zohar 2012), for instance, Mao captured kaleidoscopic feelings and sentiments of the "Japanese"— including Okinawans, the Ainu, Korean residents in Japan, *burakumin* (residents in discriminated-against settlements), and other minorities—about the rising sun flag, in a manner that revealed varied forms of constituent power within and against the national, Japanized time-space. These photos enacted her external criticism situated in the community of *nuchi du takara* against Japan. One of Mao's recent works, titled the *Dai-Ryūkyū Shashin Emaki* (Great Ryukyu Photo Scrolls) exhibition series that started in 2014, extends this line of criticism. For instance, in one of the pictures used in this series, titled *Konkurītoburokku* (A Concrete Block), ten people wearing masks representing Prime Minster Abe Shinzō were placed under a (fake) concrete block marked "45 tons," the same type of block Abe authorized for use in reclaiming land and creating a new US base, the FRF, in Henoko. The caption reads: "Prime Minster Abe, why don't you try being crushed under a block like the coral reefs? You should taste the sufferings of Okinawans and of ocean life" (Ishikawa 2015a).[8] As Mao explains, "This is my resistance as an Okinawan against the Japanese government that took the Ryukyu Kingdom in the past and continues to impose US bases on Okinawa" (Ishikawa 2015b).

In addition, Mao continued with internal criticism of Okinawa by representing through photos the lives of Okinawan "citizens" on the margins, such as the Black US Marine Myron Carr and his twin brother, whom she met in Koza in the 1970s and whose lives were captured in their native Philadelphia in 1986 (Ishikawa 2002, 84–97; Ishikawa, Kuniyoshi, and Nagamoto 1996, 110–113; Kina 2017), Filipino dancers who, replacing the "impure" Okinawan women of the past, now served US servicemen in the entertainment quarters around the bases (Ishikawa 1989), dockworkers—including her lover at the time—in Naha Port (Ishikawa 1990; 2002, 132); Okinawan actress Nakada Sachiko and her troupe (Ishikawa 1991); and members of the Self-Defense Forces in Okinawa (Ishikawa 1995), one of whom was once her husband (Ishikawa 2002, 98–105), to mention only several. In so doing, Mao subverted a lingering heterosexual taboo—a fratriarchal command—forbidding sexual interactions between Okinawan women and US servicemen (and by extension, non-Okinawan men more generally). Specifically, Mao's photos of Filipino women in bars and restaurants exposed Okinawan fratriarchy that now used "foreign" women to protect, or really control, "pure" Okinawan women. Mao's open relationship with men of varied backgrounds (e.g., Black US servicemen, dockworkers, members of the Self-Defense Forces) radically subverted the notion of "pure" Okinawan-ness altogether.

Mao no longer imposed her own view in any of these photos, in contrast to her approach in the 1970s; rather, she let photos speak positions and perspectives of diverse individuals based on the intimate and explosive communication that she had with them, showing varied life-forms that were produced by Okinawan "citizens" as much as marginalized in the community of *nuchi du takara* in post-reversion Okinawa. In so doing, Mao represented and liberated constituent power contained in the increasingly nationalized time-space, doubly criticizing Okinawan androcentrism (as a woman) and the Japanese monoethnic state (as an Okinawan "citizen") from a specific political-economic position and perspective.

From the first decade of the twenty-first century on, Mao has continued to develop her critical photography even further within and against the global time-space. While a full analysis of her work in the twenty-first century is beyond the scope of this section, I wish to comment on one specific recent work of hers (Ikiro! Tore! Ishikawa Mao! 2017) in order to pave the way for the analysis of everyday sensibilities of the Okinawan multitude that I will conduct in chapter 7. In this digitally distributed video, the viewer sees Mao, in her sixties, quietly yet fiercely taking pictures of herself, naked, reflected in a mirror. Her aged body, covered with scars of operations that she has had for the treatment of repeated cancers, may not be "beautiful" according to a received standard of aesthetics but is powerfully communicative and constituent as it subjectifies as much as objectifies violated Okinawa in a shared planetary time-space of the Okinawan multitude living in the community of *nuchi du takara*.

• • •

Henoko's *hārī* and Ishikawa Mao's photography, together with the debate over *tōtōme*, were embedded in the increasingly affluent post-reversion Okinawa (1970s–1990s), where the experience of the Battle of Okinawa among the Okinawan "people" was no longer shared with the majority of Okinawan "citizens." What emerged in the process are three threads of transformation of the community of *nuchi du takara* constructed from 1945 through the 1960s by the Okinawan "people": (*a*) women gained power vis-à-vis men by way of weakening fratriarchy (as shown by Mao's photos), (*b*) Okinawa gained power vis-à-vis the US military by way of strengthening fraternity (as shown by Henoko's *hārī*), and (*c*) Okinawan "citizens" rearticulated "something"—the cultural logic of *nuchi du takara* as the unwavering principle of life—for gradual, if not revolutionary, changes (as shown by the debate over *tōtōme*).

In the closing section of this chapter, I analyze the protest against the 1995 rape incident and a broader historical context in which the protest occurred, in order to show how these threads were tied together to complete and consummate the transformation of the community of *nuchi du takara* by Okinawan "citizens." I focus on two different yet interrelated mechanisms. On the one hand, Okinawan "citizens"—in particular, women—who experienced US rule but not the Battle of Okinawa (second generation) or even who experienced neither (third generation) critically fused internal efforts to overcome the fratriarchy of the Okinawan "people" (a process corresponding to thread (*a*)) with the external efforts to reinforce and expand fraternity (democracy and equality) that the Okinawan "people" had developed against the violence of the US military (a process corresponding to thread (*b*)). On the other hand, the older (first) generation—particularly men—who had experienced the Battle of Okinawa contributed to the construction of the collective memory that reconciled increasingly affluent and diversified post-reversion Okinawa in the 1990s with the notion of *nuchi du takara* constituted at the metaphysical level by the death of others in the war (a process corresponding to thread (*c*)). These two processes directly and indirectly interacted during and after the protest against the 1995 rape, where the three threads converged to generate a new community of Okinawan "citizens" as a mixed constitution consisting of men and women across the first, second, and third generations, a community embracing diverse and often contradictory experiences, perspectives, and attitudes regarding the US military. In the process, as I will also show, anti-base sentiments constructed in the local time-space by the Okinawan "people" through social movements in the 1950s and 1960s did not fade away; instead of being expressed by androcentric taboos against the US military, such sentiments were realigned with and anchored in the collective memory of the war against Japan in the national time-space of post-reversion Okinawa through the 1990s and were manifested "not so much as something deriving from human desires or free will, but in the form of a categorical imperative that transcends them" (Karatani [2010] 2014, 14).

5. Protests against the Rape Incident of 1995 as a Moment to Complete Okinawan Citizenship

On the evening of September 4, 1995, three US servicemen—two marines and one sailor, all Black—abducted a twelve-year-old schoolgirl in Kin Town adjacent to Camp Hansen, a US Marine Corps facility in northern Okinawa. She happened to be on her way back from a local general store after shopping. The drunken servicemen snatched her up into a car they had rented and went to a nearby beach to gang-rape her (Angst 2003, 135–136; Ryukyu Shimpo 1995, 19). Sexual crimes had been repeatedly committed by US servicemen in postwar Okinawa, as stated in chapter 3, but this incident—involving an elementary school girl—specifically highlighted the vulnerability of Okinawan life dictated by the prolonged, large-scale presence of the US military bases that still continued fifty years after the Battle of Okinawa.

If the 1995 rape incident represented the infringement of constituent power by constituted power, the political discourse that developed in Okinawa thereafter exhibits complex negotiations between constituent power and constituted power as mediated by the community of *nuchi du takara*. Construction of this community was revealed by the ways in which the rally to protest the rape, attended by some eighty-five thousand Okinawans, was organized in October 1995. For instance, the planning committee for the protest rally consisted of eighteen organizations, including not only the so-called anti-base organizations (represented by progressive parties and unions critical of the presence of the US military bases) but also the so-called pro-base organizations (represented by conservative parties and business circles that had accepted, reluctantly or enthusiastically, the presence of the US military in exchange for Tokyo's financial assistance for the development of Okinawa). The resolution adopted in the protest rally, which included a demand for reorganization and reduction—not the outright removal—of the US bases, was also generated by the collaboration between anti-base and pro-base sectors of Okinawan society.

It should be added, however, that Tochiren (Military Landowners' Association), who led the island-wide protest against the US land seizures in the 1950s (see section 1 of this chapter), declined to participate in the protest rally for fear that it would lead to the return of military land and the end of the massive rent payments they now depended on (Arasaki M. [1986] 1995, 251–252). Both the participation of diverse groups of Okinawans in the rally *and* the withdrawal of Tochiren from the rally revealed a general political vision of the citizens' community of *nuchi du takara* about Okinawa's future—to minimize, if not immediately remove, the presence of the US military. Unlike the Okinawan "people" forced to live in the base-dependent economy after their agrarian life-forms had been destroyed by the US military, the general consensus of Okinawan "citizens"—generated by the fact that base-related receipts accounted for only about 5% of gross prefectural income in the 1990s, as noted—was that Okinawa could and should manage to do without the bases. This consensus was concretized further in the two proposals announced by the Okinawa prefectural government in 1996, "Kokusaitoshi Keisei Kōsō" (International City Formation Plan) combined with "Kichihenkan Akushon Puroguramu" (Action Program for Returning US Bases to Okinawa) (Okinawaken Sōmubu Chijikōshitsu Kichitaisakushitsu 1998, 240–244).

Meanwhile, the protest displayed the socioeconomic status of affluent "citizens" in the 1970s–1990s. One of the memorable moments of the island-wide protest of the 1950s organized by the Okinawan "people" was called the "March of Beggars," in which participants showed the public that they had lost all resources to support their lives, including their own land, as noted in chapter 3, section 2. In contrast, on the stage set up for the 1995 rally, representatives were all nicely dressed (Ryukyu Shimpo 1995, 118). Okinawan intellectual Arasaki Moriteru captured the material comfort of Okinawan "citizens" by commenting that, unlike a protest rally in the 1950s that had been held under the moonlight with what he saw as an acute sense of desperation, the protest rally in 1995 had "a sense of brightness, like a picnic" ([1986] 1995, 250).

In the midst of all this, Okinawan women thematized the citizenry's sensitivity somewhat differently through their critique of the violence of the military against women (Akibayashi 2004; Akibayashi and Takazato 2009). For Okinawan androcentrism continued to play a significant role in organizing the protest, as exemplified by the facts that most members of the planning committee were men and that most of those on the stage of the protest rally were men (Ryukyu Shimpo 1995, 114, 118); in the process, the injustice of the disproportionate and prolonged presence of the US bases in Okinawa, an issue conventionally handled by men, was foregrounded in the public discourse, while the rape—the infringement of constituent power by constituted power "in a nonmediate way, outside of law" (in the form of men's violence against body and soul of the girl), to modify the words of Hardt and Negri (1994, 294)—receded into the background, as Linda Angst (2003) points out. In a manner that confirms Angst's insight, a male activist stated in a forum after the rape incident, "Do not trivialize the issues of the US bases and US-Japan security alliance into women's issues!" (Akibayashi 2004, 80).

In problematizing the continued androcentric tendency in political activism, Okinawan women expressed their constituent power to critically fuse internal efforts to overcome fratriarchy (a denial of democracy and equality) of the Okinawan "people" with the external efforts to reinforce and expand fraternity (a search for democracy and equality) against the violence of the US military. In so doing, Okinawan women rearticulated the community of *nuchi du takara* from the perspective of gender. For instance, in 1995, Takazato Suzuyo (1940–present, first generation), Itokazu Keiko (1947–present, second generation), Miyagi Harumi (1949–present, second generation) and others established the organization called Okinawa "Kichi/

Guntai o Yurusanai Kōdōsuru Onnatachi no Kai" (Acting Women's Association in Okinawa Not Allowing Bases and the Military) in the wake of the rape incident (Okinawa "Kichi/Guntai o Yurusanai Kōdōsuru Onnatachi no Kai" 1996; Miyagi H. 2006, 44–45); the Acting Women's Association collaborated with other women's groups in Okinawa to constitute a larger network, a process that resulted in a number of achievements, including a powerful demonstration in Tokyo in May 1998 to oppose the construction of the FRF (Kokoroni Todoke Onnatachi no Koe Nettowāku 1998).

Amplifying women's constituent power, Nakamura Sugako (mentioned in chapter 2, section 3), then a seventeen-year-old female high school student, most effectively fused internal efforts to overcome fratriarchy of the Okinawan "people" with the external efforts to reinforce fraternity against the violence of the US military; in educated, middle-class citizenry language, she made a speech at the protest rally that was greeted by a storm of applause from the audience of eighty-five thousand: "Allow us, the younger generation, to start a new Okinawa. I wish Okinawa to become a peaceful island in the true sense of the word. . . . Please return Okinawa to us. Return Okinawa without the military, without tragedies" (Ryukyu Shimpo 1995, 12).

It should be noted that the women's endeavors noted above were addressed not so much to Washington as to Tokyo, as confirmed by the ways in which the *Okinawa Times* and *Ryukyu Shimpo* (as newspapers and also as companies that owned TV stations) played a crucial role in conveying the anger of the community of Okinawan "citizens," in Japanese, both across Okinawa and to the rest of Japan (Yamakoshi 2011). The resentment of the community of Okinawan "citizens" directed at Tokyo became stronger (*a*) when the Supreme Court, in August 1996, dismissed an appeal made by Okinawa Prefecture, which in effect forced Governor Ōta to sign and renew leases as the authorized proxy of those Okinawans who refused to let the US military use their land, and (*b*) when Tokyo rejected Governor Ōta's request to change the Status of Forces Agreement, concluded by Tokyo and Washington in 1960, so that the Okinawa Prefectural Police would be allowed to detain the suspects in the rape incident (Ryukyu Shimpo 1995, 25–27).[9] These examples of Okinawan confrontation with Tokyo did not mean, of course, that "citizens" did not confront the US military. Governor Ōta, for instance, visited Washington a total of seven times while in office (1990–1998) to communicate Okinawa's view of the US base issues (Okinawaken Sōmubu Chijikōshitsu Kichitaisakushitsu 1998, 237–238; Sakurazawa 2015, 249). Nonetheless, as compared to the island-wide protest of the

Okinawan "people" against the US land seizure procedures in the 1950s, which had been organized in the local time-space controlled by the US military, the language of anti-base protest of Okinawan "citizens" disseminated in the analog media after the 1995 rape incident was woven into actions of resistance aimed more toward Tokyo than toward the US military, because Tokyo's policies in effect dictated the prolonged, large-scale presence of US bases in post-reversion Okinawa situated in the increasingly Japanized time-space.

An increasing importance of Tokyo as the contact point for negotiations on the US base issues coincided with the decline of the two androcentric taboos of the Okinawan "people" against the US military ("Don't develop friendship with the US military" and "Don't allow sexual relations between Okinawan women and US servicemen") created in US-ruled Okinawa. After all, in post-reversion Okinawa at the level of everyday social life, friendship of "citizens" with the US military was increasingly firm (as exemplified by Henoko's *hārī*), and the development of sexual relationships between Okinawan women and US servicemen was irreversible (as shown in Mao's photos). And yet this did not mean that the anti-base sentiments had disappeared. Rather, as shown below, anti-base sentiments for peace—as an expression of the "unwavering principle of life"—were renewed and rearticulated by Okinawan "citizens" at the institutional level externally when they anchored their subjectivity internally in collective memory of the Battle of Okinawa to reconstitute the community of *nuchi du takara* in post-reversion Okinawa against Tokyo.

• • •

The year 1995, when the rape incident occurred, marked the fiftieth anniversary of the end of the Battle of Okinawa, when the experience of this war was no longer shared among the majority of Okinawan "citizens." That is, the first generation who experienced the Battle of Okinawa (fifty years old or older) was a minority of the population (approximately 1.27 million) at approximately 27%, while the second generation who experienced the US rule (twenty-tree to forty-nine years old) and the third generation who experienced neither the war nor the US rule (under twenty-three years old) accounted for approximately 39% and 34%, respectively (Okinawaken Kikakubu Tōkeika, n.d.–d). The fading of collective memory of the war in Okinawa was intertwined with and accelerated by a series of policies and programs introduced to Okinawa by the Japanese state from the 1970s through the 1990s. Such policies and programs included (*a*) the advancement of the Self-Defense Forces—often negatively seen by Okinawans as the "descendant" (*matsuei*) of the Japanese Imperial Army (Mekaru 2021)—to Okinawa after 1972 (Arasaki M. [1982] 1992a), (*b*) visits to Okinawa by Crown Prince Akihito and Crown Princess Michiko, who attended, for instance, the opening ceremony of the 1975 Ocean Expo to restore the Japan-Okinawa relationship marred by atrocities against Okinawans by the Japanese Imperial Army that Emperor Hirohito, Akihito's father, had commanded, (c) the Ministry of Education's instruction in 1982 to eliminate descriptions in school history textbooks of the Japanese Imperial Army's atrocities against Okinawans during the Battle of Okinawa (Arasaki M. [1982] 1992c),[10] and (*d*) the Ministry of Education's "notice" in 1985 that directed Okinawa (and other prefectures) to raise the Japanese flag and sing the national anthem on ceremonial occasions at public schools (Arasaki M. [1985] 1992; Shin-Okinawa Bungaku 1986). As Gerald Figal notes, "What we witness during the run-up to and the period after Reversion is an effective nationalization of memorial space on Okinawa, presaged by Japanese interest and activity in its former prefecture" (2012, 34).

The formation and transformation of the Peace Memorial Park in southern Okinawa (where the fiercest battles took place) since the 1970s as a "sacred ground" (OPPMM 2001, 8) for peace and a site of Okinawa's annual memorial day ceremony (Figal 2003, 68–81; Ōshiro M. 1996, 110–131) can be seen as a collective response and resistance by the post-reversion community of *nuchi du takara* to the "effective nationalization of memorial space on Okinawa," an act initiated by the constituent power of the first-generation Okinawans (in the main), expressed both discursively and visually.

On the one hand, in a way that consummated preceding local projects from the late 1960s through the 1980s to record and describe experiences of Okinawans during the war,[11] the Okinawa Prefecture Peace Memorial Museum—opened in 1975 and remodeled in 2000—in the park exemplified the importance of discursive resistance to the nationalization of local memorial space by the Japanese state, by collecting, printing, and exhibiting through the analog media the testimonies of Okinawan "people" who had survived the Battle of Okinawa. An Okinawan man by the name of Kinjō Kōei (fourteen years old during the battle) left the following testimony in this museum (OPPMM 2001, 92):

I was in a cave about 50 yards east of [a community named] Maehira. There was only about two tsubo (72 sq. ft.) of floor space, but nineteen people were packed inside. It was stifling, and we went outside now and then for air. One day an old woman came with a mother and her two children of about five and three. They said they'd come from [another community named] Nakagusuku and soldiers had forced them out of their cave [where they had hidden]. Now they had no place to go and looked exhausted as they took refuge under a tree.

They'd probably stayed under this tree for about two days. After that I went outside to find that the two women had been killed by shrapnel. A shell fragment about 20 inches in diameter had opened a huge gash in the mother's ribs, probably killing her instantly. The older woman's temple had been crushed.

But the children hadn't been hit. The three-year-old was sucking at her mother's breast, and the five-year-old was clinging to her. They stayed alive like that for about three days, but the next time I went out to relieve myself, I found them both dead beside their mother, soaked in the rain that went on all night. I felt awful, wondering why human beings should have to die this way.

On the other hand, one of the new facilities in this park, the Heiwa no Ishiji (Cornerstone of Peace) memorial, which was completed in 1995, revealed the importance of visual resistance by erecting layers of stone panels inscribed with the names of all individuals—numbering in excess of 240,000 as of June 2022 ("Fusen . . ." 2022)—who died in the Battle of Okinawa and related battles, including both combatants and noncombatants, regardless of nationality. The visual resistance had global and local implications. For one thing, in a way that participated in the formation of "global memory culture," as in Hiroshima's Peace Park (Zwigenberg 2014, chap. 6), these panels spread out in a fan shape from the "flame of peace" at the center, created by merging two flames taken from Hiroshima and Nagasaki with another flame that originated on Aka Island, where the US forces landed to initiate the Battle of Okinawa in March 1945 (OPPMM 2001, 11). For another thing, the local significance is revealed by the fact that the creation of Heiwa no Ishiji was a signature project of Governor Ōta (1925–2017; in office 1990–1998). In the Battle of Okinawa, he, at the age of nineteen, fought as a recruit in Tekketsu Kin'nō Shihantai (literally, the Blood and Iron Corps of Normal School Students Dedicated to the Emperor) under the command of the Japanese Imperial Army, the emperor's army, only to witness the killing of the majority of his schoolmates—224 of 386—in the same corps (Ōshiro M. 1996, 117; Ōta M. 1972). As such, he had experientially grasped that *Guntai wa Jyūmin o Mamoranai*, "the military (the emperor's military at that) does not protect the lives of local residents," as noted in chapter 3. As Okinawa's governor, Ōta, fifty years after the war, contributed to the construction of the collective memory through the erection of Heiwa no Ishiji as a localized, visual resistance to the "effective nationalization of memorial space on Okinawa" by the Japanese state. In a way that extended the consolation of spirits enacted in memorials such as Konpaku no Tō (Tower of Souls of the War Dead), Himeyuri no Tō (Tower of Himeyuri Student Nurses Corps [see chapter 7 for further discussion on Himeyuri]), and Kenji no Tō (Tower of Blood and Iron Corps of Normal School Students), all of which were established within a year after the Battle of Okinawa (Figal 2012, 31–32), the Cornerstone of Peace, and by implication the Peace Memorial Park at large, in 1995 reconfirmed the continued presence of the ontological foundation of the community of *nuchi du takara* ("life is the ultimate treasure"), a foundation—or resistance itself—constituted by the death of others, as explained in the introduction to this book.

• • •

In sum, my analysis of the protest against the 1995 rape incident and a broader historical context in which the protest occurred reveals that in the 1990s, Okinawan "citizens" completed the transformation of the community of *nuchi du takara* once created by the Okinawan "people" in postwar Okinawa. For Okinawan "citizens"—including women and across different generations—showed explosive communication in the protest rally against the 1995 rape incident together with discursive and visual resistance to the nationalization of local memory. This explosive communication, mediated by the analog media (as in the debate over *tōtōme*, Ishikawa Mao's photography, and the display of testimonies in the Okinawa Prefecture Peace Memorial Museum provided by the Okinawan "people" who had survived the Battle of Okinawa), enabled Okinawan "citizens" to express an integrality—the power of life—not only against the US military, as in the 1950s–1960s, but increasingly against Tokyo in the national Japanized time-space of post-reversion Okinawa. By renewing the community of *nuchi du takara*, Okinawan "citizens" also demonstrated the ability to compose that community only as they decomposed it constantly in the depth of local history. Taken together, the transformation of the community of *nuchi du takara* in the 1990s revealed the constituent power of Okinawan "citizens" that was founded upon but may also have transcended their desires, projects, or free will.

Of course, the completion of Okinawan citizenship is not the completion of the community of *nuchi du takara* or the subjectivity of Okinawan social actors constituting it as "a *changing* same." Indeed, in post-reversion Okinawa (1970s–1990s), even though the citizens' community of *nuchi du takara* critically infused internal efforts to overcome the fratriarchy of the Okinawan "people" with the external efforts to reinforce and expand fraternity against the violence of the US military, that community also often projected a middle-class self-image through "pure" young women, represented by the victim of the rape incident and the high school student who made a speech at the rally (Angst 2003; Tomiyama 2006, 235–241), and in the process certain individuals might have been excluded from the category of the Okinawan "citizens." For instance, in 1995, when protests against the rape of the Okinawan schoolgirl by three US servicemen reached their peak, someone yelled, "Yankee go home!" at a sixteen-year-old mixed-race Okinawan boy (Murphy-Shigematsu 2002, 197). In other words, in the 1990s, Okinawan subjectivity was still moving toward a greater level of diversity, equity, and inclusion, a task that will be addressed by the Okinawan multitude in the twenty-first century (see part IV).

Notes

1. Until April 1946, the money economy was inoperative in Okinawa. From April 1946 through July 1948, a variety of currencies—prewar Japanese yen, B-yen, postwar Japanese yen—were used somewhat haphazardly according to three different currency policies (Ryukyu Ginkō Chōsabu 1984, 30–71).

2. Tokyo contributed an annual average of 72.6 billion yen between 1972 and 1976, 177.2 billion yen between 1977 and 1981, 197.4 billion yen between 1982 and 1986, 229.6 billion yen between 1987 and 1991, and 317.5 billion yen between 1992 and 1996—a total of 4.96 trillion yen from 1972 to 1996 (Miyamoto 2000, 6–7).

3. Tada's analysis is complicated by an insight from Gerald Figal (2012, 62), who shows that the construction of this image had already begun in the 1960s.

4. This does not mean, of course, there were no movements. For instance, in 1982, residents around Kadena Air Base instituted legal proceedings against the Japanese government to stop night flights of US military aircraft and to demand financial compensations for the damage they had caused (Sakurazawa 2015, 201).

Also in the 1980s, antiwar military landlords developed strategies to refuse to rent their land to the US military (Arasaki M. [1986] 1995). In 1987, local residents in Aha in northern Okinawa confronted MPs to oppose the construction of landing fields for Harrier aircraft; in the same year, twenty-five thousand Okinawans enclosed Kadena Air Base in "human chains" to oppose the continuing use of Okinawan land for military purposes (Sakurazawa 2015, 202–205). Furthermore, starting in 1987, residents in the Toyohara community in northern Okinawa resisted (and eventually blocked in 2008) the governmental plan to build an airport in the community for the deployment of P-3Cs, antisubmarine and maritime surveillance aircraft, by the Maritime Self-Defense Forces (Toyohara Kumin to Rentaisuru Kai 1995). In addition, as stated in chapter 1, section 1, from 1989 to 1992 the residents of Onna Village, a western coastal settlement in central Okinawa, staged sit-ins and eventually stopped the US military's attempt to develop an Urban Warfare Training Facility within the village boundaries (Ryukyu Asahi Hōsō 2014a).

5. I have collapsed the two categories, (*a*) those born in the twentieth century and (*b*) those born in the 1890s or earlier, into (*c*) a single category for those born before the Battle of Okinawa, whom I call the first generation. I differentiated (*a*) and (*b*) when I discussed the formation of the Okinawan "people" in 1955 in order to highlight the gap between (*b*), that is, those responsible for establishing an emperor-centered social order in Okinawa before and during the war, and (*a*), that is, those who were critical of the older generation (see chapter 3, section 2). In 1985, the number of people in category (*b*) (i.e., ninety-five years old or older) is small and did not constitute an independent social force to be differentiated from (*a*) those born in the twentieth century.

6. The percentage of employed women aged fifteen or older increased from 1975 (38.2%) to 2000 (46.8%), while the percentage of employed men aged fifteen or older peaked in 1990 (76.9%) and then decreased (Okinawaken Kikakubu Tōkeika, n.d.-c).

7. For the background behind this description, see Inoue 2007, 118, 242 n. 19.

8. To access some of other photos presented in the *Dai-Ryūkyū Shashin Emaki* exhibition series, see Ishikawa 2015b.

9. The Okinawan Prefectural Police could not arrest the suspects because Article 5(c) of the SOFA states: "The custody of an accused member of the United States armed forces or the civilian component over whom Japan is to exercise jurisdiction shall, if he is in the hands of the United States, remain with the United States until he is charged by Japan" (Agreement under Article VI of the Treaty of Mutual Cooperation and Security between Japan and the United States of America, Regarding Facilities and Areas and the Status of United States Armed Forces in Japan).

10. Since the late 1940s, the Japanese Ministry of Education has screened textbooks to be used in public schools across Japan (Monbu Kagakushō 1992).

11. For instance, the Government of the Ryukyu Islands and the Okinawa Prefectural Board of Education compiled twenty-four volumes of Okinawan history from 1965 through 1977 (Ryukyu Seifu/Okinawaken Kyōikuiinkai [1965–1977] 1989), including vol. 8 (originally published in 1971) on the entire history of the

Battle of Okinawa and vols. 9 and 10 (originally published in 1971 and 1974, respectively) that recorded testimonies about the Battle of Okinawaby using interviews as a main method of research. In the 1980s, extending this methodology, local municipalities produced their own volumes of history on the Battle of Okinawa (Sakurazawa 2015, 161, 226, 266).

Conclusion to Part II

Chapter 3 creolized the Freudian theory of ambivalence in the historical actualities of US-ruled Okinawa from the end of the war through 1972; in so doing, it examined the ways in which the Okinawan "people" collectively developed their subjectivity—gendered as male, racialized as non-White, and class-bound as oppressed—vis-à-vis the US military through two androcentric taboos, a homosocial taboo forbidding friendship with the US military and a heterosocial taboo forbidding sexual relations between Okinawan woman and US servicemen. These taboos, I suggest, contributed to generating the "same" in Okinawan subjectivity across the postwar period until the 1990s (and beyond, in some respects)—a form of androcentric nationalism that expressed at once *fraternity* and *fratriarchy*, democracy and oppression, the former manifested externally against the US military and the latter manifested internally against women and others such as mixed-race Okinawans.

Then, in chapter 4, I drew attention to the growth in post-reversion Okinawa through the 1990s of capitalist life-forms that undermined the androcentric taboos created by the Okinawan "people." In so doing, I explored "changes" in Okinawan subjectivity. Specifically, while intensifying the exploitation of living labor, money acted to weaken—if not dissolve—these taboos, making a positive contribution to the process whereby "the notion of human equality has . . . acquired the fixity of a popular prejudice" (Marx [1887] n.d., 41) among increasingly affluent and confident Okinawan "citizens." I investigate how this popular prejudice provided the subjectivity of these "citizens"—particularly, though not exclusively, women—with power to critically infuse internal efforts to overcome the fratriarchy (oppression) of the Okinawan "people" with external efforts to reinforce and expand fraternity (democracy) against the violence of the US military. The 1995 rape incident, in particular, prompted Okinawan "citizens" to frame both efforts, internal and external, in terms of the progressive, citizenry language on peace and the actions into which it was woven.

In exploring Okinawan subjectivity until the 1990s as "a *changing* same," Part II has also paid attention to "something" that one fails to grasp if one approaches it with a good/bad (anti-base/pro-base or conservative/progressive) dichotomy, examining how it was expressed for the formation and transformation of the community of *nuchi du takara* ("life is the ultimate treasure") in postwar Okinawa up through the 1990s. On the one hand, when constructing that community based on direct experience of the death of others in the war, the Okinawan "people" mobilized anti-American (or progressive) island-wide protests against the US military's land seizure procedures *and* allowed pro-American (or conservative) practices such as entertainment businesses to develop around the US bases. Ōshiro Tatsuhiro's *The Cocktail Party* shows precisely how the Okinawan "people" coped with contradictory perspectives, views, and sentiments for gradual yet significant social change (chapter 3). On the other hand, Okinawan "citizens" renewed the community of *nuchi du takara* by grounding new life-forms—such as the debate over *tōtōme*, Ishikawa Mao's photography, Henoko's friendly relations with Camp Schwab, and protests to the 1995 rape incident—in collective memory of the Battle of Okinawa. In so doing, the community of Okinawa "citizens" negotiated differences, tensions, and contradictions across the first, second, and third generations, between women and men, and between the anti-base and pro-base positions, to achieve gradual social change both internally (inside Okinawa) and externally (vis-à-vis the US military and Tokyo) (chapter 4).

Varied life-forms of the Okinawan multitude as the new social actor beyond the 1990s will be examined in Part IV, which, in combination with the analysis of anti-base protests in Henoko in Part I, helps extend the investigation of the community of *nuchi du takara* into the present, in a manner that confirms the validity of the concept of Okinawan subjectivity as "a *changing* same."

PART III

Empire in the Asia-Pacific Region

Between American/Global and Japanese/National

Introduction to Part III

As explained in the introduction to this book, I argue that Empire as a "new," global sovereignty in the post–World War II Asia-Pacific region has been fused into "old," internal post/colonialism, producing continued domination of Okinawa by Japan "proper" across the colonial past and the postcolonial present. In other words, Empire in the Asia-Pacific region reveals a double-sided character, both new (postmodern) *and* old (modern), imperial *and* colonialist, and American/global *and* Japanese/national. Part III scrutinizes this double-sided character of Empire.

On the one hand, chapter 5 examines five historical "moments," exploring how this global form of power has continued to internalize the "outside"—for example, Japan from 1945 on, China from the 1970s on, and the former Soviet Union and its satellite states from the 1990s on—to establish the ever-enlarging world market as its sovereign territory. In so doing, it clarifies American, global, and postmodern tendencies of Empire. Chapter 5 also serves as a background against which is presented the analysis of chapter 6, which explores how Tokyo's continued control over Okinawa since the late nineteenth century has eventually become aligned with the formation and transformation of Empire in the post–World War II Asia-Pacific region. I accomplish this task historically and ethnographically by analyzing how the term *dojin*—"a savage and inferior native race"—has been woven into Japanese nationalism against Okinawa and how this nationalism, as it is expressed digitally today, is intertwined with the rule of Empire. In so doing, chapter 6 highlights the Japanese, modern, and colonialist tendencies exhibited by Empire in the post–World War II Asia-Pacific region.

In this introduction to Part III, I examine the roles the Japanese state has played in mediating these two tendencies of Empire: new (postmodern) *and* old (modern), imperial *and* colonialist, and American/global *and* Japanese/national.

• • •

Beginning in the late nineteenth century, the Japanese state attempted to merge, absorb, and manage the nation's constituent power from above through the image of the emperor in order to develop and redevelop specific forms of "official nationalism" (Anderson 1991, 83–111). Of particular importance was the concept of *kokutai*, which referred to a "unique" form of the Japanese polity characterized by the enduring loyalty and filial piety of the unified subjects—the Japanese—toward the unbroken line of emperors from time immemorial. Discriminated against as almost but not quite "Japanese" in prewar Japan, Okinawa was eventually used by the Japanese state/emperor as a sacrifice to protect Japan "proper," where *kokutai* was to be fully expressed, against enemy attack; the result was the 1945 Battle of Okinawa, in which an estimated 150,000 Okinawans, together with approximately 66,000 Japanese troops and 12,500 American troops, were killed (Arashiro 1994, 253–254). After the war, the same Japanese state/emperor separated Okinawa, again as a sacrifice, from Japan "proper" to assist the United States in transforming it into the "Keystone of the Pacific."

In the eyes of Emperor Hirohito, the emerging Cold War in the 1940s threw war-defeated Japan into a brutal world situation in which there was war of every (capitalist) state against every (communist) state (Toyoshita 1996, 143–186, and 2008). However, due to Article 9 of the Constitution of Japan, which stipulated unarmed peace, Japan/Hirohito was, to use the words of Thomas Hobbes in his 1651 book *Leviathan*, in "continuall feare, and danger of violent death" ([1651] 2009, chap. 13), with no force to defend itself/himself. Accordingly, just as individuals in the natural state, when there was war of everyone against everyone, entered a social contract to mutually transfer their right of self-defense to construct the common power—Leviathan—for the benefit of gaining shared security (Hobbes [1651] 2009, chaps. 13, 14, and 17), Hirohito transferred what he considered "his" administrative rights over Okinawa to the common power, the United States, in order to defend Japan "by all means [it] can" use (Hobbes [1651] 2009, chap. 14). In so doing, he entered into a transnational social contract with the United States, externally, for the construction of the international Leviathan in East Asia by rearticulating, internally, an old, modern, and colonialist political control exercised by Tokyo over Okinawa since the late nineteenth century. Empire represents this new, postmodern, international Leviathan founded upon continued domination over Okinawa.

In the late 1950s, as I will discuss in chapter 5, by inventing the "administrative actions theory" (*tōchikōi-ron*), the Japanese Supreme Court legally elevated Empire to the level of the absolute, beyond and outside the Constitution of Japan—not unlike the Leviathan theorized by Hobbes, who stated: "Sovereign Power Ought In All Common-wealths To Be Absolute" ([1651] 2009, chap. 20) and "to those Lawes which the Sovereign himselfe, that is, which the Common-wealth maketh, he is not subject" ([1651] 2009, chap. 29). I call this "absolute" global power Empire version 1. The specificity of Empire v.1—operative through the 1960s—was defined by the mechanism of split governance, the economic use of Japan "proper" and the military abuse of Okinawa.

The rise of global capitalism, along with the defeat of the United States in Vietnam, introduced "reciprocity" (not equality) across the Asa-Pacific region as a new organizing principle of international relations in the 1970s through the 1980s, a process that contributed to the formation of what I call Empire version 2. My conceptualization is derived from John Locke's idea of civil government ([1690] 2010), together with Immanuel Wallerstein's model of the capitalist world-economy (Wallerstein [1974] 2000; cf. Cumings 1984, 19).

Like Hobbes, Locke used the logic of mutual transference of one's rights to the common power for the construction of the state (sec. 89). But unlike Hobbes, who as noted above theorized the common power, the Leviathan, to be absolute, beyond and outside the law, Locke highlighted that "the law of nature stands as an eternal rule to all men, legislators [composing Parliament] as well as others" (sec. 135) and that "absolute arbitrary power, or governing without settled standing laws, can neither of them consist with the ends of society and government" (sec. 137). As such, the law provides a common language that regulates a two-way reciprocity, but not equality, between the higher (the Crown) and the lower (Parliament), both of which are incorporated into the same terrain of a political/civil society. What is more, unlike Hobbes, who considered private property of subjects to be subordinate to the power of the Leviathan,[1] Locke, in a manner that acknowledged the influence of the emerging bourgeoisie (property-owning citizens) in seventeenth-century England, emphasized the protection of private property as the foundation of this reciprocity (sec. 3). In effect, Locke advanced his theory to formulate the shift from the absolutism of the Hobbesian Crown over subjects to an increase of power of Parliament/civil government (representing the interest of bourgeois/citizens) vis-à-vis the Crown as specified in the 1689 Bill of Rights in England.

I deploy Locke's insight to explain the shift from unilateral, "absolute" American hegemony over East Asia until the 1960s to the reciprocity among the United States (core), Japan (semi-periphery), and other Asian nations (periphery)—or what Bruce Cumings called "a mature hegemonic system" (1993, 61)—across Empire v.2 in the context of the 1970s and 1980s. In so doing, I show that the "imperial" political mechanism for external capitalist expansion of Empire v.2, represented by the incorporation of China within its network in the 1970s, was reinforced by above-mentioned split governance as an extension of Tokyo's internal control mechanism over Okinawa in the Cold War Asia-Pacific region. In the process, I also demonstrate how prewar official nationalism founded upon the emperor-centered ideology of *kokutai* against Okinawa was increasingly displaced by a different form of Japanese nationalism against and for Okinawa that was generated by analog capitalism.

Subsequently, across the post–Cold War Asia-Pacific region, Empire version 3, having emerged after the interlude of the 1990s, now centers on the development of the world market as its sovereign territory to which "there is no more outside" (Hardt and Negri 2000, 181). In other words, an external/outward mechanism of Empire v.1 (1945–1960s) and v.2 (1970s–1980s) to internalize the outside for capitalist development has come to an end in the twenty-first century. What has emerged instead is a new mechanism involving perpetual control of internal threats, that is, a global security apparatus under which the US military has restructured itself as a network-centric force to respond to, eliminate, and control newly emerging threats—represented by 9/11 and the rise of China—from within this sovereign territory. In the process, Empire v.3 has annihilated the distinction between economic use of Japan "proper" and military abuse of Okinawa, reformulating split governance into a generalized system of biopolitical control of everyday social life across Japan—including Okinawa—and beyond, a process that corresponded to still another form of official nationalism regulated by digital capitalism.

The beginning and closing years of Empire v.1 (1945–1960s), Empire v.2 (1970s–1980s), the interlude (1990s), and Empire v.3 (twenty-first century) are meant to be guideposts, rather than a strict periodization, to facilitate the analysis of the formation and transformation of Empire in the Asia-Pacific region. As my analysis in chapter 6 makes clear, emperor-centered official nationalism version 1 (developed from the 1880s through the end of World War II), analog-based version 2 (developed in postwar Japan, in particular from the 1970s through the 1990s), and digital-based version 3 (developed in the twenty-first century) overlap with but do not correspond to Empire v.1, v.2, and v.3, indicating an interconnection as well as the existence of separate mechanisms in operation between national and global processes.

Methodological Notes

Chapter 5 adopts methods of international relations, a historical exploration of the relations of states with one another and with international organizations such as the United Nations. It utilizes archival data collected from various sources (such as governmental documents, newspaper articles, and prior scholarly works) for a theoretical intervention into the past, present, and future of the Asia-Pacific region in light of the questions of Empire. Description and analysis in chapter 6 are prompted by my encounter with a nationalist group in the summer of 2013 in Naha and are expanded and elaborated due to the so-called *dojin* incident that occurred in 2016. Data are collected from fieldwork in both physical space and cyberspace for the analysis of contemporary digital nationalism (which I call "official nationalism version 3") and from scholarly works and archival documents of various kinds for the analysis of earlier forms of nationalism (which I call "official nationalism version 1 and version 2").

Note

1. Hobbes stated: "A . . . doctrine, that tendeth to the Dissolution of a Commonwealth, is, 'That every private man has an absolute Propriety in his Goods; such, as excludeth the Right of the Sovereign'" (chap. 29). In other words, in order to maintain the commonwealth, the right of property should be subject to the sovereign, according to Hobbes.

CHAPTER 5

American/Global/Postmodern Tendencies of Empire

Five Historical Moments of Its Formation and Transformation

Chapter 5 examines five historical moments to grasp how Empire has established the ever-enlarging world market in the Asia-Pacific region as its sovereign territory. The first moment (1945 through the early 1950s) revolves around the internalization of Japan for the formation of Empire v.1. The second moment (mid-1950s through the 1960s) involves what I call "split governance," characterized by the division between economic use of Japan "proper" and military abuse of Okinawa under the common rule of Empire v.1. The third moment (1970s–1980s) is represented by the integration of China into the world market for the transformation of Empire v.1 into Empire v.2. The fourth moment (1990s) is a transition period from Empire v.2 to Empire v.3. The fifth moment (the early twenty-first century) revolves around the formation of Empire v.3, a process that has been prompted by the incorporation of the former Soviet Union and its satellite states into the world market to which there is no more outside. In analyzing these moments, chapter 5 also underscores changing forms of conflict and tension—for example, World War II, the Cold War, 9/11, and today's US-China confrontation—associated with these historical moments.

1. The First Moment: Incorporation of Japan for the Birth of Empire in East Asia (1945 through the Early 1950s)

1.1 The "Imperialist" Model of the Occupation of Japan and Its Transformation

Annihilation of the social, economic, and political life of the Japanese through air raids on major cities (from late 1944 to August 1945), the Battle of Okinawa (March to June 1945 and beyond), and ultimately the atomic bombs dropped on Hiroshima and Nagasaki (August 1945) resulted in the Japanese Empire's unconditional surrender to the Allied powers in August 1945. The "postwar" as a specific political project was introduced by the Allied (in actuality, US) occupation (1945–1952). The primary objectives of this occupation, as laid out by Washington, were the demilitarization and democratization of Japan (Dower 1993, esp. 163–169; 1999, 73–80). Yet "MacArthur and his staff in Tokyo tended to interpret [policy directives from Washington] as a mandate for genuinely drastic reform, on occasion of a more radical nature than Washington seems to have had in mind" (Dower 1993, 165; see also Schaller 1989, 123). Accordingly, from 1945 to 1946, they implemented the "permanent and complete" disarmament of Japan (Dower 1993, 164) and introduced broad measures of democratization to promote women's participation in political processes (via women's suffrage, for instance), grow labor unions, liberate education from the state, dismantle zaibatsu (family-run conglomerates), execute land reform, purge militarist and ultranationalists from public office, abolish oppressive institutions such as the Special Higher Police, and arrest war criminals (Matsuo 1993, 31–34). In the process, the occupation resembled modern European colonial imperialism—which was "really an extension of the sovereignty of the European nation-states beyond their own boundaries" (Hardt and Negri 2000, xii)—in that MacArthur imposed policies on postwar Japan on the basis of a clearly defined political division between civilized Americans and feudalistic Japanese, a division he established to maintain his status as the ruler/victor over the ruled/loser (Katō N. 2019, 55–64; Dower 1999, chap. 6). Indeed, MacArthur noted that a Japanese people "would be like a boy of 12 as compared with our development of 45 years" "measured by the standards of modern civilization" (US Congress, Senate Committee on Armed Services 1951, 312, cited in Dower 1999, 550). The ways in which MacArthur handled issues of the emperor represent his "imperialist" approach to postwar Japan.

In a manner that extended his view about the "Oriental psychology" (Schaller 1989, viii), MacArthur suggested that "the Japanese were by nature an obedient people and used to authority" (Foreign Relations of the United States [hereafter FRUS] 1948a, 697) and considered the emperor—and his influence over the "obedient" Japanese, exemplified by the fact that more than seven million Japanese troops deployed across Japan and Asia (Matsuo 1993, 21) accepted disarmament in unison upon his command at the end of the war—to be an absolute necessity for smooth and successful occupation (Katō N. 2019, 68–93). While conservatives in Japan were relieved to see that the emperor system would not be abolished, citizens and politicians in the United States—together with other Allied powers such as China, Australia, the Philippines, and the Soviet Union—saw Hirohito as responsible for and punishable for the disasters, horrors, and atrocities the war he began had caused (Dower 1999, 299–300). MacArthur thus needed to recast the image of Hirohito in a positive light, an attempt in which Hirohito himself collaborated in order to protect *kokutai*—the "unique" Japanese polity he embodied—that presumably expressed the unbroken line of emperors from time immemorial.

For instance, the International Military Tribunal for the Far East (also known as the Tokyo Trial, May 1946–November 1948), initiated by MacArthur through a special proclamation issued in January 1946, shifted the war responsibility to Hirohito's faithful subordinate, General Tōjō, as a scapegoat to be executed in exchange for the pardon of Hirohito (Dower 1999, chaps. 11 and 15). Hirohito's declaration that he was a human and not a god in January 1946 also contributed to this rewriting (Dower 1999, 308–314). The new Constitution of Japan, drafted by MacArthur's General Headquarters, was another key tool MacArthur used to shift the image of the emperor into a democratic and peaceful one within the broader imperialist goal of replacing the old (Japanese) system of rule with the new (American) one. MacArthur created this tool in nine days in February 1946 to prevent the Far Eastern Commission—a key organization consisting of the United Kingdom, the Soviet Union, China, and eight other countries that was expected to oversee the occupation of Japan—from influencing his governance of postwar Japan (Oguma 2002, 156). The constitution came to exert enormous influence upon the shapes and directions taken thereafter by Japan, the US-Japan relationship, and Empire.

Specifically, Article 1 highlighted the principle of democratization of Japan by defining the emperor as "the symbol of the State and of the unity of the people, deriving his position from the will of the people with whom resides sovereign power." This article deprived the emperor of his transcendental power, including his power to command the military and his power to initiate and conclude war, which had been stipulated in the Meiji Constitution. In addition, Article 9 underscored the principle of demilitarization. Indeed, the first paragraph of Article 9 featured the renunciation of war by stating: "Aspiring sincerely to an international peace based on justice and order, the Japanese people forever renounce war as a sovereign right of the nation and the threat or use of force as means of settling international disputes," while Paragraph 2 of Article 9 radicalized Paragraph 1 by stipulating the nonpossession of military forces: "In order to accomplish the aim of the preceding paragraph, land, sea, and air forces, as well as other war potential, will never be maintained. The right of belligerency of the state will not be recognized." In effect, under the power of the government above the government—MacArthur and the United States—Hirohito/Japan was castrated, as it were, without a military (due to Article 9) and without sovereignty (due to Article 1).

The "imperialist" exercise of the constituted power in postwar Japan by MacArthur was shaped by his vision of postwar security in East Asia consisting of two programs. The first program concerned collective security by the United Nations, a mechanism in which "each state . . . accepts that the security of one is the concern of all and agrees to join in a collective response to threats to, and breaches of, the peace" (Hurrell 2011, 299). More specifically, until 1949 or so, MacArthur—at least officially (Oguma 2002, 452)—envisioned that postwar Japan, the former enemy now deprived of military forces due to Article 9 of the Japanese constitution he drafted, was to be collectively administered (after three to five years of occupation) as the "Switzerland of the Far East" (McEvoy 1950, 11; Toyoshita 2008, 115) by the United Nations under the extended cooperation of major powers including the United States and the Soviet Union—a cooperation that had been formed at least partially during World War II (e.g., in the Teheran Conference of November–December 1943 and the Yalta Conference of February 1945) (Igarashi 1996, 17–19; Russel 1958, esp. chaps. 7, 17, 21).

The second program was continued US military dominance in the world, made possible by the American monopoly on the nuclear arsenal at that time (Kusunoki 2009, 52–59). Accordingly, MacArthur considered US forces positioned in Okinawa as "the most advanced and vital point in [the postwar security] structure," consisting of "a U-shaped area embracing the

Aleutians, Midway, the former Japanese mandate islands, Clark Field in the Philippines, and above all Okinawa" (FRUS 1948a, 700, cited in Eldridge 2001, 207; see also Dower 1993, 171), with a plan to attack the Soviet Union with atomic bombs from Okinawa in case of a Soviet invasion in Asia, including Japan (Shibayama 2010, 21–26). In effect, in his fantastic thinking MacArthur envisaged postwar security not only against Japan (as the former enemy and a potential future threat) but also for Japan (as a new, peace-loving, castrated nation) under imminent "threats" of communism.

Meanwhile, from 1947 through 1948, the State Department under the initiative taken by George F. Kennan and others developed the policy of containment to cope with increasing communist threats in East Asia (Cumings 1993, 39–41; Igarashi 1995, 78–85; Katō N. 2019, 253–257; Kusunoki 2009, 59–73; Schaller 1986; 1997, 17), a process consummated by the approval of NSC 13/2 (October 1948) and NSC 13/3 (May 1949) concerning the US policy toward Japan by President Truman (FRUS 1948b, 1949). The US policy toward Japan was driven by a specific economic logic, as Bruce Cumings (1993, 38) noted: "In East Asia, American planners envisioned a regional economy driven by revived Japanese industry, with assured continental access to markets and raw materials for its exports." Accordingly, beginning in 1948, Washington introduced a series of measures to modify MacArthur's original, "imperialist" (or "colonialist") reform policies—which had aimed to destroy and eradicate Japan's prewar/wartime system (other than the emperor)—with alternative policies directed toward a new, "imperial" goal of redeveloping that system to integrate the economy of Japan as what Dean Gooderham Acheson (US secretary of state 1949–1953) called the "great workshop" of Asia (cited in Eldridge 2001, 262; see also Dower 1979, 416 and Schaller 1987, chap. 16). In the process, however, many projects of democratization and demilitarization implemented in occupied Japan were canceled or "reversed." This cancellation or reversal first occurred in economic and social realms.

For instance, labor movements, once actively promoted under MacArthur's policy of democratization, came to be suppressed; the dismantling of zaibatsu, also promoted for democratization in the economic sphere, came to a standstill; war criminals such as Kishi Nobusuke—a high ranking bureaucrat involved in exploitive economic development of Manchuko, the Japanese Empire's puppet state in Manchuria, who was to be punished in MacArthur's Tokyo Trial—were released in December 1948 without being indicted (Dower 1999, 268–270, 454, 533). In addition, the "reverse course" was extended into 1949 and beyond through, for instance, the Red Purge in 1949–1950 that resulted in the firing of "approximately 22,000 public and private employees" (Dower 1979, 366; cf. Dower 1999, 272).

As the reverse course—or a logic that aimed to not so much destroy and eradicate as revive and reshape Japan's prewar/wartime system—thus unfolded in the economic-social realm, the Korean War broke out on June 25, 1950. As US forces in Japan, charged with maintaining domestic security, were now deployed to the Korean Peninsula, MacArthur ordered Tokyo to create, as a compensation for diminished forces in Japan, the National Police Reserve, security forces with seventy-five thousand members (Kowalski 2013, 23; Shibayama 2010, chap. 6; Yabe 2019, 225–227 and 238–242). As Japan took a first step toward rearmament, Washington attempted to revoke MacArthur's policy of demilitarization and neutralization of Japan by formulating a mechanism to have the US military continue to stay in postwar Japan for the duration of the Korean War and beyond. In other words, in order to implement the reverse course not only economically and socially but also militarily, Washington needed to incorporate Japan, the former enemy, as a part—indeed the core—of the security apparatus in East Asia.

By this time, however, Article 9 stipulating unarmed peace had already gained broad and deep support among the Japanese people due to shared memories of the horrible war they had fought, becoming a stumbling block for Washington. Indeed, the continued stationing of the US military in Japan would not only deny the spirit of Article 9 but would also perpetuate the occupation of Japan, contradicting MacArthur's declared position that the occupation forces should withdraw as soon as the objectives of the occupation—demilitarization and democratization of Japan—were accomplished as defined by the Potsdam Declaration (FRUS 1950a, 1218) and that the United Nations should protect Japan's disarmed neutrality after occupation ended. Furthermore, there was an irreconcilable tension between the State Department, which wanted to conclude a peace treaty with Japan and end the occupation of Japan as soon as possible in order to evade criticism from other Allied powers over US "imperialism" or "colonialism" in Japan, and the Department of Defense, which wished to delay the end of occupation in order to maintain and reinforce military power over Japan and East Asia more broadly to contain the threats of communism (Eldridge 2001, chap. 7; Kusunoki 2009, 92–110). Washington overcame the multiple obstacles concerning the status of postwar Japan by establishing the "San Francisco system" (Dower 2014)—defined by the two treaties Japan signed in

September 1951 in San Francisco, the Treaty of Peace with Japan and the US-Japan Security Treaty—as the foundation of Empire v.1 in East Asia. To make this happen, John Foster Dulles implemented two different yet interrelated and critically important ideas, a process in which Emperor Hirohito was deeply involved.

1.2. The Birth of Empire in East Asia through the San Francisco System

The first idea—which was ultimately materialized by the US-Japan Security Treaty—concerned the continued use of the US bases in Japan beyond the period of occupation for "collective (or regional) self-defense" against communism (Kusunoki 2009, 115–122 and 214–228; Shibayama 2010, 268–290; Swenson-Wright 2005, chap. 2; Toyoshita 1996, 47 and 2008, 153). Collective/regional self-defense "permits a member state [of the United Nations] to intervene in the defense of another member state when that state has been subject to an unlawful armed attack" (Padmanabhan and Shih 2012, 1), and Article 51 of the United Nations Charter stipulates collective/regional (as well as individual) self-defense as "the inherent right" of the state (United Nations, n.d.). Yet, importantly, the United Nations Charter views military actions based on collective/regional self-defense as an exception and secondary to collective security (Padmanabhan and Shih 2012). For, while collective/regional self-defense presupposes the Self/Other (friend/enemy) binary and thus tends to perpetuate international tension, collective security potentially helps to deconstruct that binary and perpetuate peace instead through the formation of a democratic, supranational power.

Indeed, during World War II, Dulles had provided a vision that broadly corresponded to the notion of collective security by the United Nations (Iguchi 1998, 38) by advocating "dilution of sovereignty"—a process involving mutual transference (i.e., dilution) of state sovereignties for the construction of the common power—"to assure a constructively peaceful world order and prevent future wars" ("Dulles Outlines..." 1939). Yet, due to the deep-seated US-Soviet rivalry during and after World War II, Dulles—who played a crucial role in materializing Article 51 of the UN Charter (1950, 89-93; cf. Hida 2014)—also realistically foresaw a situation that would allow (or force) the United States (*a*) to suspend the paradigm of "collective security" by the United Nations, (*b*) to implement instead "collective/regional self-defense" against communism in East Asia, and (*c*) to continue to use bases in Japan after occupation without appearing to be imperialist or colonialist.

Accordingly, when the Korean War broke out, Dulles, who was visiting Japan as a consultant to the secretary of state (Kusunoki 2009, 111), met MacArthur seven times or so (Eldridge 2001, 335) to suggest the following: MacArthur should not abandon so much as recast his earlier position—i.e., neutralization of Japan—by using the United Nations Charter to construct a legal fiction, as it were, that the US military facilities in Japan would continue to exist after occupation, in light of the threats of communism, on behalf of the United Nations (Kusunoki 2009, 118; Yabe 2019, 195). Thus advocating the US military's involvement in collective/regional self-defense of Japan against communism, Dulles also added that these US facilities would eventually be merged into "the international security system of the United Nations [i.e., collective security] when it is finally established" (FRUS 1950b, 1230), a situation that Dulles did not think would happen but MacArthur believed (or wanted to believe) would happen. According to Dulles, MacArthur "fully agreed with such a presentation [outlined above] as being the way to make the arrangement acceptable to the Japanese people" (FRUS 1950b, 1230; cf. Yabe 2019, 232). It should be added that in the first half of 1950 (i.e., before the Korean War broke out), MacArthur—confronted by the intensification of the Cold War in East Asia (e.g., the establishment of Communist China in 1949)—had already attempted to redefine his earlier position.[1] In effect, Dulles assisted MacArthur in accomplishing that by substituting collective/regional self-defense for collective security. In the process, he appropriated MacArthur's idea as expressed latently in the early phase of occupation (1945–1946) (Schaller 1989, 125–126) and explicitly in the so-called 6/23 memorandum of 1950 (FRUS 1950c, 1227)—"The entire area of Japan must be regarded as a potential base for defensive maneuver with unrestricted freedom reserved to the United States as the protecting power"—as the guiding principle of negotiation for the US-Japan Security Treaty with the Japanese government (i.e., Prime Minister Yoshida) from January through August 1951 (Toyoshita 1996, chaps. 2 and 3; Nishimura 1971, chap. 2).

Meanwhile, Dulles, who collaborated with (or manipulated) MacArthur, also collaborated with (or manipulated and was manipulated by) Hirohito in his act of actualizing this idea—the continued use of the US bases in Japan beyond the period of occupation—as an integral element of the San Francisco system. John Dower (1979, chap. 8) noted the deep fear of communism "from outside, above, and below" (281)—that is, the Soviet

Union (outside), the Japanese military and bureaucracy (above), and the Japanese people (below)—that permeated the ruling class in pre-surrender Japan. In post-surrender Japan, the fear was retained in this class. It looks as if the fear of communism had especially intensified in the mind of Hirohito from 1950 on due to the prospect of possible defeat of South Korea in the Korean War—which could have led to the establishment of a communist regime in Japan under the Soviet Union's direct or indirect influence, to the initiation of a new military tribunal against Hirohito by the Soviet Union, and ultimately, to a new verdict on Hirohito's war responsibilities (Toyoshita 1996, 183–185; cf. Hata [1987] 2007, 244).

In response, Hirohito, against the stipulation of the new Constitution of Japan that prohibited him from conducting any political acts, established a direct path of communication with John Foster Dulles by using Matsudaira Yasumasa, the emperor's adviser. Specifically, on June 26, 1950, Matsudaira paid a visit to Compton Pakenham, Tokyo Bureau chief of *Newsweek* and a member of a Japan lobby group in Tokyo named the American Council on Japan, to ask him to relay a message containing the following point from Hirohito to Dulles (Hata [1987] 2007, 241): had the purge of wartime leaders conducted in 1945–1946 by MacArthur (noted above) been relaxed and "had such men been in a position to express their thoughts publicly, the recent mistaken controversy over the matter of bases [caused by Prime Minister Yoshida] could have been avoided through a voluntary offer [of Japan's land for the use of the US military] on the part of Japan." In so doing, Hirohito dismissed two national leaders at once. He expressed nonconfidence in Yoshida, who—apparently trying to use as a bargaining tool the matter of US bases in Japan, upon which the United States depended for the prosecution of the Korean War—was not committed to the "voluntary offer" of Japan's land to the US military, to the point of stating publicly, "I don't want the bases to be rented out [to the United States]" before the Foreign Affairs Committee of the House of Councilors on July 29, 1950 (Toyoshita 1996, 128). He also bypassed MacArthur, who used to lecture him on neutralizing postwar Japan as "the Switzerland of the Far East" without specifying how the United Nations (still unable to form its standing forces) would protect Japan, in a manner that intensified his fear of communism (Toyoshita 1996, 163–186; Yabe 2014, 257–263).

Hirohito's desire, communicated to Dulles, indeed reinforced Dulles's goal of securing "the entire area of Japan . . . as a potential base . . . with unrestricted freedom reserved to the United States"—in the above-mentioned words of MacArthur (FRUS 1950c, 1227)—in the negotiation for the conclusion of the US-Japan Security Treaty with the Yoshida administration in January–August 1951 (Toyoshita 1996, chaps. 2 and 3). Meanwhile, due to his attempt to use the matter of bases as a bargaining tool, Yoshida was most likely admonished by Hirohito through the prewar system of private consultations (*naisō*) between the emperor and governmental leaders that continued in postwar Japan (Toyoshita 1996, 201–208). Toyoshita Narahiko (1996) suggests that Yoshida, having considered himself to be the true servant of the emperor (cf. Kōsaka [1968] 2006, 22–26), accepted and endorsed Hirohito's view concerning the potentiality of the Soviet Union's invasion of Japan—which he did not share (Dower 1979, 388–391; Kusunoki 2009, 39–40, 180–182, and 268)—by following Dulles, who imposed a dual logic that defined the subordinate status of post-occupation Japan to the United States within the broader framework of "unilateral" collective/regional self-defense: (*a*) Japan should "request" and the United States with sympathy would "agree" with the stationing of the US forces to protect post-occupation Japan and the areas around it, and (*b*) in exchange, Japan should assist the US forces in case of emergency.

The second crucial idea Dulles implemented to establish the San Francisco system concerned Japan's "residual sovereignty" over Okinawa, a notion that—ultimately materialized by the Treaty of Peace with Japan—compromised a number of opposing views. On the one hand, since the early phase of the occupation, MacArthur (Eldridge 2001, 206–207; FRUS 1947, 512), along with the Defense Department and Joint Chiefs of Staff (Eldridge 2001, 177–180, 193–195, and 290–292; Igarashi 1995, 37), had insisted on permanent US control over Okinawa—"the most advanced and vital point in [the postwar security] structure," as noted. On the other hand, other members of the Allied powers, particularly the Soviet Union (but also China and India), opposed US control over Okinawa (Eldridge 2001, 285–287). The State Department also opposed it, on the basis of the principle of nonexpansion of territories as specified in the Atlantic Charter (Miyazato 1975, 5). Furthermore, Tokyo, including Prime Minister Yoshida, expressed the view that Okinawa was part of Japan (Eldridge 2001, 293–300 and 363–365).

Dulles developed the idea of Japan's residual sovereignty over Okinawa by reconciling these opposing positions about Okinawa without allowing Okinawa to express its own view on the matter.[2] Specifically, while enabling Washington to acknowledge that post-occupation Japan would retain its sovereignty over Okinawa in theory (i.e., "residually") in line with the positions of the State Department, other Allied powers, and Tokyo, this idea, in practice, let the US military control and remake Okinawa as the "Keystone of the

Pacific" according to the view of the Defense Department, Joint Chiefs of Staff, and MacArthur, in a way that would help the United States assert its hegemony in Cold War East Asia and beyond without directly infringing upon Article 9. Emperor Hirohito indeed desired this hegemony to establish postwar Japan as a "client state" (McCormack 2007), as the following information conveyed from Hidenari Terasaki (an advisor to the emperor) to W. J. Sebald (a US political advisor in Japan) in September 1947 reveals:

> The Emperor hopes that the United States will continue the military occupation of Okinawa and other islands of the Ryukyus. . . . The Emperor feels that such a move would meet with widespread approval among the Japanese people who fear not only the menace of Russia, but after the Occupation has ended, the growth of rightist and leftist groups which might give rise to an "incident" which Russia could use as a basis for interfering internally in Japan. The Emperor further feels that United States military occupation of Okinawa (and such other islands as may be required) should be based upon the fiction of a long-term lease—25 to 50 years or more—with sovereignty retained in Japan. ("Enclosure . . ." [1947] 2001, 181; cf. Shindō 1979a, 1979b)

Eventually, the concept of Japan's residual sovereignty over Okinawa was inscribed in Article 3 of the Treaty of Peace with Japan (concluded in September 1951), which reads:

> Japan will concur in any proposal of the United States to the United Nations to place under its trusteeship system, with the United States as the sole administering authority, Nansei Shoto south of 29 north latitude (including the Ryukyu Islands and the Daito Islands), Nanpo Shoto south of Sofu Gan (including the Bonin Islands, Rosario Island and the Volcano Islands) and Parece Vela and Marcus Island. Pending the making of such a proposal and affirmative action thereon, the United States will have the right to exercise all and any powers of administration, legislation and jurisdiction over the territory and inhabitants of these islands, including their territorial waters.

Of course, "the making of such a proposal and affirmative action thereon" never happened, and accordingly the United States perpetuated its direct rule of Okinawa until 1972.

In short, the San Francisco system was a two-pronged mechanism of the constituted power in East Asia involving the unrestricted use of bases in both post-occupation Japan (via the US-Japan Security Treaty) and Okinawa (via the notion of residual sovereignty as defined through the San Francisco Peace Treaty) by the United States. With this mechanism, Dulles and Washington successfully compromised Article 9—the unarmed peace of postwar Japan—and subverted the "imperialist" dream of neutralizing Japan under the United Nations and dominating East Asia by the US military that had been envisioned by MacArthur, who was ultimately dismissed from office in April 1951 (Schaller 1989, 237–240). Instead, the San Francisco system enabled Dulles/Washington to incorporate, utilize, and manage the constituent power in Japan—including Okinawa—both economically and militarily for the birth in East Asia of the capitalist sovereignty, Empire v.1, with collective/regional self-defense as the basic security paradigm of the United States against communism (cf. Sakaguchi 1998). To reinforce that paradigm, in the first half of the 1950s, the United States concluded mutual defense treaties with South Korea, the Philippines, Taiwan, and Australia/New Zealand, while establishing the Southeast Asia Treaty Organization. In the process, Dulles and Washington also contributed to keeping "history issues" (Dower 2014, 12) for which Hirohito was directly or indirectly responsible at bay—issues such as the Nanjing massacre in China and "comfort women" in Korea—while founding Empire upon "problematic legacies" (Dower 2014, 4) of the San Francisco system. As a result, until the third moment (1970s-1980s) began, historical narratives in postwar Japan tended to focus on "not the victims of Japanese aggression but the Japanese people themselves [as the victims], who, it was said, 'were embroiled' in the war by their leaders" (Gluck 1993, 83).

2. The Second Moment: The Growth of Empire Version 1 through Split Governance (Mid-1950s through the 1960s)

The Korean War, which began in June 1950, continued until July 1953, resulting in a surge of US military procurements from Japanese industries (Dower 1999, 541–542), which stimulated the economic recovery of postwar Japan more generally. This recovery, in turn, paved the way for the declaration in the Economic White Paper of 1956 (Keizai Kikakuchō) that *mohaya "sengo" dewanai*, or "we are no longer 'postwar,'" in the sense that the "postwar," defined by the US occupation together with the shortage of food, clothing, and shelter needed to satisfy basic needs of everyday life, was dissipating (Noguchi 2015, 55–64). The San Francisco system, which allowed the United States to use Japan as a base to execute the Korean War, thus generated contradiction within itself, a contradiction between the constituent power of the Japanese people who wanted to leave the "postwar" behind by continuing to improve their living conditions, on the one hand, and the constituted power of the United States to perpetuate the "postwar" by continuing to utilize Japan as a potential base with unrestricted freedom reserved to itself, on the other. In a manner that helped the United States to overcome this contradiction and to grow Empire v.1 in East Asia and beyond, the Japanese judicial system invented the so-called administrative actions theory (*tōchikōi-ron*), discussed below. Let me elaborate on the background of this "invention" first.

The desire of the Japanese people to leave the "postwar" behind was reflected in Tokyo's acknowledgment in 1955 of the "defense only" (*senshubōei*) principle (Hamaguchi 2011) that confirmed—in light of Article 9 of the Constitution of Japan—the use of Self-Defense Forces only for individual self-defense inside the territories of Japan and not for collective/regional self-defense (with the United States) outside the territories of Japan. In the process, unilaterality of the US-Japan security alliance was confirmed, where collective/regional self-defense would be exercised by the United States to protect Japan but not by Japan to protect the United States. The Japanese people's desire to leave the "postwar" behind was also acutely expressed by anti-base protests that spread across Japan "proper" in the mid-1950s, including, for example, Sunagawa Town in western Tokyo, where Tachikawa Air Base was located; Kakamigahara City in Gifu Prefecture, where Camp Gifu was located; and the Kitafuji area of Yamanashi Prefecture, where Camp Fuji McNair was located (NHK Shuzaihan 2011, 22–27). Particularly significant as a background for the rise of anti-base protests in Japan "proper" in the 1950s was the 1952 "Administrative Agreement under Article III of the Security Treaty between Japan and the United States of America" (the so-called Administrative Agreement) that defined the unequal relationship between US troops and Japanese nationals. For instance, Article 17-2 of the Administrative Agreement stated that crimes committed by US troops and related individuals would be handled not by the Japanese judicial system but by US military courts and authorities.

Accordingly, when an incident occurred in January 1957 at the US Army shooting range in Somagahara, Gunma Prefecture, the US military refused to turn the suspect over to Japanese authorities, citing the Administrative Agreement. A forty-six-year-old Japanese housewife from a farm family, the mother of six children, was collecting shell casings, precious brass, on the army shooting range to earn additional money; a twenty-one-year-old specialist third class by the name of William Girard shot and killed her after, apparently, luring her by saying in Japanese, *Mama-san daijōbu* (you are safe, come close), so that she was only 10 meters from him as a "target." In response to the outrage of the Japanese public, the US government eventually allowed him to be tried in a Japanese court (Naoshima 2000; Yamamoto Hidem. 2015).[3]

The constituent power of the Japanese expressed in protests at this time, combined with the Korean War truce in 1953, directly and indirectly impelled the US and Japanese policy planners to reduce and reorganize US bases in Japan "proper" and to reboot and stabilize the bilateral alliance (Miller 2019, chap. 2, esp. 180–185). Consequently, the total area of the US bases in Japan "proper" in 1955 (129,600 hectares) was reduced by more than 75% by 1962 (to 30,600 hectares) (Okinawaken Sōmubu Chijikōshitsu Kichitaisakuka 2020, 110).

While the dramatic reduction of the bases in Japan "proper" was made possible by a number of approaches,[4] the most important for my own analysis is the process whereby bases of the US Marine Corps in Japan "proper" were transferred to US-controlled Okinawa. As a result, the total area of US military facilities increased greatly in Okinawa, from 16,200 hectares in 1954, to 26,950 hectares in 1958, to 29,900 hectares in 1966, and to 35,300 hectares in 1971 (Okinawa Times 1997, 16–17; see also Arasaki M. 1996, 14; Oguma 2002, 497)—the opposite of the trend elsewhere in Japan. Camp Schwab in Henoko, proposed site of the Futenma Replacement Facility (FRF), was one of the US bases in Okinawa created in the late 1950s through this process (NHK Shuzaihan 2011, 56). In effect, Washington and Tokyo resolved the contradiction within the San Francisco system—between the constituent power of the Japanese who wanted to end the postwar and the constituted power of Washington to perpetuate the postwar—by imposing the bases on Okinawa. The so-called administrative actions theory provided a legal basis for this bilateral, "imperial" management of internalizing Okinawa into Empire "solely through an exclusion" (Agamben 1998, 11). It was presented in a ruling handed down by the Japanese Supreme Court in December 1959 in reference to the aforementioned anti-base protest in Sunagawa and has continued to bind Japan right up to the present time.[5]

That protest was initiated by residents of Sunagawa Town in 1955 against the planned expansion of Tachikawa Air Base, located in western Tokyo; in 1957, seven protesters were prosecuted for violation of the Special Criminal Law concerning the bilateral Administrative Agreement (Miller 2019, chap.

4). The 1959 ruling of the Japanese Supreme Court was delivered as a result of an appeal filed by prosecutors—essentially, the Japanese government—who were dissatisfied with the prior ruling of a lower court (Tokyo District Court), handed down in reference to the prosecution of the seven protesters, that the stationing of US forces in Japan violated Article 9 of the constitution. Evidence shows that Tanaka Kōtarō, the Supreme Court chief justice who presided over what came to be called the Sunagawa case, told US ambassador Douglas MacArthur II and others during an informal conversation that "it had been quite improper for Judge Date [of the Tokyo District Court] to pass on" the constitutional issue involved ("'Incoming Airgram ...'" [1959] 2013, 66). Accordingly, Tanaka rescinded the ruling of the Tokyo District Court that the stationing of US forces in Japan violated Article 9; he cited Japan's right to self-defense—to be exercised by US forces together with the Self-Defense Forces, established in 1954 as a result of the transformation of the Peace Preservation Corps[6]—as the central logic behind the decision. At the same time, he deliberately avoided judgment about whether or not the US-Japan Security Treaty was constitutional, based on what came to be known in Japanese legal circles as the "administrative actions theory," which stipulates that administrative actions of a highly political nature, when they pertain to the administrative foundations of the state, such as the presence of the US military, are to be excluded from judicial reviews (Saibansho 1959).

Since US-ruled Okinawa, over which Japan retained its sovereignty only residually, was constituted as a site of concentrated US military presence from the mid-1950s on, the administrative actions theory—established in 1959 to advance the notion that the US military presence is outside judicial review—practically designated Okinawa as an extraterritorial space for the US military. Accordingly, while in the 1950s, "The entire area of Japan ... [was regarded] as a potential base ... with unrestricted freedom reserved to the United States" (FRUS 1950c, 1227), in the 1960s, in contrast, what I call "split governance" was developed to institutionalize a division between economic use and development of Japan "proper" and military abuse and maldevelopment of Okinawa under the common rule of Empire.

On the one hand, the economic use and development of Japan "proper" from the 1960s on occurred both at the macro and micro levels in a manner that reinforced the aforementioned notion of Japan as the "great workshop" of Asia, a process made possible in part by the recycling of industrial, economic, and management policies that Japan developed before and during the war (Mimura 2011; Moore 2013, epilogue; Noguchi 2015).

At the macro level, along with disappearance of the scars and memories of World War II from the scenes of everyday social life, Japan "proper" witnessed the rising entrepreneurship of new postwar generations, cheap yet high-quality human capital with an advanced level of education, workers' increasing buying power, and a continuing US military presence that exempted Japan from high defense costs (Gordon 2014, 243–248). As these forms of the "power of life" of the Japanese were aligned, regulated, and controlled by the postwar industrial policy originated in prewar Japan through various forms of "administrative guidance" (C. Johnson 1982, chap. 7) of the state, Japan "proper" experienced an "economic miracle" of high growth from the mid-1950s through the early 1970s. During this period, Japan "proper" also constituted itself as the hub of the "processing trade" in the arena of international trade and industry managed by the Ministry of International Trade and Industry. As T. J. Pempel explains, Japan "relied heavily on importing raw materials, largely from Asia [excluding China][7] and the Middle East, and then utilizing these materials for the production of manufactured goods by a host of ever more sophisticated plants within Japan" (1997, 56). In the process, a dream of the greater East Asia co-prosperity sphere that Japan had pursued during the war returned in a different guise in postwar Empire. In the case of Indonesia, for instance, as Masashi Nishihara (1976, xiv) noted, "A trace of the Japanese occupation can be seen in the presence of certain former occupation officials, both military and civil, who returned to Japan after the war but later reemerged as 'Indonesia experts,' offering their assistance in the reparations negotiations and as intermediaries between the two sides" (cf. Hatch and Yamamura 1996, 132).

At the micro level, Japanese industrial policy from the 1960s on was intertwined with the so-called Japanese-style management, also originated in prewar Japan, that encouraged cooperation between labor and management and generated practices such as lifelong employment and promotion by seniority (Kataoka 2019; Katsube 2019). The stability in work realized by Japanese-style management, in turn, shaped specific life-forms centering on the patriarchal nuclear family consisting of the father (responsible as worker for earning money outside), the mother (responsible as housewife for raising children and handling family affairs), and two children (responsible as students for going to school to study) as an ideal type (Ueno 1990). In the process, the nuclear family was established as a basic unit of state intervention through tax, social security, and housing, in a manner that complemented the industrial policy—the state's intervention in industrial activities—it promoted at the macro level (Nakagawa 2004). The spread of TV sets among Japanese families—driven to watch national events such as the parade celebrating the marriage between the crown prince and crown princess in 1959 and the Tokyo Olympics of 1964—reinforced the normalization of the nuclear family-centered life-forms at the micro level (Okamura 1988, 16). As Kang Sang-jung and Yoshimi Shun'ya suggested (2001, 127–135), the nationalized and Japanized time-space, discussed in Part II, was generated in this process.

Meanwhile, economic use of Japan "proper" for the growth of Empire v.1 was made possible by the creation of a stable security environment in East Asia that involved military abuse of Okinawa under US rule. If the land seizure procedures in the 1950s (see chapter 3, section 2) exemplified an earlier form of encroachment on the community of *nuchi du takara*, conditions in US-ruled Okinawa in the 1960s revealed deeper encroachment on that community against the background of the revision of the US-Japan Security Treaty in 1960 combined with the intensification of the Vietnam War. For instance, when Washington developed, from the mid-1950s, a series of preparations and procedures for the deployment of nuclear weapons in Okinawa (Nakano 1969, 399–406; Miyazato 1975, 35), Tokyo tacitly participated in solidifying the state of exception—"the extension of the military authority's wartime powers into the civil sphere, and . . . a suspension of the constitution (or of those constitutional norms that protect individual libertis)" (Agamben 2005, 5)—in Okinawa through the revision of the US-Japan Security Treaty in 1960. For a stipulation in the revised treaty—which required the United States to discuss in advance with the Japanese government any plans to bring nuclear weapons into Japan—did not apply to US-controlled Okinawa (Gordon 2014, 274; Nakano 1969, 292–307; NHK Shuzaihan 2011, 60–63). Consequently, in the 1960s, without letting its residents know, the United States turned Okinawa into an island of nuclear weapons; as of 1967, thirteen hundred nuclear weapons were deployed in Okinawa against the background of the intensification of the Cold War in Asia (NHK 2017; cf. Rabson 2022).

In the process, Okinawa, along with other places in Japan that hosted US bases, such as Yokosuka and Sasebo, played a key role in the dispatch, logistics, and training of the US forces for the Vietnam War (Nakano 1969, 533–539; Yoshizawa 1988), a reality reinforced by Tokyo's decision to automatically extend the US-Japan Security Treaty for one year each year beginning in 1970 (Okinawa Times 2014). Consequently, an increasing number of crimes and accidents of US servicemen serving in Vietnam victimized

Okinawans from the second half of the 1960s onward, as noted in chapter 3, section 4.

In a broader historical context, the Vietnam War (1955–1975) represented the development of something unprecedented and unnamed—a global power that we call Empire—that began to incorporate the amorphous yet expansive realm of East Asia and beyond under its control. Washington implicated Tokyo in this process by agreeing to correct the "inequality" between the United States and Japan in the old US-Japan Security Treaty concluded in 1952—that is, it had stipulated Japan's responsibility for providing bases to the US military without specifying the duties of the United States to defend Japan. Indeed, the Japanese government, led then by Prime Minister Kishi Nobusuke (a former war criminal, as noted), proposed to revise the treaty by explicitly committing the United States to protect Japan in exchange for Japan's obligation to provide the bases for the peace and security of Japan and surrounding areas. Yet the Japanese public felt that Kishi's attempt to equalize the relationship between Japan and the United States would involve further subordination of the former to the latter, increasing the risk of Japan's participation in the US violence in the "Far East," a geopolitical concept that was presented but was not clearly defined in the revised treaty (Article 6) and could mean anywhere in the Asia-Pacific region where US interests were at stake. In spite of massive protests participated in by several million Japanese, however, the Kishi cabinet steamrolled the revision through the Diet, thereby reinforcing the "imperial" framework of collaboration between the United States and Japan against the constituent power of the Japanese public, although the revision of Article 9 (i.e., rearmament, together with the dispatching of Japanese troops outside Japan's territories) that Kishi had hoped for was left unaccomplished because his unpopularity forced him to resign from the office of prime minister (Buckley 1992, 69–98; Kapur 2018, introduction; Miller 2019, chap. 6; Oguma 2002, chap. 12; Schaller 1997, chaps. 8 and 9; Swenson-Wright 2005, chap. 6).

The violence of something unprecedented and unnamed became real through the Vietnam War. The sufferings of the Vietnamese people, as exemplified by the My Lai massacre in 1968, made this violence crystal clear (Honda 1981; "Betonamusensō no Kiroku" Henshū Īnkai 1988). The violence was multiplied by (*a*) the sufferings of US troops sent to the battlefields (Baker 2001; O'Nan 1998; Santoli 2006), who numbered more than 540,000 in 1969 ("Betonamusensō no Kiroku" Henshū Īnkai 1988, 177), and (*b*) the mobilization of troops from "friendly" countries such as South

Korea (310,000 troops [Takeda 2018]), as well as member nations of the Southeast Asia Treaty Organization, including the Philippines, Thailand, Australia, and New Zealand (Sakurai I., n.d.), against communism.

Overall, Empire v.1—"a *decentered* and *deterritorializing* apparatus of rule that progressively incorporates the entire global realm within its open, expanding frontiers" (Hardt and Negri 2000: xii)—in East Asia emerged through the San Francisco system in the early 1950s, embedded in collective/regional self-defense as the basic security paradigm of the United States against communism, the outside. As the administrative actions theory in 1959 helped solidify its internal structure through split governance, Empire v.1 also attempted to expand and reconfigure its boundaries in the 1960s by fighting the Vietnam War with techniques that were indistinguishable from imperialist/colonialist domination and exploitation (Hardt and Negri 2000, 178).

3. The Third Moment: Reciprocity as an Organizing Principle for the Formation of Empire Version 2 (1970s–1980s)

In spite of all these efforts to maintain the absolute power of Empire v.1, the United States continued to struggle in Vietnam. In 1969, President Nixon announced the so-called Guam Doctrine: the United States would provide a nuclear umbrella to defend Asia against communist threats without directly intervening in conflicts there and countries in Asia should shoulder responsibilities for their own defense (Miyazato 1975, 91–92; Yamakage 1997, 281). This was a departure from the original San Francisco system wherein the United States established itself as the sole hegemonic power in East Asia. In a manner that concretized this new doctrine, the United States not only began to withdraw its troops from Vietnam in the early 1970s but also over the course of the 1970s reduced the number of troops in the Philippines, South Korea, Thailand, and Japan "proper" (but not in Okinawa; see below) and removed troops from Taiwan altogether (Nozoe 2016a, 56–57, 134–135). Combined with this shrinking of military power overseas was an economic crisis in the United States; in 1971, President Nixon announced the end of the gold standard against the background of amassed debt, a large trade imbalance, and rampant inflation (Graeber 2011, chap. 12). These symptoms of the decline of American hegemony went hand in hand with the appearance of "reciprocity"—or mutual influence and dependence, but not equality—across the United States (core), Japan (semi-periphery), and Asia (periphery) as a new organizing principle of international relations in the 1970s through the 1980s, a process that contributed to the formation of what I call Empire v.2. I approach this process in reference to the issues of security, diplomacy, and economy.

In the realm of security and diplomacy, the principle of reciprocity was concretized through the notion of "burden sharing" (Reed 1983; General Accounting Office 1989), a notion that extended the aforementioned Guam Doctrine and the framework of collective/regional self-defense against communism more generally.

For instance, in 1978, Tokyo began paying host-nation support through the *omoiyari-yosan* ("sympathy budget"), to cover maintenance/construction expenses for houses and recreational facilities for the US military, as well as part of the personnel expenses for Japanese workers employed on the bases (Nozoe 2016a, 181–191 and 2016b, 103–105; Sonoda et al. 2020). Also, in addition to the 1973 decision to make Yokosuka the home port of the USS *Midway*, in 1978, Tokyo concluded the first *Guidelines for U.S.-Japan Defense Cooperation* ([1978] n.d.) to concretize the cooperation between the US military and Japan's Self-Defense Forces outlined in Article 3 of the revised security treaty concluded in 1960 (Nozoe 2016b, 105–106). Thus, the Self-Defense Forces began participating in the Rim of the Pacific exercise administered by the US Navy in 1980 (Maeda 1997, 77), and joint training exercises between the Ground Self-Defense Force and the Maritime Self-Defense Force, on the one hand, and the US Marine Corps and the US Navy, on the other, were institutionalized in the 1980s (Gabe M. 2007, 235–237; Maeda 1997, 77–78; Nozoe 2016a, 197 and 2016b, 102–108). The Japanese involvement in the training and operations of the US military—that is, in the scheme of "burden sharing" bordering on Japan's exercise of collective/regional self-defense outside its territories—generated tensions with Article 9 stipulating unarmed peace and raised concerns over Japan's possible path to militarization not only within Japan but also without—including in the United States, where worries about the rising power of the former "enemy" persisted against the background of the rise of *Japan as Number One*, as Ezra Vogel (1979) called it. However, Tokyo contained such tensions by emphasizing the "defense only" (*senshubōei*) principle established in the mid-1950s, noted above (Suzuki 2011). In 1976, Tokyo concretized this principle with a decision that defense spending would not rise beyond 1% of Japan's GNP (Hanai and Asakawa 1995, 139–

141). In the process, the paradigm of "burden sharing" was extended to Asia at large. For instance, in the late 1970s, the United States gave the Philippine government greater power to administer the US bases there (Yeo 2011, 37–38). In South Korea, there occurred an increasing integration of South Korean military operations into those of the US military—exemplified by the initiation of joint military exercises known as Team Spirit in 1976 and by the establishment of the US–Republic of Korea Combined Forces Command under an American general (US Forces Korea, n.d.).

Yet China represented perhaps the most important example revealing reciprocity—mutual influence and dependence (not equality)—as the organizing principle of security and diplomatic relations in East Asia in the 1970s. The United States and other countries including Japan isolated Communist China without official diplomatic relationship after it was established in 1949 (Shimizu 2001, chaps. 3 and 6); China was constituted as an "outside" of Empire. However, initiated by the visits of National Security Advisor Henry Kissinger (July 1971) and President Richard Nixon (February 1972) to Beijing and finalized by President Jimmy Carter (1979), the US-China rapprochement in the 1970s signified the broader historical process whereby Empire attempted to internalize this outside within the "free world," with a number of significant impacts on international relations across East Asia and beyond. First, the US-China rapprochement was used to seek peace in Vietnam, with which China had deep historical and political connections, and to check the Soviet Union, which China had confronted since the late 1950s (Sahashi 2010, 174). Second, in 1971, China joined the United Nations as a permanent member of its Security Council, a process that resulted in the expulsion of Taiwan (which had represented China until 1971) from the United Nations. Third, in a related development, the US-China rapprochement resulted in the withdrawal of US troops from Taiwan and the dissolution of the US-Taiwan Mutual Defense Treaty, though Washington continued its commitment to Taiwan in order to maintain stability and balance of power (Sahashi 2010, 185–190). Fourth, it triggered the economic reform of China. From 1978 on, in particular, Deng Xiaoping's administration introduced a market mechanism to attract investments from the United States, Western Europe, and Chinese abroad. The 1989 Tiananmen Square massacre crushed student movements for democratization that Deng Xiaoping's reform had triggered, but not the process of economic development (Amako 2018). Fifth, the US-China rapprochement also activated the normalization of the Japan-China relationship in 1972 and the conclusion of a peace and friendship treaty in 1978.

This normalization opened up the horizon of economic aid and investments from Japan (semi-periphery) to China (periphery) at the expense of the latter's relinquishment of the right to request war reparations from the former; it also contributed to introducing to Japan's discursive space "history issues"—such as the Nanjing massacre (Honda [1972] 1981) and Japanese war orphans left behind in China (Tamanoi 2009)—that helped the Japanese public develop awareness of the victims of Japanese aggression in China during World War II (cf. Yoshida N. 2016, 242).

The broad impacts of the US-China rapprochement in the 1970s on security, diplomatic, and historical relations cited above also show how the transformation of Empire v.1 (structured by the US hegemony) into Empire v.2 (structured by reciprocity) was linked to the overall economic development of East Asia and beyond in the 1970s–1980s. I now turn my attention to the economic dynamics of Empire v.2, especially an expansive movement toward the formation of the world market as its sovereign territory in which Japan played a significant role.

Indeed, in the 1970s–1980s, Japan became "an extraordinary corporate-centered society" (Gordon 2014, 299) accompanied by the intensification of bureaucratic control over life both at the macro and micro levels, and its industrial productivity increased at the fastest rates in the world during this period (Dore 2000, 225). In the process, the so-called trade war between the United States (the victor in the previous war) and Japan (the vanquished in that war) intensified in the areas of textiles (1972), steel (1969 and 1978), color TVs (1977), and automobiles (1981 through 1993), one after another (Gordon 2014, 290–291). One can think of this war as a process whereby the relationship between the core (the United States) and the semi-periphery (Japan) was radically rearticulated, if not reversed, within Empire v.2. This rearticulation of economic relations occurred because from the 1970s on, the sites of production of these goods were increasingly shifted from Japan (semi-periphery) to Asia at large (periphery), where the production costs were cheaper and environmental regulations were looser. While the processing trade that had used then-cheap Japan as a pivot of the production system in the 1950s–1960s thus declined from the 1970s on, keiretsu—a synergy of firms often originated in zaibatsu, centering on a main bank and engaged in diverse fields of business and trade—organized "vertically integrated production networks" (Hatch and Yamamura 1996, 28) across Asia to produce goods to be sold in the United States (and other countries). Such networks supported and were supported by the "international disciplinary order" (Hardt and Negri 2000, 261, see also 241–249) exemplified by what

Bruce Cumings (1984, 28) called the "Bureaucratic-Authoritarian Industrializing Regimes"—like the developmental dictatorships in South Korea, Indonesia, the Philippines, and Taiwan that continued in the 1980s. Against the background of the ever-stronger yen, the parent company in Japan was situated atop the hierarchy and regional subsidiaries and affiliates across Asia occupied a subordinate position within the production networks (Beeson 1999, 281; Hatch and Yamamura 1996; Pempel 1997).

In the process, the path of economic development that postwar Japan (the semi-periphery) had opened up was followed by nation-states of Asia (the periphery)—that is, by the "newly industrializing economies" of South Korea, Taiwan, Hong Kong, and Singapore in the 1960s–1970s, by the core members of the Association for Southeast Asian Nations (Thailand, Malaysia, Indonesia, and the Philippines, known as ASEAN-4) in the 1970s–1980s, and by China from the 1980s onward. Scholars explained this process by the "flying geese model" (or its variants) of economic development: "In this model, Japan was to be the 'lead goose,' the Asian originator of new industrial sectors. Heading a 'flying V' of Asian economic geese, Japan was to pull the region forward with its own success in industrialization and manufacturing" (Pempel 1997, 52; see also Watanabe To. 1985). The movement for establishing an ever-expanding transnational market of production and consumption, together with the ascendancy of Japan as an economic superpower of the world, was accelerated specifically after the 1985 Plaza Agreement that induced the bubble economy in Japan, a phenomenon that lasted until the early 1990s, when it burst. It is during this period—the 1980s—that a trans/national discursive space for debating "history issues" assumed a distinctive form in Japan (Yoshimi S. 1998) and across the Asia-Pacific region. In particular, Japan's attempts to glorify and justify the war in Asia it started provoked "outcry in Asian capitals" (Gluck 1993, 84). This "outcry" would develop further in the 1990s and beyond, as will be explained below.

Meanwhile, the expansion of the world market in Empire v.2 and its collective/regional self-defense network in East Asia and beyond generated new tensions from within and without. From within Empire v.2, for instance, oil-producing countries in the Middle East—subordinated as the periphery in the postwar world economy—began to assert their autonomy, as exemplified by the oil crises of 1973 and 1979. From without, there was a renewed "threat" of communism, the "outside," as exemplified by the Soviet Union's invasion of Afghanistan in 1979 or shooting down of Korean Air Lines flight 007 in 1983, which signaled the end of the détente of the 1970s characterized, for instance, by Strategic Arms Limitation Talks (SALT) I in 1972 and SALT II in 1979 between the United States and the Soviet Union and the beginning of the new Cold War of the 1980s. During the new Cold War, the United States and the Soviet Union fought a war of attrition, as it were, entering a seemingly endless competition in the expansion of armaments until the latter exhausted itself and collapsed in 1989–1991.

These new tensions inside and outside Empire v.2 contributed to reinforcing military abuse of Okinawa through split governance, a process that needs to be understood in three different but interrelated aspects. First, Tokyo negotiated with Washington to expand the facade of "peace and prosperity" in Japan "proper" (*a*) by reducing the total area of US military facilities in Japan "proper" from 30,500 hectares in 1966 to 19,700 hectares in 1972 and to 8,000 hectares in 1980[8] (Okinawaken Chijikōshitsu Kichitaisakuka 2020, 10 and 110) and (*b*) by enabling, in 1970, withdrawal of one-third (or approximately twelve thousand) of the US troops in Japan "proper" (Nozoe 2016b, 90). Second, in order to compensate for the reduction of the US forces in Japan "proper" (and elsewhere in East Asia after the Vietnam War), the US forces, particularly the Marine Corps, were strengthened in Okinawa in the 1970s through the 1980s due to Tokyo's desire for a continuing US military presence in Okinawa as a deterrent, a desire complemented by the wish of the US Marine Corps to maintain its influence there (Nozoe 2016b, 94–97). Third, accordingly, (*a*) marines who had returned from Vietnam were redeployed to Okinawa (Nozoe 2016b, 97–101), which contributed to increases in the number of marines stationed in Okinawa from approximately 10,000 in 1967 to more than 16,000 in 1971 and to more than 20,000 in the 1980s (Nozoe 2016a, 57–58; 2016b, 85), (*b*) Futenma Air Station was restructured as a key base for the US Marine Corps, and the number of helicopters and fixed-wing aircraft increased from four and sixteen, respectively, in 1969, to eighty and twenty-six, respectively, after 1970 (Fukumoto 2019), and (*c*) after Okinawa's reversion in 1972, about three-quarters of the facilities for the exclusive use of the US military in Japan came to be concentrated in Okinawa, which makes up only 0.6% of Japan's total land mass (Nozoe 2016a, 4 and 97). As political compensation for the continuing, indeed increasing, US military presence, Tokyo invested a huge sum of money—a total of 4.96 trillion yen from 1972 to 1996 (Miyamoto 2000, 6–7)—in Okinawa for its post-reversion development in the name of *hondonami* (catching up with the rest of Japan) (see chapter 4).

In sum, concurrent with US struggles in Vietnam together with its economic crises, Empire v.1 (structured by the US hegemony) was transformed into Empire v.2 (structured by reciprocity) in the 1970s–1980s. As "a *decentered* and *deterritorializing* apparatus of rule," Empire v.2 internalized China in the world market where "reciprocity" between the United States (core), Japan (semi-periphery), and Asia (periphery) was developed against the threats of communism. In the process, Empire v.2 reinforced the split governance to fortify Tokyo's internal control mechanism over Okinawa continuingly ab/used as the "Keystone of the Pacific."

4. The Fourth Moment: Okinawa in the 1990s at the Intersection of the Cold War and Post–Cold War Security Paradigms

Policy planners in Washington and Tokyo in the 1990s found the US-Japan security alliance to be drifting, "losing its focus and coherence" (Armitage et al., 2000; see also Funabashi 1997) without a clearly defined "enemy," a situation brought about by the collapse of the Soviet Union in 1991. The rape incident of 1995 in Okinawa occurred in this context of the drifting alliance. While Okinawa earnestly demanded the reorganization and reduction of the US bases there through protest (as discussed in chapter 4), Washington and Tokyo exploited this incident to reestablish the "focus and coherence" of their alliance. They did so by shifting the key domain of operations of the US military from the "Far East" to the "Asia-Pacific region," as indicated by the remarks of politician Yamazaki Taku: "Even though [Article 6 of] the US-Japan Security Treaty stipulates that the US military uses bases in Japan for the peace and security of [Japan and] the 'Far East,' Mr. [Kurt] Campbell [a deputy assistant secretary of defense] strongly insisted then that 'Far East' be replaced by 'Asia-Pacific.' Okinawa was indispensable for the strategies of the United States that desired the expansion of the scope of activities of the US military in Japan" (Fujita and Matsuyama 2021).

While the concept of the Far East had been deployed within the context of the Cold War security narrative on the communist threats, the notion of the "Asia-Pacific"—which had been variously and somewhat independently developed since the 1960s in Australia, Japan, and South Korea, among others—was popularized as a shared economic vision and project in the 1990s and beyond, as indicated by the establishment in 1989 of the Asia-Pacific Economic Cooperation (APEC Secretariat 2021), a forum consisting of twenty-one members including the United States, Japan, China, and the Soviet Union-turned-Russia (Ōba 2004). Concurrent is the process whereby the notion of the "Asia-Pacific War" appeared as a topic of academic debate in the 1980s Japan. Specifically, tracing how Japan's aggression from the 1930s through 1945 had been designated, studied, and debated, historians such as Soejima Shoichi (1985) proposed the use of the "Asia-Pacific War" to foreground Japan's atrocities and war responsibilities in Asia, in particular, China; in so doing, they challenged the notion of the "Pacific War," a term introduced by MacArthur's General Headquarters in postwar Japan to cancel the idea of the "Greater East-Asia War" that had been promoted by Tokyo in prewar and wartime Japan. Yamazaki's remarks above reflected how the formation of the Asia-Pacific region as an integrated market and a historical-geographical conception was directly or indirectly linked to a new security paradigm of the 1990s, a process that had already been initiated in a related geopolitical context by the Gulf War of 1990–1991, among other events.

This war was fought for the "new world order," in the words of President George H. W. Bush ([1990] 2017; see also Ismael and Ismael 1994). Indeed, if the Cold War was a global conflict of the capitalist bloc led by the United States against the communist bloc led by the Soviet Union, the overall mission of the Gulf War subverted such a grand framework; the aim was to stop the aggression of Saddam Hussein, a localized threat, so as to maintain and expand the free market and free trade of oil globally at the time of the demise of the communist regime (Nye 1991; see also Kuroda 1994). Fought *"not as a function of* [the United States'] *national motives but in the name of global right"* (Hardt and Nagri 2000, 180), the Gulf War thus expressed an emerging form of "imperial" (not "imperialist") war. The US Marine Corps—including units from Okinawa—contributed to this mission by sending ninety-three thousand troops among the overall US force consisting of five hundred thousand troops (Yara 2016, 118).

The shift of the scope and goal of the war was accompanied by the change in the methods of warfare. Toward and after the end of the Cold War (i.e., around the time of the Gulf War), the so-called Revolution in Military Affairs (RMA) (Department of Defense 2003, Hardt and Negri 2004, 41–48; Inoue 2007, 214–215) had been implemented, a broad project involving, among other programs, the transformation of the military as a hierarchically structured massive body of soldiers into a flexible and mobile network force. The Marine Corps embodied the spirit of the RMA in the Gulf War, rearticulating the Marine Air-Ground Task Force—a coordinated body of air, ground, and other forces established in the 1960s as "the principal organization for all missions across the range of military operations" (United

States Marine Corps [hereafter USMC] n.d.-a)—with new strategies based not only on a marine expeditionary brigade (or MEB, a medium-size combat power consisting of approximately fifteen thousand marines) and/or a marine expeditionary force (or MEF, the largest building block of the Marine Corps' combat power, consisting of approximately forty-five thousand marines) but also increasingly on a marine expeditionary unit (or MEU, the smallest combat power consisting of approximately two thousand marines) (Adams 2017, 3; Carns and Coerr 1994; USMC, n.d.-b; Yara 2016, 116–124). Recognized as "the operational crown jewel of the 1990s Marine Corps" (Adams 2017, 8), the MEU represented the Marine Corps as a force responsible for high-intensity police actions (or low-intensity military actions), such as "noncombatant rescue operations, humanitarian assistance, . . . maritime interdiction, . . . deception operations, . . . specialized demolition, . . . electronic warfare, amphibious raid" (Carns and Coerr 1994, 38), as compared to traditional tasks related to major combat operations, as in the Vietnam War (Millett 1991, 559–606; USMC, n.d.-c).

In a manner that reinforced the organizational-strategic change initiated around the time of the Gulf War, in September 1992, the US Marine Corps established in Okinawa the Thirty-First MEU—the successor of the Thirty-First Marine Amphibious Unit, created in Okinawa and used in Vietnam (Umebayashi 1994, 58; USMC, n.d.-c; Yara 2016, 118–119). In addition, an amphibious squadron was deployed in 1992 to the US Navy Port in Sasebo in Kyushu, in charge of the transportation of the new MEU from Okinawa to the site of an emergency (Nagasakiken Heiwa Inkai, n.d.). Furthermore, in 1996, Washington proposed the deployment to Okinawa of V-22 Ospreys,[9] tilt-rotor military aircraft with vertical takeoff and landing capabilities developed as the successor to existing (and deteriorating) military helicopters such as the CH-46, in use since the days of the Vietnam War. These developments expressed a broader shift of the basic operational paradigm of the Marine Corps in the 1990s from containment of communism in the "Far East" to distributed network presence against localized threats in the "Asia-Pacific region" (Yara 2016, 119), a shift concretized and clarified throughout the 1990s in reference to the concepts and doctrines of the US Navy and Marine Corps such as "The Way Ahead" announced in 1991, ". . . From the Sea" in 1992, "Forward . . . from the Sea" in 1994, and "Anytime, Anywhere" in 1997 (Swartz and Duggan 2020; Yara 2016). Removal of Futenma Air Station, a large immobile military base occupying 500 hectares of land in densely populated central Okinawa, and construction of the FRF in sparsely populated Henoko—originally proposed as a removable offshore military facility of 1,500 by 600 meters (90 hectares)—perfectly fit into this new operational paradigm emphasizing mobility and flexibility. Combined with existing programs—such as the Unit Deployment Program established in 1977, which allowed the US Marine Corps to rotate battalions among Okinawa, Hawaii, and the continental United States every six months and to malleably organize the Thirty-First Marine Amphibious Unit (the current Thirty-First MEU) ("Rotation System . . ." 1976; Command History Branch Office of the Joint Secretary Headquarters CINCPAC 1977, 39; Nozoe 2016b, 102–108; USMC, n.d.-c)—the ongoing organizational and operational transformations during and since the Gulf War, including the planned construction of the FRF in Okinawa, were expected to enable the US Marine Corps to redefine and enhance its role and status in the post–Cold War world (Nozoe 2019; Funabashi 1997, chap. 15).

If the above description shows the desire of Washington in the 1990s for updating the security paradigm of Empire in the emerging integrated market in the Asia-Pacific region, Tokyo joined in this broader shift through a new administrative mechanism during the same period, intensifying biopolitical control of social life in Okinawa and elsewhere in Japan. More specifically, while (as noted) split governance—the economic control of Japan "proper" and the military control of Okinawa—functioned as a basic administrative mechanism for the growth of Empire in the Cold War Asia-Pacific region until the 1980s, the 1990s, in contrast, witnessed the process whereby split governance began to be rearticulated through a double-sided process. On the one hand, the economic control of Japan "proper" was reinforced by neoliberal policies, linked with the development of Okinawa as a site of tourism and other forms of cultural industry, so that Okinawa would be used not only militarily but also, increasingly, economically in the twenty-first century, as will be fully discussed below in this chapter. On the other hand, the imperial will to continuously use and abuse Okinawa militarily was generalized by the military use of Japan at large, exemplified by the redefinition of the "defense only" principle that would allow or force Japan to exercise collective/regional self-defense outside its territories. Specifically, in April 1991, troops of the Self-Defense Forces were sent, for the first time in history, to an area outside Japan—the Persian Gulf—where they collaborated with the US military and forces of other nations in sweeping mines. After this dispatch, throughout the 1990s, Tokyo sent the Self-

Defense Forces to Cambodia, Mozambique, Rwanda, and other locations for United Nations peacekeeping operations and humanitarian assistance (Bōeishō, n.d.-a), or biopolitical engagement in everyday social life, in these places. In addition, through bilateral agreements such as the second Guidelines for US-Japan Defense Cooperation concluded in 1997 (n.d.), Washington's expectation that Japan would send Self-Defense Forces to assist US military operations outside Japan increased in the twenty-first century, as will also be fully discussed in this chapter.

• • •

Thus far, I have described how the proposed construction of the FRF was linked to the global shift of an economic-security paradigm from the Cold War era to the post–Cold War era in the 1990s. And yet I wish to note that the 1990s also observed a contradictory process that curtailed this very shift in reference to (*a*) the prevalence of the old security paradigm, and (*b*) the status of debate over "history issues."

The prevalence of the old security paradigm was exemplified by the fact that, despite the United Nations' involvement in the Gulf War of 1990–1991, military actions were actualized through the de facto command of the US military (Self) over allies (friends) against the enemy/Other, as in the Cold War era (e.g., the Korean War and the Vietnam War). The behavior of US troops (who continued to be stationed in the Middle East after the Gulf War ended) apparently revealed a Cold War mentality of US military superiority and arrogance, provoking local antipathy and leading Osama bin Laden to initiate the anti-US campaigns that ultimately resulted in the 9/11 attacks (Okamoto M. 2020). These issues were derived from the conception of the United States as the world's sole superpower during the run-up to and the period after the demise of the Soviet Union, a conception that was reinforced by the lack of a language defining the newly emerging economic-security conditions in the post–Cold War world.

In particular, in the context of the Asia-Pacific region, "threats" after the end of the Cold War were still conceptualized in the 1990s as essentially the continuation and leftovers of the Cold War. Thus, for instance, the *Japan-U.S. Joint Declaration on Security, Alliance for the 21st Century*, issued by President Bill Clinton and Prime Minister Hashimoto Ryūtarō in 1996 ([1996] n.d.), stated that, in spite of the end of the Cold War, "instability and uncertainty persist in the region. Tensions continue on the Korean Peninsula. There are still heavy concentrations of military force, including nuclear arsenals. Unresolved territorial disputes, potential regional conflicts, and the proliferation of weapons of mass destruction and their means of delivery all constitute sources of instability." Similarly, *United States Security Strategy for the East Asia-Pacific Region*, released by the Department of Defense in 1995, asserted that the United States would maintain one hundred thousand troops across the Asia-Pacific region as in the Cold War era.

Along the same lines, the governmental decision to construct the FRF in Henoko revealed the ways in which the Marine Corps and the Japanese government in the 1990s operated within the old, Cold War security paradigm. For instance, even though leaders and policy planners of the US government—such as the ambassador to Japan, Walter Mondale, and the aforementioned deputy assistant secretary of defense, Kurt Campbell—expressed their view that the FRF could be built anywhere in Japan ("Futenma Isetsusaki . . ." 2015; Henna 2015a; Yara 2016, 132–134), Tokyo insisted on constructing it within Okinawa due to the opposition of residents elsewhere in Japan to relocating it within their own prefectures, thereby contributing to the maintenance of the status quo, that is, military abuse of Okinawa. In addition, in 1995–1996 the Department of Defense took control of the FRF negotiations from the State Department by establishing direct contact with Prime Minister Hashimoto Ryūtarō and other influential politicians in Tokyo, insisting that the FRF be constructed in northern Okinawa (Henna 2015b; Funabashi 1997, chap. 15). In so doing, the Department of Defense supported the desire of the US Marine Corps—which accounted for 60% of US troops in Okinawa (16,200 of the total of 27,121) in 1995 (Okinawaken Chijikōshitsu Kichitaisakuka 2020, 24)—to place the FRF in northern Okinawa, which would allow the Marine Corps (*a*) to maintain a foothold in the place gained through victory in the hard-fought Battle of Okinawa in which 12,520 US servicemen died, (*b*) to dispel prolonged Okinawan complaints concerning Futenma Air Station, located in a congested residential area in central Okinawa, (*c*) to bury Tokyo's original proposal to integrate functions of Futenma into Kadena Air Base, an idea that generated strong opposition from the US Air Force, and (*d*) to obtain a new base for free (Tokyo would pay the cost of construction) (Miyagi and Watanabe 2016, 53, 77, and 217). When combined, these rationales helped the Marine Corps defy the argument to dismantle it that was emerging from within the US military in the 1990s (Nozoe 2019; Funabashi 1997, chap. 15). In short, the Japanese government and the Marine Corps shared the same vested interest and instinct of adhering to the Cold War security paradigm.

In a manner that echoed this particular situation whereby the transition to the post–Cold War security paradigm was at once facilitated and suspended, in the 1990s, "history issues" that had been largely silenced during the Cold War were exposed as well as suppressed. On the one hand, building on the decline of American hegemony during the age of Empire v.2 (1970s–1980s), "history issues" came to be openly discussed and debated, revealing the constituent power of social actors across the Asia-Pacific region. For instance, the issues of "comfort women" became a topic of public debate across South Korea and Japan when three former Korean "comfort women" filed a suit in the Tokyo District Court against the Japanese government in December 1991 to seek apology and indemnification (Yoshimi Y. 1995), a process that developed within the broader context of the democratization of South Korea since the late 1980s. Until 1988, South Korea was under a military dictatorship—a form of what Cumings (1984, 28) called the "Bureaucratic-Authoritarian Industrializing Regimes"—led first by Park Chung-hee (1962–1979) and then by Chun Doo-hwan (1980–1988); this dictatorship, combined with Tokyo's position that the 1965 Treaty on Basic Relations between Japan and the Republic of Korea had already completed all colonial compensations, contributed to a transnational patriarchal control system in postwar Korea and Japan that had suppressed the issues of "comfort women" and other war-related issues altogether (Ching 2019, chap. 3, esp. p. 60; Oguma 2014). Similarly, the 1989 death of Hirohito, Emperor Shōwa, triggered, at least indirectly, a debate over the Nanjing massacre in the Asia-Pacific region (e.g., Chang 1997), an issue that (as stated) had been introduced to Japan's discursive space only in the 1970s as relations between Japan and China became normalized (cf. Hayashi M. 2017). Furthermore, the Smithsonian controversy over the *Enola Gay* exhibition happened in 1995, which at least introduced a new space of discussion to question a Cold War assumption that the use of atomic bombs on Hiroshima and Nagasaki had contributed to ending the war quickly (T. Endō 1995; Hayashi Y. 1998; Yoneyama 2001; 2016, chap. 5). In spite of all these developments, however, further discussion on the "history issues"—or further advancement of the constituent power of social actors in the Asia-Pacific region—was also curtailed by the rise of nationalism within Japan and without that reinforced a Cold War paradigm of nation-centered history, represented by the activities of Atarashī Rekishikyōkasho o Tsukuru Kai (Association for History Textbook Reform), joined by well-known right-wing critics who, promoting national pride, denied or minimized atrocities of the Japanese Imperial Army during the war in Asia (Komori and Takahashi 1998; Morris-Suzuki 2013). The result was "the defeat of those who sought critical rethinking," to expand what Lisa Yoneyama (2016, 196) noted on the Smithsonian controversy over the *Enola Gay* exhibition.

In effect, responding to the changing economic-security environment—the disappearance of communist threats intertwined with the formation of the integrated market in the Asia-Pacific region—the 1990s was a period when the old and new paradigms of security coexisted and competed. Signs of a paradigm shift were observed, represented by the transformation of the Marine Corps' organizational and operational paradigm, the blurring of the boundaries between Okinawa and Japan "proper" in the structure of split governance, the dispatch of Japan's Self-Defense Forces to areas outside Japan, and the debate over "history issues" across the Asia-Pacific region. All of these reflected the formation of the world market to which there is no longer an outside, as will be explained in the next section. And yet the old Cold War paradigm still persisted, represented by the continuing military abuse of Okinawa by the Marine Corps and the Japanese government, the lack of language to describe newly emerging security conditions in the post–Cold War Asia-Pacific region, and Japanese nationalism that denied war responsibilities.

5. The Fifth Moment: The Disappearance of the Outside and the Appearance of Omni-crisis in Empire Version 3 (Twenty-First Century)

The collapse of the Soviet Union in 1991, among other events, paved the way for the formation of the integrated economy in the Asia-Pacific envisioned by Asia Pacific Economic Cooperation (APEC), having helped complete the transition from Empire v.2 in the Cold War era to Empire v.3 in the twenty-first century. As a result, we have seen emergence of the world market of economic and cultural exchanges to which there is no outside. For instance, from 2000 to 2020, trade across borders of the Asia-Pacific region and beyond has included, for instance, Japanese goods ranging from anime and manga to automobiles; electronics and high-technology products from South Korea, Singapore, and Taiwan; electronics, machinery, furniture, and clothes (among other items) from China; natural resources/materials from India, Indonesia, Australia, Russia, and Canada; and financial services, IT services, and other advanced services as well as agricultural, medical, and cultural products, among others, from the United States and other countries (ASEAN-Japan Centre 2014; Iwabuchi 2002; Kawahara, Inoue, and Akashi 2011; Keizai-Sangyōshō 2010, 2011, 2019; Oki 2022). The number of international tourists expanded from five billion in 1993 to fourteen billion in 2018 (Yamashita S. 1998, 4; Choi 2020, 193–194). Although the movement of tourists was severely restricted by the Covid-19 pandemic for a few years from 2020, this global pandemic—together with the ways in which information has continued to spread instantly across borders of the Asia-Pacific region and beyond—has itself expressed the disappearance of the outside from the world in which we live. In the process, the system of universal capitalism, which failed to materialize after World War II due to the division of the world between the capitalist and communist blocks, has finally been operative as the driving force of Empire v.3.

Significantly and ironically, the disappearance of the outside/communism/enemy has not resulted in universal peace and prosperity. Rather, it has gone hand in hand with the appearance of new threats across the sovereign territory of Empire v.3: "The clearly defined crisis of modernity gives way to an omni-crisis in the imperial world" (Hardt and Negri 2000, 190).

I identify two layers of generalized "threats"—an omni-crisis—developed on the surface of Empire v.3. The first layer is represented by the attacks on September 11, 2001, which showed the evolution of a new enemy—"the unknown, the uncertain, the unseen, and the unexpected," to use the words of the US secretary of defense, Donald Rumsfeld (2002, 23, cited in Hardt and Negri 2004, 36). In other words, new adversaries in the post–Cold War would be "not a unitary sovereign nation-state but rather a *network*" (Hardt and Negri 2004, 54; see also Metz and Johnson 2001). Exemplified by activities of Islamic fundamentalist groups such as al-Qaeda, the Taliban, ISIS, Boko Haram, and—most recently—Hamas in the context of the Israeli-Palestinian conflict, this network has exerted its influence in every corner of the post–Cold War world "based on the politicizing of religion for sociopolitical and economic goals [often] in the pursuit of establishing a divine order" (Tibi 2023, 20). Everyday social experiences of Muslims in the West—exclusion, poverty, and mistreatment, a phenomenon that needs to be grasped against the broader historical background of continued discrimination and prejudice against Islam in the West (Said 1978; Cooley 2002; Fassin 2013; Sunar 2017)—have indeed continued to directly and indirectly draw them—young Muslim men, in particular—into violent fundamentalist groups such as those noted above and to ideas (such as a radicalized and often distorted notion of jihad) that permeate such groups more broadly (Asahi Shimbun Ata Shuzaihan 2002).

The second and more recent layer of generalized "threats"—an omni-crisis—appearing on the surface of Empire v.3 specifically in the post–Cold War Asia-Pacific region is the formation of a "multipolar world order" (Clegg 2009; Turner 2009), represented by the rise of China as an economic and military powerhouse in the 2010s and beyond. While the first layer was created locally against Empire v.3 without mediation of the unitary sovereign nation-sates, the second layer of threats was generated by such nation-states, which consolidate, appropriate, and mediate local antipathy to and resentment toward American/Western-centered globalization in the post–Cold War world.

Japan rose as the "great workshop of Asia" during the 1950s–1960s in Empire v.1 and an economic powerhouse in the 1970s–1980s in Empire v.2, but its international behavior was more or less controlled within the US-centered San Francisco system, as explained in this chapter. In contrast, China in the twenty-first century is no longer regulated by the US-centered international order. Having been excluded from the "free world" system and then increasingly incorporated within it in the 1970s–1980s, the country grew, after a period of rocky takeoff in the 1990s (Castells 1998, 293–297), to produce prosperity equivalent to 12.8% of the US GNP in 2001 (when the country joined the World Trade Organization) and 62% of the US GNP in 2017 (Kondō D. 2018, 1306); in 2010, China surpassed Japan as the world's second-biggest economy ("China Overtakes..." 2011). Although America's trade volume was approximately three times as large as China's in 2000, the difference has shrunk; since 2010, the two countries' trade has been practically the same, constituting them as the two largest trading countries in the world (Keizai-Sangyōshō 2019, 164). In the process, China—along with Russia—has attempted to redefine the US-centered international order from within, with the expansive movement for establishing "socialism with Chinese characteristics" (Report of Hu Jintao to the 18th CPC National Congress 2012) which has become particularly pronounced under the leadership of Xi Jinping since 2012 (Shao 2015; Kondō D. 2018). The thrust of this movement has manifested itself in the territorial disputes in the 2010s in the South China Sea, with regard to the Senkaku (Diaoyu) Islands, and ultimately over Taiwan, together with China's increasing capability to project power near Japan in the 2010s and beyond.[10] In November 2023, during the APEC summit held in San Francisco, Xi stated,

"China will realize reunification [with Taiwan], and this is unstoppable" (Tang 2023).

The San Francisco system—together with split governance, economic use of Japan "proper" and military abuse of Okinawa—aimed to establish collective/regional self-defense across the Asia-Pacific region and was based on the binaries between Self (capitalism) and Other (communism), friends and enemies, or inside and outside. However, this system has not been able to fully respond to the omni-crisis or "a proliferation of minor and indefinite crises" (Hardt and Negri 2000, 189) in the post–Cold War Asia-Pacific region. Accordingly, Washington and Tokyo have transformed the San Francisco system into what I call the global security apparatus as the central mechanism to maintain the "peace and prosperity" of Empire v.3. The main task of the global security apparatus has been twofold: (*a*) to eliminate "threats" across its sovereign territory, the world market, for the maintenance of the smooth operation of contemporary capitalist production and accumulation, an act that requires the formation of network-centric, bilateral/multilateral security alliances in an extensive manner, and (*b*) to produce and regulate society by controlling the depths of human nature embedded in that market, an act that necessitates watching/policing of everyday life in an intensive manner. Below, I outline how Washington and Tokyo have interwoven these two tasks for development of the global security apparatus in Japan and across the Asia-Pacific region; I do so in reference to a series of documents written by a bipartisan study group in Washington that includes two key authors, Richard Armitage and Joseph Nye, both of whom have maintained close ties with the White House as policy experts on Asia-Pacific affairs. A number of policy documents released by Washington and Tokyo will also be incorporated. In doing so, the analysis below expands and elaborates on my description in chapter 1, section 2, of the global security apparatus.[11]

The first Armitage and Nye report (2000)—*The United States and Japan: Advancing toward a Mature Partnership*, to use its official title—prepared Japan for the first layer of the omni-crisis by stating that "Japan must recognize that international leadership involves risk-taking beyond its traditional donor's role." The spirit of this document was materialized in a document titled *US-Japan Alliance: Transformation and Realignment for the Future* (hereafter *US-Japan Alliance*) released in 2005 by the US-Japan Security Consultative Committee, a highest-level bilateral committee on security held at a ministerial level. Accordingly, during the first decade of the twenty-first century, Japan undertook "risk-taking beyond its traditional donor's role" by expanding what it began in the 1990s, that is, continuing to send the Self-Defense Forces to areas outside Japan for an ever wider range of missions, such as maritime transportation and logistical support operations in the Indian Ocean in support of the US-led war on terror in Afghanistan (2001–2007 and 2008–2010) and humanitarian aid operations in Iraq and neighboring regions (2003–2009) (Berdal 2008; Bōeishō, n.d.-b and 2008). Also during this period, the Self-Defense Forces performed "international peace cooperation missions" (in places such as East Timor, Nepal, and Sudan) organized by the United Nations (Bōeishō, n.d.-c), as well as "international emergency relief operations" (in places such as Indonesia, Thailand, Pakistan, and the Philippines) (Bōeishō, n.d.-d) and "anti-piracy activities" (in places such as the Gulf of Aden and the waters off Somalia), under the provisions of newly created Japanese laws (Bōeishō, n.d.-e). In the process, Tokyo also passed a series of laws to protect—or really "control," depending on the perspective—Japanese citizens in case of emergencies such as armed attack situations (Gaimushō 2005).

In order to execute these security operations across the global time-space of Empire v.3, *US-Japan Alliance*—together with an associated document titled *United States-Japan Roadmap for Realignment Implementation* (hereafter *Roadmap*) released in 2006 (US-Japan Security Consultative Committee 2006)—also highlighted the necessity for further integration of Japan's Self-Defense Forces within the US military, an idea that originated in the preamble of the revised US-Japan Security Treaty of 1960 and was subsequently laid out in the first *Guidelines for U.S.-Japan Defense Cooperation* of 1978 and updated in the second *Guidelines for U.S.-Japan Defense Cooperation* ([1997] n.d.). For instance, *US-Japan Alliance* and *Roadmap* announced the establishment of a bilateral joint operations coordination center at Yokota Air Base to support a unified command and the deployment of a new US X-band radar system in Japan to strengthen a shared weapon system.[12] In 2007, Tokyo also introduced *beigunsaihen-kōfukin* (subsidies for reorganization of US bases), to be paid to the communities that accept the planned facility, training, and operations of the US military. In effect, during the first decade of the twenty-first century, Empire v.3, at least formally, was able to subsume Japan in its network-centered security system in an extensive manner and to regulate social life in an intensive manner, even though Japan still retained a somewhat restrained posture regarding its security operations inside/outside its territories. The plan to construct the Futenma "Replacement" (not Expansion) Facility finalized in 2006 expressed this restrained posture of Japan then.

Since the 2010s, in contrast, the country has assumed an increasingly aggressive posture to engage in the second layer of the omni-crisis represented by China's maritime expansion together with North Korea's missile programs and other threats. In the process, the FRF construction plan has started to look somewhat outdated (see chapter 1, section 2), as this plan did not express Japan's willingness to fully accept the real and substantial subsumption of the entire country under the global security apparatus. The bipartisan study group led by Armitage and Nye again played an important role in the process by releasing additional reports, and Tokyo dutifully worked on the "assignments" (Satō 2020) presented in these reports both extensively and intensively.

First, at the legal level, Article 9 of the Japanese constitution has been practically abandoned through Tokyo's executive reinterpretation, rather than through democratically expressed will (e.g., a referendum), in a manner that responded to the 2012 (third) Armitage and Nye report titled *The U.S.-Japan Alliance: Anchoring Stability in Asia*, which stated: "Prohibition of collective [i.e., regional] self-defense is an impediment to the alliance" (15). More specifically, in July 2014, the Abe cabinet formalized a reinterpretation of Article 9 in order to allow the Self-Defense Forces, beyond the "defense only" principle established in the mid-1950s, to officially exercise collective/regional self-defense (in effect, to use military forces) in collaboration with the US military and others outside the territories of Japan (Abe Cabinet 2014). Obviously, this reinterpretation compromised the renunciation of war stipulated in the first paragraph of Article 9 (see section 1 of this chapter). Building on Tokyo's willingness to exercise to exercise collective/regional self-defense bilaterally (where collective/regional self-defense would be exercised by the United States to protect Japan and by Japan to protect the United States), in 2020, the Armitage and Nye group published a fifth report, titled *The U.S.-Japan Alliance in 2020: An Equal Alliance with a Global Agenda*, to recommend continued and increased security coordination among the United States, Japan, and other like-minded countries vis-à-vis China and North Korea. In the process, Tokyo has been not only deepening its alliance with the United States, as articulated below, but also promoting and enhancing (*a*) the Quadrilateral Security Dialogue (commonly known as the QUAD) with Australia, India, and the United States since 2017 (Satomi 2022), (*b*) a trilateral security cooperation with South Korea and the United States since the fall of 2022 (Kaino 2023), and (*c*) a bilateral security framework with the Philippines since the fall of 2023 (Endō and Meguro 2023).

Second, at the economic level, Tokyo has paid an increasingly large amount of money to support activities of the US military in Okinawa and elsewhere in Japan, in a way that responded to the 2007 (second) Armitage and Nye report, titled *The U.S.-Japan Alliance: Getting Asia Right through 2020*, which stated that "Japan ranks in the top five in the world in gross defense expenditures, but number 134 in the world in terms of defense budget as a percentage of GDP" (22). In actuality, Tokyo has not only covered maintenance/construction expenses for houses and recreational facilities for the US military and part of personnel expenses of Japanese workers employed on the bases through the *omoiyari-yosan* ("sympathy budget") (since 1978) but has also paid basic salaries of the Japanese workers employed in the bases (since 1987), costs for relocating training activities (since 1987), utility costs of the US bases and facilities (since 1987), costs related to activity in Okinawa (since 1995), including the construction of the FRF, and costs for reorganizing US bases in Japan (since 2007). As of 2002, Tokyo had already paid $4.4 billion, or 74% of the cost of US military activities in Japan, by far the largest contribution among allies of the United States (Sonoda et al. 2020).[13]

Third, burdens in Okinawa were often reinforced *and* spread across Japan (Bōeishō, n.d.-f). To be sure, Washington and Tokyo claimed that for the sake of "substantially reduc[ing] burdens in Okinawa" (*US-Japan Alliance*), some of the base functions in Okinawa—such as the aviator training at Kadena Air Base and the stationing of aerial refueling aircraft at Futenma Air Station—have been transferred to existing bases of the US military and the Self-Defense Forces elsewhere in Japan, such as Iwakuni, Chitose, Misawa, Komatsu, Nyūtabaru, and Tsuiki (Bōeishō, n.d.-f). However, the actuality of "substantially reducing burdens in Okinawa" is more complicated. For instance, even though after the 1995 rape incident it was decided that the US Marine Corps would "terminate artillery live-fire training over Highway 104 . . . after the training is relocated to maneuver areas on the mainland of Japan within Japanese Fiscal Year 1997" (SACO 1996), the Marine Corps relocated this training to five Ground Self-Defense Force exercise areas, with additional exercises using advanced missile launchers and drones, *and* began to conduct new training for the Expeditionary Advanced Base Operations at various US military facilities in Okinawa to overcome China's anti-access area denial strategies (Takashima et al. 2022). The V-22 Osprey—which costs approximately $94 million per aircraft—has also been deployed in Okinawa *and* across wider Japan.[14] Along the similar lines, (*a*) MQ-9 drones stationed in Maritime Self-Defense Force Kanoya Air Base in Kagoshima Prefecture were transferred to Kadena Air Base in Okinawa in November 2023 (Okinawa Terebi 2023), and (*b*) in light of the potentiality of Taiwan and related crises, the US military, together with Washington and Tokyo, seems to consider retaining Futenma Air Station semipermanently even after (and even if) the FRF construction in Henoko is completed (Yamashiro 2023a). In addition, as noted in chapter 1, section 2, Tokyo has been reinforcing the presence of the Self-Defense Forces on the neighboring islands of Okinawa near Taiwan such as Miyako, Ishigaki, and Yonaguni (Fujiwara 2020), while in November 2023, the US Marine Corps transformed the existing Twelfth Marines in Okinawa into the Twelfth Marine Littoral Regiment to develop the Expeditionary Advanced Base Operations capacity (Makino Y. 2023; Yamashiro 2023b). In effect, what has been actualized under new historical circumstances of Empire v.3 is the vision that "the entire area of Japan must be regarded as a potential base for defensive maneuver with unrestricted freedom reserved to the United States as the protecting power"—a vision originally developed by MacArthur (FRUS 1950c, 1227) and subsequently elaborated by Dulles for the continued use of the US bases in Japan beyond the period of occupation, as noted in section 1 of this chapter.

Fourth, a war-ready posture was built across Japan at the level of everyday social life and beyond. *US-Japan Alliance* (2005) had already stated that the United States and Japan "will work with local communities to ensure stable support for the presence and operations of U.S. forces in Japan." The 2012 (third) Armitage and Nye report also noted that "it would be a responsible authorization to allow our forces to respond in full cooperation throughout the security spectrum of peacetime, tension, crisis, and war" (15). In a way that expanded ideas expressed in these documents, in April 2015, the new and third *Guidelines for U.S.-Japan Defense Cooperation* (2015) stipulated collaboration between US forces and Japan's Self-Defense Forces *in times of peace*, thereby expanding the scope of application of the US-Japan security alliance from cases of emergency down to the entire time and space of everyday life of Japan. Accordingly, Tokyo now criminalizes varied forms of social contestation and resistance through a series of controversial laws such as the State Secrecy Law (2013), the revised Wiretapping Law (2016), and the Conspiracy Act (2017), which allows police to arrest people who simply discuss or plan vaguely defined "serious" criminal acts. It should be added that the new *Guidelines* (2015) also, and for the first time, stipulated US-Japan collaboration in outer space and cyberspace. In 2018, the study group led by Armitage and Nye published a fourth report, titled *More Important Than Ever: Renewing the U.S.-Japan Alliance for the 21st Century*, to recommend, against Donald Trump's isolationist "America first" policy, the further reinforcement of the US-Japan security alliance across the entire realm of social life (Saruta 2019).

It should be added that Tokyo has advanced the spirit of these reports by considering something the Armitage and Nye group did not discuss, the establishment of a capacity to attack enemy bases for self-defense ("Aratana . . ." 2020). In December 2022, the Japanese government—led by Prime Minister Kishida Fumio (1957–present; in office 2021–present) after the assassination of Prime Minister Abe in July 2022—decided to pursue this capacity by stipulating it in the new national security policy documents, a situation some critics call the "death of Article 9" of the Constitution of Japan (Komano 2023). Indeed, moving beyond the 2014 cabinet decision to allow Japan to exercise collective/regional self-defense by modifying the interpretation of Article 9 (noted above), it has now practically abandoned the nonpossession of military forces stipulated in the second paragraph of Article 9. Some politicians have even proposed the sharing of nuclear weapons with the US military for self-defense ("Beishudō . . ." 2022).

Predictably, the transformation of the US-Japan alliance in the twenty-first century outlined above has been accompanied by the reproduction of the Self/Other (friends/enemies) binary (cf. Schmitt [1932] 1976), resulting in the escalation of conflicts at multiple levels, such as continued reinforcement of the People's Liberation Army (Scobell 2010, 2017), together with the intensification of the trade war between the United States and China and of conflicts over "history issues" between Japan and China. From the perspective of China, indeed, the US-Japan alliance is a double menace in terms of which a strong nationalist sentiment has been shaped. On the one hand, the US presence in the Asia-Pacific region, as mediated by the Taiwan Strait crisis (1995–1996), the NATO bombing of the Chinese Embassy in Belgrade, Yugoslavia (1999), and the collision of US and Chinese military planes off the Chinese coast (2001), has been interpreted among the Chinese public and government as the extension of the "national humiliation" experienced since the First Opium War in the 1840s (Masuo 2019, chap. 1; Wang 2012, chaps. 2 and 7). On the other hand, the reinforcement of the US-Japan alliance has been combined with "Japan's political right-deviation"

(Shi 2015)—represented by Prime Minister Abe's visit in 2013 to Yasukuni Shrine, which commemorates "the souls of the many people who have made the ultimate sacrifice for their nation since 1853" (Yasukuni Jinja, n.d.; "Yasukuni . . ." 2021; cf. Takenaka 2015). Such "deviation" has provoked China's memories of Japan's invasion between 1931 (or earlier) and 1945, which constituted an integral, indeed a foundational, aspect of the "patriotic education campaign" organized by the Chinese Communist Party (Wang 2012, chap. 4; cf. Masuo 2019, chap. 1). Accordingly, "more and more Chinese people have come to hate Western countries, especially the United States and Japan" (Wang 2012, 190).

It should be added, however, that the deterioration of the relationship between the US-Japan alliance and China at the level of security has been complicated by the issues of economic and cultural exchanges. More specifically, while the United States has tried and may proceed with "targeted decoupling" (Segal, Reynolds, and Roberts 2021, vi) of its economic activities and technological endeavors from China, economic and related interdependence between China and Japan has remained and will remain unchanged. For instance, during the 2010s (i.e., before the Covid-19 pandemic), the growing number of increasingly affluent tourists from China visited Japan and went on buying sprees (called *bakugai* or explosive shopping) of Japanese consumer goods (e.g., medicine, electronics, cosmetics) while the money spent in their traveling helped to support the otherwise declining Japanese economy. An increasing number of Japanese companies also moved factories and offices to China, where laborers and rents were cheap, a process that facilitated the advancement of Japanese retail businesses (e.g., department stores and supermarkets) in China. Meanwhile, as Zhu Fangyue (2011) has shown, from the 1990s through the first decade of the twenty-first century, TV broadcasting and the internet helped the youth in China actively absorb Japanese popular culture in the form of manga, anime, dramas, and music, though increasing control of the media environment by the Chinese government has rapidly undermined this trend in contemporary China. For instance, the Chinese public is no longer able to watch Japanese anime on the nation's TV broadcasting system (Masuo and Hosomi 2022).

In light of the complexity of security, economic, and other relations noted above, even though *Summary of the 2018 National Defense Strategy of the United States* characterized contemporary global conditions in general and the US-China rivalry in particular as "the re-emergence of long-term, strategic competition between nations" (Department of Defense 2018, 2), as if it represented the reappearance of the Cold War, a more accurate vision would be to see it as the intensification of "global civil war" (Hardt and Negri 2004, 3) within the same sovereign territory, the world market, of Empire v.3, in which—as Zhu Feng (2015, 205) notes—"in terms of capability, will, and strategic choice, no single country is able to unilaterally lead the transformation of the East Asia security order." It is this never-ending struggle for "relative dominance within the hierarchies . . . of the [same] global system" (Hardt and Negri 2004, 4) that sustains and is sustained by the global civil war, a war one cannot win or a war that must be won every day and everywhere (Hardt and Negri 2004, 14)—as Russia's invasion of Ukraine and the Israeli-Palestinian conflict have exemplified.

How can we overcome the crises of perpetual war that the global civil war has brought about? I will explore this question in the conclusion to this book by seeking ways to move beyond the paradigm of the Armitage and Nye reports, a paradigm of Self and Other, friend and enemy, through the restoration of collective security.

Notes

1. For instance, in a memorandum written on June 14, 1950, he reinterpreted the term "irresponsible militarism" appearing in Item 6 of the Potsdam Declaration: "A new order of peace, security and justice will be impossible until irresponsible militarism is driven from the world." He insisted that the term "irresponsible militarism" should now be applied not to Japan but to new "predatory forces," i.e., communists (FRUS 1950a, 1218–1219). MacArthur had formulated this line of thought already in May 1950 (Eldridge 2001, 276).

2. Okinawa's opinion at this point (late 1940s) was moving from independence under the guidance of the United States to reversion of Okinawa to Japan, as explained in chapter 3, sections 1 and 2.

3. Evidence revealed in 1994 suggests, however, that this exceptional handling of the case was made possible by a secret agreement between Tokyo and Washington that, in exchange for the suspect being turned over to the Japanese authorities, the Japanese prosecutor would indict Girard not for murder but for a lighter offense, accidental mortality. Maebashi District Court followed this governmental agreement, giving him a light sentence of three years' imprisonment with a four years' stay of execution (Naoshima 2000).

4. For instance, the comprehensive assessment of necessity enabled the underused bases in Japan "proper" to be returned or reorganized. In addition, some of the US bases were absorbed by the bases of the newly established Self-Defense Forces of Japan (e.g., Camp Gifu, Camp Fuji McNair) (NHK Shuzaihan 2011, 27–34).

5. The analysis that follows appears in Inoue (2015). I thank H-Diplo for kind permission to reproduce portions of that article.

6. Transformation of the aforementioned National Police Reserve into the

Peace Preservation Corps occurred in 1952. The Mutual Defense Assistance Agreement between the United States and Japan led to the transformation of the Peace Preservation Corps into the Self-Defense Forces in 1954.

7. "Japan's trade with China amounted to 20.0% of its total trade from 1926 to 1930 and 18.4% from 1931 to 1936, while it amounted only to 1.3% in the period from 1951 to 1960" (T. Shiraishi 1997, 176), largely due to the embargo network directed against the People's Republic of China, which Washington had established in postwar Asia to counter a number of Sino-Japanese private sector trade accords created in the 1950s (Shimizu 2001, chaps. 3 and 6).

8. The so-called Kanto Plain Consolidation Plan played an important role in reducing the area of US bases in Tokyo and surrounding areas during the 1970s (Koyama 2008).

9. Ospreys were deployed to Okinawa in 2012.

10. Examples of this projection include (*a*) the development of a missile program consisting of nineteen hundred to two thousand medium-range ballistic missiles and intermediate-range ballistic missiles that can target US bases and Self-Defense Force bases in Okinawa and elsewhere in Japan (Doi, Satō, and Minemura 2020), (*b*) the appearance of Chinese official ships (e.g., Chinese Coast Guard ships) around the Senkaku (or Diaoyu) Islands for more than 330 days in 2020 ("Chūgoku . . ." 2020), and (*c*) the enforcement of the Coast Guard Law in 2021 that authorizes the China Coast Guard to use weapons (e.g., Article 22) (Funakoshi et al. 2021; Standing Committee of the National People's Congress 2021).

11. In chapter 1, section 2, I discussed the formation of the global security apparatus in terms of decentering and upgrading of the US Marine Corps and the US military as a whole, consolidation of US bases in Okinawa, and integration of Japan's Self-Defense Forces (and other forces) into the operations of the US Marine Corps and the US military as a whole.

12. The joint operations coordination center was established in 2011 (Bōeishō 2013b, 164–165). The X-band radar system was deployed to Shariki Air Self-Defense Force Subbase in Aomori in June 2006 and to Kyōgomisaki Air Self-Defense Force Subbase in Kyoto in December 2014 (Bōeishō 2018, 326).

13. For instance, South Korea paid $0.8 billion (40%), Germany paid $1.6 billion (32.6%), and Italy paid $0.4 billion (41.0%) of the cost of the US military's activities in the respective countries in 2002.

14. Indeed, in October 2012 and September 2013, twelve Ospreys were first deployed to Futenma Air Station in spite of sustained local opposition on the grounds of safety and noise (see chapter 2, section 2). Then, in October 2018, ten Ospreys were deployed to Yokota Air Base in western Tokyo (Ōga, Yamaura, and Furushiro 2018). Since June 2020, additional Ospreys have been deployed across Japan through the Ground Self-Defense Force (Yoshie, Fukui, and Itō 2020); one of these Ospreys has been deployed to Ishigaki, one of the neighboring islands of Okinawa near Taiwan (Taira T. 2023).

CHAPTER 6

Dojin and Okinawa

Official Nationalism Versions 1, 2, and 3

In an attempt to calm Okinawa's anger at the 1995 rape incident, Washington and Tokyo did not limit their response to the return of Futenma; they also set forth the return of a large portion of the US Marine Corps' Northern Training Area (approximately 4,000 hectares of the total area of approximately 7,900 hectares) in exchange for the construction of a total of seven (later reduced to six) new helipads for V-22 Ospreys in Takae, a small community (population: 140) in northern Okinawa (north of Nago city) located adjacent to this training area (see Figure 4 in the introduction to this book for its location) (SACO 1996).[1] As in the case of the Futenma Replacement Facility, however, the intention of Washington and Tokyo was to upgrade the functions of the US military facilities in the name of reducing the burden of their presence in and for Okinawa. In spite of villagers' repeated opposition, construction work began in 2007, but it was suspended in 2014 after the completion of two helipads. My visit to Takae and conversations with protesters there in the summer of 2015, however, made me suspect that Washington and Tokyo would soon resume the work to complete the remaining helipads. My premonition proved correct in July 2016.

On the morning of October 18, 2016, approximately seventy individuals from Okinawa and elsewhere in Japan organized public protests in front of chain-link fences erected by the Okinawa Defense Bureau around the site of the helipads under construction in Takae. In response to the protest activities, a twenty-nine-year-old sergeant of the riot squad sent from the Osaka Prefectural Police yelled at them sharply, "Don't touch [the fence], stupid! What are you holding onto, idiot? You, *dojin*!" (yanbarukanashi 2016). In a manner that reveals the power of "sousveillance"—inverse surveillance of those in power by the weak (see chapter 2, section 1)—noted Okinawan writer-activist Medoruma Shun, present at the scene, recorded this language in a video. Immediately posted on his blog (Medoruma 2016b) and reported on by local newspapers ("Doko..." 2016), the video spread across the media space, generating anger in Okinawa, wider Japan, and beyond because the word *dojin* has a discriminatory connotation of contempt and disdain with deep historical roots.

I explicate the significance of the *dojin* incident in two steps. First, I compare the way the term *dojin* is used against Okinawans today with the way it was used against them in the past. Second, in so doing, my analysis traces the transformation of what Benedict Anderson (1991, 83–111) called official nationalism—the state's attempt to merge, absorb, and manage the nation's constituent power from above—from one formed through print capitalism (plus radio) in prewar and wartime Japan, which I call "official nationalism version 1," to one formed through analog capitalism in postwar Japan (from 1945 through the 1990s), which I call "official nationalism version 2," and to one formed through digital capitalism in Japan in the twenty-first century, which I call "official nationalism version 3." I define analog capitalism and digital capitalism in the following way on the basis of the notion of "print capitalism," that is, "the convergence of capitalism and print technology on the fatal diversity of human language" (Anderson 1991, 46). That is, analog capitalism is defined as the convergence of capitalism and analog technology, including not only the press but also radio, TV, and other analog media, on the lives of increasingly affluent Japanese in postwar Japan, while digital capitalism is understood as the convergence of capitalism and digital technology on the diverse lives of precarious and atomized Japanese in the globalized time-space of Empire in the twenty-first century.

Underscoring forms of official nationalism across the ages of print capitalism (plus radio), analog capitalism, and digital capitalism, this chapter affirms but complicates and deepens the analyses presented by critics within Okinawa and without (e.g., Arakaki 2016; Yoshi'i 2016; "'Dojin' hatsugen no Dokoga..." 2016), who consider the *dojin* incident as an expression of the continuous discrimination by the Japanese nation-state against Okinawans from the late nineteenth century to the present. In the process, my analysis of official nationalism v.3 also challenges the arguments of scholars who tend to idealize the liberating potentiality of resistance by the digital-savvy cosmopolitan "multitude"—local residents with global political awareness—against an oppressive state, as in the Arab Spring (Eltantawy and Wiest 2011; Howard and Hussain 2011), China's internet nationalism (Liu 2006; Tai 2016), and the

Occupy movement (Fuchs 2014; Juris 2012). What I aim to address instead is a novel mechanism of governance embodied in official nationalism v.3, which, appearing within the specific historical context of Empire in the twenty-first century, curtails the resistance of the Okinawan multitude through the very principle of democracy they advocate.

1. A Brief History of *Dojin* Discourses: The Formation and Transformation of Official Nationalism Version 1 from the Late 1880s through 1945

In the late Meiji period (from the late 1880s to the early 1910s), in an attempt to stabilize the political and social order that had been generated during the two decades following the Meiji Restoration of 1868, the Japanese government was engaged in the making of the ideology of the emperor system. In particular, the concept of *kokutai*, which referred to a "unique" form of the Japanese polity characterized by the enduring loyalty and filial piety of the unified subjects—the Japanese—toward the unbroken line of emperors from time immemorial, played a significant role in establishing and projecting the self-image of Japan as a homogenous, harmonious, family-like nation. The notion of *kokutai* was officially presented, for instance, in the Imperial Rescript on Education (1890) (Department of Education [Japan] 1909). State directives, school textbooks, newspapers, magazines, scholarly works, and other printed materials elaborated on the notion, while a range of state ceremonies and local initiatives gave specific (and often contradictory) forms to it at the level of everyday social life (Gluck 1985, esp. chap. 5). In the process, official nationalism v.1, a merger—facilitated by print capitalism—between the state (officials, or *kan*) and the nation (the people, or *min*) began to be formed under the transcendental power of the emperor (Gluck 1985, 47).

Importantly, the late Meiji period was also a time when Japan, then a minor power of East Asia faced with the incursion of Western imperialist powers, initiated its civilizing movement by annexing or destroying the other "uncivilized" powers it faced. In effect, Japan became imperialist in its very attempt to protect itself from imperialism. In the process, the notion of *kokutai* came to contain a contradiction of sorts, because an increasing number of non-Japanese—Ainu, "Ryukyuans," Chinese residing in Taiwan, aborigines of Taiwan, Koreans, and others whose "loyalty" and "filial piety" to the emperor were uncertain at best—were incorporated into the territories of the colonialist Empire of Japan[2] over time (Kon'no 2008, 6 and 125–126; Oguma 1995, 49–72). Were they Japanese, as defined by the *kokutai* concept? The so-called Human Pavilion (Jinruikan) incident at the Fifth National Industrial Fair of 1903 became an occasion for increasingly diversified subjects of the colonialist Empire of Japan to raise, engage in, and reflect on this historically generated sociopolitical question.

Initiated in 1877, a series of national industrial fairs—a Japanese version of the World Expo—were organized in the name of the emperor, who represented progress toward Western-style civilization grounded in an enduring Japanese tradition centered on *kokutai* (Kuni 2005, 255–261). Against the historical background of Japan's victory in the First Sino-Japanese War (1894–1895) and a partial revision of the unequal treaty between Japan and Western powers in 1899, the fifth and final fair, held in Osaka in 1903, was particularly noteworthy because of its spectacular display of the industrial and technological development of the ever more "civilized" and ever more prosperous empire on a par with Western powers (Matsuda 2003, 16–17). For instance, it fully incorporated new technologies such as electricity into the exhibitions (Yoshimi S. 1992, 146–147); it was also grander than the preceding four fairs (Kuni 2005, 163–202), featuring a range of pavilions—exhibiting the accomplishments of each prefecture in agriculture, fishery, mining, chemistry, machinery, and education, among other fields—housed in magnificent European-style brick buildings (Matsuda 2003, 51, 74). The number of visitors was record-breaking—5.3 million, one-ninth of the Japanese nation at that time (Kuni 2005, 183)—due in part to the power of the print media that disseminated information about this fair (Kuni 2005, 166–167) together with the development of various means of transportation, including trains (Nakamura S. 1992, 209–216). In effect, the Fifth National Industrial Fair became a splendid pageant, constituted at the interface where state (constituted power) and nation (constituent power) met to promote official nationalism v.1 for the construction of the Japanese Self.

Various Others were brought from within the expanding Empire of Japan to facilitate the merger between state and nation. In the official exhibition area, for instance, the Taiwan Pavilion was created to display exotic items originating in Japan's new colony—such as a Taiwanese girl with bound feet serving tea for the Japanese visitors/nation (Matsuda 2003, 55–81). In addition, in the "entertainment" section set up outside the area of official exhibitions, the Human Pavilion was built, together with a range of midway features such a merry-go-round, a water chute, a mystery house, and a zoo (Kuni 2005, 186–190). A letter of intent, drafted on the initiative of Tsuboi Shōgorō, a pioneer anthropologist of the Imperial University of Tokyo (Kinjō I. 2005, 43–46), stated that the Human Pavilion would "bring to *naichi* [Japan "proper"] other races nowadays, that is, seven *dojin* including Hokkaido Ainu, aborigines of Taiwan, Ryukyuans, Koreans, Chinese, Indians, and Javanese etc., to display the most specific grades, degrees, feelings, and customs etc. of their existence" (Tokyo Jinruigaku Zasshi 1903). The practice of exhibiting the "uncivilized" did not originate in Japan, of course. The West did so from the 1850s on as a show window of imperialism, as it were, and fully developed the practice at the Paris Exposition of 1889 and after (Yoshimi S. 1992, 180–186); the Fifth National Industrial Fair became an occasion for the colonialist Empire of Japan to mimic this Western imperialist gesture. However, the gesture provoked protest from members of some of the ethnicities put on display and, in the process, exposed the problem of the notion of *kokutai*, as this fair obscured the boundaries of the Japanese Self in its very attempt to define them.

The original plan of displaying seven *dojin* in this pavilion was modified because, for instance, students from the Qing dynasty studying abroad in Meiji Japan initiated a campaign against the planned display of Chinese nationals; this campaign was linked to larger political and business circles of Qing China and eventually forced the organizer—a businessperson in the Kansai area (area around Osaka, Kyoto, and Kobe)—to cancel it in February 1903, prior to the opening of the industrial fair. After this setback, the adjective "Academic" was added to the title of the pavilion to make it sound more legitimate. However, immediately after the Academic Human Pavilion opened, the exhibition of Koreans was withdrawn because of a protest by a Korean visitor addressed to the head of the Osaka Prefectural Police Department and another protest by a Korean minister addressed to the Japanese Ministry of Foreign Affairs (Matsuda 2003, 121–124). In both cases, the complaint was that Chinese or Koreans were objectified as exotic natives—as if they were animals in a zoo—when they should be alongside the civilized Japanese subjects observing such *dojin*.

Okinawans couched their protest in the same logic (Kinjō I. 2005). In April 1903, indeed, an Okinawan who saw the display of his fellow Okinawans—two young Okinawan women (*juri*) from Tsuji, a noted entertainment quarter in Naha that I discussed in chapter 3, section 4—in this pavilion wrote a letter expressing his dismay to Okinawa's highly influential newspaper, *Ryukyu Shimpo*, and this letter generated angry protests from local readers. In a way that summarized the sentiments of Okinawans, Ōta Chōfu—a key intellectual in Okinawa and a founder of *Ryukyu Shimpo*—wrote on April 11, 1903, in the editorial titled "Jinruikan o Chūshi Seshimeyo" (Cancel the Human Pavilion) ([1903] 1995): "I am ashamed of the fact that such cruel and greedy nationals exist in the Empire of Japan. That they did not display strange customs and manners of other prefectures but chose us together with aborigines in Taiwan and Ainu in the north means that they viewed us as equal to these aborigines and Ainu. Nothing humiliates us more than this." Due to Okinawa's protest, the organizer of the pavilion removed the Okinawan women from display. After this incident, Okinawan leaders such as Ōta Chōfu intensified the effort to more fully assimilate Okinawans into the Empire of Japan, through the movement to have Okinawans—particularly schoolchildren—use "standard" Japanese rather than Okinawan "dialect" in order to eliminate Japanese discrimination against them (Kondō K. 2005, Oguma 1998, 280–319). Earlier, in 1900, Ōta had even asserted in a lecture, "One of the most urgent tasks of today's Okinawa is to make everything look as it does in other prefectures of Japan. We should even sneeze the way people in other prefectures do" (Ōta C. [1900] 1995, 58; cf. Hiyane 1996, part 2, esp. chap. 2, and Oguma 1998, 280–286).

The dissents of Chinese, Koreans, and Okinawans regarding the Academic Human Pavilion challenged the concept of *kokutai*—a unique form of the nation characterized by the enduring loyalty and filial piety of the Japanese to the emperor who progressively civilizes them—by revealing that this concept could not include Others within it even if they became the subjects of the Japanese Empire. After the Human Pavilion incident, the colonialist Empire of Japan kept expanding; specifically, in the wake of the Russo-Japanese War (1904–1905), Japan advanced into northeast China as well as controlled and eventually annexed Korea (1910), making the issue of who would be included in and excluded from *kokutai* pressing. The issue was made even more urgent because of the fact that the Japanese imitation of the Western "imperialist" gesture—the exhibition of the "uncivilized" *dojin*—reinforced the notion of "civilization" as defined by the West, thereby reproducing the very West-centered hierarchy of civilization that Japan, against the background of the rise of Yellow Peril sentiments in the West, would challenge from the late 1910s on, including wartime years of the twentieth century (Dower 1986, esp. chap. 7). Situated in this volatile historical context of the 1910s through the 1930s, a group of Japanese (including Okinawan) intellectuals/ideologues were engaged in redefining the concept of *kokutai* to incorporate non-Japanese Others in two steps; in the process, official nationalism v.1 took a new form—v.1.1.

First, they defined "Ryukyuans," Taiwanese (i.e., Chinese residing in Taiwan), and Koreans as "adopted children" (Oguma 1995, 142–151). Okinawan intellectuals such as Iha (or Ifa) Fuyū undertook a more elaborate operation by redefining Okinawans (officially incorporated into the Empire of Japan in 1879) as "the first son," Chinese residing in Taiwan (incorporated in 1895) as "the second son," and Koreans (incorporated in 1910) as "the third son" (Tomiyama 2002, 74–78; Yakabi 2003), thereby erasing the subtle quality of being alien infused in the word "adopted children" (*yōshi*), naturalizing their gender (as male), and hierarchizing them vis-à-vis the authentic Japanese subjects as "adults." All in all, by using family-related terms, Japanese (including Okinawan) intellectuals and ideologues contributed to maintaining the notion of *kokutai* (i.e., Japan as a family-like nation from time immemorial under the emperor) and to integrating as much as controlling a specific group of Others from within in it in the context of the increasingly diversified colonialist Empire of Japan. Then, in the second step, these adopted children (or first/second/third sons) were differentiated from a second group of non-Japanese, that is, *dojin* ("savage and inferior" natives) to be civilized by the caring gaze of the emperor (Nakamura J. 2000). Accordingly, (*a*) the language of "adopted children" (or "first/second/third sons") helped situate Okinawans, Taiwanese, and Koreans as more or less "insiders" of the colonialist Empire of Japan, with a sense of shaded discrimination against them as almost but not quite Japanese, and (*b*) a range of "savage and inferior" *dojin*/Others—the Ainu, aborigines of Taiwan, and Pacific Islanders, for example—were marginalized as more distant "outsiders" within the family-like nation. Print media such as school textbooks (Kondō K. 1995; Nakamura J. 2000; Oguma 1995, 160–167) and magazines and journals (Kawamura M. 2015a, 2015b; Yano Tō. 2009) played a key role in generating and differentiating these two categories of the non-Japanese Others within the concept of *kokutai*.

It should be added, however, that the boundaries between adopted children (or the first/second/third sons) more or less inside the emperor-centered family-like nation/state and the more marginalized *dojin* (outsiders) were often blurry, as exemplified by the 1935 poem titled "A Conversation" by the Okinawan poet Yamanokuchi (or Yamanoguchi)

Baku (translation by Steve Rabson [2000], which is modified by this writer). In this poem, a Japanese woman he was thinking about as a potential wife asked, "Where are you from?" Interactions between the two eventually led this woman to say, "Oh, the subtropics!" In response, Yamanokuchi wrote: "Yes, my dear can't you see 'the subtropics' right here before your eyes? Like me, the people there are Japanese, speak Japanese, and were born in the subtropics. But, viewed through popular stereotypes, that place I am from has become a synonym for chieftains, *dojin*, karate, and *awamori*." As shown below, the instability of the boundaries between inside and outside trapped Okinawans in perpetual and desperate efforts to remove their *dojin*-ness (Otherness) and become and remain Japanese, an act that was triggered by their fear or "presentiments" of discrimination against them by the Japanese (Tomiyama 2002).

From the late 1930s on, as the empire mobilized the entire nation to complete the war in the Asia-Pacific region, official nationalism v.1 took a final form, v.1.2. This transformation was carried out through discourses that refined the concept of *kokutai*, as in the case of *kōkoku-shikan*, an emperor-centered historical discourse linked to ideas such as *hakkōichiu* (eight corners under one roof) and *daitōakyōeiken* (greater East Asia co-prosperity sphere) (Sakurai S. 2001). Blending the two separate groups of Others from within—adopted children (or first/second/third sons) and *dojin*—*kōkoku-shikan* specifically insisted that the Empire of Japan would prosecute the war to liberate all ethnic groups from the yokes of Western imperialism and to actualize a great harmony among them. "The Japanese Worldview and the Construction of a New World Order," published by Monbushō (the Ministry of Education) in 1942—one of the official documents that clearly articulated *kōkoku-shikan* (Kon'no 2008, 222)—thus argued: "According to the Western worldview, the world must be conquered as a world that exists for the Westerners. Therefore, while advocating justice and humanity, the Westerners took it for granted that they were authorized to freely use the land occupied by other races in the name of 'discovery,' oppress natives, and exploit resources" (2–3). In contrast, this document continued, "the Japanese worldview [centered on the emperor] aimed at allowing the races to take forms that they should take. The races would all exist according to their true nature to concretize the world of great harmony and to co-prosper as a family" (6). *Kōkoku-shikan* thus contributed to constructing the image of the paternal, civilizing emperor also as a maternal figure who, unlike Western imperialists who were conceived in wartime

Japan in the image of the devilish-animalistic Anglo-Saxon male (*kichikubeiei*) (Dower 1986, chap. 9), would embrace, like the benevolent mother, all subjects under a hermaphroditic gaze (Kanō [1991] 1995).

As Takeyama Akiko ([1994] 2018) argued, an emperor-centered historical worldview—official nationalism v.1.2—was further promoted and reinforced in wartime Japan by the power of radio, which began to be used for propaganda in 1925 through NHK, the national broadcast station controlled by the government: "Unlike newspapers that reported events by logic, radio, a mediating human voice, appealed to emotion, thereby raising the fighting spirit of the nation" (Takeyama and Mayama 2020). Kenneth Ruoff (2010) has also shown the role that a variety of media (broadly defined)—such as newspapers, radios, department stores, and train systems—played in expanding the experiences of the Japanese and promoting tourism of historical sites across the wartime Empire of Japan in a manner that reinforced the emperor-centered worldview.

Official nationalism v.1.2, spreading the image of the civilizing-benevolent emperor, however, obscured actual violence—killing, destruction, abuse, exploitation, rape, and so on—that the colonialist Empire of Japan exercised against Others across the Asia-Pacific region in the name of harmony (Duus 2008; Oguma 1998). In light of the objective of this section, I here focus on Okinawa's struggles to become Japanese as an effect of the transformation of prewar and wartime official nationalism, a form of cultural discourse into which violence was woven.

After the Human Pavilion incident of 1903, the desire of the Okinawans to eliminate their uncivilized *dojin*-ness and become "real" subjects of the Japanese Empire unfolded in a specific political-economic context. In the aftermath of World War I, specifically, the international market price of sugar dropped sharply because of oversupply, the effect of which was devastating because income from sugar had been providing 80% of Okinawa's entire export income. The economic devastation triggered massive emigration from Okinawa to Hawaii, Peru, Brazil, Argentina, the Philippines, Saipan, and other regions and nations outside Japan. It is estimated that Okinawans constituted 10%–20% of overseas emigrants with Japanese nationality between 1923 and 1930 (Tomiyama 1990, 76–82; Arashiro 1994, 211–212). Their economic plight during this period also prompted many Okinawans to go to other parts of Japan—particularly to the Osaka area—to work as poorly paid laborers in textiles, manufacture, and other industries (Tomiyama 1990, 109–193; Rabson 2012). The emigration led not only to more contact between Okinawans and other Japanese but also to more discrimination by the latter against the former, both in Japan and abroad.

Taking this as evidence that the previous Japanization efforts had not been sufficient, during the 1930s Okinawan authorities became even further absorbed by the project of remaking Okinawans into "true" Japanese. For instance, the use of standard Japanese was thoroughly enforced (Tomiyama 2006, 80–85). In addition, the use of Okinawan toilets (used to feed pigs on human waste) and the practices of aerial sepulture, walking in bare feet, and local shamanism by *yuta* (discussed in chapter 4, section 2) were strongly discouraged to prevent the image of Okinawans as "unsanitary" and "backward" from spreading among Japanese (Tomiyama 1990, 4–5). If the official attempt to transform Okinawans into true Japanese had been centered on relatively limited locales such as schools until the 1920s, the scope of control was expanded to the entire field of everyday social life from the 1930s on (Tomiyama 2006, part 2, esp. 74–89).

Okinawans' desire to become Japanese, a desire entangled with official nationalism v.1.2, took tragic form in the Battle of Okinawa. I highlight the predicament of the Okinawans in terms of what Norma Field described as "compulsory group suicide" (1991, 61) in this battle, in a way that expands my description of compulsory group suicide on Zamami Island in chapter 3, section 1. Similar tragedies occurred in various places in Okinawa (Ōshiro M. 1996). As I stated in my first book (Inoue 2007, 61-62; see also Yomitansonshi Henshūshitsu 2002):

> More than 140 residents had taken refuge in a cave called *Chibichirigama* in Yomitan Village on the west coast of the main island of Okinawa, which the U.S. military chose as the landing spot for its operation [on April 1, 1945]. Defying the U.S. military's urgings for them to surrender, a number of men charged the enemy's position with bamboo spears, only to find themselves fatally injured [or killed] by U.S. grenades and machineguns. In spite of [the] imminent danger [posed by] staying in the cave, however, villagers were unable to leave it, because their leaders ordered them not to surrender but to maintain their honor as the imperial subjects of Japan. In an attempt to extricate themselves from this impossible situation, eighty-plus villagers killed each other with knives, sickles, stones, and other items . . . , thereby as much demolishing (by their show of loyalty to Imperial Japan) as perpetuating (by the very necessity to show their loyalty) [the Japanese] view that Okinawans were not Japanese enough.

In other words, the compulsory group suicide during the Battle of Okinawa can be seen, at least in part, as a tragic and disastrous effect of the Japanese discourse on *dojin* that defined Okinawans as Japanese with a difference, negatively defined, or lacking something Japanese should have.

2. Official Nationalism Version 2: The Rearticulation of Okinawans as Japanese with a Difference, Positively Defined (1945–1990s)

After the war, the dialectic between Okinawans as *dojin* (outsiders) and Okinawans as Japanese (insiders)—a dialectic that occurred within the historical-social context of the colonialist Empire of Japan—ceased to exist because "savage and inferior" Others from within, in relation to whom Okinawans had striven to construct themselves as Japanese, disappeared from the reduced territories of Japan. Indeed, the disappearance of *dojin*—together with the disappearance of colonies from the Empire of Japan—induced a broader rearticulation of official nationalism v.1 in prewar/wartime Japan into official nationalism v.2 in postwar Japan.

As will be elaborated below, these two forms of official nationalism were at once similar and different. They were similar in that they were both based on analog media, print and otherwise. And yet these two forms of official nationalism also differed in terms of the ways in which the Japanese Self was constituted. Through official nationalism v.1, the colonialist Empire of Japan refined the concept of *kokutai*, incorporating as much as subordinating various Others from within, that is, two groups of non-Japanese, "adopted children" (or the first/second/third sons) and *dojin*. In the process, the Japanese Self had been constructed as a multiethnic self in Asia in opposition to the West, the Other from without. In contrast, through official nationalism v.2, the Japanese Self erased the memories of itself as a colonialist empire, projecting postwar Japan instead as a peaceful and democratic nation in Asia under the authority and hegemony of the United States, as discussed in chapter 5. In so doing, postwar Japan disavowed its own past as a multiethnic empire and reimagined itself as a homogeneous nation (Oguma 1995).

In the process, significant changes in the meanings of the term *dojin* took place in the postwar media environment. Specifically, there emerged a growing recognition in the Japanese mass media that the prewar and wartime usage of *dojin*—along with certain terms that had designated *burakumin* (historically mistreated lower-class Japanese living in particular settlements), individuals with disabilities, Koreans, Chinese, and women, among others living in Japan—had been discriminatory and inadequate in light of the principles of democracy. From the 1950s on, teaching materials began to describe the Ainu people, for instance, in a less biased way slowly but surely (Aihara 2000). From the 1960s on, Japanese newspapers and TV stations also began rephrasing discriminatory terms to make nondiscriminatory representations of previously discriminated-against populations possible (Endō O. 1993; Kōriyama 2013, 148; Uji'ie 2001, 85–86). In a manner that reinforced this societal rearticulation of the meanings of Others from within, journalists and intellectuals in the postwar Japan of the 1950s–1960s started to describe Okinawans as Japanese with a difference, positively and sympathetically defined this time, within the context of official nationalism v.2, which Oguma Eiji (1998, chap. 21) defines as "progressive nationalism." Of course, this does not mean that a discriminatory view of Okinawans on the part of the Japanese completely and quickly disappeared after the war. For instance, in the midst of the island-wide protest against the US military's land seizure in the 1950s, former prime minister Ashida Hitoshi (1887–1959; in office 1948) stated that the standard of living in postwar Okinawa improved precisely because of the US occupation of Okinawa (Higa, Shimota, and Shinzato 1963, 3; Yara 2017), implying that (a) the standard of living in prewar Okinawa had been at the level of *dojin* and (b) placing Okinawa under US rule was justifiable. Nonetheless, a general tendency—to represent Okinawa as a difference in positive terms—was obvious.

The *Asahi Shimbun*'s report on the oppressive US military government in Okinawa (1955, cited in Nakano 1969, 145–148), Chūōkōron-sha's publication of avant-garde artist Okamoto Tarō's *Okinawa Bunkaron: Wasurerareta Nihon* (On Okinawan Culture: Forgotten Japan) ([1961] 2013), which (on the basis of his trip to US-ruled Okinawa in 1959) presented Okinawan culture as an archaic and unadulterated form of Japanese culture, and Iwanami Shoten's publication of Ōe Kenzaburō's *Okinawa Nōto* (Okinawa Notes) (1970), which criticized the violence of Japan from a historical perspective grounded in Okinawa, are some of the well-known examples of the transformation of the prewar and wartime meanings of Okinawa by the progressive print media in wider Japan in the search for the democratic inclusion of differences. These publications constituted an important background of Okinawa's reversion movement, a movement by the Okinawan "people" under the US control to reconstitute themselves as Japanese, as discussed in chapter 3, section 4.

Then the reversion occurred in 1972. From about the time of the reversion through the 1990s, official nationalism v.2 represented Okinawans as Japanese with a positive difference, or Okinawans having something that Japanese have lost, through analog capitalism—the convergence of capitalism and analog technology (including not only the print media but also films, radio broadcasting, and TV broadcasting) on the life of the increasingly affluent Japanese. This representation took three different yet interrelated forms. First, academic discourses in the print media in wider Japan underscored the specificity of Okinawa through the notion of culture and, in so doing, constituted Okinawa as a difference in terms of which to critique postwar materialism and modernization of Japan. Anthropologists and ethnologists from Japan "proper" came to Okinawa during this period to articulate, for instance, Okinawa's patrilineal descent groups (*munchū*; see chapter 4, section 2) as a foundation of Okinawa's social relations and spiritual universe in reference to *ie* (family or household), its counterpart elsewhere in Japan that was rapidly integrated into the corporate-centered postwar order (e.g., Higa 1983; Nihon Minzokugakkai 1962; Tokyotoritsu Daigaku Nanseishotō Kenkyū Inkai 1965). Second, the image of Okinawa as a positive difference was produced and consumed through popular culture in wider Japan, as discussed in chapter 4, section 1. Third, Okinawa came to be represented through the touristic images centering on blue ocean water and the history of the lost Ryukyu Kingdom, a process enabled by the analog media across Japan such as magazines, posters, and TV programs and commercials (Figal 2012; Tada 2004). Two exemplars of this process are the 1975 Okinawa Ocean Expo and the 1980s restoration of Shuri Castle—a symbol of the glory of the Ryukyu Kingdom that burned down during the Battle of Okinawa (Figal 2012, chap. 4; Loo 2014, chap. 5) (discussed in chapter 4, section 1).

Official nationalism v.2 did not differ from prewar nationalism v.1 (including v.1.1 and v.1.2) simply in representing Okinawa favorably. In addition, although official nationalism v.1 had allowed, under the highly abstract notion of the emperor, the presence of the distinctive local time-space of Okinawa permeated by the "strange" customs and manners Okinawan leaders had tried to eradicate, official nationalism v.2 promoted and was promoted by the homogenized national time-space across Japan (cf. Kang and Yoshimi 2001, 133–135). Put differently, from the 1970s to the 1990s—when 90% of Japanese felt that they belonged to the middle class, with a belief that "tomorrow things will be better because today things are better than yesterday" (Kanbayashi 2012)—the reintegration of post-reversion Okinawa into Japan was accomplished not through the power of the emperor, who would help remove *dojin*-ness (Otherness) from Okinawa as in prewar and wartime Japan (official nationalism v.1), but through the power of Japanese capital, of which the analog media were an integral part, to produce, consume, and manage the difference—Okinawa—within the affluent and homogeneous national, Japanized time-space.

When an Okinawan schoolgirl was raped by three US servicemen in 1995, this positively articulated difference became acutely politicized through the analog media in Okinawa (Yamakoshi 2011), against the background of the discriminatory situation that approximately 75% of the facilities in Japan for the exclusive use of the US military were concentrated in Okinawa, which constituted 0.6% of Japan's total land mass, as noted in chapter 5, section 3. The Japanese media responded to Okinawa's protest sympathetically. To be sure, the 1990s was a decade when, due in part to the decline of the population who had experienced World War II—for instance, in 1995, those born before 1945 constituted approximately 34% of the Japanese population (Sōmushō Tōkeikyoku 1996)—the transmission of the memories of the war became a social issue in Japan. There, a right-wing nationalism was on the rise, as exemplified by the attempt of a group of intellectuals to write a nationalistic history textbook that diluted atrocities of the Japanese army during World War II (Komori and Takahashi 1998), as was noted in chapter 5, section 4. And yet the influence of right-wing nationalism was still limited in Japan's media space because official nationalism v.2, as an effect of postwar Japanese efforts to pursue democratic ideals, was still operative. From the 1970s to the 1990s, indeed, critical intellectuals (e.g., Yoshimoto Taka'aki, Yamaguchi Masao, Karatani Kōjin, Asada Akira, Nakazawa Shin'ichi, Ueno Chizuko, and others who were often lumped together under a broad category of "new academism") and journalists (e.g., Honda Katsuichi and Chikushi Tetsuya)—whose works appeared in the publications of Iwanami and Asahi, among others—produced the language to challenge and control right-wing nationalism.

In so doing, they provided a broad conceptual basis for supporting the specific struggles of various minorities within Japan (e.g., Okinawans, Korean residents in Japan, Ainu, women, *burakumin*, *hibakusha* in Hiroshima and Nagasaki, the physically and mentally disabled, victims of mercury poisoning in Minamata, and "comfort women"), with an implicit call to embrace these "Japanese with differences" (and by implication, Asians victimized by the Japanese army during the war) in the now-affluent nation so as to redress the inequality of the past (Takahara 2008, 109–113; Yoneyama 2016, introduction). TV programs, as an integral component of analog capitalism, in the 1970s through the 1990s sometimes promoted—as in news and education programs of NHK—and sometimes complicated, complemented, or challenged—as in "vulgar" TV shows (S. Kim 2020)— the progressive public sphere, in a manner that extended the postwar value of democracy and demilitarization. When I conducted fieldwork in Okinawa for my dissertation research in the second half of the 1990s, therefore, I did not hear or read derogatory terms such as *dojin* directed against Okinawans. Rather, the protests were viewed as a highlight of postwar democracy in the context of official nationalism v.2 (e.g., Imai 1997; Miyamoto and Sasaki 2000).

3. The Reappearance of *Dojin* and the Rise of Official Nationalism Version 3 in the Twenty-First Century

The term *dojin*, then, has returned in the twenty-first century to rediscriminate against Okinawans, as the *dojin* incident of October 2016 shows. This incident is merely a visible signal of a more general anti-Okinawa sentiment permeating certain sectors of today's Japanese society. For instance, as noted in chapter 2, section 2, when leaders of Okinawa— including Onaga Takeshi, then mayor of Naha City and subsequently governor of Okinawa—marched on Tokyo's main street in January 2013 to oppose on the grounds of potential safety and noise issues the deployment of V-22 Ospreys (tilt-rotor military aircraft) to US bases in Okinawa, they heard bystanders yelling at them, "Traitors!" "You are selling the nation!" "Spies of China!" Some even screamed, "Get out of Japan!" (Yasuda 2016). In June 2015, a popular writer, Hyakuta Naoki, stated in an informal meeting organized by the Liberal Democratic Party, the party in power, that two Okinawan local newspapers (*Okinawa Times* and *Ryukyu Shimpo*, known for their anti-base position), because they were "biased" against the Japanese government, should be abolished ("Hyakuta Naoki . . ." 2015). In June 2016, a prefectural assemblyman in Kanagawa Prefecture commented on protesters in Henoko who came from elsewhere in Japan; he ridiculed them by calling them *kichigai*, a paronomasia meaning people coming from outside the bases and people out of their mind ("Kichihantaiha wa . . ." 2016). In October 2022, Nishimura Hiroyuki, the founder of the Japanese message board 2channel, and current administrator of the popular English message board 4chan, derided the anti-base protests in Henoko by noting that the claimed duration of sit-ins (more than three thousand days at that time) was false because no protesters were present in front of the gate on a particular day when he visited there (he apparently came in the late afternoon when the protesters had gone back home); his comment was retweeted more than three hundred thousand times ("Henoko Hōmon . . ." 2022). I wish to add one field experience of my own to illustrate the rising anti-Okinawa sentiment in wider Japan.

The sun in Okinawa was scorching at around 2:00 p.m. on Saturday, June 29, 2013. I was on my way to a favorite restaurant near the Makishi monorail station. As I got off the monorail, I heard an unfamiliar recorded chanting "Ganbare, ganbare, ganbare, Nippon!" (Hang in, hang in, hang in, Japan!) and saw a group of people gathering in a park nearby where numerous Japanese flags, together with green banners that bore the name of the organizing group—Ganbare Nippon! Zenkoku Kōdō Īinkai (Hang in, Japan! National Action Committee)—fluttered in the wind. Standing billboards and posters of varying sizes were set up on the sidewalk adjacent to the park, delivering messages that read, for instance, "Dismantle Okinawa Times and Ryukyu Shimpo!" "Support the Abe National Salvation Government!" "Stop the oppression and invasion by the Chinese government; give freedom to the Uighurs!" "We denounce Teruya Kantoku [a member of the House of Representatives of the anti-base Social Democratic Party, elected from Okinawa]!" "Employees of NHK Okinawa [said to betray the country by broadcasting pro-Okinawa news] receive an annual salary of [a staggering] 17.5 million yen (approximately $178,000 in 2013 dollars)!"

Ganbare Nippon! is closely associated with a popular, nationalist internet news station, Nippon Bunka Channeru Sakura (hereafter NBCS)—the executive director of Ganbare Nippon! is the president of NBCS—and the anti-Okinawa and nationalist-populist comments cited above have been repeatedly broadcast in their programming in order to present, they claim, "facts" that the liberal media—such as Asahi and NHK—do not report. Established in 2004 as a channel on a satellite TV station (this channel was terminated in 2017), NBCS launched its internet programming in 2007. Since then, their programs have been distributed via YouTube—where they draw more than half a million subscribers as of December 2023 (Nippon Bunka Channeru Sakura, n.d.-a)—and other online social media platforms (Nippon Bunka Channeru Sakura, n.d.-b).

The anti-Okinawa sentiment disseminated both online and offline represents Japanese discrimination against Okinawans that has continued ever since the late nineteenth century, as some critics in Okinawa and beyond have argued. However, my analysis above, in particular the minimization of derogatory representation of Okinawa in the 1950s–1990s in official nationalism v.2, indicates that the contemporary anti-Okinawa sentiment reveals something new, and I propose to read it as a symptom of official nationalism v.3. By official nationalism v.3, I mean a merger between nation and state in the age of Empire, that is, between the increasingly atomized and precarious Japanese who occupy the new media space of the twenty-first century, on the one hand, and the present-day Japanese state situated in the specific international political-economic arena of the Asia-Pacific region, on the other. I want to specify its novelty in terms of four points.

First, official nationalism v.3 expresses neither the collective self-image of the Japanese as a civilized nation on a par with Western nations, as in the case of official nationalism v.1 (including 1.1 and 1.2), nor the power of the affluent Japanese nation-state founded upon the postwar values of democracy and demilitarization, as in the case of official nationalism v.2. Instead, it expresses what Leo Ching (2019, 80) calls "postcolonial anxiety"—a collective anxiety of the Japanese Self over the economic decline of the nation, a symptom of the shift of geopolitics in the Asia-Pacific region corresponding to the formation of Empire v.3: "The modern/colonial and postwar/Cold War systems in Asia characterized by the dominance of Japan appear to have come to an end" (Ching 2019, 82). Japan's official nationalism v.3 in the twenty-first century thus needs to be grasped in the context of this long-term and irreversible globalization of economic and cultural exchanges, a process that helped the rise of China (among others) together with its anti-Japanism (Ching 2019, esp. chap. 2). As noted in chapter 5, section 5, Japan rose as the "great workshop of Asia" during the 1950s–1960s in Empire v.1 and an economic powerhouse in the 1970s–1980s in Empire v.2, but its international behavior was more or less controlled within the US-centered San Francisco system. In contrast, China in the twenty-first century is no longer regulated by the US-centered international order. With a drive to constitute a "multipolar world order" (Clegg 2009; Turner 2009), China—along with Russia—has attempted to redefine the US-centered international order from within, with the expansive movement for establishing "socialism with Chinese characteristics" (Report of Hu Jintao to the 18th CPC National Congress 2012) which has become particularly pronounced under the leadership of Xi Jinping since 2012 (Shao 2015; Kondō D. 2018), as also noted in chapter 5, section 5.

Second, official nationalism v.3 has been substantiated and reinforced by the consciousness of those who constitute *Precarious Japan* (Allison 2013). As noted in chapter 2, section 2, under the regime of neoliberalism, the power of capital has undermined established labor policies and practices in postwar Japan—including the lifelong employment system and labor-management cooperation. When combined with the narrative of personal responsibility and the technology of evaluation and assessment, capital has transformed postwar Japanese society in the 1970s–1990s into a site of perpetual competition of everyone against everyone. In the process, many Japanese have come to possess the mentality of the "underclass" (Hashimoto 2018) or "precariat," deprived of stability or guarantee of safety in work and life (Standing 2011; Allison 2013), even if they do not belong to it, for what happens to the underclass today—joblessness, lack of savings, illness—could happen to them tomorrow. Not surprisingly, the precarious Japanese no longer share postwar Japan's self-image—official nationalism v.2—of the 1970s to the 1990s as an affluent, stable, democratic nation that includes and protects minorities within it and without (Takahara 2008, 109–113). Rather, today, the precarious Japanese resentfully view minorities—including not only Okinawans but also Koreans and Chinese residing in Japan, *burakumin*, and even Fukushima residents in the disaster-stricken area after the great earthquake and tsunami in eastern Japan in 2011—as *han'nichi* (anti-Japanese), that is, unpatriotic traitors who complain with selfish economic motives to demand subsidies from the state, which the precarious/underclass Japanese are not qualified to obtain in spite of their precarious lives and economic uncertainties. In effect, Okinawans and other oppressed minorities in Japan are seen as the "privileged" groups of people entitled to have money (subsidies) simply because of their common status as minorities.

Meanwhile, voices of the precarious Japanese are no longer silenced by the "establishment"—represented by Asahi, Iwanami, and NHK as well as by intellectuals, critics, and journalists affiliated with them—who used to control the analog media to shape the basic contour of official ("progressive") nationalism v.2 in the 1970s–1990s by promoting peace, democracy, and other liberal causes such as gender equality. Against the background of a further decrease in the population who experienced World War II—in 2015, those born before 1945 constituted approximately 19% of the Japanese population (e-Stat 2015)—it has become increasingly difficult to relay the memories of the war across generations, and voices of the precarious Japanese dismissing peace and democracy (and other liberal causes more generally) are openly expressed in the new media space, in a way that echoes what Marx and Engels ([1848] n.d.) predicted when they wrote of the "dangerous class" that "its conditions of life . . . prepare it . . . for the part of a bribed tool of reactionary intrigue." I cite two examples of such "reactionary intrigue."

In 2005, a former Japanese commander at the Battle of Okinawa and a sibling of another former Japanese commander (deceased) sued Ōe Kenzaburō, together with Iwanami, claiming that a false characterization in Ōe's aforementioned *Okinawa Nōto* (Okinawa Notes) published by Iwanami in 1970—that the commanders forced Okinawans to commit "compulsory group suicide"—defamed them. Support for the plaintiffs has spread, despite the fact that the Supreme Court dismissed their claim in 2011 (Ōe Kenzaburō/Iwanami Shoten Okinawasen Saiban Shienrenrakukai, n.d.). Likewise, in December 2011, a work titled *Statue of a Girl of Peace* by Korean sculptors Kim Seo-kyung and Kim Eun-sung generated controversy as it was installed in front of the Japanese Embassy in Seoul to commemorate the one-thousandth Wednesday rally by former comfort women and their supporters. The bronze statue represented the sufferings of the women (many of them Korean) mobilized to sexually "comfort" soldiers of the Japanese Imperial Army during World War II. However, Fujimura Osamu, the Japanese government's main spokesman, "called the installation of the statue 'extremely regrettable' and said that his government would ask that it be removed" (Ching 2019, 75; cf. Yoneyama 2016, 171–172; see also Morris-Suzuki 2013). Yet, since then, copies of this statue have been created and installed within Korea and in countries such as the United States, Canada, Australia, and China. Then, in August 2019, a copy of this statue was exhibited at the Aichi Triennale in Nagoya City, and a man in his fifties threatened the organizer by sending a fax that said that he would come to the exhibition with gasoline, and he was arrested (Tanaka and Yamamoto 2019). The mayor of Nagoya City, Kawamura Takashi, supported, if only tacitly, such an act by stating that while the city contributed two hundred million yen of taxpayers' money to the Aichi Triennale, the exhibition of this statue and of works criticizing the emperor "trampled on the heart of the Japanese and was unacceptable" (Kawamura T. 2019). In September 2019, the Agency of Cultural

Affairs decided to withdraw subsidies it had committed to pay to the organizer, though in March 2020 it revised this decision and paid part of the subsidies after public criticism ("Aichi . . ." 2020).

Third, populist resentment is explicitly digitalized, linked to a process whereby the "imagined community" of official nationalism v.3 has become increasingly virtual, as illustrated by the fact that the term *dojin* has been utilized to describe Okinawans throughout cyberspace. For instance, a comment submitted to Yahoo Japan's online forum Chiebukuro on April 1, 2008, titled "On recent discrimination against Okinawa in Japanese society and Okinawa bashing . . . ," reads: "How do the Okinawans feel? I have read comments such as: 'You are *dojin*, so do not complain; simply shut up. . . . Okinawans lie. I wish the US bases would never disappear from Okinawa. Okinawans are like Chinese and Koreans. I wish Okinawans died in the Battle of Okinawa. . . . They are foreigners after all'" ("Saikin'no . . ." 2008). On April 7, 2015, a comment was posted on 5 Chan'neru, an online bulletin board, stating: "The Okinawa *dojin* are complaining again. Do they want more money? I wish they were dead" ("Okinawa-dojin ga . . ." 2015). If one searches the internet for the words "Okinawa, anti-base movements" (in Japanese), one will see all kinds of virtual abuse against Okinawans, a distorted form of "constituent power," appropriated and absorbed by nationalism and in cyberspace, as in programs on NBCS. Given the centrality of the internet today to the everyday life of the Japanese, particularly the youth, it would not be surprising if the riot police sergeant from Osaka had picked up the *dojin* vocabulary against Okinawa from cyberspace and allowed it to spill over into physical space through his offensive statement of October 2016.

Subways, barbershops, coffee shops, and residential neighborhoods used to provide the public with a space for reading newspapers (Anderson 1991, 35). Having once constituted a major forum for official nationalism v.1 and v.2, these locations have today—as indeed have all physical locations—been reconstructed as abstract "access points" linked by Wi-Fi or the 5G network to the broader cyberspace where the communicant, "in silent privacy, in the lair of the skull" (Anderson 1991, 35), checks the news, responds to emails, reads blogs, tweets and retweets, texts, post pics and videos, presses "like" buttons, and performs all sorts of virtual activities with little or no face-to-face interaction with other communicants. In the process, this communicative ceremony, now conducted, not daily or twice daily as in the age of print capitalism, but incessantly throughout the day and the night, is being replicated simultaneously by the population of "digital classes," which is significantly larger than that of the "reading classes" (Anderson 1991, 76) once created by print/analog capitalism in the age of official nationalism v.1 and v.2. Countless instances of praise or agreement expressed in cyberspace for the *dojin* statement of the riot police sergeant from Osaka in 2016 reveal the reach of the digitally mediated imagined community today, which communicants believe exists even though they have "not the slightest notion" of the identities of others in the community (Anderson 1991, 35).

My fourth and last point is that official nationalism v.3 is not linked with the idea of *kokutai* in general or with the emperor-centered worldview of *kōkoku-shikan* or related concepts such as *hakkōichiu* (eight corners under one roof) and *daitōakyōeiken* (greater East Asia co-prosperity sphere) in particular, as in the case of official nationalism v.1. Nor is it linked with the national, Japanized time-space organized by the analog media, as in the case of official nationalism v.2. Rather, it is embedded in the "homogeneous, empty time [and space]" (Benjamin [1942] 1968, 264; see also Anderson 1991, 24) of Empire. In this globalized time-space, issues of China, North Korea, the Middle East, and Russia are flattened to the language of "threats" without any historical sensibilities or place-based imaginations (Dirlik 1999), while the image of unpatriotic, traitorous Okinawans is reinforced because, by opposing the US military presence, such Okinawans allegedly jeopardize the security of Japan, the inside, against external threats, the outside, when the world market has already annihilated such boundaries. Boundaries between the inside and the outside, Self and Other, friends and enemies, in other words, are produced today within the same world market, within the global time-space.

Official nationalism v.3 becomes "official" as the state appropriates populist anger and resentment to undermine Okinawa's anti-base voices in this homogenous and empty, digitized time-space without history. Accordingly, politicians commented on the *dojin* incident not to criticize but to justify, if not praise, the riot police sergeant from Osaka. For instance, Tsuruho Yōsuke, then the minister of state for special missions concerning Okinawa and the Northern Territories (in office 2016–2017), stated that everybody has a right to speech and that he was not at all certain whether *dojin* is a discriminatory word ("Tsuruho Tantōsō . . ." 2016). Suga Yoshihide, then chief secretary of the Abe administration (in office 2012–2020) and later prime minister himself (in office 2020–2021), supported Tsuruho's comments by stating that the government shares the understanding that *dojin* cannot be considered a discriminatory word ("Suga-shi . . ." 2016). Matsui Ichirō, then prefectural governor of Osaka (in office 2011–2019), also stated that though the expression may not be appropriate, it is also true that the riot police from Osaka and across Japan were working extremely hard to prevent unnecessary conflicts from happening for the sake of Okinawa; he added that the protesters had become extreme, leaving an impression that protesters themselves were responsible for the *dojin* remark ("'Dojin' hatsugen mondai . . ." 2016).

・・・

Situating the *dojin* incident in the above four features of official nationalism v.3 (i.e., the fall of Japan and the rise of China in the Asia-Pacific region, the formation of the precarious Japanese, the digitalization of their anger, and the state's appropriation of such anger in the homogeneous and empty global time-space), my analysis reveals the ways in which Okinawa's antibase voice—the constituent power of the Okinawan multitude—has been systematically silenced by a peculiar mechanism that I call official nationalism v.3. That is, contemporary nationalism has not excluded Okinawa's anti-base voice. Rather, it has included such a voice while at the same time misrecognizing, trivializing, and controlling it as a voice of *dojin* in the new media space regulated by digital capitalism. The power and effectiveness of Okinawa's anti-base voice has thus been dramatically reduced precisely when the democratic potential of the digital time-space—inclusion of all voices (even hate speech, if taken as free speech)—has been materialized.

In the process, official nationalism v.3 has been fused with the rule of a broader security apparatus of Empire v.3, the objective of which is to eliminate "threats" from the global time-space for the maintenance of the smooth operation of contemporary capitalist production and accumulation, on the one hand, and to manipulate and regulate social life in the depths of human nature, on the other (see chapter 5, section 5).

For instance, in order to eliminate Okinawa's anti-base movements, understood as a "threat" to imperial security embedded in the capitalist global time-space, Tokyo has biopolitically disintegrated democracy further by taking advantage of the *dojin* incident. Indeed, after the *dojin* incident, Sakaguchi Masayoshi, secretary of the National Police Agency, stated, "The [*dojin*] statement made by a member of the riot police [in October 2016] was inappropriate and extremely regrettable." He added, "We will take all possible measures to eliminate incidents of this kind and will provide thorough instruction so that adequate security activities are conducted" ("'Dojin' Hatsugen no Kidōtai'in . . ." 2016). In line with this "democratic" (or egalitarian) statement, the tactics that the riot police have developed to manage anti-base protesters and that I discussed in chapter 1, particularly the deployment of digital cameras combined with the use of force, have been since then more orderly yet severely applied in Okinawa and elsewhere in Japan, to watch both the citizens (nation) *and* the police (state). In effect, Sakaguchi represented the global security apparatus of Empire v.3 beyond or behind the nation-state, constraining at once the constituent/democratic power of the nation over the police (state) and the constituted, tyrannical power of the police (state) over the nation—or really intensifying tyranny through the very principles of democracy Okinawa has sought—by way of radically inclusive digital technologies of watching, such that there is "watching of everyone against everyone," to modify Hobbes. In so doing, the global security apparatus has effectively rendered the existing binaries—such as "democracy and tyranny"—obsolete, preserving merely the appearance of democracy while destroying its substance.

Meanwhile, in order to manipulate and regulate Okinawa's social life in the depths of human nature, Tokyo has been using money, a process intertwined with the rise of official nationalism v.3. For instance, in a manner that has reinforced the anti-Okinawa sentiment brewed in official nationalism v.3, Tokyo reduced the Okinawa development budget by more than 20%, from 350.1 billion yen in 2014 to 268.4 billion yen in 2022 ("Okinawashinkōyosan . . ." 2021), as a punishment, as it were, for the anti-Tokyo attitude assumed by governors such as Onaga Takeshi (in office 2014–2018) and Tamaki Denny (in office 2018–present), as well as by the Okinawan "multitude" who have supported them, as explicated in Part I. Accordingly, in spite of the development of tourism in contemporary Okinawa (see chapter 2, section 2), the reality of the everyday work and life of the majority of the Okinawan multitude has increasingly become bleak. Uema Yōko (2017) analyzes the ways in which domestic violence has been produced and reproduced against women who, often with small children, supported themselves by doing night work in service industries of various kinds, for which wages are higher than for day work. Fujii Seiji (2018) explores the predicaments of sex workers in Okinawa from a historical and ethnographic perspective. Uchikoshi Masayuki (2019) documents the work and life of young, undereducated Okinawan males in the construction industry. In a way that confirms the distress of the Okinawan multitude described in these and other works, the number of contingent workers in Okinawa increased steadily, from 75,000 (17.7% of the employed labor force) in 1992 to 238,000 (43.0%) in 2012, to 253,800 (43.1%) in 2017, and to 247,000 (39.7%) in 2022, a higher percentage than any other prefecture in Japan ("Hiseiki . . ." 2015; Yagi 2018; Okinawaken Kikakubu Tōkeika 2022). As elsewhere in Japan, women in Okinawa have been particularly vulnerable (especially during the Covid-19 pandemic), because the majority of female workers (e.g., 82.8% in the hotel/restaurant service industry) are contingent workers without job security ("Kankōgyō . . ." 2018; Tamaki 2021). The poverty rate of children in Okinawa, an estimated 30%, has also been the highest in the nation ("Okinawa no Kodomo . . ." 2016). The average per capita income in Okinawa is still one of the lowest, or often the lowest, of any area in the nation. In effect, Tokyo has been using money as a method of manipulating and regulating social life in Okinawa in the process whereby it suppresses democracy.

The ways in which official nationalism v.3 has blended into the global security apparatus confirms my argument in Part III that Empire in the Asia-Pacific region reveals a double-sided character, both new (postmodern) *and* old (modern), imperial *and* colonialist, and American/global *and* Japanese/national. Implications of this "blending" will be explained in the conclusion to Part III.

Notes

1. The portion of the Northern Training Area was returned in December 2016 (Bōeishō, n.d.-g); the newly constructed helipads began to be used in July 2017 (Ryukyu Shimpo 2017).

2. The adjective "colonialist" is inserted in the term "colonialist Empire of Japan" in order to make explicit that the Empire of Japan at that time is to be differentiated from "Empire," defined in this study as "a *decentered* and *deterritorializing* apparatus of rule that progressively incorporates the entire global realm within its open, expanding frontiers" (2000: xii). Rather, the colonialist Empire of Japan was a variant of imperialism that was "really an extension of the sovereignty of the . . . nation-states beyond their own boundaries" (Hardt and Negri 2000, xii).

Conclusion to Part III

By showing that Empire in the Asia-Pacific region reveals a double-sided character, both new (postmodern) *and* old (modern), imperial *and* colonialist, and American/global *and* Japanese/national, Part III has complicated Hardt and Negri's proposition that "imperialism [i.e., colonialism] is over" (2000, xiv) in the age of Empire. I hasten to add that I deliberately misread what Hardt and Negri intend to convey by writing that "imperialism is over." Their intention is to argue that "no nation will be world leader in the way modern [imperialist] European nations were" (Hardt and Negri 2000, xiv), a claim with which I agree. Rather, Part III has shown that, even though Japan in the twenty-first century is not a "world leader," its imperialism/colonialism over Okinawa—ingrained in the form Japan has taken since the late nineteenth century—continues today in a different form and is fused with the rule of Empire, a rule that feels like an impeccably designed nightmare for Okinawan social actors held captive inside. For Okinawa has been trapped in Empire as "the most advanced and vital point in [the postwar security] structure" (FRUS 1948a, 700) and yet excluded from the constitutional norms of Japan, including Article 9. Not unlike a bare life in ancient Rome characterized by "its capacity to be killed" (Agamben 1998, 8), Okinawa's "capacity to be killed" has been ominously revealed beyond the threshold of possibility today, as the voice of Okinawa for peace has been continually silenced because of its inclusion by Empire combined with its exclusion by Tokyo, in the midst of the increasing danger that the US bases in Okinawa may become the target of China's missile attacks over issues concerning Taiwan.

This nightmare has continued ever since World War II. After surviving the disastrous Battle of Okinawa, Okinawa was excluded from the negotiations between John Foster Dulles (winner) and Hirohito, Emperor Shōwa (loser), who co-decided that the same Japanese state that had discarded

Okinawa as a sacrifice to protect Japan in that war would separate Okinawa from Japan "proper" to assist the United States in transforming Okinawa into the "Keystone of the Pacific" for the development of Empire v.1 between 1945 and the 1960s. Then, this separation—or the alienation of Okinawa from the rest of Japan—was reinforced for the formation of Empire v.2 from the 1970s to the 1990s through what I call "split governance" cogenerated by Washington and Tokyo, a form of rule enabled by the economic development of Japan as the "great workshop of Asia" and the military abuse of Okinawa as the "Keystone of the Pacific." Furthermore, the mechanism of split governance has been transformed in the twenty-first century into a generalized system of biopolitical control over everyday social life—the global security apparatus—across Japan as a whole *and* Okinawa in particular while perpetuating the unequal relations of power between them, a process that coincided with the formation of Empire v.3.

How might Okinawa be able to exit the nightmare of Empire in which it has become trapped? I will explore this question in Part IV.

PART IV

A Paradigm beyond Self and Other

The Okinawan Multitude within and against Empire in the Asia-Pacific Region

Introduction to Part IV

Pulling together key threads of analysis developed in Part I (anti-base struggles in Henoko and the formation of the Okinawan multitude), Part II (Okinawan subjectivity as "a *changing* same" and the historicity of the community of *nuchi du takara*), and Part III (formation and transformation of Empire in the Asia-Pacific region), Part IV investigates how the Okinawan multitude constructs its community and subjectivity and deploys a specific institutional mechanism in the planetary time-space to confront and negotiate with Empire. Two notions—"mimesis" and the "general will"—will conceptually structure my descriptions, analyses, and arguments in Part IV in search of a paradigm beyond Self and Other. While the notions of mimesis and general will will be fully elaborated in chapter 7 and chapter 8, respectively, this introduction explains the passage to this new paradigm—a paradigm beyond Self and Other—from the argument that I have developed in Part II.

In Freud's theorization, the sons are afflicted by the sense of guilt (ambivalence) due to their patricide; to overcome the ambivalence, they introduce and observe two taboos—"not to kill the totem and not to have sexual relations with a woman of the same totem" (Freud [1913] 1950, 132)—which is psychoanalytically equivalent with identifying with the father and redirecting sexual desires for the mother to other women. However, in this act of identification, I suggest, the Freudian sons accept, internalize, and institutionalize the violence of the father against women and thus reproduce patriarchy, a process captured in an ironic way in Frantz Fanon's *Black Skin, White Masks* ([1952] 1967).

For Fanon, the White man was the sublime object of identification: "I wish to be acknowledged not as *black* but as *white*" ([1952] 1967, 63; cf. Chen 2010, 77–78). The identification with the White man was made possible by Fanon's privilege as the "postcolonial bourgeois" (Bhabha 1994, 50), a medical doctor (a psychiatrist) educated in France. And yet this privilege also introduces a contradiction and split in his selfhood (cf. Bhabha 1994, 50): "As I begin to recognize that the Negro is the symbol of sin, I catch myself hating the Negro. But then I recognize that I am a Negro" (197). He tried to overcome this contradiction of self through a White woman: "By loving me she proves that I am worthy of white love. I am loved like a white man.... When my restless hands caress those white breasts, they grasp white civilization and dignity and make them mine" (63); "By marrying [a White woman], who [is] a European, I may ... appear to be making a show of contempt for the women of my own race and, above all, to be drawn on by desire for that white flesh that has been forbidden to us Negros as long as white men have ruled the world" (Maran 1947, 185, cited in Fanon [1952] 1967, 69–70). However, while a White woman may allow him to behave as if he were a White man, as if he replaced the father, and as if the father were dead, the act of sleeping with a White woman violates the heterosocial taboo instituted by this absent father, not to have sexual relations with the father's woman. The consequence—or perhaps, punishment—of violating the taboo was "psychopathology" (Fanon [1952] 1967, chap. 6). For Fanon demolished (by his act of breaking the taboo) as much as perpetuated (by the very necessity to break the taboo) the institution of "white men [who] have ruled the world." Fanon was haunted and controlled by the father in his very attempt to replace him through identification.

In contrast, Part II has shown that the Okinawan "people" were not able to replace the violent and omnipotent father, the US military; instead, they had to accept the father in exchange for money. It is this acceptance that generated Okinawa's ambivalence toward the US military. The Okinawan "people"—gendered as male, racialized as non-White, and class-bound as oppressed—coped with their ambivalence by establishing the homosocial taboo (forbidding friendship with the US military) and the heterosocial taboo (forbidding sexual relations between Okinawan women and US servicemen). In so doing, they constituted the androcentric community of *nuchi du takara* ("life is the ultimate treasure") in the local time-space, characterized by the *fraternal* bond of the poor/oppressed against the US military and the *fratriarchal* control over women and others such as mixed-race Okinawans.

Significantly, as Part II has also shown, the presence of the US military in postwar Okinawa was accompanied by the expansion of the commodity economy made possible by money as the "universal equivalent" (as Marx called it). Specifically, in the 1970s–1990s when money undermined the two androcentric taboos, Okinawan subjectivity was set in motion, and its androcentric structure was transformed into "a *changing* same," a historical-social-cultural movement for the expansion of equality and actualization of democracy, externally vis-à-vis the US military *and* internally within increasingly diversified Okinawa. Affluent and confident Okinawan "citizens"—in particular, women, in collaboration with the "people"—concretized this movement, reformulating the community of *nuchi du takara* in the national/Japanized time-space as they anchored the anti-base sentiments against the US military in the collective memory about the war, now projected against Japan.

The analysis of Okinawan subjectivity in Part II has begun to present the possibility of new life-forms and social relations in a manner that challenges what Freud theorized through his model of the Oedipus complex, the possibility of anti-Oedipus (Deleuze and Guattari 1983). Instead of deploying the taboos as a mechanism for the identification with and internalization of the father and for the reproduction of his power founded upon the distinction between men and women, White and Black, colonizer and colonized, as in Fanon, the Okinawan multitude, grounding itself in the depth of local history, constitutes the community of *nuchi du takara* within and against Empire through a different paradigm, a paradigm beyond Self and Other that undoes "colonial identification" (Chen 2010, 68).

To shed light on this paradigm, chapter 7 explores the mimetic faculty—the faculty of "becom[ing] and behav[ing] like something else," as Walter Benjamin ([1933] 1978, 333) defined it—of the Okinawan multitude at the level of everyday social life. I conceptualize the mimetic faculty of the Okinawan multitude as an expression of their constituent power to produce *not* an "essence" or an "identity" of Okinawa that is shared by all social actors *but rather* overlapping similarities and crisscrossing differences—"family resemblances" (Wittgenstein [1953] 2001, 27e)—whereby some life-forms, experiences, visions, and perspectives are shared by *some* (but not all) social actors for the construction of the community of *nuchi du takara*. What emerges in this community is a broader desire of the Okinawan multitude for universal peace, global democracy, and shared affluence. Articulating this desire in terms of what Jean-Jacques Rousseau called the "general will"—"the constant will of all the members" ([1762] 2014, book 4, chap. 2)—of this community, chapter 8 then seeks ways to materialize that will at an institutional level through collective security, to be exercised by a yet-to-come democratic supranational power that I call the World Republic of *nuchi du takara*. In so doing, I present a policy proposal to challenge, critique, and undermine the practice of collective (or regional) self-defense founded upon the binary between Self and Other, friend and enemy (see Part III). Indeed, this binary was deployed in the wars in the past (see chapter 5) and has been redeployed in the wars that we witness today, both actually (e.g., the Russian invasion of Ukraine and the Israeli-Palestinian conflict) and possibly (e.g., the Chinese invasion of Taiwan), as well as in other forms of violence that prevent us from actualizing universal peace, global democracy, and shared affluence.

Ultimately, what Part IV imparts is the planetary consciousness—or a critical perspective in the planetary time-space—beyond the paradigm of Self and Other, conveyed by the remarks of an undergraduate student that I quoted in the introduction to this book (A. Johnson 2023). To requote: "One day a few billion years from now, the earth will be swallowed by the sun as it begins to die. What is the point of killing innocents [in wars] when we can just live our lives in peace?"

Methodological Notes

Part IV utilizes methods of anthropology, cultural studies, and international relations. Data and information are thus collected from diverse sources, including but not limited to newspapers, magazines, video clips on the internet, films, music, photography, governmental documents, and prior scholarly works, as well as interview procedures that I conducted at various points in time. The interview dates will be noted in the text.

CHAPTER 7

The Mimetic Production of the Okinawan Multitude in the Planetary Time-Space

In analyzing the mimetic faculty of the Okinawan multitude, this chapter at once builds on and departs from postcolonial studies on mimesis. It builds on postcolonial studies on mimesis (Bhaba 1994; Chen 2010, esp. 96–101; Ōsugi 1999; Taussig 1993) by situating the mimetic faculty of the Okinawan multitude within specific relations of power and history. My analysis departs from postcolonial studies on mimesis, however, by overcoming the Self/Other (civilized/savage, West/rest, inside/outside) binary in which these studies were trapped.

Michael Taussig's anthropological study (1993), for instance, explores the two-way process whereby (*a*) the "savage" mimic the "civilized" externally to strengthen their internal substance (e.g., chaps. 1, 9, 10, and 13) and (*b*) the civilized contain and control the mimetic faculty of the savage though colonialism (chaps. 5, 6, 7, 11, 12, 13, and 14) and commodification (chap. 15). In spite of its breadth and depth, however, Taussig's analysis mostly stays within the Self/Other, West/rest, or inside/outside binary. To be sure, Taussig proposes "mimetic excess" as a strategy for subverting this binary, recognizing "the fact that the self is no longer clearly separable from its Alter" (1993, 252). And yet, this "self" remains a Western, White, male self vis-à-vis the Other, as Taussig himself acknowledges. For instance, Taussig states the following: "I am, as a 'European type,' brought to confront my cultured self in the form of an Indian figurine" (1993, 8); and

> For the white man, to read this face [of a mud sculpture of a white man made by natives in northern Iboland, Nigeria] means facing himself as Others read him, and the "natives' point of view" can never substitute for the fact that now the native is the white man himself, and that suddenly,

woefully, it dawns that the natives' point of view is endless and myriad. The white man as viewer is here virtually forced to interrogate himself, to interrogate the Other in and partially constitutive of his many and conflicting selves, and as yet we have few ground rules for how such an interrogation should or might proceed. (1993, 238)

In the end, it seems as if the authority of the West was reinserted precisely when it is deconstructed, a situation indicated by the passage where he states that "mimetic excess as a form of human [read "Western, White, male"] capacity potentiated by post-coloniality provides a welcome opportunity [for the Western White male like Taussig] to live subjunctively as neither subject nor object of history but as both, at one and the same time" (1993, 255). Here Taussig presents an anti-colonialist position, but this position is still based on "a theory of segregation [if] not a theory of hierarchy" (Hardt and Negri 2000, 193). For the West/Tausig embodies Self and Other but keeps them separated within it/him.

In contrast, I substantiate this mimetic excess in the planetary time-space against Empire, a time-space where Okinawan social actors in the twenty-first century reorganize the segregation between Self and Other, the West and the rest, into family resemblances, a perpetual dialogue of the Okinawan multitude to co-produce overlapping similarities and crisscrossing differences of life-forms, experiences, and perspectives in the community of *nuchi du takara*. Reminding that we are living on the planet Earth to which there is no more outside, a planet in which we are already connected as "travelers on the same boat" (Da Pump 2018, 1:04)[1] beyond the paradigm of Self and Other, I highlight that diverse individuals in twenty-first-century Okinawa not only "subjectively" or privately but also socially, politically, and planetarily enact mimetic excess at an intersection of gender, sexuality, race, class, age, and geography, among other attributes, as Heidi Safia Mirza (2013), among others, conceptualized it. In the process, as I will show, the Okinawan multitude expresses singularities of social actors—including nonhumans and the dead—by traversing three distinctive ontological layers of the community of *nuchi du takara* ("life is the ultimate treasure") explored in this book. More specifically, the Okinawan multitude expands the second layer of face-to-face communication into the third layer of global and virtual communication, while grounding these two layers in the first layer constituted by the death of others in the past and at present.

This chapter explores overlapping similarities and crisscrossing differences—family resemblances—of the Okinawan multitude by looking at the lives and works of (*a*) Cocco, an Okinawan female artist, (*b*) US servicemen stationed in Okinawa and long-marginalized mixed-race Okinawans as well as their mothers, together with sexual minorities such as gay US servicemen and queer Okinawans, and (*c*) Emperor Akihito and Empress Michiko. I choose these individuals for three different yet related reasons. First, they engage in, though they do not necessarily resolve, varied contradictions of postwar Okinawa identified in this book. Chief among these are a contradiction between the anti-base and pro-base sectors of Okinawa, noted in Part I and other parts of this book, in which Cocco engages; a contradiction in the very efforts to construct the Okinawan identity, which continue to exclude certain individuals, noted in Part II, a process mixed-race Okinawans and diverse US servicemen, among others, confront; and a contradiction of globalization (Empire), which reinforces nationalism (imperialism/colonialism), noted in Part III, which former Emperor Akihito and Empress Michiko address. Second, in so doing, these social actors reinforce the community of *nuchi du takara*, a cultural cushion between constituent power and constituted power, which has enabled them to externally engage in complex negotiations with the Empire on the basis of their internal capacities to embrace diverse and often contradictory attitudes, experiences, and perspectives regarding the US military and bases. Third, in the process, life-forms—the totality consisting of languages and actions into which they are woven—of these social actors throw into relief the general will of *nuchi du takara*, that is, a collective will of the Okinawan multitude for universal peace, global democracy, and shared affluence. It is by investigating this general will that I wish to capture what Gayatri Chakravorty Spivak (2003, chap. 3) calls *planetarity*, a time-space beyond—or, perhaps, across, within, beside, against, and prior to—the capitalist time-space Empire has controlled locally, nationally, and globally.

1. Cocco as an Artist Capturing Utopia from within the Contradictions of Everyday Life

1.1. Cocco as an "Artist"

Cocco is known as a musician, but in actuality she has not only produced music but also written books, taken photos, drawn pictures, initiated an environmental movement, and been featured in films and magazines as an actor and a model.[2] To capture her perpetual creativity, perhaps the category of "artist" may better define her life and work, part of which I analyze here to examine the ways in which she has contributed to producing the planetary time-space through her arts of capturing utopia from within contradictions of everyday life. Situating herself in the totality of the web of all life on this planet, she mediates a tension between those who participate in the protest movement in Henoko and those who do not or cannot, in a manner that shows the immense scale and depth of the community of *nuchi du takara* constructed by the Okinawan multitude.

Cocco originally came from Okinawa to Tokyo after graduating from high school intending to become a ballerina, not a singer; she considered music to be a sideline at that time (Cocco and Shibuya 2006, 20–27). However, this sideline activity caught the attention of some producers, and upon her debut in 1996 in Tokyo, Cocco became known as an Okinawan singer with an inimitable artistic sensibility, conveying a gamut of emotions in songs that are both disturbing and beautiful. For instance, in "Kubi" (Head) (1997a), the very first song of her debut album, titled *Būgenbiria (Bougainvillea)*, Cocco sang about a violent love to the beat of contemporary rock, expressing desire for destruction of a loved one. Yet juxtaposed with the sense of violence in "Head" and other songs of a similar nature was Cocco's expression of fragility and affection in a number of tranquil ballads such as "Hikōkigumo" (Winter Cloud) (Cocco 1997b) included on the same album. These songs exemplify a key theme in Cocco's early songs, the contradiction of love or the coexistence of possibility and impossibility in love: a longing for pure love makes life unbearably painful due to the impossibility of completely satiating this longing, which brings in the opposite drive for destruction of oneself as well as those one loves. It is by situating herself in this contradiction that she catches a glimpse of the utopia of love in the planetary time-space beyond the received boundaries of love.

Meanwhile, her sense of Okinawanness was relegated to the background, being only subtly evoked by such images as ocean, wind, flowers (such as bougainvillea), rain, and other elements of Okinawa's natural environment. Local musical instruments such as the *sanshin*, the Okinawan dialect, and the Ryukyuan musical scale—used in much of contemporary Okinawan popular music by artists such as Kina Shōkichi, the Nēnēzu, the Begin, the Rinken Band, and Natukawa Rimi, as anthropologist James Roberson (2009) insightfully noted—were not employed on *Būgenbiria* (Cocco 1997c). Cocco's translocal aspirations have been revealed also by the facts that all the lyrics on her debut album (together with lyrics on her other albums and her books and official website created later) have been translated and printed in English, a language imposed by Empire yet creolized by Cocco for communication in the planetary time-space, and that she even sings some songs in English, even though her English may contain grammatical errors and awkward turns of phrase. Cocco's cosmopolitanism, along with her talent as a singer-songwriter and the tasteful arrangement of her songs by her supporting band based in Tokyo, a global city created and recreated by the multitude, may explain the popularity of her music in wider Japan. Cocco's first album sold extremely well. Her second and third albums, released in 1998 and 2000, sold even better, each ranking number one for a few weeks on the nation's album chart (Youtaijyu 2009).

In 2001, at the peak of her fame, Cocco released her fourth album successfully. Shortly thereafter, however, she discontinued her activities and returned to Okinawa. The reason for her sudden withdrawal from the music scene was revealed in a conversation with noted journalist Chikushi Tetsuya. In a documentary titled *Heaven's hell* (2003), she told him, "I began singing not necessarily because I liked music. But as I sang, I found that I really loved singing, so I didn't want to make it a business" (35:15–35:20). What frustrated her specifically was the fact that due to the logic of the music industry centered on profit-making, she was not allowed to sing all the songs that constantly welled up from within her; she experienced this as "murdering" (Cocco and Shibuya 2006, 41) newly born songs. She quit singing to save these songs and to sing/release them on the beaches of Okinawa even if nobody—other than the ocean—would hear them (Cocco and Shibuya 2006, 44–45).

For two years after returning to Okinawa, Cocco maintained a low profile while drawing and publishing two picture books that shed light on her evolving emotional states. In the first picture book, entitled *Minami no Shima no Hoshi no Suna* (Star Sands in the South Ocean) (Cocco 2002), she used a lot of dark colors in a way that suggests the despair she felt at that time (ooba 2004; Cocco and Shibuya 2006, 45–48). However, her second picture book, published in 2004 and entitled *Minami no Shima no Koi no Uta* (Love Songs from the South Ocean) (2004), signaled Cocco's artistic renewal with its range of bright colors (ooba 2004). Subsequently, she released two new albums, one (her fifth) in 2006 and the other (her sixth) in 2007, while also appearing in numerous concerts, TV programs, radio programs, newspapers, and magazines in wider Japan as well as in Okinawa. The floodgates of her musical productivity had fully opened (Lycoris 2004–2010). She explained this change by referring to her awareness of being accepted, embraced, and loved by Okinawa (Lycoris 2004). This awareness seems to have constituted an important turning point in her artistic endeavor, in which Cocco found ways to ground and anchor her cosmopolitanism in a specific locality, as exemplified by the "Zero Trash Operations" discussed below.

As Manuel Castells (1997, 110–133) argued, concern about the environment has become a global issue since the 1970s. In post-reversion Okinawa, too, issues of environment—such as the disappearance of coral reefs, increase of garbage and waste, deterioration of Okinawan landscapes, and so on—have come to be widely recognized as a negative consequence of post-reversion Okinawa's economic development, conducted in the name of *hondonami* (catching up with the rest of Japan) and as political compensation for the continuing, indeed increasing, US military presence, as noted in chapter 5, section 3. Concerns over the environment have been intensified also due to the continuing presence of the US military bases, which has generated problems such as water pollution, soil pollution, and noise pollution, as noted in chapter 2, section 2.

After returning to Okinawa in 2001, Cocco became involved in issues of the environment by picking up trash that littered Okinawa's beaches. In 2003, as she began to regain her artistic strength, Cocco sublimated this personal effort into a social project titled the "Zero Trash Operations." In order to make her "operations" effective, Cocco decided to hold a miniconcert. This was not a "business," so she made it a volunteer-based concert without relying on any corporate sponsor. There she would sing "Heaven's hell," a song she had written that she referred to as "the song for picking up trash" (Cocco 2003, 11), accompanied by a high school brass band with more than sixty members and a chorus of about 140 Okinawan students and their parents, in order to deliver a message to Okinawa at large: "If this song reaches you, please pick up trash, even if it's just one piece" (Cocco 2003, 10). To highlight the significance of her endeavor, Cocco chose August 15, the anniversary of the end of World War II, as the concert date. In a conversation with Chikushi Tetsuya in *Heaven's hell* (2003, 33:10–34:15), Cocco explained that even though wars had been waged in the name of justice and that she was at a loss as to what she could do, "I pray for world peace. . . . On [August 15] when all people in Japan wish for world peace, I wanted to do something to concretize this prayer. I decided that I would pick up trash [and sing] on August 15."

The process of planning and organizing the concert was not necessarily easy, but her strenuous efforts bore fruit. On August 15, 2003, the concert venue—the schoolyard of a junior high school in Naha—was filled with an audience of two thousand people chosen by lottery from about seven thousand applications,[3] along with camera crews from the local and national TV stations (which broadcast the concert) and a movie company (which created a DVD of the concert). Before an expectant audience, Cocco appeared, dressed in a pink camisole and a white skirt and barefoot and looking utterly overwhelmed and almost in tears. Cheers of support came from the audience. Cocco, still shaking, took her place in front of the microphone, and the moment she began to perform, her timidity faded into calm. With a voice clear and pure, she sang "Heaven's hell" (*Heaven's hell* 2003, 48:50–59:10).

I hear this song—a prayer for peace—as an artistic intervention in a tension in the community of *nuchi du takara*, a tension between heaven and hell, life and death, or nature and history, revealing how the act of constructing peaceful postwar Okinawa (heaven/nature/life) has gone hand in hand with creating a heap of trash (hell/history/death), on the one hand, and with commemorating the war dead of the Battle of Okinawa (hell/history/death), on the other. Through this prayer as intervention, Cocco's performance merged with the shimmering band and the powerful chorus, transforming the ordinary schoolyard into the extraordinary, a site of what Christopher Small (1998) called "musicking," a complex and dynamic assemblage of actions, emotions, memories, dreams, images, and thoughts of all the people involved in a music event. When the song/prayer ended, many, including Cocco herself, burst into tears, suggesting the planetary, utopian time-space of the community of *nuchi du takara* that had been created out of the contradictions between heaven and hell, nature and history, and life and death within and against Empire.

Cocco repeated "Zero Trash Operations" in subsequent summers. In 2004, she even got the Okinawa prefectural government involved, mobilizing more than ten thousand people to collect 108 tons of trash across Okinawa (Lycoris 2004). Yet Cocco became increasingly disillusioned by her own success. In a 2006 concert, Cocco said from the stage, "Without knowing it, I was made to become an 'advertisement tower' for the ecological movement, and I question that" ("Cocco Hatsu . . ." 2006). After the mini-concert for "Zero Trash Operations" in the summer of 2003, indeed, she lived in England for five years (until 2008) to create a certain distance from Okinawa. Intertwined with this distancing is the sense of helplessness. Referring to her work as a whole, Cocco stated, "Things were making steady progress irrespective of my will, and I was more and more alienated from them" (2009, 34), adding, "Nothing changes no matter how much I sing" (2009, 35). The distancing from Okinawa has made her "a rootless wanderer" (Cocco 2007b, 30), but it also appears to have helped shape and reshape her critical, cosmopolitan consciousness as revealed in her engagement in questions of memory (hell/history/death), on the one hand, and the issue of the dugongs (heaven/nature/life), on the other.

1.2. Himeyuri: Bridging the Past, the Present, and the Future

In Okinawa and elsewhere in Japan, stories of the Himeyuri Gakutotai (Lily Princess Student Corps or Lily Student Corps) have been told and retold as the ultimate tales of victimization. Originally consisting of 222 students (between the ages of fifteen and nineteen) of the Okinawa Women's Normal School and the First Prefectural Girls School who had been mobilized as medical aides for the Japanese Imperial Army and the eighteen teachers who led them, the Corps lost 123 students and thirteen teachers in the Battle of Okinawa (Himeyuri Heiwa Kinen Shiryōkan 2006; Yoshida N. 2016, 240). One survivor, Kinjō Motoko, described what she experienced in a cave—used as an improvised "hospital" in the battlefield for accommodating more than three thousand wounded soldiers (Nakasone 1982, 95)—as follows:

> Due to the shortage of medical supplies . . . , soldiers' wounds were full of wiggling maggots. The cave was filled with groans of the soldiers in pain and sounds of the saws used for amputating their limbs. When I heard a soldier yelling, "I will curse the Yankees even after I die," I kept my blanket over me, covering my ears with my hands. When he became quiet, I found him dead. As the number of wounded soldiers increased, the regular nurses became too busy, and we helped them dispose of the soldiers' feces and urine. We were only fifteen to sixteen years old and were extremely embarrassed. (Nakasone 1982, 385–386)

On August 15, 2006, before the first solo concert she ever held in Okinawa, Cocco visited the Himeyuri Memorial, created in 1946 to commemorate Himeyuri students and their teachers. From the stage, as Cocco states in a collection of her essays and photos titled *Omoigoto* (Things I Contemplate):[4]

> I tried to explain to people about the meaning of Himeyuri. I still vividly remember the wind that blew just then. I remember how lashes of wind gathered under the flower-patterned silk dress I was wearing. How they gathered and swirled around me over and over again. I cannot but believe it was the wind of Himeyuri. The wind was there as if it were to support me, struggling to explain with words my innermost feelings. I was definitely feeling the wind of Himeyuri that night. (Cocco 2007a, 64)

After 2006, Cocco extended her involvement in Himeyuri issues by helping to promote a documentary titled *Himeyuri* (dir. Shibata Shōhei, 2007), which I watched in Okinawa in May 2010. Noting that the real voices of the survivors were seldom represented in the commercial films about the Lily Student Corps, Japanese director Shibata Shōhei spent thirteen years and interviewed twenty-two survivors to create the film as a synopsis of "true" Himeyuri experiences ("Eiga 'Himeyuri' . . ." 2007; Shibata 2009). The film has been highly acclaimed, receiving a number of prestigious awards in Japan and abroad. On August 15, 2007, in a small municipal all-purpose hall in Tokyo where the film was being shown, Cocco made a public appearance with two survivors, Shimabukuro Toshiko and Miyagi Kikuko, both featured in the film. Onstage, Cocco, along with Shibata as host, discussed Himeyuri experiences with the two survivors and then held a miniconcert for the audience. Let me focus on this event, documented in "Hōkoku: Tokubetsu Jōeikai 'Himeyuri no Kaze'" (Report: Special Screening, "The Wind of Himeyuri") (2007), to highlight how Cocco intervened in the everyday collective dilemma and contradiction over memory, where history has presented itself as something Okinawa cannot entirely forget or completely remember. Cocco, as an "artist," again situated herself in this dilemma and contradiction to capture utopia.

On the one hand, Cocco adamantly refused to let the memory of Okinawa's wartime experiences fade away. Cocco spoke specifically to the young audience, saying, "We should know about [these facts shown in the film]. That is our duty. . . . There are a lot of things we can learn from those survivors whom we can still touch." In so saying, Cocco actually extended her hands to touch Shimabukuro Toshiko sitting next to her, symbolically connecting the present to the past. In *Omoigoto* (2007a, 66), Cocco also wrote, "Thank you for telling us the harrowing story we should never forget."

On the other hand, however, Cocco also challenged and complicated the stereotypical narrative of victimization that the film might have reinforced. She did so in three different ways, while using Okinawa as a mirror, as it were, upon which her cosmopolitan consciousness was articulated. First, Cocco underscored the agency of the survivors to discover the joys of life in spite of (or precisely because of) the unspeakable experiences of the war, by composing a beautifully cheerful song titled "Sweets and the Girls" for the survivors. This song, included in the miniconcert at the municipal hall as well as on her sixth album, was inspired by one brief line in the film *Himeyuri* spoken by a survivor, Miyagi Kikuko, who talked about the pleasurable memory of hearing, in the cave, a song titled "A Parisian Girl Who Likes Sweets," sung by a young woman teacher. Cocco stated, "When I watched this movie, I thought about how I could make the survivors laugh. They must have been asked so many times, 'How was the war?' My concern was for them to have a good time after talking about their experiences of the war."

Second, Cocco illuminated the active role the audience plays in the construction of memory, by saying, "It is understandable that the younger generation does not fully understand the war experiences. Do not feel guilty just because you don't understand them. . . . [But it is important to know about them because] if we know, we may be able to understand them later on and may get connected to those who experienced them." Put differently, against the tendency to privilege the film as an authentic representation of the truth flowing to the audience in a one-way system of communication, Cocco emphasized that the truth is constructed intersubjectively through dialogue between the survivors and the audience.

Third, she marked the unmarked position of the film by interjecting that "survivors were made to talk about the war over and over again, and were made to cry over and over again." In so saying, Cocco shed light on memory as a performance, enacted by the survivors (women/Okinawa) on a stage set up by the director (a man/Japan) and sold as a commodity for the audience (young Japanese/Okinawans without war experiences). Indeed, though the film was inspired by a request from one of the survivors to document Himeyuri experiences truthfully, director Shibata Shōhei discarded the script prepared by the survivors. Instead, he chose to have them talk about their experiences at the sites where the tragedies of the killing and dying occurred, in order to dramatize the totality of the Himeyuri experiences as he saw them ("Eiga 'Himeyuri' . . ." 2007). I do not mean to accuse Shibata of manipulating the survivors' will. Rather, with Cocco, I simply want to highlight memory as commodified performance, shedding light on how this "documentary"—like other commercial films about Himeyuri—was implicated in specific relations of power, money, and history.

As Linda Angst (1997) has noted, the narrative of Himeyuri survivors has often manifested a problematic tendency to highlight personal experiences of victimization without critically scrutinizing the issues of the larger sociopolitical structure, such as the responsibility of the prewar Japanese state, of the emperor, and—if I may add—of Okinawa's own participation in the prewar ideology surrounding the emperor, as noted in chapter 6. Indeed, a memorandum of eight students who had evacuated to Japan "proper" instead of joining the Himeyuri Corps revealed that although the majority of the teachers and parents had been opposed to sending the students to the battlefield as medical aides because of the anticipated risk of death and injury, their opinion was suppressed by the executive members of the school who, having connections to the Imperial Army, threatened these teachers and parents with a demand that scholarships the students had received be returned. While most parents tearfully agreed to send their daughters to the battlefield due in part to this threat, some students, under the subtle encouragement of their teachers, ended up evacuating in spite of being called "anti-Japanese" and "cowards" ("Arekara 30nen" 1975).

Through the very act of her involvement in Himeyuri, Cocco may have unwittingly reinforced the tendency to victimize and idealize Himeyuri students and teachers. Nonetheless, she also illuminated the memory not as a finished text detached from specific sociohistorical contexts but as a process involving dynamic negotiations of diverse positions and perspectives—the Okinawan multitude—within such contexts. In working through the questions of memory, Cocco established a historical agency that has actively opened up, through the mimetic faculty—the faculty of becoming and behaving like the Other/Himeyuri, of producing similarities with rather than differences from the Other/Himeyuri—the possibility of dialogue across generations for the past, present, and future of the Okinawan multitude in a way that manifested the planetary time-space against Empire.

1.3. "The Hill of Dugongs": Overcoming the Ambivalence toward the US Military in the Planetary Time-Space

It is with this historical agency that Cocco has intervened in the questions of the US military bases in Okinawa and, in so doing, has engaged in the questions of nature in order to assemble her planetary consciousness.

As discussed in chapter 1, since 1996 the debate over the US military presence in Okinawa has centered on the controversy over the proposal to construct a new facility in Henoko, Nago City, as a replacement for Futenma Air Station, the Futenma Replacement Facility (FRF). Due to sustained local social movements in Henoko/Nago against the proposal, the plan changed again and again—from building an offshore facility in 1996, to reclaiming land from the sea and making it into a commercial-military airport in 1999, to creating a V-shaped airport inside Camp Schwab in 2006. By 2007, Cocco could say, "The situation is so complicated that one cannot simply say no [or yes] to the base. Everybody wishes to make Okinawa better, but sadly, everybody's [wishes clash]" (Lycoris 2007). She also stated in *Omoigoto*: "I never publicly gave my yes or no to [the matters of the US bases in Okinawa] . . . I want people to know that forcing a yes or no from a person can be cruel" (Cocco 2007a, 16), adding, "Getting Okinawa back from the American military forces would simply kick-start endless relocations, a baton relay in search of another site. We would be simply passing on the struggle to others" (Cocco 2007a, 16). Via dugongs, however, Cocco was led to articulate herself in this contradiction between yes and no to the US military, that is, yes in terms of friendships and relationships at the level of everyday social life with American military personnel and their families (such as her first boyfriend, see below) but no in terms of the violence the military exercises at the level of global politics and history and in which Okinawa has been implicated.

In June 2007, in the midst of the complications of the Futenma relocation issue, two swimming dugongs were videotaped by an Okinawan TV crew flying in a helicopter over the cape of Henoko at Camp Schwab, the planned site of the new military base (Neko3_Paradisez 2016). Having watched this news on TV with tears, Cocco (2007c) composed a song titled "Jyugon no Mieru Oka" (The Hill of Dugongs) in order to express her wish to protect Okinawa's ocean in spite of the complexity of the US base problems ("Okinawa no Umi . . ." 2009). Cocco (2007a, 16) wrote in *Omoigoto*, "Suddenly, for the first time in my life, I had a clear wish in my mind . . . a wish to see the beautiful islands once more, an Okinawa without any military existence [as a political institution inflicting violence]."

In this song, which became an immediate hit in Okinawa and elsewhere in Japan, Cocco attempted to overcome the ambivalence, or "the simultaneous existence of love and hate," as Freud ([1913] 1950, 157) defined it, toward the US military that I discussed in Part II—in which an "anti-base" desire to remove the US bases for peace clashes with another, "pro-base" desire to use revenues generated by the bases for happiness and a better life—by introducing and utilizing the mimetic faculty of presenting the perspective of the dugongs. Cocco commented in one of the concerts that "even though we may not be able to judge everything in terms of yes or no, I would like us to think about what is necessary and right from the dugongs' perspective" (Lycoris 2007). In other words, she relativized and decentered this human dilemma by situating it in the totality of the web of *all* life on this planet in a manner that highlighted *nuchi du takara*, "life is the ultimate treasure." Indeed, this song can be heard as one subverting the human-centered notion of ecology—such as "sustainable development" and "coexistence with nature," both of which often prolonged and reinforced capitalist exploitation of nature, after all—if one takes into consideration her essay, in which she stated that she wants to offer herself as a sacrifice in order to settle the US base problems, adding that "this ocean is the dugongs' ocean" (Cocco 2010).

A telling anecdote to be added here—one that shows her affinity to such subversively spiritual sensibilities of Okinawan women—is that Cocco almost became a *yuta* (a shaman healer; most *yuta* are women) at the age of sixteen in obedience to the will of ancestry gods after becoming temporarily possessed, an experience referred to locally as *kamidāri* (Cocco 2009, 38–39). As noted in chapter 4, section 2, the *yuta*, whose presence dates back to the age of the Ryukyu Kingdom, have continued to exercise their influences as "folk counselors" (*no no kaunserā*) (Ōhashi 1983, 14) to the present time in spite of repeated attempts of authorities (men) to suppress and control them; they have healed, consoled, and counseled families and individuals under stress and despair by uniting the living with the dead, humans with nature, and here with there through the act of possession. Like these shamans, Cocco, with the faculty of becoming and behaving like the Other, has given voices to those who do not have voices, such as the war dead and the dugongs, through her songs and other activities as an "artist." Or rather, the dugongs, the rain, the wind, and the ocean—as well as the dead—spoke *through* her in a range of artistic activities and performances. As Cocco stated, "When I sing my songs, I often wonder . . . whose songs these are, because I [often feel like something possessing me and] don't realize these are the songs of my own making" (Cocco and Shibuya 2006, 34). In chapter 4, section 2, in reference to debate over *tōtōme*, I presented *yuta* in part as an obstacle to women's liberation. Here I complicate my own analysis by discussing transformative potentialities of their presence.

Indeed, as a woman situated in the totality of the web of all life on this planet, Cocco, like *yuta*, has crossed multiple borders. Namely, she has traversed local (via Himeyuri), national (via "Zero Trash Operations"), and global time-space (via the US military issues) to open up possibilities for social change in the planetary time-space (via the dugongs), possibilities—like dreams—that may vanish as soon as they are materialized as an explicit political program but that may nonetheless contribute to transforming the existing order from a hinterland of political and social struggles.

Such possibilities are felt by many of those who listen to her music. A male Japanese fan wrote, for example, "A verse in her song titled *Fūkafūsō* (Weathering and Disposition of a Dead Body) says, 'That's all right / You will soon / Forget me,' but I will never forget. That's why I have written this passage here and left it [in this site permanently]" (Tomii 2001). Another Japanese fan posted a message on YouTube that reads, "I just want to thank the fact that a being like her exists in this world" (chohsuke 2009). Still another Japanese fan stated on Amazon.co.jp, "It feels as if God spoke to me through her music.... It's riveting" (postman 2019). From outside Japan, a Korean fan wrote (in Japanese) on Amazon.co.jp about how Cocco's music made her (most likely her) sense something she was not aware of but nonetheless exists (Kasutamā 2004), while an individual who appears to be a native speaker of English wrote on YouTube, "I'm so deeply touched [by 'Heaven's hell'], simple yet profound" (erbeeflower 2009).

• • •

A disclaimer needs to be inserted before completing this section, for my analysis on Cocco may confuse abstract possibility with concrete reality, imaginative cultural practices with actual political changes. For instance, when observing that Cocco's visions, actions, and prayers have been reduced to T-shirts, handkerchiefs, cell phone straps, and other commodities, all available online through her own official website run by Cocco Co., Ltd. (2010), one cannot help feeling that her utopian agency—exemplified by her statement, cited previously, that "I [don't] want to make [music] a business"—has been controlled, reshaped, and even erased by the power of capital. Cocco's then recurrent eating disorder (Cocco 2009) may have something to do with this power of capital. Her anorexic body vis-à-vis the ever "fattening" music industry can be seen as a symptom of larger social processes whereby the body—the very site of our constituent power—is not liberated for love and peace as Cocco envisions but is always already appropriated and extracted by the constituted power of capital for the global game of profit, marketability, and instant consumption. The potency of Cocco's artistic intervention in the US base problems has thus remained ambiguous, as she herself noted in *Omoigoto*: "[If the bases are removed from Okinawa,] then, who on earth is going to carry the burden? I cried out of helplessness, as I knew my emotions were totally lacking any sense of responsibility. Somebody, please help!" (Cocco 2007a, 16).

But I want to argue, with Slavoj Žižek (2008, 4), that the very confusion, inconsistency, and ambiguity—even failure—of Cocco's intervention "is part of the solution." For it makes her music truthful, helping us catch a glimpse of a form of everyday violence at work, violence that has sustained and reproduced the US base problems in her/our very effort to settle them. It is within and against this violence that Cocco has shown how art has become part of the very real, though ultimately unavowable, community of *nuchi du takara* of the Okinawan multitude in search of love and peace.

2. Mixed-Race Okinawans and US Servicemen: Negotiating the Contradiction of the Okinawan Identity

Allow me to add one more piece of analysis on Cocco to create a transition to the investigation about experiences of mixed-race Okinawans and US servicemen as integral constituents of the community of *nuchi du takara*, as they occupy and produce the planetary time-space by expressing the general will of the Okinawan multitude for not only love and peace (as shown above) but also democracy and the shared affluence they produce as living labor.

In the "Zero Trash Operations" concert, Cocco extended the community of the Okinawan multitude by inviting mixed-race children born to US servicemen and Okinawan women and their mothers to be members of the chorus (*Heaven's hell* 2003, 15:30–19:20). As noted in chapter 3, section 2, mixed-race Okinawans were harshly discriminated in postwar Okinawa. Exercising the mimetic faculty of becoming and behaving like the Other/mixed-race Okinawans, Cocco also wrote:

> Everybody experiences life-changing encounters with special individuals. Without them, or this person I am going to talk about, I am not sure if I could exist. He was somebody who existed beyond the boundaries of "I love you" and meant absolutely everything to me, who had no means but to

"love" somebody. He was an Amerasian, who had only distant memories of his father, born between an American serviceman and an Okinawan woman.

Okinawans are known to be gentle in nature.

Compassionate and generous, that's how people describe us.

However, through this person, who was also my first boyfriend, I witnessed an entirely different Okinawa. My beloved Okinawa acting in the most unforgivable way to him. I don't know how to say this, but the rejection of American military bases, to me, was tantamount to rejecting who he was. (Omoigoto 2007a, 16)

As discussed in Part II, discrimination against mixed-race children in postwar Okinawa unfolded hand in hand with the two androcentric taboos, a homosocial taboo forbidding friendship with the US military and a heterosocial taboo forbidding sexual relationships between Okinawan women and US servicemen. More specifically, in postwar Okinawa through the 1960s, while the former may have enabled the Okinawan "people" to establish Okinawan fraternity, the latter contributed to internal gender and class oppression and exclusion. In an NHK TV program titled "Uchinā o Toru: Shashinka Ishikawa Mao" (Capturing Okinawa: Photographer Ishikawa Mao) (PMG5 2016), Higa Maria, a woman born to a White serviceman and an Okinawan woman working for a bar in Henoko toward the end of the 1960s, thus explained to Mao (whose work and life is analyzed in chapter 4) that Okinawan men had called her "a child of *panpan*" (a derogatory term meaning prostitute) when she was young, adding: "My heart aches for the suffering of these men. They had a fear or something that they would lose their own position if they did not make fun of me.... It was only by ridiculing me and my mother that they were able to puff out their chests as Okinawan men" (21:10–21:30). In post-reversion Okinawa (1970s–1990s), the status of women improved but mixed-race Okinawans—together with their mothers and fathers, among others—were continuingly excluded from the community of the Okinawan "citizens," as also noted in Part II.

This does not mean that the issues of discrimination against mixed-race children were completely ignored in postwar Okinawa. For instance, at the institutional level, International Social Service Okinawa (ISSO)—established in 1958 under International Social Service, an international NGO created in 1924—was instrumental in providing legal and social services to mixed-race children and their mothers over issues such as international adoption, marriage, divorce, and abandonment in US-ruled Okinawa. In April 1972, right before reversion, ISSO was reorganized as International Social Assistance Okinawa (ISAO) to expand the services provided by ISSO (Oyakawa 2019). One of ISAO's key accomplishments was its 1979 proposal concerning mixed-race Okinawans who had no citizenship, an issue generated by the paternalism of the Japanese citizenship law—that is, children were legally recognized as Japanese only when their fathers were Japanese. Accordingly, many mixed-race Okinawans were left citizenshipless because their fathers were not Japanese (so they could not get Japanese citizenship) and they were often abandoned by their American fathers or did not know who their fathers were in the first instance (so they could not get American citizenship). ISAO's 1979 proposal contributed to a change in the Japanese citizenship law in 1986, which now recognizes children as Japanese if either their fathers or mothers are Japanese (Ōshiro M. 1985, 215–221). ISAO was absorbed by the Okinawa prefectural government's Women's Center in 1998 after having handled more than fifteen thousand cases in its forty-year history. Meanwhile, in the second half of the 1990s, in a way that extended the efforts of ISSO/ISAO, mothers of mixed-race children and others took the lead to establish a school for them, Amerasian School in Okinawa (Uezato K. 1998). It was students of this school and their mothers who joined the chorus for Cocco's "Zero Trash Operations" concert.

That mixed-race Okinawans were legally and socially recognized as citizens in post-reversion Okinawan society has not resolved issues of their vulnerability at the level of everyday life, however. For one thing, those in power appropriated them as a convenient symbol of internationalization and multiculturalism as well as a fashionable commodity of difference to be sold and bought on the culture market. For instance, for the 2000 G-8 Okinawa Summit, Tokyo designated Amuro Namie—a popular female Okinawan singer with mixed-race heritage—as the representative of Okinawa and Japan at large, having her express the ideal of global connectedness with the theme song of this political show at a reception to welcome world leaders (Inamasa Channel 2017). The situation was highly "imperial" (not "imperialist"), in that mixed-race Okinawans, gendered as female, were not excluded and oppressed but actively incorporated and celebrated in the representation of Okinawa and Japan at large, but nonetheless, as Shimabukuro Maria (2002) has suggested, their agency was erased in the binary between the local impulse to marginalize them (often even in the act of rescuing them) and the global strategy to idealize and commodify them.

The use of Amuro effectively reproduced the Orientalist binary of Self (Okinawa and Japan at large) and Other (the "world" represented by the Group of Eight), in which those in power, over the shoulder of the mixed-race Okinawan woman, "interpellated" or "hailed" (Althusser 1970, 37 and 40) the subject (Okinawans) as the subject (Japanese)—or gave identity to Okinawans as Japanese—as part of a larger global mechanism to produce, integrate, and orchestrate a spectrum of cultural differences in the system of control and management. In so doing, ideology—a system of ideas and ideals produced by those in power—"*subjects* the subjects [Okinawans as Japanese] to the Subject [the state/Empire]" (Althusser 1970, 45).

In a way that defies this erasure of agency, however, diverse voices of mixed-race Okinawans from below have also become more forcefully expressed and positively recognized in twenty-first-century Okinawa, as represented by the election of Tamaki Denny, who has a mixed-race background—his father was a marine he never met ("Ano . . ." 2020)—as the new governor of Okinawa in 2018. Governor Tamaki emphasizes not so much the identity of Okinawa as the diversity of Okinawa (or diversity as Okinawa's identity) in his political platform (Higa Mo. 2018). Put differently, mixed-race Okinawans have asserted their singularities even as they are commodified, objectified, and exchanged on the culture market, as Shimoji Lawrence Yoshitaka (2018, 229–232) noted in the context of twenty-first-century Japan at large. Combined with other publications about her life, my interview in January 2020 with Ms. O., a mixed-race Okinawan woman in her mid-thirties fathered by a Black US serviceman, confirms this point. (January 2020 is the present time in the description about Ms. O. below.)

Ms. O. is the wife of an Okinawan man and the mother of four small children; she lives in a town in northern Okinawa and, as a designer, runs a clothing and accessory shop in a market with her husband, a dyer. Her father had been stationed at a base in northern Okinawa when he met Ms. O.'s mother, who had run a barbershop, but he left Okinawa when she was four years old. While she was able to maintain a correspondence with him until she finished middle school—he even came to Okinawa when she was fifteen—Ms. O. came to know that he was married to another woman in the United States and had become the father of three children (Agarie 2017, 76).

She is painstakingly aware of the contradiction that the very presence of US bases that has affirmed and enabled her life has also become the cause of discrimination that has denied her life (Hatachi 2018). This contradiction manifested itself specifically and acutely in the case of mixed-race Okinawans with Black backgrounds, as a novella titled *Aru Hizumi* (A Strain) by Fukumura Takeshi (1962) shows. This novella describes the ways in which a traditional Okinawan family handles the birth of a mixed-blood child born to one of its daughters (Saeko) and a Black serviceman. The father of the family has died in the war and, judging from a somewhat vague description in the text, Saeko appears to be working in a pleasure quarter around a major US base to support the family. In the meantime, the mother, Kane, unaware of Saeko's situation, is openly quite critical of young women who have relationships with servicemen, "as if she instinctively expressed a sense of disgust at such relationships" (12), in a manner that reveals Okinawa's two taboos noted above, "Do not develop friendship with the US military" and "Do not allow sexual relationship between Okinawan women and US servicemen." However, eventually, Kane learns of Saeko's pregnancy, a fact that prompts Kane to reposition herself vis-à-vis the collective taboos: "The premature baby safely delivered [in the US military hospital] was neither black nor yellow; depending on the viewer's perspective it could be both, a real half-breed boy with a smooth skin. . . . [Kane and Saeko's sister] felt somehow relieved. They looked in each other's eyes to share their sentiment, 'This sort of color is all right'" (15) (see also Nakahodo 2008, 222).

The 1995 rape of an Okinawan schoolgirl by two marines and one sailor (discussed in the introduction to this book and in chapter 4, section 5) and the 2016 rape and murder of a twenty-year-old Okinawan woman by a former marine (noted in chapter 1, section 2), among other crimes, may have reinforced the negative images of US servicemen, particularly Black servicemen, because these crimes were committed by men with Black racial backgrounds. Ms. O.'s experience indeed reveals the continuity of discriminations against mixed-race Okinawans in general and against those with Black backgrounds in particular, as she has encountered hateful comments concerning her appearance, such as *amerikā* (American), *kuronbō* (Black), and *kawaikunai* (unattractive) ever since she was little, as well as seemingly innocent comments by adults to describe her children, such as "They look different." Ms. O. is sensitive to such comments because they are often tied to "a human emotion that constitutes the foundation of war, the use of weapons" (Agarie 2017, 79)—an emotion that is based on the binary between Self and Other, or "friend and enemy," as Carl Schmitt put it ([1932] 1976).

Yet, in a manner that would enable her to build on and overcome the experiences of mixed-race Okinawans having lived in the age of the Okinawan "people" (1950s–1960s), as in the family described in *Aru Hizumi*) or of Okinawan "citizens" (1970s–1990s, as in the example of Higa Maria), F. A. has devised a number of strategies to express "something" that one fails to grasp if one approaches it with an anti-base/pro-base (or progressive/conservative, good/bad) dichotomy, as she opposes the US military (or military violence more generally) at the institutional level *and* accepts the US military and embraces mixed-race Okinawans like herself at the level of everyday life.

Accordingly, she has been involved in anti-base activities such as (*a*) becoming an editorial member of a grassroots magazine titled *Pikunikku* (Picnic) published to raise questions and awareness about the US base issues in Okinawa, (*b*) joining rallies, sit-ins, and meetings (including those held in Henoko) together with her husband and children to oppose the construction of the FRF in Henoko, and (*c*) participating in photographer Ishikawa Mao's anti-base photo exhibition series titled *Dai-Ryūkyū Shashin Emaki* (The Great Ryukyu Photo Scrolls) (see chapter 4, section 4). Ms. O.'s engagement in the US base issues has not been confrontational or agitative but rather dialogic and inclusive in that she has sought circuits of conversation—that is, the community of *nuchi du takara*—across difference, even with US servicemen, at the level of everyday social life. In pursuing an approach that simultaneously opposes and embraces the presence of the US military in Okinawa, Ms. O. asserts that she is not a *hāfu* (mixed-race person) or a *daburu* (double-race person), or even an "Amerasian," the term popularized in the 1990s in the movement for establishing a school for mixed-race Okinawans noted above, because these are the categories provided and imposed by society. Rather, "I am me" (*watashi wa watashi*), not fully contained by any of these imposed social categories, as she produces herself as a singularity, part of the Okinawan multitude (see also Hatachi 2018 and Higa Mo. 2018).

She claims her cosmopolitan aspiration as a singularity—"I am me"—in two additional yet interrelated ways. First, she radically grounds this aspiration in local cultural practices, a strategy developed by mixed-race Okinawans such as (*a*) Byron Fija, a well-known advocate of the identity he calls "American-Okinawans," who is more fully versed than many contemporary Okinawans in the Okinawan language ("dialect"), *sanshin* (a three-stringed musical instrument), and other forms of traditional "Ryukyuan" culture (yuken teruya studio 2014), and (*b*) informants anthropologist Mitzi Uehara Carter studied, who "are proud of their detailed knowledge of Okinawan ancestral religious practices and incorporate this into their rooted sense of belonging to the island" (2014, 658). For Ms. O., Okinawa has already been diluted or contaminated due to excessive Japanization. She has tried to reclaim the "rooted sense of belonging" *against* diluted or contaminated Okinawan identity through her work, for instance, in which she uses authentic Okinawan dying materials—known as Ryukyu indigo—handmade by her husband to color the clothes and accessories that she produces for her shop. In a way that reinforces her attempt to protect—or really produce—her rooted sense of belonging, Ms. O. added in my interview, categorically, "I don't like Japanese," including those "sympathizers" who have migrated to Okinawa to go native: they would dilute or contaminate Okinawa further in their very goodwill, in their very attempt to sympathize with Okinawa.

Second, Ms. O. has extended her cosmopolitan aspiration as a singularity—"I am me"—by coming to understand her father and his current family in a positive light, in a manner that challenges and complicates stereotypically negative images of US servicemen, particularly Black servicemen, in Okinawa. That is, even though she had lost contact with her father after he came to Okinawa when she was fifteen, Ms. O. has recently reconnected with him and with his family through social media, a method of global communication that allows her to mimetically construct a "family" across the Pacific in the planetary time-space, a family that is situated on the border of reality and virtuality, presence and absence.

More specifically, Ms. O. searched for her half-siblings on Facebook on the basis of her father's family name and found a woman whose physical features resembled hers. Ms. O. contacted her, confirmed she was her half sister, obtained her father's telephone number from her, and talked with him on the phone. Even though limited contact (e.g., letters and gifts) had made his presence "abstract" when she was young, fresh conversation with him, together with these letters and gifts she had received in the past, helped her to comprehend, if not to fully accept, the fact that the father could not get in touch with Ms. O. even though he loved her (Agarie 2017, 75–77). She even communicated to him her wish that he should or could live in Okinawa for the rest of his life, an act that would make up for his absence while young, but he declined her request by citing discrimination against foreigners in Okinawa and the business he had run in the United States as some of the key reasons. Meanwhile, Ms. O. has been video chatting with her half sister more than once a month. Furthermore, she has come to know that her half brother served in the US Air Force and was deployed to Iraq and Afghanistan for specific missions. While she cannot possibly accept his institutional military actions (involving, possibly, destruction, or worse, killing), Ms. O. is sympathetic with the general socioeconomic situation in the United States, where many young people join the military due to poverty.

・・・

In order to complicate and challenge the negative images of the US servicemen further, to include them in the category of the Okinawan multitude, and to situate their lives in the planetary time-space of their community of *nuchi du takara* within and against Empire, I proceed to analyze the experiences of some veterans who have been stationed in Okinawa and elsewhere. Allow me to emphasize that I introduce their life histories not to deny, erase, or ignore crimes and atrocities of the US military and some of its servicemen. Indeed, the life stories below show that US servicemen are often themselves critical of military violence as a form of institutional violence.

Mr. G. is a former marine.[5] In my interview with him in May 2013, he explained that he was born in an eastern Kentucky town with a population of ten thousand, "which has pretty much nothing except coal mines, fast-food restaurants, and . . . a small community college." Many residents used drugs. Out of sheer desire to get out of that town and to "be [his] own man," he joined the US Marine Corps after graduating from high school. In a manner that confirms Ms. O.'s insight above, poverty—or, lack of resources, opportunities, and hopes, more broadly—became one of the basic motivations for him to join the Marine Corps. This is an observable pattern among other veterans that I interviewed. It should be added that the lives of veterans are often difficult even after being discharged from the military. When I interviewed him, Mr. G. continued his night work from 10:00 p.m. through 8:00 a.m. at a lightbulb factory to support himself.

Upon completing basic training, Mr. G., at the age of nineteen, chose to go to Okinawa in June 2007 to "experience something new." He was stationed at a base in northern Okinawa. At first, he regretted coming to Okinawa because he found the new surroundings, the weather in particular, difficult to adapt to, but before long, in a movie theater in a shopping district in central Okinawa, he met an Okinawan who became his girlfriend (and became his wife in 2010). He was liberated from the stifling lifestyle of many servicemen—getting stuck on the base all the time, as another serviceman from Kentucky, C. B., noted in an interview I conducted in March 2019—and became better situated in Okinawan life and society. Even though he does not "want to say they accepted me as one of their own," interactions with Okinawans did help him see that "there is more than the United States, more than Kentucky."

Then, for nine months from March 2008, Mr. G. was deployed to Iraq as a member of a gunfire support unit. He thought at that time that he came to Iraq for freedom, but at the time of the interview (May 2013) he was no longer sure. The area was dangerous. Bombs were hidden by the side of the road or behind trash bags; in one situation, two Iraqis blew themselves up apparently by mistake right before Mr. G.'s truck drove by. He saw their blown-up bodies "crispy." He was in charge of a machine gun on the truck, often standing up eighteen to nineteen hours straight, through heat and cold. When I asked if he had ever used that machine gun, he responded, "I don't feel comfortable answering that question." Iraqi people earned $2 an hour by hauling trash at the station, while the contractor from a major American development company earned $80,000–$90,000 by "sitting and sleeping" there. "I am a little bit bitter about them." At the station, he took boxes of candy bars (which no service member would eat because they did not taste good) with him, stuck them together with duct tape, and tossed them from the truck onto the street, where adult residents pushed kids away—even grabbing a girl by the hair and pulling her down on one occasion—to get these boxes. The situation in Iraq was far from the vision of "freedom."

In effect, Okinawa and Iraq helped him to relativize his perspective as an American: "I don't say necessarily that I was a racist before, but I just wanted to hang out with people like me"; but having interacted with different kinds of people in Iraq and Okinawa, he recognized that "America is not the best with everything," a statement that reminds me of journalist Takamine Chōichi's observation of US servicemen during the Vietnam War, one of whom said, "Vietnamese too have rights to live freely. . . . I don't want to kill enemies and don't want to be killed by them" (1984, 30). In the act of relativizing ethnocentrism, Mr. G. imagined Okinawa and wider Japan as an idealized sanctuary ("Japan shaped my life probably more than any other event ever. . . . I would like to go back"), while Iraq is seen as a sort of dystopia ("They shoot each other, blow each other up. Let them do that, I don't want to be there"). I pay special attention here to the idealization of Okinawa and wider Japan, for it became radicalized to such an extent that Mr. G., in Taussig's terms, "exists not just as a subject [American] but also as a mimeticised Other [Okinawan]" (Taussig 1993, 106).

The 1995 rape of a twelve-year-old Okinawan schoolgirl by three US servicemen is well documented, but in addition, in February 2008, a fourteen-year-old Okinawan schoolgirl was raped by a marine sergeant. Immediately after this incident, Mr. G.'s nineteen-year-old fellow marine, X, who had recently been deployed to Okinawa, became heavily drunk and ended up breaking into a civilian's house in the entertainment quarter near the base to look for a woman. It so happened that Mr. G. and his friends, also walking in this entertainment quarter, saw X coming out of the house. While sympathizing with X's feeling of isolation and confusion, caused by being in a place so different from what he was used to, Mr. G. did not tolerate this blunder, because if publicized, this would intensify the anti-base sentiment of Okinawans further and make the already difficult life of marines—confinement to the base in the name of improving the US military's relationship with local communities—even more difficult. While in actuality X's incident was not publicized, Mr. G., together with fellow marines, punished X by administering fist-law—that is, using their fists on X as punishment. I interpret this as an act that was facilitated by Mr. G.'s understanding of and empathy with Okinawa's predicaments, made possible by his engagement with Okinawan society through marriage; in other words, Okinawa has become part of who he was through his mimetic faculty. Indeed, while the act reminds me of the hazing rituals of the military, it also looks as if Mr. G. let the anger of Okinawa possess him and he mimetically became and behaved like Okinawans who might want to express their anger and frustration toward the US military with fists, if that were at all possible.

Experiences of Mr. H., a former marine from central Kentucky whom I interviewed online in June 2020, also reveal the ways in which the mimetic faculty of the Okinawan multitude like him produces similarities and resemblances across difference in the planetary time-space of the community of *nuchi du takara*. He developed a mimetic faculty as a marine who was deployed to Afghanistan as a combatant (2013–2014) and to Okinawa as a trainer (2015–2016), constructing a subjectivity that consists of three different yet interrelated threads. The first is his class background as an individual born in a family living in near poverty. As he stated, "I went many years without hot water.... I did not really realize that being hygienic is a thing until the seventh grade." In his teenage years, he did a lot of work at a farm to get needed cash. Combined with the fact that he was able to spend, with his father and a group of close friends, what he considers a "normal" life in the family and school without using any drugs, his early relationship with money, or lack thereof, seems to have contributed to forming his moral scrupulousness. Indeed, in his attempt to disentangle himself from the world of civilian life dictated by money, Mr. H. imitated (or mimicked) what he considered to be the "true" marine way of life by declining—like his comrades—to apply for a range of benefits in spite of his combat experience in Afghanistan (see below). He feels that his service involves something—constituent power itself—that cannot and should not be exchanged for money, thereby situating himself outside the capitalist ways of life that permeate the global time-space of Empire.

The second thread is his subjectivity as an American man. Mr. H. does not remember the details of events on September 11, 2001, because he was in the first grade when they happened. Nonetheless, the images of America being attacked projected on TV screens upset him as a child and remained deep in his consciousness, constituting one of the motivations for serving the nation as a marine. Mr. H. thus noted, "Most marines would tell you this . . . it feels like a right thing to do. . . . It's a weird thing inside you . . . you don't wanna be a guy that do not do it." In effect, he mimeticized, as a man, the "true" American ways of life by enthusiastically and dedicatedly joining the Marine Corps at the age of seventeen, immediately after he graduated from high school. He observed that this desire to serve the nation was shared by the leaders of his unit in Afghanistan, all coming from "that part of the country"—including Kentucky, Tennessee, Georgia, upstate New York, and Illinois—that upholds, in his view, the authentic American ways of life.

The third thread is his experience as a combatant. Having barely internalized the core value of the Marine Corps, willingness to obey, at the boot camp—where Mr. H. regretted his decision to join the Marine Corps the whole time, as he understood for the first time what being a marine, willingness to obey, would really entail—he was immediately deployed to Afghanistan in June 2013. His battalion stayed in Afghanistan until September 2014 to oversee a presidential election there. He summarized his experience by saying, "Loss of life [across the boundaries of marines and local residents], I guess, is what I remember the most," as he was involved in combat on a daily basis. As a lance corporal, part of his duty was to "locate, close with, and destroy the enemy by fire maneuver or repel the enemy's assault." He was shot once and "blown away" twice during his deployment.

The situation was volatile because of the tension caused by the presence of Taliban soldiers in the community of non-Taliban residents. In his own words, "They did not ask for us to come there . . . and then we came to help them, but I am not certain we did," citing an experience, for instance, in which members of his unit helped residents dig an irrigation channel for their crops, and then, as his unit walked just fifty feet away from it, they were shot at by the local residents themselves, apparently under pressure from the Taliban. When he lost his best buddy in one of these conflicts, he wondered if his presence in Afghanistan was really worth it, though he was then convinced that it was, with a sense that he did this for "something bigger than myself." This sense was sustained and reinforced by the camaraderie and friendship of his unit, which was "the most incredible thing in the world to me." He did not regret joining the Marine Corps once he arrived at the battlefield, even for a second, although there was hazing, which he considered might have been necessary in that it did contribute to creating a sense of order, cohesion, and camaraderie in the fighting unit.

His subjectivity as a marine is constructed where these three threads of his life are tied together. Significantly, this subjectivity is often used not to create a wall between Self and Other but to bridge and overcome it. For instance, reflecting on the meaning of the loss of his comrades on the battlefield, Mr. H. understands and accepts, although he does not endorse, anti-marine, anti-base sentiments in Okinawa, by noting that "years ago [during the Battle of Okinawa] we went [and] slaughtered the whole island when the people did not do anything wrong." Ironically, when his mimetic faculty of becoming and feeling like Okinawans was exercised based on the shared experience of loss of life, the division was created not between him and Okinawans but between his world and the civilian world within the United States. For instance, he noted that many of his comrades killed themselves after coming back to the United States. He also stated that his return from Afghanistan was "terrifying. . . . I wanted to be back in Afghanistan." Everyday civilian life appeared strange and unfamiliar, and "it still does today." After coming back from Okinawa, he tried some civilian jobs that did not work out, so he returned to work for the Marine Corps until June 2020 as a valued trainer and recruiter with combat experience. At the moment I conducted the interview, he was still at a loss as to what he would do with his life in the civilian world.

I hypothesize that, engaged in the planetary time-space of life and death outside the American society controlled by the empty capitalist time-space of Empire, Mr. H., as a marine, mimetically participated in the community of *nuchi du takara* of the Okinawan multitude, a network of irreducible singularities across Okinawa and beyond who, linked through US base issues in the past and at present, act in common for peace, democracy, and shared affluence they produce as living labor. This hypothesis is confirmed by a similar mimetic process observed in the intercultural encounter of gay men in the contact zone between Okinawa and the US military, as insightfully discussed by Okinawan critic Shinjō Ikuo (2006) in reference to a novella titled *Sāchiraito* (Searchlight) written in 1956 by Toyokawa Zen'ichi, a student at the University of the Ryukyus.

In this novella, Shinkichi—an orphan who, having survived the Battle of Okinawa, lived in sheer poverty in postwar Okinawa—was raped by a Black gay serviceman in the summer of 1948 when he was sixteen, a humiliating experience that turned him gay. Now, at the age of nineteen, Shinkichi "wears dark red lipstick unlike a man, puts on a very special and most expensive poplin dress shirt with a loud necktie, and slicks down his hair shining brightly like a dragonfly—in short, he dresses up very queerly" (Toyokawa 1956, 29, cited in Shinjō 2006, 102); and on the increasingly turbulent Keystone of the Pacific now used as a launching base for the Korean War, Shinkichi has a relationship with a (seemingly) White serviceman by the name of Kennedy-san.

Shinjō (2006) analyzes the encounter among the constituents of the Okinawan multitude—in this case, Black/White gay servicemen and Shinkichi—where the occupier (America) homo-sexually/socially desires the occupied (Okinawa) who mimics the lifestyle/materialism of the occupier (through the lipstick, dress shirt, and shining hair, etc.); in so doing, he highlights the crisis of the occupier's sexuality. If following the Oedipus formula (i.e., internalizing the father and renouncing his sexual desires for the mother), the occupier is to direct his sexual desire toward the occupied women; numerous cases of rape that happened in the early phase of US control over Okinawa (see chapter 3, section 1) indeed reveals how this Oedipus formula penetrated the depth of the sexuality of the US military. However, this novella shows an irony; that is, when the colonizer is controlled by nothing in the colony—occupied Okinawa—and enjoys absolute freedom beyond the limit prescribed by the Oedipus formula, his sexuality is queerly directed toward the Self who is the Other, or the Other (Shinkichi) who becomes and behaves like the Self (America). In the process whereby the boundaries between Self and Other dissolve, Shinjō (2006) suggests, the occupier is on the verge of disintegrating his masculine subjectivity, thereby contributing to dismantling Empire from within. Issue 11 of *Ryūdai Bungaku* (University of Ryukyus Literature), which included this novella and other writings, was placed under a ban by the US authority in Okinawa due to the anti-US sentiments directly and indirectly expressed in this issue (Shinjō 2006, 94 and 106; Gabe S. 2013, 67–77).

In effect, in spite of (or precisely because of) all contradiction and inconsistency, the Okinawan multitude or those who have been excluded from the category of the Okinawan "people" and "citizens"—such as US servicemen stationed in Okinawa and long-marginalized mixed-race Okinawans as well as their mothers, together with sexual minorities such as gay US servicemen and queer Okinawans, among others—express "something" that one fails to grasp if one approaches it with an anti-base/pro-base (or progressive/conservative, good/bad) dichotomy. For this "something"—that is, *nuchi du takara* as the shared "unwavering principle of life"—allows these social actors to engage in a series of complex negotiations that, though they often involve compromises and concessions of constituent power vis-à-vis constituted power, nonetheless have generated varied life-forms for small yet significant and incremental social changes. In the process, the principle of *nuchi du takara* ("life is the ultimate treasure") shapes the general will of the community of the Okinawan multitude for peace, democracy, and shared affluence as a form of what Naoki Sakai and Hyon Joo Yoo (2012) call the "trans-Pacific imagination," an imagination that "encompasses discrete nations, nationalities, and societies, as well as specific ethnographizations and political interventions" (viii). By conducting the analysis of the mimetic faculty of Emperor Akihito and Empress Michiko in becoming and behaving like Okinawans, I want to make this imagination take a clearer shape; to that end, the next section explores how they addressed, negotiated, and transformed still another contradiction that this book has identified, that globalization—the formation of Empire—reinforces nationalism (see Part III).

3. Emperor Akihito, with Empress Michiko, from/with Okinawa against Empire: Overcoming the Contradiction That Globalization Reinforces Nationalism

Japanese war criminals were indicted for the Tokyo Trial on April 29, 1946, the forty-fifth birthday of Emperor Hirohito, and seven of them were executed on December 23, 1948, Crown Prince Akihito's fifteenth birthday, in a way that sent a message of MacArthur's General Headquarters that the Imperial House should never forget the meaning of the lost war (Yabe 2015,

17). This section explores the process whereby Akihito—the emperor from 1989 to 2019 (i.e., during the Heisei era)—conformed to but ultimately subverted this message, or really intimidation, by establishing himself, together with his wife Michiko, as the democratic symbol of the nation committed to the ideal of unarmed peace, as defined in Articles 1 and 9 of the new Constitution of Japan (see chapter 5, section 1).

Okinawa has played a special role in this entire process, which began to take shape in July 1975, when Akihito, then the crown prince, visited Okinawa as the honorary president of the Ocean Expo—one of the key events organized by Tokyo to celebrate the reversion of Okinawa and promote post-reversion development. Before delivering the opening address for the Ocean Expo on July 19, Akihito and Michiko were scheduled to visit on July 17 the Himeyuri Memorial and other southern battle memorial sites, among other places in Okinawa. This was the first visit to Okinawa by any member of the Imperial House since 1921, when Crown Prince Hirohito, later Emperor Showa and the father of Akihito, came there in the age of official nationalism v.1.1 when Okinawans were at once included and excluded as the adopted child or the first son of the Japanese Empire conceptualized as a family-like nation from time immemorial under the emperor, as noted in chapter 6. After the war, although he visited each and every prefecture of wider Japan to reassert his authority, Hirohito was unable to come to US-ruled Okinawa, which the administrative power of Japan did not reach, a condition shaped by Hirohito's own message in 1947 that he wanted Okinawa to be occupied by the US military for twenty-five to fifty years or more, as analyzed in chapter 5, section 1. After the Okinawan reversion of 1972, Hirohito was still not able to come because of Okinawa's bitter resentment at him as the individual responsible for the war he initiated, in which Okinawa, used as a sacrifice to protect Japan "proper," lost an estimated 150,000 residents due to the barrage of the US military's indiscriminate bombing and artillery fire together with other causes such as atrocities of the Japanese soldiers against Okinawans. The local saying—that "the military (the emperor's military at that) does not protect the lives of local residents"—was the result of this collective Okinawan experience, as noted in chapters 3 and 4. Due to Okinawa's antipathy to Hirohito, it was decided that Hirohito's son and his wife would visit Okinawa after reversion, a plan that generated equivocal responses there.

On the one hand, conservative politicians and pro-Japan business leaders in Okinawa expressed their enthusiasm for welcoming the crown prince and crown princess, reasoning that their visit—symbolizing the reunification of Okinawans and Japanese who had been separated for twenty-seven years due to US rule—would promote the commercial success of the Ocean Expo. Governor Yara Chōbyō's position was close to, though not identical with, this stance, which however risked undermining his reformist electoral base (Komatsu 2019a). On the other hand, Okinawa's reformist groups—such as labor unions, teachers' unions, and student organizations, as well as reformist political parties—expressed their criticisms regarding the visit of Akihito and Michiko on the basis of the broad grassroots feeling of discontent against the Imperial House derived from the experience of the Battle of Okinawa. Still, they could not form a unified front, as that would have contradicted and ruined the welcoming position of Governor Yara, whom they supported. Therefore, there was a shading of oppositional positions among reformist groups, ranging from a moderate, wait-and-see posture to a firm, stop-the-visit stance. Critical intellectuals represented the latter position by issuing a statement denouncing the visit as an attempt "to reintegrate Okinawa under imperial control" ("Ten'nōsei . . ." 1975). Opinions of ordinary Okinawans, as revealed in newspapers' letters-to-the-editor columns, were also diverse, ranging from enthusiastic welcome ("Kaiyōhaku . . ." 1975) to vague antagonism ("Sunaoni . . ." 1975) to absolute opposition ("Gunkokushugi . . ." 1975). Due to the mounting yet equivocal tension across Okinawa, Prime Minister Miki Takeo (1907–1988; in office 1974–1976) called for "thoroughgoing security" for this imperial visit ("Shushō Banzen . . ." 1975); in light of signs of violent protest by extremist groups, the Okinawa Prefectural Police implemented an "unprecedented security system" that mobilized fourteen hundred prefectural police officers together with an additional twenty-four hundred riot police from thirty prefectures across wider Japan ("Kōtaishi Gofusai . . ." 1975). As the date of the planned visit of Akihito and Michiko drew near, the atmosphere of the island became increasingly tense and "indescribable" (*iyōna*) ("Iyōna . . ." 1975).

The incident happened on July 17, 1975, the first day of their three-day visit. Akihito and Michiko arrived at Naha Airport a little after noon and then began to tour the southern battle memorial sites in a car under the scorching sun. While a large number of Okinawans stood on streets with the rising sun flag in their hands to welcome the crown prince and crown princess on their way to the Himeyuri Memorial, two extremist students—one from Okinawa and the other from Japan "proper"—who had been feigning illness in order to stay in a hospital situated along the route came out onto a balcony of the hospital on the third floor and threw at the line of cars and motorcycles two bottles containing disinfectant, two bottles of milk, an adjustable wrench, a square timber, etc., which hit cars that were following Akihito and Michiko's car ("Keikakuteki . . ." 1975). Then, at around 1:20 p.m., the crown prince and crown princess arrived at the Himeyuri Memorial site, which was packed with spectators and security forces; they dedicated flowers to the victimized student medical aides and their teachers to console their spirits. As they listened to an explanation from Minamoto Yuki, a former teacher and the president of the Himeyuri Memorial alumni association, another pair of extremist students—one from Okinawa and the other from Japan "proper"—who had been hiding in a cave next to the memorial tower, a cave where student medical aides had cared for injured and dying imperial soldiers during the Battle of Okinawa, emerged from that cave using a ladder, set off firecrackers, and threw a Molotov cocktail toward the crown prince and princess, screaming, "We oppose the visit of the crown prince!" The Molotov cocktail broke open and went up in flames two meters away from the couple ("Okinawasen no Hisan . . ." 1975). Governor Yara, who had accompanied Akihito and Michiko, was in great shock (Komatsu 2019b). The Himeyuri Memorial area was in chaos as the police arrested the suspects. Meanwhile, the crown prince spoke words of appreciation to the governor, made sure that Ms. Minamoto was safe, and requested that the security forces receive no punishment for this incident. He and the crown princess went on to complete their scheduled visits to other battle memorial sites (Takeuchi M. 2018, 61). At the Konpaku no Tō (Tower of Souls of the War Dead) memorial created in 1946 in the center of the battlefield in southern Okinawa (mentioned in chapter 4, section 5), Akihito sang a poem in the Okinawan language (*ryūka*) to console the spirit of the war dead and pray for peace (Yabe 2015, 25).

At a press conference held in the evening of that day, Katō Akira, the prefectural director of the Ocean Expo Special Police Forces, explained with apologies that they had not checked the inside of the cave where the suspects had hidden because "the Himeyuri Memorial, among other memorials, is the symbol of the tragedy of the Battle of Okinawa, and in light of the feeling of prefectural residents (*kenmin kanjō*), we judged it inappropriate to check the inside of the cave [an act that would profane the victims]. This decision brought about the unfortunate result" ("Keibitaisei . . ." 1975). The principal suspect, Chinen Isao, an Okinawan college student who belonged to an extremist group, stated in his memoir, published in 1995, that the purpose of throwing a Molotov cocktail was not to injure the crown prince and princess—he threw the bottle at the two stone monuments a short distance from them (Chinen 1995, 79). Rather, the purpose was to draw public attention to the question of the war responsibility of Hirohito, the father of Akihito, and of the Japanese government (Chinen 1995, 10–11).

As if responding to what Katō called "the feeling of prefectural residents" in general, and Chinen's question, or really accusation, in particular, Akihito, together with Michiko, composed the following message and delivered it to the public in the evening of the same day, an act that had never been done in the history of imperial visits (Takeuchi M. 2018, 61–62):

> That Okinawa, which has been seeking peace in spite of many difficulties, became our nation's sole battleground in the last world war and has made numerous sacrifices to this day, is an unforgettable, grave misfortune. It pains and grieves me most deeply when I think about the victims and surviving families.... Countless precious lives that had been sacrificed cannot be expiated by a passing act or word. The only way to atone for these lives is that we remember them by spending an extended period of time; and each and every one of us, through deep reflection, continues to direct one's attention to this place. ("Kōtaishi no . . ." 1975)

In this request for prayer, publicly enacted at the depth of Okinawan history, it seems that Akihito, together with Michiko, as "the symbol of the State and of the unity of the people" (Article 1 of the Constitution of Japan), approached Okinawa at the closest point possible by exercising his capacity to become, feel, and behave like the Other/Okinawans.

Their mimetic commitment to Okinawa was extended through Akihito's and Michiko's continuing study of Okinawan language, culture, and history (Takara 2019), as well as by their ten additional official visits to Okinawa. More specifically, after the first visit in July 1975, they came to Okinawa in (*a*) January 1976, to attend the closing ceremony of the Ocean Expo, (*b*) July 1983, to attend the national convention for the campaign promoting blood donation, (*c*) October 1987, to attend the National Athletic Meet, (*d*) November 1987, to attend the National Sports Meet for the Physically Disabled, (*e*) April 1993, to attend the National Tree-Planting Ceremony, (*f*) August 1995, as part of their trip to Hiroshima, Nagasaki,

Okinawa, and Tokyo to console the spirits of the war dead at the fiftieth anniversary of the end of World War II, (*g*) January 2004, to watch the opening performance at the National Theater Okinawa, a mecca of traditional performing arts of Okinawa, (*h*) November 2012, to attend the National Meeting for a Healthy Ocean, (*i*) June 2014, to console the spirits of the victims of *Tsushima Maru*, a ship—carrying close to seventeen hundred Okinawans including more than eight hundred children planning to evacuate from Okinawa to Kyushu—that was sunk by torpedoes from a US submarine (Tsushima Maru Kinenkan, n.d.), and (*j*) March 2018, to make a last visit before Akihito's abdication in April 2019 (Takeuchi M. 2018).

Akihito's mimetic commitment to Okinawa was founded upon his "profound regret about the previous war" (saki no taisen ni taisuru fukai hansei, in Japanese) (Hirokawa 2015), which was expressed, for instance, by his actions on what he considered to be the four important dates that the Japanese should never forget—June 23 (the official date on which the systematic military operations of the Japanese Imperial Army ended in Okinawa), August 6 (the date on which an atomic bomb was dropped on Hiroshima), August 9 (the date on which an atomic bomb was dropped on Nagasaki), and August 15 (the date on which the war ended). On these four days, all members of the family of Akihito and Michiko had been directed to dedicate prayers in the palace (Hosaka 2014, 273–276). Prayer—a mimetic dialogue with the dead—represents "a simultaneity of past and future in an instantaneous present" (Anderson 1991, 24), thereby producing the planetary time-space, the outside that Empire cannot internalize.

This planetary time-space multiplied publicly as Akihito, together with Michiko, continually expressed the same profound regret by visiting, as the emperor and empress, various places around the world, including Thailand (1991), Malaysia (1991), Indonesia (1991), China (1992), the United States (1994),[6] the United Kingdom (1998),[7] the Netherlands (2000), Saipan (2005), Palau (2015), and the Philippines (2016), though not South Korea, despite Akihito's wish to visit that country (Takeuchi M. 2018). In these and other places, they demonstrated their mimetic capacity to the Other and war victims by delivering speeches, offering silent tributes, and/or praying for peace perhaps more seriously than anybody else in contemporary Japan (Ōsawa 2019). In the Netherlands, for instance, there had been a strong anti-Japanese sentiment because the Japanese Imperial Army took prisoner some forty thousand soldiers and ninety thousand civilians in the Dutch

East Indies (present-day Indonesia, then a colony of the Netherlands), twelve thousand of whom died in captivity. Some of them were forced to work as "comfort women"—to serve Japanese soldiers sexually ("Emperor..." 2000). Therefore, when Hirohito, Akihito's father, visited the Netherlands in 1971, his car was struck by a thermometer thrown by a protester, and two hours before the arrival of Akihito and Michiko at the National Monument on Dam Square in Amsterdam in 2000, a group of former prisoners conducted an anti-Japanese demonstration around it. When Akihito and Michiko placed flowers and offered a one-minute prayer in the square, silence permeated the entire space as if to assuage the historical anger (Kitano et al. 2019). Later at the dinner organized by Queen Beatrix at the Royal Palace, Akihito delivered a statement that included the sentiment, "It grieves our hearts to think that so many people were victimized in their respective ways during that war and that there are still those who continue to bear unhealed scars from it" ("Emperor . . ." 2000). The address was favorably received in the Netherlands.

Akihito and Michiko tried to link their status as the symbol of the nation with not only the ideal of peace but also the ideal of democracy, by mimetically experiencing but not absorbing the everyday life of the Japanese, particularly the weak. For instance, as if to atone for the historical process whereby the Imperial House, particularly the empress, had been politically utilized as the "merciful benefactor" since the early twentieth century to promote the state policy of isolating leprosy patients and former leprosy patients in national sanatoriums—a policy that was concretized in the 1907 Law concerning the Prevention of Leprosy, reinforced in the 1931 Leprosy Prevention Law, and extended by the 1953 Leprosy Prevention Law, which was abolished in 1996 and subsequently declared unconstitutional in 2001—Akihito and Michiko visited all fourteen of the national sanatoriums to console such patients ("Kōgō . . ." 2017), including Okinawa Airakuen Sanatorium in Nago City, which I visited with my friend and informant Kinjō Hatsuko (see chapter 2, section 3). In 2013, they also visited Minamata City, noted for mercury poisoning from a chemical factory that killed or disabled numerous residents in the 1950s and beyond (Takeuchi M. 2018, 221–228; Ishimure [1969] 2004). Furthermore, during the thirty years of Akihito's reign (1989–2019), Akihito and Michiko visited sites of natural disasters at least forty-two times. For instance, in 1991, they visited the site of the volcanic eruption of Mount Unzen in Nagasaki Prefecture, where they dressed casually and knelt down to talk with victims evacuated to a community center. They ate the same retort-pouched heat-and-eat curry for lunch as the afflicted. This "democratic" style of visit was extended on other occasions, including their repeated visits to the areas devastated by the great earthquake and tsunami in eastern Japan in 2011(Takeuchi M. 2018, 12–15, 46).

The ideal of democracy—in the sense of psychological or symbolic reciprocity and proximity between the Imperial House and the Japanese people—had been expressed ever since 1959, when Akihito married Michiko, the first time in modern imperial history that a woman outside the network of imperial families married an heir to the throne, an act enthusiastically received by the Japanese public at that time (Hosaka 2014, 193–199). In order to reinforce the ideal of democracy, Akihito also proposed to open the Imperial Palace to the public and even dreamed of living outside the palace; while that dream was not realized until his abdication, Kōkyo Higashi Gyoen (the East Garden of the Imperial Palace) was opened to the public in 1968 (Yabe 2015, 12). In turn, Michiko, together with Akihito, raised their children by themselves against an established imperial practice of separating children from the emperor and empress by using wet nurses. Michiko also cooked meals for them as the "housewife" according to the standard of the "ordinary" family that came to be established in the high-growth era of postwar Japan (Hosaka 2014, 201–204; "Kōgō-sama ni . . ." 2017).

In effect, Akihito responded to, or really subverted, the message of MacArthur's General Headquarters—"Never forget about the meaning of the lost war for the Imperial House"—by seeking and materializing the principles of peace and democracy stipulated in the Constitution of Japan often beyond the US-centered peace and democracy MacArthur and others envisioned. In a manner that undermined the vision that Okinawa should be controlled by the US military semi-permanently—a vision shared by his father Hirohito and MacArthur and refined by Dulles (as analyzed in chapter 5)—Akihito specifically expressed his desire to settle the Okinawa base issue for the happiness and well-being of Okinawans in 1996 when he met with President Bill Clinton (Yabe 2015, 100). Of course, as the "mere" symbol of the nation to whom "political" acts are prohibited by the Constitution, Akihito never criticized the government even as it exploited Okinawa. Yet Akihito's statements of profound regret about the previous war for the people in Okinawa and elsewhere in the Asia-Pacific region became a counterpoint to nationalism brewed within Japan in the age of Empire (see chapter 6).

The actions of Akihito and Michiko did not pass without criticism, however. In particular, Okinawa was a contested place where, until the 1990s or so, there remained a palpable tension between pro-Imperial House and anti-Imperial House sentiments, a tension increased by the excessive security measures implemented due to the "failure" of security on their 1975 visit. In October 1987, for instance, in anticipation of a visit during the National Athletic Meet of Crown Prince Akihito and Crown Princess Michiko (acting on behalf of the emperor, who could not come due to illness), a group of more than thirty-one hundred Okinawans collectively took out a full-page advertisement in local newspapers to state: "We oppose the visit to Okinawa by the emperor (members of the Imperial House) and inquire into [his/their] war responsibility" and "We oppose the participation of the emperor/Self-Defense Forces (Japanese army) in the National Athletic Meet" (Ten'nō (Ichizoku) no Raioki ni Hantaishi, Sensō Sekinin o Tsuikyūsuru Ikenkōkoku Undō 1987). During this visit, Chibana Shōichi, who owned a grocery store in Yomitan Village, pulled down a national flag displayed at a softball stadium and burned it. He justified his action by invoking the tragedy of "compulsory group suicide" (Field 1991, 61) at Chibichirigama that I noted in chapter 6, section 1 ("'Watashiga . . .'" 1987). In addition, Okinawan intellectuals expressed antipathy to, and sometimes insisted on the outright abolishment of, the Japanese imperial system (e.g., Arasaki and Kawamitsu 1988, authors of *Okinawakara Tennōsei o Kangaeru* 1988; cf. Rabson 2008). In his novel titled *Heiwadōri to Nazukerareta Machi o Aruite* (Walking the Town Named Peace Street) ([1986] 1990), Okinawan writer Medoruma Shun depicted an almost senile old Okinawan woman, who, having lost her son in a cave during the Battle of Okinawa, acted out profanity against the crown prince and crown princess, who were visiting Okinawa in 1983 for a national blood donation campaign, by banging on the window of their car with hands covered in her own feces on the main street of Naha.

Nonetheless, overall, the negative sentiment toward the Imperial House in Okinawa waned during Akihito's reign. In February 1989, immediately after the enthronement of Akihito as emperor, 53% of Okinawans surveyed in a poll expressed a positive feeling toward him. In April 2019, immediately before the abdication of Akihito, 87% of those surveyed in a poll expressed a positive feeling toward him ("Ten'nōheika ni kōkan 87%"). Already at the 1987 National Athletic Meet (the fourth visit of Akihito and Michiko to Okinawa), Okinawa enthusiastically sought to take the Emperor's Trophy, the highest honor, awarded to the prefecture whose athletes perform the best among all athletes from prefectures across Japan; when this feat was accomplished, Okinawa seethed with excitement ("Okinawa Ten'nōhai..." 1987). Okinawa's governor, Nishime Junji (1921–2001; in office 1978–1990), reflected on the success of the 1987 National Athletic Meet, stating that "Okinawa's postwar has come to an end" ("Sengowa..." 1987). Indeed, from the 1990s on, the tension between pro-imperial House and anti-imperial House sentiments in Okinawa has been increasingly inconspicuous. On their last visit in 2018, the ways in which Emperor Akihito and Empress Michiko candidly talked with survivors of the Battle of Okinawa in plain language favorably impressed many, if not all, Okinawans ("Okinawasen no Kioku..." 2018). With continuing prayers showing their mimetic faculty of becoming and behaving like the Other, Akihito and Michiko were true to the message delivered in 1975 after the Molotov cocktail incident cited above: "The only way to atone for these [lost] lives is that we remember them by spending an extended period of time; and each and every one of us, through deep reflection, continues to direct one's attention to this place" ("Kōtaishi no..." 1975). Even Kawano Jyunji, a Nago City assembly member and one of the students who in July 1975 had thrown objects at Akihito and Michiko from the hospital balcony when they were on their way to the Himeyuri Memorial, positively evaluated their commitment to Okinawa as emperor and empress in my interview with him in Nago City in January 2020.

The change of Okinawa's sentiments toward the Imperial House corresponded with a shift of social actors from the Okinawan "citizens" who played a key role in constructing the collective memory of the war (see chapter 4, section 5) to the Okinawan multitude whose sensibilities have been shaped increasingly by the generations who experienced neither the Battle of Okinawa nor the US occupation of Okinawa. While the sample size is limited, of five Okinawan subjects in their twenties and thirties (three women and two men) whom I interviewed in Okinawa in January 2020, two expressed strong feelings toward the Imperial House—one (woman) positively and one (woman) negatively—while the sentiments of each of the remaining subjects was equivocal, expressing an amalgam of somewhat negative, somewhat positive, neutral, and/or indifferent feelings toward it (e.g., negative toward the Japanese imperial system but positive toward Akihito and Michiko). The diversity of responses among the young generation is contrasted with the responses of the older generation who expressed their negative views in the 1980s, as noted above.

How should we interpret this change? Instead of simply reading this as the disappearance or erasure of Okinawa's collective memory against the Imperial House that goes hand in hand with Japanese containment and control of the subjectivity of post-reversion Okinawa, I pay attention to what Okinawa has produced—that is, how the Okinawan multitude has negotiated with the Imperial House for the rearticulation of the community of *nuchi du takara*. Indeed, unlike Hirohito (Emperor Showa), who presented himself as the "Oriental" monarch from above and manipulated Okinawa before, during, and after the war (see Part III), Akihito resolved the tensions and conflicts Hirohito had generated with Okinawa by redefining the emperor as the antiwar-democratic symbol from below, to the point that Akihito, together with Michiko, embedded, dissolved, and dispersed himself in the everyday social life of the Okinawan multitude, not to control them but to become part of their community of *nuchi du takara* at the depth of history. Empress Michiko reinforced this process—the dispersion of the Imperial House in the network of the Okinawan multitude—by stating, "I believe that everyone lives one's own life with a core that resists the understanding and help of others. Therefore, rather than entering that core when I meet with people, I always keep in mind the fact that one has one's own life. Everyone is ashamed of one's own weakness and yet lives without giving up all hope. When I meet with people, I wish we would mutually acknowledge, think fondly of, and encourage such our existences" (cited in Yabe 2015, 112). Her stance is confirmed by the fact that Michiko, let alone Akihito, never showed tears in their public performances in Okinawa (or anywhere else, for that matter). Tears would dissolve the distance between Self and Other, the Imperial House and the community of *nuchi du takara* in postwar Okinawa, reintegrating the pains and sufferings of the latter (caused by the war the Imperial House—Akihito's father—had initiated) in the existing structure of the former. What Akihito and Michiko did instead was to use their mimetic faculty to stand by this community without absorbing it; it is in their act of declining to absorb, internalize, and integrate the Other that they constituted and reinforced the general will in the community of the Okinawan multitude—including the war dead of the Asia-Pacific region and beyond—through the "trans-Pacific imagination" (Sakai and Yoo 2012) for peace, democracy, and shared affluence across the planetary time-space.

Though often confronted by public criticism that he lacked the charisma that Hirohito was said to have had (Hosaka 2014, 194, 204–209, 239–240), Akihito, together with Michiko, pursued the vision of the emperor as the antiwar-democratic symbol of the nation in a manner that revealed a possibility of casting out the "ghost" (Gluck 1993, 89) of Emperor Showa, Dulles, and MacArthur from the historical stage of postwar Japan. This section has explained this possibility. Whether or not and how the current emperor (Naruhito) and empress (Masako), enthroned in 2019, may extend what Akihito and Michiko accomplished remains to be seen, in light of the fact that today's Imperial House has been increasingly consumed, like comfort food, as an icon of Japan or else utilized by the state as a buffer, so to speak, for the management of crises and contingencies of various kinds within Japan and without.

4. The General Will in the Community of *Nuchi Du Takara*

By looking at the lives and works of Cocco, mixed-race Okinawans together with their mothers, US servicemen stationed in Okinawa and elsewhere, and Emperor Akihito and Empress Michiko, among others, this chapter has shown overlapping similarities and crisscrossing differences—family resemblances—in the community of *nuchi du takara* constructed through the mimetic faculty of the Okinawan multitude. To conclude this chapter, I wish to note how they have traversed the three ontological layers of this community that this study has explored, that is, the first, oldest and metaphysical layer constituted by the death of others, the second, newer layer of everyday social life centered on face-to-face communication, and the third, newest layer of global and virtual communication among those separated from each other across time and space (see the introduction to Part I). Tied to the exploration of the protest movements in Henoko in Part I, this concluding description and analysis will help us identify how the general will of the Okinawan multitude for universal peace, global democracy, and shared affluence, shapes and is shaped by the community of *nuchi du takara* characterized by explosive communication, integrality against power, and absence/presence of structural permanency.

For instance, Cocco has immersed herself in the first, metaphysical layer of this community constituted by the death of Okinawans in the war— through her "Heaven's hell" as a prayer for world peace and her engagement in the Himeyuri issues; in so doing, she has situated herself in the network of explosive communication, both real (e.g., her concerts, writings, and drawings; the second layer) and virtual (e.g., DVDs and YouTube videos distributed to fans across Japan and beyond; the third layer). Similarly, US servicemen such as Mr. G., Mr. H., and the fictional gay servicemen came into contact with the first, metaphysical foundation of the community of *nuchi du takara* through their combat experience in Iraq (Mr. G.), Afghanistan (Mr. H.), and (perhaps) Okinawa or Korea (the gay servicemen), while negotiating their perspectives and positions through explosive communication in the second layer centering on face-to-face interactions (e.g., Mr. G., who married an Okinawan woman, Mr. H., who struggled to establish his position in the civilian world, and the gay servicemen who had sexual interactions with Shinkichi) and in the third layer centering on global/virtual interactions (e.g., allowing me to conduct an online interview in the case of Mr. H.).

Ms. O., a mixed-race Okinawan woman fathered by a Black US serviceman, was also situated in the metaphysical foundation of the community because of her connection to the military, an institution of destruction. Indeed, her life is an effect of this institution, an effect characterized by the contradiction that the very presence of US bases that has affirmed and enabled her life has also become the cause of discrimination that has denied her life. Ms. O. has engaged in and overcome this contradiction (*a*) through her work and life as a designer, as a peace activist, and as a woman/mother with Black background in the second layer of face-to-face communication and (*b*) through her efforts to construct a virtual family with her father and half sister via Facebook in the third layer of global communication, in a manner that reveals an integrality against power of the Okinawan multitude.

In addition, former emperor Akihito, together with Empress Michiko, has been confronted by the "history issues" (see chapter 5)—the death of 150,000 Okinawans, together with the death of both combatants and noncombatants in Japan as a whole (numbering more than three million) and across the Asia-Pacific (numbering more than twenty million). The death or absence of these singularities, caused by the war initiated in the name of Akihito's own father, Hirohito, has been compensated for, at least to a certain degree, by Akihito and Michiko's public acts for peace, their presence. Specifically, represented by their repeated visits to and face-to-face communication with Okinawa (the second layer), which have been virtually disseminated to the world via archives on the internet (the third layer), Akihito and Michiko's public presence has been associated with the "profound regret about the previous war" that envelops the absence—that is, the war dead—in the community on a metaphysical level (the first layer). In so doing, Akihito and Michiko highlighted the absence/presence of structural permanency of the community of *nuchi du takara*, a characteristic derived from the ability of this community to constantly renew and rearticulate itself as a "*changing* same."

In the process, these social actors—together with all other actors that this study has examined—have engaged in a perpetual dialogue across differences to generate the general will to universal peace, global democracy, and shared affluence, which appears "not so much as something deriving from human desires or free will, but in the form of a categorical imperative that transcends them" (Karatani [2010] 2014, 14). If my analyses in this and other chapters have helped reveal the virtuality of this general will in the changing-same community of *nuchi du takara*, "The passage from the virtual through the possible to the real is the fundamental act of creation" (Hardt and Negri 2000, 357). I accomplish this "act of creation" in chapter 8, the concluding chapter of this book, through a specific policy proposal for global social change.

Notes

1. The expression "travelers on the same boat" is taken from the lyrics of "U.S.A.," a song by Da Pump, the Japanese hip-hop group led by Hentona Issa, a mixed-race Okinawan male mentioned in the introduction to this book.

2. A substantial portion of the following analysis on Cocco's work appeared in Inoue 2011, which focuses on what I consider the formative years of her life as an artist (ca. 1996–2010). I thank Taylor & Francis for kind permission to reproduce portions of that article published in *Inter-Asia Cultural Studies*. In the 2010s and beyond, Cocco has continued to be actively engaged in a variety of artistic activities, the analysis of which is beyond the scope of this chapter. To access examples of Cocco's work, see her official YouTube site (Cocco, n.d.).

3. Cocco wrote five thousand postcards by hand and sent them to those who were not chosen, with her signature, as an expression of apology (*Heaven's hell* 2003, 36:25–36:30).

4. All translations of *Omoigoto* were made by Chieko Kamei. I have modified her translations as I saw fit.

5. Part of the analysis of the life history of Mr. G. that follows was originally presented by this writer (Inoue 2014) at the American Anthropological Association Annual Meeting that took place in Washington, DC, between December 3 and 7, 2014.

6. Akihito and Michiko also visited the United States in 1997 and 2009 (as well as in 2005, if one counts Saipan, a commonwealth of the United States in the western Pacific Ocean).

7. Akihito and Michiko also visited the United Kingdom in 2007 and 2012.

CHAPTER 8

Conclusion

Collective Security from an Okinawan Perspective

Fundamental to the development of Empire in the Asia-Pacific region is the notion of "collective (or regional) self-defense"—of defending the interests, safety, and security of friends (Self) against enemies (Other) (cf. Schmitt [1932] 1976). Defined as an "inherent right" of the state by the United Nations Charter's Article 51, collective/regional self-defense framed the Self/Other (friend/enemy) binary across the capitalist and communist states during the Cold War and has reproduced it anew across the United States and China today—and more broadly across the so-called democratic and authoritarian states, often with the "Global South" situated in between (see Part III).

In contrast, the conclusion to this study proposes an alternative paradigm of "collective security"—a paradigm adopted by the United Nations as its fundamental principle of operation and one to which collective/regional self-defense is deemed secondary and an exception. Collective security involves the process whereby all states transfer their "inherent right" of collective/regional self-defense (but not their right of individual self-defense, as discussed below) to a democratic supranational power; it is this democratic supranational power that collectively copes with threats to the peace and security of the world, on the basis of the notion that the security of one state is the concern of all and the security of all is the concern of each state (Hurrell 2011, 299). I argue that collective security is possible and necessary under new historical circumstances of globalization that already connect us as earthlings beyond the paradigm of Self and Other, friend and enemy. Combining the insight of Karatani Kōjin (2006, [2010] 2014) with the analysis developed in this book, I call this democratic supranational power the World Republic of *nuchi du takara*—currently approximated by but also disrupted by the United Nations. Grounded broadly in the premise that "life is the ultimate treasure"—a premise shared by Okinawan and other social actors across the globe—the World Republic of *nuchi du takara* helps to envision, from a planetary perspective, how we could (*a*) restore the principle of unarmed peace stipulated in Article 9 of the Constitution of Japan, (*b*) link that principle to shared management and use of military forces against common threats, and (*c*) reconcile, from a fresh perspective, modern Asia's "history issues" (Dower 2014, 12)—the Nanjing massacre, "comfort women," Okinawa, and other problematic legacies of Imperial Japan's colonial dominations across Asia before and during World War II that have been long silenced by postwar American hegemony. Complementing the right of individual self-defense of all states (United Nations, n.d.), collective security exercised by the World Republic aims at achieving "perpetual peace" envisioned by Immanuel Kant ([1795] 2016). As such, collective security is closely tied to the outlawry of war, a concept developed since the late nineteenth century to stipulate that "war is in principle forbidden and permitted only as a reaction against a delict" (Wright 1953, 367; see also Mimaki 2014).

To articulate the significance of collective security, I first review the works of some scholars who engage the problems of Empire—a global sovereignty with a double-sided character, both new (postmodern) *and* old (modern), imperial *and* colonialist, and American *and* Japanese. I argue, however, that their insights, though valuable, are ultimately insufficient because they do not offer a vision by which to move beyond the paradigm of collective/regional self-defense, of Self (friend) and Other (enemy).

• • •

Critically redeveloping Takeuchi Yoshimi's ([1961] 1966) idea of "Asia as Method" in the context of late twentieth-century and early twenty-first-century East Asia, Taiwanese critic Kuan-Hsing Chen advocates three different yet interrelated projects of reversal in East Asia: decolonization, de–Cold War, and de-imperialization. Decolonization aims to dismantle the mechanism of "colonial identification" (2010, 68) through "a critical syncretism"—a strategy to "generate a system of multiple reference points" (2010, 101) beyond the West/rest binary. De–Cold War aims at "establishing mutual recognition of each other's history of suffering" (2010, 156) across East Asia and, by extension, at redressing "history issues" (2010, chap. 3) within it. De-imperialization involves critical examination of "the presence of the United States in East Asia as an imperial power" (2010, 173) that has controlled the politics, economy, and culture of this region since the end of World War II. I fully agree with all these notions.

Yet I remain unconvinced by the idea of the global formation of regional blocs that he advocates as a solution to the problems of continued colonization, Cold War, and imperialism in East Asia: "If all of Asia can be integrated as other regions have started to do through organizations such as the African Union, the European Union, and the Association of South East Asian Nations, that integration would increase the likelihood that the global balance of power vis-à-vis the US military empire could shift. At this historical moment, the global formation of regional blocs seems necessary to prevent the United States from continuing to abuse its position as the single superpower" (2010, 15; see also 209 and 213). His proposal, situated in the period of transition from the Cold War to the post–Cold War, does not seem to fit the contemporary context of the twenty-first century Asia-Pacific region and beyond, where regionalism has been rampant in the name of a multipolar world order: "Economic globalisation is a major driver of political multipolarisation since it promotes the diversification of centres of industrial production and accumulation with economic integration mainly on a regional basis" (Clegg 2009, 76; see also Turner 2009).

For instance, against the background of this economic globalization, China as a new center of industrial production and accumulation reinstitutes its regional boundaries based on the afterimage of Imperial China (Self) against the United States and Japan (Other/enemy) (Hayashi N. 2022; Wang 2012). Similarly, Russia has advanced the logic of regionalism to restore old borders of Imperial Russia and justify its invasion of Ukraine as a form of resistance to the liberal Westernizing project since the 1990s. In turn, the planned construction of the Futenma Replacement Facility (FRF) in Henoko, together with the buildup of the US-Japan security alliance, is now being justified by Washington and Tokyo for the promotion of collective/regional self-defense of the democratic bloc in the Asia-Pacific region (see chapter 5). In effect, as regionalism has been revived to turn an old binary between the capitalist bloc and the communist bloc during the Cold War into a new binary between the democratic bloc and the authoritarian bloc (with the "Global South" often situated in between) in the post–Cold War multipolar world, Kuan-Hsing Chen's proposal, significant as it may be in its call for the three reversals in the Asia-Pacific region already mentioned, would ironically add fuel to the flames of Self/Other (friend/enemy) confrontations in "global civil war" (Hardt and Negri 2004, 3).

Meanwhile, Okinawan critic Nomura Kōya has problematized the prolonged, disproportionate burden of the US military that has been placed on Okinawa as an extension of modern Japan's colonial domination over Okinawa into the postcolonial present (i.e., into the age of Empire); in so doing, he proposes a more equal distribution of US bases across Japan through *kengai isetsu*, that is, relocation of US bases in Okinawa to prefectures elsewhere in Japan (2019, 47–52). Evidence shows, however, that transferring parts of functions of the US bases from Okinawa to mainland Japan has already become an administrative tactic Washington and Tokyo have established to control Okinawa's frustration at the presence of the US military. Importantly, this tactic has been linked to the reinforcement of the central role Okinawa is expected to continue to play in the security of the Asia-Pacific region, as explicated in chapter 5, section 5. Indeed, in the name of collective/regional self-defense, the military abuse of Okinawa (e.g., the construction of the FRF no matter what) has gone hand in hand with today's increased collaboration between the US military and the forces of not only Japan but also Taiwan, South Korea, the Philippines, India, and Australia, among others, to securitize the Asia-Pacific region against China within the same sovereign territory, the world market, of Empire v.3, with added squadrons from European countries (the United Kingdom, France, and Germany, among others) in that region. Nomura's proposal, in spite of (or precisely because of) its admirable call for shifting the unequal relations of power and history in the context of modern Japan, exhibits a nation-bound tendency in his approach to the US base issues in Okinawa. It misses the global nature of the issues, ironically assisting the US-Japan alliance in confronting China in a manner that reinforces the friend/enemy binary in the global civil war, as in Kuan-Hsing Chen's proposal.

The following is an attempt to overcome the limitations of Chen's globalist/regionalist approach and Nomura's localist approach to the shared issue pertaining to a contemporary global order, Empire, by introducing an alternative paradigm of collective security.

1. Suppressing the General Will: The Displacement of Collective Security with Collective/Regional Self-Defense

In eighteenth-century Europe, Jean-Jacques Rousseau ([1762] 2014) developed the notion of the general will—"The constant will of all the members of the State" (book 4, chap. 2), a will that is "inalienable" (book 2, chap. 1) and "indivisible" (book 2, chap. 2)—to theorize the popular sovereignty, that is, to designate the will of the people as the source of authority and power of the state.[1] In the twenty-first century, following and developing the usage of Karatani Kōjin (2006, esp. 219–225; [2010] 2014, part 4, chap. 2),[2] I redefine the concept of popular sovereignty to explore the general will of the multitude as the source of authority and power of the yet-to-come World Republic of *nuchi du takara*. This redefinition enables us to grasp the World Republic as a form of the community of *nuchi du takara* expanded across the globe and to achieve the conceptual rearticulation of the general will within and against Empire in the twenty-first century by modifying Rousseau ([1762] 2014):

> The general will alone can direct the [World Republic of *nuchi du takara*] according to the object for which it was instituted, *i.e.* the common good: for if the clashing of particular interests [among the multitude across the globe] made the establishment of [the World Republic of *nuchi du takara*] necessary, the agreement of these very interests made it possible. The common element in these different interests is what forms the [global] social tie; and, were there no point of agreement between them all, no [global] society could exist. It is solely on the basis of this common interest that [the World Republic of *nuchi du takara*] should be governed. (Book 2, chap. 1)

In effect, the "common good" in the World Republic is life as *takara* ("the ultimate treasure"). The common interest is thus "the preservation of the contracting parties" (book 2, chap. 5; see also book 1, chap. 5), such that "*we cannot work for others without working for ourselves*" (book 2, chap. 4, emphasis mine). Reminding us of the fact that today, we are living on the planet Earth to which there is no more outside (as evidenced by climate change, the Covid-19 pandemic, and global civil wars such as Russia's invasion of Ukraine and the Israeli-Palestinian conflict), the notion that "we cannot work for others without working for ourselves" is particularly helpful for grasping the role the state is to play in collective security—a system in which "each state ... accepts that the security of one is the concern of all and agrees to join in a collective response to threats to, and breaches of, the peace" (Hurrell 2011, 299).

More specifically, I use Rousseau to conceptualize the state as a mediator of the general will of *nuchi du takara* between the multitude and the World Republic: "The essence of the [global] body politic [i.e., the World

Republic] lies in the reconciliation of obedience [i.e., "working for others"] and liberty [i.e., "working for ourselves"], and the words subject [read the "multitude"] and Sovereign [read the "World Republic"] are identical correlatives the idea of which meets in the single word 'citizen' [read the "state"]" ([1762] 2014, book 3, chap. 13). Through this synthesis between "from above" (obedience) and "from below" (liberty), collective security allows the state to be regulated by the World Republic from above *and* the multitude from below. In effect, collective security—as an expression of the general will of *nuchi du takara*—is to be actualized through the trinity of the multitude (local), the state, and the World Republic (global).

Violently imperialistic though it is, MacArthur's vision in search of the US-centered one-world system—a vision founded on the US military presence in Okinawa as a base for the launching of nuclear weapons against the Soviet Union—helps us catch a glimpse of how the trinity could work. For, as elaborated in chapter 5, section 1, the postwar constitution MacArthur created for Japan—specifically, Article 1 defining the popular sovereignty—contributed to transforming Japan from a nation defined by the absolute power and authority of the state and emperor over the subjects before 1945 to one defined by the power of the people/Japanese (local) to control, shape, and govern the state from below after the war. It is the will of the people/Japanese that renounced part of the sovereignty of their state—the right of collective/regional self-defense—to generate Article 9 stipulating the principle of unarmed peace. Meanwhile, Article 9 was connected to the power of the United Nations as an approximation of the World Republic (global) to exercise collective security from above "for" the Japanese state (confronted by the new "threats" of communism) and, if necessary, "against" the Japanese state (as a former enemy that may return to militarism to become a new threat).

In actuality, however, against the background of the intensification of the Cold War, what spread was not collective security but a different premise, that of collective/regional self-defense—the premise that the United Nations Charter viewed as secondary and an exception to collective security, as noted in chapter 5, section 1—according to which "we work for ourselves (friends) without working for others (enemies)." One of the decisive moments for the development of this premise in the Asia-Pacific region is the time when Hirohito, Emperor Shōwa, chose to have postwar Japan enter a transnational "social contract" to transfer part of what he considered "his" rights, including the administrative right over Okinawa, to the United States; in an attempt to defend it against communism, Hirohito constituted postwar Japan as a client state of the United States (see chapter 5, section 1). To modify Rousseau, collective security, "to be really such, must be general in its object as well as its essence; . . . it must both come from all [states] and apply to all [states]; and . . . it loses its natural rectitude when it is directed to some particular and determinate object, because in such a case we are judging of something foreign to us [within the paradigm of Self and Other, friends and enemies], and have no true principle of equity to guide us" ([1762] 2014, book 2, chap. 4). Hirohito's desire "directed toward some particular and determinate object," namely the United States the conqueror, was sublimated through John Foster Dulles, the key architect of the San Francisco system that implemented a paradigm of collective/regional self-defense as the norm of security in the postwar Asia-Pacific region and beyond.

Accordingly, we have observed, for instance, how the United States, to overcome the crisis of the Korean War, displaced collective security by the United Nations with collective/regional self-defense by the United States to establish Empire v.1 against communism across the Asia-Pacific region (chapter 5, section 1). We have also seen how, after the Vietnam War, the United States promoted the notion of "burden sharing" to continue to cope with the crisis of the Cold War, reinforcing the network of collective/regional self-defense to generate Empire v.2, governed by reciprocity across the United States (core), Japan (semi-periphery), and other Asian nations (periphery) against the "threats" of communism (chapter 5, section 2). Furthermore, as discussed in chapter 5, section 5, to cope with the crisis of US-China rivalry, Empire v.3 has expanded the concept of collective/regional self-defense even further, as exemplified by the Abe cabinet's 2014 reinterpretation of Article 9 of the Constitution of Japan, together with the repeated and ongoing buildup of the US-Japan security alliance to reinforce the global security apparatus. In effect, one can see a broader historical process whereby the notion of collective/regional self-defense, founded upon the Self/Other (friend/enemy) dichotomy, has been normalized for the development of Empire in the Asia-Pacific region across the Cold War and post–Cold War periods. Japan's participation in the United Nations since 1956 has not altered this general trend.

In the meantime, the ab/use of collective/regional self-defense has effectively paralyzed collective security. For instance, the veto power of the Soviet Union prevented the United Nations from exercising collective security when the Soviet military intervened in Hungary (1958), Czechoslovakia (1968), and Afghanistan (1979) for collective/regional self-defense of the communist bloc. Similarly, the United States exercised its veto against the United Nations' attempts to utilize collective security when the United States (*a*) invaded Grenada in 1980 and intervened in Panama in 1989 for collective/regional self-defense of Latin America (Mogami 2006, 156–159) and (*b*) endorsed Israel's actions in the Middle East in and after 1972 in light of Israel's right to defend itself (Newton 2021). On the basis of these examples, Gary Wilson (2014, 45) concludes that "during the cold war, collective security cannot be said to have operated on anything more than a very limited level, and essentially gave way to a balance of power system." This is not surprising because, as Inis L. Claude Jr. had already noted in the early 1960s, "The United Nations has never been intended or expected to apply the principle of collective security on a universal scale" (1962, 172). Accordingly, as Hans Kelsen predicted back in 1948, it has become "inevitable to substitute collective [i.e., regional] self-defense for collective security as established by the Charter, but such substitution would be the bankruptcy of that political and legal system for which the United Nations was created" (796).

2. Reinventing Collective Security within and against Empire from an Okinawan Perspective

Today, the changing historical context has made the reinvention of collective security necessary and possible. On the one hand, it is necessary because further reinforcement of the logic of collective/regional self-defense (the friend/enemy binary) as the solution to the crises in the Asia-Pacific region—as suggested by Armitage and Nye's study group (see chapter 5, section 5)—would have the United States, China, Russia, and others risk destroying each other and the entire world. What is at stake is "the development of [global] community consciousness which overrides the divisiveness of national interests," as Claude noted in the early 1960s (1962, 199). More specifically: "It requires a conception of national interest which identifies the destiny of the state so closely with the order of the global community as to make participation in the safeguarding of that order a virtually automatic response to any disturbances. . . . This is not a matter of repudiating the national interest, or of neglecting it, but of defining it in terms of, and identifying it with, the international interest in peace and order" (1962, 199).

On the other hand, the salvation and reinvention of collective security is possible because the general will of *nuchi du takara* shared by the global multitude has taken clearer shape in the planetary time-space. Historically, in the 1970s–1980s, due to the dysfunction of the Security Council caused by the intensification of the Cold War, there emerged signs of a shift of influence within the United Nations from the Security Council, controlled by the five permanent members, to the General Assembly, governed by all member nations, whose collective will came to be broadly expressed through its "norm-formation" function (Peterson 2006, 144) on issues such as women, children, indigenous populations, democracy, peace, and human rights across and beyond various United Nations organs (Peterson 2006, 100–102; Mogami 2005, 124). The shift of influence from the Security Council to the General Assembly together with varied entities of the United Nations and beyond has been accelerated by the new security environment of the post–Cold War era, characterized by the metamorphoses of "the enemy," communism, into amorphous threats and contingencies across nations, regions, and continents (see Part III), such that (*a*) climate change has necessitated annual United Nations climate change conferences since 1995, resulting in the international adoption of the Kyoto Protocol in 1997 and of the Paris Agreement in 2015 (United Nations Framework Convention on Climate Change 2022), (*b*) the Treaty on the Prohibition of Nuclear Weapons, an international treaty adopted by the United Nations General Assembly in 2017 and ratified by fifty-nine countries and regions as of January 2022, came to be supported by more than 520 cities across the world (such as Hiroshima, Nagasaki, Paris, Glasgow, Washington, DC, Los Angeles, and Boston), owing in part to the campaign developed by the International Campaign to Abolish Nuclear Weapons (ICAN, n.d.; Miyake, Fukutomi, and Okada 2022), and (*c*) local conflicts necessitate a wide range of activities for humanitarian assistance and disaster relief by the United Nations (as noted in chapter 5, sections 4 and 5).

If these efforts represent the expansion of the concept of collective security into that of human security (Nasu 2013), collective security proper has also been invoked continuingly even as it has remained unexercised, as exemplified by the ways in which the United Nations has responded to the Russian invasion of Ukraine in 2022. For instance, by invoking the mechanism of the emergency special session—established by the Uniting for Peace resolution issued in 1950 in the midst of the Korean War in response to the failure of the Security Council to act as required to restore international peace and security owing to the US-Soviet rivalry (United Nations General Assembly, n.d.)—the General Assembly adopted a resolution to condemn the Russian invasion of Ukraine in 2022, based on the approval of 141 (of a total of 193) member nations. Two days before this resolution was adopted, the Security Council turned down a resolution drafted under the leadership of Albania, a nonpermanent member of the Security Council, in a way that highlighted Russia's veto (which was expressed by the show of a hand by the Russian representative). In effect, the United Nations was able to demonstrate, in the eyes of the world, that "Russia destroys international peace and security by invading Ukraine *and* makes the normal functioning of the Security Council—collective security—impossible through veto" (Hoshino 2022). The international community (the Arab-Islamic world in particular) has developed a similar criticism against Israel, which justifies its military actions in Gaza in the name of self-defense, and against the United States that approves them, though the situation is murky at the time of this writing (December 2023).

The following is a policy proposal for collective security from an Okinawan perspective (hereafter PPCSOP). It is developed in light of contemporary global conditions that have made collective security both necessary and possible in the Asia-Pacific region. Specifically, this proposal aims to materialize the general will of the community of *nuchi du takara* for peace, democracy, and shared affluence in the planetary time-space of the yet-to-come World Republic in the twenty-first century via the following three mechanisms.[3]

First, PPCSOP asserts mutual transference of the rights of collective/regional (not individual) self-defense by all states to the World Republic of *nuchi du takara*, which in turn integrates *all* national militaries in the Asia-Pacific region, including not only the US military and its allies such as Japan's Self-Defense Forces and the Republic of Korea National Military, but also (eventually) China's People's Liberation Army, North Korea's People's Army, and the Armed Forces of the Russian Federation, among others, and reorganizes them into what one might call the Asia-Pacific security forces. Its basic function is to "take effective collective measures for the prevention and removal of threats to the peace, and for the suppression of acts of aggression or other breaches of the peace," as defined by United Nations Charter Article 1(1). The World Republic of *nuchi du takara* will deem existing weapons of mass destruction—including nuclear and chemical weapons—completely contradictory to the mission of the Asia-Pacific security forces and will reduce, manage, and ultimately remove such weapons from the region and from the planet.

Second, PPCSOP maintains that bilateral alliances like the US-Japan security alliance, the US–South Korea security alliance, and the Australia, New Zealand, United States Security Treaty, created during the Cold War to contain and intimidate the "enemy," are to be restructured as a forum of multilateral security dialogues across the Asia-Pacific region. It is in this forum that the US-China dialogue will be expanded and "history issues" of the Asia-Pacific region, including the war responsibilities of Japan and the Imperial House, as touched on in Part III, will be discussed and debated with what Tessa Morris-Suzuki calls "reconciliation as method"—that is, reconciliation "not as an end-point in which consensus on history is achieved, but rather as sets of media, skills and processes that encourage the creative sharing of ideas and understandings of about the past" (2013, 13) in the Asia-Pacific region and across state and nonstate realms (see also Chen 2010, chap. 3; Ching 2019; Fujitani, White, and Yoneyama 2001).

Third, PPCSOP envisions that a basic principle of the Constitution of Japan—unarmed peace, as stipulated in Article 9—will be restored, for Japan will have two limited forces, one for the World Republic of *nuchi du takara*'s collective security and the other for individual self-defense in case of an unlawful armed attack from outside. More specifically, this is a mechanism that will enable Japan simultaneously to exit the existing US-centered collective/regional self-defense system and to actively participate in the collective security missions of the Asia-Pacific security forces of the World Republic of *nuchi du takara*, such as peacekeeping and humanitarian operations. In so doing, Japan will be able to achieve the vision expressed in Paragraph 1 of Article 9: "Aspiring sincerely to an international peace based on justice and order, the Japanese people forever renounce war as a sovereign right of the nation and the threat or use of force as means of settling international disputes." The notion of individual self-defense, as acknowledged in Article 51 of the United Nations Charter as an "inherent right" of the state, will be strictly conceived and applied and thus will square with Paragraph 2 of Article 9, which stipulates: "In order to accomplish the aim of the preceding paragraph, land, sea, and air forces, as well as other war potential, will never be maintained. The right of belligerency of the state will not be recognized."

"The more thoroughly these three mechanisms are implemented, the less U.S. bases in Okinawa/Japan, a symbol of the Cold War logic of containment and intimidation, will be necessary. As an increasing number of U.S. bases become inessential and are returned to Okinawa/Japan, the U.S.

military presence will decline until no U.S. troops are permanently stationed in Okinawa/Japan. It follows that construction of the FRF in Henoko will become unnecessary" (Inoue 2017b, 54–55)—the plan has already begun to look outdated anyway (see chapter 1, section 2)—and that Futenma should be returned unconditionally. This is where the general will of *nuchi du takara* shared by the Okinawan multitude is materialized as a policy principle of collective security for the shaping of the future.

. . .

I develop PPCSOP in reference to a number of efforts made in Okinawa and Japan as a whole in the 1990s and beyond to change the US-dependent security paradigm that had been adopted by Japan ever since 1945 (see Part III). For instance, a group of legal scholars in Japan connected the principle of collective security by the United Nations with Article 9 of the postwar Japanese constitution (Kozeki et al. 1993). From an Okinawan perspective, in 1996, in response to the 1995 rape incident, the Okinawa prefectural government proposed the Kichihenkan Akushon Puroguramu (Action Program for Returning US Bases to Okinawa) under the leadership of Governor Ōta Masahide, which charted the reorganization and reduction and ultimate removal of the US bases in Okinawa, as noted in chapter 4, section 5. Meanwhile, the center-right Liberal Party, under the leadership of Ozawa Ichirō, advocated a shift from the US-centered collective/regional self-defense paradigm to the UN-centered collective security paradigm as part of its own diplomatic platform in the late 1990s (Sakaguchi 1999; Takano H. 2012, 211–225). Ozawa's Liberal Party joined the center-left Democratic Party of Japan (DPJ) in 2003. By the time the DPJ came to power in 2009 by defeating the Liberal Democratic Party—a conservative, pro-American party in power in much of post–World War II Japan after 1955 (when it was formed)—it no longer openly promoted this paradigm shift (which was viewed as "too radical" by the public); nonetheless, the DPJ attempted to accomplish a change in postwar Japan's security system to actively reduce the burden of the US military bases in Okinawa (Democratic Party of Japan 2008), although the political failure of Prime Minister Hatoyama Yukio of the DPJ, as discussed in chapter 1, section 1, made it impossible to actualize this change.

Situated in the above genealogy of ideas about international security, PPCSOP is also grafted onto and creolized by the current of Okinawa's radical thought on *nuchi du takara*. For instance, in the midst of the reversion movement (discussed in chapter 3, section 4), writers such as Arakawa Akira, Kawamitsu Shin'ichi, and Okamoto Keitoku, in their critical analyses of the reversion of Okinawa as a historical process that would perpetuate control of Okinawa by the Japanese state, radicalized the logic of reversion by situating Okinawa beyond and outside the nation-state of Japan in the spirit of what Hardt and Negri called "altermodernity," which is "two removes from" the nation-state (Hardt and Negri 2009, 114). First, their criticisms were grounded in the anti-base struggles undermining the transnational unity of the two nation-states, the United States and Japan; second, their criticisms broke with the nation-state paradigm itself. In the process, their ideas highlighted the indigenous concept of *nuchi du takara* as the unwavering principle of life.

More specifically, Okinawan critic/poet Arakawa Akira (1931–present) ([1970] 1992; cf. Oguma 1998, chap. 23)—who belonged to the first generation of Okinawan social actors having experienced both the Battle of Okinawa and the US rule of Okinawa—developed the concept of "anti-reversion" (*han-fukki*), arguing, correctly from the perspective of the 2020s, that the reversion would forever trap Okinawa in a situation where Okinawa would no longer be excluded from Japan but subordinated within it politically, economically, and culturally, not unlike the Ryukyu Measures in the 1870s, by which Meiji Japan abolished and integrated the Ryukyu Kingdom. In so doing, Arakawa—as a singularity preceding the Okinawan multitude—resituated Okinawa through what Naoki Sakai and Hyon Joo Yoo (2012) call the "trans-Pacific imagination," outside the time-space of Japan, the US-Japan alliance, and Empire. From a slightly different perspective, Okinawan literary critic Okamoto Keitoku (1934–2006) proposed *sui-heijiku*, or a community of copresence, against the individualism that had functioned as a driving force of Japanese modernity founded on the institution of the emperor: "I think that a direction of Okinawa's possibility may lie in refusing to mold Okinawa according to the fictive image of 'modernity' and instead harnessing the difference of Okinawa [i.e., the community of copresence] freely and critically" ([1970] 1992, 161).

In a way that extended the thoughts of Arakawa and Okamoto, Kawamitsu Shin'ichi (1932–present), another noted Okinawan critic/poet and contemporary of Arakawa and Okamoto, also published a draft of the "Constitution of the Ryukyu Republic Society" ([1981] 2014) on the basis of deep disillusionment with the consequence of the 1972 Okinawa reversion—that is, the continued presence of the US military in exchange for money, resulting in destruction of life, at once social, spiritual, and natural. Subverting the conventional notion of a constitution as a foundational legal framework that defines the role, scope, and power of a state controlling its subjects from above, Kawamitsu drafted this constitution to conceptualize Okinawa as an open, heterogeneous "society," a vision that represents the community of *nuchi du takara* that we have explored in this study. In other words, Kawamitsu's constitution sought to express and protect the constituent power of the Okinawan multitude, not the constituted power of the state as in the case of conventional constitutions.

Accordingly, while this constitution designates the Ryukyu archipelago as the locus of the Ryukyu Republic Society, all people, insofar as they are willing to approve and observe this constitution, are qualified as its constituents, regardless of race, ethnicity, gender, and nationality (Articles 8 and 11). It declares unarmed peace (Article 13), together with the abolition of the military, the police, the courts, and other centralized, bureaucratic systems of constituted power. At the level of everyday life, no discrimination is allowed in this society (Article 18), a principle extended to the stipulation about shared ownership and management of social infrastructure and the means of production for the enhancement of the common/shared wealth (Articles 6, 7, and 19), which regulates, if it does not eliminate, private property (Article 18). Locally grounded visions of the community of *nuchi du takara* as formulated by Arakawa, Okamoto, and Kawamitsu, among others, when complemented by other ideas about international relations developed in Okinawa and wider Japan and cited above, help develop PPCSOP in a historical context in which amorphous contingencies—an omni-crisis—in the Asia-Pacific region and beyond require global yet grounded response and in which "we cannot work for others without working for ourselves."

• • •

Allow me to express some hesitation about advancing PPCSOP—and collective security, more generally—before I conclude this study. Observing that the United Nations has been collaborating with groups of powerful global capitalists such as the World Economic Forum for "strategic partnership" (World Economic Forum 2019) and that its projects, such as Sustainable Development Goals, are highly Euro-centric (Hickel 2020), my suspicion lingers that the World Republic of *nuchi du takara*, if constructed on the basis of the reform of the United Nations, would be hijacked by "the power over life" (constituted power) exercised by Empire from above, rather than authentically representing and embodying "the power of life" (constituent power) of the multitude from below. In other words, collective security may simply contribute to the dictatorship of the supranational common power that would monopolize all the security/military forces globally, a process that would be facilitated by mutual transference of the rights of collective/regional self-defense by all states to the World Republic.

I raise this concern because I worry that the idea of collective security—the use of the armed forces—may promote idealization of the military as a hero (as it were) who would protect the peace, by ignoring and slighting the lesson of Okinawan pacifism—"The military does not protect the lives of local residents"—that Okinawa collectively drew from the Battle of Okinawa, as noted in chapters 3, 4, and 7. This indeed is the lesson that I have learned, over and over again, from elderly men and women who were my friends and informants as I have conducted fieldwork in Henoko and greater Nago City ever since the late 1990s. It should be remembered that during this battle, instead of protecting Okinawans, Japanese soldiers, in the name of the emperor, ordered them (Okinawans) to kill themselves and their families, obtained food from them by force, exploited them and others sexually by establishing "comfort stations," kicked them out of shelters, fled to Japan "proper," and in some cases, executed them, saying that they were spies of the US military (Okinawa Times 1950). Okamoto Tarō, a Japanese artist known for his avant-garde paintings, constructions, and sculptures, visited US-ruled Okinawa in 1959 (as noted in chapter 6), commenting—on the basis of his own experience as a lowest-rank soldier sent to China during World War II (Yamamoto A. 2023)—that "irredeemable stupidity and inhumanity of the Japanese Imperial Army, together with its shame and humiliation, were condensed here [in Okinawa]" ([1961] 2013, 20). More recently, an argument that "the military does not protect the lives of local residents" has been supported through allegations of sexual exploitation and abuse and other misconduct made against United Nations peacekeepers (Wheeler 2020; UN News, n.d.). Indeed, instances of sexual violence against women exercised by the military (men) to conquer and control the "enemy" have been too numerous to fully document, exemplified by the acts of not only Japanese but also American, Korean, Russian, Rwandan, and Serbian troops in zones of conflict in the recent past and at present (Akibayashi 2017; Kim K. 2006; Takano Y. 2022).

To this concern over the military as an institution of violence rather than of peace, I respond by insisting on the role the "multitude-states" should play in conceiving and establishing a planetary system of collective security built on the aforementioned trinity of the multitude (local), the state, and the World Republic (global), in which the military *does* protect the lives of the multitude. More specifically, I suggest that the multitude will continue to transform nation-states—"imagined communities" (Anderson 1991) characterized by the homogenization of the inside as well as the division of the inside (Self) and the outside (Other/enemy)—into "multitude-states." Unlike the nation (citizens/subjects) in a nation-state, the multitude in a multitude-state is neither homogenous nor demarcated by national boundaries but is always and already united by the general will of *nuchi du takara* across the planet. As such, the multitude in the multitude-state is not oriented solely toward generating and regenerating the World Republic of *nuchi du takara* to exercise collective security "from above" to complement the rights of individual self-defense of multitude-states. In case of tyranny of the supranational common power (the World Republic), the multitude-states will also collectively perform self-defense "from below" against the collective security forces of that common power. In other words, the same general will of *nuchi du takara* that has enabled the multitude-states to create the World Republic will also oblige them to overthrow the World Republic if it does not protect the common good, life. Accordingly, I am skeptical of Hardt and Negri's call to dismantle the state apparatuses, regarding "the state as not the realm of freedom but the seat of domination" (2009, 355). The state can be the seat of domination (over the multitude) *and* the realm of freedom (against the tyranny of the supranational power), depending on the context.

For I consider humanity—including us, the multitude—to be fundamentally contradictory and ambiguous: in that we need to eat (i.e., kill) to live, our creativity can readily turn exploitative and destructive, and our sublime acts of love are often dictated by selfishness and inseparable from violence against others. In other words, we may never be able to eradicate our own evilness, violence, and selfishness, even as we perform honorable deeds by constructing the World Republic of *nuchi du takara*. To cope with such evilness, ultimately, the global multitude may need to align or reconcile its constituent power with the realm of divine power, broadly conceived, a realm that appears and reappears "not so much as something deriving from human desires or free will, but in the form of a categorical imperative that transcends them" (Karatani [2010] 2014, 14), just as the Okinawan multitude has constructed the changing-same community of *nuchi du takara* on a metaphysical ground that has appeared and reappeared as "resistance itself" (Nancy [1983] 1991, 35) often beyond human desires or free will, as noted in chapters 2, 4, and 7. Meanwhile, the World Republic of *nuchi du takara*, the agent of collective security against threats to the peace, also needs to have a built-in mechanism—the military—to defend itself from the possibility that the World Republic could turn into a threat to the peace in spite of itself. In effect, we may need to control the violence, either against the World Republic or by the World Republic, by using the very violence we intend to control, until "one day a few billion years from now, the earth will be swallowed by the sun as it begins to die." Instead of generalizing and projecting the historical truth that "the military did not protect the lives of local residents" into the future, I thus propose, with some hesitation, that the multitude actively and wisely manage, use, and control the military through the trinity of the multitude, multitude-states, and the World Republic of *nuchi du takara* precisely because the military did not protect the lives of local residents in the past.

Notes

1. Rousseau (1762 [2014]) asserted "that the institution of government is not a contract, but a law; that the depositaries of the executive power are not the people's masters, but its officers; that it can set them up and pull them down when it likes; that for them there is no question of contract, but of obedience; and that in taking charge of the functions the State imposes on them they are doing no more than fulfilling their duty as citizens, without having the remotest right to argue about the conditions" (book 3, chap. 18).

2. Karatani follows the usage of Immanuel Kant in *Perpetual Peace* ([1795] 2016, esp. 136) to develop the notion of the World Republic.

3. PPCSOP elaborates on, rearticulates, and ultimately overcomes *jōji-chūryūnaki anpo* (a security alliance without permanent stationing of US forces in Okinawa or elsewhere in Japan), discussed in Inoue 2017b, 54–55.

REFERENCES

When dates for an old edition in brackets [ ] and a new edition without brackets are juxtaposed, citations refer to the new edition unless otherwise noted.

This section contains bibliographical information about books, articles, DVDs, films, videos, blogs, websites, TV programs, newspaper articles written by specified authors, and other related materials. Bibliographical information about newspaper articles written by unspecified authors, the newsletter titled *No Base*, and governmental documents is inscribed under different headings that follows this section.

Abe Shinzō. n.d. *Jiyūminshutō Abe Shinzō* [Liberal Democratic Party Abe Shinzō] (homepage). Accessed March 31, 2024. https://www.s-abe.or.jp/

Abe Takashi. 2021. "Henoko, Rikuji mo Jyōchū" [Japan Ground Self-Defense Force Will Also Be Permanently Stationed in Henoko]. *Okinawa Times*, January 25, page 1.

Abe Takashi, and Akamine Yukiko. 2016. "Henoko Kaijōkeibi, Kōgishimin o Tokutei Kōdōkiroku o Bōeikyoku e Hōkoku" [Coastal Patrol in Henoko Identifies Protesting Citizens, Records of Activities Submitted to the ODB]. *Okinawa Times*, May 14, 2016. Accessed November 3, 2020. https://www.okinawatimes.co.jp/articles/-/30740

Adams, Eric. J. 2017. *United States Marine Corps Post-Cold War Evolutionary Efforts: Implications for a Post-Operation Enduring Freedom/Operation Iraqi Freedom Force*. Fort Leavenworth, KS: School of Advanced Military Studies United States Army Command and General Staff College. Accessed March 30, 2024. https://apps.dtic.mil/sti/tr/pdf/AD1038855.pdf

Agamben, Giorgio. 1998. *Homo Sacer: Sovereign Power and Bare Life*. Stanford, CA: Stanford University Press.

Agamben, Giorgio. 2005. *State of Exception*. Chicago: University of Chicago Press.

Agarie Akiko. 2017. *Watashi no Pojishon* [My Position]. Naha, Okinawa: Ryukyu Shimpo-sha.

Ahagon Shōkō. 1973. *Beigun to Nōmin* [The US Military and the Peasantry]. Tokyo: Iwanami Shoten.

Ahagon Shōkō. 1992. *Inochi koso Takara: Okinawa Hansen no Kokoro* [Life Is the Ultimate Treasure: The Heart of Okinawa's Pacifism]. Tokyo: Iwanami Shoten.

Aihara Masayoshi. 2000. "Sengochiri/Chiri Kyōiku o Torimaku Ainu Minzoku Kijytsu no Kentō" [An Investigation of Description about the Ainu People in Postwar Geography and Geography Education]. *Hekichikyōiku Kenkyū* 55: 67–78. Accessed March 30, 2024. https://hokkyodai.repo.nii.ac.jp/records/9769

Akibayashi Kozue. 2004. "Anzenhoshō to Jendā nikansuru Kōsatsu: Okinawa 'Kichi Guntai o Yurusanai Kōdōsuru Onnatachi no Kai' no Jireikara" [A Gender Perspective on Security: A Case Study of the Okinawa Society of Acting Women Who Do Not Accept the Military and Bases]. *Jendā Kenkyū* 7: 73–85. Accessed December 20, 2020. http://hdl.handle.net/10083/35596

Akibayashi Kozue. 2017. "Guntai to Seibōryoku: Kokusaikihan toshiteno Buryokufunsōka no Seibōryoku to Shiminshakai" [The Military and Sexual Violence: Sexual Violence in the Areas of Conflict and Civil Society]. In *Okinawa nimiru Seibōryoku to Gunjishugi* [Sexual Violence and Militarism in Okinawa], authored by Miyagi Harumi et al., 111–128. Tokyo: Ochanomizu Shobō.

Akibayashi Kozue, and Suzuyo Takazato. 2009. "Okinawa: Women's Struggle for Demilitarization." In *The Bases of Empire: The Global Struggle against U.S. Military Posts*, edited by Catherine Lutz, 243–269. New York: New York University Press.

Akutibu Myūjiamu Onnatachi no Sensō to Heiwa Shiryōkan (wam). 2020. *Nihongun Ianjo Mappu, Okinawa* [A Map of Military Comfort Stations, Okinawa]. Accessed December 11, 2020. https://wam-peace.org/ianjo/area/area-jp/area-jp-47/

Allen, David. 2004. "Helo Crashes on Okinawa Campus." *Stars and Stripes*, August 15. Accessed October 29, 2020. https://www.stripes.com/news/helo-crashes-on-okinawa-campus-1.23241

Allen, Matthew. 2002. *Identity and Resistance in Okinawa*. Lanham, MD: Rowman & Littlefield Publishers.

Allen, Mathew. 2016. "The shaman hunts and the postwar revival and reinvention of Okinawan shamanism." Japan Forum, 29:2, 218–235. https://doi.org/10.1080/09555803.2016.1189447

Allison, Anne. 2013. *Precarious Japan*. Durham, NC: Duke University Press.

Althusser, Louis. 1970. *Ideology and Ideological State Apparatuses*. Translated by Ben Brewster. Marxists.org. Accessed December 1, 2020. http://www.marxists.org/reference/archive/althusser/1970/ideology.htm

Amako Satoshi. 2018. "Kaikakukaihō" [Reform and Opening of China]. *Nihon Daihyakka Zensho*, April 18. Accessed December 21, 2020. https://kotobank.jp/word/%E6%94%B9%E9%9D%A9%E9%96%8B%E6%94%BE-456883

Amamiya Karin, and Kayano Toshihito. 2008. *"Ikizurasa" ni Tsuite: Hinkon, Aidentiti, Nashonarizumu* [On the Hardness of Life: Poverty, Identity, Nationalism]. Tokyo: Kōbunsha.

Ames, Christopher 2010. "Crossfire Couples: Marginality and Agency among Okinawan Women in Relationships with U.S. Military Men." In *Over There: Living with the U.S. Military Empire from World War Two to the Present*, edited by Maria Höhn and Seungsook Moon, 176–202. Durham, N.C.: Duke University Press.

Anderson, Benedict. 1991. *Imagined Communities: Reflections on the Origin and Spread of Nationalism*, Revised edition. London, New York: Verso.

Angst, Linda Isako. 1997. "Gendered nationalism: the Himeyuri Story and Okinawan Identity in Postwar Japan." *Political and Legal Anthropological Review* 20(1): 100–113. Accessed December 27, 2020. https://www.jstor.org/stable/24497988

Angst, Linda Isako. 2003. "The Rape of a Schoolgirl: Discourses of Power and Women's Lives in Okinawa." In *Islands of Discontent: Okinawan Responses to Japanese and American Power*, edited by Laura Hein and Mark Selden, 135–157. Lanham, MD: Rowman & Littlefield.

APEC Secretariat. 2021. *Homepage*. Accessed July 30, 2021. https://www.apec.org/

Arakaki Reo, and Agarie Ikuka. "Daishikkōsoshō Ken Haiso" [Okinawa Prefecture Lost the Subrogation Case]. *Okinawa Times*, December 21, page 1.

Arakaki Tsuyoshi. 2016. "'Okinawa Dojin' Hatsugen, Yamato wa 'Heisei no Jinruikan' da." [The Statement about Okinawans as "Dojin": Japan Is the Human Pavilion of the Heisei Era]. *Ronza*, November 8. Accessed October 14, 2018. http://webronza.asahi.com/politics/articles/2016110700009.html

Arakawa Akira. [1970] 1992. "'Hikokumin' no Shisō to Ronri: Okinawa niokeru Shisō no Jiritsu nitsuite" [The Thought and Logic of the Nonnational: On the Autonomy of Thought in Okinawa]. In *Okinawa Bungaku Zenshū Dai 18-kan, Hyōron II* [Complete Works of Okinawan Literature, Volume 18, Criticisms II], edited by Okinawa Bungaku Zenshū Henshū Īnkai, 61–116. Tokyo: Kokusho Kankōkai.

Arasaki Kyōtarō. 1980. "Kanettai: Ōbāhīto Zōn" [Exceedingly Tropical: An Overheated Zone]. Serialized from February 12, 1980, 49 times in the *Okinawa Times*. Citations refer to the 26th episode, appearing in the *Okinawa Times* on March 13, 1980.

Arasaki Moriteru, ed. 1969. *Dukyumento Okinawa Tōsō* [Documenting Okinawa Struggles]. Tokyo: Aki Shobō.

Arasaki Moriteru. [1973] 1992. "Hōkaisuru Okinawa" [Decaying Okinawa]. In *Okinawa Dōjidaishi Dai 1-kan, 1973–1977: Yogawari no Uzu no Nakade* [Contemporary History of Okinawa, 1973–1977: As We Are Drawn into the Vortex of Changes], 16–26. Tokyo: Gaifūsha.

Arasaki Moriteru. [1982] 1992a. "'Hondoka' no Honryū ni Teikō" [Resisting the Torrents of "Japanization"]. In *Okinawa Dōjidaishi Dai 2-kan, 1978–1982: Ryūkyūko no Shiten kara* [Contemporary History of Okinawa, 1978–1982: From the Perspective of the Arc of Ryukyus], 196–200. Tokyo: Gaifūsha.

Arasaki Moriteru. [1982] 1992b. "Okinawa deno Jyūmin Gyakusatsu to Kyōkasho Kentei" [Massacres of Residents in Okinawa and the Screening of School Textbooks]. In *Okinawa Dōjidaishi Dai 2-kan, 1978–1982: Ryūkyūko no Shiten kara* [Contemporary History of Okinawa, 1978–1982: From the Perspective of the Arc of Ryukyus], 184–187. Tokyo: Gaifūsha.

Arasaki Moriteru. [1985] 1992. "Okinawa wa Naze 'Hinomaru' o Kakagerarenaika" [Why Okinawa Cannot Hoist the National Flag]. In *Okinawa Dōjidaishi Dai 3-kan, 1983–1987: Shōkokushugi no Tachiba de* [Contemporary History of Okinawa, 1983–1987: From the Viewpoint of a Small Nation], 61–66. Tokyo: Gaifūsha.

Arasaki Moriteru. [1986] 1995. *Okinawa Hansen Jinushi* [Okinawa's Anti-military Landlords]. Tokyo: Kōbunken.

Arasaki Moriteru. 1996. *Okinawa Gendaishi: Shinpan* [Modern History of Okinawa: New Edition]. Tokyo: Iwanami Shoten.

Arasaki Moriteru. 2014. *Okinawa o Koeru: Minshūrentai to Heiwasōzō no Kakushingenbakara* [Overcoming Okinawa: From the Site of Solidarity of the People and Construction of Peace]. Tokyo: Gaifūsha.

Arasaki Moriteru, and Kawamitsu Shin'ichi, eds. 1988. *Okinawa: Ten'nō-sei eno Gyakkō* [Okinawa: A Backlight against the Emperor System]. Tokyo: Shakaihyōronsha.

Arasaki Moriteru, Okamoto Keitoku, Asato Eiko, Ui Jyun, and Takara Ben. [1989] 2016. "Zadankai: Sorezore ni Totteno Jyūmin Undō—Honnne de Kataru" [Roundtable: Local Residents' Campaigns for Each of Us—an Open and Honest Talk]. *Ryūkyūko no Jyūmin Undō* Fukkan 7 (Tsūkan 32): 20–30. In *Ryūkyūko no Jyūmin Undō, Fukkokuban* [Social Movements of the Residents in the Ryukyu Arc], edited by "Ryūkyūko no Jyūmin Undō" Fukkokuban Kankō Īnkai, 749–759. Tokyo: Gōdō Shuppan.

Arashiro Toshiaki. 1994. *Kōtō Gakkō Ryukyu-Okinawa Shi* [High School History of the Ryukyus and Okinawa]. Ginowan, Okinawa: Okinawaken Rekishi Kyōiku Kenkyūkai.

Arce, Moisés, and Robert Rice, eds. 2019. *Protest and Democracy*. Calgary: University of Calgary Press. Accessed May 6, 2022. ProQuest Ebook Central.

Armitage, Richard L., Dan E. Bob, Kurt M. Campbell, Michael J. Green, Kent M. Harrington, Frank Jannuzi, James A. Kelly, Edward J. Lincoln, Robert A. Manning, Kevin G. Nealer, Joseph S. Nye Jr., Torkel L. Patterson, James J. Przystup, Robin H. Sakoda, Barbara P. Wanner, and Paul D. Wolfowitz. 2000. *The United States and Japan: Advancing Toward a Mature Partnership*. Accessed December 21, 2020. http://www.ne.jp/asahi/nozaki/peace/data/data_inss_sr.html

Armitage, Richard L., and Joseph S. Nye. 2007. *The U.S.-Japan Alliance: Getting Asia Right through 2020*. Washington, DC: Center for Strategic and International Studies. Accessed December 22, 2020. https://csis-website-prod.s3.amazonaws.com/s3fs-public/legacy_files/files/media/csis/pubs/070216_asia2020.pdf

Armitage, Richard L., and Joseph S. Nye. 2012. *The U.S.-Japan Alliance: Anchoring Stability in Asia*. Washington, DC: Center for Strategic and International Studies. Accessed December 22, 2020. https://csis-website-prod.s3.amazonaws.com/s3fs-public/legacy_files/files/publication/120810_Armitage_USJapanAlliance_Web.pdf

Armitage, Richard L., and Joseph S. Nye. 2018. *More Important Than Ever: Renewing the U.S.-Japan Alliance for the 21st Century*. Washington, DC: Center for Strategic and International Studies. Accessed December 22, 2020. https://csis-website-prod.s3.amazonaws.com/s3fs-public/publication/181011_MorethanEver.pdf

Armitage, Richard L., and Joseph S. Nye. 2020. *The U.S.-Japan Alliance in 2020: An Equal Alliance with a Global Agenda*. Washington, DC: Center for Strategic and International Studies. Accessed December 26, 2020. https://csis-website-prod.s3.amazonaws.com/s3fs- public/publication/201204_Armitage_Nye_US_Japan_Alliance_1.pdf

Asahi Shimbun. [1955] 1969. *Asahi Hōdō* [Asahi Report]. In Nakano Yoshio, *Sengo Shiryō Okinawa* [Historical Records of Postwar Okinawa], 145–148. Tokyo: Nihon Hyōronsha.

Asahi Shimbun Ata Shuzaihan. 2002. *Terorisuto no Kiseki: Mohamedo Ata o Ou* [The Trajectory of a Terrorist: Following Mohamed Atta]. Tokyo: Sōshisha.

Asato Eiko. 2000. "Beigunseika ni miru Kodomo to Josei no Jinken" [Human Rights of Children and Women under the US Military Rule]. *People's Plan Forum* 3(4) (September). Accessed December 12, 2020. http://www.jca.apc.org/ppsg/News/3-4/F03-4-08.htm

Asato Eiko. 2009. "'Fukki'-go no Kaihatsu Mondai" [Environmental Problems after "Reversion"]. In *Okinawa: Toi o Tateru 5: Imo to Hadashi—Senryō to Genzai* [Okinawa: Establishing Questions, Volume 5: Potatoes and Barefoot—the Occupation and the Present], edited by Toriyama Atsushi, 109–144. Tokyo: Shakai Hyōronsha.

Asato Keinosuke. 1989. *Hōsō Yobun: Sōsōki no Rajio/Terebi* [Tidbits of Broadcasting: The Beginning of Radio and TV]. Okinawa: Unknown.

Authors. 1988. *Okinawakara Tennōsei o Kangaeru* [Thinking the Emperor System from Okinawa]. Tokyo: Shinkyō Shuppansha.

Azusawa Noboru. 2012. "Shinyaku Kankō ni Atatte—Yakusha Atogaki ni Kaete" [On the Occasion of Publishing a New Translation—in Place of Afterword by the Translator]. In *Hachigatu Jyūgoya no Chaya, Okinawa Senryō Tōchi 1945* [The Teahouse of the August Moon, Occupying and Ruling Okinawa in 1945], translated by Azusawa Noboru, 320–334. Tokyo: Sairyūsha.

Baker, Mark. *Nam: The Vietnam War in the Words of the Men and Women Who Fought There*. New York: Cooper Square Press.

Barske, Valerie H. 2010. "'Dancing Through' Historical Trauma: Okinawan Performance in Post-Imperial Japan." *Intersections: Gender and Sexuality in Asia and the Pacific Issue 24: Special Issue on Trauma*. Accessed December 13, 2020. http://intersections.anu.edu.au/issue24/barske.htm#t44

Barske, Valerie H. 2013. "Visualizing Priestesses or Performing Prostitutes?: Ifa Fuyu's Depictions of Okinawan Women (1913–1943)." *Studies on Asia: Interdisciplinary Journal of Asian Studies* Series IV Vol. 3:1 (March): 65–108. Accessed December 13, 2020. https://castle.eiu.edu/studiesonasia/documents/seriesIV/Barske_Studies_March2013_001.pdf

Bataille, Georges. [1949] 1976. "Existence des sociétés au niveau de la mort." In *Œurvres Completes* VII, 245–246. Gallimard. Accessed May 22, 2022. https://fdocuments.us/document/georges-bataille-oeuvres-completes-tome-7.html?page=121

Bataille, Georges. [1952] 1973. "Notes." In *Œurvres Completes* V, 419–579. Paris: Gallimard.

Bataille, Georges. [1956] 1989. "Madame Edwarda." In *My Mother, Madame Edwarda, the Dead Man*, translated by Austryn Wainhouse, 135–159. London/New York: Marion Boyars.

Beeson, Mark. 1999. "The End of the Miracle? Japan and the East Asian Crisis." *Political Science* 50(2): 274–84. https://doi-org.ezproxy.uky.edu/10.1177/003231879905000211

Benjamin, Walter. [1921] 1996. "Critique of Violence." In *Selected Writings, Volume 1 1913–1926*, edited by Marcus Bullock and Michael W. Jennings, 236–252. Cambridge, MA: Belknap Press of Harvard University Press.

Benjamin, Walter. [1933] 1978. "On the Mimetic Faculty." In *Walter Benjamin: Reflections*, translated by Edmund Jephcott, 333–336. New York: Schocken Books.

Benjamin, Walter. [1942] 1968. "Theses on the Philosophy of History." In *Walter Benjamin: Illuminations*, translated by Harry Zohn, 253–264. New York: Schocken Books.

Berdal, Mats. 2008. "The Security Council and Peacekeeping." In Vaughan Lowe, Adam Roberts, Jennifer Welsh, and Dominik Zaum (eds.), *The United Nations Security Council and War: the Evolution of Thought and Practice Since 1945*, 175–204. Oxford: Oxford University Press.

"Betonamusensō no Kiroku" Henshū Īnkai. 1988. *Betonamusensō no Kiroku* [Records of the Vietnam War]. Tokyo: Ōtsuki Shoten.

Bhabha, Homi K. 1994. *The Location of Culture*. London/New York: Routledge.

Bhowmik, Davinder. 2008. *Writing Okinawa: Narrative Acts of Identity and Resistance*. London and New York: Routledge.

Binnendijk, Johannes A. 1973. "Part I: The Dynamics of Okinawan Reversion, 1945–69." In *Public Diplomacy and Political Change; Four Case Studies: Okinawa, Peru, Czechoslovakia, Guinea*, edited by Gregory Henderson, 1–188. New York: Praeger.

Blanchot, Maurice. [1984] 1988. *The Unavowable Community*. Translated by Pierre Joris. New York: Station Hill Press.

Bōeichō Bōeikenshūjo Senshishitsu. 1968. *Senhi Sōsho: Okinawa Hōmen Rikugun Sakusen* [A Series of War History: Army Operations in the Okinawa Area]. Tokyo: Asagumo Shimbunsha.

Buckley, Roger. 1992. *US-Japan Alliance Diplomacy, 1945–1990*. New York: Cambridge University Press.

Bush, George H. W. [1990] 2017. "The other 9/11: George H.W. Bush's 1990 New World Order Speech." *Dallas Morning News*, September 8. Accessed December 21, 2020. https://www.dallasnews.com/opinion/commentary/2017/09/08/the-other-9-11-george-h-w-bush-s-1990-new-world-order-speech/

Cancian, Mark F. 2020. *U.S. Military Forces in FY 2021: Marine Corps.* Accessed December 15, 2020. https://www.csis.org/analysis/us-military-forces-fy-2021-marine-corps?fbclid=IwAR0bz2Gt_86m3rMkghJiS94dhkb44QKEHMm-FLJHbN1k06qS0VMXyQ64rTg

Carns, Neil C., and Stanton S. Coerr. 1994. "A True Force in Readiness." *Proceedings* (August) 120/8/1,098: 35–38

Castells, Manuel. 1997. *The Power of Identity, The Information Age: Economy, Society and Culture Volume II.* Malden, MA: Blackwell.

Castells, Manuel. 1998. End of Millennium, The Information Age: Economy, Society and Culture Volume III. Malden, MA: Blackwell.

Castells, Manuel. 2015. *Networks of Outrage and Hope: Social Movements in the Internet Age.* Second edition. Cambridge, UK: Polity Press.

Chang, Iris. 1997. *The Rape of Nanking: The Forgotten Holocaust of World War II.* New York: Basic Books.

Chen, Kuan-Hsing. 2010. *Asia as Method: Toward Deimperialization.* Durham, NC: Duke University Press.

Chiba Takurō. 2016. "Dentsū no Josei Shin'nyūshain Jisatsu, Rōsai to Nintei, Zangyō Tsuki 105-jikan" [The Suicide of a Newly Employed Woman of Detsū is Acknowledged as a Work-Related Accident, 105 Hours of Overwork a Month]. *Asahi Shimbun*, October 8. Accessed December 20, 2020. https://digital.asahi.com/articles/photo/AS20161007005365.html

Chigakudantai Kenkyūkai. 2019. *Henoko Shinkichi Kensetsu ni Hantaisuru Seimei* [Statement to Oppose the Construction of a New Base in Henoko]. Issued on August 24. Accessed December 10, 2020. https://www.chidanken.jp/DL_storage/01_General/2019_Tokyo/statement_2019Henoko.pdf

Chinen Isao. 1995. *Himeyuri no Ininbi* [The Deep-Seated Grudge of Himeyuri]. Tokyo: Inpakuto Shuppankai.

Ching, Leo T. 2019. *Anti-Japan.* Durham, NC: Duke University Press.

Chohsuke. 2009. "Comment on: Cocco – Jyugon no Mieruoka" [Comment on: Cocco - *The Hill of Dugongs*]. Accessed July 19, 2010. http://www.youtube.com/watch?v=wNKg-qjv5_I&feature=related

Choi Keumjin 2020. "Ōbātsūrizumu no Hassei to Jizoku Kanō na Kankōhatten no Kadai" [The Appearance of Over-Tourism and the Tasks for Sustainable Tourism development]. *Kyūshū Kokusai Daigaku Kokusai/Keizai Ronshū* 5: 193–206. Accessed December 22, 2020. http://id.nii.ac.jp/1265/00000715/

Claude, Inis L., Jr. 1962. *Power and International Relations.* New York: Random House.

Clegg, Jenny. 2009. *China's Global Strategy: Towards a Multipolar World.* London: Pluto Press. Accessed May 24, 2023. https://doi.org/10.2307/j.ctt183p561

Cocco. n.d. *Cocco.* Accessed October 22, 2023. https://www.youtube.com/user/Coccochannelofficial

Cocco. 1997a. "Kubi" (Head). In *Būgenbiria* [*Bougainvillea*]. Tokyo: Victor Entertainment.

Cocco. 1997b. "Hikōkigumo" (Winter Cloud). In *Būgenbiria* [*Bougainvillea*]. Tokyo: Victor Entertainment.

Cocco, 1997c. *Būgenbiria [Bougainvillea]*. Tokyo: Victor Entertainment.
Cocco. 2002. *Minami no Shima no Hoshi no Suna* [Star Sands in the South Ocean]. Tokyo: Kawaideshobō-Shinsha
Cocco. 2003. *Heaven's hell* (booklet accompanying the DVD). Tokyo: Victor Entertainment.
Cocco. 2004. *Minami no Shima no Koi no Uta* [Love Songs from the South Ocean]. Tokyo: Kawaideshobō-Shinsha.
Cocco. 2007a. *Omoigoto* [Things I Contemplate]. Tokyo: Mainichi Shimbunsha.
Cocco. 2007b. "Utautai no Ibasho wa Dokoni" [Where is the place for a singer to be in?]. *Papyrus* 13: 18–40.
Cocco. 2007c. *Jugon no Mieru Oka* [The Hill of Dugongs]. Tokyo: Victor Entertainment.
Cocco. 2009. "Ai to Zaiakukan no Yukue" [Future of Love and the Sense of Guilt]. *Papyrus* 26: 14–54.
Cocco. 2010. "Moshimo Negaiga Kanaunara" [If I Had One Wish]. 2010. *Okinawa Times*, January 5. Accessed July 19, 2010. https://www.okinawatimes.co.jp/article/2010-01-05_1267
Cocco and Shibuya Yōichi. 2006. "Kanzen Dokusen! Katsudō Chūshikarano 5nenkan o Subste Kataru" [Scoop! Discussing everything she did for 5 years after the discontinuance of activities]. *bridge* 49: 8–55.
Cocco Co., Ltd. (2010) *Cocco Official Site*. Accessed. July 19, 2010. http://www.cocco.co.jp/contents/index.html
Cooley, John. 2002. *Holy Wars: Afghanistan, America and International Terrorism* (New Edition). London: Pluto Press.
Cumings, Bruce. 1984. "The Origins and Development of the Northeast Asian Political Economy: Industrial Sectors, Product Cycles, and Political Consequences." *International Organization* 38(1) (Winter): 1–40. Accessed December 6, 2018. http://www.jstor.org/stable/2706600
Cumings, Bruce. 1993. "Japan's Position in the World System." In *Postwar Japan as History*, edited by Andrew Gordon, 34–63. Berkeley: University of California Press.
Da Pump. 2018. *U.S.A.* Accessed May 15, 2022. https://www.youtube.com/watch?v=sr--GVIolu
Deleuze, Gilles, and Félix Guattari. 1983. *Anti-Oedipus: Capitalism and Schizophrenia*. Translated by Robert Hurley, Mark Seem, and Helen R. Lane. Minneapolis: University of Minnesota Press.
Democratic Party of Japan. 2008. *Minshutō: Okinawa Bijyon* [Democratic Party of Japan: The Okinawa Vision]. Tokyo: DOP. Accessed on October 29, 2020. http://www1.dpj.or.jp/news/files/okinawa%282%29.pdf
Derrida, Jacques, 1978. "Violence and Metaphysics: An Essay on the Thought of Emmanuel Levinas." In *Writing and Difference*, translated by Alan Bass, 79–152, Chicago: University of Chicago Press.
Derrida, Jacques. [1994] 2005. *The Politics of Friendship*. London/New York: Verso.

Dirlik, Arif. 1999. "Place-Based Imagination: Globalism and the Politics of Place." *Review (Fernand Braudel Center)* 22(2): 151–87.
Doi Takaki. 2017. "Nihonban Kaiheitai, 2020nendai Zenhan ni Okinawa e, Beibutai Itengo" [The Japanese Marine Corps, to be deployed to Okinawa in the first half of the 2020s, after the American units move to Guam]. *Asahi Shimbun*, October 31. Accessed November 29, 2020. https://digital.asahi.com/articles/ASKBW53J7KBWUTIL034.html
Doi Takaki, Satō Taketsugu, and Minemura Kenji. 2020. "Okinawa Jyōkūni Chūgokuki, Kyōi no Misairu Nōryoku Gunkaku no Ashioto" [Chinese Planes over Okinawa, Threats of Missile Capacity, Steps toward the Expansion of Armaments]. *Asahi Shimbun*, March 23. Accessed December 23, 2020. https://digital.asahi.com/articles/ASN3Q74KPN3KUTFK01X.html?iref=pc_rellink_03
Doi Takeo. 1971. 'Amae' no Kōzō [The Structure of 'Dependence']. Tokyo: Kōbundō.
Dore, Ronald. 2000. *Stock Market Capitalism, Welfare Capitalism: Japan and Germany versus the Anglo Saxons*. Oxford: Oxford University Press.
Dower, John W. 1979. *Empire and Aftermath: Yoshida Shigeru and the Japanese Experience, 1878–1954*. Cambridge, MA: Council on East Asian Studies, Harvard University.
Dower, John W. 1986. *War without Mercy: Race and Power in the Pacific War*. New York: Pantheon Books.
Dower, John W. 1993. "Occupied Japan and the Cold War in Asia." In *Japan in War and Peace: Selected Essays*, 155–207. New York: The New Press.
Dower, John W. 1999. *Embracing Defeat: Japan in the Wake of World War II*. New York: W.W. Norton.
Dower, John W. 2014. "The San Francisco System: Past, Present, Future in U.S.-Japan-China Relations." *The Asia-Pacific Journal/Japan Focus* 12(8), Number 2: 1–41 (Article ID 4079). Accessed December 17, 2020. https://apjjf.org/2014/12/8/John-W.-Dower/4079/article.html
Dulles, John F. 1950. *War or Peace*. New York: Macmillan.
Duras, Marguerite. [1982] 1986. *The Malady of Death*. Translated by Barbara Bray. New York: Grove Press.
Duus, Peter. 2008. "The Greater East Asian Co-Prosperity Sphere: Dream and Reality." *Journal of Northeast Asian History* 4 (1): 143–154.
Eldridge, Robert D. 2001. *The Origins of the Bilateral Okinawa Problem: Okinawa in Postwar U.S.-Japan Relations, 1945–1952*. New York, NY: Garland Publishing.
Eltantawy, Nahed, and Julie B. Wiest. 2011. "Social Media in the Egyptian Revolution: Reconsidering Resource Mobilization Theory." *International Journal of Communication* 5: 1207–1224. Accessed October 12, 2018. http://web.b.ebscohost.com.ezproxy.uky.edu/ehost/detail/detail?vid=0&sid=773561a4-cc0d-424d-a80d-2d00674a7f53%40sessionmgr101&bdata=JnNpdGU9ZWhvc3QtbGl2ZSZzY29wZT1zaXRl#db=ufh&AN=97317275
Endō Orie. 1993. '*Sabetsugo/Fukaigo no Nagare to Ima.*' [Trends of Discriminatory Words/Unpleasant Words and Their Current Situations.] *Kokubungaku* 38(12): 110–115.

Endō, Takashi. 1995. "The Enola Gay—the Smithsonian controversy." *Hokkaido Tōkai Daigaku Kiyō, Jinbun Shakaikagakukei* 8: 125–135.

Endō Seiji, and Meguro Takayuki. 2023. "Amerika Ipponashi-dahō ga Nihon no Risuku" [One-Sided Reliance on the United States is Japan's Risk]. *Asahi Shimbun*, November 4. Accessed November 4, 2023. https://digital.asahi.com/articl es/ASRC36QW3RC2UTFK027.html?iref=comtop_7_01

Erbeeflower. 2009. "Comment on: Cocco – Okinawa Gomizero Raibu, Love" [Comment on: Cocco—A Live Concert for Zero Trash in Okinawa, Love]. Accessed July 19, 2010. http://www.youtube.com/watch?v=xAsfuji-gSE&feature=related

Esashi Hidenobu, and Miyashita Yoshitaka. 2015. "Saikin no Seiki/Hiseiki Koyō no Tokuchō" [Characteristics of Recent Non-Fulltime and Fulltime Employment]. *Tōkei Today* 97, July 24. Accessed December 22, 2020. http://www.stat.go.jp/in fo/today/097.html#k2

Fanon, Frantz. [1952] 1967. *Black Skin, White Masks*. Translated by Charles Lam Markmann. New York: Grove Press.

Fassin, Didier. 2013. Enforcing Order: An Ethnography of Urban Policing. Cambridge: Polity Press.

Field, Norma. 1991. *In the Realm of a Dying Emperor*. New York: Pantheon Books.

Fifield, Anna. 2016. "In Okinawa, Protesters Dig in as Work Proceeds to Relocate U.S. Marine base." *Washington Post*, February 7. Accessed January 16, 2021. https://www.washingtonpost.com/world/asia_pacific/in-okinawa-protesters -dig-in-as-work-proceeds-to-relocate-us-marine-base/2016/02/06/82d05264 -c481-11e5-b933-31c93021392a_story.html?utm_term=.965b2c296f26

Figal, Gerald. 2003. "Waging Peace in Okinawa." In *Islands of Discontent: Okinawan Responses to Japanese and American Power*, edited by Laura Hein and Mark Selden, 65–98. Lanham, MD: Rowman & Littlefield.

Figal, Gerald. 2012. *Beachheads: War, Peace, and Tourism in Postwar Okinawa*. Lanham, MD: Rowman & Littlefield.

Fisch, Arnold G., Jr. 1988. *Military Government in the Ryukyu Islands, 1945–1950*. Center of Military History, United States Army. Washington, D.C. Accessed December 11, 2020. https://history.army.mil/html/books/030/30-11-1/CMH_Pub_30-11 -1.pdf

Forgash, Rebecca. 2020. *Intimacy across the Fencelines: Sex, Marriage, and the U.S. Military in Okinawa*. Ithaca, NY: Cornell University Press.

Foucault, Michel. [1961] 1988. *Madness and Civilization: A History f Insanity in the Age of Reason*. Translated by Richard Howard. New York: Vintage Books.

Foucault, Michel. [1975] 1977. *Discipline and Punish: The Birth of Prison*. Translated by Alan Sheridan. New York: Vintage Books.

Foucault, Michel. 1977. "Nietzsche, Genealogy, History." In *Language, Counter-Memory, Practice: Selected Essays and Interviews*, edited by Donald F. Bouchard, and translated by Donald F. Bouchard and Sherry Simon, 139–164. Ithaca, NY: Cornell University Press.

Foucault, Michel. [1978] 1990. *The History of Sexuality: An Introduction, Volume I*. Translated by Robert Hurley. New York: Vintage Books.

Freud, Sigmund. [1913] 1950. *Totem and Taboo: Some Points of Agreement between the Mental Lives of Savages and Neurotics*. Translated by James Strachey. New York: W.W. Norton.
Fuchs, Christian. 2014. *OccupyMedia!: The Occupy Movement and Social Media in Crisis Capitalism*. Winchester, UK: Zero Books.
Fujii Seiji. 2018. *Okinawa Andāguraundo* [Okinawa's Underground]. Tokyo: Kōdansha.
Fujimoto Yukihisa, and Asako Kageyama, dirs. 2014. *Assatsu no Umi: Okinawa, Henoko* [The Ocean where Freedom is Suppressed: Henoko, Okinawa]. Hokkaido: Mori no Eigasha.
Fujita Naohisa, and Matsuyama Naoki. 2021. "Futenma 25-nen, Botan Kakechigai no Renzoku, Yamazaki Taku-shi no Keishō" [25 Years of Futenma Problems: A Cycle of Misunderstandings]. *Asahi Shimbun*, May 6. Accessed May 7, 2021. https://digital.asahi.com/articles/ASP4X4H51P4GUTFK00Z.html?iref=com_rnavi_rensai_2
Fujita Naohisa, and Teramoto Daizō. 2021. "Hatoyama Seiken de Fujō, 'Beigunkichi no Nichibei Shiyō'" [Idea that US Bases are to be Shared by the US and Japan Emerged during the Hatoyama Administration]. *Asahi Shimbun*, May 6. Accessed November 6. https://digital.asahi.com/articles/ASP5F6345P4GUTFK01L.html?iref=pc_rensai_article_short_1237_article_9
Fujitani, Takashi, Geoffrey M. White, and Lisa Yoneyama. 2001. *Perilous Memories: The Asia-Pacific War(s)*. Durham, NC: Duke University Press.
Fujiwara Shin'ichi. 2020. "Dan mo Danyakuko mo Nai Saizensen, 'Osomatsu' Haibi Maneita Kuni no Shittai" [Frontline without Ammos and Ammunition Depos, Poor Equipment Causing National Embarrassment]. *Asahi Shimbun*, April 16. Accessed November 29, 2020. https://digital.asahi.com/articles/ASN4G4T26N49TPOB004.html
Fujiwara Shin'ichi. 2021. "Miuchi no Ikotsu Haitteitara? Henoko Umetate Doshameguri Kakuchi de Ikensho" [What if the Sediment Contained the Bones of Your Dead Family Members? A Note of Protest is Adopted in Many Places]. *Asahi Shimbun*, September 9. Accessed June 14, 2022. https://digital.asahi.com/articles/ASP986RSZP98TIPE01K.html
Fukawa Reiko, and Niihara Shoji. 2013. *Sunagawa Jiken to Tanaka Saikōsai Chōkan: Beikaikin Bunsho ga Akirakanishita Nihon no Shihō* [The Sunagawa Case and Chief Justice of the Supreme Court Kotaro Tanaka: Japanese Judicial Practice Debunked by Declassified US Government Documents]. Tokyo: Nihonhyōronsha,
Fukuchi Hiroaki. [1977] 1995. *Okinawa ni Okeru Beigun no Hanzai* [Crimes Committed by the US Military in Okinawa]. Tokyo: Dōjidaisha.
Fukuchi Hiroaki. 1980. *Okinawa no Konketsuji to Hahatachi* [Mixed-Race Children in Okinawa and their Mothers]. Naha, Okinawa: Aoiumi Shuppansha.
Fukuma Yoshiaki. 2010. "Sengo Okinawa to Sensō Taikenron no Henyō (1)—Shūsen kara 'Tetsu no Bōfū' made" [Postwar Okinawa and the Transformation of Narratives on War (1): From the End of the War to the Publication of 'The Typhoon of Steel and Bombs']. *Ritsumeikan Sangyōshakai Ronshū* 45(4): 31–44.

Fukumoto Daisuke. 2019. "Naze Futenma wa Kiken ni Natta? Heisa Itten, Hondokara Butaizō" [Why has Futenma Become Dangerous? The Closing Plan was Cancelled, Replaced by the Increase of the Power of its Units]. *Okinawa Times*, February 13. Accessed December 21, 2020. https://www.okinawatimes.co.jp/articles/-/384323

Fukumura Takeshi. 1962. *Aru Hizumi* [A Strain]. *Ryūdai Gungaku* 3(2): 6–15.

Funabashi Yōichi. 1997. *Dōmeihyōryū* [Drifting of the US-Japan Security Alliance]. Tokyo: Iwanami Shoten.

Funakoshi Gishō. 1990. "Uema Ikuko no Zō" [Uema Ikuko's Images]. In *Uema Ikuko to Otohime Gekidan no 40-nen: Hana to Moete* [Uema Ikuko and 40 years of the Otohime Troupe: Glowing like Flowers], edited by Ōshiro Tatsuhiro, Kayō Yasuo, Funakoshi Gishō, Kōki Yoshihide, Hazama Yoshiko, Henna Tsunetsugu, and Fujimura Yoshiki, 20–23. Okinawa: Otohime Gekidan.

Funakoshi Takashi, Niekawa Shun, Itō Yoshitaka, and Teramoto Daizō. 2021. "Kaikeihōde Takamaru Atsuryoku, Nicchū Haiiro no Fune o Seni Shiroi Funega Kensei" [Increasing Tensions between China and Japan due to the enforcement of the Coast Guard Law]. *Asahi Shimbun*, February 24. Accessed July 11, 2021. https://digital.asahi.com/articles/ASP2R735WP2RUHBI00R.html?iref=pc_rellink_01

Futenma-Henoko Mondai o Kangaeru Kai. 2016. "'Futenma-Henoko Mondai o Kangaeru Kai' Kyōdōseimeibun" [Joint Statement of the Group That Considers Futenma-Henoko Issues]. *Global Ethics* (blog), September 20. Accessed November 4, 2020. https://globalethics.wordpress.com/2016/09/20/%E2%97%86%E3%80%8C%E6%99%AE%E5%A4%A9%E9%96%93%E3%83%BB%E8%BE%BA%E9%87%8E%E5%8F%A4%E5%95%8F%E9%A1%8C%E3%82%92%E8%80%83%E3%81%88%E3%82%8B%E4%BC%9A%E3%80%8D%E5%85%B1%E5%90%8C%E5%A3%B0%E6%98%8E%E5%85%A8/

Gabe Masaaki. 2007. *Sengo Nichi-Bei Kankei to Anzen Hoshō* [Postwar US-Japan Relations and Security]. Tokyo: Yoshikawa Kōbunkan.

Gabe Satoshi. 2013. "Senryōsha no Manazashi o Kugurinukeru Kotoba" [The Language that Escapes the Gaze of the Occupier]. In *Senryōsha no Manazashi: Okinawa/Nihon/Beikoku no Sengo* [The Gaze of the Occupier: Postwar Okinawa/Japan/US], edited by Tanaka Yasuhiro, 63–85. Toyo: Serika Shobō.

Gibney, Frank. 1949. "Forgotten Island." *TIME Magazine* 54(22) (November 28 issue): 24–27. Accessed March 24, 2020. http://search.ebscohost.com.ezproxy.uky.edu/login.aspx?direct=true&db=a9h&AN=54763248&site=ehost-live&scope=site

Gilroy, Paul. 1993. *The Black Atlantic: Modernity and Double Consciousness*. Cambridge, MA: Harvard University Press.

Gluck, Carol. 1985. *Japan's Modern Myths: Ideology in the Late Meiji Period*. Princeton, NJ: Princeton University Press.

Gluck, Carol. 1993. "The past in the present" In *Postwar Japan as History*, edited by Andrew Gordon, 64–95. Berkeley, CA: University of California Press.

Gordon, Andrew. 2014. *A Modern History of Japan. From Tokugawa Times to the Present, Third Edition*. Oxford: Oxford University Press.
Graeber, David. 2011. *Debt: The First 5,000 Years*. Brooklyn, NY: Melville House.
Hamaguchi Kazuhisa. 2011. "Senshu Bōei toiu Gensō (Zen): Jieitai no Sonzaiigi o Tou" [The Illusion of Defense-Only: Questioning the Meaning of the Existence of the Self-Defense Forces]. *NetIB News*, September 13. Accessed June 27, 2022. https://www.data-max.co.jp/2011/09/13/post_16251.html
Hammersley, Martyn, and Paul Atkinson. 2007. Ethnography: Principles in Practice. London/New York: Routledge.
Hanai Hitoshi, and Asakawa Kōki, ed. 1995. *Sengo Nichibei Kankei no Kiseki* [Trajectories of the Postwar Japan-US Relationship]. Tokyo: Keisō Shobō.
Hardt, Michael. 2009. "Forward: Three Keys to Understanding Constituent Power." In Antonio Negri, *Insurgencies: Constituent Power and the Modern State*, vii-xiii. Minneapolis, MN: University of Minnesota Press. Accessed September 9, 2023. https://www-jstor-org.ezproxy.uky.edu/stable/10.5749/j.ctttv1x6.3
Hardt, Michael, and Antonio Negri. 1994. *Labor of Dionysus: A Critique of the State-Form*. Minneapolis, MN: University of Minnesota Press.
Hardt, Michael, and Antonio Negri. 2000. *Empire*. Cambridge, MA: Harvard University Press.
Hardt, Michael, and Antonio Negri. 2004. *Multitude: War and Democracy in the Age of Empire*. New York: The Penguin Press.
Hardt, Michael, and Antonio Negri. 2009. *Commonwealth*. Cambridge, MA: Belknap Press of Harvard University Press.
Hardt, Michael, and Antonio Negri. 2017. *Assembly*. New York: Oxford University Press.
Harvey, David. 1990. *The Conditions of Postmodernity*. Cambridge, MA: Blackwell.
Harvey, David. 2005. *A Brief History of Neoliberalism*. Oxford: Oxford University Press.
Hashimoto Kenji. 2018. *Shin, Nihon no Kaikyū Shakai* [A New Class Society of Japan]. Tokyo: Kōdansha.
Hata Ikuhiko. [1987] 2007. *Hirohito: The Shōwa Emperor in War and Peace*. Translated by Marius B. Jansen. Leiden, Netherlands: Brill.
Hatachi Kota. 2018. "'Hāfu demo, Daburu demo nai. Watashi wa watashi" [I am Neither a Half nor a Double. I am Me]. *BuzzFeed News*, October 10. Accessed December 28, 2020. https://www.buzzfeed.com/jp/kotahatachi/okinawa-roots
Hatch, Walter, and Yamamura Kozo. 1996. *Asia in Japan's Embrace: Building a Regional Production Alliance*. New York: Cambridge University Press.
Hattori Asako. 2014. "Henoko/Shin'kichikensetu Hantaiundō Sankashajosei no Raifu Hisutorī [The Life History of a Female Participant in the Protest Movement to the Construction of a New Military Base in Henoko]." *Senshū Jinbun Ronshū* 94: 1—19. Accessed October 29, 2020. https://senshu-u.repo.nii.ac.jp/?action=pages_view_main&active_action=repository_view_main_item_detail&item_id=2230&item_no=1&page_id=13&block_id=21
Hayashi Michiyoshi. 2017. "Nihongun Ianfu Mondai no Kaiketsu o Habandekita

Higashi Ajia no Reisen Kōzō" [The Structure of East Asian Cold War Blocking the resolution of Japanese Army's Comfort Women Issues]. Accessed November 22, 2020. http://hayashihirofumi.g1.xrea.com/paper117.htm

Hayashi Nozomu. 2022. "'Kokuchichizu' ni Himerareta Teikoku no Kioku Sekai Chitsujo Yusaburu Chūgoku no Rekishikan" [Memories of the Empire in the 'National Humiliation Map,' China's Historical Perspective Shaking the World Order]. *Asahi Shimbun*, April 21. Accessed April 22, 2022. https://digital.asahi.com/articles/ASQ4C5VLKQ3ZUHBI01W.html?iref=pc_rensai_short_1474_article_1

Hayashi Yoshikatsu. 1998. "'Enora Gei' Ronsō' to Rekishi no Kioku" [The 'Enola Gay' Controversy and Memories of History]. *Rekishigaku Kenkyū* 714: 29–38.

Heaven's hell. 2003. A documentary film of Cocco's "Zero Trash Operations" concert, generated by Inoue Nami and a production group consisting of diverse individuals. Tokyo: Victor Entertainment.

Hein, Laura, and Mark Selden, eds. 2003. *Islands of Discontent: Okinawan Responses to Japanese and American Power*. Lanham, MD: Rowman and Littlefield.

Henna Sumiyo. 2015a. "Futenma Henkan Kyōgi, Nichibei ga Okinawa ni Koshitsushita Wake, Moto Bei-Kōkan ga Kaiko" [Reasons Japan and the US Clung to Okinawa, A former American High-Rank Office Reflected]. 2015. *Okinawa Times*, July 29. Accessed December 21, 2020. https://www.okinawatimes.co.jp/articles/-/17031

Henna Sumiyo. 2015b. "Anpo Hōan ni Tsunagaru Omowaku, Futenma Henkan Kōshō no Butaiura" [Expectations leading to the legislations concerning the Security Treaty; the backstage of Futenma negotiations]. *Okinawa Times*, August 3. Accessed December 21, 2020. https://www.okinawatimes.co.jp/articles/-/17211

Henna Sumiyo. 2016a. "Henoko Wakai, Andosuru Beikoku, Jizen ni Nihon to Kyōgishiteita" [Compromise over Henoko, the United States is relived, as it negotiated with Japan beforehand]. *Okinawa Times*, March 6. Accessed October 31, 2020. https://www.okinawatimes.co.jp/articles/-/24903

Henna Sumiyo. 2016b. "Henoko Shinkichi, Kassōro Chakkō wa 2024nendo Futenma Henkan wa 25nendo Ikōka" [A New Base in Henoko, the Start of the Runway Construction Would Be during 2024 and Return of Futenma Would Be during or after 2025]. *Okinawa Times*, January 23. Accessed October 31, 2020. https://www.okinawatimes.co.jp/articles/-/23060

Henoko Dosha Hanshutsu Hantai Zenkoku Renraku Kyogikai. 2019. *Stop Henoko!* Accessed November 4, 2020. http://stophenoko.html.xdomain.jp/

Henoko Kikin. n.d. *Anata no Omoi ga Min'i o Sasae, Chikara ni Kawaru* [Your Thoughts/Prayers Support the Will of the People and Turn into Power]. Accessed December 10, 2020. http://henokofund.okinawa/

Henokoku Hensan Īnkai. 1998. *Henoko-shi* [Descriptions of Henoko Culture and History]. Nago, Okinawa: Henokoku Jimusho.

Herikichi Hantaikyōgikai. 2022. "No. 489 Usoga Makaritōru" [No. 489 Lies Go Unpunished]. Blog. June 1. Accessed June 30, 2022. https://lovehenoko.org/%e2

%84%96489%e3%80%80%e3%82%a6%e3%82%bd%e3%81%8c%e3%81%be
%e3%81%8b%e3%82%8a%e9%80%9a%e3%82%8b%e3%80%82/

Herikichi Hantaikyōgikai. 2019–2020. n.d.-a. *Herikichi Hantakyō Burogu*. Accessed December 8. 2020. http://www.mco.ne.jp/~herikiti/blog.html

Herikichi Hantaikyōgikai. n.d-b. Homepage. Accessed May 6, 2022. https://lovehenoko.org/

Hickel, Jason. 2020. "The World's Sustainable Development Goals Aren't Sustainable" *Foreign Policy*, September 30. Accessed October 1, 2023. https://foreignpolicy.com/2020/09/30/the-worlds-sustainable-development-goals-arent-sustainable/

Hida Susumu. 2014. "Kokuren Kenshō Dai-51jyō no Seiritsukatei karamita Shūdantekijieiken no Imi to Dōjyōyakuseiritukatei eno Daresu no Kakawari (2)" [Meaning of the Right of Collective Self-Defense judging from the Establishing Process of Article 51 and Dulles' involvement in that process (2)]. *Meijyō Hōgaku* 63(4), 37–93. Accessed December 20, 2020. http://law.meijo-u.ac.jp/staff/contents/63-4/630402_hida.pdf

Higa Masao. 1983. *Okinawa no Monchū to Sonraku Saishi* [Munchū and Village Rituals]. Tokyo: San'ichi Shobō.

Higa Masao. 1987. *Josei Yūi to Dankei Genri* [Predominance of Women and the Principle of Agnation]. Tokyo: Gaifūsha.

Higa, Mikio. 1963. *Politics and Parties in Postwar Okinawa*. Vancouver, Canada: University of British Columbia.

Higa Momono. 2018. "'Denī Carā' Tayōna Okinawa Shintō e Ippo" [Deny's Color, a Step toward Diverse Okinawa]. *Okinawa Times*, October 15. Accessed December 28, 2020. https://www.okinawatimes.co.jp/articles/-/327122

Higa Shunchō, Shimota Seiji, and Shinzato Keiji. 1963. *Okinawa* [Okinawa]. Tokyo: Iwanami Shoten.

Higashionna Takuma, and Gigi Maki. 2015. "Shinkichi Kensetsu de Yureru Okinawaken Henoko: Kanūtai o Hatsuanshita Higashionna Takuma Nagoshigi ni Kiku" [Henoko, Okinawa, Where Citizens Are Divided over the Question of Whether the New Base is to be Constructed: Interviewing Nago City Assemblyman Higashionna Takuma]. 2015. *Independent Web Journal*, March 7. Accessed November 3, 2020. https://iwj.co.jp/wj/open/archives/237450

Higuchi Kōtarō. 2014. "Okinawa kara Kichi ga Nakunaranai Hontō no Riyū: Okinawa Senkyoku de Tōhyō suru Mae ni Kangaetaikoto" [The True Reason Why US Bases Do Not Disappear from Okinawa: What I Would Like Us to Consider before the Election in the Okinawa Electoral District]. *Okinawa Times*, December 19. Accessed December 23, 2020. https://www.okinawatimes.co.jp/articles/-/50244

Hikarizumi Shōgo, and Itō Kazuyuki. 2022. "Kokyō no Umi o Umeru Dosha, Danpu de Hakobu Hibi, 25-man'en no Gesshū to Yureru Kokoro" [The days when he carried sediment to charge into the ocean of his hometown, in exchange for the monthly salary of 250,000 yen]. *Asahi Shimbun*, January 14. Accessed January 15, 2022. https://www.asahi.com/articles/ASQ1F66JYQ1DUTIL03B.html?iref=pc_ss_date_article

Himeyuri Heiwa Kinen Shiryōkan. 2006. *Himeyuri o Manabu* [Leaning Himeyuri]. Accessed December 27, 2020. http://www.himeyuri.or.jp/JP/himeyuri.html

Hirokawa Takashi. 2015. "Ten'nōheika: Okotoba de 'Fukai Hansei' ni Genkyū—Zenkoku Senbotsusha Tsuitōshiki" [The Emperor: Spoke about his "Profound Regret" about the Previous war, in the National Memorial Service for the War Dead]. *Bloomberg*, August 15. Accessed December 28, 2020. https://www.bloomberg.co.jp/news/articles/2015-08-15/--idcnq59m

Hirsch, Marianne. 2008. "The Generation of Postmemory." *Poetics Today* 29:1 (Spring 2008): 103–128.

Hiyane Teruo. 1996. *Kindai Okinawa no Seishin-shi* [A Spiritual History of Modern Okinawa]. Tokyo: Shakai Hyōronsha.

Hobbes, Thomas. [1651] 2009. *Leviathan*. The Project Gutenberg E-book. Accessed December 20, 2020. https://www.gutenberg.org/files/3207/3207-h/3207-h.htm

Hokama Yoneko. 2007. "Senryōka no Joseitachi." In *Sengo o Tadoru: 'Amerika-yo' kara 'Yamato no Yo' e* [Tracing the Postwar: From the 'World of US rule' to the 'World of Japanese Rule'], 34–39. Edited by Nahashi Rekishi Hakubutsukan. Naha, Okinawa: Ryukyu Shimpo-sha.

Honda Katsuichi. [1972] 1981. *Chūgoku no Tabi* [Traveling in China]. Tokyo: Asahi Shimbunsha.

Honda Katsuichi. 1981. *Senjō no Mura* [Villages in the Battlefield]. Tokyo: Asahi Shimbunsha.

Horiba Kiyoko. 1990. *Inaguya Nanabachi: Okinawa Joseishi o Saguru* [Seven Curses of Being a Woman: Exproing Okinawan Women's History]. Tokyo: Domesu Shuppan.

Hosaka Masayasu. 2014. *Ten'nō: 'Kunshu' no Chichi, 'Minshu' no Ko* [The Emperor: The Father in Monarchy, the Son under Democracy]. Tokyo: Kōdansha.

Hoshino Toshiya. 2022. "Tomaranu Roshia ni Kokuren ga Dekirukoto, Kyohiken o Tsukawaseta Nerai, Tsugi no Tewa [What the United Nations Can Do to Russia that Doesn't Stop; the Purpose of Letting Russia Use the Veto Right; What's Next?]." *Asahi Shimbun*. May 30, 2022. Accessed June 10, 2022. https://digital.asahi.com/articles/ASQ3B41XLQ37UHBI01X.html?iref=comtop_7_03

Hosoi Naoko. 2014. "Okinawa Shibai no Shōkai." Accessed May 15, 2022. https://www.rikkyo.ac.jp/research/institute/caas/qo9edr000000ml88-att/o_42.pdf

Howard, Philip N., and Muzammil M. Hussain. 'The Role of Digital Media.' *Journal of Democracy* 22(3): 35–48. Accessed October 12, 2018. DOI:10.1353/jod.2011.0041

Hurrell, Andrew. 2011. "Collective Security." In *International Encyclopedia of Political Science*, edited by Bertrand Badie, et al., 299–302. Los Angeles: SAGE Publications.

ICAN (International Campaign to Abolish Nuclear Weapons). n.d. *Homepage*. Accessed May 15, 2022. https://www.icanw.org/

Igarashi Takeshi. 1995. *Sengo Nichibei Kankei no Keisei: Kōwa/Anpo to Reisengo no Shiten ni Tatte* [The Formation of Postwar Japan-US Relationship]. Tokyo: Kōdansha.

Iguchi Haruo. 1998. "Jon Fosutā Daresu no Gaikōshisō: Senzen Sengo no Renzokusei" [John Foster Dulles's Diplomatic Thought: Continuity between the Prewar and Postwar Periods]. *Dōshisha Amerika Kenkyū* 34: 33–48. Accessed April 9, 2024. https://doshisha.repo.nii.ac.jp/search?page=1&size=50&sort=controlnumber&search_type=0&q=%E3%82%B8%E3%83%A7%E3%83%B3%E3%83%BB%E3%83%95%E3%82%A9%E3%82%B9%E3%82%BF%E3%83%BC%E3%83%BB%E3%83%80%E3%83%AC%E3%82%B9%E3%81%AE%E5%A4%96%E4%BA%A4%E6%80%9D%E6%83%B3

Iha Fuyū (also known as Ifa Fuyū). [1927] 1973a. "Onarigami" [Sister-Goddess]. In *Onarigami no Shima 1* [Islands of Sister-Goddess, Volume 1], 3–22. Tokyo: Heibonsha.

Iha Fuyū. [1936] 1973b. "Hinokami-kō" [Analysis of the God of Fire]. In *Onarigami no Shima 2* [Islands of Sister-Goddess, Volume 2], 3–23. Tokyo: Heibonsha.

Iha Yōichi. 1993. "Kichiato Riyō" [Use of the Former Military Land]. In *Shinpojiumu Okinawa Senryō: Mirai e Mukete* [Symposium on Okinawa Occupation: Toward the Future], edited by Miyagi Etsujirō, 151–157. Naha, Okinawa: Hirugisha.

Ikemiya, Masaharu. 1990. "Otohime Gekidan no Omoide" [Memories of the Otohime Troupes]. In *Uema Ikuko to Otohime Gekidan no 40-nen: Hana to Moete* [Uema Ikuko and 40 years of the Otohime Troupe: Glowing like Flowers], edited by Ōshiro Tatsuhiro, Kayō Yasuo, Funakoshi Gishō, Kōki Yoshihide, Hazama Yoshiko, 43. Okinawa: Otohime Gekidan.

Ikiro! Tore! Ishikawa Mao! 2017. *Okinawa no Shashinka Ishikawa Mao no Gan Chiryōhi to 'Dai-Ryūkyū Shashin Emaki 4 Tenjikai Kaisai Hiyō o Tsunoru Purojekutodesu* [This is a Project to Cover the Costs of Okinawan photographer Ishikawa Mao's Cancer Treatments and of the Exhibition of the Great Ryukyu Photo Scrolls 4]. Accessed December 16, 2020. http://crowdmonstar.com/project/_9456/ (Citations refer to the first video of this webpage.)

Ikusabanu Tudumi program production editor. 2015. *Ikusabanu Tudumi*. Tokyo: Tōfū.

Imai Hajime. 1997. *Jyūmin Tōhyō* [Referendum]. Osaka: Nikkei Osaka PR Kikaku Shppanbu.

Inagaki Masami. 1990. *Onna dakeno 'Otohime Gekidan' Funtōki* [Struggles of the Women-Only 'Otohime Troupe']. Tokyo: Kōdansha.

Inamasa Channel. 2017. "Amuro Namie 'Never End,' Okinawa Samitto Imējisongu, Komuro Tetsuya san mo Tōjō" [Amuro Namie's 'Never End,' Okinawan G-8 Summit's Image Song, Komuro Tetsuya also Made Appearance]. YouTube. Video, 12:56. Accessed December 28, 2020. https://www.youtube.com/watch?v=uTBQOZgSrtU

Inamine Kei'ichi. 1999. "Shibai Bunka no Hatten Keishō o" [Wishing the further Development of Okinawa's theater culture]. In *Sōritsu 50-shūnen Kinen-shi, SHIBAI: Ikuko, Yoshiko Onna Ichidaiki* [To Commemorate the 50th Anniversary of the Establishment of the Otohime Troupes, STAGE PERFORMANCES: Ikuko and Yoshiko—Biographies of Women], edited by Otohime Gekidan, 3. Naha, Okinawa: Omoro Shuppan.

Inoue, Masamichi. 2002. "Gurōbaruka no Nakano Okinawa Inishiachibu Ronsō: Kioku, Aidentitī, Kichimondai" [The Debate over the 'Okinawa Initiative' in the Age of Globalization: Collective Memory, Identity, and the Base Problems]. *Shisō* 933: 246–267.

Inoue, Masamichi. 2007. *Okinawa and the U.S. Military: Identity Making in the Age of Globalization*. New York: Columbia University Press.

Inoue, Masamichi. 2011. "Cocco's Musical Intervention in the US Base Problems: Traversing a Realm of Everyday Cultural Sensibilities in Okinawa." *Inter-Asia Cultural Studies* 12(3): 321–340. https://doi.org/10.1080/14649373.2011.578789

Inoue, Masamichi. 2014. "Japan as a Global Sanctuary: Mimetic Production of the Other in the Age of Empire." Presented at the American Anthropological Association Annual Meeting, December 3–7, Washington, DC.

Inoue, Masamichi. 2015. Review of an article titled "Fractured Alliance: Anti-Base Protests and Postwar U.S.-Japanese Relations" by Jennifer M. Miller. *H-Diplo Article Reviews*, Number 558. Accessed December 20, 2020. http://tiny.cc/AR558

Inoue, Masamichi. 2017a. *Okinawa and the U.S. Military: Identity Making in the Age of Globalization*, with New Preface. New York: Columbia University Press.

Inoue, Masamichi. 2017b. "On the Okinawan Multitude: Toward a New Policy Paradigm for Reorganization-Reduction of the U.S. Bases in Okinawa." *Georgetown Journal of Asian Affairs* 3(2): 47–57.

Inoue, Masamichi. 2019. "Between Surveillance and Sousveillance: Or, Why Campus Police Feel Vulnerable Precisely Because They Gain Power." *Journal of Contemporary Ethnography*, 49(2): 229–256. https://journals.sagepub.com/eprint/IY7RQBPQEAKF6EGNDFYG/full

Ishikawa Mao. 1982. *Atsuki Hibi in Kyampu Hansen!!* [Blazing Days in Camp Hansen!!]. Okinawa: Āman Shuppan.

Ishikawa Mao. 1989. *Firipin* [The Philippines]. Okinawa: Ishikawa Mao.

Ishikawa Mao. 1990. *Minatomachi Erejī* [An Elegy of a Port Town]. Okinawa: Ishikawa Mao.

Ishikawa Mao. 1991. *Nakada Sachiko Ikkō Mongatari* [A Story of the Nakada Sachiko's Troupe]. Okinawa: Ishikawa Mao.

Ishikawa Mao. 1995. *Okinawa to Jieitai* [Okinawa and the Self-Defense Forces]. Tokyo: Kōbunken.

Ishikawa Mao. 2002. *Okinawa Souru* [The Okinawan Soul]. Tokyo: Ōta Shuppan.

Ishikawa Mao. 2011. *Hinomaru o Miru Me* [Here's What the Japanese Flag Means to Me]. Tokyo: Miraisha.

Ishikawa Mao. 2015a. *Konkurītoburokku* [A Concrete Block]. A photo used in a poster for the *Dai-Ryūkyū Shashin Emaki* [Great Ryukyu Photo Scrolls] exhibition, held in Nakano Zero in July 2015. The poster is cited in Nakatsu (2015). Accessed October 27, 2023. http://www.magazine9.jp/wp-content/uploads/2015/07/mao.jpg

Ishikawa Mao. 2015b. *Dai-Ryūkū Shashin Emaki Pāto 1 & Pāto 2, Ishikawa Mao* [The Great Ryukyu Photo Scrolls by Mao Ishikawa, Parts 1 and 2]. *Fraction*

Magazine Japan 18. Accessed December 16, 2020. https://fractionmagazinejap an.asia/archive/jpne/cn108/pg1019.html

Ishikawa Mao. 2017. *Red Flower: The Women of Okinawa*. New York City: Session Press.

Ishikawa Mao, Kuniyoshi Kazuo, and Nagamoto Tomohiro. 1996. *Korega Okinawa no Beigunda: Kichi ni Ikiru Hitobito* [This Is the US Military in Okinawa: People Living in the Island of Bases]. Tokyo: Kōbunken.

Ishikawa Ryōta and Chinen Yutaka. 2022. "Keizaihakyūkōka 1-chōen, Dētademiru 50-nen" [1 Trillion Yen of Economic Impacts, 50 Years After Reversion as Data Show]. *Okinawa Times*, May 15, page 10.

Ishimure Michiko. [1969] 2004. *Kukai Jōdo: Waga Minamatabyō* [Paradise in the Sea of Sorrow: Our Minamata Disease]. Tokyo: Kōdansha.

Ismael, Tareq Y., and Jacqueline S. Ismael. 1994. "Introduction." In *The Gulf War and the New World Order: International Relations of the Middle East*, edited by Tareq Ismael and Jacqueline S. Ismael, pp. 1–21. Gainesville: University Press of Florida.

Issa, and Hikarizumi Shōgo. 2022. "'Da Pump' Issa-san, Hittokyoku ni Kometa 'Kyōzon' eno Omoi" [Issa of "Da Pump," Hope of Co-existence Put into a Hit Tune]. *Asahi Shimbun*, May 9. Accessed May 15, 2022. https://digital.asahi.com /articles/ASQ56627WQ51TPOB001.html?iref=pc_ss_date_article

Itō Kanji. 1962. "Yaeyamaguntō ni Okeru Kyōdai-Shimai o Chūshin to Shita Shinzoku Kankei" [Kinship Relations, Especially Brother-Sister Relations, in Yaeyama]. *Minzokugaku Kenkyū* 27(1): 7–12.

Itō Kazuyuki. 2019. "'Kaiho no Taiho wa Ihō' Naha Chisai, Sakka no Medoruma-san Shōs" [JCG's Arrest Was Illegal, Naha District Court, Writer Medoruma Won His Case]. *Asahi Shimbun*, March 19. Accessed November 3, 2020. https:// digital.asahi.com/articles/ASM3L6Q8NM3LTPOB00B.html

Iwabuchi, Kōichi. 2002. *Recentering Globalization: Popular Culture and Japanese Transnationalism*. Durham: Duke University Press.

Iwata Katsuhiko, Kashiwabara Tadasuke, and Gigi Maki. 2015. "10nenmae no Kaiho wa Bōeikyoku to Shimin no Chūsaiyaku datta" [10 Years Ago, JCG was a Mediator between the ODB and Citizens]. *Independent Web Journal*, March 18. Accessed October 30, 2020. https://iwj.co.jp/wj/open/archives/239674

Johnson, Archie. 2023. Class assignment. September 13.

Johnson, Chalmers. 1982. *MITI and the Japanese Miracle: The Growth of Industrial Policy, 1925–1975*. Stanford, CA: Stanford University Press.

Junkerman, John, dir. 2015. *Okinawa: Urizun no Ame* [Okinawa: The Rain of Early Summer]. Tokyo: MAXAM.

Juris, Jeffrey S. 2012. "Reflections on #Occupy Everywhere: Social media, public space, and emerging logics of aggregation." *American Ethnologist* 39 (2): 259–279. Accessed October 13, 2018. https://doi.org/10.1111/j.1548-1425.2012.013 62.x

Jyugon Hogo Kikin. n.d. *Tomoni Ikiru Jyugon Hogo Kikin* [Co-Existing with the Dugongs: Dugong Protection Fund]. Accessed December 10, 2020. http://sea -dugong.org/kikin.html

Kabira Chōshin. 1997. *Shūsengo no Okinawa Bunka Gyōseishi* [A History of Cultural Administration after the War]. Naha, Okinawa: Gekkan Okinawa-sha.

Kabira Nario. 2011. *Okinawa Kūhaku no Ichinen: 1945–1946* [Okinawa, One Blank Year: 1945–1946]. Tokyo: Yoshikawa Kōbunkan.

Kaino Hiroyuki. 2023. "Nichi-Bei-Kan Shunōkaidan, Kyōryokubunya no Kakudai de Icchi, Keizaianzenhoshōdemo Renkeikyōka" [Leaders' Summit of the United States, Japan, and the Republic of Korea, Expansion of Cooperation is Confirmed, Economic-Security Collaboration Will be Reinforced]. *JETRO Bijinesu Tanshin*, August 22. Accessed November 10, 2023. https://www.jetro.go.jp/biznews/2023/08/83316eacf4fccf98.html

Kameya Chizuko. 1950. *Sumire Niou* [A Violet That Smells Good]. *Uruma Shunjyū* 2(5) (June/July Issue): 13–25.

Kanbayashi Hiroshi. 2012. '"*Sōchūryū*" to Fubyōdō o Meguru Gensetsu: Sengonihon ni Okeru Kaisō Kizokuishiki ni Kansuru Nōto (3)'. ['Everybody Belongs to the Middle-Class' and Discourses on Inequality: Notes about the Social Class Consciousness in Postwar Japan (3).]. *Tōhoku Gakuin Daigaku Kyōyōgakubu Ronshū* 161: 67–90. http://www.tohoku-gakuin.ac.jp/research/journal/bk2012/pdf/bk2012no03_06.pdf

Kanegae Haruhiko. 2007. "Henoko Kaijōkichi Kensetsuhantaiundō no Keika to Tokushitsu" [Development and Characteristics of the Movement to Oppose the Construction of a Sea-Based Military Base in Henoko]. *Senshū Daigaku Shakaikagaku Nenpō* 41: 103–123. Accessed October 29, 2020. http://www.senshu-u.ac.jp/~off1009/PDF/n41_103-124.pdf

Kang Sang-jung, and Yoshimi Shun'ya. 2001. *Gurōbaru-ka no Enkinhō: Atarashii Kōkyō Kūkan o Motomete* [Perspective of Globalization: In Search of a New Public Space]. Tokyo: Iwanami Shoten.

Kano Masanao. 1987. *Sengo Okinawa no Shisōzō* [Thoughts in Postwar Okinawa]. Tokyo: Asahi Shimbunsha.

Kano Masanao, Tobe Hideaki, Tomiyama Ichirō, and Mori Yoshio. 2015. "Sengo Okinawa Rekishi Ninshiki Apīru" [Historical Understanding of Postwar Okinawa, an Appeal]. 2015. Accessed November 4, 2020. https://www.change.org/p/%E6%B2%96%E7%B8%84%E7%9C%8C%E6%B0%91-%E6%97%A5%E6%9C%AC%E5%9B%BD%E6%B0%91-%E4%B8%96%E7%95%8C%E3%81%AE%E4%BA%BA%E3%81%B3%E3%81%A8-%E6%88%A6%E5%BE%8C%E6%B2%96%E7%B8%84-%E6%AD%B4%E5%8F%B2%E7%A0%94%E7%A9%B6%E3%82%A2%E3%83%94%E3%83%BC%E3%83%AB#petition-letter

Kanō Mikiyo. [1991] 1995. "'Bosei' no Tanjō to Ten'nō sei" [The Birth of 'Motherhood' and the Emperor System]. In *Bosei* [Mother-ness], edited by Inoue Teruko, Ueno Chizuko, and Ehara Yumiko, 56–61. Tokyo: Iwanami Shoten.

Kanū Chīmu Henoko Burū. 2018. "Ankēto Happyō" [Announcing the Results of Questionnaires]. Accessed December 9, 2020. https://henokoblue.wixsite.com/henokoblue/single-post/2018/05/11/Untitled

Kanū Chīmu Henoko Burū. n.d.-a. Blog. Accessed November 3, 2020. https://henokoblue.wixsite.com/henokoblue

Kanū Chīmu Henoko Burū. n.d.-b. Facebook. Accessed November 3, 2020. https://www.facebook.com/henokoblue/

Kant, Immanuel. [1795] 2016. *Perpetual Peace: a Philosophical Essay*. The Project Gutenberg E-book. Accessed May 30, 2022. https://www.gutenberg.org/files/50922/50922-h/50922-h.htm

Kapur, Nick. 2018. *Japan at the Crossroads: Conflict and Compromise after Anpo*. Harvard University Press.

Karatani Kōjin. 2006. *Sekai Kyōwakoku e—Shihon=Nēshon=Kokka o Koete* [Toward the World Republic: Beyond Capital=Nation=State]. Tokyo: Iwanami Shoten.

Karatani Kōjin. [2010] 2014. *The Structure of World History*. Translated by Michael K. Bourdaghs. Durham, NC: Duke University Press.

Kariyushi Okinawa. n.d. "Ryukyu Nanbangame Kariyushi Puremiamu" [Ryukyu Kariyushi Premium Vessel]. Accessed September 8, 2023. https://kariyusi-okinawa.com/user_data/nanbangame

Kasutamā. 2004. "Costumer Reviews: Kumui-uta" [Costumer Reviews: Lullaby]. Posted on December 31. Accessed May 29, 2022. https://www.amazon.co.jp/-/en/Cocco/product-reviews/B00005GXLS/ref=cm_cr_getr_d_paging_btm_next_2?ie=UTF8&reviewerType=all_reviews&pageNumber=2

Kataoka Nobuyuki. 2019. "'Nihonteki Keiei'-Ron no Shatei" [The Theory of the Japanese-Style Management and Its Scope]. *Keieigaku Ronshū* 89: 19–28. https://doi.org/10.24472/abjaba.89.0_19 Accessed June 27, 2022. https://www.jstage.jst.go.jp/article/abjaba/89/0/89_19/_article/-char/ja/

Katō Masahiro. 2014. "Koza no Toshikeisei to Kanrakugai—1950nendai ni Okeru Shōchūshinchi no Sōsei to Henyō" [Formation of the City and the Entertainment Sector in Koza—Birth and Transformation of a Small Center in the 1950s]. *Ritsumeikan Daigaku Jinbunkagaku Kenkyūjo Kiyō* 104: 41–70.

Katō Norihiro. 2019. *9-jō Nyūmon* [Introduction to Article 9]. Osaka: Sōgensha.

Katsube Nobuo. 2019. "Nihonteki Keiei no Genzai" [The Present of the Japanese Style Management]. *Senshū Bijinesu Rebyū* 14(1): 23–34. Accessed June 27, 2022. https://www.senshu-u.ac.jp/albums/abm.php?d=1599&f=abm00001956.pdf&n=%E5%8B%9D%E9%83%A8%E4%BC%B8%E5%A4%AB.pdf

Kawada Fumiko. 1987. *Akagawara no Ie: Chōsen kara Kita Jyūgun Ianfu* [The House of Red Roof Tiles: A Military Comfort Woman from Korea]. Tokyo: Chikuma Shobō.

Kawahara Shōichirō, Inoue Sōtarō, and Akashi Kōichirō. 2011. "Ajia-Taiheiyōchiiki no Bōeikikōzō" [Trade Structure of the Asia-Pacific Region]. In *Ajia-Taiheiyōchiiki no Bōeikikōzō to ASEAN+1-gata FTA* [The Trade Structure of the Asia-Pacific Region and the ASEAN+1-type FTA], 1–36. Tokyo: Nōrinsuisan Seisaku Kenkyūjo. Accessed May 28, 2022. https://www.maff.go.jp/primaff/kanko/project/attach/pdf/110328_23asipaci1_01.pdf

Kawakita Satoshi. 2011. *Beigunjkichi ga Motarashita Mono: Kichi no Shima no Minzokushi* [What Has the US Military Brought About? An Ethnography of a Community of a Base]. Master's Thesis, Submitted to the Sociology Program, Hitotsubashi University.

Kawamitsu Shin'ichi. [1981] 2014. "Ryūkyū Kyōwa Shakai Kenpō, C(Shi/Shi)an" [The Constitution of Ryukyu Republic Society, C-Plan (private draft)]. In *Ryūkyū Kyōwa Shakai Kenpō no Senseiryoku* [Potentiality of the Constitution of Ryukyu Republic Society], edited by Kawamitsu Shin'ichi and Nakazato Isao, 9–26. Tokyo: Miraisha.

Kawamura Minato. 2015a. "Koroniarizumu to Orientarizumu: 'Bōken Dankichi' no Chikyūgi" [Colonialism and Orientalism: Adventurer Dankichi's Globe.] In *Kawamura Minato Jisenshū Dai 4kan Ajia/Shokuminchi Bungaku Hen* [Kawamura Minato's Own Selection of Writings Volume 4: Volume on Asia and Colonial Literature], 140–172. Tokyo: Sakuhinsha.

Kawamura Minato. 2015b. "'Minami' e Mukau Bungaku: Nihon Kindaibungaku ni okeru Nanpō" [Literature that Goes 'South': The South in Modern Japanese Literature]. In *Kawamura Minato Jisenshū Dai 4kan Ajia/Shokuminchi Bungaku Hen* [Kawamura Minato's Own Selection of Writings Volume 4: Volume on Asia and Colonial Literature], 173–193. Tokyo: Sakuhinsha.

Kawamura Takashi. 2019. "Aichi Torien'nāre 2019 'Hyōgen no Fujiyūten, Sonogo' nitsuite" [On Aichi Triennale 2019, the Exhibit, 'After Freedom of Expression'] (A Memorandum written by Kawamura Takashi addressed to Ōmura Hideaki). Accessed March 30, 2024. https://www.city.nagoya.jp/kankobunkakoryu/cmsfi les/contents/0000123/123556/23.pdf. https://www.city.nagoya.jp/kankobunka koryu/cmsfiles/contents/0000119/119833/webc.pdf

Kawase Shin. 1954. "*Nagaregi*" [Driftwood]. *Ryūdai Bungaku* 5, 34–44.

Kayō Yasuo. 1990. "Otohime Gekidan no Hanayakasa" [The Splendor of the Otohime Troupes]. In *Uema Ikuko to Otohime Gekidan no 40-nen: Hana to Moete* [Uema Ikuko and 40 Years of the Otohime Troupe: Glowing like Flowers], edited by Ōshiro Tatsuhiro, Kayō Yasuo, Funakoshi Gishō, Kōki Yoshihide, Hazama Yoshiko, Henna Tsunetsugu, and Fujimura Yoshiki, 44. Okinawa: Otohime Gekidan.

Kelsen, Hans. 1948. "Collective Security and Collective Self-Defense under the Charter of the United Nations." *American Journal of International Law* 42(4): 783–796.

Kenheiwa Sentā. 2015. "Shōkai, Henoko Kanūtai (Zen'nikken) no Tatakai to Heiwa F ni Ishikawaken Umare no Katsuhima Jimukyokuchō" [Announcement: Struggles of the Henoko Canoe Team (All Japan Construction and Transport Solidarity Labor Union) and Mr. Katsushima from Ishikawa becomes Deputy Director General of the Peace Forum]. Accessed December 9, 2020. https://i-pe ace-ishikawa.com/2015/10/09/%E3%80%90%E7%B4%B9%E4%BB%8B%E3 %80%91%E8%BE%BA%E9%87%8E%E5%8F%A4%E3%82%AB%E3%83%8C %E3%83%BC%E9%9A%8A%EF%BC%88%E5%85%A8%E6%97%A5%E5 %BB%BA%EF%BC%89%E3%81%AE%E9%97%98%E3%81%84%E3%81%A8 %E5%B9%B3%E5%92%8C/

Kim, Seong Un. 2020. "Performing Democracy: Audience Participation in Postwar Broadcasting." *The Journal of Japanese Studies*, 46(1): 61–89. Accessed December 26, 2020. https://doi.org/10.1353/jjs.2020.0004

Kim Kioku. 2006. "Chōsen Sensō to Josei: Senjikokka niyoru Seibōryoku no Ruikei to Sōten" [The Korean War and Women: Types of Sexual Violence by the State at War and Issues of Controversy]. Translated by Cho Kyonhi. In *Okinawa no Senryō to Nihon no Fukkō: Shokuminchi-shugi wa ikani Keizokushitaka* [Occupation of Okinawa and Recovery of Japan: How Colonialism has Continued], edited by Nakano Toshio, Namihira Tsuneo, Yakabi Osamu, Lee Hyoduk, 59–84. Tokyo: Seikyūsha.

Kina, Laura. 2017. "The Black Pacific Through Okinawan Eyes: Photographer Mao Ishikawa's 'Hot Days in Camp Hansen!!' and 'Life in Philly.'" In *Rethinking Postwar Okinawa: Beyond American Occupation*, edited by Pedro Iacobelli and Hiroko Matsuda, 149–168. Lanham, Maryland: Lexington Books. Lexington Books.

Kinjō Isamu. 2005. "*Gakujyutu-jinruikan Jiken to Okinawa: Sabetsu to Dōka no Rekishi*" [The Academic Human Pavilion Incident and Okinawa: A History of Discrimination and Assimilation]. In *Jinruikan: Fūinsareta Tobira* [The Human Pavilion: The Door That Has Been Closed], edited by Engeki 'Jinruikan' Jōen o Jitsugensasetai Kai, 27–69. Osaka: Attowākusu.

Kinjō Masaki. 2010. "Bōryoku to Kanki—Furantsu Fanon no Jojyutsu to Medoruma Shun no 'Niji no Tori' kara" [Violence and Rejoicing: In reference to Franz Fanon's Descriptions and Medoruma Shun's 'Niji no Tori']. In *Gendai Okinawa no Rekishi Keiken: Kibō, aruiwa Miketsusei ni Tsuite* [Historical Experiences of Contemporary Okinawa: On Hope, or Undecidability], edited by Tomiyama Ichirō and Mori Yoshio, 319–358. Tokyo: Seikyūsha.

Kinjō Yoshiko. 1977. *Naha Onna Ichidaiki* [A Life of a Naha Woman]. Naha, Okinawa: Okinawa Times-sha.

Kishaba Jun. 1955. *Kurai Hana* [A Dark Flower]. *Ryūdai Bungaku* 10: 25–33.

Kishaba Naoko. [1985] 1990. "Onna Ayaoriuta" [Songs of Women Who Weave]. In *Okinawa Bungaku Zenshū Dai 9-kan, Shōsetsu IV* [Complete Works of Okinawan Literature, Volume 9, Literary Works IV], edited by Okinawa Bungaku Zenshū Henshū Īnkai, 178–207. Tokyo: Kokusho Kankōkai.

Kishi Masahiko, and Manabe Hiroki. 2022. "Ikiteiru Ningen ga Okinawa ni Irukoto, Wasurenaide, Sensō kara Hitotsuzuki no Ima" [Don't Forget that Living People Exist in Okinawa: The Present Directly Extended from the War]. *Asahi Shimbun*. February 22. Accessed April 15, 2022. https://digital.asahi.com/articles/ASQ213R4CQ1LUPQJ012.html?iref=comtop_Opinion_01

Kitano Ryūichi. 2015. "Henoko Isetsu, Hōgakushara ga Kōgiseimei, Ichiren no Tetsuzuki 'Ihō'" [Statement of Protest by Legal Scholars and Others; Procedures of the Transference of Futenma to Henoko are Illegal]. 2015. *Asahi Shimbun*, December 14. Accessed November 4, 2020. https://digital.asahi.com/articles/ASHDG53MDHDGUTIL01K.html

Kitano Ryūichi, Shima Yasuhiko, Tada Akiko, Nakada Jyunko, and Ogata Yūdai. 2019. "2000.5.23–26, Oranda" [The Netherland, May 23–26, 2000]. In *Inori no Tabi* [Travels of Prayers]. *Asahi Shimbun*, April 19. Accessed December 28, 2020. https://www.asahi.com/special/heisei-inori/05/

Kitaueda Takeshi. n.d. *Choisan no Okinawa Nikki* [Mr. Choi's Okinawa Diary] (blog). Accessed November 3, 2020. https://blog.goo.ne.jp/chuy

Kitaueda Takeshi. 2015. "Shuwabu Kichi Gētomae, 'Henoko Sōgō Daigaku' Kōgi Ichiran" ["In front of the Gate of Camp Schwab, a List of Lectures at 'Henoko Comprehensive University'"]. *Choisan no Okinawa Nikki* [Mr. Choi's Okinawa Diary] (blog), August 27. Accessed November 3, 2020. https://blog.goo.ne.jp/chuy/e/5a8544cf431b381b7939e2ea67e7598c

Kitaueda Takeshi. 2018. *Henoko Shinkichi Kensetsu wa izure Tonza suru* [Construction of the New Base in Henoko Will Falter Soon or Later]. Accessed October 31, 2020. https://www.foejapan.org/aid/henoko/pdf/180427_1.pdf

Kitazawa Takuya. 2019. "Henoko Isetsu Hantai Rīdā, Yūzaikakutei e Shōgai nado no Tsumi" [The Leader of the Movement to Oppose the Transference of Futenma to Henoko was Convicted of Bodily Injury and Other Crimes]. *Asahi Shimbun*, April 25. Accessed November 3, 2020. https://digital.asahi.com/articles/ASM4T3GD5M4TUTIL00M.html

Kobayashi Masato. 2014. "Ensōba no Sui'i (Tai-doru), 1973–2002" [Changes of the Japanese Yen's Exchange Rate (against the US dollar), 1973–2002]. Accessed December 16, 2020. https://www.komazawa-u.ac.jp/~kobamasa/reference/gazou/yenrate/yenrate1.pdf

Koikari, Mire. 2015. *Cold War Encounters in US-occupied Okinawa: Women, Militarized Domesticity, and Transnationalism in East Asia*. Cambridge, UK: Cambridge University Press.

Koiso Kazuo. 1990. "Shukuji" [Congratulatory Message]. In *Uema Ikuko to Otohime Gekidan no 40-nen: Hana to Moete* [Uema Ikuko and 40 years of the Otohime Troupe: Glowing like Flowers], edited by Ōshiro Tatsuhiro, Kayō Yasuo, Funakoshi Gishō, Kōki Yoshihide, Hazama Yoshiko, Henna Tsunetsugu, and Fujimura Yoshiki, 6. Okinawa: Otohime Gekidan.

Kojima Yoshiyuki. 1990. "Minshū no Yume no Butai—Otohime Gekidan to Watashi" [The People's Dream Stage—the Otohime Troupes and I]. In *Uema Ikuko to Otohime Gekidan no 40-nen: Hana to Moete* [Uema Ikuko and 40 years of the Otohime Troupe: Glowing like Flowers], edited by Ōshiro Tatsuhiro, Kayō Yasuo, Funakoshi Gishō, Kōki Yoshihide, Hazama Yoshiko, Henna Tsunetsugu, and Fujimura Yoshiki, 42. Okinawa: Otohime Gekidan.

Kokoroni Todoke Onnatachi no Koe Nettowāku. 1998. *Mō Gamanshinai! Onnatachi wa Subete no Kichi o Kyohisuru!—Tokyo Daikōdō Kirokushū, 1998nen 5gatsu 8-10nichi* [We will not Put Up! Women Reject all the Bases—A Record of Tokyo Great Actions, May 5–10, 1988]. Naha, Okinawa: Kokoroni Todoke Onnatachi no Koe Nettowāku.

Kokuba, Kōtarō. [1973] 2019. *Okinawa no Ayumi* [Footsteps of Okinawa], edited by Arakawa Akira and Kano Masanao. Tokyo: Iwanami Shoten.

Kokuritsu Gekijō Okinawa. 2023. *Kōenkirokukanshō to Kōza: Okinawashibai o Shiru— Otohime Gekidan* [Viewing of a Recorded Performance and a Lecture: Understanding Okinawan Plays—Otohime]. poster. Accessed October 27, 2023. https://www.nt-okinawa.or.jp/images/tyosa/kouza/R5.2_otohimegekidan/R52_otohimegekidanomote.jpg

Komamura Kōhei. 2015. *Chūkansō Shōmetsu* [Disappearance of the Middle Class]. Tokyo: Kadokawa Shoten.
Komano Tsuyoshi. 2023. "'Kenpō9jyō wa Shinda'; Moto-Hōseikyoku Chōkan ga Kataru Seifukenkai no Kiben to Ayausa ['Article 9 is dead,' Former Director General of the Legislative Bureau Criticizing the Governmental View]." *Asahi Shimbun*, April 14. Accessed May 2, 2023. https://digital.asahi.com/articles/AS R4F62NSR31UPQJ00F.html?iref=pc_photo_gallery_bottom
Komatsu Hiroshi. 2019a. "'Yara Chōbyō Nisshi' ni Miru Kōtaishi Akihito no Okinawa Hatsu-hōmon, Jyō" [The Crown Prince's first visit to Okinawa as seen in 'Yara Chōbyō Diary' 1]. *Okiron*, June 8. Accessed December 28, 2020. https://okiron.net/archives/1340
Komatsu Hiroshi. 2019b. "'Yara Chōbyō Nisshi' ni Miru Kōtaishi Akihito no Okinawa Hatsu-hōmon, Ge" [The Crown Prince's first visit to Okinawa as seen in 'Yara Chōbyō Diary' 2]. *Okiron*, June 9. Accessed December 28, 2020. https://okiron.net/archives/1358
Komori Yōichi, and Takahashi Tetsuya. 1998. *Nashonaru Hisutorī o Koete* [Beyond National History]. Tokyo: Tokyo Daigaku Shuppankai.
Kondō Daisuke. 2018. *Shū Kinpei to Beichūshōtosu: "Chūkateikoku" 2021nen no Yabō* [Xi Jinping and the US-China Clash: The Ambition in 2021 by the "Chinese Empire"]. Tokyo: NHK Shuppan.
Kondō Ken'ichiro. 1995. "Kokutei Kyōkasho no Okinawazō: Rekishi, Chiri o Chūshin ni" [Images of Okinawa in School Textbooks Compiled by the State, with a Focus on History and Geography]. *Hokkaidō Daigaku Kyōiku-gakubu Kiyō* 68: 161–175. Accessed December 26, 2020. http://hdl.handle.net/2115/29482
Kondō Ken'ichiro. 2005. "Kindai Okinawa ni okeru Hōgenfuda no Jittai: Kinjirareta Kotoba" [Actual Conditions of the Dialect Placard in Okinawa: A Forbidden Language]. *Aichi Kenritsu Daigaku Bungakubu Ronshū* 53: 3–14. https://doi.org/10.15088/00000969. Accessed December 26, 2020. https://core.ac.uk/download/pdf/228932525.pdf
Kon'no Nobuyuki. 2008. *Kindai Nihon no Kokutairon: 'Kōkokushikan' Saikō* [Discourses on Kokutai in Modern Japan: Rethinking the Emperor-Centered Historical View]. Tokyo: Perikansha.
Kōriyama Mitsuru. 2013. "*Kotoba no Tabū to Sono Īkae*" [Taboos of Words and their Rephrasing]. *Kokubungaku* 97:29–49. Accessed December 26, 2020. http://hdl.handle.net/10112/9219
Kōsaka Masataka. [1968] 2006. *Saishō Yoshida Shigeru* [Prime Minister Yoshida Shigeru]. Tokyo: Chūōkōron-sha.
Koshi'ishi Tadashi. 2009. *Tōga: Kinjō Yūji-san: Henoko 'Inochi O Mamoru Kai' no Nemoto niwa* [Mourning Mr. Kinjō Yūji: What Exists at the Root of Henoko's Society for the Protection of Life]. Nago, Okinawa: Jinbun Kikaku.
Kowalski, Frank. 2013. *An Inoffensive Rearmament: The Making of the Postwar Japanese Army*, edited and annotated by Robert D. Eldridge. Annapolis, MD: Naval Institute Press.

Koyama Takashi. 2008. "Kantokeikaku no Naritachi ni Tsuite" [On the Establishment of the Kanto Plain Consolidation Plan]. *Senshi Kenkyū Nenpō* [NIDS Military History Studies Annual] 11: 1–20. Accessed December 20, 2020. http://www.nids.mod.go.jp/publication/senshi/pdf/200803/02.pdf

Kozeki Shōichi, Suzuki Yūji, Takahashi Susumu, Takayanagi Sakio, Maeda Tetsuo, Yamaguchi Yasushi, Yamaguchi Jirō, Wada Haruki, and Tuboi Yoshiaki. 1993. "'Heiwa Kihon-hō o Tsukurō: Heiwa Kenpō no Seishin ni Sotte Jieitai Mondai o Kaiketsusuru Tameni" [Let Us Make the Basic Law for Peace: For Resolving the Issues of the Self-Defense Forces in Accordance with the Spirit of the Peace Constitution]. *Sekai* 580 (April), 52–67.

Kudō Takaharu and Shimizu Yasunobu. 2015. "Henoko Fushin no Uzu, Hantaiha/Kaiho Ryōsha ni Intabyū" [Vortex of Mistrust in Henoko, Interviewing both protesters and JCG]. 2015. *Asahi Shimbun*, March 28. Accessed March 29, 2015. http://www.asahi.com/articles/ASH3V6DZ0H3VTPOB006.html

Kugai Ryōjun. 1990. "Sengo Okinawa ni Okeru Hōtaikei no Seibi—Tōkibo/Kosekibo o Fukumete" [The Reform of the Legal System in Postwar Okinawa, including the Registration Systems of Land and Family]. *Okidai Hōgaku* 9: 83–121. Accessed December 12, 2020. http://hdl.handle.net/20.500.12001/6547

Kumamoto Hiroyuki. 2014. "Dai 8-sshō, Beigun Kichi o Ukeireru Ronri—Kyampu Shuwabu to Henoko Shakai no Henbō" [Chapter 8, A Logic to Accept the US Base—Camp Schwab and the Changes of the Henoko Community]. In *Sōsho: Sensō ga Umidasu Shakai III, Beigun Kichi Bunka* [Series: Cultures that Wars Produce III, Cultures of the US Military], edited by Nanba Kōji, pp. 253–277. Tokyo: Shinyōsha.

Kumamoto Hiroyuki, Andō Yumi, Yamane Kiyohiro, Tanabe Shunsuke, Matsutani Mitsuru, Yoneda Sachihiro, and Takayashi Junko. 2023. *Seijisanka to Okinawa ni Kansuru Yoronchōsa: Chōsahōkokusho (Sokuhōbam)* [A Public Opinion Poll on Political Participation and Okinawa (Preliminary Report)]. Accessed September 15, 2023. https://w3.waseda.jp/prj-ipa/wp-content/uploads/sites/187/2023/06/ReportOkinawa2022compressed2.pdf

Kumashiro Tatsumi, dir. 1987. *Beddotaimu Aizu* [Bedtime Eyes]. Nagoya: Herarudo Eiga.

Kuni Takeyuki. 2005. *Hakurankai no Jidai: Meiji Seifu no Hakurankai Seisaku*. [The Age of Exhibitions: The Meiji Government's Exhibition Policy]. Tokyo: Iwata Shoin.

Kuniyoshi Mika. 2022. "Henoko Isetsu ni 'Hantai' 54%, Zenkai no 63% kara Genshō, Yoronchōsa" [54% of People 'Oppose' the FRF Construction, Reduced from 63% in the Previous Poll]. *Asahi Shimbun*, January 17. Accessed May 7, 2022. https://digital.asahi.com/articles/ASQ1K6X5PQ1KUZPS002.html?iref=pc_ss_date_article

Kuniyoshi Takumi. 2023. "Okinawaheno Kankōkyaku Kyūzō 2.06-bai, 2022-nendo 677-man'nin" [The Number of Tourists to Okinawa Rapidly Increased by 206%, 6.77 Million People in 2022]. *Okinawa Times*, April 28. Accessed October 25, 2023. https://www.okinawatimes.co.jp/articles/-/1142921

Kurima Yasuo. 1998. *Okinawa Keizai no Gensō to Genjitu* [Myths and Realities of the Okinawan Economy]. Tokyo: Nihon Keizaihyōronsha.

Kuroda, Yasumasa. 1994. "Bush's New World Order: A Structural Analysis of Instability and Conflict in the Gulf." In *The Gulf War and the New World Order: International Relations of the Middle East*, edited by Tareq Ismael and Jacqueline S. Ismael, pp. 52–76. Gainesville: University Press of Florida.

Kuroshima Minako. 2022. "'Sensō to Heiwa' Jyūminshiten de, Ken Heiwashiryōkan" ['War and Peace' from the Residents' Perspective, Okinawa Prefectural Peace Memorial Museum]. *Okinawa Times*, September 7, p. 17.

Kushi Fusako. [1932] 1993. "Horobiyuku Ryūkyū Onna no Shuki" [A Memoire of a Decaying Ryukyuan Woman]. In *Okinawa Bungaku Zenshū Dai 6-kan, Shōsetsu I* [Complete Works of Okinawan Literature, Volume 6, Literary Works I], edited by Okinawa Bungaku Zenshū Henshū Īnkai, 96–103. Tokyo: Kokusho Kankōkai.

Kusunoki, Ayako. 2009. *Yoshida Shigeru to Anzen Hoshō Seisaku no Keisei: Nichi-Bei no Kōsō to sono Sōgo Sayō, 1943–1952-nen* [Yoshida Shigeru and the Formation of Security: US-Japan plans and their Mutual Influences]. Kyoto: Mineruva Shobō.

Kyan Yukio. 1994. "Kyan Yukio (Aishō: Oyuki) hen" [A Chapter on Kyan Yukio (nickname: Oyuki)]. In *Rokku to Koza* [Rock and Koza], edited by Ishihara Masaie, 134–195. Okinawa: Okinawa Shiyakusho.

Levinas, Emmanuel. [1954] 1998. "The Ego and the Totality." In *Collected Philosophical Papers, Emmanuel Levinas*, translated by Alphonso Lingis, 25–45. Pittsburgh, PA Duquesne University Press.

Liu, Shih-Diing. 2006. 'China's Popular Nationalism on the Internet. Report on the 2005 anti-Japan Network Struggles 1.' *Inter-Asia Cultural Studies*, 7(1), 144–155. Accessed October 12, 2018. http://web.b.ebscohost.com.ezproxy.uky.edu/ehost/pdfviewer/pdfviewer?vid=1&sid=8756a8c0-b962-4929-a023-6411dd244baa%40pdc-v-sessmgr02

Locke, John. [1690] 2010. Book 2, *Two Treatise of Government*. The Project Gutenberg E-book. Accessed December 21, 2020. https://english.hku.hk/staff/kjohnson/PDF/LockeJohnSECONDTREATISE1690.pdf

Loo, Tze May. 2014. *Heritage Politics: Shuri Castle and Okinawa's Incorporation into Modern Japan, 1879–2000*. Lanham, MD: Lexington Books.

Lummis, C. Douglas. 2015. "The Bus to Henoko: Riot Police and Okinawan Citizens Face-Off over New Marine Base." *Asia-Pacific Journal/Japan Focus* 13(3), Number 1: 1–5 (Article ID 4816). Accessed October 30, 2020. http://www.japanfocus.org/-C.-Douglas-Lummis/4816/article.html

LunaticEclipseHenoko5. 2015. "Sakareru Umi" [The Sea that is Torn Apart]. YouTube. Video, 11:07. Accessed December 10, 2020. https://www.youtube.com/watch?v=F1do

Lycoris. 2004. "About Cocco, 2004." Accessed December 27, 2020. http://www.eonet.ne.jp/~derzirin/Cocco/04.htm

Lycoris. 2004–2010. "About Cocco." Accessed December 27, 2020. http://www.eonet.ne.jp/~derzirin/Cocco/about.htm

Lycoris. 2007. "About Cocco, 2007." Accessed December 27, 2020. http://www.eon et.ne.jp/~derzirin/Cocco/07.htm

Maeda Hisao. 1997. "Kaisetsu: Gaidorain towa" [Commentary: What is the 'Guidelines']. *Sekai* 641 (Bessatsu): 75–82.

Makiminato Tokuzō, Ōshiro Tatsuhiro, Kawamitsu Shin'ichi, Kōki Yoshihide, Asato Susumu, and Arasaki Moriteru. 1975. "Okinawa nitotte Sengo towa Nanika" [What is Postwar for Okinawa]. *Shin Okinawa Bungaku* 27: 98–124.

Makino Hirotaka. 1987. *Sengo Okinawa no Tsūka* [Currencies in Postwar Okinawa]. Naha, Okinawa: Hirugisha.

Makino Yoshihiro. 2023. "Kawaru Beigun, Chūgoku Nentō ni Nichibeikan de Kyōryoku Kyōka" [The Changing US Military, Strengthening Cooperations among the US, Japan, and South Korea to Confront China]. *Asahi Shimbun*, May 5. Accessed May 5, 2023. https://digital.asahi.com/articles/ASR4Y64R7R4 SUPQJ00J.html?iref=comtop_Opinion_01

Makishi Kisako. 2016. "Otohime Gekidan to Tsuji Bunka" [The Otohime Troupes and Tsuji Culture]. *Shinasaki no Umi e*, March 21. Accessed December 13, 20020. https://blog.goo.ne.jp/nasaki78/e/f2e350bc8d280429276703891846 b1c0

Mann, Steve, Jason Nolan, and Barry Wellman. 2003. "Sousveillance: Inventing and Using Wearable Computing Devices for Data Collection in Surveillance Environments." *Surveillance & Society* 1(3): 331–355. Accessed November 3, 2020. https://doi.org/10.24908/ss.v1i3.3344

Maran, René. 1947. *Un homme pareil aux autres*. Paris: Editions Arc-en-Ciel.

Marx, Karl. [1887] n.d. *Capital: A Critique of Political Economy, Volume I*. Translated by Samuel Moore and Edward Aveling and edited by Frederick Engels. Marxist Internet Archive. Accessed December 11, 2020. https://www.marxists .org/archive/marx/works/download/pdf/Capital-Volume-I.pdf

Marx, Karl, and Friedrich Engels. [1848] n.d. *Manifesto of the Communist Party*. Marxist Internet Archive. Accessed December 30, 2020. https://www.marxists .org/archive/marx/works/1848/communist-manifesto/ch01.htm

Masagata. n.d. *Okinawa Henoko Shōsetsu "Henoko Bā Seijyōki" Dai 1shō Sensō o Shiranai Watashitachi* [A Fiction about Henoko, Okinawa "A Henoko Bar, the Stars and Stripes" Chapter 1 We who Don't Know War]. Blog. Accessed November 10, 2023. https://masagata.exblog.jp/31003860/

Masubuchi Asako. 2013. "'Hachigatsu Jyūgoya no Chaya' o meguru Manazashi no Seijigaku" [The Politics of Gaze concerning *The Teahouse of the August Moon*]. In *Senryōsha no Manazashi: Okinawa/Nihon/Beikoku no Sengo* [The Gaze of the Occupier: Postwar Okinawa/Japan/US], edited by Tanaka Yasuhiro, 14–38. Toyo: Serika Shobō.

Masuo Chisako. 2019. *Chūgoku no Kōdōgenri* [Action Principles of China]. Tokyo: Chūōkōron-sha.

Masuo Chisako, and Hosoi Takuji. 2022. "Hanyu Yuzuru senshu nimiru Nicchūyūkō no Yoin, Ryōkokumin ga Ōen 'Saigo no Kōkei kamo'" [Afterglow of Japan-China Friendship in HanyuYuzuru, Both Nations Support, 'Could be the Last

Chance']. *Asahi Shimbun*, February 22. Accessed April 3, 2022. https://digital.asahi.com/articles/ASQ2151Z0Q1XUCVL00K.html?iref=pc_ss_date_article

Matsubara Kōji. 2016. *Hankotsu: Onagake Sandai to Okinawa no Ima* [Defiance: Three Generations of the Onaga Family and the Present of Okinawa]. Tokyo: Asahi Shimbun Shuppan.

Matsuda Kyōko. 2003. *Teikoku no Shisen: Hakurankai to Ibunka Hyōshō.* [The Gaze of the Empire: Exhibitions and Representations of Different Cultures.] Tokyo: Yoshikawa Kōbunkan.

Matsumura, Wendy. 2015. *The Limits of Okinawa: Japanese Capital, Living Labor, and Theorizations of Community.* Durham, NC: Duke University Press.

Matsuo Takayoshi. 1993. *Nihon no Rekishi 21: Kokusai Kokka eno Shuppatsu* [Japanese History Volume 21: Departure for the International State]. Tokyo: Shūeisha.

Matsushita Yūichi. 2011. "Sakka Ōshiro Tatsuhiro no Tachiba Kettei: 'Bungaku-ba' no Shakaigaku no Shiten kara" [Sociological Analysis of Position-Taking in the Literary Field: A Case of Oshiro Tatsuhiro]. *Mita Shakaigaku* 16: 104–117. Accessed March 2024. https://koara.lib.keio.ac.jp/xoonips/modules/xoonips/detail.php?koara_id=AA11358103-20110709-0104

McClintock, Anne. 1995. *Imperial Leather: Race, Gender, and Sexuality in the Colonial Contest.* New York: Routledge.

McCormack, Gavan. 2007. *Client State: Japan in the American Embrace.* New York: Verso.

McCormack, Gavan, and Satoko Oka Norimatsu. 2018. *Resistant Islands: Okinawa Confronts Japan and the United States* (2nd edition). Lanham, MD: Rowman & Littlefield.

McEvoy, J. P. 1950. "General MacArthur Reports on Japan." *Reader's Digest* (May), 9–14.

Mead, George H. 1934. *Mind, Self, and Society: From the Standpoint of a Social Behaviorist.* Chicago: University of Chicago Press.

Medoruma Shun. n.d. *Uminari no Shimakara: Okinawa/Yanbaru yori* [The Island Filled with Sea Roars: from Yanbaru, Okinawa] (blog). Accessed November 3, 2020. https://blog.goo.ne.jp/awamori777

Medoruma Shun. [1986] 1990. *Heiwadōri to Nazukerareta Machi o Aruite* [Walking the Town Named Peace Street]. In *Okinawa Bungaku Zenshū Dai 9-kan, Shōsetsu IV* [Complete Works of Okinawan Literature, Volume 9, Literary Works IV], edited by Okinawa Bungaku Zenshū Henshū Īnkai, 74–115. Tokyo: Kokusho Kankōkai.

Medoruma Shun. 1999. *Kibō* [Hope]. In Medoruma Shin Tanpen Shōsetsu Senshū 3: *Umukaji tou Chirete* [Selected Short Stories of Medoruma Shun Volume 3: Together with What It Used to be], 103–106. Tokyo: Kage Shobō.

Medoruma Shun. [2004] 2017. *Niji no Tori* [A Bird of Rainbows]. Tokyo: Kage Shobō.

Medoruma Shun. 2005. *Okinawa Sengo Zero-nen* [Zero Year after the War]. Tokyo: Nihon Hōsō Shuppan Kyōkai.

Medoruma Shun. 2014a. "Kono Tatakai wa Kateru! Kyampu Shuwābu no Gētomae ni 3600nin ga Atsumaru" [We Can Win This Struggle! 3,600 People Gathered in front of the Gate of Camp Schwab]. *Uminari no Shimakara: Okinawa/Yanbaru yori* [The Island Filled with Sea Roars: from Yanbaru, Okinawa] (blog), August 24. Accessed October 30, 2020. https://blog.goo.ne.jp/awamori777/e/29b42447 b8cef43cabb8598ea3ef34ac

Medoruma Shun. 2014b. "50mei-ijō no Sankaniyori Okonawareta Kaijyōdaikōdō" [Great Protest on the Sea Joined by More Than 50 Individuals]. *Uminari no Shimakara: Okinawa/Yanbaru yori* [The Island filled with Sea Roars: from Yanbaru, Okinawa] (blog), August 30. Accessed October 30, 2020. http://blog.goo.ne.jp/awamori777/e/1cca7a63e5c13195aa7801ffc0435f05

Medoruma Shun. 2014c. "Betanagi no Umi demo Nami wa Sawagu . . . 'Anzenkakuho' o Kōjitu Nishita Futōna Kōsoku" [The Quiet Ocean Can Stir Waves . . . Unjust Detention in the Name of Safety]. *Uminari no Shimakara: Okinawa/Yanbaru yori* [The Island filled with Sea Roars: from Yanbaru, Okinawa] (blog), August 21. Accessed December 10, 2020. https://blog.goo.ne.jp/awamori777/e/ac14a790fcd73d852bec03bcabd99e8b

Medoruma Shun. 2014d. "Kyanpu Shuwābu no Gētomae Kōgikōdō to Henoko no Hama no Beigunkunren" [Protest Activities in front of the Gate of Camp Schwab and US Military's Training on the Beach of Henoko]. *Uminari no Shimakara: Okinawa/Yanbaru yori* [The Island filled with Sea Roars: from Yanbaru, Okinawa] (blog), July 16. Accessed December 10, 2020. https://blog.goo.ne.jp/awamori777/e/8b09bf3a2d97a181403a3ad0bad965a0

Medoruma Shun. 2015. "Shōkai: 'Henoko ni Kichi o Tsukurasenai Burū no Fune' Shinsuishiki ni Atari" [Introduction: Upon launching "the Blue Ship that Blocks the Construction of a Base in Henoko"]. 2015. *Uminari no Shimakara: Okinawa/Yanbaru yori* [The Island Filled with Sea Roars: from Yanbaru, Okinawa] (blog), November 8. Accessed November 3, 2020. https://blog.goo.ne.jp/awamori777/e/38b9731158d1745c658395aef7ba7223

Medoruma Shun. 2016a. "Oirufensu Secchisoshi to Kaitei Bōringuchōsa no Jyunbi" [Preventing the Installation of Oil Fence and the Preparation for Boring Survey]. *Uminari no Shimakara: Okinawa/Yanbaru yori* [The Island Filled with Sea Roars: from Yanbaru, Okinawa] (blog), February 17. Accessed October 30, 2020. https://blog.goo.ne.jp/awamori777/e/47ca9ea664b51778cdc813bf664a 8d92

Medoruma Shun. 2016b. 'Okinawa-Kenmin o 'Dojin' Yobawarisuru Kidōtai'in' [A Riot Policeman Who Called Okinawans 'Dojin.']. Accessed on October 13, 2018. *Uminari no Shimakara: Okinawa/Yanbaru yori* [The Island Filled with Sea Roars: from Yanbaru, Okinawa] (blog), October 18. https://blog.goo.ne.jp /awamori777/e/93cd24d10a5c21f3dde2c5aac97e2eec

Mekaru Ittetsu. 2021. "'Sakimoro' no shōzō, Jieitai Okinawa ijyū 50nen 1" [The Portrait of the "Guardians," 50 Years since the Moving of the Self-Defense Forces to Okinawa 1]. *Okinawa Times*, January 4, page 21.

Metz, Steven, and Douglas V. Johnson II. 2001. *Asymmetry and U.S. Military Strat-*

egy: Definition, Background, and Strategic Concepts. Carlisle, PA: U.S. Army War College Strategic Studies Institute.
Mikami Chie. 2006. *Umi ni Suwaru: Hankichi 600 nichi no Tatakai* [Sitting In on the Sea: 600 Days of an Anti-base Struggle in Henoko]. Broadcast March 25 by Ryukyu Asahi Hōsō.
Mikami Chie, dir. 2014. *Ikusabanu Tudumi* [Bringing the War to the End]. Tokyo: Kinokuniya Shoten.
Miller, Jennifer M. 2019. *Cold War Democracy: The United States and Japan.* Cambridge, MA: Harvard University Press.
Millett, Allan Reed. 1991. *Semper Fidelis: The History of the United States Marine Corps, Revised and Expanded Edition.* New York: Free Press.
Mimaki Seiko. 2014. *Sensō Ihōka Undō no Jidai: 'Kiki' no 20-nen no Amerika Kokusai Kankei Shisō* [The Era of the Outlawry of War Movement: The Development of International Political Thought during the "Twenty Years' Crisis" in the United States]. Nagoya: Nagoya Daigaku Shuppankai.
Mimura, Janis. 2011. *Planning for Empire: Reform Bureaucrats and the Japanese Wartime State.* Ithaca, NY: Cornell University Press.
Mirza, Heidi Safia. 2013. "'A Second Skin': Embodied Intersectionality, Transnationalism and Narratives of Identity and Belonging Among Muslim Women in Britain." *Women's Studies International Forum* 36: 5–15.
Mitchell, Jon. 2010. "Beggars' Belief: The Farmers' Resistance Movement on Iejima Island, Okinawa." *Asia-Pacific Journal/Japan Focus* Volume 8, Issue 23(2). Accessed December 12, 2020. https://apjjf.org/-Jon-Mitchell/3370/article.html
Miyagi Eishō. 1967. *Okinawa Joseishi* [A History of Okinawan Women]. Naha, Okinawa: Okinawa Times-sha.
Miyagi Etsujirō. 1982. *Senryōsha no Me: Amerikajin ha Okinawa o dō Mitaka* [The Gaze of the Ruler: How Did Americans see Okinawans?]. Naha, Okinawa: Naha Shuppansha.
Miyagi Etsujirō. 1994. *Okinawa/Sengo Hōsōshi* [Okinawa/A History of Postwar Broadcasting]. Naha, Okinawa: Hirugisha.
Miyagi Harumi. 2006. "Okinawa no Amerikagunkichi to Seibōryoku: Americagun Jyōrikukara Kōwajōyaku Hakkōmae no Seihanzai no Jittai wo Tōshite" [US Bases in Okinawa and Sexual Violence: In light of Actuality of Sexual Crimes between 1945 and 1951]. In *Okinawa no Senryō to Nihon no Fukkō: Shokuminchishugi wa ikani Keizokushitaka* [Occupation of Okinawa and Recovery of Japan: How Colonialism has Continued], edited by Nakano Toshio, Namihira Tsuneo, Yakabi Osamu, Lee Hyoduk, 42–58. Tokyo: Seikyūsha.
Miyagi Harumi. 2008a. *Shinpan: Haha no Nokoshita Mono* [What My Mother Left Behind, new edition]. Tokyo: Kōbunken.
Miyagi Harumi. 2008b. "Zamami-jima no Shūdanjiketsu: Jendā no Shiten kara 'Shiron'" [Group Suicide in Zamami: An Attempt from a Perspective of Gender]. In *Okinawa: Toi o Tateru 4: Yūgun to Gama—Okinawasen no Kioku* [Okinawa: Establishing Questions Volume 4: The Japanese Army and Caves—Memories of the Battle of Okinawa], edited by Yakabi Osamu, 75–106. Tokyo: Shakai Hyōronsha.

Miyagi, Hiroya, and Shihoko Abe. 2019. "203,800 Signatures Collected for White House Petition to Halt US Base Work in Okinawa." *The Mainichi*, January 9. Accessed December 9, 2020. https://mainichi.jp/english/articles/20190109/p2a/00m/0na/007000c

Miyagi Taizō, and Watanabe Tsuyoshi. 2016. *Futenma/Henoko: Hizumerarate 20nen* [Futenma/Henoko: Distorted 20 years]. Tokyo: Shūeisha.

Miyake Risako, Fukutomi Tabifumi, and Okada Shōhei. 2022. "Kakukin-Jōyaku o Atooshisuru Sekai no 524-toshi, NY 'Tokubetsuna Sekininga aru'" [524 Cities in the World that Support the Treaty on the Prohibition of Nuclear Weapons; NY City Says, 'We Have a Special Responsibility']. *Asahi Shimbun*, January 22. Accessed May 15, 2022. https://digital.asahi.com/articles/ASQ1Q4CDGQ1PPITB00N.html?iref=comtop_ThemeRightS_01

Miyamoto Ken'ichi. 2000. "Okinawa no Ijikanō na Hatten no tameni" [For the Sustainable Development of Okinawa]. In *Okinawa: 21-seiki eno Chōsen* [Okinawa: Challenges to the Twenty-First Century], edited by Miyamoto Ken'ichi and Sasaki Masayuki, 1–30. Tokyo: Iwanami Shoten.

Miyamoto Ken'ichi, and Sasaki Masayuki, eds. 2000. *Okinawa: 21-seiki eno Chōsen* [Okinawa: Challenges to the Twenty-First Century]. Tokyo: Iwanami Shoten.

Miyanishi, Kaori. 2012. *Okinawa Gunjinzuma no Kenkyū* [A Study of Okinawan Wives of US Servicemen]. Kyoto: Kyotodaigaku Gakujutsushuppankai.

Miyara Tamotsu. 1950. "*Kami no Shisha*" [A Messenger of God]. *Uruma Shunjyū* 2(5) (June/July Issue): 1–12.

Miyasaka Tōru. 2005. "Bokuga Mita Henoko: Shinkichikensetsuhantai Hibōryokuteikōundō ni Sankashite" [Henoko that I Saw: Participating in the Non-Violent Resistance to the Construction of a New Base]. *Gekkan Shakai Kyōiku* (Social Education Monthly) 598 (August 2005 Issue): 28–32.

Miyazaki Hayao, dir. 1988. *My Neighbor Totoro*. Tokyo: Tohō.

Miyazaki Hayao, dir. 1997. *The Princess Mononoke*. Tokyo: Tohō.

Miyazaki Hayao, dir. 2001. *Spirited Away*. Tokyo: Tohō.

Miyazato Seigen. 1975. "Amerika no Tai-Okinawaseisaku no Keisei to Tenkai" [Formation and Development of the US Policies over Okinawa]. In *Sengo Okinawa no Seiji to Hō, 1945nen-1972nen* [Politics and Law in Postwar Okinawa, 1945–1972], edited by Miyazato Seigen, 3–116. Tokyo: University of Tokyo Press.

MMproton. 2014. "Okinawa/Henoko Kanūtai Rirē" [A Relay of the Okinawa/Henoko Canoe Team]. YouTube. Video, 14:34. Accessed December 10, 2020. https://www.youtube.com/watch?v=6g8p2VejeXQ

MMproton. 2015. "20150208 Henoko Burū Kanūtai Rīda Sasaki Kōbun san ni Kiku Ima no Genjō" [February 8, 2015: Current Conditions as Addressed by Mr. Sasaki Kōbun, a Leader of Henoko Blue]. YouTube. Video, 8:39. Accessed December 9, 2020. https://www.youtube.com/watch?v=3WI_JkS8wNo

Mogami Toshiki. 2005. *Kokuren to Amerika* [The United Nations and the United States]. Tokyo: Iwanami Shoten.

Molasky, Michael S. 1999. *The American Occupation of Japan and Okinawa: Literature and Memory*. New York: Routledge.

Moore, Aaron Stephen. 2013. *Constructing East Asia: Technology, Ideology, and Empire in Japan's Wartime Era, 1931–1945*. Stanford, CA: Stanford University Press.

Mori Yoshio. 2010a. "Okinawa Sengoshi towa Nanika: Ken'nai Isetsu Hantai Undō no Haigo niaru Rekishiishiki" [What is Postwar Okinawan History?: Historical Consciousness behind the Movement against the Construction of the FRF in Okinawa]. In *Gendai Okinawa no Rekishi Keiken: Kibō, aruiwa Miketsusei ni Tsuite* [Historical Experiences of Contemporary Okinawa: On Hope, or Undecidability], edited by Tomiyama Ichirō and Mori Yoshio, 159–206. Tokyo: Seikyūsha.

Mori Yoshio. 2010b. *Tsuchi no Naka no Kakumei: Okinawa Sengoshi ni okeru Sonzai no Kaihō* [A Revolution from Below: The Liberation of Being in the History of Postwar Okinawa]. Tokyo: Gendai Kikakushitsu.

Mori Yoshio. 2016. *Okinawa Sengo Minshū-shi: Gama kara Henoko made* [Postwar History of the Okinawan People: From Caves to Henoko]. Tokyo: Iwanami Shoten.

Morris-Suzuki, Tessa. 2013. "Introduction: Confronting the Ghosts of War in East Asia." In *East Asia Beyond the History Wars: Confronting the Ghosts of Violence*, authored by Tessa Morris-Suzuki, Morris Low, Leonid Petrov, and Timothy Y. Tsu, 1–26. London/New York: Routledge.

Motohama Hidehiko. 2003. "Kaisetsu" [Commentary]. In *Okinawa Bungaku-sen: Nihon Bungaku no Ejji kara no Toi* [Selections of Okinawa Literature: Questions from the Edge of Japan], edited by Okamoto Keitoku and Takahashi Toshio, 130–132. Tokyo: Bensei Shuppan.

Murakami Ryū. 1976. *"Kagirinaku Tōmei ni Chikai Burū"* [Almost Transparent Blue]. In *Murakami Ryū Jisen Shōsetsu-shū 1* [Self-Selected Works of Murakami Ryu, Volume 1], 281–369. Tokyo: Kōdansha.

Murase Haruki. 1970. *Dareka Okinawa o Shiranaika* [Does Anybody Know Okinawa?]. Tokyo: San'ichi Shobō.

Murphy-Shigematsu, Stephen. 2002. *Amerajian No Kodomotachi: Shirarezaru Mainoriti Mondai* [Amerasian Children: An Unknown Minority Issue]. Translated by Sakai Sumiko. Tokyo: Shūeisha.

Nagadō Eikichi. 1985. *Cijin Taiheiki: Monogatari, Sengo Okinawa Engekishi* [Chijin Taiheiki: A Narrative on Postwar Okinawan Performing Arts History]. Naha, Okinawa: Gekkan Okinawasha.

Nagai Yoshikazu. 2011. *Minami Saori ga Ita Koro.* [Where Minami Saori Was There]. Tokyo: Asahishinbun Suppan.

Nagasakiken Heiwa Īnkai. n.d. "Sasebo o Bokō tosuru Bei Kantei" [American Naval Vessels that Use Sasebo as Their Home Port]. Accessed December 21, 2020. http://www7b.biglobe.ne.jp/~chi-tan/usship.html

Nahashi Rekishi Hakubutsukan. 2015. *Konbu no Tochitōsō* [Struggles to Protect the Land in Konbu]. Accessed on October 29, 2020. http://www.rekishi-archive.city.naha.okinawa.jp/archives/item3/22345

Nakachi Hiroshi. 2001. "Sengo Okinawa Jichiseido-shi (ichi)" [A history of postwar

Okinawa's self-governing system (1)]. *Ryūdai Hōgaku* 65: 83–114. Accessed December 11, 2020. http://hdl.handle.net/20.500.12000/1793

Nakae Yūji, dir. 1999. *Nabī no Koi* [Nabī's Love]. Tokyo: Office Shirous.

Nakagawa Kiyoshi. 2004. "Kazoku o Meguru Shakaiseisaku no Tenkai to Genkyokumen" [The Development of Social Policies concerning Family in Japan]. *Mita Shakaigaku* 9: 15–30. Accessed June 27, 2022. https://core.ac.uk/download/pdf/145719493.pdf

Nakahodo Masanori. 2008. *Amerika no Aru Fūkei: Okinawa Bungaku no Ichiryōiki* [The Scenery Where America Exists: A Domain of the Okinawa Literature]. Naha, Okinawa: Niraisha.

Nakamatsu, Yashū. 1990. *Kami to Mura* [Gods and Villages]. Tokyo: Fukurōsha.

Nakamura Jun. 2000. "'Dojin'-ron: 'Dojin' Imēji no Keisei to Tenkai" [Discourses on *Dojin*: Formation and Transformation of the Images of *Dojin*]. In *Kindai Nihon no Jikozō to Tashazō* [Images Self and Other in Modern Japan], edited by Shinohara Tōru, 85–128. Tokyo: Kashiwa Shobō.

Nakamura Satoshi. 1992. *Nihon no Rekishi 16: Meiji Ishin* [Japanese History Volume 16: The Meiji Restoration]. Tokyo: Shūeisha.

Nakandakari Hatsu. [1981] 1993. "Yakusoku" [A Promise]. In *Okinawa Tanpen Shōsetsu-shū* [A Collection of Okinawan Short Stories], edited by Ryukyu Shimpo-sha, 145–160. Naha, Okinawa: Ryukyu Shimpo-sha.

Nakano Yoshio. 1969. *Sengo Shiryō Okinawa* [Historical Records of Postwar Okinawa]. Tokyo: Nihon Hyōronsha.

Nakao Takumi. 1990. "Iwayuru Okinawa Zenesuto Keisatukan Satugaijiken Kunibaishō Soshō Jōkokushin Hanketsu ni Tsuite" [On the Ruling at the Court of Final Appeal in the Lawsuit demanding Damage Recovery from the State for the so-called Police Officer Murder Case that Occurred during the Okinawa General Strike]. *Keisatugaku Ronshū* 43(3): 50–65.

Nakasone Seizen. 1982. *Himeyuri no Tō o Meguru Hitobito no Shuki* [Memoranda of the People Related to the Himeyuri Memorial]. Tokyo: Kadokawa Shoten.

Nakatsu Jyūzō. 2015. "Okinawajin no Ikari to Iji ga Tsutawattekuru 'Dai-Ryūkyū Shashin Emaki'" [The *Dai-Ryūkyū Shashin Emaki* Exhibition Communicates Anger and Pride of Okinawans]. *Magazine 9*, July 8. Accessed October 27, 2023. http://www.magazine9.jp/article/biboroku/20510/

Nakazato Kazuka. 2013. "Okinawaken Zaijyū Filipinjin Josei no Seikatsujittai Chōsa" [Research on Actual Living Conditions of Filipino Women Living in Okinawa]. *Kyushu Communication Studies* 11: 31–57. Accessed December 16, 2020. http://www.caj1971.com/~kyushu/KCS_11_05_Nakazato.pdf

Nakazato Isao. n.d. "(4) 'Hachigatsu Jyūgoya no Chaya' Kutsujoku o Meguru Rongi/Senryōsha no Dokuzensei o Warau" [(4) "'The Teahouse of the August Moon': Discussion on Humiliation, Laughing at the Self-Righteousness of the Occupier"]. In *Ryūkyū Denei Retsuden/Kioku to Yume no Sukuranburu* [Stories of Great Ryukyuan Films/Scrambling Memories and Dreams]. Accessed December 12, 2020. http://www7b.biglobe.ne.jp/~whoyou/retsuden.htm#%EF%BC%94

Namihira Isao. 1970. "Konketsuji no Kenkyū (1)" [A Study of Mixed-Race Children]. *Okidai Ronsō: The Journal of the Okinawa University* 10(1), 77–160.
Nancy, Jean-Luc. [1983] 1991. "The Inoperative Community," translated by Peter Conner. In *The Inoperative Community*, edited by Peter Conner, Translated by Peter Connor, Lisa Garbus, Michael Holland, and Simona Sawhney, 1–42. Minneapolis: University of Minnesota Press.
Nanseichi'iki Sangyō Kasseika Sentā. 2015. *Okinawaken Oyobi Kennai Shichōson no Jinkōdōkō, Heisei 27nen 7gatsu* [Changes of Populations in Okinawa Prefecture and the Municipalities in the Prefecture, July 2015]. Accessed December 21, 2020. https://niac.or.jp/topix/population_1st_H27.pdf
Naoshima Masao. 2000. "Jirādo Jiken no Shinsō: Nichibei Seiji Mitsuyaku" [The truth about the Girard incident: A secret agreement between the US and Japanese governments]. In *60nen Anpo/Mi'ike Tōsō: Ishihara Yūjirō no Jidai, 1957–1960* [Struggles over the Security Treaty and the Mi'ike Coal Mine: The Age of Ishihara Yūjirō, 1957–1960], edited by Nishi'i Kazuo, 16. Tokyo: Mainichi Shimbunsha.
Nasu, Hitoshi. 2013. "The Place of Human Security in Collective Security." *Journal of Conflict and Security Law* 18(1): 95–129. Accessed May 15, 2022. https://doi.org/10.1093/jcsl/krs026
National Diet Library. 2020. "Nuchi Du Takara no Shutten o Shiritai" [Wanting to Know the Origin of *Nuchi Du Takara*]. *Referensu Kyōdō Dētabēsu*. Accessed September 8, 2023. https://crd.ndl.go.jp/reference/modules/d3ndlcrdentry/index.php?page=ref_view&id=1000272426
Negri, Antonio. 1999. *Insurgencies: Constituent Power and the Modern State*. Translated by Maurizia Boscagli. Minneapolis, MN: University of Minnesota Press.
Neko3_Paradisez. 2016. "'Jyugon no Mieru Oka' Supesharu Eizō: Ātisuto Cocco" [A Special Video, 'The Hill of Dugongs' by Cocco]. YouTube. Video, 10:56. Accessed December 27, 2020. https://www.youtube.com/watch?v=JAYJgrLOcyg
Nelson, Christopher T. 2008. *Dancing with the Dead: Memory, Performance, and Everyday Life in Postwar Okinawa*. Durham, NC: Duke University Press.
Nelson, Christopher T. 2015. "Listening to the Bones: The Rhythms of Sacrifice in Contemporary Japan." *boundary* 2 42:3, 143–155. https://doi.org/10.1215/01903659-2919549
Newton, Creede. 2021. "A history of the US blocking UN resolutions against Israel." *Aljazeera*, May 19. Accessed October 22, 2023. https://www.aljazeera.com/news/2021/5/19/a-history-of-the-us-blocking-un-resolutions-against-israel
NHK. 1993. *Ryukyu no Kaze* [The Wind of the Ryukyu Kingdom]. Broadcast January 10–June 13. Tokyo: NHK.
NHK. 2001. *Churasan* [Beauty]. Broadcast April 2-September 29. Tokyo: NHK.
NHK. 2017. *NHK Supesharu, Sukūpu Dokyumento Okinawa to Kaku* [NHK Special, A Scoop Documentary: Okinawa and Nuclear Weapons]. Broadcast September 10. https://www.nhk-ondemand.jp/goods/G2017080831SA000/
NHK Shuzaihan. 2011. *Kichi wa Naze Okinawa ni Shūchūshite Irunoka* [Why Have the Bases been Concentrated in Okinawa]. Tokyo: NHK Shuppan.

Nihon Minzokugakkai. 1962. *Minzokugaku Kenkyū* 27(1).
Nihonshizenhogo Kyōkai. 2001. "IUCN no Kankoku o Sonchōshita Seisaku o Sakkyūni Jikkoōsurukoto o Yōsei suru" [We Request that the Policy Respecting the IUCN's Advice be Promptly Implemented]. Issued on July 6. Accessed December 10, 2020. https://www.nacsj.or.jp/archive/2001/07/231/
Nihonshizenhogo Kyōkai. 2004. "'Jyugon, Noguchigera, Yanbarukuina no Hozen o Motomeru Kankoku' Saitakusareru" [Recommendation for the 'Conservation of Dugongs, Okinawa Woodpeckers and Okinawa Rails in Japan' Adopted]. Issued on November 26. Accessed December 10, 2020. https://www.nacsj.or.jp/archive/2004/11/309/
Nippon Bunka Channeru Sakura. n.d.-a. *Nippon Bunka Channeru Sakura* [Japan Culture Channel Sakura]. Accessed December 23, 2023. https://www.youtube.com/user/SakuraSoTV
Nippon Bunka Channeru Sakura. n.d.-b. "Channeru Sakura Shichōhōhōno Goan'nai [Guides to how to watch Channeru Sakura]." Accessed September 29, 2023. http://www.ch-sakura.jp/1012.html
Nishihara, Masashi. 1976. *The Japanese and Sukarno's Indonesia: Tokyo-Jakarta Relations, 1951–1966*. Honolulu: University Press of Hawai'i.
Nishimura Kumao. 1971. *Nihon Gaikō-shi Dai 27-kan: San Furanshisuko Heiwa Jyōyaku* [Japanese Diplomatic History Volume 27: San Francisco Peace Treaty]. Tokyo: Kashima Kenkyūjo Shuppankai.
Nishitani Osamu. 1997. "Yakuchū" [Translator's Notes]. In *Akashienu Kyōdōtai* [The Unavowable Community], 119–163. Tokyo: Chikuma Shobō.
Nishitani Osamu. 2001. "'Bunyū,' Sonzai no Fukusūsei no Shikō—Atogaki ni Kaete" ["Sharing," Thought on the Multiplicity of Being—In place of Afterword]. In *Mui no Kyōdōtai—Tetsugaku o Toinaosu Bunyū no Shikō* [The Inoperative Community—Thought on the Multiplicity of Being where Philosophy is Reexamined], translated by Nishitani Osamu and Yasuhara Shin'ichirō, 277–291. Tokyo: Ibunsha.
Noguchi Yukio. 2015. *Sengo Keizaishi: Watakushitachi Wa Doko De Machigaetanoka*. Tokyo: Tōyō Keizai Shinpōsha.
Nomura Kōya, ed. 2007. *Shokuminsha e: Posutocoroniarizumu toiu Cōhatsu* [To the Colonizer: A Provocation named Postcolonialism]. Tokyo: Shōraisha.
Nomura Kōya. 2019. *Zōho Kaiteiban Muishiki no Shokuminchi-shugi: Nihonjin no Beigun Kichi to Okinawajin* [Unconscious Colonialism: Japanese US Bases and Okinawans, expanded and revised edition]. Tokyo: Shōraisha.
No Osprey Okinawa Kenmintaikai Jimukyoku. 2013. *Kenpakusho* [Petition]. Accessed October 31, 2020. https://kenmintaikai2012.ti-da.net/e4331515.html
Nozoe Fumiaki. 2016a. *Okinawa Henkango no Nichi-Bei Anpo: Beigun Kichi o Meguru Sōkoku* [The US-Japan Security Alliance after Okinawa Reversion: Struggles over the US Bases]. Tokyo: Yoshikawa Kōbunkan.
Nozoe Fumiaki. 2016b. "1970nendai kara 1980nendai ni Okeru Zaioki Kaiheitai no Saihen/Kyōka" [Reorganization and Reinforcement of the US Marine Corps in Okinawa from the 1970s to the 1980s]. In *Okinawa to Kahieitai: Chūryū no Rekishiteki Tenkai* [Okinawa and the US Marine Corps: Historical Develop-

ment of Stationing], authored by Yara Tomohiro, Kawana Shinji, Saitō Kōsuke, Nozoe Fumiaki, and Yomamoto Akiko, 85–113. Tokyo: Jynpōsha.

Nozoe Fumiaki. 2019. "Okinawa no Beigun Heri Tsuiraku no Haikei ni Kaiheitai no Shinsenryaku ari" [There Exists a New Strategy of the US Marine Corps against the Background of Recent Accidents of its Helicopters]. *Ronza*, September 6. Accessed December 21, 2020. https://webronza.asahi.com/politics/articles/201 9090200004.html?page=4

Nye, Joseph S., Jr. 1991. "Why the Gulf War Served the National Interest." *The Atlantic Monthly* (July) 268(1): 56–64. Accessed December 21, 2020. https://www.theatlantic.com/past/docs/issues/91jul/nye.htm

Ōba Mie. 2004. *Ajia Taiheiyō Chiki Keisei eno Dōtei: Kyōkaikokka Nichi-Gō no Aidentiti Mosaku to Chikishugi* [The Road to the Formation of the Asia-Pacific Region: Identity and Regionalism of Marginal Nation-States of Japan and Australia]. Kyoto: Mineruba Shobō.

Obutsudan no Akamine. n.d. "Nananin-dachi, M01-7S-MK." Accessed December 14, 2020. http://www.okinawabutudan.jp/item/a096/

Odagiri Makoto. 2012. "Dokuji no Rekishi o Tadotta Okinawa no Media Jijyō" [A Distinctive History of the Okinawan Media Environment]. In *Wedge Infinity*, July 11. Accessed December 13, 2020. https://wedge.ismedia.jp/articles/-/2063?page=2

Ōe Kenzaburō. 1970. *Okinawa Nōto* [Okinawa Notes]. Tokyo: Iwanami Shoten.

Ōe Kenzaburō and Iwanami Shoten Okinawasen Saiban Shienrenrakukai. n.d. *Kiroku*. [Archives]. Accessed October 14, 2018. https://osaka-rekkyo.org/okinawasen/

Ōga Yukiko, Yamaura Masataka, and Furushiro Hirotaka. 2018. "'Okinawa no Itami, Watashitachimo.' Osupurei Tokyo Haibi, Fuan no Koe" ['We Share Okinawa's Pains.' Ospreys are Deployed to Tokyo, Voices of Concerns Spread]. *Asahi Shimbun*, August 22. Accessed December 22, 2020. https://www.asahi.com/articles/ASL8Q61HZL8QUTIL03G.html?iref=comtop_8_02

Ogden, David Ayres Depue. 1954. "Keystone of the Pacific." *Army Information Digest* 9(1):42–48. Accessed December 11, 2020. https://books.google.com/books?id=6vO9KeM-RrAC&pg=PA42&lpg=PA42&dq=Ogden,+the+keystone+of+the+pacific&source=bl&ots=hvUhIsrw8T&sig=ACfU3U3P9aqXp-cvH_axUuIFY_Gl1nOVfA&hl=en&sa=X&ved=2ahUKEwisjJiJjcroAhUZLs0KHST2D2QQ6AEwA3oECA8QKQ#v=onepage&q=Ogden%2C%20the%20keystone%20of%20the%20pacific&f=false

Oguma Eiji. 1995. *Tan'itsu Minzoku Shinwa no Kigen* [The Origin of the Myth of Homogeneous Japan]. Tokyo: Shinyōsha.

Oguma Eiji. 1998. *Nihonjin no Kyōkai: Okinawa, Ainu, Taiwan, Chōsen—Shokuminchi Shihai kara Fukki Undō made* [The Boundaries of the Japanese: Okinawa, Ainu, Taiwan, Korea—From Colonial Control to the Reversion Movement]. Tokyo: Shinyōsha.

Oguma Eiji. 2002. *"Minshu" to "Aikoku": Sengonihon no Nashonarizumu to Kōkyōsei* ["Democracy" and "Patriotism": Nationalism and the Public Sphere in Postwar Japan]. Tokyo: Shinyōsha.

Oguma Eiji. 2014. "Garapagosuteki Giron kara Dakkyaku o" ["Exiting the Old Ways of Discussing the Matter"]. *Asahi Shimbun*, August 6, 2014. Accessed November 22, 2020. https://digital.asahi.com/articles/ASG814WQLG81PTIL00V.html

Ōhashi Hideshi. 1983. "Gairai Bunka no Shinkō to Dochaku Shāmanizumu no Teikō" [Invasion of Foreign Culture and Resistance of Indigenous Shamanism]. *Shin-Okinawa Bungaku* 57: 2–14

Ōhashi Hideshi. 1998. *Okinawa Shāmanizumu no Shakai-Shnrigakuteki Kenkyū* [A Sociopsychological Studies of Okinawan Shamanism]. Tokyo: Kōbundō.

Okamoto Keitoku. [1970] 1992. "Suiheijiku no Hassō" [The Idea of a Horizontal Axis]. In *Okinawa Bungaku Zenshū Dai 18-kan, Hyōron II* [Complete Works of Okinawan Literature, Volume 18, Criticisms II], edited by Okinawa Bungaku Zenshū Henshū Īnkai, 144–192. Tokyo: Kokusho Kankōkai.

Okamoto Keitoku. 1986. "'Kakuteru Pāthī' no Kōzō" [The Structure of *The Cocktail Party*]. *Okinawa Bunka Kenkyū* 12: 59–91. Accessed December 12, 2020. http://doi.org/10.15002/00015616

Okamoto Keitoku. 1990. "'Okinawa henkan'-go no Bungaku Tenbō" [The Prospect of Okinawan Literature after Reversion]. In *Okinawa Bungaku Zenshū Dai 9-kan, Shōsetsu IV* [Complete Works of Okinawan Literature, Volume 9, Literary Works IV], edited by Okinawa Bungaku Zenshū Henshū Īnkai, 414–422. Tokyo: Kokusho Kankōkai.

Okamoto Michirō. 2020. "Wangan Kiki/Sensō kara 30-nen, Chūtō-Daihenbō o Yomitoku" [30 years after the Gulf Crisis/War: Interpreting Drastic Transformation of the Middle East]. *Yomiuri Shimbun*, October 31. Accessed May 30, 2022. https://www.yomiuri.co.jp/choken/kijironko/ckworld/20210201-OYT8T50099/

Okamoto Tarō. [1961] 2013. *Okinawa Bunkaron: Wasurerareta Nihon* [On Okinawan Culture: Forgotten Japan]. Tokyo: Chūōkōron-sha.

Okamura Reimei. 1988. *Terebi no Shakai-shi* [Social History of Television]. Tokyo: Asahi Shimbunsha.

Okazaki Akiko, and Sakaguchi Kyōhei. 2020. "Shinitaitoki wa Oreni Denwashiro, 2man'nin o Ronpa, Sakaguchi Kyōhei san." *Asahi Shimbun*, November 1. Accessed November 29, 2020. https://digital.asahi.com/articles/ASNBV4T4BNBHULBJ00R.html?iref=comtop_7_07

Oki Hiromi. 2022. "Reisen-shūengo no Gurōbarizēshonka niokeru Roshia no Keizai/Bōeki" [Russia's Economy and Trade under Globalization after the End of the Cold War]. *Kokusai Bōeki to Tōshi* 129: 1–37.

Okinawa "Kichi/Guntai o Yurusanai Kōdōsuru Onnatachi no Kai." 1996. *Buki niyoranai Kokusaikankei: Amerika Pīsu Kyaraban Hōkokushū* [International Relations without Depending on Weapons: Collected Reports of the Peace Caravan to the United States]. Naha, Okinawa: Okinawa "Kichi/Guntai o Yurusanai Kōdōsuru Onnatachi no Kai."

Okinawa "Kichi/Guntai o Yurusanai Kōdōsuru Onnatachi no Kai." 2021. "Webuseminā no Goan'nai: Feminisuto ga Kōsōsuru Shin'no Anzenhoshō to Seimei o Tōtobu Bunka no Sōzō" [Invitation to a Webinar: A True Security

Feminists Envision and the Culture that Respects Life]. Accessed May 14, 2023. https://space-yui.com/?p=179

Okinawa Prefectural Archives. n.d. "Okinawans jining a rally to protest the U.S. land seizures." 1956. Accessed November 15, 2023. http://www2.archives.pref.okinawa.jp/opa/SearchPicsDetail2.aspx?pid=41186&kword=%E8%BB%8D%E7%94%A8%E5%9C%B0

Okinawa Terebi. 2023. "Beign MQ-9 no Kadenahaibi Kanryō" [The US Military Completed Deployment of MQ-9 Drones]. Web, November 8. Accessed November 10, 2023. https://www.youtube.com/watch?v=LlN66HTw9wE

Okinawa Terebi Hōsō Sōgōkikakushitsu. 1989. *Okinawa Terebi 30-nenshi* [A 30-Year History of Okinawa TV Station]. Naha, Okinawa: Okinawa Terebi Hōsō.

Okinawa Times, ed. 1950. *Okinawasenki Tetsu no Bōfū* [The Typhoon of Steel and Bombs]. Naha, Okinawa. Okinawa Times-sha.

Okinawa Times, ed. 1971. *Okinawa no Shōgen: Gekidō no 25nenshi, Jō* [Testimonies of Okinawa: A History of Turbulent 25 Years, Volume 1]. Naha, Okinawa: Okinawa Times-sha.

Okinawa Times, ed. 1973. *Okinawa no Shōgen: Gekidō no 25nenshi, Ge* [Testimonies of Okinawa: A History of Turbulent 25 Years, Volume 2]. Naha, Okinawa: Okinawa Times-sha.

Okinawa Times, ed. 1997. *Okinawa kara: Beigunkichimondai Dokyumento* [From Okinawa: Documenting US Military Base Issues]. Tokyo: Asahi Shimbunsha.

Okinawa Times, ed. 1998. *Shomin ga Tsuzuru Okinawa Sengo Seikatsu-shi* [Postwar Social Life Histories from the Perspective of the Ordinary People]. Naha, Okinawa: Okinawa Times-sha.

Okinawa Times, ed. 2014. *Kichi de Hataraku* [Working in the Bases]. Naha, Okinawa: Okinawa Times-sha.

Okiron. 2017. Accessed December 10, 2020. https://okiron.net/

Ōmine Sawa. 2008. "Uragaesukoto, Omotegaesukoto: 1999nen-ikō no Okinawa no Hyōshō" [Reversing and Re-reversing: Representations of Okinawa after 1999]. In *Okinawa Eiga-ron* [Discussions on Okinawan Films], edited by Yomota Inuhiko and Ōmine Sawa, 139–190. Tokyo: Sakuhinsha.

Onaga Takeshi. 2015a. *Onaga Okinawaken Chiji no Kokuren supīchi* [A Speech at the United Nations by Okinawa Governor Onaga]. *Hi-hyou.com*. Accessed October 31, 2020. https://hi-hyou.com/archives/3337

Onaga Takeshi. 2015b. *Daishikkōsoshō Onagachiji Chinjyutusho Zenbun* [Governor Onaga's Statement at the Naha branch of Fukuoka High Court for a Case regarding a Forceful Execution of the Governmental Order Filed against Him]. Accessed December 9, 2020. http://ryukyushimpo.jp/pages/entry-181721.html

Onaga Takeshi. 2015c. *Tatakau Min'I* [Fighting for Public Will]. Tokyo, Kadokawa Shoten.

O'Nan, Stewart, ed. 1998. *The Vietnam Reader: The Definitive Collection of American Fiction and Nonfiction on the War*. New York: Anchor Books.

Onga, Hisashi. 2017. "Dai4shō Senryō to Jyūmin." In *Okinawakenshi, Kakuronhen Dai-6-kan: Okinawasen* [Okinawa Prefectural History, Itemized Analyses, Vol-

ume 6: The Battle of Okinawa], edited by Okinawaken Kyōikuchō Bunkazaika Shiryōhenshūhan, 407–419. Haebaruchō, Okinawa: Okinawaken Kyōikuiinkai.
Onosaka Gen. 2019. "Gaka no Yonaha Taichi-san ga Henoko no Genjō o Tēma ni Sakuhin o Seisakuchū!" [Artist Yonaha Taichi is Producing Art Works with Current Conditions of Henoko as a Main Theme!]. 2019. *Independent Web Journal*, January 12. Accessed November 3, 2020. https://iwj.co.jp/wj/open/archives/439527
ooba. 2004. "Kyōwa Cocco no Gomizero Daisakusen 2004@News23" [Today is the date for Cocco's Trash Zero Actions to be broadcast at News23]. Accessed July 19, 2010. *bricklife.weblog**, http://www.bricklife.com/weblog/000413.html
OPPMM (Okinawa Prefectural Peace Memorial Museum). n.d.-a. "American battleships gathering around the Island of Okinawa." Itoman, Okinawa: Okinawan Prefectural Peace Memorial Museum.
OPPMM (Okinawa Prefectural Peace Memorial Museum). n.d.-b. "An Okinawan girl carrying a white flag." Itoman, Okinawa: Okinawan Prefectural Peace Memorial Museum.
OPPMM (Okinawa Prefectural Peace Memorial Museum), ed. 2001. *Okinawaken Heiwakinen Shiryōkan Sōgōan'nai* [Okinawa Prefectural Peace Memorial Museum Comprehensive Guide]. Itoman, Okinawa: Okinawan Prefectural Peace Memorial Museum.
Oroku Kunio. 1990. "40-shūnen ni Yosete" [On the occasion of the 40th anniversary]. In *Uema Ikuko to Otohime Gekidan no 40-nen: Hana to Moete* [Uema Ikuko and 40 years of the Otohime Troupe: Glowing like Flowers], edited by Ōshiro Tatsuhiro, Kayō Yasuo, Funakoshi Gishō, Kōki Yoshihide, Hazama Yoshiko, Henna Tsunetsugu, and Fujimura Yoshiki, 7. Okinawa: Otohime Gekidan.
Ōsawa Masachi. 2019. "Heisei no Owari, Reiwa no Kadai" [The end of the Heisei era, Tasks of the Reiwa era]. *Okinawa Times*, June 6, page 13.
Ōshiro Daisuke, and Kara Kentarō. 2021. "Ken, Fushōnin'e Riron Kōchiku" [The Okinawa Prefectural Government Develops an Argument for Rejecting Tokyo's Application for Changes to the Planned Work in Henoko]. *Okinawa Times*, July 7, p. 3.
Ōshiro Masayasu. 1985. *Okinawa karano Kokuhatsu, Kokuseki no Nai Seishun: Konketsuji* [An Indictment from Okinawa, the Springtime of Life without Citizenship, Children of Mixed Races]. Tokyo: Kokusai Jyōhōsha.
Ōshiro Masayasu. 1996. "II. Okinawasen no Ato o Tadoru" [Tracing the Battle of Okinawa]. In *Shinpan Kankō Kōsu denai Okinawa: Senseki, Kichi, Sangyō, Bunka* [New Edition, Okinawa Not for Tourism: War Ruins, Bases, Industry, and Culture], authored by Arasaki Moriteru, Ōshiro Masayasu, Takamine Chōichi, Nagamoto Tomohiro, Yamakado Ken'ichi, Nakasone Masaji, Kinjō Asao, Asato Eiko, Miyagi Harumi, and Kuniyoshi Kazuo, 51–155. Tokyo: Kōbunken.
Ōshiro Tatsuhiro. [1967] 1989. "The Cocktail Party." In *Okinawa: Two Postwar Novellas by Ōshiro Tatsuhiro and Higashi Mineo*, translated with an introduc-

tion and afterword by Steve Rabson, 33–80. Berkeley, CA: Center for Japanese Studies.

Ōshiro Tatsuhiro. [1970] 1992. "Okinawa de Nihonjin ni Narukoto" [Becoming Japanese in Okinawa]. In *Okinawa Bungaku Zenshū Dai 18-kan, Hyōron II* [Complete Works of Okinawan Literature, Volume 18, Criticisms II], edited by Okinawa Bungaku Zenshū Henshū Īnkai, 31–60. Tokyo: Kokusho Kankōkai.

Ōshiro Tatsuhiro. 1990a. "Hōgen Shibai Zanmai" [Giving all my time to Okinawan plays performed in Okinawa dialect]. In *Okinawa Engeki no Miryoku* [Appeals of Okinawan Performing Arts]. Naha, Okinawa: Okinawa Times-sha.

Ōshiro Tatsuhiro. 1990b. "Okinawa Engeki niokeru Otohime Gekidan no Yakuwari (Ichi)" [The Position (role) of the Otohime Troupe in Okinawan Performing Arts]. In *Uema Ikuko to Otohime Gekidan no 40-nen: Hana to Moete* [Uema Ikuko and 40 years of the Otohime Troupe: Glowing like Flowers], edited by Ōshiro Tatsuhiro, Kayō Yasuo, Funakoshi Gishō, Kōki Yoshihide, Hazama Yoshiko, Henna Tsunetsugu, and Fujimura Yoshiki, 18–20. Okinawa: Otohime Gekidan.

Ōshiro Tatsuhiro, Kayō Yasuo, Funakoshi Gishō, Kōki Yoshihide, Hazama Yoshiko, Henna Tsunetsugu, and Fujimura Yoshiki, eds. 1990. *Uema Ikuko to Otohime Gekidan no 40-nen: Hana to Moete* [Uema Ikuko and 40 years of the Otohime Troupe: Glowing like Flowers]. Okinawa: Otohime Gekidan.

Ōshiro Yukie. 2013. "Okinawa/Beikokuminseifuka no Rajio Tōsei to 1950-nendai Gunyōchi Sesshū Tōsō—Henoko Jinushi ni Your Tēpu Shiryō no Kaiseki o Tōshite" [Control of Radios in Okinawa under the USCAR and the Struggles over Military Land Seizures—by way of Analyzing Recorded Tapes by Henoko's Landowners]. *Nihon Bunkaron Nenpō* 16: 99–123.

Ōsugi Takashi. 1999. *Mui no Kreōru* [Inoperative Creole]. Tokyo: Iwanami Shoten.

Ōta Chōfu. [1900] 1995. "Joshi Kyōiku to Okinawaken [Women's Education and Okinawa Prefecture"]. In *Ota Chōfu Senshū, Chūkan* [Selected Works of Ota Chōfu, Volume 2], edited by Hiyane Teruo and Isa Shin'ichi, 57–59. Tokyo: Dai'ichi Shobō.

Ōta Chōfu. [1903] 1995. "Jinruikan o Chūshi Seshimeyo [Make the Human Pavilion Cancelled]." *Ryukyu Shimpo*. April 11. In *Ota Chōfu Senshū, Chūkan* [Selected Works of Ota Chōfu, Volume 2], edited by Hiyane Teruo and Isa Shin'ichi, 213–214. Tokyo: Dai'ichi Shobō.

Ōta Masahide. 1972. *Okinawa no Kokoro* [Okinawa's Heart]. Tokyo: Iwanami Shoten.

Ōta Masahide. 1976. *Okinawa no Minshūishki* [The Popular Consciousness of Okinawa]. Tokyo: Shinsensha.

Ōta Seisaku. 1980. *Rekishi no Shōgen: Bei-Senryōka niokeru Okinawa no Ayumi* [Testimonies of History: Progress of Okinawa under US-Rule]. Tokyo: Rikitomi Shobō.

Ōta Seisaku. 1990. "Oiwai" [Celebration]. In *Uema Ikuko to Otohime Gekidan no 40-nen: Hana to Moete* [Uema Ikuko and 40 years of the Otohime Troupe: Glowing like Flowers], edited by Ōshiro Tatsuhiro, Kayō Yasuo, Funakoshi

Gishō, Kōki Yoshihide, Hazama Yoshiko, Henna Tsunetsugu, and Fujimura Yoshiki, 9. Okinawa: Otohime Gekidan.

Otohime Gekidan, ed. 1999. "Onaha Būte" [Onaha Būten]. In *Sōritsu 50-shūnen Kinen-shi, SHIBAI: Ikuko, Yoshiko Onna Ichidaiki* [To Commemorate the 50th Anniversary of the Establishment of the Otohime Troupes, STAGE PERFORMANCES: Ikuko and Yoshiko—Biographies of Women], edited by Otohime Gekidan, 58. Naha, Okinawa: Omoro Shuppan.

Oyadomari Kōsei. 1990. "Shukuji" [Congratulatory Message]. In *Uema Ikuko to Otohime Gekidan no 40-nen: Hana to Moete* [Uema Ikuko and 40 years of the Otohime Troupe: Glowing like Flowers], edited by Ōshiro Tatsuhiro, Kayō Yasuo, Funakoshi Gishō, Kōki Yoshihide, Hazama Yoshiko, Henna Tsunetsugu, and Fujimura Yoshiki, 5. Okinawa: Otohime Gekidan.

Oyakawa Yūko. 2019. "Mainorithi Josei, Fukugō Sabetsu to Okinawa—Mukokusekiji Mondai kara" [Minority Women, Layered Discriminations and Okinawa—in reference to Issues of Children without Citizenship]. *Peace Studies Association of Japan*, May 18. Accessed March 30, 2024. https://heiwagakkai.jimdo.com/20 19/05/18/%E3%83%9E%E3%82%A4%E3%83%8E%E3%83%AA%E3%83%86 %E3%82%A3%E5%A5%B3%E6%80%A7-%E8%A4%87%E5%90%88%E5%B7 %AE%E5%88%A5%E3%81%A8%E6%B2%96%E7%B8%84-%E7%84%A1%E5 %9B%BD%E7%B1%8D%E5%85%90%E5%95%8F%E9%A1%8C%E3%81%8B %E3%82%89/

Padmanabhan, Aadhithi, and Michael Shih. 2012. "Collective Self-Defense: A Report of the Yale Law School Center for Global Legal Challenges." Accessed December 20, 2020. http://docplayer.net/155032495-Aadhithi-padmanabhan-michael-shih-1-december-10-2012.html

Peace Studies Association of Japan. 2015. "Okinawa Henoko Beigun Kichi Kensetsu no Sokuji Chūshi o Motomeru Seimei" [A Statement Demanding Immediate Cancellation of the Construction of a US Military Base in Henoko, Okinawa]. Accessed March 2024. https://heiwagakkai.jimdo.com/%E8%AB%96%E8%AA %AC-%E5%A3%B0%E6%98%8E/%E6%B2%96%E7%B8%84%E8%BE%BA %E9%87%8E%E5%8F%A4%E5%A3%B0%E6%98%8E/

Pempel, T. J. 1997. "Transpacific Torii: Japan and the Emerging Asian Regionalism." In *Network Power: Japan and Asia*, edited by Peter J. Katzenstein and Takashi Shiraishi, 47–82. Ithaca, NY: Cornell University Press.

Peterson, M. J. 2006. *The UN General Assembly*. London: Routledge.

PMG5. 2016. "Uchinā o Toru: Shashinka Ishgikawa Mao" ["Recording Okinawa: Photographer Ishikawa Mao"]. Daily Motion. Video, 29:00. Accessed December 16, 2020. https://www.dailymotion.com/video/x5rimc5 Originally broadcast through *Hātonetto TV*, NHK, on June 20, 2016.

Pitts, Forrest Ralph, William P. Lebra, and Wayne P. Suttles. 1955. *Post-war Okinawa*. Washington, DC: Pacific Science Board, National Research Council.

postman. 2019. "Customer Reviews: *Kumui-ita*" [Customer Reviews: *Luluby*]. Posted on October. Accessed May 29, 2022. https://www.amazon.co.jp/-/en/Co ccco/product-reviews/B00005GXLS/ref=cm_cr_getr_d_paging_btm_prev_1?ie =UTF8&reviewerType=all_reviews&pageNumber=1

Purves, John M. 1995–2019. "The Melvin Price Report." In *The Contemporary Okinawa Website*. Accessed December 12, 2020. https://ryukyu-okinawa.net/pages/archive/price.html

Rabson, Steve. 1989. "Afterword." In *Okinawa: Two Postwar Novellas by Ōshiro Tatsuhiro and Higashi Mineo*, translated with an introduction and afterword by Steve Rabson, 121–136. Berkeley, CA: Center for Japanese Studies.

Rabson, Steve. 1993. "'Kakuteru Pāthī' no Uketorikata" [Ways to read *The Cocktail Party*]. In *Shinpojiumu Okinawa Senryō: Mirai e Mukete* [Symposium on Okinawa Occupation: Toward the Future], edited by Miyagi Etsujirō, 32–39. Naha, Okinawa: Hirugisha.

Rabson, Steve. 2008. "Okinawan Perspectives on Japan's Imperial Institution." *The Asia-Pacific Journal: Japan Focus* 6(2): 1–23. Accessed December 29, 2020. https://apjjf.org/-Steve-Rabson/2667/article.html

Rabson, Steve. 2012. *The Okinawan Diaspora in Japan: Crossing the Borders Within*. Honolulu, HI: University of Hawai'i Press.

Rabson, Steve. 2022. *Training and Deployment of America's Nuclear Cold Warriors in Asia: Keepers of Armageddon*. Newcastle upon Tyne: Cambridge Scholars Publishing.

Reed, Robert F. 1983. *The US-Japan Alliance: Sharing the Burden of Defense*. Washington, DC: National Defense University Press. Accessed March 31, 2024. https://apps.dtic.mil/sti/citations/ADA135527

Rimpeace. n.d. *Sasebo Kichi*. Accessed November 3, 2020. http://www.rimpeace.or.jp/jrp/sasebo/saseboindex/sind.html

Roberson, James E. 2009. "Memory and Music in Okinawa: The Cultural Politics of War and Peace." *positions* 17(3): 683–711.

Rousseau, Jean-Jacques. [1762] 2014. *The Social Contract & Discourses*. Translated by George Douglas Howard Cole. The Project Gutenberg E-book. Accessed December 27, 2020. http://www.gutenberg.org/files/46333/46333-h/46333-h.htm

Rumsfeld, Donald. 2002. "Transforming the Military." *Foreign Affairs* 81(3): 20–32.

Ruoff, Kenneth. 2010. *Imperial Japan at Its Zenith: The Wartime Celebration of the Empire's 2,600th Anniversary*. Ithaca, NY: Cornell University Press.

Russell, Ruth B. 1958. *A History of the United Nations Charter; The Role of the United States, 1940–1945*. Washington, DC: Brookings Institution.

Ryujin Mabyer Official Website. n.d. "Intorodakushon" [Introduction]. Accessed September 8, 2023. http://mabuyer.com/introduction/

Ryukyu Asahi Hōsō. 2006. "QAB seisaku 'Umi ni Suwaru' Gyarakushī-shō Senshō o Jyushō" [Sitting In on the Seaproduced by QAB receives a Galaxy Award]. *QAB News Headlines*, June 1. Accessed May 6, 2022. https://www.qab.co.jp/news/200606017130.html

Ryukyu Asahi Hōsō. 2014a. *Q+Ripōto: Arekara 25nen: Onnasonmin no Tatakai* [Q+ Report: 25 Years after the Struggle of Onna Villagers]. Broadcast March 26. Accessed October 28, 2020. http://www.qab.co.jp/news/2014032651522.html

Ryukyu Asahi Hōsō. 2014b. "Kenshō Ugokanu Kichi 139kai: Okizari ni Sareru Jimoto no Ishi" [Examining the Base that Does not Move Volume 139: Will of the Local Community that is Forgotten]. Broadcast September 3, 2014. Accessed

December 22, 2015. https://www.youtube.com/watch?v=Xx6aIFlV2_g. For a transcript of the program, see https://www.qab.co.jp/news/2014090357964.html (accessed December 2020).
Ryukyu Asahi Hōsō. 2017. "Yara Chiji no Genten to Fukke eno Omoi" [The Starting Point of Governor Yara and his Desire for Reversion]. Broadcast May 15, 2017. Accessed September 8, 2023. https://www.qab.co.jp/news/2017051590499.html
Ryukyu Ginkō Chōsabu, ed. 1984. *Sengo Okinawa Keizaishi* [Postwar Okinawan Economic History]. Naha, Okinawa, Ryukyu Ginkō Chōsabu.
Ryukyu Hōsō Kikakubu. 1965. "Ryukyu Hōsō 10-nenshi" [A 10-Year History of Ryukyu Broadcasting]. Naha, Okinawa: Ryukyu Hōsō
Ryukyu Shimpo, ed. 1980. *Tōtōme-kō: Onna ga Tuide Naze Warui!?* [Thinking *Tōtōme*: What's Wrong about Women Inheriting *Tōtōme*!?]. Naha, Okinawa: Ryukyu Shimpo-sha.
Ryukyu Shimpo, ed. 1995. *Igi-Mōshitate Kichi Okinawa* [Objections to the Bases from Okinawa]. Naha, Okinawa: Ryukyu Shimpo-sha.
Ryukyu Shimpo. 2015. "Kenkei Kidōtai, Kōgi no shimin Gobōnukim Henoko Gētomae" [Prefectural Riot Squad Forcibly Removing Demonstrators, in front of the Gate of Camp Schwab]. November 2. Accessed June 30, 2022. https://ryukyushimpo.jp/news/entry-164734.html#prettyPhoto[164734]/0/
Ryukyu Shimpo. 2017. "Osupurei N1, H-chiku no Heripaddo de Richakuritsu o Hajimete Kaishi" [Ospreys Began Taking off and Landing on a Helipad in H-Area]. YouTube. Video: 1:41. Accessed December 23, 2020. https://www.youtube.com/watch?v=yJNlFcZDr00
Sahashi Ryo. 2010. "Beichūwakai Purosesu no Kaishi to Taiwan Mondai: Amerika niyoru Shinraisei to Kinkō no Tsuikyū" [Initiation of the US-China Rapprochement Process and the Taiwan problem: Pursuit of Trust and Balance of Stability by the United States]. *Nihon Taiwangaku Kaihō* 12: 173–198. http://www.jats.gr.jp/journal/journal_012.html
Said, Edward, W. 1978. *Orientalism*. New York: Vintage Books.
Sakaguchi Kiyoshi. 1998. "Sengonihon no Anzenhoshōkōsō to Kokuren, 1945–1952" [Conceptions of Postwar Japanese Security Policy and the United Nations, 1945–1952]. *Kokusai Kōkyōseisaku Kenkyū* 3(1), 63–92. Accessed December 19, 2020. http://hdl.handle.net/11094/8789
Sakaguchi Kiyoshi. 1999. "Wangansensōgo no Nihon no Anzenhoshōronngi nikannsuru Ichikōsatsu: Ozawa Ichirō Jiyūtōtōshu no Anzenhoshōron wo Megutte" [Japanese Security Debate after the Gulf Crisis: A study of Security Policy of Ichiro Ozawa]. *Kokusai Kōkyōseisaku Kenkyū* 4(1), 203–219. Accessed October 1, 2023. https://hdl.handle.net/11094/9248
Sakai, Naoki, and Hyon Joo Yoo. 2012. "Preface" and "Introduction: The Trans-Pacific Imagination—Rethinking Boundary, Culture and Society." In *The Trans-Pacific Imagination: Rethinking Boundary, Culture and Society*, edited by Naoki Sakai and Hyon Joo Yoo, v–xi and 1–44. Singapore: World Scientific Publishing.
Sakiyama Tami. [1989] 1994. "*Suijō Ōkan*" [Coming and Going on the Water]. In *Furusato Bugakukan, Dai 54-kan: Okinawa* [The Pavilion of Local Literature, Volume 54: Okinawa], edited by Okamoto Keitoku, 42–62. Tokyo: Gyōsei.

Sakurai Izumi. n.d. "Kankoku, Gun mo Kigyō mo Betonamu Sansen" [Both the Military and the Industry in South Korea Participated in the War]. *Asahi Shimbun* "Rekishi wa Ikiteiru, Dai 8-shō, Chōsen Sensō to Betonamu Sensō," n.d. Accessed December 20, 2020. http://www.asahi.com/international/history/chapter08/02.html

Sakurai Susumu. 2001. '*Teikoku eno Yokubō: "Kokutai no Hongi," "Kōkokushikan," "Daitōa Kyōeiken."'* [Desire for the Empire: 'The Underlying Principle of National Polity,' 'the Emperor-Centered Historical View,' 'Greater East Asia Co-Prosperity Sphere.'] *Gendai Shisō* 29(16): 114–124.

Sakurazawa Makoto. 2012. *Okinawa no Fukki Undō to Hokaku Tairitsu: Okinawa Chiiki Shakai no Hen'yō* [Okinawa's Reversion Movement and Confrontation of Conservatives and Progressives: Transformation of Okinawa Regional Society]. Tokyo: Yūshisha.

Sakurazawa Makoto. 2015. *Okinawa Gendaishi: Beikoku Tōchi, Hondo Fukki kara "Ōru Okinawa" made* [A Modern History of Okinawa: From US Rule and Reversion to "All-Okinawa"]. Tokyo: Chūō Kōron Shinsha.

Santoli, Al. 2006. *Everything We Had: An Oral History of the Vietnam War.* New York: Ballantine Books.

Saruta Sayo. 2019. "Dai 4-ji Āmitēji/Nai Hōkoku Bunseki: Saranaru Nichibei Ittaika eno Yōkyū" [An Analysis of the Fourth Armitage and Nye Report, Which Demands Further Unification between the US and Japan]. *New Diplomacy Initiative*, May 14. Accessed December 22, 2020. https://www.nd-initiative.org/research/6411/

Sasagawa Shōhei, Tajima Nobuhiko, and Watanabe Takashi. 2023. "Henoko Isetsu, Daishikkō Chiratsukaseru Seiken" [The Futenma Replacement Facility, Tokyo Insinuates Execution by Proxy]. *Asahi Shimbun*, September 4. Accessed September 10, 2023. https://digital.asahi.com/articles/ASR946F8HR91UTIL026.html?iref=comtop_7_01

Satō Taketsugu. 2020. "Shūsen, Reisen, Kawaru Sekai: Hitosujinawadewanai Nichibeianpo no Kongo" [End of the war, the Cold War, and the changing word: The future of the US-Japan alliance that is difficult to predict]. *Asahi Shimbun*, July 20. Accessed July 30, 2020. https://digital.asahi.com/articles/ASN7V64GHN7DULZU002.html?iref=pc_ss_date_article

Satomi Minoru. 2022. "Kuaddo te Ittai Nani" [What is the QUAD?]. *Asahi Shimbun*, May 22. Accessed November 4, 2023. https://digital.asahi.com/articles/ASQ5P6T97Q5NUTFK00P.html

Sawada Kayo. 2014. *Sengo Okinawa no Seishoku o Meguru Poritikusu: Beigun Tōchika no Shusseiryoku Tenkan to Onnatachi no Kōshō* [The Politics of Reproduction in Postwar Okinawa: Transformation of Fertility under US Rule and Women's Negotiation]. Tokyo: Ōtsuki Shoten.

Schaller, Michael. 1986. "MacArthur's Japan: The View from Washington." *Diplomatic History* 10(1): 1–23.

Schaller, Michael. 1987. *The American Occupation of Japan The Origins of the Cold War in Asia.* New York: Oxford University Press.

Schaller, Michael. 1989. *Douglas MacArthur: The Far Eastern General*. New York: Oxford University Press.
Schaller, Michael. 1997. *Altered States: The United States and Japan since the Occupation*. New York: Oxford University Press.
Schmitt, Carl. [1932] 1976. *The Concept of the Political*. Translated by George Schwab. New Brunswick, NJ: Rutgers University Press.
Scobell, Andrew. 2010. "China's Rise: How Peaceful?" In *The Routledge Handbook of Asian Security Studies (Routledge Handbooks) 1st Edition*, 11–22.
Scobell, Andrew. 2017. "Wither China's 21st Century Trajectory?" In *The Routledge Handbook of Asian Security Studies (Routledge Handbooks) 2nd Edition*, 11–20.
Segal, Stephanie, Matthew Reynolds, and Brooke Roberts. 2021. *Degrees of Separation: A Targeted Approach to U.S.-China Decoupling—Final Report*. Washington, DC: Center for Strategic and International Studies. Accessed November 6, 2021. https://csis-website-prod.s3.amazonaws.com/s3fs-public/publication/21 1021_Segal_DegreesSeparation_Final.pdf?ivhSdtS5EaN75MV.21FWz4KnCO ypU1Al
Sered Susan. 1995. "Jyūzokusha ga Rīdosuru Toki: Okinawa to Isuraeru ni Okeru Jyosei no Shyūkyōteki Rīdāshhipu no Paradokkusu" [When the Subjugated Leads: A Paradox of Women's Religious Leadership in Okinawa and Israel], translated by Akamine Masanobu. *Okinawa Minzoku Kenkyū* 15: 1–10.
Sered, Susan. 1999. *Women of the Sacred Groves: Divine Priestesses of Okinawa*. Oxford: Oxford University Press.
Shao Binhong. 2015.*China under Xi Jinping: Its Economic Challenges and Foreign Policy Initiatives*. Boston: BRILL.
Shi Yinhong. 2015. "Japan's Political Right-deviation, and the Issue of Way of Thinking and Strategic Approach to Sino-Japanese Relations" In *China under Xi Jinping: Its Economic Challenges and Foreign Policy Initiatives*, Shao Binhong, 255–271. Boston: Brill.
Shibasoromon. 2019. "Sugawara Bunta Saigo no Enzetsu, Okinawaken Chiji Senkyo 2014-nen 11gatsu Tuitachi" [The Last Speech of Sugawara Bunta, Okinawa Gubernatorial Election, November 1, 2014]. YouTube. Video, 11:12. Published by Shiba Soromon. Accessed November 4, 2020. https://www.youtube.com/watch?v=5WYE18mE9Jk
Shibata Shōhei, dir. 2007. *Himeyuri* [Himeyuri]. Tokyo: ASIA Documentary Productions.
Shibata Shōhei. 2009. "Director's notes." Accessed December 27, 2020. http://www.himeyuri.info/himeyuri_english_top.html
Shibayama, Futoshi. 2010. *Nihon Saigunbi eno Michi, 1945–1954-nen* [The Road to Re-Arming Japan]. Kyōto: Mineruva Shobō.
Shigemori Akira. 2000. "*Okinawa Keizai no Jiritsuteki Hatten to Ken Zaisei*" [Autonomous Development of the Okinawan Economy and Prefectural Finance]. In *Okinawa: 21-seiki eno Chōsen* [Okinawa: Challenges to the Twenty-First Century, edited by Miyamoto Ken'ichi and Sasaki Masayuki,] 79–104. Tokyo: Iwanami Shoten.

Shih, Shu-mei, and Françoise Lionnet. 2011. "Introduction: The Creolization of Theory." In *The Creolization of Theory*, edited by Françoise Lionnet and Shu-mei Shih, 1–33. Durham, NC: Duke University Press.

Shimabuku, Annmaria M. 2019. *Alegal: Biopolitics and the Unintelligibility of Okinawan Life*. New York: Fordham University Press.

Shimabukuro Maria (also known as Annmaria M. Shimabuku). 2002. "Okinawa no 'Konketsuji to sono Haha o Kataru Seijisei" [The Politics of Discussing Mixed-Race Children and their Mothers]. In *Ajia Shinseiki Dai 3-kan: Aidenthithi* [Asia in the New Century Volume 3: Identity], edited by Aoki Tamotsu and others, 85–100. Tokyo: Iwanami Shoten.

Shimada Hisanori. 2001. "*Okinawa Shinkōseisaku no Koremade to Korekara*" [The Past and Future of Okinawa Development Policies]. *Kaigin Ekomaga* 6–9. Accessed December 21, 2020. http://www.kaiho-ri.jp/wp-content/uploads/2011/05/kri-outlook003.pdf

Shimanaka Kensei. 1982. "Okinawa ni Okeru Saishi Shōkei no Mondaiten ni Tsuite" [On the Problems of the Inheritance of Religious Services]. *Okinawa Hōgaku* 4: 25–49. Accessed December 16, 2020. http://hdl.handle.net/20.500.12001/6489

Shimizu, Sayuri. 2001. *Creating People of Plenty: The United States and Japan's Economic Alternatives, 1950–1960*. Kent, Ohio: Kent State University Press.

Shimoji, Lawrence Yoshitaka. 2018. *'Konketsu' to 'Nihonjin':Hāfu, Daburu, Mikkusu no Shakaishi* ['Mixed-Race' and the 'Japanese': Social History of Half-breeds, Double-breeds, and Mixed-breeds]. Tokyo: Seidosha.

Shimota Seiji. [1952] 2005. "Okinawa" [Okinawa]. In *Sengo Shoki Okinawa Kaihō Undō Shiryōshū Dai 3-kan: Okinawa Higōhō Kyōsantō to Amami/Nihon* [Materials regarding Postwar Okinawa's Early Liberation Movements, Vol. 3: Okinawa's Underground Communist Party and Amami/Japan], edited by Mori Yoshio and Kokuba Kōtarō, pp. 80–85.

Shimota Seiji. [1954] 2005. "Kotō no Hitobito" [People on an Isolated Island]. In *Sengo Shoki Okinawa Kaihō Undō Shiryōshū Dai 3-kan: Okinawa Higōhō Kyōsantō to Amami/Nihon* [Materials regarding Postwar Okinawa's Early Liberation Movements, Vol. 3: Okinawa's Underground Communist Party and Amami/Japan], edited by Mori Yoshio and Kokuba Kōtarō, pp. 94–101.

Shindō Ei'ichi. 1979a. "Bunkatusareta Ryōdo: Okinawa, Chishima, soshite Anpo" [Divided Territories: Okinawa, Krill Islands, and the Security Treaty]. *Sekai* (April), 31–51.

Shindō Ei'ichi. 1979b. "Ten'nō-messēji Sairon: Sengo Gaikō Shiryō no Yomikata [Rediscussing the Emperor's message: How to read postwar diplomatic archives]. *Sekai* (October), 104–113.

Shinjō Ikuo. 2006. "Okinawa Senryō to Gei Shintai-Seiji: Shokuminchi no Dansei Sekushuaritī" [Occupation of Okinawa and the Body Politics of Gay Men: Masculine Sexality in the Colony]. In *Okinawa no Senryō to Nihon no Fukkō: Shokuminchi-shugi wa ikani Keizokushitaka* [Occupation of Okinawa and Recovery of Japan: How Colnialism has Continued], edited by Nakano Toshio, Namihira Tsuneo, Yakabi Osamu, Lee Hyoduk, 85–107. Tokyo: Seikyūsha.

Shin-Okinawa Bungaku, ed. 1986. *Rinji Zōkango: Okinawa—A Hinomaru/Kimigayo* [Special Issue: Okinawa—The Japanese Flag and the National Anthem]. Okinawa: Okinawa Times-sha.

Shiraishi Takashi. 1997. "Japan and Southeast Asia." In Network Power: Japan and Asia, edited by Peter J. Katzenstein and Takashi Shiraishi, 169–194. Ithaca, NY: Cornell University Press.

Shiraishi Yayoi. [1986] 1990. "Wakanatsu no Raihōsha" [A Visitor in the Early Summer]. In *Okinawa Bungaku Zenshū Dai 9-kan, Shōsetsu IV* [Complete Works of Okinawan Literature, Volume 9, Literary Works IV], edited by Okinawa Bungaku Zenshū Henshū Īnkai, 323–351. Tokyo: Kokusho Kankōkai.

Shiraishi Yayoi. [1987] 1990. "Toshibī" [Celebration of the Seventy-Third Birthday]. In *Okinawa Bungaku Zenshū Dai 9-kan, Shōsetsu IV* [Complete Works of Okinawan Literature, Volume 9, Literary Works IV], edited by Okinawa Bungaku Zenshū Henshū Īnkai, 352–374. Tokyo: Kokusho Kankōkai.

Silveria, Paige. 2017. "mao ishikawa's stunning photographs of her friends in 70s Okinawa" *i-D*, March 27. Accessed December 16, 2020. https://i-d.vice.com/en_us/article/papddk/mao-ishikawas-stunning-photographs-of-her-friends-in-70s-okinawa

Small, Christopher. 1998. *Musicking: The Meanings of Performing and Listening*, Hanover, NH: Wesleyan University Press.

Sneider, Vern. 1951. *The Teahouse of the August Moon*. New York: G. P. Putnam's Sons.

Sonoda Kōji, Suzuki Takuya, Satō Taketsugu, Takeshita Yuka, and Doi Takaki. 2020. *Nichibei Anpo 60-nen*, "Dai 8-kai 'Kimitachi wa Yūfukudarō' Beigun Chūryūhi, Futanzō e Takamaru Atsuryoku [60 years after the Implementation of the Revised US-Japan Security Treaty, Volume 8: 'You Are Rich, Aren't You?' Growing Pressure to Shoulder More Host Nation Support]." *Asahi Shimbun*, March 2. Accessed June 8, 2020. https://digital.asahi.com/articles/ASN162SY7N16ULZU002.html?iref=pc_rensai_article_short_1053_article_1

Spivak, Gayatri Chakravorty. 2003. *Death of a Discipline*. New York: Columbia University Press.

Standing, Guy. 2011. *The Precariat: The New Dangerous Class*. New York: Bloomsbury Academic.

sunao999. 2012a. "Henoko, Sit-in on the Sea P1." YouTube. Video, 12:09. Accessed October 28, 2020. https://www.youtube.com/watch?v=fy296RaZEa0

sunao999. 2012b. "Henoko, Sit-in on the Sea P2." YouTube. Video, 12:03. Accessed October 28, 2020. https://www.youtube.com/watch?v=WMmbFViet0A

sunao999. 2012c. "Henoko, Sit-in on the Sea P3." YouTube. Video, 12:44. Accessed October 28, 2020. https://www.youtube.com/watch?v=g_y5qLiCSxI

sunao999. 2012d. "Henoko, Sit-in on the Sea P4." YouTube. Video, 10:19. Accessed October 28, 2020. https://www.youtube.com/watch?v=2nxwweu2RBI

Sunar, Lütfi. 2017. "The Long History of Islam as a Collective 'Other' of the West and the Rise of Islamophobia in the U.S. after Trump." *Insight Turkey* 19(3): 35–51. https://doi.org/10.25253/99.2017193.03. Accessed October 24, 2023. https://

www.insightturkey.com/commentaries/the-long-history-of-islam-as-a-collecti
ve-other-of-the-west-and-the-rise-of-islamophobia-in-the-us-after-trump

Suzuki Takahiro. 2011. "Kenpō Dai 9-jō to Shūdanteki Jieiken—Kokkai Tōben kara Shūdanteki Jieiken Kaishaku no Hensen o Miru" [Article 9 of the Constitution and Collective Self-Defense: Examining the Changes of the Interpretation of Collective Self-Defense through Answers at the Diet]. *Referensu Heisei 23nen 11gatsu gō*: 2–47. Accessed December 21, 2020. https://dl.ndl.go.jp/view/down load/digidepo_3194045_po_073002.pdf?contentNo=1

Suzuki Takuya, Katōno Akira, Okumura Satoshi, and Yoshida Takushi. 2015. "'Jijik-okukoku': Kyokusetu 19nen, Chakkō Oshikiru 2013nen, Obama-shi ni Henoko Isetsu Semarareta Shushō" [From Moment to Moment: 19 Years of Twists and Turns, Commencement of Work Pushed Through, the Prime Minister Pressed by Mr. Obama to Transfer Futenma to Henoko in 2013]. *Asahi Shimbun*, October 30. Accessed October 29, 2020. https://digital.asahi.com/articles/DA3S120 42003.html

Swartz, Peter M., and Karin Duggan. 2020. "US Navy Capstone Strategies and Concepts (1991–2000): Strategy, Policy, Concept, and Vision Documents." *Naval History and Heritage Command*, June 22. Accessed December 21, 2020. https:// www.history.navy.mil/research/library/online-reading-room/title-list-alphabe tically/u/us-navy-capstone-strategies-concepts-1991-2000.html

Swenson-Wright, John. 2005. *Unequal Allies?: United States Security and Alliance Policy toward Japan, 1945–1960*. Stanford, CA: Stanford University Press.

Taba Mitsuko. [1985] 1990. "Kaminshitsu" [A Nap Room]. In *Okinawa Bungaku Zenshū Dai 9-kan, Shōsetsu IV* [Complete Works of Okinawan Literature, Volume 9, Literary Works IV], edited by Okinawa Bungaku Zenshū Henshū Īnkai, 208–245. Tokyo: Kokusho Kankōkai.

Tada Osamu. 2004. *Okinawa Imēji no Tanjō: Aoi Umi no Karuchuraru Sutadīzu* [The Birth of the Okinawa Image: Cultural Studies of the Blue Ocean]. Tokyo: Tokyo Keizai Shinpōsha.

Tai, Zixue. 2015. 'Networked Resistance: Digital Populism, Online Activism, and Mass Dissent in China.' *Popular Communication* 13 (2): 120–31. https://doi.org /10.1080/15405702.2015.1021469

Taira Chōkei. 2014. "Keizaiteki Gunjiteki Kankyō wa kawatta. Dōdō to Kichi Tekkyo o Ieru Jidai ga Kita" [Economic and Military Environments Have Changed: The Time Has Come When We Can Advocate the Removal of the Bases Openly]. *Rentai-Kyōdō 21*, July 14. Accessed November 3, 2020. http://rentai21 .com/?p=1749

Taira Natsume. n.d. *Firia no Nikki* [A Diary of Philia]. Accessed December 10, 2020. http://blog.livedoor.jp/natsumetaira/

Taira Takaharu. 2023. "Rikuji Osupurei Hatsuhirai" [An Osprey of the Ground Self-Defense Force Arrived for the First Time]. *Okinawa. Times*, October 20, page 1.

Tajima Nobuhiko, Sasagawa Shōhei, Tanasaki Satsuki, and Yajima Daisuke. 2023. "Daishikkō made 'Dondon Susumeru': Okinawa no Handan wa Sōteizumi, Tsukisusumu Seiken" ['Steadily Proceeding' to Execution by Proxy: Tokyo Takes Okinawa's Judgment into Consideration and Heads Straight Down the

Road to Construction of the FRF]. *Asahi Shimbun*, October 5. Accessed October 8, 2023. https://digital.asahi.com/articles/ASRB56RWLRB3UTIL03N.html?iref=comtop_7_04

Takahara Motoaki. 2008. "*Nikkan no Nashonarizumu to Radhikarizumu no Kōsaku: Kankoku no Shinpo Ideorogī to Nihon no Ajia-kan o Jirei toshite*" [The Interplay between Nationalism and Radicalism of Japan and South Korea: Case Studies of South Korea's Progressive Ideology and Japan's View of Asia]. *Shisōchizu* 1: 87–118. Tokyo: NHK Shuppan.

Takahashi Mirai. 2020. "Korona-shitsugyō suru Hiseiki no Josei 'Onaji Ningentomo Omowarenai.' [Non-fulltime Female Workers, Laid Off due COVID Pandemic; 'We are not Considered as the Same Human Beings]." *Asahi Shimbun*, July 20. Accessed October 28, 2021. https://digital.asahi.com/articles/ASN7C77KSN7BULFA044.html?iref=pc_ss_date_article

Takahashi, Shinnosuke. 2017. "Beyond Minority History: Okinawa Korea People's Solidarity and Internationalization of the Okinawa Struggle." In *Rethinking Postwar Okinawa: Beyond American Occupation*, edited by Pedro Iacobelli and Hiroko Matsuda, 81–102. Lanham, Maryland: Lexington Books. Lexington Books.

Takamine Chōichi. 1984. *Shirarezaru Okinawa no Beihei* [Unknown US Servicemen in Okinawa]. Tokyo: Kōbunken.

Takano Hajime. 2012. *Okinawani Kaiheitaiwa Iranai!* [The Marine Corps Are Not Needed in Okinawa!]. Tokyo: Ningenshuppan.

Takano Yūsuke. 2022. "Ie ni Shin'nyūshita Roshiahei, 'Ore no Aite o'" [A Russian Soldier Broke into the House, Saying "Have Sex with me"]. *Asahi Shimbun*, June 23. Accessed June 29, 2022. https://digital.asahi.com/articles/ASQ6R31T1Q6GUHBI03D.html?iref=pc_ss_date_article

Takara Kurayoshi. 1983. "Yuta Kinatsu no Zentei" [The Premise of Prohibiting Yuta]. *Shin-Okinawa Bungaku* 57: 15–25.

Takara Kurayoshi. 1987. *Ryūkyū Ōkoku no Kōzō* [Structure of the Ryukyu Kingdom]. Tokyo:Yoshikawa Kōbunkan.

Takara Kurayoshi 2017. *Okinawa Mondai: Riarizumu no Shitenkara* [Okinawa Problems: From the Perspective of Realism]. Tokyo: Chūōkōron-sha.

Takara Kurayoshi. 2019. My own interview in Naha, Okinawa on June 8.

Takara Kurayoshi, Ōshiro Tsuneyoshi, and Maeshiro Marisada. 2000. "Okinawa Inishiatibu: Ajia/Taiheiyou de Hatasu Yakuwari [Okinawa Initiative: The Role Okinawa Should Play in the Asia-Pacific Region]." *Okinawa Times*, May 3, 4, 5, 7, 8, 10, and 11, 2000. The article can be accessed also at: *Fūyū: Okinawa no Jiritsu-Kaihō ni Rentaisuru Fūyū Saito!* https://www7b.biglobe.ne.jp/~whoyou/initia-honbun.htm

Takashima Ken, Shiraishi Msayuki, Kuratomi Ryūta, and Fujiwara Shin'ichi. 2022. "Renya Hibiku Hōgekion, Saishinheiki mo, Zenoku ni Hirogaru Beigunkunren, Kasumu Futankeigen" [Sound of Shooting Heard Every Night, Updated Weapons Used as well; US Military Trainings Spread across the Nation, Reduction of Burden almost Forgotten]. *Asahi Shimbun*, April 25. Accessed May 12,

2022. https://digital.asahi.com/articles/ASQ4R5QYFQ4NTIPE045.html?iref=comtop_7_01

Takeda Hajime. 2018. "Kankoku Daitōryō ga Ikan no I" [The Korean President Expressed Regret]. *Asahi Shimbun*, March 24. Accessed December 20, 2020. https://digital.asahi.com/articles/ASL3S4CMNL3SUHBI00Q.html?iref=pc_rellink_01

Takenaka, Akiko. 2015. *Yasukuni Shrine: History, Memory, and Japan's Unending Postwar*. Honolulu: University of Hawai'i Press.

Takeuchi Akinori. 2020. "Uchināguchi to Yamatoguchi, Jimoto no Takara Arinkurin (12)" [The Okinawan Language and the Japanese Language: Local Treasures (12)]. Accessed September 5, 2023. https://fun.okinawatimes.co.jp/columns/life/detail/9552

Takeuchi Masahiro. 2018. *Tabisuru Ten'nō: Heisei 30nenkan no Tabi no Kiroku to Hiwa* [The Travelling Emperor: Records of Travels and Unknown Episodes during 30 years of the Heisei Era]. Tokyo: Shōgakukan.

Takeuchi Yoshimi. [1961] 1966. "Hōhō toshiteno Ajia" [Asia as Method]. In *Nihon to Ajia: Takeuchi Yoshimi Hyōron-shū Dai 3kan* [Japan and Asia: Collected Works of Essays by Takeuchi Yoshimi, volume 3], 396–420. Tokyo: Chikuma Shobō.

Takeyama Akiko. [1994] 2018. *Sensō to Hōsō*. Tokyo: Yoshikawa Kōbunkan.

Takeyama Akiko, and Mayama Hitoshi. 2020. "Sensō to Medhia" [War and the Media]. *Asahi Shimbun*, November 28. Accessed December 26, 2020. https://digital.asahi.com/articles/DA3S14711628.html?iref=comtop_Opinion_03

Tamaki Hinako. 2021. "'Shigotonaiyo' Rishokuhyō ni Sainsemarare ['There are No Jobs for You': Forced to Sign the Documentation of Unemployment]." *Okinawa Times*, February 16. Accessed October 28, 2021. https://www.okinawatimes.co.jp/articles/-/708079

Tamanoi, Mariko Asano. 2009. *Memory Maps: The State and Manchuria in Postwar Japan*. Honolulu: University of Hawai'i Press.

Tan, Rubin. 2023. "Why Guam? Reactivation of Marine Corps Base Camp Blaz." *Defense Visual Information Distribution Service*, January 25. Accessed November 15, 2023. https://www.dvidshub.net/news/437182/why-guam-reactivation-marine-corps-base-camp-blaz#:~:text=The%20Marine%20Corps%20is%20reactivating,of%20the%20Northern%20Mariana%20Islands

Tanahashi Satsuki, Watanabe Takashi, Tajima Nobuhiko, Ono Tarō, and Itō Kazuyuki. 2023. "Henoko Isetsu, Ukabu Gōrisei no Toboshisa" [Relocation to Henoko throws the lack of rationality into relief]. *Asahi Shimbun*, December 18. Accessed December 20, 2023. https://digital.asahi.com/articles/ASRDK73VDRD9TPOB001.html?iref=pc_politics_top#expertsComments

Tanaka Kyōta, and Yamamoto Chika. 2019. "Hyōgen no Fujiyūten ni Kyōhaku Fakkusu o Okutta Utagai, Kaishain o Taiho" [Suspicious of sending a threatening fax to the exhibition thematizing the lack of freedom of expression, a company employee was arrested]. *Asahi Shimbun*, August 8. Accessed December 26, 2020. https://digital.asahi.com/articles/ASM8777BYM87OIPE028.html

Tanaka Tōko. and Itō Maniji. 2020. "Kodomono 7-nin ni Hitoriga Hinkon Jyōtai, 18nen-chōsa de Takai Suijyun ni" [1 out of 7 Children live in Poverty]. *Asahi Shimbun*, July 17. Accessed December 22, 2020. https://digital.asahi.com/articl es/ASN7K6WFPN7KUTFL00K.html?iref=comtop_8_05

Tanaka Yasuhiro. 2010. *Fūkei no Sakeme: Okinawa, Senryō no Ima* (A Rift in the Scenery: Okinawa, Occupied Today). Tokyo: Serika Shobo.

Tang, Didi. 2023. "Taiwan Envoy Says He's Hopeful Biden-Xi Meeting Will Reduce Tensions in the Asia-Pacific Region." *Associated Press*, November 17. Accessed November 18, 2023. https://apnews.com/article/apec-taiwan-morrischang-chi na-united-states-1767d84366607bbf9e2d93a65892b4f2

Tanji, Miyume. 2008. U.S. Court Rules in the "Okinawa Dugong" Case: Implications for U.S. Military Bases Overseas. *Critical Asian Studies* 40:3, 475–487. Accessed October 29, 2020. https://doi.org/10.1080/14672710802274094

Tanji, Miyume, and Daniel Broudy. 2017. *Okinawa Under Occupation: McDonalization and Resistance to Neoliberal Propaganda*. Singapore: Palgrave MacMillan.

Taussig, Michael T. 1993. *Mimesis and Alterity: A Particular History of the Senses*. London/New York: Routledge.

Ten'nō (Ichizoku) no Raioki ni Hantaishi, Sensō Sekinin o Tsuikyūsuru Ikenkōkoku Undō. 1987. Advertisement. *Okinawa Times*, October 22, page 9.

Theory Out of Bounds Series Editors (Michael Hardt, Brian Massumi, and Sandra Buckley). 1999. In Antonio Negri, *Insurgencies: Constituent Power and the Modern State*, vii-ix. Minneapolis, MN: University of Minnesota Press. Accessed September 9, 2023. https://www-jstor-org.ezproxy.uky.edu/stable/10.5749/j.ctt tsnjz.3

Tibi, Bassam. 2023. *The Challenge of Fundamentalism: Political Islam and the New World Disorder*. University of California Press, 2023.

Tokuda Tomoko. 1989. "Shinjō Matsu no Tenshi" [An Angel of Shijō Matsu]. *Shin-Okinawa Bungaku* 82: 168–184.

Tokyo Jinruigakkai Zasshi. 1903. "*Jinruikan Kaisetsu Shuisho*" [A Letter of Intent to Create the Human Pavilion]. *Tokyo Jinruigakkai Zasshi* 18(203). In *Jinruikan: Fūinsareta Tobira* [The HumanPavilion: The Door That Has Been Closed], edited by Engeki 'Jinruikan' Jōen o Jitsugensasetai Kai, 33–34. Osaka: Attowākusu.

Tokyotoritsu Daigaku Nanseishotō Kenkyū Īnkai, ed. 1965. *Okinawa no Shakai to Shūkyō* [Okinawan Society and Religion]. Tokyo: Heibonsha.

Tomii. 2001. "Cocco no Ongakukatsudō Chūshi ni Tsuite Kataru" [Talking about Cocco who has Discontinued her Music Activities]. Accessed July 19, 2010. http://www7.plala.or.jp/tomikyu/cocco/chushi.html

Tomikawa, Moritake. n.d. "Okinawa's economic future and Asia: Looking beyond the U.S. Military Presence." A paper distributed in GWU Okinawa Collection Strategy Workshop, held on February 3, 2017, at George Washington University, Washington DC.

Tomiyama Ichirō. 1990. *Kindai Nihonshakai to 'Okinawajin': 'Nihonjin' ni Naru to Iukoto* [Modern Japanese Society and 'Okinawans': The Meaning of Becoming 'Japanese']. Tokyo: Nihon Keizai Hyōronsha.

Tomiyama Ichirō. 2002. *Bōryoku no Yokan: Iha Fuyū ni okeru Kiki no Mondai* [Presentiments of Violence: Ifa Fuyu and Okinawa's Crisis]. Tokyo: Iwanami Shoten.
Tomiyama Ichirō. 2006. *Zōho: Senjō no Kioku* [Memories of the Battlefield, expanded edition]. Tokyo: Nihon Keizai Hyouronsha.
Tomiyama Ichirō. 2010. "Rekishi Keiken, aruiwa Kibō nitsuite" [On Historical Experiences, or Hope]. In *Gendai Okinawa no Rekishi Keiken: Kibō, aruiwa Miketsusei ni Tsuite* [Historical Experiences of Contemporary Okinawa: On Hope, or Undecidability], edited by Tomiyama Ichirō and Mori Yoshio, 13–58. Tokyo: Seikyūsha.
Torikobori Jō. 1949. *Iwa'ana no Tenshi* [An Angel in a Cave]. *Gekkan Taimusu* 1(10) (November Issue): 27–28.
Toriyama Atsushi. 2007. "Fukkō eno Maishin—Gunsagō o Meguru Hitobito no Ugoki" [Striving towards Recovery—Movements of the People in Relation to Military Work]. In *Sengo o Tadoru: 'Amerika-yo' kara 'Yamato no Yo' e* [Tracing the Postwar: From the 'World of US rule' to the 'World of Japanese Rule'], 92–97. Edited by Nahashi Rekishi Hakubutsukan. Naha, Okinawa: Ryukyu Shimpo-sha.
Toriyama Atsushi. 2013. *Okinawa: Kichi Shakai no Kigen to Sōkoku, 1945–1956* [Okinawa: The Origin and Tensions of the Base Society]. Tokyo: Keisō Shobō.
Toyohara Kumin to Rentaisuru Kai, ed. 1995. *P-3C o Buttobase: Okinawa, Toyohaara Kumin no Tatakai* [Knock Down P-3C: Struggles of Residents in the Toyohara Community]. Tokyo: Gaifūsha.
Toyokawa Zen'ichi. 1956. "Sāchiraito" [Searchlight]. *Ryūdai Bungaku* 11: 20–29.
Toyoshima Tetsuhiro. 2017. "'Shīruzu Ryukyu—Koremade/Korekara, Jō': Kibishisa Masu Okinawa no Genjō, Seikaku na Jyōhōteikyō ga Jyūyō" [SEALDs-Ryukyu—the Past and the Future, 1: Okinawa's Situations Have Become Difficult; Importance of Accurate Information]. *Okinawa Times*, March 21. Accessed November 3, 2020. https://www.okinawatimes.co.jp/articles/-/89453
Toyoshita Narahiko. 1996. *Anpojyōyaku no Seiritu: Yoshida Gakiō to Ten'nō Gaikō* [The Establishment of the US-Japan Security Treaty: Diplomacies of Yoshida and the Emperor]/ Tokyo: Iwanami Shoten.
Toyoshita Narahiko. 2008. *Shōwa Ten'nō/Makkāsā Kaiken* [The Meetings of the Shōwa Emperor and MacArthur]. Tokyo: Iwanami Shoten.
Tsushima Maru Kinenkan n.d. "Tsushima-maru ni Kansuru Kisodēta" [Basic Data about Tsushima Maru]. Accessed December 28, 2020. http://tsushimamaru.or.jp/?page_id=72
Turner, Susan. "Russia, China, and a Multipolar World Order: The Danger in the Undefined." 2009. *Asian Perspective* 33:1, 159–184. Accessed May 24, https://www.jstor.org/stable/42704667
Uchikoshi Masayuki. 2019. *Yankī to Jimoto* [Delinquencies in Okinawa and Their Local Communities]. Tokyo: Chikuma Shobō.
Uchinā Kana Nikki [Okinawan Diary]. n.d. Blog. Accessed November 3, 2020. https://www.nuchigusui-kikou.com/

Uechi Ichirō. 2008. "Dai 2-shō Okinawa no Kyūkan Tochiseido no Bunseki" [Chapter 2. Analysis of Okinawa's Old Land System]. In *Okinawa Shakai no Kindaihōseido heno Hōsetsu to sono Eikyō: Rekishi Hōshakagakuteki Bunseki* [Incorporation of Okinawan Society into the Modern Legal System and its Impacts: A Historical Legal Sociological Analysis]. Ph.D. dissertation submitted to Waseda University. Accessed December 15, 2020. https://waseda.repo.nii.ac.jp/?action=repository_action_common_download&item_id=9378&item_no=1&attribute_id=20&file_no=7

Uehara Eiko. 1976. *Tsuji no Hana: Kuruwa no Onnatachi* [The Flowers of Tsuji, Women in the Pleasure Quarter]. Tokyo: Jiji Tsūshinsha.

Uehara Carter, Mitzi. 2014. "Mixed Race Okinawans and Their Obscure In-Betweeness." *Journal of Intercultural Studies* 35(6): 646–661. https://doi.org/10.1080/07256868.2014.963531

Uema Ikuko. 1981. "Watashi no Sengoshi" [My Postwar History]. In *Watashi no Sengoshi Dai 4-shū* [My Postwar History, Vol. 4], edited by Okinawa Times-sha, 105–137. Naha, Okinawa: Okinawa Times-sha.

Uema Yōko. 2017. *Hadashi de Nigeru: Okinawa no Your no Machi no Shōjotachi* [Escaping barefoot: Okinawan Girls in Nightlife Districts]. Tokyo: Ōta Shuppan.

Ueno Chizuko. 1990. *Kafuchōsei to Shihonsei* [Patriarchy and Capitalism]. Tokyo: Iwanami Shoten.

Uezato Kazumi. 1998. *Amerajian—Mōhitotsu no Okinawa* [Amerasians—Another Okinawa]. Kyoto: Kamogawa Shuppan.

Uezato Takashi. 2007. "Buki no nai Kuni, Ryukyu?" [Ryukyu, a Nation without Weapons?]. In *Mekara Uroko no Ryukyu/Okinawa-shi* [Eye-opening History of Ryukyu and Okinawa]. Accessed September 8, 2023. http://okinawa-rekishi.cocolog-nifty.com/tora/2007/11/post_08c5.html and http://okinawa-rekishi.cocolog-nifty.com/tora/2007/11/post_99eb.html

Uji'ie Yōko. 2001. "'Sabetugo'-gari no Jittai: Kyōkahso kara Kieru 'Sabetsu'" [Actual Conditions of Hunting Discriminatory Words: Discrimination that Has Disappeared from Textbooks]. *Nihongogaku* 20(7):79–93.

Umebayashi Hiromichi. 1994. *Jyōhō Kōkaihō de Toraeta Okinawa no Beigun* [The US military in Okinawa revealed by the Furnishing of Information Act]. Tokyo: Kōbunken.

UN News. n.d. "Fresh Allegations of Sexual Abuse made against UN Peacekeepers in Central African Republic." *Africa Renewal*. Accessed December 29, 2020. https://www.un.org/africarenewal/news/fresh-allegations-sexual-abuse-made-against-un-peacekeepers-central-african-republic

Urashima Etsuko. 2005. *Henoko: Umi no Tatakai* [Henoko: A Struggle on the Sea]. Tokyo: Inpakuto Shuppankai.

Vogel, Ezra F. 1979. *Japan as Number One: Lessons for America*. Cambridge, MA: Harvard University Press.

Wakabayashi Chiyo. 2015. *Jīpu to Sajin: Beigun Senryōka Okinawa no Seiji-shakai to Higashiajia Reisen, 1945–1950* [Jeeps and Dust: Okinawa's Political Society under US Rule and the East Asia Cold War]. Tokyo: Yūshisha.

Wakao Noriko. 2012. "Dai IV-shō: 1980nendai no Okinawa—'Hakken'-sareru Jinkenmondai" [Chapter 4: Okinawa in the 1980s—Human Rights Issues 'Discovered']. In *Sengo Okinawa no Jinkenshi: Okinawa Jinken Kyōkai Hanseiki no Ayumi* [A History of Human Rights in Postwar Okinawa: Steps taken by the Okinawan Association for Human Rights over Half a Century], edited by Okinawa Jinken Kyōkai, 113–141. Tokyo: Kōbunken.

Wallerstein, Immanuel. [1974] 2000. "5. The Rise and Future Demise of the World Capitalist System: Concepts for Comparative Analysis." In *Essential Wallerstein*, 71–105. New York: The New Press.

Wang, Zheng. 2012. *Never Forget National Humiliation: Historical Memory in Chinese Politics and Foreign Relations*. New York: Columbia University Press.

Watanabe Toshio. 1985. *Seichō no Ajia, Teitai no Ajia* [Asia Representing Growth, Asia Representing Stagnation]. Tokyo: Tōyō Keizai Shinpō-sha.

Watanabe Tsuyoshi. 2008. *Ame to Muchi no Kōzu: Futenmaisetsu no Uchimaku* [The Composition of the Carrot and the Stick: Inside the Transference of Futenma]. Naha, Okinawa: Okinawa Times-sha.

Wheeler, Skye. 2020. "UN Peacekeeping has a Sexual Abuse Problem." *Human Rights Watch*, January 11. Accessed December 29, 2020. https://www.hrw.org/news/2020/01/11/un-peacekeeping-has-sexual-abuse-problem#

Wilson, Alex. 2023. "Thousands of Marines wrap up 6-month rotation to Australia marked by loss." *Stars and Stripes*, October 31. Accessed November 15, 2023. https://www.stripes.com/branches/marine_corps/2023-10-31/marines-rotational-force-darwin-australia-11890074.html#:~:text=Marine%20Corps-,Thousands%20of%20Marines%20wrap%20up%206%2Dmonth,to%20Australia%20marked%20by%20loss&text=U.S.%20Marines%20deployed%20to%20Australia,since%202012%20%E2%80%94%20officially%20ended%20Oct.

Wilson, Gary. 2014. *The United Nations and Collective Security*. London/New York: Routledge.

Wittgenstein, Ludwig. [1953] 2001. *Philosophical Investigations: The German Text, with a Revised English Translation, Third Edition*, translated by G. E. M. Anscombe. Malden, MA: Blackwell Publishing.

World Economic Forum. 2019. "World Economic Forum and UN Sign Strategic Partnership Framework." Accessed May 15, 2022. https://www.weforum.org/press/2019/06/world-economic-forum-and-un-sign-strategic-partnership-framework

World Wildlife Fund–Japan. 2004. "Futenma Hikōjōdaitaishisetsu Kensetsujigyō ni kakawaru Kankyōeikyō Hyōkahōhōsho" *ni taisuru Ikensho* [Out Opinion against "the Scoping Documents for the Futenma Replacement Facility Construction Project"]. Accessed October 29, 2020. https://www.wwf.or.jp/activities/activity/267.html

World Wildlife Fund–Japan. n.d. "'Henoko' ni kansuru Kiji" [Articles concerning 'Henoko']. Accessed December 10, 2020. https://www.wwf.or.jp/tags_k_373/

Wright, Quincy. 1953. "The Outlawry of War and the Law of War." *The American Journal of International Law* 47(3): 365–376. Accessed December 29, 2020. https://www.jstor.org/stable/2194678?seq=1

Yabe Kōji. 2014. *Nihon wa Naze 'Kchi' to 'Genpatsu' o Tomerarenainoka* [Why Japan Cannot Stop the US bases and the Nuclear Plants]. Tokyo: Shūeisha.
Yabe Kōji. 2015. *Sensō o Shinai Kuni: Akihito Ten'nō Messēji* [The Country that Does Not Wage Wars: Emperor Akihito's Messages].]. Tokyo: Shōgakukan.
Yabe Kōji. 2019. *Nihon wa Naze 'Sensō ga Dekiru Kuni' ni Nattanoka* [Why Japan Has Become a Country that Can Wage Wars]. Tokyo: Kōdansha.
Yae Sakura. 1950. *Azami to Seppun* [Thistles and Kisses]. *Gekkan Taimusu* 12 (January Issue): 30–35.
Yagi Nanako. 2018. "Okinawa no Hiseiki Rōdōsha, Kakosaita 25man3800nin, Wariai 43% wa Zenkokuichi" [Number of Non-Fulltime Workers in Okinawa Reaches the Record High, 253,800; Percentage of Non-Fulltime Workers is the Highest among Prefectures in the Nation]. *Okinawa Times*, July 15. Accessed December 22, 2020. https://www.okinawatimes.co.jp/articles/-/283567
Yakabi Osamu. 2003. '*Kindai Okinawa ni okeru Mainoritī Ninshiki no Hensen*.' [Changes of Minority Perception in Modern Okinawa]. *Fūyū: Okinawa no Jiritsu-Kaihō ni Rentaisuru Fūyū Saito!* Accessed on October 13, 2018. http://www7b.biglobe.ne.jp/~whoyou/yakabi.htm
Yakabi Osamu. 2009. *Okinawasen, Beigunsenryō-shi o Manabinaosu—Kioku o Ikani Keishōsuruka* [Relearning the Battle of Okinawa and the History of US Occupation—How to Inherit Memories]. Yokohama: Seori Shobō.
Yamada Eimi. 1985. *Beddotaimu Aizu* [Bedtime Eyes]. Tōkyō: Kawade Shobō Shinsha, 1985.
Yamakage Susumu. 1997. "Japan's National Security and Asia-Pacific's Regional Institutions in the Post-Cold War Era." In *Network Power: Japan and Asia*, edited by Peter J. Katzenstein and Takashi Shiraishi, 275–305. Ithaca, NY: Cornell University Press.
Yamakoshi Shūzō. 2011. "Okinawa Shakai ni Okeru Hankichi Kanjō no Media Hyōshō: Okinawa Chihōshi no Gensetu Bunseki (1995nen 9gatu-11gatu) o Chūshini" [The Media Representation of Anti-base Sentiments in Okinawa: A Discourse Analysis of Local Newspapers in Okinawa (Sep.-Nov. 1995)]. *Keio Media and Communications Research* 61: 149–160.
Yamamoto Akiko. 2018. "Kenmintōhyō to Rendō? Okinawa no Seikaisaihen no Yukue" [Linked to the Prefectural Referendum? The Future of Reorganization of Okinawa's Political Arena]. *Ronza*, June 8. Accessed December 10, 2020. https://webronza.asahi.com/politics/articles/2018060600002.html
Yamamoto Akiko. 2023. "Okinawasen o Shiranai wakamono ni Dō Rekishi o Hikitsuguka, Ge" [How can we transfer history to the youth who did not experience the Battle of Okinawa? (Volume 2)]. *Okinron*. June 23. Accessed October 26, 2023. https://okiron.net/archives/2764
Yamamoto Hidemasa. 2015. "'Jirādo Jiken' Tsuikō 4" [Additional thoughts on the Girard incidents]. *Mathesis Universalis* 16(2): 1–30. Accessed December 20, 2020. https://dokkyo.repo.nii.ac.jp/?action=pages_view_main&active_action=repository_view_main_item_detail&item_id=381&item_no=1&page_id=13&block_id=17

Yamamoto Hideo. n.d.-a. *Yamahide no Okinawadayori* [Letters from Okinawa by Yamahide] (blog). Accessed November 3, 2020. photoyamahide.cocolog-nifty.com/

Yamamoto Hideo. n.d.-b. *Yamahide no Okinawadayori II* [Letters from Okinawa by Yamahide II]. Accessed November 3, 2020. http://poyamahide.cocolog-nifty.com/blog/#_ga=2.67017449.613460305.1582051528-243529013.1582051528

Yamamoto Hideo. n.d.-c. *Yamahide no Okinawadayori III* [Letters from Okinawa by Yamahide III]. Accessed November 3, 2020. http://ponet-yamahide.cocolog-nifty.com/

Yamanoha Nobuko. [1984] 1990. "Kokū Yasha" [Demons in the Empty Air]. In *Okinawa Bungaku Zenshū Dai 9-kan, Shōsetsu IV* [Complete Works of Okinawan Literature, Volume 9, Literary Works IV], edited by Okinawa Bungaku Zenshū Henshū Īnkai, 116–131. Tokyo: Kokusho Kankōkai.

Yamanoha Nobuko. [1985] 1990. "Onibi" [A Fireball in the Air]. In *Okinawa Bungaku Zenshū Dai 9-kan, Shōsetsu IV* [Complete Works of Okinawan Literature, Volume 9, Literary Works IV], edited by Okinawa Bungaku Zenshū Henshū Īnkai, 132–160. Tokyo: Kokusho Kankōkai.

Yamanokuchi Baku (also known as Yamanoguchi Baku). [1935] 2000. 'A Conversation.' Translated by Steve Rabson. In *Southern Exposure: Modern Japanese Literature from Okinawa*, edited by Michael S Molasky and Steve Rabson, 47. Honolulu, HI: University of Hawai'i Press.

Yamashiro Hibiki. 2023a. "Zaioki Beigun Kanbu Kenen Shimesu" [Top Executives of the US Military Expressed Concerns]. *Okinawa Times*, November 8, page 1.

Yamashiro Hibiki. 2023b. "Tōsho Sentōbutai ga Hossoku" [An Island Fighting Unit Established]. *Okinawa Times*, November 16, page 1

Yamashita Ryūichi. 2018. "Henoko deno Kōji, Seifu ga Saikai" [The Government Resumes Construction Works in Henok]. *Asahi Shimbun*, November 1. Accessed October 31, 2020. https://digital.asahi.com/articles/ASLB06FMYLB0TPOB00B.html?iref=comtop_8_01

Yamashita Shinji. 1998. *Kankō Jinruigaku* [Anthropology of Tourism]. Tokyo: Shinyōsha.

Yamazato Teiko. [1984] 1990. "Uchiumi no Kaze" [The Wind of an Inland Sea]. In *Okinawa Bungaku Zenshū Dai 9-kan, Shōsetsu IV* [Complete Works of Okinawan Literature, Volume 9, Literary Works IV], edited by Okinawa Bungaku Zenshū Henshū Īnkai, 6–28. Tokyo: Kokusho Kankōkai.

Yamazato Teiko. [1989] 1994. "Souru Torippu" [Soul Trip]. In *Furusato Bugakukan, Dai 54-kan: Okinawa* [The Pavilion of Local Literature, Volume 54: Okinawa], edited by Okamoto Keitoku, 393–416. Tokyo: Gyōsei.

yanbarukanashi. 2016. "Okinawakenmin o Dojin Yobawarisuru Osaka Fukei no Kidōtai'in" [A Riot Police from Osaka Prefectural Police Who Called Okinawans a Dojin]. YouTube. Video, 0:41, October 18. Accessed October 12, 2018. https://www.youtube.com/watch?v=zm6NbNKIayk&feature=youtu.be

Yano Teruo. 1974. *Okinawa Geinō Shiwa* [Narratives on the History of Okinawan Performing Arts]. Tokyo: Nihon Hōsō Shuppankai.

Yano Tōru. 2009. *Nanshin no Keifu: Nihon no Nanyōshikan* [The Genealogy of

South-Bound Expansion: Japan's View of the South-Sea History]. Tokyo: Chikura Shobō.

Yara Tomohiro. 2016. "Posuto-Reisen to Zaioki Kaiheitai" [Post–Cold War and the US Marine Corps in Okinawa]. In *Okinawa to Kahieitai: Chūryū no Rekishiteki Tenkai* [Okinawa and the US Marine Corps: Historical Development of Stationing], authored by Yara Tomohiro, Kawana Shinji, Saitō Kōsuke, Nozoe Fumiaki, and Yomamoto Akiko, 115–141. Tokyo: Jynpōsha.

Yara Tomohiro. 2017. "Naze Beigunkichi was Okinawa ni Shūchūshiteirunoka—'Jyūken to Burudōzā de Tochi o Ubai, Hondo no Kichi o Okinawa e" [Why have the US Bases Been Concentrated in Okinawa—Usurping Land with 'Bayonets and Bulldozers' and Transfer Bases from Mainland Japan to Okinawa]. *ND Initiative*, June 16. Accessed May 31, 2022. https://www.nd-initiative.org/research/5906/

Yasuda Kōichi. 2016. "Okinawa Heito o Kangaeru (Jō)" [Thinking Hate Speeches against Okinawa]. *Okinawa Times*, August 3. Accessed December 9, 2020. https://www.okinawatimes.co.jp/articles/-/55260?page=2

Yasuda Kōichi. 2018. "38sai, Josei Uyoku Katsudōka ga Amerika to Danko Tatakai Tsuzukeru Riyū" [Reasons why a 38-Years-Old Woman Right-Wing Activist Resolutely Has Continued to Fight against the United States]. *Kodansha Gendaishinsho*, July 14. Accessed November 4, 2020. https://gendai.ismedia.jp/articles/-/56511

Yasukuni Jinja. n.d. "History." Accessed October 25, 2021. https://www.yasukuni.or.jp/english/about/history.html

Yeo, Andrew. 2011. *Activists, Alliances, and Anti-U.S. Base Protests*. New York: Cambridge University Press.

Yomitansonshi Henshūshitsu. 2002. "Chibichirigama deno Shūdanjiketsu" [Compulsory Collective Suicide in Chibichirigama.] In *Yomitansonshi Dai 5kan Shiryōhen 4, Senjikiroku Jyōkan* [History of Yomitan Village 5, Historical Materials 4, Records of the Battle of Okinawa 1]. Okinawa: Yomitanson. Accessed on October 13, 2018. http://www.yomitan.jp/sonsi/vol05a/index.htm

Yonaha Keiko. 2016. "Beikaigunseifu no Gunseiyōin: Hanna to Watoson" [Civil Affairs Officers of the US Navy Government: Hanna and Watkins]. *Meiō Daigaku Kiyō* 21: 29–40. Accessed December 11, 2020. http://hdl.handle.net/20.500.12001/21951

Yonaha Shoko. 2016. *'Tsuji Yūkaku' ni Miru Kindai Okinawa Geinōshi Kenkyū: Yūkaku, Juri, Geinō (Yōyaku)* [A Study of the History of Modern Okinawan Performing Arts as Seen through the Tsuji District: Entertainment Quarters, Juri, and Performing Arts (digest)]. Ph.D. dissertation submitted to the Humanities and Social Sciences Program, University of Ryukyus Graduate School. http://hdl.handle.net/20.500.12000/35405

Yonaha Shoko. 2019. "'Hachigatsu Jyūgoya no Chaya' no Genfūkei: Jyuri to Tsujibunka to Okinawa no Aidentiti" [The Primary Scene of 'The Teahouse of the August Moon': Juri, Tsuji Culture, and Okinawan Identity]. Accessed December 12, 2020. https://blog.goo.ne.jp/nasaki78/e/4f47b47d6d831fdeabe36d0ca41f3d46

Yoneda Sachihiro, and Tanizu Norio. 2022. "Nago Shichōsen, 'Chinmoku' Tsuranuku Genshoku no Saisen o Kangaeru, Kichimondai ni 'Sedaisa'" [Thinking the re-election of the imcumbent mayer in Nago City Mayoral Election; Generational Gaps on the US base issues]. *Asahi Shimbun*, January 24. Accessed May 7, 2022. https://digital.asahi.com/articles/ASQ1R4F5TQ1PULZU009.html?iref=comtop_7_02

Yoneyama, Lisa. 2001. "For Transformative Knowledge and Postnationalist Public Spheres: The Smithsonian *Enola Gay* Controversy." In Takashi Fujitani, Geoffrey M. White, and Lisa Yoneyama, eds. *Perilous Memories: The Asia-Pacific War(s)*, 323–346. Durham, NC: Duke University Press.

Yoneyama, Lisa. 2016. *Cold War Ruins: Transpacific Critique of American Justice and Japanese War Crimes*. Durham, NC: Duke University Press.

Yoshida Naoko. 2016. "'Ikinobitekita' Sensō no Kioku o Keishōsuru: 'Sei no Ayausa' ni Nezasu Heiwakyōiku no Saikōchiku nimukete" [Inheriting the Memories of 'Surviving' the War: Toward Rebuilding Peace Education Based on 'Precariousness of Life']. *Tokyo Daigaku Daigakuin Kyōikugaku Kenkyūka Kiso Kyōikugaku Kenkyushitsu Kiyō* 42: 239–247. Accessed March 30, 2024. https://repository.dl.itc.u-tokyo.ac.jp/records/17374

Yoshida Sueko. [1984] 1990. "Kamāra Shinjū" [Suicide at Kamāra]. In *Okinawa Bungaku Zenshū Dai 9-kan, Shōsetsu IV* [Complete Works of Okinawan Literature, Volume 9, Literary Works IV], edited by Okinawa Bungaku Zenshū Henshū Īnkai, 161–177. Tokyo: Kokusho Kankōkai.

Yoshie Nobuyuki, Fukui Maho, and Itō Yoshitaka. 2020. "Osupurei, Muika Kisarazu e, 5nengo no Isō Mitōsenumama" [Ospreys will be deployed to Kisarazu on the 6th, the locations of their deployment in the future unknown]. *Asahi Shimbun*, July 4. Accessed December 22, 2020. https://digital.asahi.com/articles/ASN737KC6N6TUTIL024.html?iref=pc_extlink

Yoshi'i Masami. 2016. "'Dojin' Hatsugen o Kabau, Kono Kuni no Kūkitowa" [What's the Atmosphere of this Nation that Protects the 'Dojin' Statement?]. *Mainichi Shimbun*, December 2. Accessed on December 3, 2016. https://mainichi.jp/articles/20161202/dde/012/040/009000c

Yoshikawa Yuki. 2017. "Dai 1-shō, dai 3-setsu: Hansenbyōsha" [Chapter1, Section 3: Lepers]. In *Okinawakenshi Kakuronhen 6* [Okinawa Prefectural History 6], "Okinawasen" [The Battle of Okinawa], edited by Okinawaken Kyōikuiinkai, 310–314. Naha, Okinawa: Okinawaken Kyōikuiinkai.

Yoshimi Shun'ya. 1992. *Hakurankai no Seijigaku* [The Politics of Exhibitions]. Tokyo: Chūōkōron-shinsha.

Yoshimi Shun'ya. 1998. "Zasshi Medhia to Nashonarizumu no Shōhi" [The Media Journalism and the Consumption of Nationalism]. In *Nashonaru Hisutorī o Koete* [Beyond National History], edited by Komori Yōichi and Takahashi Tetsuya, 195-212. Tokyo: Tokyo Daigaku Shuppankai.

Yoshimi Yoshiaki. 1995. *Jyūgun Ianfu* [Comfort Women]. Tokyo: Iwanami Shoten.

Yoshioka, Itaru. 2021. "Min'i to Medhia—'Henoko' Kenmintōhyō nikansuru Shinbunhōdō o Jireitoshite" [People's Will and the News Media: A Case Study Analyzing the News Reports of 'Henoko' Prefectural Referendum in Okinawa].

Kansaidaigaku Shakaigakubu Kiyō 52(2): 65-92. Accessed March 15, 2024. https://kansai-u.repo.nii.ac.jp/record/19077/files/KU-1100-20210331-03.pdf

Yoshizawa Minami. 1988. "Shōgen, Tōi Senjyō, Chikai Sensō: Okinawa no Hitobito" [Testimonies: The Distant Battlefield and the War That was Close]. In *Betonamusensō no Kiroku* [Records of the Vietnam War], edited by 'Betonamusensō no Kiroku' Henshū Īnkai, 202–205. Tokyo: Ōtsuki Shoten.

Youtaijyu. 2009. "Orikon Rankingu Jōhōsābisu" [Providing Orikon's Information about Ranking of Album Sales]. Accessed July 19, 2010. http://ranking.oricon.co.jp/free_contents/search/ranking_list.asp?itemcd=288151&samecd=1&chart_kbn=11A&linkcd=30041108, and http://ranking.oricon.co.jp/free_contents/search/ranking_list.asp?itemcd=288475&samecd=1&chart_kbn=11A&linkcd=30049387

Yui Akiko. 2007. "Haikyokara no Shuppatsu—Kokyōkikan de yomigaeru." In *Sengo o Tadoru: 'Amerika-yo' kara 'Yamato no Yo' e* [Tracing the Postwar: From the world of US rule to the world of Japan], edited by Nahashi Rekishi Hakubutsukan, 23–33. Naha, Okinawa: Ryukyu Shimpo-sha.

yuken teruya studio. 2014. "A performance of Fija Byron: Part 1 of 4." Vimeo. Video, 8:20. Accessed December 28, 2020. https://vimeo.com/116880049

Zhu Fangyue. 2011. "Chūgoku no Wakamono ni okeru Nihon Popyurābunka no Jyuyō: Anime fan no Jyuyōtaido karano Kōsatsu" [Acceptance of Japanese Popular Culture among the Chinese Youth: An examination of the Acceptance Attitude of Animation Fans]. *Shidai Shakaigaku* 12: 45–63. Accessed April 3, 2022. https://dlisv03.media.osaka-cu.ac.jp/il/meta_pub/G0000438repository_111E0000011-4

Zhu Feng. 2015. "Sino-U.S. Strategic Rivalry and Evolution of the East Asian Security Order." In *China under Xi Jinping: Its Economic Challenges and Foreign Policy Initiatives*, edited by Shao Binhong, 186–219. Boston: BRILL.

Žižek, Slavoj. 2008. *Violence: Six Sideways Reflections*, New York: Picador.

Zohar, Ayelet. 2012. "Okinawa-Philadelphia-Tokyo: The Specificity and Complexity of Mao Ishikawa's Photographic Work." *Women's Camera Work: Asia* 2(2). Accessed December 16, 2020. http://hdl.handle.net/2027/spo.7977573.0002.204

Zwigenberg, Ran. 2014. *Hiroshima: The Origins of Global Memory Culture*. Cambridge, UK: Cambridge University Press.

Newspapers, Magazines, Websites, and Other Forms of Publication by Unidentified Authors

"Aichi Torienāre Hojokin Kōfu Hōshin Katameru" [Subsidies for the Aichi Triennial Will Be Paid]. *NHK Seiji Magajin*, March 23. Accessed December 26, 2020. https://www.nhk.or.jp/politics/articles/lastweek/32262.html

"Aidoru 'Seifukukōjō-Īnkai' ga Kokkai Hōi Yobikake" [Pop Idol group 'Seifukukōjō-Īnkai' Calling out to Surround the National Diet Building]. 2015. *Ryukyu Shimpo*, May 24. Accessed November 4, 2020. https://ryukyushimpo.jp/news/prentry-243309.html

"Aikokusha Dantai 'Issuikai'ga Onaga Chiji Chinjyutusho o Zenbunkeisai shita Wake" [Reasons why Issuikai, a Nationalist Group, Has Posted the Entire Statement of Governor Onaga]. 2016. Okinawa Times, January 10. Accessed November 4, 2020. https://www.okinawatimes.co.jp/articles/-/22591

"Akutagawashō Sakka Medoruma Shun-san Shakuhō" [Medoruma Shun, Who Received the Akutagawa Prize, Was Released]. 2016. *Okinawa Times*, April 3. Accessed November 3, 2020. https://www.okinawatimes.co.jp/articles/-/26573

"'Amerika yori Okinawa ni Omoiyari wo'" [Give Consideration to Okinawa rather than the United States]. 2017. *Okinawa Times*, December 20. Accessed November 4, 2020. https://www.okinawatimes.co.jp/articles/-/185395

"Ankēto Happyō~Dai 4kai Kaijō Suwarikomi" [Results of Questionnaires Filled Out by those Who Participated in the 4th Sit-in on the Sea]. n.d. *Kanū Chīmu Henoko Burū* [Canoe Team Henoko Blue] (blog). Accessed November 4, 2020. https://henokoblue.wixsite.com/henokoblue/single-post/2018/07/07/%E3%82%A2%E3%83%B3%E3%82%B1%E3%83%BC%E3%83%88%E7%99%BA%E8%A1%A8%E3%80%9C%E7%AC%AC%EF%BC%94%E5%9B%9E%E6%B5%B7%E4%B8%8A%E5%BA%A7%E3%82%8A%E8%BE%BC%E3%81%BF%E3%80%9C

"Ano Sensō o Fūkasasenai" [Will not let the memories of that war fade]. 2020. *Okinawa Times*, June 23, page 4.

"Aratana Anposeisaku Giron e" [Toward Discussing New Security Policies]. 2020. *Okinawa Times*, June 19, page 3.

"Arekara 30nen" [30 years after]. 1975. *Okinawa Times*, July 14, page 1.

"Bakushōmondai no Futari ga Henoko Tento ni Shuzai ni Kimashita" [Two Comedians of Bakusōmondai Came to the Tent in Henoko]. 2009. *Henokohama Tsūshin* [Newsletters from Henoko's beach] (blog), November 2. Accessed November 4, 2020. https://henoko.ti-da.net/e11631971.html

"Bei, Nanjyakukjiban o Kenen" [US has Concerns about Fragile Ground]. 2020. *Okinawa Times*, June 25, p. 1

"Beishudō IPEF, Nihon de Hossoku Hyōmei, Baiden Daitōryō 22-nichi ni Rainichi" [US-led IPEF, to be Declared in Japan when President Biden will visit Japan]. 2022. *Asahi Shimbun*, May 19. Accessed May 31, 2022. https://digital.asahi.com/articles/DA3S15298244.html?iref=pc_ss_date_article

"Bōeikyoku Henoko Umetate Kojichakushu, Ken ya Nagoshi wa Tsuyokuhanpatsu" [ODB began reclamation work; Okinawa Prefecture and Nago City strongly opposed]. 2015. *Asahi Shimbun*, October 29. Accessed October 29, 2015. http://digital.asahi.com/articles/ASHBY2TN5HBYTPOB002.html?_requesturl=articles%2FASHBY2TN5HBYTPOB002.html&rm=295

"Bui, Henoko ni Han'nyū Kyōnimo Ukisanbashi o Secchi" [Buoys Transported to Henoko, Floating Docks May Be Set Up Even Today]. 2014. *Rhyukyu Shimpo*, July 21. Accessed October 30, 2020. https://ryukyushimpo.jp/movie/prentry-228840.html

"China Overtakes Japan as World's Second-Biggest Economy." 2011. *BBC*, February 14. Accessed May 28, 2022. https://www.bbc.com/news/business-12427321

"Chūgoku, Senkaku e Kansen 332-nichi" [China sent Vessels to Senkaku for 332 days]. 2020. *Okinawa Times*, December 29, page 3.

"Cocco Hatsu no Okinawa Tandoku Raibu, 'Gomi Zero' Sanka, Uta de Arigatō" [Cocco's First Solo Concert in Okinawa, Thanking People for Participating in the "Trash Zero" Operation with the Song]. 2006. *Ryukyu Shimpo*, August 24. Accessed July 19, 2010. http://ryukyushimpo.jp/news/storyid-16593-storytopic-6.html

"'Dojin' hatsugen mondai Matsuji Chiji 'Urikotobani Kaikotoba'" [The Issue concerning the 'Dojin' Statement, Governor Matsui, "They only Gave them Tit for Tat"]. 2016. *Okinawa Times*, October 21. Accessed October 14, 2018. http://www.okinawatimes.co.jp/articles/-/67516

"'Dojin' Hatsugen no Dokoga Mondai Nanoka" [What are the Problems of the 'Dojin' Statement?]. *Okinawa Times*, October 20. Accessed October 14, 2018. http://www.okinawatimes.co.jp/articles/-/67368

"'Dojin' Hatsugen no Kidōtai'in o Chōsa e, Betsu no Tai'in wa 'Shinajin' Hatsugen" [The Riot Police Officer Made a Statement about 'Dojin' Will be Investigated, Another Riot Policeman Made a Statement about 'Chinaman.'] 2016. *Asahi Shimbun*, October 20. Accessed October 21, 2018. http://www.asahi.com/articles/ASJBN3J51JBNPTIL00D.html

"'Doko Tsukandonja Boke, Dojinga' Kidōtai'in ga Okinawa de Bōgen, Herripaddo Hantai no Akutagawashō Sakkani" ['What are you Holding onto, Idiot. You, Dojin.' A Riot Police Used Offensive Language to an Akutagawa-Prize Writer Who Opposed the Helipads]. 2016. *Okinawa Times*, October 19. Accessed October 12, 2018. http://www.okinawatimes.co.jp/articles/-/67175

"Dulles Outlines World Peace Plan: He Tells Y.M.C.A. Council Dilution of Sovereignty Idea Is Needed." 1939. *New York Times*, October 29. Accessed April 9, 2024. https://www.proquest.com/docview/102774525?_oafollow=false&accountid=11836&pq-origsite=primo&sourcetype=Historical%20Newspapers

"Eiga 'Himeyuri' Intabyū" [Interviewing the director of the film 'Himeyuri']. 2007. *Okinawa Web Magazine ryuQ*, June 22. Accessed December 27, 2020. https://ryuqspecial.ti-da.net/e1621970.html

"11gatsu15nichi Henoko Gētomae aru Kanūmenbā no Kiroku" [Henoko on November 15: A Report by a Member of the Canoe Team]. 2015. *Kanū Chīmu Henoko Burū*, not dated. Accessed October 30, 2020. https://henokoblue.wixsite.com/henokoblue/single-post/2015/12/14/11%E6%9C%8815%E6%97%A5%E8%BE%BA%E9%87%8E%E5%8F%A4%E3%82%B2%E3%83%BC%E3%83%88%E5%89%8D%E3%80%81%E3%81%82%E3%82%8B%E3%82%AB%E3%83%8C%E3%83%BC%E3%83%A1%E3%83%B3%E3%83%90%E3%83%BC%E3%81%AE%E8%A8%98%E9%8C%B2

"Emperor Expresses Grief over War with Dutch." 2000. *Japan Times*, May 25, page 1 and page 3.

"Fusen Chikai Arata" [Renewing the Pledge of Peace]. 2022. *Okinawa Times*, June 23. Accessed June 26, 2022. https://epaper.okinawatimes.co.jp/hv/index_viewer.html?pkg=jp.co.okinawatimes.viewer.pc&mcd=G0&npd=20220623&pn=1&uid=unknow&tkn=unknow

"Futenma Isetsu de Jimin 5shi Henoko Yōnin Kenranmo Tenkan e" [5 LDP Assemblypersons Accept the Construction in Henoko, Prefectural Chapter also Converts]. 2013. *Ryukyu Shimpo*, November 26. Accessed on October 29, 2020. https://ryukyushimpo.jp/news/prentry-215810.html

"Futenma Isetsusaki 'Okinawa to Itteinai' Mondēru Moto-Chūnichitaishi Nihon ga Kettei to Kyōchō" [We Didn't Say that the Site of Relocation of Futenma is Okinawa; Former Ambassador Mondale Emphasizes that it was Japan's Decision]. 2015. *Ryukyu Shimpo*, November 9. Accessed December 20, 2020. https://ryukyushimpo.jp/news/entry-168306.html

"Gunkokushugi no Fukkatsu" [Restoration of Militarism]. 1975. *Okinawa Times*, July 5, page 8.

"Hankichi no Shōchōdatta Kōkōsei 'Okinawa no Kunō, Imamo Kawarazu" [A High School Student That Symbolized the Anti-base: "Agonies over the Bases Have Not Changed"]. 2015. *Asahi Shimbun*, October 18. Accessed December 21, 2015. https://asyagi.exblog.jp/24582945/

"Henoko de Yamashiro Gichōra 4nin o Taiho" [4 Individuals including Chairman Yamashiro arrested]. 2016. *Okinawa Times*, November 29. Accessed October 30, 2020. https://www.okinawatimes.co.jp/articles/-/73388

"Henoko 8gatsu ni Doshatōnyū, Sango Hozensaku de Okure" [Charging of Sediment in August in Henoko, Delay due to the Necessity to Take Measures to Protect Coral Reefs]. 2018. *Okinawa Times*, June 8. Accessed October 31, 2020. https://www.okinawatimes.co.jp/articles/-/264143

"Henoko Hōmon '0-nichi Ni Shitahōga" [Visiting Henoko to Ridicule, 'You'd Better Change the Duration of Sit-Ins to a Zero Day]. 2022. *Okinawa Times*, October 6, page 28.

"Henoko Isetsu—Kore ga Netsubōshita Sokokuka" (Transference to Henoko—Is this the Homeland Okinawa Desired?). 2014. *Asahi Shimbun*, May 17. Accessed on June 5, 2014. http://www.asahi.com/articles/ASG5J35ZBG5JUSPT003.html

"Henoko Kikin 1oku 1900man en ni, 7wari ga Kengaikara" [Donation for the Henoko Fund has Reacheed 119,000,000 yen, 70% of which Comes from outside Okinawa]. 2015. *Okinawa Times*, May 1. Accessed December 10, 2020. https://www.okinawatimes.co.jp/articles/-/13811

"Henoko Kōgitento, Kuni ga Tekkyoshidō Kyōseihaijyo mo Shiya" [Tents for Opposition in Henoko, Government Gave Guidance to Remove, a Possibility of Forceful Removal]. 2015. *Okinawa Times*, February 20. Accessed on October 30, 2020. https://www.okinawatimes.co.jp/articles/-/11153

"Henoko Kōji Saikai" [Resuming the construction work in Henoko]. 2016. *Ryukyu Shimpo*, Special Edition, December 27. Accessed October 31, 2020. http://ryukyuheiwa.blog.fc2.com/img/201612290210235a2.jpg/

"Henoko Kōki wa 12nen, Seifu ga Mitōshi" [The Expected Period of Work for Constructing the Base in Henoko is 12 years, Tokyo Predicted]. 2019. *Okinawa Times*, December 25. Accessed October 31, 2020. https://www.okinawatimes.co.jp/articles/-/515316

"Henoko Kyōgiketsuretsu Songenkake Shukushuku to Torikse" [Negotiation over

Henoko broke down; Solemnly revoke the permit to maintain the dignity of Okinawa]. 2015. *Ryukyu Shimpo*, September 8. Accessed October 31, 2020. http://ryukyushimpo.jp/news/storyid-248548-storytopic-11.html

"Henoko Niramiau Umi, Kaiho ga Hantaiha no Kanū o Renjituhaijo" [Confrontation on the sea of Henoko, JCG removes protesters consecutive days]. 2015. *Asahi Shimbun*, February 9. Accessed December 23, 2015. http://digital.asahi.com/articles/ASH2K7521H2KTPOB007.html

"Henoko no Shin'kichi 'Hitsuyōna Chōsa sareteinai'" ['Necessary Investigations Have Not Been Conducted' for Henoko's New Base]. 2021. *Okinawa Times*, November 25. Accessed May 8, 2022. https://www.okinawatimes.co.jp/articles/-/868978

"Henoko o BBC ga Shuzai" [BBC Collects News Materials at Henoko]. 2005. *Watching*, May 10. Accessed November 5, 2020. https://blog.goo.ne.jp/turn_turn_turn/e/38f10d38c45628c49dd9e00709cb3930

"Henoko Saidaikyū 500-nin ga Suwarikomi" [In Henoko, 500 People sat-in, One of the Largest Numbers since the Protest Began]. 2015. *Okinawa Times*, November 11. Accessed October 30, 2020. https://www.okinawatimes.co.jp/articles/-/20742

"Henoko Shinkichi: Gyōseihō Kenkyūsha 110nin no Seimeibun zenbu" [The Complete Text of Statement by 110 Researchers of Administrative Laws]. 2018. *Okinawa Times*, October 26. Accessed November 4, 2020. https://www.okinawatimes.co.jp/articles/-/336001

"Henoko Shinkichi: Kanehide Gurūpu Shinyūshain ra Shimin Gekirei" [New Base in Henoko: New Employees of Kanehide Visited to Support Citizens]. 2015. *Okinawa Times*, April 9. Accessed November 3, 2020. https://www.okinawatimes.co.jp/articles/-/13015

"Henoko Shinkichi Kensetsu no Kyōkō ni Hantai suru Kenpō Kenkyūsha Seimei" [Statement by Researchers of Constitution Who Oppose the Forceful Execution of the Construction of a New Base in Henoko]. 2019. *Okinawa Times*, January 25. Accessed November 4, 2020. https://www.okinawatimes.co.jp/articles/-/376924

"Henoko Shinkichi Kensetsu Soshi! Doyōbi Kenmin Daikōdō" [Stop the Construction of a New Base in Henoko! Saturday Great Actions for Okinawans]. 2017. *Independent Web Journal*, October 7. Accessed October 31, 2020. https://iwj.co.jp/wj/open/archives/400200

"'Henoko Shinkichi Soshi' 22000nin Kokkai Hōi" [Stop the new base in Henoko' 22,000 people surrounded the National Diet building]. 2015. *Ryukyu Shimpo*, September 13. Accessed November 4, 2020. https://ryukyushimpo.jp/news/prentry-248817.html

"Henoko Suishin Nichibei de Saikakunin, Fukki 50-nen" [Washington and Tokyo reconfirmed the FRF construction in Henoko, 50 years after Reversion]. 2022. *Okinawa Times*, May 5. Accessed May 31, 2022. https://www.okinawatimes.co.jp/articles/-/953820

"Henoko Umetate Chakkō 5gatsu nimo Doshatōnyū" [Land Reclamation Work

Initiated, Charging of Sediment Possibly in May]. 2017. *Okinawa Times*, February 7. Accessed October 31, 2020. https://www.okinawatimes.co.jp/articles/-/83079

"Henoko Umetate Hajimaru, Gogagnkōji, Ken wa Hanpatsu, Fukkigo Saidai no Kichikensetsu e" [Land Reclamation Began in Henoko, Okinawa Prefecture Opposed the Shore Protection Works; toward the Construction of a Largest Base after Reversion]. 2017. *Okinawa Times*, Special Edition, April 25. Accessed October 31, 2020. https://www.okinawatimes.co.jp/articles/-/94777

"Herikichi Hantaikyō Seigiheiwashō Jushō" [COOBC received the Justice Peace Award]. 2017. *Okinawa Times*, November 24. Accessed November 5, 2020. https://www.okinawatimes.co.jp/articles/-/174997

"Hiseiki Koyōsha 30nen de 2.7bai, Seiki Kyūjin, Izen Hikuku" [The number of non-Fulltime Workers Increased by 270% in 30 years. Recruitment of Fulltime Workers Remains Low]. 2015. *Ryukyu Shimpo*, November 1. Accessed December 22, 2020. http://ryukyushimpo.jp/news/entry-164213.html

"Hōkoku: Tokubetsu Jōeikai 'Himeyuri no Kaze'" [Report: Special Screening, "The Wind of Himeyuri"]. 2007. Accessed December 27, 2020. http://www.himeyuri.info/event/20070815_16/kaze.html

"Hyakuta Naoki Shi 'Okinawa no Shinbun Tsubuse,' Jimin Benkyōkai de Hatsugen." [Mr. Naoki Hyamuta said, "Abolish Okinawa's Newspapers," in a Liberal Democratic Party Study Meeting]. 2015. *Okinawa Times*, June 26. Accessed October 14, 2018. https://www.okinawatimes.co.jp/articles/-/15792

"Iyōna Fun'iki Tadayō" [Indescribable atmosphere permeates]. 1975. *Okinawa Times*, July 15, page 11.

"Jitakunai o yaku1jikan-han Kakete Sōsaku, Beigun no Haikibutsu Kōgide" [Police Investigated the House for one Hourand a Half, in Relation to the Protest using the Military Waste]. 2021. *Okinawa Times*. Accessed June 25, 2021. https://www.okinawatimes.co.jp/articles/-/765815

"Jyugonsoshō Genkoku Haiso" [The Plaintiffs Lost the Dugong Case]. 2020. *Okinawa Times*, May 8, page 23.

"Kaiho no Bōryoku Hyōmenka, Osaetsuke Odoshi, Keganinmo" [JCG's Violence Exposed, Protesters Forced Down, Threatened, and Injured]. 2014. *Ryukyu Shimpo*, September 11. Accessed on October 30, 2020. https://ryukyushimpo.jp/movie/prentry-231432.html

"Kaiho, Seigensui'ikigai de Kōgi no Shimin o Kyōseihaijo" [JCG Eliminates Protesters Forcefully Outside the No Admittance Zone]. 2014. *Okinawa Times*, August 16. Accessed October 30, 2020. https://ryukyushimpo.jp/movie/prentry-230221.html

"Kaiketsusaku 'Henokogai' ga 6wari, Nagoshi Kube 2ku Jyūmin Ankeēto" [60% of Residents Think of Moving the Base "outside Henoko," Results of the Questionnaires of 3 Districts around Henoko in Nago City]. 2016. *Ryukyu Shimpo*, April 12. Accessed December 9, 2020. https://ryukyushimpo.jp/news/entry-255026.html

"Kaiyōhaku Mokuzen ni Shite Watashimo Hitokoto" [I too Want to Comment on the Ocean Expo that will Begin soon]. 1975. Okinawa Times, July 4, page 10.

"Kankōgyō no Josei Jyūgyōin, 8wari ga Hiseiki Koyō" [80% of women employed in the tourist industry are non-fulltime workers]. 2018. *Okinawa Times*, December 5. Accessed December 20, 2020. https://www.okinawatimes.co.jp/articles/-/354737

"Keibitaisei ni Oten Nokosu" [Leaving an Indelible Stain on the Security System]. 1975. *Okinawa Times*, July 18, page 10.

"K8 Gogan nimo Daisen Kakunin" [Pontoons are being set up at K8-Seawall as well]. 2020. *Okinawa Times*, December 15, page 2.

"Keikakuteki na Hankōka" [Could be a planned crime]. 1975. *Okinawa Times*, July 18, page 11.

"Keishichō Kidōtai o Hatsutōnyū Shuwābu Gētomae Shōtotsugekika de Taihosha" [The First Usage of the Riot Squad by the Tokyo Metropolitan Police Department, Some Arrested due to the Escalation of the Crash]. 2015. *Ryukyu Shimpo*, November 5. Accessed October 30, 2020. https://ryukyushimpo.jp/movie/entry-166256.html

"Kenmin wa Akiramenai! Shurijyō mo Henoko mo; Henoko Shūchū Kōdōbi ni 1000nin" [Okinawans will not give up Shuri Castle or Henoko!: 1000 people gathered for a Henoko action day]. 2019. *Uchinā Kana Nikki* [Okinawan diary], November 2. Accessed October 31, 2020. https://www.nuchigusui-kikou.com/?p=20482

"Kichihantaiha wa 'Kichigai; Jimin Kojima Kengi "Shitsugendenai."" [Those Who Opposed the Base are Out of the Bases and Out of Mind; "It Was Not a Slip of the Tongue," said LDP Prefectural Assemblyman Kojima.] *Kanaroko*, May 24. Accessed December 26, 2020. https://www.kanaloco.jp/news/government/entry-76197.html

"Kichi Nakunaruto Okinawa Keizai wa Hatansuru?" [Will the Okinawan Economy Collapse without Bases?]. 2019. *Ryukyu Shimpo*, February 22. Accessed February 22, 2019. https://ryukyushimpo.jp/news/entry-879144.html

"Kisha Kōsoku 'Kiken na Senrei o Tsukutta' Kokkyōnaki Kikshadan no Okinawa Seimei Zenjbun" [Detaining of a Journalist, 'A Dangerous Precedent being Created; the entire 'Okinawa Statement' by Reporters Without Borders]. 2016. *Okinawa Times*, October 23. Accessed December 9, 2020. https://www.okinawatimes.co.jp/articles/-/67867

"Kiteihōshindōri Kyōchō, Futenmaisetsu de Koizumi Shushō" [As Scheduled, Prime Minister Koizumi Emphasized]. 2005. *Ryukyu Shimpo*, January 27. Accessed December 22, 2015. http://ryukyushimpo.jp/news/prentry-120240.html

"Kōgō Jikei no Ninaite; Hansenbyō Mimai Sossen, Kokusaku to Kankei no Kakomo" [The Empress in Charge of Charity: Took the Initiative in Visiting Lepers; Connection with the State Policy in the Past]. 2017. *Mainichi Shimbun*, May 29. Accessed July 25, 2020. https://mainichi.jp/articles/20170529/ddm/003/040/122000c

"Kōgō-sama ni Akogare to Shin'ai, Kōdoseichōki, Kazoku no Moderu, Ippankatei no Kosodate Tori'ire" [Admiration and Affection with the Empress; During the High-Growth Era, She Became a Role Model for the Family; Incorporating the

Methods of Childrearing used in the Ordinary family]. 2017. *Mainichi Shimbun*, May 29. Accessed July 25, 2020. https://mainichi.jp/articles/20170527/ddm/002/040/102000c

"Kokkai Hōikōdō ni 28000nin, 'Henoko ni Kichi Tsukuruna' Uttae" [28,000 people Participated in the Action to Surround the National Diet Building, to Demand 'Do Not Build a Base in Henoko']. 2016. *Ryukyu Shimpo*, February 21. Accessed November 4, 2020. https://ryukyushimpo.jp/news/entry-225471.html

"Kokusaku Min'i o Shingai, Henoko Sagyōsaikai" [The State's Policy Violated the People's Will, the Construction Work in Henoko Resumed]. 2015. *Okinawa Times*, January 16. Accessed October 30, 2020. https://www.okinawatimes.co.jp/articles/-/21312

"Koronagono Henoko, Kawaru Kōgino Genba, Swarikomi Sankasha wa Fueru" [Henoko after the COVID Pandemic; Situations Have Changed at the Site of Protest; the Number of Participants Has Increased]. 2020. *Okinawa Times*, July 12. Accessed October 31, 2020. https://www.okinawatimes.co.jp/articles/-/599681

"Kōtaishi Gofusai Asu Raioki" [The Crown Prince and Princess visit Okinawa Today]. 1975. *Okinawa Times*, July 16, page 1.

"Kōtaishi no Okotoba" [The Crown Prince's comments]. 1975. *Okinawa Times*, July 18, page 1.

"Kunino Shakkin Saidai 114chōen" [The Nation's Debts Have Reached 1,140 trillion yen]. 2020. *Okinawa Times*, May 9, page 6.

"Kussakusagyō ni Chakushu, Henoko Daisen o Setcchi" [Starting the Drilling Operation, Installing the Pontoons in Henoko]. 2014. *Ryukyu Shimpo*, August 17. Accessed October 30, 2020. https://ryukyushimpo.jp/news/prentry-230259.html

"Kyokuchōkyū ya Yōjin to Mendan" [Meetings with Top Officials and Important Persons]. 2018. *Okinawa Times*, November 18, page 2.

"Kyō no Henoko, Hirogaru Okinawa eno Kyōkan" [Today's Henoko, Expanding Sympathy to Okinawa]. 2015. *Uchinā Kana Nikki*, April 25. Accessed December 9, 2020. https://www.nuchigusui-kikou.com/?m=201504&paged=2

"Map of Okinawa Island 02.svg." 2021. *Wikimedia Commons, the free media repository*. Accessed November 15, 2023. https://commons.wikimedia.org/wiki/File:Map_of_Okinawa_Island_02.svg?uselang=en

"Map of the World with Countries—Single Color." n.d. *FreeVectorFlags.com*. Accessed November 15, 2023. https://freevectormaps.com/world-maps/WRLD-EPS-01-0011?ref=atr

"Miyazaki Hayao-shi 'Henoko Kikin Kyōdōdaihyō e, Shinkichi Soshi, Naigai ni" [Miyazaki Hayao will Join the 'Henoko Fund' as a Codirector; Expressing the Will to Stop the New Base Construction Internally and Externally]. 2015. *Ryukyu Shimpo*, May 8. Accessed November 4, 2020. https://ryukyushimpo.jp/news/prentry-242675.html

"Ōbeishikisha Henoko Isetsu Hantai de Seimei, Stōn Kantokura 109nin" [Statement by Critics in Europe and the United States to Oppose the Relocation of the Base to Henoko, Director Stone and other Individuals Numbering 109]. 2015. *Chiba Nippō*, August 31. Accessed December 9, 2020. http://www.chibanippo.co.jp/newspack/20150831/275351

"Ōe Kenzaburō san Henoko o Hōmon, 'Shimingawa ga Katsu'" [Ōe Kenzaburō Visited Henoko and Said 'Citizens Will Win']. 2015. *Ryukyu Shimpo*, June 21. Accessed November 4, 2020. https://ryukyushimpo.jp/movie/prentry-244574.html

"Okinawa Beigun de Aratani Hitori Kansen" [One more individual in the US military in Okinawa was infected]. 2020. *Okinawa Times*, July 12. Accessed October 31, 2020. https://www.okinawatimes.co.jp/articles/-/599875

"Okinawa Beigun, Kōgisankasha o Kanshi Kojinjōhōshūshūshi Hōkoku" [The US Military Monitors Those Participating in Protests; Personal Information Collected and Reported]. 2016. *Okinawa Times*, October 7. Accessed November 3, 2020. https://www.okinawatimes.co.jp/articles/-/65504

"Okinawa-dojin ga Mata Gonetemasukedo, Mata Kanedesue? Shineba Īnoni" [The Okinawa *dojin* are complaining again. Do they want more money? I wish they were dead]. 2015. *5 Chan'neru*, April 6. Accessed October 14, 2018. https://viper.5ch.net/test/read.cgi/news4vip/1428272654/

"Okinawa/Henoko Isetsumondai ni Oribā Stōn Kantoku, Chomusukī san ra Hantai Seimei (Zenbun)" [Director Oliver Stone, Mr. Chomsky, and Others Issued a Statement of Opposition to the Relocation of a Base to Henoko/Okinawa (Full Text)]. 2014. *Huffington Post* (Japanese edition), January 8. Accessed December 9, 2020. https://www.huffingtonpost.jp/2014/01/08/okinawa-henoko_n_4559609.html

"'Okinawa-kenmin mo Kokumin dewananinoka' Osupurei Saikai, Fukuchiji ga Kuni ni Kōgi" ['Are Okinawan prefectural residents also not the Japanese nation?' Vice Governor lodged a complaint against the national government]. 2016. *Okinawa Times*, December 20. Accessed May 7, 2022. https://www.okinawatimes.co.jp/articles/gallery/76625?ph=1

"Okinawa no Kankyō o Kangaeru: Okinawa Kankyō Nettowāku Kessi 20-shūnen Kinen Shinpojiumu" [Thinking Okinawa's Environment: A Symposium to Commemorate the 20th Anniversary of the Establishment of the Okinawa Environmental Network]. 2018. *Independent Web Journal*, October 27. Accessed December 10, 2020. https://iwj.co.jp/wj/open/archives/434644

"Okinawa no Kodomo 30% ga Hinkon Zenkoku no 2bai" [30% of Okinawan Children Live in Poverty, Twice as High as the National Average]. 2016. *Okinawa Times*, January 30. Accessed December 23, 2020. https://www.okinawatimes.co.jp/articles/-/23335

"Okinawa no Umi o Mamoritai: Cocco 'Jyugon no Mieru Oka'" [Wishing to Protect Okinawa's Ocean: Cocco, 'The Hill of Dugongs']. 2009. *Asahi Shimbun*, October 6. Accessed December 27, 2020. http://www.asahi.com/video/eco/TKY200910060156.html

"Okinawasen no Hisan ni Kokoroitameru" [Heartbroken by the Tragedy of the Battle of Okinawa]. 1975. *Okinawa Times*, July 18, page 11.

"Okinawasen no Kioku Kōsaku" [Memories of the Battle of Okinawa Interacts with the Present]. 2018. *Okinawa Times*, March 27, page 28.

"Okinawashinkōyosan 3000-okuen ware, 10-nen buri" [Okinawa development budget reduced below 300,000,000,000 yen, for the first time in 10 years]. 2021. *Asahi Shimbun*, December 23. Accessed October 22, 2023. https://digital.asahi.com/articles/DA3S15151770.html

"Okinawa Ten'nōhai o Kakutoku" [Okinawa achieved the Emperor's Trophy]. 1987. *Okinawa Times*, October 29, page 1.

"Onaga Takeshi-shi o Zenmenshien shita Kanehide Gurūpu ni Ihen" [Changes in the Kanehide Group that uniformly supported Mr. Onaga Takeshi]. 2021. *Okinawa Times*, September 15. Accessed May 7, 2022. https://www.okinawatimes.co.jp/articles/-/830986

"On Okinawa, Many Locals Want U.S. Troops to Leave." 2017. *PBS NewsHour*, September 16. Accessed December 9, 2020. https://www.pbs.org/newshour/show/okinawa-locals-want-u-s-troops-leave

"Osupurei 'Kiken' 72% Haibi 5nen Yoron Chōsa" [72% of Okiinawans oppose MV-22 Ospreys, An Opinion Poll 5 years after the deployment shows]. 2017. *Ryukyu Shimpo*, September 28. Accessed November 4, 2020. https://ryukyushimpo.jp/news/entry-584346.html

"Rola Hatsugen ni Kurūnī Kasane Sakamoto Ryūichi san no Kanaria-ron" [Overlapping the Statement of Rola with that of George Clooney, Sakamoto Ryuichi's Idea on Okinawa as a Canary]. 2019. *Asahi Shimbun*, January 9. Accessed November 4, 2020. https://digital.asahi.com/articles/ASM184TCNM18UTIL026.html

"Rotation System Studied." 1976. *Marine Corps Gazette* 60(3): 2. Accessed December 21, 2020. http://ezproxy.uky.edu/login?url=https://www-proquest-com.ezproxy.uky.edu/trade-journals/rotation-system-studied/docview/206269600/se-2?accountid=11836

"Saikin'no Nihonshakai no Okinawa Sabetsu to Okinawa Tataki nitsuite . . ." [On recent discrimination against Okinawa in Japanese society and Okinawa bashing . . .]. 2008. *Yahoo Chiebukuro*, April 1. Accessed October 14, 2018. https://detail.chiebukuro.yahoo.co.jp/qa/question_detail/q1415682459?__ysp=5pyA6L%2BR44Gu5pel5pys56S%2B5Lya44Gu5rKW57iE5beu5Yil44Go5rKW57iE5Y%2Bp44GN44Gr44Gk44GE44Gm

"Sano Motoharu san, Henoko Otozure 'Dare ga Kizuna Kowashiteiruka to tou" [Sano Motoharu Visited Henoko and Asked 'Who Destroys Human Connections']. 2015. *Ryukyu Shimpo*, May 9. Accessed November 4, 2020. https://ryukyushimpo.jp/news/prentry-242722.html

"'Sayokuzasshi' to Kōgeki o Uketemo Hirumanakatta 'Tsūhan Seikatsu' ni Kandō! Sono Hankotsu no Rekishi o Aratamete Furikaeru" [Impressive! 'Tsūhan Seikatsu' Undaunted by the verbal attack calling it 'Leftist.' Reflecting on its Oppositional History]. 2016. *Litera*, November 21. Accessed November 5, 2020. https://lite-ra.com/2016/11/post-2715_4.html

"Seifu Henoko Enganbu e Doshatōnyū o Kaishi" [Government Began Charging Sediment in the Coastal Area]. 2018. *Asahi Shimbun*, December 14. Accessed October 31, 2020. https://digital.asahi.com/articles/ASLDG35NJLDGTIPE008.html

"Sekai no Wakamono ga Henoko Gētomae ni" [Young People across the World Came to the Gate of Camp Schwab in Henoko]. 2015. *Ryukyu Shimpo*, April 12. Accessed November 3, 2020. https://ryukyushimpo.jp/news/prentry-241717.html

"Sengowa Owatta" [Okinawa's postwar has come to an end]. 1987. *Okinawa Times*, October 30, page 1.

"Shinkichi 100nen Tattemo Kanseishinai'? Doshatōnyū Hitsuyōryō no 1%" ['It would not be Completed even after 100 years'? The Amount of Sediment Charged is 1% of What is Needed]. 2019. *Okinawa Times*, December 15. Accessed October 31, 2020. https://www.okinawatimes.co.jp/articles/-/510552

"Shinkichi Hantai, Uchū no 7mannin" ["Opposing the New Base, 70,000 People Gathered in Spite of the Rain"] 2018. *Okinawa Times*, August 12. Accessed December 9, 2020. https://www.okinawatimes.co.jp/articles/-/297964

"Shushō Banzen no Keibi o Shiji" [Prime Minister Directed Thorough Security]. 1975. *Okinawa Times*, July 15, page 1.

"Shuwābu Ichibu Chiryō Neage, Bōeishō, Satei Minaoshi 65% Mashi" [Rent of Camp Schwab Partially Raised; Ministry of Defense Revises the Evaluation Criteria for Increase by 65%]. 2015. *Ryukyu Shimpo*, January 11. Accessed December 9, 2020. https://www.ryukyushimpo.jp/news/prentry-237150.html

"Sōdōmae Beiheijiken Nen1000kenchō" [More than 1,000 Crimes Were Committed by US Servicemen before the Koza Riot]. 2020. *Okinawa Times*, December 16, page 29.

"Sonmin no Ishi ni Shitagau" [I will follow the will of villagers]. 1956. *Ryukyu Shimpo*, December 22. Accessed on December 12, 2020. In ayirom-net, *Ore ga Chōshi ni Notte Okinawa/Ryukyu no Rekishi o Kataru Burogu*, May 11, 2018. http://www.ayirom-uji-2016.com/%E3%80%90%E5%86%8D%E8%80%83%E3%80%91-%E3%82%AD%E3%83%A3%E3%83%B3%E3%83%97%E3%83%BB%E3%82%B7%E3%83%A5%E3%83%AF%E3%83%96%E8%AA%95%E7%94%9F%E3%81%AE%E7%B5%8C%E7%B7%AF-%E3%81%9D%E3%81%AE2

"Suga-shi Hatsugen ni 'Chotto Chigau,' Henoko Kuchōra 'Jimotomo Sandō' o Hitei" ["That is Not What We Meant," Responding to Mr. Suga's Comment; Mayors of Henoko and nearby Districts Denied the View that 'Local Communities Have Given Approval']. 2015. *Okinawa Times*, November 20. Accessed March 31, 2024. https://www.okinawatimes.co.jp/articles/-/21098

"Suga-shi 'Ssabetsu to Danteidekinu.'" [Mr. Suga stated, 'Unable to Conclude that it is Discriminatory']. 2016. *Okinawa Times*, November 22. Accessed October 14, 2018. http://www.okinawatimes.co.jp/articles/-/72243

"Suidōsui kara Zanteichigoe no PFAS Kenshutsu wa Renraku o: Okinawaken, Beigunkichi no Shūhen Shichōson ni Yōsei e" [Contact if the PFAS Level is beyond the Standard Value: Okinawa Prefectural Government will Request Cities/Towns/Villages surrounding US Bases]. 2021. *Okinawa Times*, October 14. Accessed June 26, 2022. https://www.okinawatimes.co.jp/articles/-/846536

"Sunaoni Yorokobenai Kōtaishi Raioki" [I Should be but Cannot be Happy with Crown Prince's Visit to Okinawa]. 1975. *Okinawa Times*, July 9, page 4.

"Taieki Beigunjinra Rentai no Suwarikomi Kōgi" [Veterans and Others Sat in for Solidarity]. 2015. *Ryukyu Shimpo*, December 11. Accessed November 3, 2020. https://ryukyushimpo.jp/news/entry-186778.html

"Ten'nōheika ni Kōkan 87%" [87% of Okinawans Have a Positive Feeling toward the Emperor]. 2019. *Okinawa Times*, April 29, page 1.

"Ten'nōsei Shihai o Nerau" [Attempting to Control Okinawa through the Emperor System]. 1975. *Okinawa Times*, July 17, page 1.

"Tochikiseihō ga Seiritsue, Kokkaimae dewa Hantai-shūkai" [Land Control Act is to be Passed, Protests in front of the Diet]. 2021. *Okinawa Times*, June 16. Accessed November 6, 2021. https://www.okinawatimes.co.jp/articles/-/770839

"Tsuruho Tantōsō 'Sabetsu towa Danteidekinai'" [Unbale to Conclude that it is Discriminatory]. 2016. *Mainichi Shimbun*, November 8. Accessed October 14, 2018. https://mainichi.jp/articles/20161108/k00/00e/010/265000c

"Uehara Eiko" [Uehara Eiko]. n.d. *Kotobanku*. Accessed October 27, 2023. https://kotobank.jp/word/%E4%B8%8A%E5%8E%9F%20%E6%A0%84%E5%AD%90-1639556

"'Watashiga Yatta' to Shuttō" [A Suspect Reported to the Police, Saying, 'I did it']. 1987. *Okinawa Times*, October 27, page 23.

"Watashi no Iken." 1956. Unpublished manuscript written by a Henoko leader that I received in Henoko in March 1998.

"Yasukuni Sanpai, Abeshi no Kyōkō to Fūin, 'Shitubō' Beiseimei no Urade" [Mr. Abe's Yasukuni visit and discontinuation, against the background of American "disappointment"]. 2021. *Asahi Shimbun*, May 28. Accessed October 25, 2021. https://digital.asahi.com/articles/ASP5P4R1GP4NUTFK00S.html

"Yowagoshi Gaikō no Shiritataku" [Spanking Week-kneed Diplomacy]. 1956. *Ryukyu Shimpo*, June 26.

"Yui Akiko-san Shikyo." 2020. *Okinawa Times*, April 16, p. 23.

No Base

No Base is a newsletter published by the Tent Village in Henoko. It is archived at http://henoko.blog110.fc2.com/. Accessed March 31, 2020.

7/21/2014, #1065b, http://blog-imgs-63-origin.fc2.com/h/e/n/henoko/1065b.jpg
8/4/2014, #1072b, https://blog-imgs-63-origin.fc2.com/h/e/n/henoko/1072b.jpg
10/23/2014, #1107a, https://blog-imgs-46-origin.fc2.com/h/e/n/henoko/1107a.jpg
11/7/2014, #1113a, http://blog-imgs-46-origin.fc2.com/h/e/n/henoko/1113a.jpg
11/7/2014, #1113b, http://blog-imgs-46-origin.fc2.com/h/e/n/henoko/1113b.jpg
11/20/2014, #1118a, http://blog-imgs-46-origin.fc2.com/h/e/n/henoko/1118a.jpg
12/11/2014, #1126b, http://blog-imgs-46-origin.fc2.com/h/e/n/henoko/1126b.jpg
12/27/2014, #1132b, https://blog-imgs-77-origin.fc2.com/h/e/n/henoko/1132b.jpg
1/3/2015, #1134b, https://blog-imgs-77-origin.fc2.com/h/e/n/henoko/1134b.jpg
1/14/2015, #1137b, http://blog-imgs-77-origin.fc2.com/h/e/n/henoko/1137b.jpg
1/16/2015, #1138a, http://blog-imgs-77-origin.fc2.com/h/e/n/henoko/1138a.jpg

1/16/2015, #1138b, http://blog-imgs-77-origin.fc2.com/h/e/n/henoko/1138b.jpg
2/18/2015, #1153b, https://blog-imgs-77-origin.fc2.com/h/e/n/henoko/1153b.jpg
2/19/2015, #1154b, http://blog-imgs-77-origin.fc2.com/h/e/n/henoko/1154b.jpg
3/2/2015, #1159a, https://blog-imgs-73-origin.fc2.com/h/e/n/henoko/1159a.jpg
3/5/2015, #1161b, http://blog-imgs-73-origin.fc2.com/h/e/n/henoko/1161b.jpg
4/28/2015, #1184a, https://blog-imgs-73-origin.fc2.com/h/e/n/henoko/1184a.jpg
5/16/2015, #1191b, https://blog-imgs-73-origin.fc2.com/h/e/n/henoko/1191b.jpg
5/28/2015, #1196a, https://blog-imgs-73-origin.fc2.com/h/e/n/henoko/1196a.jpg
6/27/2015, #1208a, https://blog-imgs-76-origin.fc2.com/h/e/n/henoko/1208a.jpg
7/4/2015, #1211b, https://blog-imgs-80-origin.fc2.com/h/e/n/henoko/1211b.jpg
7/7/2015, #1212b, https://blog-imgs-80-origin.fc2.com/h/e/n/henoko/1212b.jpg
2/25/2016, #1301a, https://blog-imgs-88-origin.fc2.com/h/e/n/henoko/1301a.jpg
3/31/2016, #1314b, https://blog-imgs-84-origin.fc2.com/h/e/n/henoko/1314b.jpg
5/4/2016, #1326b, https://blog-imgs-94-origin.fc2.com/h/e/n/henoko/1326b.jpg
6/1/2016, #1335b, https://blog-imgs-94-origin.fc2.com/h/e/n/henoko/1335b.jpg
8/8/2016, #1360b, https://blog-imgs-94-origin.fc2.com/h/e/n/henoko/1360b.jpg
1/11/2017, #1414b, https://blog-imgs-98-origin.fc2.com/h/e/n/henoko/1414b.jpg
1/17/2017 #1416b, https://blog-imgs-98-origin.fc2.com/h/e/n/henoko/1416b.jpg
1/31/2017, #1422b https://blog-imgs-98-origin.fc2.com/h/e/n/henoko/1422b.jpg
2/13/2017, #1427a, https://blog-imgs-121-origin.fc2.com/h/e/n/henoko/1427a.jpg
2/19/2017, #1429a, https://blog-imgs-121-origin.fc2.com/h/e/n/henoko/1429a.jpg
3/7/2017, #1435b, https://blog-imgs-121-origin.fc2.com/h/e/n/henoko/1435b.jpg
4/4/2017, #1445b, https://blog-imgs-121-origin.fc2.com/h/e/n/henoko/1445b.jpg
4/24/2017, #1452a, https://blog-imgs-121-origin.fc2.com/h/e/n/henoko/1452a.jpg
4/29/2017, #1454b, https://blog-imgs-121-origin.fc2.com/h/e/n/henoko/1454b.jpg
5/9/2017, #1457b, https://blog-imgs-108-origin.fc2.com/h/e/n/henoko/1457b.jpg
6/13/2017, #1469a, https://blog-imgs-108-origin.fc2.com/h/e/n/henoko/1469a.jpg
8/12/2017 #1490b, https://blog-imgs-108-origin.fc2.com/h/e/n/henoko/1490b.jpg
9/4/2017, #1498b, https://blog-imgs-108-origin.fc2.com/h/e/n/henoko/1498b.jpg
9/30/2017, #1507a, https://blog-imgs-108-origin.fc2.com/h/e/n/henoko/1507a.jpg
10/11/2017, #1511b, https://blog-imgs-108-origin.fc2.com/h/e/n/henoko/1511b.jpg
11/11/2017, #1521b, https://blog-imgs-108-origin.fc2.com/h/e/n/henoko/1521b.jpg
11/14/2017, #1522b, https://blog-imgs-108-origin.fc2.com/h/e/n/henoko/1522b.jpg
11/21/2017, #1525b, https://blog-imgs-108-origin.fc2.com/h/e/n/henoko/1525b.jpg
11/30/2017, #1528a, https://blog-imgs-108-origin.fc2.com/h/e/n/henoko/1528a.jpg
12/3/2017, #1529b, https://blog-imgs-108-origin.fc2.com/h/e/n/henoko/1529b.jpg
1/11/2018, 1541b, https://blog-imgs-108-origin.fc2.com/h/e/n/henoko/1541b.jpg
1/27/2018, #1546a, https://blog-imgs-108-origin.fc2.com/h/e/n/henoko/1546a.jpg
1/31/2018, #1547b, https://blog-imgs-108-origin.fc2.com/h/e/n/henoko/1547b.jpg
2/13/2018, #1551b, https://blog-imgs-120-origin.fc2.com/h/e/n/henoko/1551b.jpg
2/14/2018, #1554b, https://blog-imgs-120-origin.fc2.com/h/e/n/henoko/1554b.jpg
3/8/2018, #1558a, https://blog-imgs-120-origin.fc2.com/h/e/n/henoko/1558a.jpg
3/11/2018, #1559b, https://blog-imgs-120-origin.fc2.com/h/e/n/henoko/1559b.jpg
3/14/2018, #1560b, https://blog-imgs-120-origin.fc2.com/h/e/n/henoko/1560b.jpg

3/18/2018, #1561a, https://blog-imgs-120-origin.fc2.com/h/e/n/henoko/1561a.jpg
3/22/2018, #1562b, https://blog-imgs-120-origin.fc2.com/h/e/n/henoko/1562b.jpg
4/7/2018, #1567b, https://blog-imgs-77-origin.fc2.com/h/e/n/henoko/1567b.jpg
5/9/2018, #1576a, https://blog-imgs-77-origin.fc2.com/h/e/n/henoko/1576a.jpg

Governmental Publications

Abe Cabinet. 2014. *Kuni no Zonritsu o Mattōshi, Kokumin o Mamorutame no Kiremenonai Anzenhoshō Hōsei no Seibi ni Tsuite* [Cabinet Decision on Development of Seamless Security Legislation toEnsure Japan's Survival and Protect its People]. Tokyo: Kantei. Accessed December 22, 2020. http://www.cas.go.jp/jp/gaiyou/jimu/pdf/anpohosei.pdf

"Administrative Agreement under Article III of the Security Treaty between Japan and the United States of America." Accessed October 21, 2023. https://worldjpn.net/documents/texts/docs/19520228.T1E.html#:~:text=The%20facilities%20and%20areas%20used,a%20view%20toward%20such%20return

"Agreement under Article VI of the Treaty of Mutual Cooperation and Security between Japan and the Unites States of America, Regarding Facilities and Areas and the Status of United States Armed Forces in Japan" (also known as SOFA). Accessed December 16, 2020. https://www.mofa.go.jp/mofaj/area/usa/sfa/pdfs/fulltext.pdf

ASEAN-Japan Centre. 2014. ASEAN Information Map. Accessed May 28, 2022. https://www.asean.or.jp/ja/wp-content/uploads/sites/2/2013/08/70d02737c4a8e9ae30da2654c2c6e4ee1.pdf

Bōeishō. n.d.-a. "Katsudō Shūryōshita PKO Katsudō (1992nen~2000nen)" [Completed PKO missions, 1992–2000]. Accessed December 21, 2020. https://www.mod.go.jp/j/approach/kokusai_heiwa/pko/1992_2000.html

Bōeishō. n.d.-b. "Iraku Jindō Fukkōshien Tokusohō ni Motozuku Taiōsochi" [Measures based on a Special Law for the Humanitarian Support Mission in Iraq]. Accessed December 22, 2020. https://www.mod.go.jp/j/approach/kokusai_heiwa/terotoku/iraq/index.html

Bōeishō. n.d.-c. "Katsudō Shūryōshita PKO Katsudō (2001nen-2010nen)" [Completed PKO missions, 2001–2010]. Accessed December 22, 2020. https://www.mod.go.jp/j/approach/kokusai_heiwa/pko/2001_2010.html

Bōeishō. n.d.-d. "Kokusai Kinkyūenjo Katsudōnado" [International Emergency Relief Operations]. Accessed December 22, 2020. https://www.mod.go.jp/j/approach/kokusai_heiwa/kokusai_enjyo/index.html

Bōeishō. n.d.-e. "Somaria-oki/Aden-wan ni Okeru Kaizokutaisho" [Anti-piracy activities in places such the waters off Somalia and the Gulf of Aden]. Accessed December 22. 2020. https://www.mod.go.jp/j/approach/kokusai_heiwa/somaria/index.html

Bōeishō. n.d.-f. "Beigunsaihen no Omona Shinchoku Jyōkyō" [Progression Status of the Restructuring of the US Forces]. Accessed December 22, 2020. https://www.mod.go.jp/j/approach/zaibeigun/saihen/sintyoku.html#sintyoku05

Bōeishō. n.d.-g. "Hokubu Kunrenjō no Kahan no Henkan/Hikiwatashi ni Tsuite"

[On the Return of more than Half of the Northern Training Area]. Accessed December 23, 2020. https://www.mod.go.jp/j/approach/zaibeigun/saco/hokubu_henkan.html

Bōeishō. 2008. *'Tero tono Tatakai' to Jieitai no Katsudō* ['War on Terrorism' and Activities of the Self-Defense Forces]. Accessed December 22, 2020. https://www.mod.go.jp/j/approach/kokusai_heiwa/terotoku/pdf/tatakai_katsudou.pdf

Bōeishō. 2013a. "Kadena Hikōjō-inan no Tochi no Henkan" [Returning of Land south of Kadena]. Accessed November 15, 2023. https://www.mod.go.jp/j/approach/zaibeigun/saihen/pdf/20130405_fig_j.pdf

Bōeishō. 2013b. *Heisei 25nen-ban Bōei Hakusho* [Defense White Paper 2013]. Accessed December 22, 2020. http://www.clearing.mod.go.jp/hakusho_data/2013/2013/pdf/index.html (Citations refer to Part II, Chapter 3, Section 5.)

Bōeishō. 2016. *Heisei 28nen-ban Bōei Hakusho* [Defense White Paper 2016]. Accessed December 22, 2020. https://warp.da.ndl.go.jp/info:ndljp/pid/11502835/www.mod.go.jp/j/publication/wp/wp2016/pdf/index.html (Citations refer to Part II, Chapter 4, Section 4.)

Bōeishō. 2018. *Heisei 30nen-ban Bōei Hakusho* [Defense White Paper 2018]. Accessed December 22, 2020. http://www.clearing.mod.go.jp/hakusho_data/2018/pdf/index.html (Citations refer to Part III, Chapter 1, Section 2.)

Clinton, William J. 2000. "Remarks at the National Peace Memorial Park in Okinawa, Japan." Delivered July 21. Accessed September 8, 2023. https://www.presidency.ucsb.edu/documents/remarks-the-national-peace-memorial-park-okinawa-japan

Command History Branch Office of the Joint Secretary Headquarters CINCPAC. 1977. "Forces and Basing in Japan." In *Commander in Chief Pacific Command History*, Volume 1, 37–41. Camp H. M. Smith, HI: Command History Branch Office of the Joint Secretary Headquarters CINCPAC.

Department of Defense. 1995. *United States Security Strategy for the East Asia-Pacific Region*. Washington, DC: Office of International Security Affairs.

Department of Defense. 2003. *Military Transformation: A Strategic Approach*. Washington, DC: Office of the Secretary of Defense.

Department of Defense. 2018. *Summary of the 2018 National Defense Strategy of the United States*. Accessed December 22, 2020. https://dod.defense.gov/Portals/1/Documents/pubs/2018-National-Defense-Strategy-Summary.pdf

Department of Education [Japan]. 1909. *The Imperial Rescript on Education: Translated into Chinese, English, French, & German*. Tokyo: Department of Education. Accessed October 13, 2018. https://babel.hathitrust.org/cgi/pt?id=ucl.ax0000968321;view=1up;seq=7

"Enclosure to Dispatch No. 1293 dated September 22, 1947, from the United States Political Adviser for Japan, Tokyo, on the subject 'Emperor of Japan's Opinion Concerning the Future of the Ryukyu Islands.'" [1947] 2001. In *Okinawaken Heiwakinen Shiryōkan Sōgōan'nai* [Okinawa Prefectural Peace Memorial Museum Comprehensive Guide], edited by Okinawa Prefectural Peace Memorial Museum (OPPMM), 181. Itoman, Okinawa: Okinawan Prefectural Peace Memorial Museum.

e-Stat. 1950. *Shōwas 25nen Kokusei Chōsa: 100 Zen-Ryukyu, Sangyōdaibunruibetu, Nenreikaikyūbetsu, 14sai-ijō Ryukyu Shyūgyō Jinkō (Danjo)* [National Census 1950, 100 All Ryukyus, Employed Ryukyuan Nationals 14 years of age and over, by industry and by age group]. Accessed December 12, 2020. https://www.e-st at.go.jp/stat-search/files?page=1&layout=datalist&toukei=00200521&tstat=00 0001036869&cycle=0&tclass1=000001038722&result_page=1&tclass2val=0

e-Stat. 1955. *Shōwa 30nen Kokusei Chōsa: 2. Nenrei Kakusai oyobi Danjobetsu Jinkō, Zen-Ryukyu* [National Census 1955, 2. population by age and by sex, all Ryukyus]. Accessed December 12, 2020. https://www.e-stat.go.jp/stat-search ?page=1&query=%E6%98%AD%E5%92%8C30%E5%B9%B4%E5%9B%BD %E5%8B%A2%E8%AA%BF%E6%9F%BB%20%2F%20%E3%80%90%E6%B2 %96%E7%B8%84%E3%80%91&layout=dataset&metadata=1&data=1

e-Stat. 1960. *Shōwa 35nen Kokusei Chōsa:Okinawa, Jinkō-hen, Dai 1-kan Sōkatsu-hen Sono1; 13 Sangyō, Nenrei (5sai Kaikyū) oyobi Danjobetsu 15sai-ijō Shūgyōsha* [National Census 1960: Okinawa, Population; 13 Employed Ryukyuan Nationals 15 years of age and over, by industry, by age group (5 years), and by sex]. Accessed December 12, 2020. https://www.e-stat.go.jp/stat-search/files?page=1 &layout=datalist&toukei=00200521&tstat=000001036867&cycle=0&tclass1=0 00001038757&tclass2val=0

e-Stat. 2010. *Kokuseichōsa Heisei 22nen Kokuseichōsa Jinkōnadokihontōkei: Hyō Bangō 00310* [2010 National Census, Basic Statistics about Population and Other Items, Table Number 00310]. Accessed October 27, 2020. https://www .e-stat.go.jp/dbview?sid=0003038588

e-Stat. 2015. *Heisei 27nen Kokusei Chōsa Jinkō nado Kihon Shūkei, Hyō Bango 00310* [2015 National Census, Basic Statistics about Population and Other Items, Table Number 00310]. https://www.e-stat.go.jp/dbview?sid=0003149249

FRUS (Foreign Relations of the United States). 1947. "General of the Army Douglas MacArthur to the Secretary of State." In *The Far East Volume VI*, 512–515. Accessed December 19, 2020. https://history.state.gov/historicaldocuments/frus1 947v06/pg_512

FRUS (Foreign Relations of the United States). 1948a. "Report by the Director of the Policy Planning Staff (Kennan)." In *The Far East and Australasia, Volume VI*, 691–719. Accessed March 27, 2022. https://history.state.gov/historicaldocu ments/frus1948v06/d519

FRUS (Foreign Relations of the United States). 1948b. NSC 13/2 "Report by the National Security Council on Recommendations With Respect to United States Policy Toward Japan." In *The Far East and Australasia, Volume VI*, 857–862, and 877. Accessed December 19, 2020. https://history.state.gov/historicaldocumen ts/frus1948v06/pg_858

FRUS (Foreign Relations of the United States). 1949. NSC 13/3 "Report by the National Security Council on Recommendations With Respect to United States Policy Toward Japan." In *The Far East and Australasia, Volume VII, Part 2*, 730–735. Accessed December 10, 2020. https://history.state.gov/historicaldocumen ts/frus1949v07p2/d70

414   REFERENCES

FRUS (Foreign Relations of the United States). 1950a. "Memorandum by the Supreme Commander for Allied Powers." In *East Asia and the Pacific, Volume VI*, 1213–1221. Accessed December 19, 2020. https://history.state.gov/historicaldo cuments/frus1950v06/pg_1213

FRUS (Foreign Relations of the United States). 1950b. "Memorandum by the Consultant to the Secretary (Dulles)." In *East Asia and the Pacific, Volume VI*, 1229–1230. Accessed December 19, 2020. https://history.state.gov/historicaldocume nts/frus1950v06/pg_1229

FRUS (Foreign Relations of the United States). 1950c. "Memorandum by the Supreme Commander for the Allied Powers (MacArthur)." In *East Asia and the Pacific, Volume VI*, 1227–1228. Accessed December 19, 2020. https://history.st ate.gov/historicaldocuments/frus1950v06/pg_1227

Gaimushō. 2005. "Yūji Hōsei." In *Dai 48-gō, Heisei 17nen-ban Gaikō Seisho* [2005 Diplomacy Blue Book Volume 48]. Accessed May 28, 2022. https://www.mofa .go.jp/mofaj/gaiko/bluebook/2005/html/honmon3106.html

General Accounting Office. 1989. *U.S.-Japan Burden Sharing: Japan Has Increased Its Contributions but Could Do More*. Washington, DC: General Accounting Office. Accessed December 21, 2020. https://www.gao.gov/assets/150/148034 .pdf

Ginowanshi. 2020. *Ginowanshi no Gaiyō* [An Overview of Ginowan City]. Accessed November 7, 2020. https://www.city.ginowan.lg.jp/shisei/shokai/2/3427.html #:~:text=%E3%81%BE%E3%81%9F%E6%99%AE%E5%A4%A9%E9%96%93 %E3%82%92%E4%B8%AD%E5%BF%83%E3%81%AB,%E5%B8%82%E3%80 %8D%E3%81%8C%E8%AA%95%E7%94%9F%E3%81%97%E3%81%BE%E3 %81%97%E3%81%9F%E3%80%82

"Guidelines for U.S.-Japan Defense Cooperation." [1978] n.d. Accessed December 21, 2020. https://www.mod.go.jp/e/d_act/us/anpo/19781127.html

"Guidelines for U.S.-Japan Defense Cooperation." (Second Edition). [1997] n.d. Accessed December 21, 2020. https://www.mod.go.jp/e/d_act/us/anpo/19970923 .html

"Guidelines for U.S.-Japan Defense Cooperation." (Third Edition). [2015] n.d. Accessed December 21, 2020. https://www.mod.go.jp/e/d_act/us/anpo/shishin _20150427e.html

Hatoyama Cabinet. 2009. "Ajia eno Atarashī Komittomento: Higashi Ajia Kyōdōtai Kōsō no Jitsugen ni Mukete" [New Commitment to Asia: Toward Realization of the Conception of the Community of East Asia]. *Shushō Kantei*, November 15. Accessed May 31, 2022. https://www.kantei.go.jp/jp/hatoyama/statement/2009 11/15singapore.html

"'Incoming Airgram: Department of State, Number G-230,' U.S. Ambassador Douglas MacArthur II to the Secretary of State, 5 November 1959." [1959] 2013. In Fukawa Reiko and Niihara Shoji, *Sunagawa Jiken to Tanaka Saikōsai Chōkan: Beikaikin Bunsho ga Akirakanishita Nihon no Shihō* [The Sungawa Case and Chief Justice of the Supreme Court Kotaro Tanaka: Japanese Judicial Practice Debunked by Declassified US Government Documents], 64–67. Tokyo: Nihonhyōronsha,

Japan-U.S. Joint Declaration on Security, Alliance for the 21st Century. [1996] n.d. Accessed December 21, 2020. https://www.mofa.go.jp/region/n-america/us/security/security.html

Keizai Kikakuchō. 1956. "Ketsugo" [Conclusion]. In *Shōwa 31nen Nenji Keizai Hōkoku* [1956 Economic White Paper]. Accessed October 21, 2023. https://www5.cao.go.jp/keizai3/keizaiwp/wp-je56/wp-je56-010501.html

Keizai Kikakuchō. 1972. *Nenji Keizai Hōkoku: Atarashii Fukushishakai no Kensetsu* [Annual Economic Report; Toward Construction of a New Welfare Society]. Accessed December 11, 2020. https://www5.cao.go.jp/keizai3/keizaiwp/wp-je72/wp-je72-s0030.html

Keizai-Sangyōshō. 2010. *Tsūshō Hakusho 2010, Dai2-sho* [Trade White Paper 2010, chapter 2]. Accessed May 28, 2022. https://dl.ndl.go.jp/info:ndljp/pid/3487788/11?tocOpened=1

Keizai-Sangyōshō. 2011. *Tsūshō Hakusho 2011, Dai2-shō, dai1-setsu-2* [Trade White Paper 2011, chapter 2, section 2–1]. Accessed May 28, 2022. https://www.meti.go.jp/report/tsuhaku2011/2011honbun/html/i2120000.html

Keizai-Sangyōshō. 2019. *Tsūshō Hakusho 2019, Dai2-shō* [Trade White Paper 2019, chapter 2]. Accessed June 29, 2021. https://www.meti.go.jp/report/tsuhaku2019/pdf/02-01-01.pdf https://www.meti.go.jp/report/tsuhaku2019/pdf/02-01-02.pdf

Kinchō to Kichi Henshū Īnkai. 1991. *Kinchō to Kichi* [Kin Town and the Base]. Kinchō, Okinawa: Kinchō to Kichi Henshū Īnkai.

Kōsei-Rōdōshō. n.d. *Hiseikikoyō no Genjō to Kadai* [Current Conditions and Challenges concerning Non-Fulltime Employment]. Accessed August 11, 2023. https://www.mhlw.go.jp/content/001078285.pdf

Kōsei-Rōdōshō. 2015. "Kakushusetai no Shotokunado no Jyōkyō" [The Situation of Income and Other Conditions of a Variety of Households]. In *Heisei 27-nen Kokumin Seikatsu Kisochōsa no Gaikyō* [General Situations of the Living Conditions of the Nation, 2015]. Accessed December 22, 2020. https://www.mhlw.go.jp/toukei/saikin/hw/k-tyosa/k-tyosa15/dl/03.pdf

Kōsei-Rōdōshō. 2019. "Kakushusetai no Shotokunado no Jyōkyō" [The Situation of Income and Other Conditions of a Variety of Households]. In *2019-nen Kokumin Seikatsu Kisochōsa no Gaikyō* [General Situations of the Living Conditions of the Nation, 2019]. Accessed December 22, 2020. https://www.mhlw.go.jp/toukei/saikin/hw/k-tyosa/k-tyosa19/dl/03.pdf

Monbu Kagakushō. 1992.*Gakusei 120-nenshi* [A 120-Years History of the Education System]. Tokyo: Gyousei. The citation comes from the following link. https://www.mext.go.jp/b_menu/hakusho/html/others/detail/1318346.htm

Monbushō. 1942. "Nihon Sekaikan to Sekai Shinchitsujo no Kensetsu" [The Japanese Worldview and the Construction of a New World Order]. In *Shūhō* 292 (May 14 Issue): 2–8.

Naikakufu. 2013. *Kokuei Okinawa Kinen Kōen Shurijōchiku Seibi Keikaku* [National Okinawa Commemorative Park, the Shuriō Area Development Plan]. Accessed December 14, 2020. http://www.dc.ogb.go.jp/kouen/shurijo/pdf/H2503syuri_seibikeikaku.pdf

Okinawa Kenritsu Maizō Bunkazai Sentā and Nago City Kyōiku Īinkai. 2020.

Kyampu Shuwabu Kaiikibunkzai Bunpu Chōsa [A Study of Distribution of Cultural Property in the Camp Schwab Ocean Area]. Okinawa: Okinawa Kenritsu Maizō Bunkazai Sentā and Nago City Kyōiku Iīnkai. Accessed October 31, 2020. https://sitereports.nabunken.go.jp/en/70238

Okinawa Prefectural Government. 2018. *What Okinawa Wants You to Understand about the U.S. Military Bases*. Naha, Okinawa. Accessed March 31, 2024. https://storage.googleapis.com/studio-design-asset-files/projects/8dO8BMJran/s-1x1_9c23c775-11dd-463e-9814-47ab30f2d811.pdf

Okinawaken Chijikōshitsu Kichitaisakuka. 2017a. "FAC6051 Futenma Hikōjō" [FAC6051 Futenma Air Station]. Accessed February 13, 2017. https://www.pref.okinawa.jp/site/chijiko/kichitai/1224.html

Okinawaken Chijikōshitsu Kichitaisakuka. 2017b. "FAC6009 Kyanpu Shuwābu" [FAC6009Camp Schwab]. Accessed February 13, 2017. https://www.pref.okinawa.jp/site/chijiko/kichitai/1185.html

Okinawaken Chijikōshitsu Kichitaisakuka. 2020. *Okinawa no Beigun oyobi Jieitai Kichi (Tōkeishiryō-shū)* [Bases of the US Military and Self-Defense Forces in Okinawa (Statistics)]. Naha, Okinawa: Okinawaken Chijikōshitsu Kichitaisakuka. Accessed May 15, 2022. https://www.pref.okinawa.jp/site/chijiko/kichitai/syogai/toukeishiryousyur2.html

Okinawaken Chijikōkōshitsu Kōhōka. 1996. *Okinawa karano Messēji* [A Message from Okinawa]. Naha, Okinawa: Okinawaken Chijikōkōshitsu Kōhōka.

Okinawaken Kikakubu Tōkeika. n.d.-a. *Nenrei (5sai-Kaikyū), Danjobetsu Jinkō oyobi Seihi (Taishō 9nen-Shōwa 10nen, Shōwa 30nen-Heisei 17nen)* [Population of Okinawa Prefecture by 5 Years of Age and Sex, from 1920–1935 and from 1955 to 2005]. Accessed June 25, 2022. https://www.pref.okinawa.jp/toukeika/pc/jinkou/okinawa_jinkou.html

Okinawaken Kikakubu Tōkeika. n.d.-b. *Rōdōryoku Chōsa Dai-2hyō* [Survey of Labor Power, Table #2]. Accessed December 15, 2020. https://www.pref.okinawa.jp/toukeika/long-term/longterm_index.html#2

Okinawaken Kikakubu Tōkeika. n.d.-c. *Rōdōryoku Chōsa Dai-1hyō* [Survey of Labor Power, Table #1]. Accessed December 15, 2020. https://www.pref.okinawa.jp/toukeika/long-term/longterm_index.html#2

Okinawaken Kikakubu Tōkeika. n.d.-d. Heisei 7nen Kokusei Chōsa [National Census]. Accessed September 23, 2023. https://view.officeapps.live.com/op/view.aspx?src=https%3A%2F%2Fwww.pref.okinawa.jp%2Ftoukeika%2Fpc%2F1995%2Fpc1995_2_47_03r.xls&wdOrigin=BROWSELINK

Okinawaken Kikakubu Tōkeika. 2022. *Rōdōryoku Chōsa: Reiwa 4nen Heikin* [Survey of Labor Power: 2022 Average]. Accessed September 29, 2023. https://www.pref.okinawa.jp/toukeika/lfs/2022/2022y/lfs2022a.pdf

Okinawaken Kōbunshokan. n.d. *Navy Military Government Proclamation Number 1*. Accessed December 11, 2020. https://www3.archives.pref.okinawa.jp/RDA/ryusei/RDAP000031/index.html?title=%E6%B5%B7%E8%BB%8D%E8%BB%8D%E6%94%BF%E5%BA%9C%E5%B8%83%E5%91%8A%2FNavy%20Military%20Government%20Proclamation%20%E7%AC%AC001%E5%8F%B7

Okinawaken Kyōikushinkōkai. 1976. *Konketsuji Jittai Chōsa Houkokusho* [A Report on Actual Conditions of Mixed-Race Children]. Okinawa: Okinawa Kyōkai.

Okinawsken Sōmubu Chijikōshitsu Kichitaisakushitsu. n.d. *Okinawa no Beigunkichi* [US Bases in Okinawa] (pamphlet). Naha, Okinawa: Okinawsken Sōmubu Chijikōshitsu Kichitaisakushitsu.

Okinawaken Sōmubu Chijikōshitsu Kichitaisakushitsu. 1998. *Okinawa no Beigun Kichi* [US Bases in Okinawa]. Naha, Okinawa: Okinawaken Sōmubu Chiji Kōshitsu Kichitaisakushitsu.

Okinawaken Sōmubu Chijikōshitsu Kichitaisakuka. 2022. *Okinawa no Beigun oyobi Jieitai Kichi (Tōkeishiryōshū Reiwa 4nen 7gatsu)* [Bases of US Military and Japan's Self-Defense Forces in Okinawa (Statistical Materials), July 2022]. Naha, Okinawa: Okinawaken Sōmubu Chijikōshitsu Kichitaisakuka. Accessed March 31, 2024. https://www.pref.okinawa.jp/heiwakichi/kichi/1017273/1017274/1025057/1017275.html

Report of Hu Jintao to the 18th CPC National Congress. 2012. *Firmly March on the Path of Socialism with Chinese Characteristics and Strive to Complete the Building of a Moderately Prosperous Society in All Respects*, Report to the Eighteenth National Congress of the Communist Party of China, November 8, 2012. China.org.cn, November 16. Accessed December 22, 2020.

Ryukyu Seifu/Okinawaken Kyōikuiinkai. [1965-1977] 1989. Okinawakenshi 23-kan, Bessatsu 1 [Okinawa Prefectural History 23 Volumes and One Separate Volume]. Tokyo: Kokusho Kankōkai.

Saibansho. 1959. "Saikōsai Hanrei Jiken Bangō Shōwa 34 (A)710 [Supreme Court Decisions, Case Number Shōwa 34(A)710]," December 16. Accessed December 20, 2020. http://www.courts.go.jp/app/hanrei_jp/detail2?id=55816

Sōmushō Tōkeikyoku. 1996. "96nen 11gatsu 29nichi zuke Tōkeikyoku Infomēshon (NO. 141)" [Statistical Bureau Information issued on 11–29-1996 (Number 141)]. Accessed October 14, 2018. https://view.officeapps.live.com/op/view.aspx?src=https%3A%2F%2Fwww.stat.go.jp%2Fdata%2Fkokusei%2F1995%2Fzuhyou%2F06273.xls&wdOrigin=BROWSELINK

SACO (Special Action Committee on Okinawa). 1996. "Final Report." Ministry of Foreign Affairs. Accessed on December 21, 2015. http://www.mofa.go.jp/region/n-america/us/security/96saco1.html

Standing Committee of the National People's Congress. 2021. "Coast Guard Law of the People's Republic of China." Accessed July 11, 2021. https://www.lawinfochina.com/display.aspx?id=34610&lib=law&SearchKeyword=&SearchCKeyword=

Treaty of Peace with Japan. Accessed December 20, 2020. https://treaties.un.org/doc/publication/unts/volume%20136/volume-136-i-1832-english.pdf

United Nations. n.d. The Charter of the United Nations. Accessed December 19, 2020. https://www.un.org/en/charter-united-nations/

United Nations Framework Convention on Climate Change. 2022. Accessed May 15, 2022. https://unfccc.int/process-and-meetings/conferences/the-big-picture/what-are-united-nations-climate-change-conferences

United Nations General Assembly. n.d. "Emergency Special Sessions." Accessed May 15, 2022. https://www.un.org/en/ga/sessions/emergency.shtml

United States. Congress. Senate. Committee on Armed Services. 1951. *Military Situation in the Far East: Hearings Before the Committee on Armed Services and the Committee on Foreign Relations, United States Senate, Eighty-second Congress, First Session, to Conduct an Inquiry Into the Military Situation in the Far East and the Facts Surrounding the Relief of General of the Army MacArthur from His Assignments in that Area, Part 1*. Accessed December 29, 2020. https://books.google.com/books?id=mjc13Io6FkoC&printsec=frontcover&source=gbs_ge_summary_r&cad=0#v=onepage&q&f=false

United States Forces Korea. n.d. *Combined Forces Command, Mission of the ROK/US Combined Forces Command*. Accessed December 21, 2020. https://www.usfk.mil/About/Combined-Forces-Command/#:~:text=Established%20on%20November%207%2C%201978,outside%20aggression%20against%20the%20ROK

United States Navy Department. 1944. *Civil Affairs Handbook: Ryukyu (Loochoo) Islands*. Washington, DC: Office of the Chief of Naval Operations.

US-Japan Security Consultative Committee. 2005. *US-Japan Alliance: Transformation and Realignment for the Future*. Accessed October 29, 2020. http://www.mofa.go.jp/region/n-america/us/security/scc/doc0510.html

US-Japan Security Consultative Committee. 2006. *United States–Japan Roadmap for Realignment Implementation*. Accessed October 29, 2020. https://www.mofa.go.jp/region/n-america/us/security/scc/doc0605.html

USMC (United States Marine Corps). n.d.-a. "What is a MAGTF?" Accessed December 21, 2020. https://www.26thmeu.marines.mil/About/MAGTF/

USMC (United States Marine Corps). n.d.-b. "Types of MAGTFs." Accessed December 21, 2020. https://www.candp.marines.mil/Organization/MAGTF/Types-of-MAGTFs/

USMC (United States Marine Corps). n.d.-c. "The 31st MEU." Accessed December 21, 2020. https://www.31stmeu.marines.mil/About/History/

USMC (United States Marine Corps). n.d.-d. "Expeditionary Advanced Base Operations (EABO)." Accessed March 31, 2024. https://www.marines.mil/News/News-Display/Article/2708120/expeditionary-advanced-base-operations-eabo/

USMC (United States Marine Corps). 2020. *Force Design 2030*. Accessed December 23, 2020. https://www.hqmc.marines.mil/Portals/142/Docs/CMC38%20Force%20Design%202030%20Report%20hase%20I%20and%20II.pdf?ver=2020-03-26-121328-460

INDEX

Abe cabinet, 57, 78, 86
Abe Shinzō, 49, 50, 182, 242, 246
accidents, 135
Acheson, Dean Gooderham, 210
activism. *See* anti-base protests; sit-ins
administrative actions theory (*tōchikōi-ron*), 203, 218, 219–20
Administrative Agreement under Article III of the Security Treaty between Japan and the United States of America (1952), 218
"adopted children" in *kokutai* concept, 255
aerial sepulture (wind burial), 258
Afghanistan, 228, 305–6
Agamben, Giorgio, 93
age. *See* generations
Agency of Cultural Affairs, 267–68
Agreement under Article VI of the Treaty of Mutual Cooperation and Security between Japan and the United States of America, Regarding Facilities and Areas and the Status of United States Armed Forces in Japan (SOFA), 194n9
agriculture, 123
Ahagon Shōkō, 20
Aichi Triennale (2019), 267–68
Ainu people, and nationalism/*dojin* discourse, 252, 253, 254, 255, 260
Airakuen Sanatorium, 96–97, 120, 154n7
Aka Island, 191
Akihito and Michiko (emperor and empress), 26, 190, 308–19; anti-imperial sentiments in Okinawa and, 315–17; democratic ideals and, 314–15, 318–19; general will/mimetic faculty of Okinawan multitude and, 320–21; marriage, 315; visits to Okinawa, 309–13, 316, 317, 320; visits to other countries, 313–14, 321nn6–7
Akutagawa Prize, 136, 148

Al Jazeera, 80
Allen, Matthew, 95, 170
All-Okinawa Council to Realize the "Okinawa Petition," 57–58
All-Okinawa movement against the FRF construction, 4
ambivalence, 196; Freud on, 14, 107, 277; internal capacity of community of *nuchi du takara* to embrace contradictory perspectives, 6, 18–19, 21, 33–34, 39, 65, 115, 133, 134, 283. *See also* constituent and constituted power, *nuchi du takara* mediates contradiction; US military, ambivalence toward
Americanization, dream of, 136
Ames, Christopher, 177
Amuro Namie, 297–98
analog capitalism, 250, 261
ancestor worship. *See tōtōme* (Okinawan-style mortuary tablet)
Anderson, Benedict, 250
androcentric community, formation of, 112–53, 278; ambivalence toward US military (1950–1957), 112, 122–34; deepening ambivalence toward US military (1958–1966), 112, 134–41; formation of Okinawan "people," 112, 122–34; formation of two taboos, 112, 134–41; local time-space, transition to national time-space, 112, 141–53; love and trust toward US military (1945–1949), 112, 113–22, 132. *See also* heterosocial taboo (sexual relationships between US servicemen and Okinawan women); homosocial taboo (friendship with US military)
androcentric taboos. *See* heterosocial taboo (sexual relationships between US servicemen and Okinawan women); homosocial taboo (friendship with US military)

419

420 INDEX

androcentrism, 15–16, 107, 109, 133–34; androcentric nationalism, 14, 196; in Blanchot's writings, 35, 68; "changing sames" and, 171, 279; "first/second/third son" in *kokutai* concept, 255; Ishikawa's criticism of, 183; money and, 162, 279; preservation of, through rewriting homosocial taboo, 172–77; at protests, 68, 71, 103, 187; *tōtōme* practices, 164–72. See also androcentric community, formation of

Angst, Linda, 187, 291

anti-base/pro-base binary: collaboration between, 70; overlap across, 4, 17–23, 34, 70, 83

anti-base protests, 3–5, 36–37, 38–63, 124, 218–19; androcentrism of, 68, 71, 103, 187; arrests of protesters, 53–54, 71–72, 76; businesses in support of, 69–70; Camp Schwab fortification plan, 49–50, 57–58; canoes and fishing boats used in, 45–46, 54–56, 70–71, 72, 81; debates on rationale for building FRF, 38, 48–50; decline in, 4–5, 102, 103; *dojin*/official nationalism and, 263–64; draining of oppositional energy, 84–85; during Covid-19 pandemic, 102; feminist global network of, 79–80; financial contributions to, 92; first period in Henoko (2004-2005), 38–48; impact of, 56–57; lawsuits as protest tactics, 47, 58, 60, 63n4; maintaining US bases in post-reversion Okinawa, 178; manipulation of, by Washington/Tokyo, 39–40, 136, 153, 161; music, art, and education at, 68–69, 72–73, 74–75, 78; "no admittance" zone, 54–55, 71–72; Others in, 81–83; protesters from Japan "proper," 46–47, 48, 66, 81, 83; second period in Henoko (2013-2023), 50–63; sites of, 51, 54–55, 65, 67–70, 76–77, 87–88, 102; solidarity protesters, 46–47, 80; sousveillance by protesters, 77–81; surveillance of, 75–76, 77, 82; Tent Village, 51, 52, 71, 72–75, 88; violent intervention of, 53–54. See also community of *nuchi du takara*, formation of; generations, at anti-base protests; Inochi o Mamoru Kai (Society for the Protection of Life); rape incident of 1995, protest against; sit-ins

anti-base sentiments, 2–5, 17–23, 34, 102–4; Battle of Okinawa as grounding for, 110; disappearance of, in post-reversion Okinawa, 104, 161–62; dugongs' importance in, 47, 63n4, 85–86, 91–93, 94; feminist global network, 79–80; land seizures as grounding for, 124, 127. See also heterosocial taboo (sexual relationships between US servicemen and Okinawan women); homosocial taboo (friendship with US military); pro-base sentiments

"anti-piracy activities," by Self-Defense Forces, 241

"anti-reversion" *(han-fukki)*, 334

antiwar movements, 193n4

Arakawa Akira, 156n18, 334

Arasaki Kyōtarō, 173–74

Arasaki Moriteru, 80, 84, 91, 187

ARD (consortium of public broadcasters in Germany), 80

Armitage, Richard, and Joseph Nye, 240, 242, 243, 244, 245

arrests: jurisdiction and legality of, 135, 178, 194n9; of Okinawa People's Party activists, 125; of protesters, 53–54, 71–72, 76. See also police

art. See music, art, and culture

ARTE (Franco-German television network), 80

Article 1 of the Constitution of Japan (popular sovereignty), 208–9, 327

Article 9 of the Constitution of Japan (unarmed peace), 202; abandonment/reinterpretation in Empire v3, 242, 245; administrative actions theory and, 220; collective security paradigm and, 327, 332; demilitarization and, 209; occupation of Japan and, 211; San Francisco system and, 217; self-defense and, 218, 220, 223

artillery live-fire training, 243

Aru Hizumi (A Strain) (novella, Fukumura), 298–99

Asahi Shimbun (newspaper), 98, 260, 262, 266

Ashida Hitoshi, 260

Ashitomi Hiroshi, 41, 69, 99

Asia-Pacific Economic Cooperation (APEC), 230–31, 237–38

Asia-Pacific region: Cold War intensification in, 121; concept of, and US-Japan security alliance, 230–31; policy proposal for collective security from an Okinawan perspective (PPCSOP), 331–38

"Asia-Pacific War," 28n1, 231

Asō Tarō, 49

Assatsu no Umi: Okinawa, Henoko (The Ocean Where Freedom Is Suppressed: Henoko, Okinawa; documentary), 78

assimilation. *See* Japanization
Association for Southeast Asian Nations (ASEAN), 228
Atarashī Rekishikyōkasho o Tsukuru Kai (Association for History Textbook Reform), 237
Atlantic Charter (1941), 154n4, 215
Atsuki Hibi in Kyampu Hansen!! (Blazing Days in Camp Hansen!!; Ishikawa), 180
August 6, 313
August 9, 313
August 15, 286–87, 313
Australia, 238, 242
Azami to Seppun (Thistles and Kisses; Yae), 120

Bakushōmondai (comedy duo), 78
"bare life," 93
Barske, Valerie, 144
Bataille, Georges, 34, 35, 37n1
Battle of Okinawa (Operation Iceberg, 1945), 1, 14, 28n1, 102, 194n11; compulsory group suicide during, 17, 113–14, 133–34, 258; Governor Ōta during, 191–92; as grounding for anti-base sentiments, 110; Himeyuri Corps, 288; OPPMM, 190–91; postmemory and intergenerational recall, 93–94, 97–99. *See also* World War II
BBC, 80
Beddotaimu Aizu (Bedtime Eyes; Yamada), 180
beigunsaihen-kōfukin (subsidies for reorganization of US bases), 241
Benjamin, Walter, 5, 33, 279
bilateral alliances, 240, 242–43. *See also* US-Japan security alliance; to be restructured as multilateral, 332
binaries, 21–22. *See also* anti-base/pro-base binary; Self/Other binary
Binnendijk, Johannes, 149
biodiversity. *See* non-human creatures, included in Okinawan multitude
A Bird of Rainbows (Niji no Tori) (Medoruma), 5
Black servicemen, 116, 121; discrimination against mixed-race Okinawans and, 298–99; Ishikawa Mao's photography, 179–80, 183; rape incident of 1995, 185
Black Skin, White Masks (Fanon), 277–78
Blanchot, Maurice, 68; on community, 34, 35, 37nn1–3, 75
Broudy, Daniel, 161

Būgenbiria (Bougainvillea) (album, Cocco), 284–85
burakumin (historically mistreated lower-class Japanese living in particular settlements), 259, 266
"burden sharing," 225–26, 243–44
B-yen currency, 136, 158–59, 193n1

Campbell, Kurt, 230, 235
Camp Hansen, 130
Camp Schwab, 2, 4; creation of, 130, 219; Henoko's "friendship" with, 84, 174–75, 197; job site yard in, 44, 45, 51; layoffs at, 173; protests at gate of, 52–56, 65, 67–70, 76, 77, 102; protests on the sea, 70–72, 77, 102
Camp Schwab fortification plan, 38, 48–50, 51; opposition to, 49–50, 57–58
Canada, 163, 238
Cancian, Mark F., 63
canoes and fishing boats, in protests, 45–46, 54–55, 70–71, 72, 81
Capital (Marx), 157
capitalism, 157, 196; analog and digital, 250; Cocco's artistic interventions and, 294–95; reintegration of post-reversion Okinawa into Japan and, 261–62. *See also* money
Caraway, Paul, 130, 135
Carr, Myron, 183
Carter, Jimmy, 226
Carter, Mitzi Uehara, 300
Castells, Manuel, 91, 286
"changing sames," Okinawan subjectivity as, 14–16, 104, 193, 196–97, 321, 337–38; androcentrism and, 171, 279; Gilroy on changing sames, 14, 107; mimetic faculty of Okinawan multitude and, 15, 279; money and, 164
Chen, Kuan-Hsing, 323–24
Chibana Shōichi, 316
Chigasaki Beach protest, 218
Chikushi Tetsuya, 285, 286
children: language of, in official nationalism, 255; mixed-race, 132–33; poverty rate of, 89–90, 272; sexual violence and rape against, 127, 154n9, 185
China: Cold War and, 121; economy of, 239, 246; Imperial House visits to, 313; Japan's trade with, 248n7; maritime expansion of, 60; as part of Higashi Ajia Kyōdōtai (Community of East Asia), 49; reciprocity and, 226–27; regionalism and, 324; rise of in

China (continued)
multipolar world order, 90, 239–40, 265–66; Ryukyu Kingdom subordinated by, 155n14; Taiwan conflict, 240, 244, 325; tourists from, 85; US-China rapprochement, 226–27; US-Japan security alliance against, 50, 245–46, 273
Chinen Isao, 311–12
Chinese Communist Party, 246
Ching, Leo, 265
Choisan no Okinawa Nikki (Mr. Choi's Okinawa Diary; Kitaueda), 77
Chomsky, Noam, 80
Chūōkōron-sha, 260
Churasan (Beauty; TV drama series), 161
citizenship status, 297. *See also* Okinawan "citizens"
Civil Affairs Handbook: Ryukyu (Loochoo) Islands (US Navy Department 1944), 117–18
Civil Code of Japan (1868), 166
Civil Code of Japan (1957), 134, 169
Claude, Inis L., Jr., 329
climate change, 85–86, 330
Clinton, Bill, 21, 234
Coalition for Opposing the Offshore Base Construction (COOBC), 41, 56, 69, 74, 77, 80
Cocco (artist), 283–95; background, 283–84; *Būgenbiria* (album), 284–85; capitalism and, 294–95; fans, 294; "Heaven's hell" (song), 286, 287; "Hikōkigumo" (song), 284; Hill of Dugongs and ambivalence toward US military, 291–94; Himeyuri and, 288–91; "Jyugon no Mieru Oka" (song), 292–93; "Kubi" (song), 284; layers of *nuchi du takara* community and, 319; *Omoigoto* (book), 289, 292, 295–96; picture books, 285; as singer, 284–85; spiritual sensibilities, 293; "Sweets and the Girls" (song), 290; Zero Trash Operations project, 286–87, 295
The Cocktail Party (Ōshiro), 136–41, 148, 155n13
Cold War, 121, 202, 229; de-Cold War, 323; shift in global security paradigm and, 234
collective/regional self-defense, 10–11, 322; San Francisco system and, 212–15; substituted for collective security, 212–13, 325–29
collective security paradigm, 11, 279–80, 322–38; collective/regional self-defense displacing, 212–13, 325–29; policy proposal for collective security from an Okinawan perspective (PPCSOP), 331–38; reinventing from Okinawan perspective, 329–33; UN use of, 11, 209, 212–13, 322–23, 327
colonialism, 272n2; decolonization, 323; Empire's difference from, 8; postcolonial scholarship, 15–16. *See also* Empire; imperialism
comfort facilities. *See* entertainment quarters
comfort women, 236, 267, 314; women's work addresses, 167. *See also* heterosocial taboo (sexual relationships between US servicemen and Okinawan women)
commercialization, 149
communication. *See* explosive communication; face-to-face communication
communism, threats of, 125, 210, 213–14, 224, 228–29
community, theoretical scholarship, 22, 23, 34–36, 37nn1–3, 75
community of *nuchi du takara*. *See* androcentric community, formation of; anti-base protests; community of *nuchi du takara*, formation of; Okinawan multitude
community of *nuchi du takara*, formation of, 38–63, 65–100; disappearance, questions of, 103, 104; everyday/social layer, 35–36, 66–67, 68–69, 70–71, 72, 145, 176, 319–21; global/virtual layer, 36, 66–67, 75–81, 282, 319–21; horizontal expansion, 34, 41–42; metaphysical layer, 34–35, 67, 192, 282, 319–21; as multigenerational and diverse, 41, 65–66, 69, 94; Onaga and, 4, 58, 59, 86–87, 101; Others incorporated into, 81–83, 87, 94; postmemory in, 93–100; through sit-ins, 40–41; Washington/Tokyo response, 39, 40, 48, 101. *See also* anti-base protests
compulsory group suicide (Battle of Okinawa), 17, 113–14, 133–34, 258–59
Conspiracy Act (2017), 244–45
constituent and constituted power, *nuchi du takara* mediates contradiction, 5–6, 17, 21, 39, 101; ambivalence toward US military, 115, 124, 131, 147–48; Camp Schwab negotiations, 49–50, 51; manipulation by Washington/Tokyo, 40, 58. *See also* rape incident of 1995
constituent power ("power of life"), 9, 39, 110, 130, 192–93. *See also* anti-base protests; Okinawan multitude; in anti-base protests, 219; defined, 33–34; *dojin* term used in

cyberspace and, 268–69; silencing of, by official nationalism, 3, 90, 270; sit-ins, 41; successes of, 47; suppression of, 43, 160; women's, in dispute over *tōtōme*, 164–72
constituted power ("power over life"), 110, 130; *Civil Affairs Handbook* as administrative tool of, 117–18; defined, 33–36; JCG as, 55–56; Okinawan Prefectural Police as, 53. See also Okinawan "citizens"
Constitution of Japan, 151, 169. See also Article 9 of the Constitution of Japan (unarmed peace); Article 1 (popular sovereignty), 208–9, 327; MacArthur's influence on, 208–9
"Constitution of the Ryukyu Republic Society" (Kawamitsu), 13, 334–35
containment, policy of, 210
contingent workers, 272
"A Conversation" (poem, Yamanokuchi), 256
Cornerstone of Peace (Peace Memorial Park), 21, 192
Covid-19 pandemic, 84, 85, 90; effect on tourism, 103, 238; Onaga's death and, 101; protests during, 102
creolization of theory, 21
crime, 135, 151, 161–62, 178. See also arrests; police; rape incident of 1995; sexual violence and rape
cultural cushion of *nuchi du takara*. See constituent and constituted power, *nuchi du takara* mediates contradiction
Cultural Property Protection Act, 57
culture. See literary works; music, art, and culture; Okinawan cultural practices
Cumings, Bruce, 7, 210, 228, 236
currency: B-yen, 136, 158–59, 193n1; exchange rates, US dollar, 158, 163, 172, 176–77; Japanese yen, 158, 172, 193n1. See also money
cyberspace, 301; *dojin* in, 268–69; resistance in, 75–81; US-Japan collaboration in, 245

Dai-Ryūkyū Shashin Emaki (Great Ryukyu Photo Scrolls; Ishikawa), 182, 300
daitōakyōeiken (greater East Asia co-prosperity sphere), 256, 269
Da Pump (hip-hop group), 17, 321n1
Days at No Base Gallery (blog, Ms. S.), 76
death, 37n1, 95–98, 191; in metaphysical layer of *nuchi du takara*, 34–35, 66–67, 97, 192, 282, 319–21. See also *tōtōme* (Okinawan-style mortuary tablet)

"de-Cold War," 323
decolonization, 323
defense only *(senshubōei)* principle, 218, 225
de-imperialization, 323–24
demilitarization of Japan, 207, 209, 210–11. See also Article 9 of the Constitution of Japan (unarmed peace)
Democratic Party of Japan (DPJ), 49, 50, 333
democratization of Japan; Okinawan multitude: Article 1 (defining emperor's power) and, 208–9; ideals of democracy, and Imperial House, 314–15, 318–19; as objective of US occupation, 207; reversals of, 210–11; USMGR and, 117. See also fraternity/fratriarchy duality
Deng Xiaoping, 226
depopulation, 129
Derrida, Jacques, 34, 35–36, 75
Diaoyu (Senkaku) Islands, 240
digital capitalism, 250
digital resistance, 76
digital technology/media, 36, 75–81, 301
dilution of sovereignty, 212
diplomacy: DPJ/Camp Schwab fortification plan and, 49–50; reciprocity/formation of Empire v.2 and, 225, 226–27. See also Empire
dojin, Japanese discourse on: defining Okinawans as Japanese with a negative difference, 258–59; defining Okinawans as Japanese with a positive difference, 259–60, 261. See also nationalism
dojin incidents: Human Pavilion incident at Fifth National Industrial Fair (1903), 252–54; at protest in Takae (2016), 249–50, 268, 269–71
domestic violence, 271
donkakuteki taisei ("obtuse-angle attitude"), 18
Dower, John, 213
drones, 244
dugongs, importance of, 85–86, 91–93; Cocco and, 292–93; lawsuit, 47, 63n4, 94. See also anti-base sentiments
Dulles, John Foster, 9; Hirohito and, 213–14; MacArthur and, 213; San Francisco system and, 212–17

eating disorders, 294
Economic White Paper of 1956, 217
economy, global. See world market, and Empire

economy of Japan: economic recovery, 217–18, 221; in Empire v.2, 227–29; national debt, 62; split governance and, 220–22, 229–30; US policy and, 210–11
economy of Okinawa, 122, 124; agriculture, 123; base-dependent, 14, 123, 130, 136, 158, 186; entertainment quarters' impact on, 125; gross prefectural income, 130, 136, 163, 166, 173, 186; human labor in, 158–59, 169; money economy, expansion of, 159, 166, 193n1; in 1957, 130; in 1960s, 148–50; in 1990s, 163; per-capita income, 150; post-reversion, 162, 166–67, 169, 173, 177; poverty, 90, 100n7, 144; pro-base view of, 18, 19, 84, 85, 86, 175; Tokyo funds for development, 3, 39, 160, 162, 193n2; US bases depress, 69–70, 85; USCAR's role in, 123, 125, 129, 130; US military influence, decline in, 173–74; Washington/Tokyo's development promises in exchange for FRF building, 39, 175. *See also* labor market
education, 122
elections, concerns about impact on, 52, 58
emperor, powers of, 208–9. *See also* Akihito and Michiko (emperor and empress); Hirohito (emperor)
Empire, 5; complex negotiations with, 18; concept defined, 8–10; double-sided character of, 201, 273; expanding security apparatus of, 61–62; Okinawa Initiative and, 103; versions of, 9–10, 11–12
Empire version 1 (1945–1960s), 9, 203, 224, 328; formation of, through internalization of Japan (first moment), 206, 207–17; growth of through split governance (second moment), 217–24
Empire version 2 (1970s–1980s), 9, 203, 328; economic dynamics of, 227–30; formation of, 206; formation of through reciprocity (third moment), 224–30; security and diplomatic dynamics of, 225–27
Empire version 3 (21st c.), 9, 204, 328; characterization of, 237–38; formation of (fifth moment), 206, 237–47; official nationalism and, 265; transition to (fourth moment), 206, 230–37
Empire version 3, omni-crisis in, 9, 238–45; first layer of (new adversaries), 238–39; global security apparatus and, 240–45; second layer of (multipolar world order), 239–40, 242, 265–66

employment. *See* labor market
Engels, Friedrich, 267
Enola Gay exhibition, 236, 237
entertainment quarters: ambivalence toward US military and, 131–33, 197, 304; comfort facilities, 117, 140–41; cost of services, 172–73; formation of, in Koza, 117; Okinawa's income and, 130, 271; Tsuji, 142–45; USCAR bans military personnel from patronizing, 125
environmentalism, 85–86, 91–93, 286–88
everyday/social layer of *nuchi du takara*, 319–21; Blanchot's theorization and, 35–36; *harī* festival as, 176; refugee camps and, 145; resistance and, 66–67, 68; at Tent Village, 72
exception, state of, 222
Expeditionary Advanced Base Operations (EABO), 243, 244
explosive communication, 13, 127–28, 192; Blanchot on, 35, 36, 68; as characteristic of *nuchi du takara*, 36, 68, 71, 127, 319–20; digital resistance as, 76; Ishikawa's photography demonstrates, 183; *No Base* as form of, 74, 76

face-to-face communication, 35, 36, 75, 282, 319–21. *See also* explosive communication; at Tent Village, 73–74
family, nuclear, centering of, 221–22, 315
family-related terms, and official nationalism, 255, 256–57, 261
Fanon, Frantz, 277–78
"Far East," concept of, and US-Japan security alliance, 230
Far Eastern Commission, 208
Far East Network radio broadcast (1956), 129–30
father/son/patricide taboos: Freud on, 14, 107–8, 132, 277; Oedipus myth, 27, 108; paternal figure, US military as, 107–108, 115, 117, 131–132, 138, 155n15
fiction. *See* literary works
Field, Norma, 258
Fifth National Industrial Fair (1903), Human Pavilion incident at, 252–54
Figal, Gerald, 190, 193n3
Fija, Byron, 300
Filipino workers, 159, 173, 183
Fisch, Arnold, 121
flag burnings, 316
flexible conservatism, 86

INDEX   425

"flying geese model" of economic development, 228
Force Design 2030 (USMC 2020), 61
Ford, Clellan S., 117–18
foreign media, 80
Forgash, Rebecca, 177
Foucault, Michel, 13–14
fraternity/fratriarchy duality, 14, 278; anti-base protests, 71; depicted in *The Cocktail Party*, 139, 140, 141; heterosocial taboo, as fratriarchal protection, 139–40, 141; Ishikawa Mao's photography, 178, 179, 181, 182, 183, 184; reversion movement and, 147–48, 152, 193; transformation of community of *nuchi du takara* and, 109, 184; women's constituent power and, 187–88. *See also* democratization of Japan; heterosocial taboo; homosocial taboo
free speech, 269–70
Freud, Sigmund, 14, 132; on patricide, 14, 107–8, 132, 277, 277; *Totem and Taboo*, 107–8
"friendship without presence," 76–81
Fujii Seiji, 271
Fujimoto Yukihisa, 78
Fujimura Osamu, 267
Fukkikyō (the Association for the Reversion of Okinawa Prefecture to the Homeland), 149, 151
Fukuda Yasuo, 49
Fukumura Takeshi, 299
Funakoshi Gishō, 146
Futenma Air Station, 2–3, 104, 229, 233, 235, 244
Futenma Replacement Facility (FRF), 2–5; completion date and cost estimates, 62, 63; controversy over, 292; cultural artifacts discovered during survey work, 57; debates on rationale for building, 38, 48–50; generating support for construction of, 175; grassroots resistance organizations, 21, 41; Okinawa's alternative plan for, 39–40; plans for, 39, 83–84; political will to construct, 4–5, 55–56, 60, 62; pro-base movements for, 3–4, 81–82, 83–87, 88; referendum to express Okinawans' opinions (2019), 101–2, 103; regionalism and, 324; "scoping document" published, 42; security paradigm and, 61–62, 233, 235–36, 333; Self-Defense Forces' use of, 60–61, 64n7. *See also* anti-base protests; anti-base sentiments; pro-base sentiments

G-8 Okinawa Summit (2000), 40, 297–98
Ganbare Nippon!, 264
gay men, 307
gender inequality, 2, 169. *See also* androcentric community, formation of; androcentrism; men; *tōtōme* (Okinawan-style mortuary tablet); women
genealogy of ideas, 13–14, 15, 333–35
general will: collective security and, 325–29; in community of *nuchi du takara*, 319–21; concept of, 279, 325–26. *See also* Okinawan multitude, mimetic faculty of
generations: anti-base sentiment among, 102–4, 124–25; differentiation of, 12, 41, 93–94, 194n5, 197; memory of war, 93–94, 124–25, 184–85, 189–90; "postgeneration," 162–63
generations, at anti-base protests, 41, 45, 47–48, 65–66, 69–70, 98–99; digital resistance, by younger generations, 76; memory and postmemory, 93–94, 99
Germany, 80, 248n13
ghosts, presence of, 94–95, 96
Gibney, Frank, 117
Gilroy, Paul, 14, 107
Ginowan Village, 125, 154n8
Girard, William, 218–19, 247n3
"global civil war," 247, 324–25
global communication, 301. *See also* explosive communication
global security apparatus, 10, 204, 240–45, 248n11, 271, 328
"global sovereign state," 8–9. *See also* Empire
global/virtual layer of *nuchi du takara*, 36, 66–67, 75–81, 282, 319–21. *See also* community of *nuchi du takara*, formation of
gold standard, ending of, 172, 224
governance of Okinawa: Government of the Ryukyu Islands (GRI), 123, 124, 129, 150, 152; political autonomy as "myth," 135; self-governance, 117, 122, 129; split governance, 10, 204, 220–22, 224, 229–30, 233–34, 325; USMGR, 114, 115, 117–118, 123; US rule, 1–3, 93–94, 122–24. *See also* US Civil Administration of the Ryukyu Islands (USCAR)
Government of the Ryukyu Islands (GRI), 123, 124, 129, 150, 152
Greek society, ancient, 157
Greenpeace, 47
gross domestic product (GDP). *See* economy of Okinawa

Guam Doctrine, 224, 225
Guidelines for U.S.-Japan Defense Cooperation (1978), 225, 241
Guidelines for U.S.-Japan Defense Cooperation (1997), 234, 241
Guidelines for U.S.-Japan Defense Cooperation (2015), 244, 245
Gulf War, 231–32, 234
Gushikawa Village, 41

hakkōichiu (eight corners under one roof), 256, 269
Hamas, 238
Hanaui nu In (Connections of the Flower Vendor; play), 119
Hanna, Willard Anderson, 118
Hardt, Michael, and Antonio Negri, 5, 8, 12; call to dismantle state apparatuses, 337; constituent and constituted power and, 33, 39; "imperialism is over," 273; on multitude, 26, 26; rape incident of 1995 and, 187; on reform and revolution, 26, 27, 27; on tendency, 13
hārī (dragon boat festival), 174–77, 184
Harvey, David, 110
Hashimoto Ryūtarō, 235
Hatoyama Yukio, 49–50
heaven/nature/life, 287, 288
Heaven's hell (2003) (documentary), 285, 286–87
"Heaven's hell" (song, Cocco), 286, 287
Hein, Laura, 104
Heiwadōri to Nazukerareta Machi o Aruite (Walking the Town Named Peace Street) (novel, Medoruma), 316
Heiwa no Ishiji (Cornerstone of Peace) memorial, 191, 192
helicopter crashes, 43, 59, 100n6
helipads, 59, 60
hell/history/death, 287, 288
Henoko Blue (canoe team) blog, 81
Henoko Kikin (Henoko Fund), 71, 92
Henoko: Umi no Tatakai (Henoko: A Struggle on the Sea) (Urashima), 36
Hentona Issa, 17, 321n1
Herikichi Hantaikyōgikai (Coalition for Opposing the Offshore Base Construction; COOBC), 41, 56, 69, 74, 77, 80
heterosocial taboo (sexual relationships between US servicemen and Okinawan women), 109, 112, 155n13, 189, 196; consequence for violation, 278; decline of, 163, 172, 177–84; as fratriarchal protection, 139–40, 141; homosocial taboo, synchronization with, 141, 142, 152; marriage and, 177, 181–82; mixed-race children and, 141, 152, 154n11, 296; Otohime Troupe and, 141–48; perspective of women undermines, 163, 177–84; race and, 278. *See also* fraternity/fratriarchy duality; homosocial taboo (friendship with US military)
Higa Mikio, 136, 154n12
Higashi Ajia Kyōdōtai (Community of East Asia), 49
Higashionna Takuma, 41, 47, 70, 71, 82, 99
Higa Shunchō, 15
Higa Takahiro, 129
Higa Toyomitsu, 179
high commissioner position (USCAR), 135
"Hikōkigumo (Winter Cloud)" (song, Cocco), 284
Himeyuri (documentary, 2007), 289–91
Himeyuri Gakutotai (Lily Princess Corps or Star Lily Corps), 288–91
Himeyuri Memorial, 288, 310–12
Hinomaru o Miru Me (Here's What the Japanese Flag Means to Me; Ishikawa), 182
Hirohito (emperor), 9; Dulles/San Francisco system and, 213–15, 216; MacArthur's handling of image of, 208–9; Nanjing massacre debate and, 236; sentiments toward Imperial House and, 318; social contract with US and, 202, 327–28; visits to Netherlands, 314; visits to Okinawa, 309
Hiroshima's Peace Park, 191
"history issues"/historical narratives, 217, 227, 228, 236–37
history textbooks, 190, 262
Hobbes, Thomas, 9, 202, 203, 205n1
homosocial taboo (friendship with US military), 108–9, 112, 147, 178, 189, 196; *The Cocktail Party* depicts, 139–41; decline of, 163, 172; heterosocial taboo, synchronization with, 141, 142, 152; mixed-race Okinawans and, 154n13, 196; Okinawa reversion as expression of, 152; rewriting, to preserve androcentrism, 172–77. *See also* fraternity/fratriarchy duality; heterosocial taboo (sexual relationships between US servicemen and Okinawan women)
hondonami (catching up with the rest of Japan), 229

INDEX   427

Hope (Kibō) (Medoruma), 5
human equality, notion of, 14, 109, 157–60
humanitarian aid operations, by Self-Defense Forces, 234, 241
Human Pavilion at Fifth National Industrial Fair (1903), 252–54
Hyakuta Naoki, 263
Hyon Joo Yoo, 8

identity, 87, 91, 92, 96, 300–301
Ie Island, 20
Iha (or Ifa) Fuyū, 15, 255
Ikiro! Tore! Ishikawa Mao! (video, Ishikawa), 184
Ikusabanu Tudumi (Bringing the War to an End; documentary), 78
Imperial House. *See* Akihito and Michiko (emperor and empress); Hirohito (emperor)
imperialism: de-imperialization, 323–24; Empire's difference from, 8; of Japanese Empire, 254, 272n2; *kokutai* and, 251–52, 254–57; of MacArthur's approach/US occupation, 207–10, 327. *See also* colonialism; Empire
Imperial Palace, 315
Inamine Kei'ichi, 39, 40, 49, 146–47
Inamine Susumu, 49, 57
income, Japanese household, 100n7. *See also* economy of Okinawa
income inequality, 159
incremental change, 6, 33, 36
India, 215, 238, 242
Indonesia, 221, 228, 238, 313
Inochi o Mamoru Kai (Society for the Protection of Life), 41, 84, 91; Kinjō Yūji as leader of, 21, 42, 88, 95–96; struggle hut built by, 87–88
inoperative community, 34–35
"The Inoperative Community" (Nancy), 34
International Military Tribunal for the Far East (May 1946–November 1948), 208
International Social Assistance Okinawa (ISAO, previously ISSO), 297
International Social Service Okinawa (ISSO, later ISAO), 296–97
International Union for Conservation of Nature, 92
intersectionality, 14, 136–37
interviews: with mixed-race Okinawans, 298, 299–302; with protest participants, 36, 67, 74–75, 76, 81; with US servicemen, 302–7

Iraha Inkichi, 20
Iraq, 241, 303
Iraq War, 43, 44
Ishiba Shigeru, 50
Ishigaki Island, 244, 248n14
Ishikawa Mao, 167, 172, 177–84, 300; internal and external criticisms of, 182; works by, 180–81, 182–83
Islamic fundamentalist groups, 238–39
Islands of Discontent: Okinawan Responses to Japanese and American Power (Hein and Selden), 104
Israel-Palestine conflict, 331
Issuikai (right-wing nationalist group), 79
Italy, 163, 248n13
Itokazu Keiko, 187
Iwa'ana no Tenshi (An Angel in a Cave; Torikobori), 121
Iwanami Shoten, 260, 262, 266, 267

Japan: defense spending, 243; idealization of by US servicemen, 303; "residual sovereignty" over Okinawa, 215–16, 217; US military occupation of, 207, 211–12. *See also* economy of Japan; Empire; Japan "proper"; nationalism
Japan-China relationship, normalization of, 226–27
Japan Coast Guard (JCG), 55–56, 71–72, 77
Japanese flag, 150, 178, 190
Japanese Imperial Army, 113, 117, 153n1, 190, 192, 313; Himeyuri Corps and, 288, 291
"Japanese" Marine Corps, 61
Japanese/Okinawan postcolonial scholarship, 15–16
"The Japanese Worldview and the Construction of a New World Order" (Monbushō, Ministry of Education), 256
Japanese yen, 158, 172, 193n1
Japanization, 118, 120, 178, 254, 258; mixed-race Okinawans and, 300–301
Japan "proper," 28n2; anti-base protesters from, 46–47, 48, 66, 81, 83; anti-base protests in, 218–19; cultural interface with Okinawans, 91–93, 148; economic use and development of, 220–21, 222, 233; Okinawa as sacrifice for, 202; reduction of US bases/troops in, 219, 224, 229; use of term, 28n2; US military goal of separating Okinawan culture from, 146. *See also* split governance of Okinawa

Japan-U.S. Joint Declaration on Security, Alliance for the 21st Century (1996), 234–35
JCG. *See* Japan Coast Guard (JCG)
jobs. *See* labor market
Johnson, Archie, 20, 280
jōji-chūryūnaki anpo (security alliance without permanent stationing of US forces in Okinawa or elsewhere in Japan), 338n3
June 23, 313
Junkerman, John, 78
juri (women entertainers), 142–45
Jyugon Hogo Kikin (Dugong Protection Fund), 92
"Jyugon no Mieru Oka" (The Hill of Dugongs) (song, Cocco), 292–93

Kabira Chōshin, 146
Kadena Air Base, Okinawa, 151, 152, 154n9, 193n4, 235, 244
Kageyama Asako, 78
Kagirinaku Tōmei ni Chikai Burū (Almost Transparent Blue; Murakami), 180
Kajiwara, Robert, 80
Kakamigahara City protest, 218
Kakazu Chiken, 174
Kameya Chizuko, 120
Kami no Shisha (A Messenger of God; Miyara), 120
Kanehide Holdings, 69–70, 81
Kanehide Supermarket, 73
Kanettai: Ōbāhīto Zōn (Exceedingly Tropical: An Overheated Zone; Arasaki), 173–74
Kang Sang-jun, 78, 222
Kanū Chīmu Henoko Burū (Canoe Team Henoko Blue), 77
Karatani Kōjin, 11, 35, 322, 338n2
Kariyushi Hotel Group, 69, 73, 81
Katō Akira, 311
Kawabata Yasunari, 146
Kawamitsu Shin'ichi, 13, 156n18, 334–35
Kawamura Takashi, 267
Kawano Jyunji, 317
Kawase Shin, 128
Kayō Yasuno, 146
keiretsu (synergy of firms), 227
Kelsen, Hans, 329
kengai isetsu (relocation of US bases in Okinawa to mainland Japan), 325
Kennedy, John F., 148, 150
Kerama Islands, 113, 153n2
Kichi/ Guntai o Yurusanai Kōdōsuru Onnatachi no Kai (Association of Women Acting against Military Bases and Forces in Okinawa), 37n4
Kichihenkan Akushon Puroguramu (Action Program for Returning US Bases to Okinawa), 186, 333
Kim Seo-kyung and Kim Eun-sung, 267
Kina, Laura, 180
Kinjō Hatsuko, 95, 96–97, 99, 154n7
Kinjō Kōei, 190–91
Kinjō Motoko, 288
Kinjō Yoshiko, 167
Kinjō Yūji, 16, 21, 42, 95–96, 99; death of, 88
Kin Town, 130, 159
Kishaba Jun, 128
Kishaba Naoko, 167
Kishida Fumio, 245
Kishi Masahiko, 17
Kishimoto Tateo, 39, 174
Kishi Nobusuke, 210, 223
Kissinger, Henry, 226
Kitaueda Takeshi, 62, 77
Koikari, Mire, 148, 150
Koiso Kazuo, 147
Koizumi Jun'ichirō, 46, 89
kōkoku-shikan (emperor-centered worldview), 256–57, 269
Kokoroni Todoke Onnatachi no Nettowāku (Women's Network to Reach the People's Heart), 41
Kokuba Kōtarō, 124, 125–26
"Kokusaitoshi Keisei Kōsō" (International City Formation Plan), 186
kokutai (loyalty/filial piety of Japanese subjects toward emperors), 202, 208, 251–52; Human Pavilion incident and, 252–54; redefinitions of in official nationalism, 255–57
Konkurītoburokku (A Concrete Block; Ishikawa), 182
Korea. *See* North Korea; South Korea
Korean Broadcasting System, 80
Koreans, and official nationalism, 252, 255
Korean War, 122–23, 211, 213, 217
Korega Okinawa no Beigunda: Kichi no Shima ni Ikiru Hitobito (This Is the US Military in Okinawa: People Living on the Island of Bases) (Ishikawa, Kuniyoshi, and Nagamoto), 181
Koza riot (1970), 152
"Kubi (Head)" (song, Cocco), 284

INDEX 429

Kumashiro Tatsumi, 180
kumiodori court performance, 156n16
Kurai Hana (A Dark Flower; Kishaba), 128
Kushi Village, 130
Kyan Yukio, 131–32

labor, 13; division of, 221; official nationalism and, 266
labor market, 169; layoffs at Camp Schwab, 173; Okinawa as site of human labor, 157–59; promises of preferential employment on bases, 129; slavery, 157; women's labor, 89–90, 109–10, 166–67, 271, 272. *See also* economy of Okinawa
labor movements, 124, 210
labor policies, in Japan, 89–90
land, four principles for protecting, 159–60
Land Acquisition Ordinance, 124
land reclamation permit, 50, 51, 58, 82, 87
land reclamation work, 53, 59; difficulty of, 62
land seizures, 5, 41, 154n4, 159; as grounding for anti-base sentiments, 124, 127; land enclosures by US military, 115–16; protests, 125–30, 159, 186; Tochiren leads, 159, 162, 186; by USCAR, 124, 125–30, 159
law of nature, 203
Lebra, William, 121
Le Figaro (newspaper), 80
leprosy and ex-leprosy patients, 96–97, 120, 314
Leviathan (Hobbes), 202, 203
Levinas, Emmanuel, 36, 37n3
Liberal Democratic Party (LDP), 46, 49, 263, 333; Okinawa chapter, 50, 86
Liberal Party, 333
liberation, from Japanese government, 115, 117, 118, 120
literary works: anti-imperial sentiments in, 316; *The Cocktail Party*, 136–141, 148, 155n13; construction of community of *nuchi du takara* and, 120–21, 128, 136–37; on entertainment quarters, 173–74; exploring relationships between Japanese women and Black men, 128, 180, 298–99; intercultural encounter of gay men in, 307; revolutionary violence in, 5; *The Teahouse of the August Moon*, 144, 155nn13, 15; women writers, 167. *See also* music, art, and culture
Locke, John, 203
Lummis, Douglas, 53, 67
lump-sum payment method, 159

MacArthur, Douglas, 123; demilitarization of Japan and, 209, 211; drastic reforms implemented by, 207–9; Dulles/San Francisco system and, 213, 215, 217; Hirohito's image and, 208–9; imperialist approach of, 207–10, 247n1; vision of defense security as Empire v3, 244, 327
Malaysia, 228, 313
management, Japanese-style, 221
manufacturing, 221
maps of Okinawa, 6, 7
"March of Beggars," 187
Maritime Self-Defense Force Kanoya Air Base, Kagoshima Prefecture, 244
marriage, mixed-race, 177, 180, 181–82
Marx, Karl, 267; *Capital*, 157; on money as universal equivalent, 109
Matenkō port, 44
maternal figures, 150, 256–57
Matsudaira Yasumasa, 214
Matsui Ichirō, 270
Matsumura, Wendy, 157–58
McClintock, Anne, 110
media: analog, 163, 192; Chinese consumption of, 246; digital, 36, 75–81, 301; foreign, 80; official nationalism and, 257, 260–61, 264; reversion movement and, 149, 260–61; television broadcasting, 148–49, 180; US military controls in order to suppress Okinawans' freedom of speech, 125
Medoruma Shun: arrest of, 71–72, 76; *dojin* incident and, 249–50; *Heiwadōri to Nazukerareta Machi o Aruite*, 316; *Kibō*, 5; *Niji no Tori*, 5; on postmemory, 98–99; *Uminari no Shimakara: Okinawa/Yanbaru yori*, 77
Meiji period, 165, 251–52
memory: Himeyuri experiences and, 289–91; postmemory, 93–100
men, 15; cultural celebration of Otohime Troupe by, 146–47; as *kumiodori* performers, 156n16; in organization of protest of rape incident of 1995, 187; political-economic power of, 164, 166; postwar Okinawa, 168. *See also* androcentrism
metaphysical layer of *nuchi du takara*, 34–35, 66–67, 97, 282, 319–21. *See also* community of *nuchi du takara*, formation of
methodologies, 27–28, 36–37, 111, 205, 280
Michiko (empress). *See* Akihito and Michiko (emperor and empress)
microwave circuit system, 148–49

middle class, 89, 90, 193, 261
Middle East, and world economy, 228
Mikami Chie, 37, 63n3, 78
Miki Takeo, 310
military. *See* Japanese Imperial Army; Self-Defense Forces; US military
military, abuses by, 336
"mimetic excess," 281–82
mimetic faculty of Okinawan multitude. *See* Okinawan multitude, mimetic faculty of
Minami no Shima no Hoshi no Suna (Star Sands in the South Ocean) (picture book, Cocco), 285
Minami no Shima no Koi no Uta (Love Songs from the South Ocean) (picture book, Cocco), 285
Minami Saori, 161
Minamoto Yuki, 311
Ministry of Education, 178, 190, 194n10, 256
Mirza, Heidi Safia, 282
mixed-race Okinawans. *See* Okinawans, mixed-race
Miyagi Ayano, 76
Miyagi Eishō, 142
Miyagi Etsujirō, 150
Miyagi Harumi, 113, 187
Miyagi Kikuko, 289, 290
Miyako Island, 244
Miyanishi Kaori, 177
Miyara Tamotsu, 120
Miyazaki Hayao, 78–79, 92
Miyume Tanji, 161
modernity, 334
Molotov cocktail incident, at crown prince visit to Himeyuri Memorial (1975), 310–12
moments, historical. *See* Empire
Mondale, Walter, 235
money, 14–15; androcentrism and, 162, 279; for damages, 82; government aid, 51, 119–20, 122; guilt and ambivalence about, 132–33; reduction of Okinawa development budget, 271; taboo and, 22, 107–9, 112; as universal equivalent, 109, 278–79. *See also* currency; economy of Okinawa; Okinawan "citizens," money and development of
More Important Than Ever: Renewing the U.S.-Japan Alliance for the 21st Century (Armitage and Nye, 2018), 245
Mori Yoshio, 15
Morris-Suzuki, Tessa, 332
Motoyama Jinshirō, 103

Mr. B. (protest participant), interview with, 67
Mr. G. (former US Marine), interview with, 302–4, 320
Mr. H. (former US Marine), interview with, 304–6, 320
Ms. O. (mixed-race Okinawan woman), interview with, 298, 299–302, 320
Ms. S. (Tent Village volunteer), interview with, 36, 74–75, 76, 81
multitude, concept of, 26, 337
multitude, the. *See* Okinawan multitude
"multitude-states," 336–37
munchū (patrilineal descent groups), 164, 176, 261
Murakami Ryū, 180
Muramoto Daisuke, 78
Murase Haruki, 179
murder of Okinawan woman (2016), 58–59
Murdock, George, 117–18
music, art, and culture; literary works: at anti-base protests, 68–69, 72–73, 74–75, 78; *kumiodori* court performance, 156n16; Otohime Troupe, 142–48, 156n17; post-reversion, 161; in refugee camps, 118–19, 142, 145, 155n15; *The Teahouse of the August Moon*, 144, 155nn13, 15. *See also* Cocco

Nabī no Koi (Nabī's Love; film), 161
Nagadō Eikichi, 146
Nagaoka Chitarō, 15
Nagaregi (Driftwood; Kawase), 128
Nagayama Yumiko, 154n9
Naha, Okinawa, 7
Naha Bōeishisetsukyoku (Naha Defense Facilities Administrative Agency; NDFAA), 40, 42–48. *See also* Okinawa Bōeikyoku (Okinawa Defense Bureau, ODB, formerly NDFAA)
Naha Family Court, 169
Nakada Sachiko, 183
Nakaima Hirokazu, 49, 51, 58
Nakamura Midori, 79
Nakamura Sugako, 98, 99, 188
Nakandakari Hatsu, 167
Nancy, Jean-Luc, 34–35, 96
Nanjing massacre, 217, 227, 236
Naoki Sakai, 8
National Athletic Meet (1987), 316–17
nationalism, 86, 90, 204–5; androcentric, 14, 196; Chinese, vs US-Japan alliance, 245–46; right-wing, 79, 262; rise of, and "history

INDEX 431

issues," 236–37. *See also* nationalism, versions of, and *dojin* discourses
nationalism, versions of, and *dojin* discourses, 249–72; version 1 (1880s–1945), 250, 251–59; version 2 (1945–1990s), 250, 259–63; version 3 (21st c.), 250, 263–70
National Police Reserve, 211, 247n6
Negri, Antonio. *See* Hardt, Michael, and Antonio Negri
Nelson, Christopher, 97
neoliberalism, 89–91, 266
Netherlands, the, 313–14
New China News Agency, 80
New York Times, 80
NHK (national broadcast radio station), 149, 161, 257, 263, 266
Nimitz, Chester W., 114
Nippon Bunka Channeru Sakura (NBCS), 264
Nishihara, Masashi, 221
Nishime Junji, 124, 317
Nishimura Hiroyuki, 263–64
Nixon, Richard, 172, 224, 226
"no admittance" zone, 54–55, 71–72
No Base (newsletter, Ms. S.), 36, 74, 100n4
Nomura Kōya, 325
non-human creatures, included in Okinawan multitude, 12; dugongs, importance of, 47, 63n4, 85–86, 91–93, 94, 292–93
nonviolence, 47, 67, 68, 88
Northern Training Area, 59, 76; return of, 60, 249, 272n1
North Korea, 50, 60, 242
novels. *See* literary works
NSC 13/2 (October 1948), 210
NSC 13/3 (May 1949), 210
nuchi du takara ("life is the ultimate treasure"), 6; androcentrism characterized by fraternity/fratriarchy duality, 278; anti-/pro-base complexities reflected in, 17–20; concept defined, 8, 17–23; as cushion between constituent and constitutive power, 33; everyday/social layer of, 35–36, 66–67, 68–69, 72, 145, 176; explosive communication within, 35; "friendship without presence" within, 36; general will in, 319–21; global/virtual layer of, 36, 66–67, 75–81, 282, 319–21; internal capacity of community to embrace contradictory perspectives, 6, 18–19, 21, 33–34, 39, 65, 115, 133, 134, 283; metaphysical layer of, 34–35, 66–67, 97, 282, 319–21; origin of, 20; radical thought on, 333–35; three layers of, 34–36, 66–67, 282, 319–21; World Republic of, 11, 26, 280, 322–23, 326–27, 335–38. *See also* androcentric community, formation of; community of *nuchi du takara*, formation of; constituent and constituted power, *nuchi du takara* mediates contradiction; Okinawan "citizens," money and development of; Okinawan multitude, mimetic faculty of
nuclear weapons: abolition of, 330, 331; in US-controlled Okinawa, 222; use of in WWII, 207, 236, 313; US monopoly on, 209–10
Nye, Joseph. *See* Armitage, Richard, and Joseph Nye

Obama, Barack, 50
Obama administration, 49
obedience, 208, 327, 338n1
Ocean Expo (1975–1976), 160, 190, 261, 309
Ochiai Keiko, 78
Oedipus complex, 277, 279
Oedipus myth, 27, 108
Ōe Kenzaburō, 78, 260, 267
official nationalism. *See* nationalism, versions of, and *dojin* discourses
Oguma Eiji, 260
Ōhashi Hideshi, 171
Okamoto Keitoku, 156n18, 167, 334
Okamoto Tarō, 260, 336
Okinawa: development budget, reduction of, 271; emigration from, 257–58; in global market, 257; Imperial House visits to, 309–12; as Japanese with a negative difference, 258–59; as Japanese with a positive difference, 259–60, 261; as sacrifice, 1, 202. *See also* economy of Okinawa; governance of Okinawa
Okinawa, US military occupation, 202; administrative actions theory and, 220; military abuse of through split governance, 222, 229–30, 325; residual sovereignty and, 215–16
Okinawa Advisory Committee, establishment of, 117
Okinawa and the U.S. Military: Identity Making in the Age of Globalization (Inoue 2007), 2–4, 140–41, 258
Okinawa Bōeikyoku (Okinawa Defense Bureau, ODB, formerly NDFAA), 51–56, 58; construction work begun by, 97–98; as NDFAA, 40, 42–48; surveillance of protesters by, 75–76

Okinawa Bunkaron: Wasurerareta Nihon (On Okinawan Culture: Forgotten Japan) (Okamoto), 260
Okinawa Development Plans, 160
Okinawa Ham, 69, 73, 81
Okinawa Initiative (2000), 103
Okinawa-Japan relations, 10, 202, 215–16
Okinawa Kankyō Nettowāku (Okinawa Environmental Network), 92
Okinawa "Kichi/Guntai o Yurusanai Kōdōsuru Onnatachi no Kai" (Acting Women's Association in Okinawa Not Allowing Bases and the Military), 187–88
Okinawan "citizens," 12–14, 107, 112; protests of rape of 1995 and, 185–93; sentiments toward Imperial House and, 317. *See also* Okinawan "citizens," money and development of; Okinawan subjectivity
Okinawan "citizens," money and development of, 157–93, 196; demographic makeup, 162–63, 189; *hārī* festival and, 174–77; heterosocial taboo and, 164, 177–85; homosocial taboo and, 164, 172–77; Marxism, relevance to, 157–58; money economy and, 157–62; nationalization of memorial space and, 189–92; rape incident of 1995, protests, 164, 185–89; women's constituent power in dispute over *tōtōme*, 164–72
Okinawan Communist Party, 125
Okinawan cultural practices, 118, 146. *See also* music, art, and culture; Imperial House studying/embracing, 312–13; mixed-race Okinawans emracing, 300–301
Okinawan multitude: articulations of constituent power of, 34, 51; concept defined, 8, 10–16; formation of, 38; general will of, 319–21, 325–29; paradigm beyond Self/Other and, 279; periodization of ("people," "citizens," multitude), 11–14; political engagement by, 26; race, gender, and class coding of, 14–15; sentiments toward Imperial House and, 317–18. *See also* Okinawan multitude, mimetic faculty of
Okinawan multitude, mimetic faculty of, 15, 279, 281–321; Akihito/Michiko and, 308–19; Cocco and, 283–95; general will in community of *nuchi du takara* and, 319–21; mixed-race Okinawans and, 295–302; US servicemen in Okinawa and, 302–7
Okinawa Nōto (Okinawa Notes) (Ōe), 260, 267
Okinawan "people," 12–14, 107–9; in contrast to "citizens," 163; formation as key social actor, 112, 122–34; first generation of social actors, 124–25, 194n5; land seizures, 125–30; land seizure protests organized by, 186–87; money and guilt, 132–33; race, gender, and class coding of, 278; subjectivity of, *The Cocktail Party* and, 137; subjectivity shaped against US military, 163, 196. *See also* Okinawan subjectivity
Okinawans, mixed-race, 134, 295–302, 320; anti-base activities and, 300; attitudes toward, and ambivalence toward US military, 132–33, 193; citizenship status of, 297; Cocco and, 295–96; commodification of, 297–98; in fiction, 298–99; heterosocial taboo and, 141, 152, 154n11, 296; homosocial taboo and, 154n13, 196; identity of, 300–301; interview with, 298, 299–302; Ishikawa Mao's photography, 179
Okinawan subjectivity, 110, 163; *The Cocktail Party* and, 137. *See also* "changing sames," Okinawan subjectivity as
Okinawa People's Party, 118, 124, 125
Okinawa Prefectural Peace Memorial Museum (OPPMM), 19–20, 28n1, 190–91
Okinawa Prefectural Police, 53, 161–62, 188, 194n9
Okinawa reversion, 19, 112, 142, 148–53; day of reversion (May 15, 1972), 153; fraternity and, 147–48, 152, 193; human equality notions expressed through, 160; increased desire for, 135–36; media spread of, 149, 260–61; radical thought on, 333–35; struggle for, 125; violence in protests surrounding, 178; Washington/Tokyo finalize details on, 152
Okinawa Socialist People's Party, 124
Okinawa Teachers' Association (OTA), 124, 151–52
Okinawa Television Broadcasting, 147
Okinawa Times (newspaper), 37, 149, 167, 188, 263
Okinawa: Urizun no Ame (Okinawa: The Rain of Early Summer; documentary), 78
OKIRON (online journal), 79
Ōmine Sawa, 150
omni-crisis, 238–39
Omoigoto (Things I Contemplate) (book, Cocco), 289, 292, 295–96
omoiyari-yosan ("sympathy budget"), 225, 243
Onaga Takeshi, 4, 99, 263; anti-base movement

INDEX   433

in Henoko and, 58, 59, 73; death of, 87, 101; flexible conservatism of, 86–87
Onaha Būten, 147
Onna Village, 41, 194n4
OPPMM. *See* Okinawa Prefectural Peace Memorial Museum (OPPMM)
Orientalism, 92–93, 208
Oroku Kunio, 147
Ōshiro Tatsuhiro, 136, 146, 147, 148
Ōta Chōfu, 254
Ōta Masahide, 2, 188, 191–92, 333
Ōta Seisaku, 146, 147
Others. *See* Self/Other binary
Otohime Troupe (Otohime Gekidan), 141–48, 156n17
outer space, US-Japan collaboration in, 245
Oyadomari Kōsei, 146
Ozawa Ichirō, 333

pacifism, 18–19, 20–21, 336–38. *See also nuchi du takara*
Pakenham, Compton, 214
Palau, 313
paternal figures: emperor as, 255, 256; US military as, 107–8, 115, 117, 131–32, 138, 155n15
patricide. *See* father/son/patricide taboos
Patrick, John, 155n15
patrilineal descent groups *(munchū)*, 164, 176, 261
PBS, 80
peacekeeping operations, by Self-Defense Forces, 234, 241
Peace Memorial Park, Okinawa, 21, 190, 192
Peace Preservation Corps, 220, 247n6
Pempel, T. J., 221
performing arts. *See* music, art, and culture
"personal responsibility" narrative, 89
Philippines, the, 226, 228; bilateral security cooperation with, 243; Filipino workers, 159, 173, 183; Imperial House visits to, 313; US reduction of troops in, 224
Philippine Scouts, 121
Pikunikku (Picnic) (magazine), 300
Pitts, Forrest, 121
planetarity. *See* time-space, planetary
planetary consciousness, 20, 280, 293, 326
Plaza Agreement (1985), 228
police, 55–57. *See also* arrests; cybersurveillance informs actions of physical, 76; jurisdiction and legality of arrests, 135, 178, 194n9; riot police, 53–54, 67–68, 178, 271

policy proposal for collective security from an Okinawan perspective (PPCSOP), 331–38; genealogy of ideas for, 333–35; hesitations about, 335–37; mechanisms of, 331–33
political will, 4–5, 55–56, 60, 62, 68. *See also* general will
postcolonial anxiety, 265
postmemory, 93–100
Post-war Okinawa (Pitts, Lebra, and Suttles), 121
Potsdam Declaration (1945), 211, 247n1
poverty, 90, 100n7, 144, 272; of US servicemen, 302, 304
power. *See* constituent and constituted power, *nuchi du takara* mediates contradiction; constituent power; constituted power
PPCSOP. *See* policy proposal for collective security from an Okinawan perspective (PPCSOP)
prayers, 96, 286–87, 312, 313, 317
precariat, mentality of, 88–90, 266–67
Price Report (1956), 126–27
primogeniture, 164
print capitalism, 250
privatization, 89
pro-base movements for FRF, 3–4; current number of supporters, 88; decline of logic of, 83–87; former FRF supporters become anti-base, 81–82; *nuchi du takara* perspective in, 84
pro-base sentiments: economy of Okinawa and, 18, 19, 84, 85, 86, 175; in post-reversion Okinawa, 161–62
processing trade, 221, 227
property rights, 169, 203. *See also tōtōme* (Okinawan-style mortuary tablet)
prostitution. *See* entertainment quarters
protests. *See* anti-base protests; anti-base sentiments; community of *nuchi du takara*, formation of; rape incident of 1995, protest against; sit-ins

Quadrilateral Security Dialogue, 242

race: Black US servicemen, 116, 121, 179–80, 183, 185, 298–99; Fanon on, }277–78. *See also* Okinawans, mixed-race
radar system, 241, 248n12
radio, 149, 257
Radio France, 80

rape incident of 1995, 1–2, 3, 19; media and, 262; *nuchi du takara* and, 39; political context for, 230. *See also* sexual violence and rape
rape incident of 1995, protest against, 79, 98, 164, 184–93; directed toward Tokyo, 189; issues of US-Japan security foregrounded in, 187. *See also* anti-base protests
rape incident of 2008, 304
reciprocity, 203, 224–30
reconciliation, 332
Red Flower: The Women of Okinawa (Ishikawa), 180
Red Purge (1949–1950), 211
reform, 27
refugee camps, 115–19, 132; number of, 153n3; Otohime Troupe originates in, 142, 145; *The Teahouse of the August Moon* and, 155n15
regional blocs, global formation of, 324
rent, 123–24, 159; military landowners' dependence on, 186; military landowners stop agitating for return of their land, 162; Tokyo increases land rent for bases in Okinawa, 160
Reporters without Borders, 80
resistance, criminalization of, 244–45
resistance movements, 13; digital resistance, 76; Okinawa People's Party's involvement in, 118; scholarship on Okinawan, 15–16. *See also* anti-base protests
Reuters, 80
reversal, projects of, 323–24
reversion. *See* Okinawa reversion
revolution, 5–6, 27, 33
Revolution in Military Affairs (RMA), 231–32
riot police, 53–54; protesters block, 67–68; tactics of, 271; violence toward, 178
Roberson, James, 284
Rousseau, Jean-Jacques, 279, 325, 326–27, 328, 338n1
Rumsfeld, Donald, 238
Ruoff, Kenneth, 257
Russia, 238, 239; invasion of Ukraine (2022), 330–31; regionalism and, 324
Ryūdai Bungaku (University of Ryukyu Literature), 128, 307–8
Ryujin Mabyer, 21
Ryukyuan culture. *See* Okinawan cultural practices
Ryukyuan Police, purview of, 178
Ryukyu Broadcasting, 147

Ryukyu Islands, governance of. *See* governance of Okinawa
Ryukyu Kingdom, 20, 29n8; androcentrism of, 133; feudalistic class system, 157; subordination of, 155n14; Tsuji entertainment district, 142, 145
Ryukyu no Kaze (The Wind of the Ryukyu Kingdom; historical drama), 161
Ryukyu Republic Society, 13
Ryukyu Shimpo (newspaper), 37, 149, 168–70, 188, 254, 263

Sāchiraito (Searchlight) (novella, Toyokawa), 307
Saipan, 313
Sakaguchi Masayoshi, 270–71
Sakai, Naoki, 8, 308, 334
Sakamoto Ryūichi, 78
Sakiyama Tami, 167
sanatoriums, 314; Airakuen, 96–97, 120, 154n7
San Francisco Peace Treaty (Treaty of Peace with Japan, 1951), 212, 215, 216, 217
San Francisco system, 212–17; contradiction within itself, 217–18, 219; Japan's residual sovereignty over Okinawa and, 215–17; transformation into global security apparatus (in Empire v3), 240; use of US bases in Japan for collective/regional self-defense and, 212–15
Sano Motoharu, 78
sanshin music, 119, 146
Satō Eisaku, 151
scholarship: critical dialogue with *nuchi du takara*, 22; Japanese/Okinawan postcolonial, 15–16; scholars against FRF construction, 79
sculpture, 267
Sea Stallion helicopter crash (2004), 43
security: alliances in Empire v3, 241–43; bilateral alliances to be restructured as multilateral, 332; FRF construction and, 61–62, 233, 235–36, 333; global security apparatus, 10, 204, 240–45, 248n11, 271, 328; MacArthur's vision for, 209–10, 244, 327; reciprocity and, 225–27; US-Japan security alliance, 50, 230–34, 240–45, 324, 325. *See also* collective security paradigm
security studies, 77
segregation, theory of, 282. *See also* West/rest binary
Seifukukōjō-Īnkai (pop idol group), 78–79
Selden, Mark, 104

self-defense, collective/regional. *See* collective/regional self-defense
Self-Defense Forces, 190; administrative actions theory and, 220; cooperation/reciprocity with US military and, 225, 233–34, 241–42; "defense only" principle and, 218; establishment of, 248n6; FRF construction and, 60–61, 62, 64n7; sent to other nations, 233–34, 241
self-governance, 117, 122, 129. *See also* governance of Okinawa
Self/Other binary; *dojin*, Japanese discourse on: death and, 97; in Empire, 9–11, 201, 245–46, 280; environmentalism and, 91–93; formation of community of *nuchi du takara* and, 81–83, 94; gay men in military contact zone and, 307; mixed-race Okinawans and, 297–98, 299; in official nationalism, 259–60; San Francisco system and, 240; West/rest binary, 21, 254–55, 281–82. *See also* collective/regional self-defense
Senaga Kamejirō, 124, 125
Senkaku (Diaoyu) Islands, 240
senkwa-agiyā (people who obtained "war booty"), 119
September 11th, 2001 attacks, 234, 238, 305
sexism, 46
sexual relations, between Okinawan women and US servicemen, 109; mixed-race children, Okinawan attitude toward, 132–33; Otohime Troupe and, 142–48; as taboo, 139–40, 141–48. *See also* heterosocial taboo
sexual violence and rape, 127, 336; during Battle of Okinawa, 114; against children, 127, 154n9, 185; in *The Cocktail Party*, 138, 139; in post-reversion Okinawa, 162; race and, 116, 121; in refugee camps, 116–17, 132. *See also* rape incident of 1995
sex workers. *See* entertainment quarters
shamanism, 170–71, 258, 293
Sheetz, Josef Robert, 122
Shibata Shōhei, 289, 290
Shimabuku, Annmaria, 180
Shimabukuro Fumiko, 97–98, 99
Shimabukuro Maria, 297
Shimabukuro Toshiko, 289
Shimoji Lawrence Yoshitaka, 298
Shimota Seiji, 128
Shinjō Ikuo, 307
Shin-Nihonbungaku (New Japanese Literature), 128

Shiraishi Yayoi, 167
Shuri Castle, 160–61, 261
sit-ins, 264, 300; historical context, 40–41, 47; protesting land seizures, 41, 126; protesting survey work, 40, 45, 52–53, 56, 102; protesting Urban Warfare Training Facility, 41, 194n4; sites of, 45, 52–53, 56, 102, 126. *See also* anti-base protests
6/23 memorandum (1950), 213
slavery, 157
Small, Christopher, 287
Sneider, Vern, 155n15
social change: in Henoko, 87–88; national, 88–91; policy proposal for global, 331–38
social class, 89–91, 100n7, 193, 261; *burakumin*, 259, 266; feudalistic class system, 157
social media, 77, 301
social problems in postwar Okinawa, 1–2
Society for the Protection of Life. *See* Inochi o Mamoru Kai (Society for the Protection of Life)
Soejima Shoichi, 231
soft ground issue, 57, 62–63, 101
Sokoku Fukki Kyōgikai (also known as Fukkikyō, or the Association for the Reversion of Okinawa Prefecture to the Homeland), 135
Somagahara, incident at shooting range in (1957), 218–19
sons, 164, 168, 255. *See also* androcentrism; father/son/patricide taboos
sousveillance, 77–81, 249
South China Sea, territorial disputes in, 240
Southeast Asia Treaty Organization, 224
South Korea, 85; Cold War and, 121; comfort women issue and, 236; expenditures on US military activities, 248n13; fear of communism and, 214; reciprocity and, 224, 226; trilateral security cooperation with, 242; Vietnam War and, 224
sovereignty, 209; dilution of, 212
sovereignty, global. *See* Empire
sovereignty, popular: in Article 1 of Constitution, 208–9, 327; general will of multitude and, 326–27
sovereignty, residual, over Okinawa, 215–16, 217
Soviet Union: collapse of, 237; formation of Empire v.3 and, 206; opposed US control over Okinawa, 215; postwar security and, 209, 210, 328–29

Special Action Committee on Okinawa (SACO), 2
Spivak, Gayatri Chakravorty, 283
split governance of Okinawa, 10, 204, 224; development of, 220–22; military abuse of occupation and, 222, 229–30, 325; rearticulation of in 1990s, 233–34
standard of life, currency and, 158
state, the, 22, 26, 203, 336–37. *See also* collective security paradigm; constituted power; Empire; nationalism; Okinawan multitude; World Republic of *nuchi du takara*
State Secrecy Law (2013), 244
Statue of a Girl of Peace (sculpture, Kim Seo-kyung and Kim Eun-sung), 267
Stone, William Oliver, 80
Strategic Arms Limitation Talks (SALT), 229
struggle hut, 87–88, 91, 94–95
Students Emergency Action for Liberal Democracy (SEALDs), 77–78
Studio Ghibli, 92
Subcommittee on Readiness of the Armed Service Committee, 62–63
subrogation, 63
sugar, 257
Sugawara Bunta, 65–66, 79
Suga Yoshihide, 82, 269–70
suicide: compulsory group, during Battle of Okinawa, 17, 113–14, 133–34, 258–59; Japan's rate of, 89; by US servicemen, 306
Sumire Niou (A Violet That Smells Good; Kameya), 120
Summary of the 2018 National Defense Strategy of the United States (Department of Defense), 246
Sunagawa Town protest (1955), 218, 219–20
Supreme Court (Japan), 58, 60, 62–63, 203, 219–20
surveillance, 75–76, 77, 82
Suttles, Wayne, 121
"Sweets and the Girls" (song, Cocco), 290

Taba Mitsuko, 167
taboos, 134–41, 154n13, 163. *See also* father/son/patricide taboos; Freud, Sigmund; heterosocial taboo; homosocial taboo
Tachikawa Air Base, 218, 219
Tada Osamu, 160, 193n3
Taira Natsume, 41, 43–44, 99
Taira Tomi, 161
Taiwan: China conflict/Empire v3 and, 240, 244, 325; *dojin* discourse/official nationalism and, 252, 253, 254, 255; Empire v2 and, 224, 226; tourism from, 85
Takae, Okinawa, 7, 249–50
Takamine Chōichi, 152, 303
Takara Kurayoshi, 19–20
Takazato Suzuyo, 187
Takeuchi Yoshimi, 323
Takeyama Akiko, 257
Taliban, 238, 305–6
Tamaki Denny, 59–60, 63, 298
Tanaka Kōtarō, 220
Taussig, Michael, 281–82, 303
The Teahouse of the August Moon ("Uehara Eiko," novel, play, and movie), 144, 155nn13, 15
The Teahouse of the August Moon (Sneider), 155n15
television broadcasting, 37, 143, 148–49, 180, 246, 263
television sets, spread of, 222
tendency, concept of, 13
Tent Village (*tentomura*; protest site), 51, 72–75, 88; canoe parking annex, 71; removal ordered, 52
Tetsu no Bōfū (The Typhoon of Steel and Bombs) (Okinawa Times 1950), 114
Thailand, 224, 228, 313
Time magazine, 117
time-space, 110–11
time-space, globalized, 110–11, 269–70. *See also* Empire version 3
time-space, local, 110, 178; transition to national (in formation of androcentric community), 112, 141–53
time-space, nationalized/Japanized, 110, 178, 222, 261
time-space, planetary, 20, 93, 95, 280, 281, 283, 330
tochikiseihōan (Land Control Act, 2021), 76
Tochiren (Military Landowners' Association), 159, 162, 186
Toguchi Taketoyo, 102
toilets, 258
Tōjō Hideki, 208, 308
Tokuda Tomoko, 167
Tokugawa Japan, 155n14
Tokyo District Court, 220, 236
Tokyo Metropolitan Police Department, 53
Tokyo Olympics (1964), 148–49
Tokyo Trial (1946), 308

Tomiyama Ichirō, 15–16, 95, 157–58
Torikobori Jo, 121
Totem and Taboo (Freud), 107–8
totemism, Freudian model of, 107–9
tōtōme (Okinawan-style mortuary tablet), 164–72, 184; historical context, 165–67; *Ryukyu Shimpo* series on, 168–70; spiritual-social customs, 164, 165, 170. *See also* androcentrism
tourism industry, 85, 160–61; Covid's effect on, 103, 238; impact on women, 167; official nationalism and, 261; Self/Other binary and, 246
Toyokawa Zen'ichi, 307
Toyoshita Narahiko, 215
trade wars, 227, 245
"trans-Pacific imagination," 308, 334
Treaty of Peace with Japan (San Francisco Peace Treaty, 1951), 212, 215, 216, 217
Treaty on Basic Relations between Japan and the Republic of Korea (1965), 236
Treaty on the Prohibition of Nuclear Weapons (2017), 330
trinity of the multitude, the state, and the World Republic, 327, 337
Truman, Harry S., 121
Tsuboi Shōgorō, 253
Tsūhan Seikatsu, 79
Tsuji (entertainment district), 142–45
Tsuruho Yōsuke, 269
two taboos. *See* heterosocial taboo; homosocial taboo
typhoons, 57

Uchikoshi Masayuki, 271–72
Uchinā Kana Nikki (Okinawan Diary), 77
"Uchinā o Toru: Shashinka Ishikawa Mao" (Capturing Okinawa: Photographer Ishikawa Mao) (NHK TV program), 296
Uehara Eiko, 144
Uema Ikuko, 142–44
Uema Yōko, 271
Ui Jun, 91
Uminari no Shimakara: Okinawa/Yanbaru yori (The Island Filled with Sea Roars: From Yanbaru, Okinawa; Medoruma), 77
Umi ni Suwaru: Hankichi 600 nichi no tatakai (Sitting In on the Sea: 600 Days of an Anti-base Struggle in Henoko) (documentary), 36–37, 37n4, 63n3
Unai Fesutyibaru (Okinawa Sisters' Festival), 167

The Unavowable Community (Blanchot), 35
unavowable community theory, 35, 36
Unit Deployment Program (of USMC), 233
United Kingdom, Imperial House visits to, 313
United Nations, 26; as approximation of World Republic (and collective security), 11, 327; China's membership in, 226; collective security by, 209, 322–23; Eurocentrism/Empire of, 335–36; shift of influence within, 330
United Nations Charter, 212, 331
United Nations General Assembly, 330–31
United Nations Human Rights Council, 58
United Nations Security Council, 226, 330–31
United States: collective security and, 329; Empire paradigm of rule, 8–9; Imperial House visits to, 313; trade war with Japan, 227
The United States and Japan: Advancing toward a Mature Partnership (Armitage and Nye, 2000), 240–41
United States-Japan Roadmap for Realignment Implementation (US-Japan Security Consultative Committee, 2006), 48, 241
United States Security Strategy for the East Asia-Pacific Region (Department of Defense, 1995), 235
universal capitalism, system of, 238
University of the Ryukyus, 103, 122
Urashima Etsuko, 36, 38
US Air Force, 28n3, 61, 135, 235
US Army, 28n3, 61. *See also* US military
US bases in Japan: continued use of for collective/regional self-defense, 212–15, 217, 325; decreasing need for in PPCSOP, 332–33; Japan's expenditures on, 243; reduction of total area in Japan "proper," 219, 247n4; transfer of to Okinawa, 219. *See also* anti-base protests
US bases in Okinawa, 2–3; consolidation of, 60, 62; disproportionate burden of, 96; economy of Okinawa depressed by, 69–70, 85; effect on Okinawan gross income (1957), 130; Futenma Air Station, 2–3, 104, 229, 233, 235, 244; Northern Training Area, 59, 60, 76, 249, 272n1; number of, 28n3; younger generations' acceptance of, 103–4
USCAR. *See* US Civil Administration of the Ryukyu Islands (USCAR)
US-China rapprochement, 226–27
US-China rivalry, 245–47, 328

US Civil Administration of the Ryukyu Islands (USCAR): arrests and land seizures by, 124, 125–30, 159; Camp Schwab deal, 130; establishment of, 123–24; GRI as subordinate to, 123, 124, 129, 135, 138; money infusion by, 128–29; Okinawan "people" and, 125, 135–36
US Department of Defense, 61, 211, 235
US dollar, 158, 163, 172, 176–77
US Government Appropriation for Relief in Occupied Area (GARIOA) Fund, 119
The US-Japan Alliance: Anchoring Stability in Asia (Armitage and Nye, 2012), 242, 244
The US-Japan Alliance: Getting Asia Right through 2020 (Armitage and Nye, 2007), 243
The US-Japan Alliance in 2020: An Equal Alliance with a Global Agenda (Armitage and Nye, 2020), 242
US-Japan Alliance: Transformation and Realignment for the Future (US-Japan Security Consultative Committee, 2005), 48, 241, 244
US-Japan security alliance: in 1990s (fourth moment, transition to Empire v.3), 230–34; against China and North Korea, 50; in Empire v.3, 240–45; regionalism and, 324, 325
US-Japan Security Consultative Committee, 63n5, 241
US-Japan Security Treaty (1951–1960), 212, 213, 214–15, 217, 220, 223
US-Japan Security Treaty (1960–), 222, 223, 230, 241; Article 3, 225
US Marine Corps (USMC), 60–61, 218; burdens in Okinawa spread across Japan and, 243–44; construction of FRF and, 235–36; cooperation/reciprocity with, 225; facilities used by, 28n3; Gulf War and, 231–32; shift in operational paradigm of, 232–33; split governance and, 229; upgrading capabilities of, 61. *See also* US bases in Japan
USMGR. *See* US Military Government of the Ryukyu Islands (USMGR)
US military: Air Force, 28n3, 61, 135, 235; Army, 28n3, 61; construction of refugee camps in Okinawa, 115–17; cooperation/reciprocity with, 225–26; damage compensation by, 159; decentering, 61–62; Japanese government's justification for continued presence of, 60; Navy, 28n3, 48, 61, 225; Okinawan media control by, 125; other nations' expenditures on, 243, 248n13; as paternal figure, 107–8, 115, 117, 131–32, 138, 155n15; problems derived from presence of, 85–86; rape incident of 1995, 1–2, 3; reasons for joining, 302, 304–5; rent payments by, 159; Sea Stallion helicopter crash incident (2004), 43. *See also* US Marine Corps
US military, ambivalence toward, 108, 112, 122–41, 278; androcentric community, deepening (1958-1966) and, 112, 134–41; androcentric community (1950–1957) and, 112, 122–34; Cocco/Hill of Dugongs and, 291–93; *The Cocktail Party* depicts, 136–41; mixed-race children, Okinawan attitude toward, 132–33, 193; San Francisco system and, 217–18, 219
US military, love and trust toward, 112, 113–22, 136; *The Cocktail Party* depicts, 138; paternalism and liberation context, 115–22, 132
US Military Government of the Ryukyu Islands (USMGR), 114, 115, 117–18, 123
US Navy, 28n3, 48, 61, 225
US rule of Okinawa, 1–3, 122–23; experience transformed through postmemory, 93–94; US rent payments to landowners, 123–24
US servicemen: Black servicemen, 116, 121, 179–80, 183, 185, 298–99; general will/mimetic faculty of Okinawan multitude and, 320; *hārī* participation by, 174–77; interviews with, 302–7; marriage to Okinawan women, 177; protests and, 75; salaries of, 172–73
US State Department, 210, 211, 215

V-22 Ospreys, 86, 232, 244, 248n14; crash, 59, 100n6
Vietnam War, 112, 131, 151, 222–24

Wallerstein, Immanuel, 203
war, outlawry of, 323
"war booty," 119–20
war criminals, 210
war memorials, 190–92, 288, 310–11
Watkins, James Thomas, 118
West/rest binary, 21, 254–55, 281–82. *See also* Self/Other binary
We the People (online petition system), 80
Whispers (band), 131

Whiting, John W. M., 117–18
Wilson, Gary, 329
Wiretapping Law (2016), 244
Wittgenstein, Ludwig, 12, 66
women: constituent power of, 164–72, 188; economic advancement of, 166–67; heterosocial taboo, dissolving, 163, 177–84; *juri*, 142–145; labor of, 89–90, 109–10, 166–67, 271, 272; mother-child relationship, 150; Otohime Troupe, 141–48, 156n17; *yuta*, 170–71, 293. *See also* androcentrism
women, violence against. *See* sexual violence and rape
women's organizations, 41
women's suffrage, 117, 134
world market, and Empire, 9, 158, 201, 204, 206, 224–25; economic globalization, 324; in Empire version 2, 227–28, 230; in Empire version 3, 237–38, 240, 247
World Republic of *nuchi du takara*, 26, 280, 322–23; concerns over military as institution of violence and, 335–38; general will of multitude and, 326–27; UN as approximation of, 11, 327
World War II, 1; air raids during, 95; Imperial House regrets, 312, 313–14, 315, 320; Japanese surrender, 153n1; memory of, 93–94, 97, 124–25, 184–85, 189–90; use of nuclear weapons in, 207, 236, 313; use of term, 28n1. *See also* Battle of Okinawa (Operation Iceberg, 1945)
World Wildlife Fund–Japan, 42, 92

X-band radar system, 241, 248n12
Xi Jinping, 239–40

Yae Sakura, 120
Yamada Eimi, 180

Yamahide no Okinawadayori (Yamahide's Letters from Okinawa; blogs by Yamamoto), 77
Yamamoto Hideo, 77
Yamamoto Taro, 78
Yamanoha Nobuko, 167
Yamanokuchi (or Yamanoguchi) Baku, 15, 256
Yamashiro Hiroji, 54, 67, 72, 76, 99
Yamashiro Yoshikatsu, 45–46, 99
Yamazaki Taku, 230
Yamazato Teiko, 167
Yara Chōbyō: *donkakuteki taisei* ("obtuse-angle attitude"), 18; on human labor, 158–59; Imperial House visit and, 310, 311; mobilizing anti-base spirit in community of *nuchi du takara*, 124, 128; reversion movement and, 149, 152, 153
Yasukuni Shrine, 246
yen. *See* currency
Yokota Air Base, 241, 248n14
Yonaguni Island, 244
Yoneda Sachihiro, 102–3
Yoneyama, Lisa, 237
Yoo, Hyon Joo, 8, 308, 334
Yoshida Shigeru, 214, 215
Yoshida Sueko, 167
Yoshimi Shun'ya, 222
yosomono ("outsiders"), 87–88
Yui Akiko, 167
yuta (female shamans), 170–71, 293

zaibatsu (family-run conglomerates), 207, 210, 227
Zamami Island, 113
"Zero Trash Operations" (project/concert, Cocco), 286–87, 295
Zhu Fangyue, 246
Zhu Feng, 247